New Realities of the Twenty-first Century, Part 1
A Psychic's View of the Supernatural, Parapsychic, and Religion, Including Prophecy Prediction!

by

Prophet Wildman

The contents of this work including, but not limited to, the accuracy of events, people, and places depicted; opinions expressed; permission to use previously published materials included; and any advice given or actions advocated are solely the responsibility of the author, who assumes all liability for said work and indemnifies the publisher against any claims stemming from publication of the work.

All Rights Reserved
Copyright © 2017 by Prophet Wildman

No part of this book may be reproduced or transmitted, downloaded, distributed, reverse engineered, or stored in or introduced into any information storage and retrieval system, in any form or by any means, including photocopying and recording, whether electronic or mechanical, now known or hereinafter invented without permission in writing from the publisher.

Dorrance Publishing Co
585 Alpha Drive
Suite 103
Pittsburgh, PA 15238
Visit our website at *www.dorrancebookstore.com*

ISBN: 978-1-4349-2804-7
eISBN: 978-1-4349-2156-7

A Prayer Dedication

Above all, this book is dedicated to the Glory, Power, Majesty, Love, Forgiveness, Infinite Wisdom, and Compassion of God. To his spiritual son, Jesus Christ, Lord and Savior of all mankind, the One True Messiah, and the sacred holy Bible.

Special thanks to my guardian angel, servant of the Kingdom of heaven, and my personal protector. One who has helped me, guided me, and certainly many times intervened to save my life; perhaps with knowledge of worthwhile purpose and contribution on this Earth yet to come and unfulfilled. Without such intervention, this book would not have been written.

To the memory of my parents' spirits, now in heaven's hand, I dedicate this book. I also dedicate this book to their memory and their love shown to me in their lifetime.

To my two daughters and grandchildren: May you walk in and are forever protected by our heavenly Father's holy light, knowing also that you are loved.

Praise God Almighty

Praise Jesus, our Lord, and Savior

I hold these to be truths in Jesus' name. Amen.

In Memoriam

To all the civilians, New York City police, and rescue firefighters lost by the evil, criminal, and murderous acts of foreign terrorists on September 11, 2001; to all their families who still grieve; to all the valiant armed forces services personnel who sacrificed in service of their country through America's response to this immense and senseless tragedy; and to those wounded and fallen in Iraq and Afghanistan, as well as those grieving families forever scarred. Our nation truly thanks and appreciates you. We will remember this sacrifice and loss.

A special thanks is given to Philip Imbrogno, author of *Interdimensional Universe* (Llewellyn Publications, 2008). Since the early days of Roswell and U.F.O.-logy, he has played an active role in the inner circle of investigational research, as both a scientist and a consultant for the government. His many personal experiences and perspectives encompass a wide case file.

Although my own psychic experiences date way back, my U.F.O. encounters are much more recent. It was these encounters that prompted me to do six months of exhaustive research extending to many related topics.

Remarkably, the conclusions drawn by Philip Imbrogno seem to match my own in virtually all subject areas. There are nearly identical conclusions, even though he approaches these subjects from the scientific side, while I approach mine from the psychic/spiritual side.

Thus, readers of this book who seek additional comparative information and subject matter accounts are advised that I recommend his book highly as additional, supplemental reading. It is when people begin to hear the same explanations of similar, bizarre supernatural stories from different authors that they can then allow it to become accepted belief. Realization that the supernatural realm is comprised of multiple dimensions is a good point to start, and his *Interdimensional Universe*, both qualitatively and (in paperback format) quantitatively, is an exceptional read.

Foreword

With both of my daughters graduating magna cum laude, I would like to think that at least a little of their genius might have rubbed off on their Dad. This book is a chance for you to evaluate my first literary effort, while learning secrets of some supernatural discoveries and enjoying some accounts uniquely my own.

Astonishingly, as I was preparing this book, new entries that I didn't even need to dig for came to me, as if to say: *In your book about us and our world (the supernatural), include this, too!* Like some spirit entities had just picked this information off some supernatural vine; fresh this morning and quite authentic!

Perhaps angels are making things interesting; angel sightings, as well, beyond my normal invisible angel psychic message delivery. Did Prophet Wildman (as I refer to myself in this book) actually get to view the face of Gabriel? Or later, were the four, circulating orbs of white light in the night sky angel orbs (Occurring upon completion of matching all future Apocalyptic prediction through history along with my own to Bible Book of Revelation!)? This is documented in the Lie-Detection section, also.

Not only does this book give the Bible Tribulation period awareness, but in parapsychic, supernatural, religious relevance, and other future prediction discussions, much is revealed! This book thrusts light into many dark places and corners of these realms; sending, in some cases, the sewer rats scurrying as the secrecy lid is blown off their cover. Even some two-legged creatures exposed as this light of new awareness pours in.

There are (totally real) dark, evil forces you probably aren't even fully aware of, working to intercept your spiritual well-being and suppress it in an effort to block your soul's salvation. Although in a different dimension, Hell is quite real (In contrast verifying the holy Bible that such.). Not only does this book provide you with counter measure advice but, perhaps, through awareness gained, allow you to devise a plan for your own spiritual well-being; not to mention physical survival relative to future predictions.

In the original version of this book, there was a great deal more humor and fiction, but that didn't mix well with convincing you to believe many bizarre occurrences which are true, or the most holy and serious topic within the Religion section. In that version, I was out to show that one's sanity is equivalent to their faith. Readers would have felt as they neared the conclusion of the book that they were down on all fours and climbing an incredibly steep, mental cliff. Clutching the draw strings of a sack they were pulling behind them containing their sanity and thinking they needed to hold on extra tight because they had made it this far on such a demandingly steep climb; almost to the summit.

Others of strong faith would have regarded the seemingly endless shock and awe, and assaults on their sanity as increasingly humorous as they realized how badly a toll this must be having on those with less spiritual fortitude and mental stamina. It occurred to me about then that it does no good to lead a person to Christ if you drive them insane or they die of a heart attack along the way!

I had concocted a broad array of (quite humorous) fictional mental illness and, as that version progressed, the reader is periodically told that other readers are falling by the wayside, driven right into the mental ditch, and worse was yet to come! My book kept reinforcing the idea that slope was just getting mentally steeper and steeper, turning the book into an endurance mountain climb. As it went, it kept reporting on how it was the cause of an epidemic of mental illness. While some readers increasingly would have been roaring with laughter, knowing they were fine, but seeing right through to the comedy, others would have been taking it all a bit too seriously and would have actually begun to feel a bit mentally threatened and challenged by incessant jolts of shock and awe, coupled with reports of rampant insanity breaking out.

It was, in fact, my own faith and sense of humor that had seen me through some of unexpected, mentally harrowing circumstances, the ones I was relating. So that was the reason behind focusing on those aspects in that version. In rewriting in a different style (this version), I didn't want a dry read, so I tried to allow just enough humor to remain in order to achieve that. Fiction that had been the vehicle by which to deliver the humor was greatly reduced, except by metaphor. The final resulting writing style works well, and heads off an epidemic of insanity before it ever has a chance to get started! Or does it?

Part I uses some people's brains like they were Frisbees, ironically resembling Grey's U.F.O.s, but providing necessary understandings of the supernatural described here, required as background understanding in the Part II religious commentary. Anyone finding their mental stability challenged by Part I are asking for trouble to then venture into Part II. Unless your relatives are already coming to see you at the asylum on Thursdays and Saturdays, Part II could be the final nudge over the mental precipice. And that's not exaggerated characterization! If anyone finds Part I rough, don't go anywhere near part II.

The high seas of religion in Part II are churning so violently that even the clergy, metaphorically speaking, will need lifejackets to go up on deck for clearly one intense reading adventure; very highly informative, not to be missed, and if you don't brace yourself, your sanity could get swept overboard quite seriously. Yes, a one-two punch exactly.

Literary jabs to shock you are here in Part I, with a couple of upper cuts and a left hook. And then in Part II, an explosive right hook, and other literary informational blows you never expected to stagger you! Some people knocked out with incredibly positive take aways, while in other cases simply getting blown away! Mental hatches not battened down and simply swept overboard with overpowering waves of truth more than they were mentally prepared to handle, their sanity swept overboard potentially! That intense a reality brass knuckles blow.

So if you care to venture out to sea in Part II with captain Wildman, come prepared for heavy seas and stormy weather. An outstanding reading adventure packed with factual information regarding the future! We are sailing ahead on into a little hurricane known as Tribulation, only then to examine the eye of that storm. Part II is a classic before it ever leaves port; one engaging read not to be missed. Not a single reader is likely to be disappointed, and any time clergy reading religious topic have to wear life vests, prepared for the eye of the storm (the heart of this book), you can pretty well tell what the reading voyage will be like. Prohibited reading at all mental institutions already overcrowded from people unable to handle Part I? I'll let you decide. No big deal for some, hopefully you; I realize, but for others, perhaps a bit intense. Fact can be far stranger than fiction, and this is all fact. Incident and circumstance described is one side of the knife, but the reality fact side of that blade can seem even sharper.

Full transparency in the Truth Verification/Lie Detection section exhibits all questions asked and passed so the reader can examine how the questions were worded. There are similar questions in exam offered in Part II, with some overlap; perhaps the tip of that same sharp-bladed knife. I'm hopeful I can establish full belief acceptance with my readers in Part I, so that Part II won't even be an issue. They know I'm dead serious, and they need to believe me for their own good (and survival!).

Introduction

It is my hope that this book will succeed in expanding awareness horizons for readers. All aspects of the supernatural realm are deeply intertwined and interrelated as influencing forces upon each other. No sections of this book stand by themselves, are independent of the others, or are unaffected by them. Even religion, and especially so, can be seen dividing the others along lines of good (holy) and evil (unholy).

Here I should mention I have no formal theological training background other than my Protestant roots, yet I think here even theologians will be interested in my free and unencumbered viewpoint and comments. Opinions based on a lifetime of experiences, accumulated wisdom, and quite unique psychic insights and awareness.

As if not to be denied inclusion, in readying this manuscript for publishing, additional strange events suddenly occurred! When I was a little boy, early in the morning I'd cross the street and knock on a neighbor's door to see if my playmate friend could come out to play. A little older, kids would come knocking for extra players for baseball, basketball, or football games. In college I went exploring into the supernatural realm to see if it would come out to play. Then married and settled, I stopped knocking for many years. However, by midlife, it came knocking on my door and, without much choice in the matter, I was now receiving psychic play. The supernatural knocking on Wildman's door, wanting me to come out and play, and this psychic play has continued to retirement age!

Psychic prediction and awareness still coming to me are quite alarming and disturbing, but allowing me time to make people aware well in advance of what I see ahead, and this could be lifesaving. Please take these comments seriously because I do, and I plan my own future around them. The term psychic is used loosely to describe varied sets of skills, as you will read later in that Section, although mine is pre-cognitive (future prediction).

Just as I credit the Kingdom of heaven and angels as my source, I should also point out I suspect God's involvement behind the scenes, as well. It might seem a bit tongue-in-cheek coy to say God is my Senior Editor, but frankly I have no other way to explain certain events other than to label them as acts of God. My Senior Editor wants certain descriptions and/or occurrences to be discussed in this book, and faster than Emeril can say *BAM!*, guess what? It is another new topic or incident. Try to imagine the supernatural coming at you as if the *on* switch were stuck or something. Not to leave out several events, I can explain in no other way than to call them acts of God, and they, too, for purpose of inclusion in this book!

I'm quite serious, not to mention being repeatedly awe struck. So much so I had to abandon the expression/exclamation, *Wow, nothing can top this!* Because it seemed every time I said that, something came along that did, and even more outrageously, extraordinarily, incredible! As you will read later, there is without question a destiny involved here, as well! That's pretty incredible in a book with an entire Psychic section in description of fate and destiny that also pop within later chapter discussions.

Make no mistake, all of the described events are real and factual, except where for purposes of humor a small amount of obvious fiction is allowed to co-exist. It was only with help from my own sense of humor (and faith) that enabled me to bounce back from the shock and awe of some of these experiences. It gets a bit rough when you start experiencing things a crazy person might describe, except you know you are not crazy! A big credit line of bizarre now fully maxed out, or at least you start hoping it is!

Is this payback for all the times when I was younger and I kicked in the imaginary side door of the supernatural building, looking for answers? Those hidden secrets and answers now looking for me? My mental door getting kicked in for all the imaginary split-door-jamb repairs I caused back then? Twilight Zone University alumni practical goof on, certainly, but not as much for my benefit, but for yours! For the All-Terrain Vehicle ride through the bumpy roads of the Twilight Zone you are about to take! It's all about this book, and certain things that needed to be in a book itself riding a destiny to describe to you! Yes, that's right, it's all your fault (just joking, my humor off the leash again.)! Your

AT.V. ride includes the Tribulation Trail in later chapters; yes, something to do with those one-hundred-pound hailstones, perhaps.

All right, supernatural world, your guests have arrived. Try to be better behaved this time and not eat the minds of so many alive like you did that last group of readers. Do you think these readers are your personal hors devours or something? Apparently so!

Be nice this time; be polite, behave yourselves (like that is ever going to happen), and stop handing out complimentary nightmares, will you? I told you before about that; you never listen! Yes, you may be surprised with what falls out of the supernatural bag when Wildman shakes it; almost to the point to begin finding out.

You can skip past the inspirational stuff in Chapter 1, An Open Mind, and even past the first section, if you prefer, as these are there mainly for background reference (although the aliens chapter could prove helpful later). You can, if you wish, jump all the way up to Chapter 8. Begin there, and come back later to read the other Entities in that section; or straight through, your option.

Darkness and storms (my old girlfriends as you will later read) moving in; perfect reading conditions for reading about this subject with lightning crashing down. Figurative jolts of shock and awe, of which this book has abundant supply.

Don't even think of reading this book if you have any kind of heart condition or are on any kind of heart medication. You don't want a "New Reality" that this was the last book you never finished reading. No, not even with a defibrillator right next to your chair. How do you think you are going to operate it on yourself, anyway?

Others might consider pushing their chair up against a wall so it doesn't go over backwards with them in it. Women currently taking panic or anxiety medication should consult with their doctor before attempting to read this book (which will probably result in increased dosage to your existing prescription.). Women who are nursing or pregnant should wait until their pregnancy comes to term. Otherwise, your child could be born with a crash helmet already in place and, in rare cases, knee or elbow pad protectors pre-strapped on, as well. What were you thinking, wanting to go AT.V.ing on bumpy roads in the Twilight Zone's Tribulation Trail during pregnancy, anyway?

All others check the manual override switch on your mental circuit breaker box in case things start to overload later, just to make sure it's working. Realize, too, this book may introduce nausea and vomiting as your preconceived notion of things goes right out the window along with lunch! Expect your imagination to ask for, and receive, a pay raise from all the extra workout, overtime, and wear and tear. What have you gotten yourself in to? Hopefully a great read, exceeding expectations.

Secrets certain entities have managed to keep secret and hidden from accurate human awareness have now had their cover blown. Even a likeness image brought to daylight along with new details! A huge jailbreak is like a security breach for them. Sirens, horns, whistles, and alarm bells are all going off! This book represents mass exposure. An entire alien saucer air wing is scrambled, while all manner of other beings are running for cover from the supernatural darkness. They know you are about to penetrate their world!

This book is your passport; luxury accommodations reserved for you at the Twilight Zone Inn; complementary mental stimulation; and a room with a panoramic view just as wide as your imagination will allow. You are all checked in; welcome to my world and have a great read! Enjoy.

When you are ready to begin this reading adventure, Chapter 1 can be skipped over and returned to later, if you wish. Its primary, but not sole, purpose is to convince you to reserve your opinions, take time to evaluate new evidences, and reach decisions slowly after thoughtful evaluation, rather than snap reaction decisions. Many things said in later chapters have relevance in early chapters and vice-versa, so perhaps waiting until the book is fully completed to see what new realities develop for you is best. Think spiritually and look to find hidden answers in that realm. Understanding the supernatural, you will see sometimes science as void as a desert in that realm as far as answers. See the invisible supernatural also as a connected extension of the natural (visible reality).

A good analogy: my (2004) first U.F.O. sighting, (later detailed) where the windows on the saucer rim were only lit on the south side. The window on the other sides certainly there, but invisibly cloaked in darkness. A sort of microcosm of the supernatural itself; invisible, yet there. Third, not unlike George Lucas/Star Wars Jedi force of the Light, and Dark side forces of evil in parallel with the Bible do in fact exist! That is God and Christianity as the Bible stated, and it is no myth. (This the posse that I ride with you could say). It is invisible, yet there, and by the time that you complete this book, if I've done my job, I will have convinced you of this with both certainty and conviction to this awareness (So perhaps save Chapter 1 for last). Now if you are ready to start, go to Chapter 2, if you wish, The Entities Section, and get my viewpoint on these supernatural groups (cast of characters). We'll inspect each one of them at this supernatural Zoo, as if from inside the cages, for an up close inspection, including those hostile to humans. Perspective on these is essential as background information later. What about your reading adventure author/guide; Wildman? Why that pen name?

It seemed appropriate for this book, in multiple ways. In real life it was a name assigned to me as a nickname at least three times, and years apart, by people not realizing I'd had that moniker before! Later in this book the word Prophet is added because in over fifty years of future prediction wise. Then in 2008/2009 receiving prophecy no longer on general subject, but on holy subject; the Coming Tribulation. Wildman also because there is clearly destiny involvement, and in as much as there was still some unfulfilled prediction, (representing a promise from God to do so) God found it necessary to intervene or intercede several times in my life to block my death! Had he not, you would not be reading this. Praise the Lord, both the Father and the Son for those. More than two dozen brushes with death near miss/close calls I'll mention again later in the book.

Angels guarding me, angels delivering prophecy to me, and holy angels revealing themselves to me on separate occasion in that 2008/2009 time period conjunctive to the writing of this book, as well. As you will read, they can assume different forms.

So I mention this now because that awareness that this identity is not random, but dates back at least as far as 1970, and is genuinely appropriate, almost particularly so for this book's author/guide. There is no fiction in this book whatsoever; the exception being humor that is either obvious, or so noted. Please realize as an anointed, saved, Christian, my faith as the Bible directs it; demands that I witness to you with complete truth and accuracy within honesty. I have done so, but be prepared that some things are so astonishingly amazing and incredible, your first impression is likely that it couldn't be truth, or that I must be crazy or delusional, or something along those lines. Some are literally acts of God, and wherever God is involved, the incredible should be expected, or at least accepted as reasonable belief conclusion. Just don't make a judgment too quickly, but instead keep an open mind and perhaps reserve judgment until later.

Table of Contents

Chapter 1: Keeping an Open Mind and Other Notes and Inspirations 1
Chapter 2: Entities Section: Ghosts, Jinn, and Holy Angels 4
Chapter 3: Monsters 18
Chapter 4: Extraterrestrial Aliens and Ultraterrestrials 26
Chapter 5: Humans Possessed/Vampires 38
Chapter 6: Other Phenomena 42
Chapter 7: U.F.O. Section: Main Theories 48
Chapter 8: South Florida (1990s) U.F.O. Infestation and a 2004 Sighting 56
Chapter 9: A U.F.O. Psychic Dream: 2008 U.F.O. Premonition 68
Chapter 10: 1988 Particle Beam Premonition: 2008 Fulfillment Sighting 78
Chapter 11: Busting the Star Pretenders 86
Chapter 12: U.F.O. Craft Characteristics 94
Chapter 13: U.F.O.s and E.T.s Government Cover-Up 101
Chapter 14: Psychic Section: The Majors 123
Chapter 15: Describing My Own Personal Psychic Experience 138
Chapter 16: Hallucination 154
Chapter 17: Leys, Dark Leys, and Psychic Leys 164
Chapter 18: Portals: High Strangeness: Dimensional Warps 168
Chapter 19: The 1988 T.V. Show and Particle Beam Premonition 174
Chapter 20: Metaphysical Section: Time Warps 181
Chapter 21: Astrology/Astronomy: Pre-Statement Comments 186
Chapter 22: Cosmic Model 193
Supplement Section: Two Riders Knowing God: Poetic Justice to Divine Destiny in Matrix Convergence 200
Conclusion, Part I: Preview, Part II 206
Bibliography by Chapter 210
General Bibliography 214
Lie Detection Section 217
Lie Detection Variations (as stated) 219

Chapter 1
Keeping an Open Mind and Other Notes and Inspirations

No, airhead is something different. This has to do with not coming to snap-reaction judgments too rapidly, but instead making a reserved until all evidence is presented and a wisely based conclusion is made. Try to accept that not one, but several, things I will make you aware of are on the needle indicator end of gauge, pointing at beyond extraordinarily incredible. Not one experience, but multiple! Literally God's hand is on my shoulder involvements, Twilight Zone receipted deliveries of shockmaximus proportion. Choice reading all true factual accounts, but my point is you will have to drag your brain, (at least some people) into complete acceptance, rather than it co-operating willingly!

It is only fair that I warn people, but I promise you, although I have a robust sense of humor, if I use the word God in conjunction with anything I explain, I am stone-cold somberly, seriously truthful in using my words. This is all supernatural, paranormal, and often in my case, as psychic medium, paranormal interaction with holy angel activity that I've experienced over a fifty-year lifetime of holy angel-sourced premonitions and psychic experiences. I simply filed it under acts of God; and probably the best approach you can use in accepting what I explain. God rolling up his sleeves, so to speak; shock and awe in over dosage amounts and in multiple account experiences. You can handle that, I hope. Part I of this book is to prepare people for Part II, where general subject shifts to holy subject, and a whole new level layer of shock and awe is encountered. I actually have to start this book (and that one, too, by making sure people are wearing their mental crash helmets and have their mental safety harnesses properly fastened). You might think it is exaggeration now, but you haven't completed both halves of this book yet, and you need to reserve perhaps your overall reaction until then, even if reacting as you go to these separate instances. Some rather bumpy trail bike trails ahead, and as much as some people will want to dismiss what I say as an easy way out of coping with wise for their minds, (for those who still have one) I state again, all testimony statements are truthful (Transparent Lie-Detection exams all Passed, for further exhibited evidence). It is when you combine statements from both Part I and Part II that you then realize God's direct involvement, as claimed, is the only logical and reasonable explanation to accept. So, please reserve immediate judgment, and I think you will then find yourself realizing that I speak the truth, and the accounts given are all true.

The supernatural just needing someone over in this Dimension to put it into words for them—guess who! There is the Twilight Zone return address on many of these psychic deliveries, too.

But I don't want to hold you from discovering the rest of the book because you, too, will experience second hand what it's like to get your mental side door kicked in just from reading about it! The asylums are filling fast, make reservations early for best accommodations (just joking). Wildman is one of the few who can literally watch an entire Star Trek episode for real off his front patio; that seems to be a protectorate colony or something of the Twilight Zone. Then, on another night, witness angel orbs of white light swirling overhead in a dancing quartet pattern. You mean that's not normal? This is exactly what I'm referring to; stuff that sounds like a statement issued from the mouth of a lunatic, just trying to prepare you. As weird, strange, bizarre, incredibly extraordinary, ultra amazing that stretches your imagination to the breaking point, you must realize that most things paranormal or parapsychic are this way. It would be less believable if it wasn't. I will try to get you through this book with your sanity intact, but I make no guarantees! Realize that some will tell you later that to accept an invitation to go AT.V.ing with Wildman over in the Twilight Zone only proves you were crazy to start with! Remember what I told you though; no matter how extreme, I speak the truth!

Paranormal Kids

Often people with parapsychic gifts begin experiencing *introductions* to their hidden talents at an early age. This subject departs a bit, but I want to remind all, society should not disrespect or ridicule any child who experiences these occurrences. Their gift is normal, it just seems to be abnormal, but truly is a gift from the spirit world. Children with these gifts, including adults, are sometimes referred to as *sensitives* because of elevated psychic sensitivity levels. Whether they see auras, ghosts, telepathically read other humans living, or humans non-living, have channeling skills, receptivity, or predict future event, they should never be made to feel ashamed for not being normal like other kids; otherwise they are vulnerable to being psychologically damaged and that can then cause them to suppress their gift. A gift from God is not to be ridiculed. Open mindedness brings wisdom, and wisdom is the beginning of knowing God. These children are blessed; please treat them so.

For my readers of advanced awareness: In this book whenever I use the Twilight Zone as an acronym reference, it is related to the psychological/parapsychic type of zone, which is similar to the popular 1960s television show of the same name. For those not old enough to remember, it was a way ahead of its time. Rod Sterling hosted and produced a show dealing with anomalies and phenomenon of the supernatural paranormal; and the human mind's perceptions and reactive explanation in coping with it; both in terms of the actors portrayal, and then the viewer's reaction to the reaction, often with a suspenseful or surprise ending.

There was an original lead in theme, then in later episodes, a revised version. Number one: You unlock this door (door pictured floating in space) with your imagination as the key.
You are traveling through another dimension; not just of sight and sound, but of mind. It is a dimension of both shadow and substance; a journey into a wondrous land whose boundaries are those of imagination. Your next stop: the Twilight Zone.

Number two: You are traveling through another dimension. A fifth dimension that lies beyond that which is known to man. As vast as space, as timeless as infinity. In a place between light and shadow, between science and superstition, and it lays between the pits of man's fears, and the summit of his knowledge. This is the dimension of imagination. It's an area we call The Twilight Zone.

Picture this, if you will; a signpost up ahead. You've just crossed over. Your next stop: The Twilight Zone.

Because in more recent years, a *Twilight Zone* movie, saga, and series have hijacked the name and taken it to mean a bloodsucking vampire-like entity or demonic dimension in general, I feel it necessary to make a distinction/differentiation between the two. All of my references in this book relate to more of original context. A parapsychic episode type of meaning toward the supernatural, in general; not demonic specific. My a bit-tongue-in-cheek reference to T.Z.U. or Twilight Zone University relates both to my former college days as a heavy hallucinogenic drug user, but a holy angel psychic training course with an entire personal lifetime archives reference library of Parapsych: fortold then later fulfilled events upon future arrival.

Keeping an Open Mind (In the Supernatural World): The Rules of Engagement

In the supernatural realm very little is proven, and anything (almost anything) and most everything is possible. Therefore, the word impossible is treated like it doesn't exist. Belief in God means even the perceived impossible can, at times, be possible. Miracles do happen. Things unexplained do happen.

Keep the possibility of new information arising, and regard subject matter as a constant consideration. Changes can change your mind. No conclusion should ever be so final as to be exempt from future re-evaluation.

Truth is a virtue in God's universe. Facts can change or dissolve. Truth itself is constant and indestructible; a virtue in God's care.

Accept the Bible as truth until shown otherwise. It is the one otherwise which will never come.

There are varied dimensions which are constant; there are scientific properties which can be constant or change depending on the dimension; there are dimensions that can be altered to change perceptions; and altered perceptions can cause altered dimensions, as well in some cases (See also Cosmic Model chapter).

Not all answers are found in the scientific realm; some are found spiritually in these realms. At times knowledge of the scientific and wisdom of the spiritual are both required. That is the fabric of God's universe.

In developing an opinion, examine, contemplate, and try to develop more than one perspective at the same time. Remember: Not all aspects of what you are focused on might develop simultaneously. For example, a criminal investigation can move in a totally new direction when new information is learned. You can be focused while remaining open-minded at the same time.

Though invisible, evil is a powerful, negative force in this world. Be wary and vigilant against harm. demons are real and will always seek your demise. Arm yourself with Faith. Faith equals Sanity. Faith will deliver you from harm if you believe in Jesus.

More Thoughts

Perception through a dimensional looking glass
We see this world as Reality,
The afterlife almost an illusion.
When in fact once we pass on to that world,
A spirit/spiritual one becomes Reality,
And this one a distant delusional memory of a Ghost.
Sometimes these theories can seem like peculiar, strange
Little birdhouses that reality cannot support, and all
Wisdom working contrary will not past, present or future
Ever support. Nothing will ever be seen living inside.
Then just when you assume such to be so, some equally
Strange, weird-looking bird, in fact, will fly in from
Nowhere, never before seen, and take up residence. Thus
Proving our conclusion based on conventional knowledge to
Be wrong, and that at least the possibility for exceptions
To the rules should never be dismissed.

Some say there is a thin line between Genius and insanity
actually, insanity will only allow fleeting glimpse of the
Concepts a Genius firmly grasps.
One's faith equals Sanity; Sanity won't make you a Genius by
Itself, but without the stability it provides, Genius
Becomes totally out of reach.

A Modest Genius
It's tough being a Genius, but I've learned to compensate
For that handicap.

Chapter 2
Entities Section: Ghosts, Jinn, and Holy Angels

In this chapter, after discussing the subject in general terms, I thought I'd relate some personal experiences. These other dimensions not only interconnect with us, but there appears to be inter-connect there, also.

The prevailing belief is that immediately after death, we (our spirit) pass through a tunnel and toward a bright light. This after-life is said to something like a border immigration check point when you first arrive; being sorted, separated, and quite organized. This is the description by some who have experienced NDEs (near death experiences) and afterlife itself being similar to the Biblical description. Paradise or heaven is also known as the Garden of Righteousness. Most do not immediately enter; very few, in fact. Final judgment will not come until the end time (that we are now approaching, as described later in this book) when all who have ever lived shall be judged by what Christians call the white Throne Judgment.

So there is an entry sorting point, then what is described by many as a kind of limbo state; very pleasantly described, but not the space of heaven proper itself. The entry point sorts out obvious bad apples (by varying degree) shortly after arrival. Aside from the most wicked, sinful, or criminal, most others move to separate spaces, and are said to reunite with deceased loved ones and family. These loved ones are said to appear in their prime years (early thirties to forties), rather than their age at time of death.

While these visions vary from person to person, there is a good bit of similarity. Sometimes they are described as being seen by one's mind's eye, rather than with their normal eyes. Beautiful meadows, hills, fields, waters, and waterfalls. Pleasant music, flowers, angels, cherubs, people in robes, and lights of unknown sources. A very peaceful, tranquil feeling of harmony and pleasantness with multicolors in background atmosphere are similarly described from different accounts.

Some return to their bodies here on Earth, stating that they were given the choice, the decision, to return back to life and that it was theirs to make. While others report deceased relatives telling them to return so as they might complete unfinished business, or being told they still had further work left to be completed (No dessert until you eat your vegetables). In examining such accounts, we should all realize this could be some sort of transitory conceived space, rather than afterlife after death in actuality. There is simply no way to verify any of this. A person only recently dead still often at some level does have some functioning brain capacity left, and therefore perception could be a distortion of the living mind moving toward shutdown. Or, you could argue that one's soul (mind's eye) transcends all of this and is immune from the physical, and its transmitting this back to the still functioning brain, but at a reduced level amperage, you might say. While a hospital monitor may be showing a flat line, perhaps one's spiritual circuitry is still functioning beyond that for a short time. That provides argument both for and against these descriptions being what actually transpires immediately after death.

We know the spirits who do not move on, do not go into the light, or perhaps decide to remain Earthbound as spirits for a time, having perhaps been granted permission to return, all qualify as ghost spirits. Those who once lived are now Earthbound spirits. All other spirits that have never lived are demonic spirits and seem to circulate in close quarters within other dimension (other than Holy Spirit entity).

Almost all Earthbound ghosts fall into one of the following categories:

1. They were murder victims, their normal lives cut short (their spirit does not feel ready to move on).
2. They died accidentally, their normal lives cut short (their spirit does not feel ready to move on).
3. They have an attachment to relatives, a spouse, children, etc. (their spirit does not feel ready to move on).
4. They died naturally, but perhaps led a shortened life (their spirit does not feel ready to move on).

5. They fear punishment in the afterlife (they remain Earthbound to avoid/delay eventual punishment for wrongdoings).
6. They have an obsession with completing unfinished business (whether they actually can or not). It can be a personal, family, or other matter. They seek completion or closure before moving on.
7. Some Native Americans (and other Indian spirits) for whatever reason, do remain Earthbound.

In the case of number five on the list, what are commonly referred to as shadow people, and a ghost, a recognized subcategory by ghost paranormal investigators, is a likely fit. These are generally considered evil spirits, even considered by some as the spirits of the damned; afraid to move on. They cast dark shadow on a ceiling or wall where no one is present to leave a shadow. It is seen outdoors, as well, a shadow where there shouldn't be any.

Keep in mind, most Earthbound spirits are not evil or malevolent, and many never make their presence known, or do so only subtly and thus unconvincingly. Most are harmless even if they do make their presence known. Such spirits are generally active at night, especially late night. Daytime ghost events do occur, although less frequently.

Ghosts give off high electromagnetic discharge, and they create a lot of positively charged ions, which can drop surrounding air temps significantly and can draw electricity from batteries or other electrical currents.

Levitation and teleportation of solid objects have been associated with ghosts and are well documented over many centuries. Places of former residence, employment, burial, or the scene of one's death are common haunt sites. However, they can move about and are not restricted to just these places, yet they most often do stay localized.

In other forms, these spirits commonly exhibit something known as ghost orbs. At night, they appear as glowing particle balls of light (blue/green or yellowish/white are most common coloration). These are also referred to as Ghost Lights, Ghost Globules, Will O' the Wisps, and transit spirits.

Foxfire or Elves Lights, also termed Corpse Candles, are said to be omens of death/and or bad luck. There are documented cases where a flame or fire seen in the middle of such a glowing orb did shortly thereafter result in the death of someone viewing it. Thus, there seems to be some fact to this belief, substantiating such claims.

Later in this book I will discuss orbs of white light that I witnessed following me! I like to think they were angels revealing themselves, since orbs of white light is a documented angel form. The number four and an angel are an associated number, but in trying to remain subjectively objective, leave U.F.O. Oz orb open as possibility (Chapter 18 discusses in greater detail this occurrence). They are clearly intelligently guided.

In these cases, you are seeing spirit energy visible in this dimension, but existing also within parallel space of a different dimension. The ghost realm limit does not limit itself to humans, either.

Pet dogs, for example, in the Hound of Goshen, and even ghost dogs in the presence of their ghost masters, have been witnessed. Solid physical objects, which also include backdrops, are often referred to as spectors. Boats, ships, cars, trains, and trucks all occasionally are witnessed as a replay of what once was reality. The white ghost dog of Goshen was seen around Newbury, South Carolina, in the 1850s.

While some psychics seem to be able to tap right in and read the thoughts of spirits no differently than if they were still living, others can physically see spirits that others cannot. A few can do both, but this is rare to begin with, even to be able to do one.

Both ghosts and guardian angels occasionally have the one action in common in that they both will try to gain the attention of a living person. I don't have a lot of ghost experiences to tell you about, but an encounter with an Indian ghost? You can decide after hearing the story. I'm still not certain myself on this one.

Indian tribes in Florida date back further than most even realize, into the B.C. time frame. As a matter of fact, on May 5, 2008, one of the national T.V. networks evening news reported that, due to a reduced drought/water table level on Lake Okeechobee, the lake bottom had exposed artifacts of inhabitants dating back to around 6,000 B. C. Up until then, it was believed to be the oldest recovered artifacts, but divers had just recovered (in Northwest Central Florida) an ancient spear that dated back twelve thousand years, or around 10,000 B.C. Found in a freshwater pool spring, it was well-preserved due to mineral and lower oxygen content of the water (It also correlates Native American presence during the time of the lost continent of Atlantis!).

Here on the Southeast coast, the 6,000 B.C. timeframe was clearly established, and thus Indian burial sites existence, as well. In other chapters, I re-examine a particular roadway (State Road 809) that, when widened, had disturbed several ancient Indian burial sites. Even sightings of Indian ghosts had been reported. Since I do come back to this subject (Psychic section, Chapter 17) later, I will limit my comment here to saying, on two separate occasions, my windshield wiper electrical connection may have had a ghost siphoning off the current. No way of proving it, but the next day after the first time, they worked fine. Two months go by, they work fine, and then on that roadway again, it starts to rain, and once again they don't work, but since then they have worked fine! An Indian windshield wiper ghost? Chief Pesumpsud from the Twilight Zone, my old fishing guide buddy from over there playing pranks on me (A fictitious character I made up to give this ghost a name.)? You'll encounter *Pesu* again in the Psychic section, admittedly a bit tongue in cheek. There is little fiction in this entire book, so when I introduce any you need to take seriously. Although it is pretty apparent and transparent where it is used, at times I will so note it (I've made a reasonably successful effort in preventing a book containing factual content from being a dry read, something most will appreciate.).

Waking dreams, also referred to as hypnopompic imagery, offer another experience I can relate to first-hand. One morning, upon just opening my eyes, in the flash of a split second, I saw four, young (middle age) ladies, shoulder to shoulder, (in miniature about two inches wide and eight or nine inches tall) at the foot of and to the right of my bed. They were dressed in business dressy, but casual, attire, like four ladies might be on a break in a large office building might look. I started to say, *Good morning ladies*, but before I could even begin to speak they had already vanished. Ghosts? Angels? I think angel is more likely, as four is a number associative to angels (This was about nine or ten months prior to the four overhead orbs of white light seen February 2009). Regardless of how much validity someone else might place in these waking dreams, I did see this image, and I am not one prone to such, and in fact can't ever remember having had one such episode before. Certainly in another dimension, but there in my opinion, regardless! Apparently it was a heavier security detail assigned to the author, in stealth, or at least a possibility of a squad of angels (great protection). Did my guardian angel call for back up?

In the ghost realm, or at least other dimension, there is a whole assortment of wee folk, or little people; all are a varied size of miniature. Stories and legends of dwarfs, leprechauns, gnomes, pixies, elves, little gentry, trolls, hobbit, fairies, munchkins, and more. Nobody ever said other dimensions have to scale the same as ours, and apparently some don't. If you watch a small screen T.V., a person you know in reality is a full adult size, but on the screen, it is on a miniature scale. It might be something similar; an illusion of scale perception, the explanation.

Previously I mentioned that most ghosts make their presence known as being harmless; they are, in some way, connected to the particular site. However, this is not always so. In the Metaphysical section more is said about what could be described as two orders, levels, or planes, as you might wish to categorize them. The higher spiritual order is the one you could call the Christian/angelic order. Beneath is an Earthbound realm (within the spiritual dimension) of non-living human spirits. Therein lay deceased animal spirits, non-living human spirits (ghosts), never-lived demon spirits, perhaps even shape-shifting entities, and even E.T. transients. Demons having rankings, it is said, similar to holy angels in terms of rankings and strengths/malevolent capabilities and powers.

Encounters with ghosts can often be innocent, and they seldom escalate to malevolent levels. They, however, you should be aware, are by their very presence creating a doorway or gateway opening between dimensions. This portal can lead to the entrance of other not-so-friendly hostile-to-human spirit entity to enter, once this conduit conductor is created interdimensionally. This lower spirit level is then linked with the dimension of human living. Torment, psychological invasion with attempt at thought control, then leads to possession, destructive purpose, destructive command, all negatively form, and dark spirit focus. In many cases, the original ghost is pushed aside and has nothing to do with what is now taking place, but a dark force spirit instead. Keep in mind, it has been shown that they, too, can also become influenced, manipulated, and controlled, as well, in some instances.

In my view, all sites exhibiting such categorizations, at the first signs of any unfriendly to human activity or presence, should be immediate cleansed through clergy summoning of holy angel to assist in dispelling evil entity; and this process repeated if not first successful. Simply having a ghost presence doesn't mean this is going to be necessary, but the chances of it elevating into a problem at some future point in time is most definitely greater than at a site without ghost presence/portal.

Chapter 5 will pick up again with the discussion of human possession. With other dimensions layered very closely with our own, in your lifetime you have likely passed very close to many of these entities invisible to you without even knowing it. A wispy thin, *Interdimensional* wall is all that was separating you; the human mind a component of the connectivity, even when not engaged in such, since the human mind both in sending and receiving thoughts is our link to the spiritual realm on all levels, good or bad.

I've taken a diagram chart from the Supplement section and moved it up here to give you a sort of organizational layout perspective of how different components of the afterlife might relate compartmentally to each other, but within different dimensions. Do not consider these aspect areas to be all within the same afterlife spirit dimension. It is more likely a different dimension, especially as I've defined lower Earthbound spirit realm and upper holy/angelic kingdom. Clearly the demonic dimension has subway stations within the lower ghostly Earthbound spirit realm, but not penetrating into the holy/angelic realm whatsoever. I originally drew this chart to explain or help some people visualize the rapture pathway as opposed to the normal death entrance into the spiritual dimension. It is based on what is known, and it is certainly not too far off from actuality. The lower Earthbound ghost spirit realm can be thought of as the natural lower order, or metaphysical realm (just different phraseology).

Later when you get to the discussion on rapture, remember this diagram is in the front of the book in case you want to refer back to it. The reason I place it here is because in many religions, paradise and heaven are different words for the same destination. However, only one God and only one faith can be the correct God and faith, and that faith I tell you with total certainty is the Christian faith. You will notice in the chart that the Garden of Righteousness, or Paradise, is lower and separate from heaven. How so you ask? Because it is Bible that mentioned that Christ, upon entrance into the spirit realm, descended into hell to both retrieve and pardon some souls, taking them out of there with him. He also entered this Garden of Righteousness, bringing some souls from there and raising these souls up to heaven with him. This delineates that paradise and the Garden of Righteousness are both separate from heaven and lower in presence, as well. Only the Judeo-Christian model represents this. By knowing the Christian faith is true and correct, I can state to you then that this also must be the correct afterlife description; Paradise then is highly overrated. I will also tell you that the horror and severity of hell is extremely underestimated by most people, and why, sadly, many of them will come to the realization the hard way.

Now how can I tell you with certainty that the Christian faith is, with certainty, true and correct? It is because as a psychic with a lifetime of experience that I credit to the holy angel, foretelling to me future awareness/even fulfillments, that all of this is happening exactly as predicted when the time arrived. What I didn't understand was that I was a Christian psychic in basic training, who one day would receive prophecy on the holy subject rather than general or personal subject related. All of it is important to a book that it, too, predicted I would one day write this book, with God as my contributing and senior editor. You don't believe me? By the time you finish this book, if I were you, I'd start preparing myself to totally believe me. And, while you're at it, just toss out any resistance you have to Christianity being the correct faith. Your author provides the month and the year dating to the entire seven-year Tribulation. It's all there and all provided by the kingdom of heaven source (full details supplied in Part II).

As most know, Yahweh, or Jehovah, the God of the Jewish faith, is one and the same with the Christian Old and New Testament Bible (I recommend using only one standard KJV Bible; not some of the newer translations). As I will discuss later, many of the old testament prophets echo precisely the same second coming of Christ and even mentioned it repeatedly in the New Testament. A good investment is a Bible commentary like the one that I used extensively in the writing of this book. It machetes its way right through those vine-snarled phrasing confusions. Let's see here: The Bible's Old and New Testament prophets in identical speak, and now a twenty-first-century one calling himself the Prophet Wildman; writing a book with direct kingdom of heaven help information-wise, not only confirming these two-thousand-year-old prophecy groups being correct, but also when to expect fulfillment.

Could the Prophet Wildman be a false prophet, some wonder? Not a chance. How can you be sure? Because a false prophet will contradict the statements of the Bible by definition within the Bible. Wildman, in his younger days, earned this nickname several times, and escaped death more than two dozen times, on a couple of occasions likely through divine assistance. God would likely only do that for a true prophet. The pen name is used to direct as much attention to Christ and deflect attention from my personal self. Awareness I've received merely reconfirmed Bible statement and predictions of those prophets, but also now with timing awareness given, and urgently important as they related to the Tribulation period. It's hard to be a false prophet when your message is, *Believe in Jesus, believe in the Bible.* You would have to arrest all Christian clergy guilty if that were the case.

By psychic means, described in Part II (Saints Covenant Prophecy), Wildman will prove the validity of the Christian faith as supreme. How you wish to regard the other religions of the world after that, especially if you are non-Christian, is your choice or decision. In view of the information with which this book will present you, it is my sincere hope that Christians will deepen their faith conviction, and non-Christians will simply decide to change and come out with their hearts and minds in the air in complete surrender to the Lord. He has them surrounded, and you can run, but not hide from God. If you are smart, you won't want to run and hide.

Here I've explained paradise being overrated and mentioned how hell's severity is underestimated. It is too late to change the course then; all over except for the screams. It's inside our planet, just in a different dimension. I will show you a peek at what the *corrections officers* actually look like when you read about extraterrestrials. Wildman is walking the cutting edge of psychic parapsychology, U.F.O.-logy, and theology to bring you that depiction of an angel's rendition of a demon that was contained in a psychic dream sleep vision (in psychic high-megapixel resolution HD quality). Although it was only a fraction of a second glimpse, it was enough. An all-angel-delivered vision is about as reliable as reliable gets. When you couple that with one of my other dream sleep psychic dream messages, it becomes locked in solid certainty. A psychic human named Wildman catching a demon in a snare! Now that's an interesting twist, and it explains why my pen name has just been rocketing up on the demons' Most Dangerous Humans list, and why my house seems to be under *Don't let him out of your sights* U.F.O. watch. It would certainly explain the U.F.O. tailing me in recon as I traveled upstate one morning when it wasn't quite light yet because I decided to get an early start, and why on nights when there are no stars at all in the night sky for ten miles in any directions, I'll have a number of *stars* directly above and in immediate vicinity of my home (what I call the lopsided chocolate chip cookie effect; astronomers take note). More on this in later chapters, but I also know because of this book, God actually does have me under an angelic witness protection program, and I am totally serious on all these points. They definitely know where Wildman lives, in that end unit, writing about end times, and just compromising the demons' top-secret security to shreds! It may sound a little psycho rather than psychic, but Wildman's sanity is all there. If I told you I was on a special ops assignment from God, I hope you would believe that, too, and it doesn't sound so strange when you realize many clergymen make the same claim. I don't see you questioning their sanity, right? If I'm to deliver you the *Interdimensional* New Realities then just accept that God has Wildman on special ops assignment, I'll retrieve that awareness information for you from behind enemy lines, so to speak. I don't see your name moving higher on the demon's Most Dangerous Humans list; well, alright then.

Now getting back to the paradise versus heaven comparison: A righteous, God-fearing person technically cannot be denied a spiritual resting place free from torment if they have lived a life that is deemed worthy of praise and respectable in the eyes of God, even if the person actually incorrectly perceived the true God. The man had, in fact, lived a godly life and did believe in a God Almighty, but for whatever reason had perceptions incorrect in the direction of faith. If paradise, in fact, simply means an afterlife destination for one's spirit that is peaceful, pleasant, and free from torment, then hypothetically righteous persons of any faith might find it their afterlife destination.

A couple of analogies I can use for you would be the garden grounds outside God's mansion as the Bible describes. It is the mansion for those worshiping the sacrificed Jesus Christ made for them personally as their Lord and Savior. Only Christians abide inside this mansion, while others deemed righteous by God who were not Christians take peace and comfort on the garden grounds, which are quite majestically beautiful.

Or you could think of paradise as the mezzanine lobby of a tower inhabiting the Christian righteous. Only Christians can go up the elevator because a redeemed (validated) faith pass is required to do so. Others (non-Christian) must stay on the afterlife ground floor. Still it is far better than going to a place of eternal afterlife where torture and punishment are carried out by demon correction officers, and horrors that defy the imagination are perpetual. Dark and distanced from God for eternity, or being confined to stand inside endless flames of fire in complete surround are hardly the desirable alternative, but the outcome variables are limited, and other than possibly a temporary limbo, you will continue to spiritually exist after death in at least one of those destinations. I will present it to you in several different ways and go to great lengths to convince you on the validity of Christian faith. Yes, the Bible and the clergy express the very same, but I come at this from a totally different witness experience approach. Yet the fact that those conclusions of mine and theirs' being the same, are why you should place additional weight and commitment toward Christian beliefs. Certainty is certainty no matter the subject, and this is re-proven certainty.

Now is the analogy of the paradise garden, and non-Christian righteous not being allowed beyond the ground floor of a building in afterlife in which Christians occupy the penthouse suites is figurative to make the understanding analogy. The living of this dimension have conceptual awareness (hypothetical only), based on what is suspected of being the true picture potentially, but confined to this dimension, none of us will know for sure until we become confined to that dimension.

The Bible speaks of streets of gold in heaven, and structures of the most precious gemstones and crystal are prevalent. Yet it seems many redeemed souls will inhabit Christ's Millennial Reign Kingdom in a completely transformed time/space/matter plane of existence on planet Earth post Armageddon. Even clergy are not all in agreement on this, as if that were anything new; yet others argue if ascending to a plane of spiritual heaven means being in the company of Jesus, then perhaps it is meant heaven itself will have an Earthly branch office, as well as the ethereal other dimensional main office it has now, so to speak.

The Bible makes it clear that the Millennial Reign Temple will descend from heaven for the Throne of Christ's Millennial Reign from the holy land. This is literal, but descriptions of Earth also indicate transformational changes and why possibly the dimensional space/time/matter change is an integral part. In Chapters 26 and 27, as well as the Supplement section discussion, I mention Millennial Reign, but I don't get into extended discussion of it, which is why I'm making some mention here (Part II).

You can point to scriptural evidence to make arguments for several different interpretations, but ultimately no one will know until they are participants what will really transpire then. The greater message is: Don't worry about that stuff, because if you don't focus on yourself within this dimension in the here and now, you may never get to experience the other anyway.

Even though I bring a lot of new and better U.F.O. understanding to the Tribulation awareness situation table, in post-Armageddon my understanding is limited to comments of others. I mention some at the conclusion of Chapter 27, but as if holy angels are only releasing what secrets they have security clearance to do so upon, and non-essential information has not been cleared for release, at least not yet. Perhaps it never will, or some other psychic/prophet might find those missing awareness puzzle pieces included in his awareness portfolio. Wildman receives on a need-to-know basis, with nothing new from the holy angel since 2008/2009.

There are other terms applied to describe the unsaved dead who are yet to receive final judgment. Hollywood has portrayed them at times using the term zombies; the dead who come to life at night to walk together in a trance-like state, with arms outstretched as if sleepwalking, in over-dramatic Hollywood fashion. But is there partial basis of fact involved?

Long before movies, around the world and in places quite distant from each other on different continents, legends, rumors, and mythology believe that when the condition was right (metaphysical/astronomic, etc.), very late at night, and usually unseen to this dimension of the living, the dead, sometimes in large numbers as dark, silhouetted spirits, would walk the Earth. They are referred to as the Legion of the Dead, or the Cadre of the Dead, or labeled as the Army of the Dead (Unsaved), or simply the shadow souls of the unrighteous (shadows of the shamed). Is there any measure of truth to this?

Personally, I think there is. Ghost investigators have numerous, documented accounts of sightings of what are referred to as shadow people, so the existence of such entity then in larger numbers is hardly a very sizeable stretch. Larger numbers of shadow people walking could easily be an interdimensional fact. The condemned, *en masse,* all out for late night walks across an open area.

Consider elsewhere in this book, whenever I seemed to reach an impasse where my contemplative wheels were spinning without gaining forward traction on one subject or another, my subconscious psyche, it seems, at night would go running off like a hunting dog retriever to find the answer. Or perhaps a holy angel would deliver a psychic dream containing the answer sought or hand the answer over to my psyche retriever subconscious brain for a dreamscape message conveyance (as you will read in the Psychic section of other instances). Did it run through briars and brambles to retrieve the answer from some other astral psychic plane, or was retrieval less problematic? I can't be sure.

However, much later in the book and while in deep contemplation (while awake) on the subject of the saved and spiritually righteous, I was led to a dream sleep relative to the unsaved. As if the spirit world was instructing me that the quickest route to understanding of the saved was to envision these unsaved! Yes; picture a large, open field, like something similar to a soccer field; perhaps even more wide open. There were hundreds of ghostly dark silhouettes (souls) of humans non-living, all walking across this field in darkness; they themselves just dark human form silhouettes without features; just dark shadowy ghosts! What I was seeing, no question about it, was this Legion of the Dead in a psychic dream, imparted to me either through my subconscious, or by the holy angel, or both in collaborative endeavor. Not only was there this image, but a sensing of these unsaved, doomed souls having a feeling or an overriding mood of gloom, hollowness, and perhaps all of them fully aware of their personal damnation, being found guilty, yet prior to final judgment condemnation sentencing! Not so different from what Bible scripture denotes, so everything seems consistent.

Did my hunting dog retriever subconscious psyche or holy angel lend an assist toward confirmation? I have to think so, and if I was to name that dog, message retriever Psyche would be a good fit. The Prophet Wildman and his trusty retriever named Psyche seem to fit all the way around. So, I do think Psyche did find that mystical puzzle piece confirmation answer for you. Apparently this inter-dimension, legion of the dead, comprised of shadow people actually does exist!

By the time you read both Part I and Part II of this book (assuming that you do), you'll have had the Bible's connection to the supernatural confirmed to you sixteen ways from Sunday, sixteen more from Monday, and a couple of thousand walking dead confirming it is for you late night Tuesday. It is a statement from a prophet, no less, and don't even get me started on Wednesday or Thursday. Otherwise I'll have your mind running through briars and brambles out of sheer shock and awe, with some prickling all the way down your spine, as well. Reading a book written with the Wildman as your guide, this is just a taste of what lies ahead in this supernatural exploration reading adventure. Aren't you the brave one sitting there on your all-terrain vehicle?

Some people need the Devil frightened out of them first in order to receive Jesus. Finish this entire book, and I'll likely accomplish that first part and cause you to desire hanging on to your faith with both spiritual faith hands tightly to that second part. Jesus is the way, the truth, and the life, both in this life and in afterlife, and the light to cut through spiritual darkness there, as well.

Relative to judgment in the afterlife, opinion/interpretation even among all clergy is inconsistent and variable. The Bible seems to indicate all unredeemed souls both prior to Tribulation and beyond the Rapture occurring during Tribulation must wait the full one thousand years for the final White Throne Judgment scheduled at the end of Millennial Reign. These would be all those unsaved and unredeemed souls we were discussing. Most of the interpretation variable among theologian relates to the aspects of the rapture itself, such as when and how many Rapture point occurrences, or the afterlife current pre-Tribulation mechanisms. It is important to allow all opinion/interpretations to be tolerated, even if it contradicts to that which one personally holds.

In this book I try to explain why I hold to interpretation like I do, but no one is infallible, especially on a subject as intangible as theology. I fully respect the right of anyone to disagree, as long as they respect my right to do the same. The foundation base of all of my explanation of the supernatural is deep-rooted, staunch Christian Bible/Holy Trinity belief, yet I'm sure many who might have alternate viewpoints on nuances or details relative to mechanisms pertaining to afterlife also equally agree; coming off that same foundation cornerstone we both agree is solid and correct spiritual/faith placement.

So, while some might not be in full agreement of my interpretational explanations of mechanisms defined and described, likely they do agree, even if only in principle, that such a legion of the dead/unsaved exists of those people who walked to the beat of a different drummer, except it was the Devil who was drumming. Now the afterlife consequences being despair, regret, heartbreak, hopelessness, un-fulfillment, spiritually missing, a sense of being outcast, aimlessly walking and seeking something lost that can never be found (their soul unbroken), now broken in darkness forever. Does any of this have any attractive appeal? If so, then you've just been diagnosed with Legionnaire's disease (Yeah, better stay off the sport field late at night and get more rest or the Devil might call you up to the majors. Joking)!

When a righteous person dies, even a non-Christian, if you can, envision a sort of afterlife intake center (so to speak) where some initial sorting takes place. Righteous souls are allowed to remain; the non-righteous may not even make it through the door or, if so, shortly instructed that they must return to Earthbound spiritual domain.

The Garden of Righteousness or Paradise is merely pleasant surroundings, and the joy and peace having to do with absence of fear from future punishment or torture in one level of hell or another. It is merely a peaceful limbo state, but definitely not the same as heaven, which is a true spiritual paradise that is much more wonderful, but reserved exclusively for devout/righteous Christians because that is what the Bible says. Now some wonder about Millennial Reign and these righteous. Only God knows who might ascend into heaven from this lower-level Paradise, and who might be reassigned to return to Earth to take part in this new Millennial Reign existence. I do think most pre-existing humans left surviving the full seven years could technically, on paper, carry into this new Kingdom; yet theoretically, more likely, it is a total plane of existence reset intentionally conducted so that a makeover, spiritual righteousness upgrade in caliber of all new humans of the Millennial Reign can occur. Out with the old plane of existence, and in with a one-thousand-year-new one, under Christ's iron rod rule. This is explained more later in the Religion and Supplement section of Part II, but that is what it sounds like is in store. I wouldn't worry about it; cross that spiritual plane of existence when you get there, or if you get there. Wildman is predicting an epidemic worldwide outbreak of Legionnaire's disease between now and then, and walking in darkness for eternity without a flashlight amongst thousands of others is a serious avoidance goal in the interim. I don't know about you, but paradise just has a much more favorable ring to the word accompanying the impression.

Apostle Paul's comments in Corinthians 15:51–52 and in combination with Thessalonians 4:16–17 believe that the dead in Christ shall rise first out of the Earthly ground from graves worldwide, upon Christ's second coming (Part II explains when I believe this event will happen). However, nowhere does it say from the Earth, and thus the raising up of the righteous could just as easily be from such a spiritual limbo/state to an even higher plane, as it could from this Earthly realm as from some cold, damp, dark cemetery. Such a limbo *Interdimensional* state doesn't necessarily have to be far removed from the living dimension we live in, but even in a protective dimension close by. It hardly would seem like Christ would treat his righteous no different than the unsaved, and do so in a prolonged fashion for centuries. While we might be lacking all the details until a better explanation arrives, I like the concept of this spiritual garden of righteousness/limbo state being, perhaps, part way between upper heaven and Earth. It's clearly not the same as the Christian heavenly Kingdom, yet works with the explanation, concept-wise, where it states in Corinthians 15:51–52, the dead will be raised imperishable or in Thessalonians 4:16–17, that the raptured shall meet up with (those righteous dead now raised) will be caught up with them in the clouds to meet the Lord in the air. Now I'm not trying to say that such is not definitely so, all I'm trying to say is that it should not be assumed that these righteous already dead in Christ spirits did not enter such an intermediate spiritual state even prior.

If theologians can't disprove my point, maybe they should at least consider it a valid argument, especially where I'm not trying to say it with certainty. Theological dispensation from the Reverend Wildman now, they are saying (joking here). Twilight Zone University doesn't even have a theology/seminary department, except as a figure of speech, speaking credential- wise, they argue. Yes, that only proves I might have been a figure of speech speaking admitted under full scholarship. Why is Wildman so rarely incorrect? They wonder who is this masked Wildman is anyway. Tell 'em Tonto. Tonto isn't sure either, actually, but he can vouch for Kemosabe's expertise on the supernatural subject, especially when it comes to riding off into the sunset!

Readers, please note: Contention among clergy exists over how many Rapture points the Tribulation contains, which is from two usually, although a minority claim one, to three or more, and the timing for the raising of the dead in Christ, usually assigned to just prior to the first or second rapture point.

In both Part I and Part II, I make it known here that your author believes in at least three Raptures, and have a very compelling case to evidencing the dead in Christ being raised at the second rapture point rather than the first, and will occur at the sounding of the seventh Tribulation trumpet (as discussed thoroughly in Part II, but essentially confirmed to me by the Holy Angel!). Pretty compelling confirm!

While the White Thrown Judgement for the Unsaved, and unrighteous, will arrive at the end of Millennial Reign, it must be mentioned as well that the Saved and righteous shall experience a judgement of sorts of their own. Not for meeting out punishment, but rather determining extent of reward for the faithful, deemed deserving. It shall arrive after the end of the "Church Age", but prior to Millennial Reign as to "official start". It is known as the Judgement Seat of Christ, and as referenced in Romans 14: 10-12, as well as I Corinth. 3:13-14, but with ties to Galatians 6:7, Eph. 6:8, and I Samuel 16:7 and elsewhere also.

One's "heart" and one's "works" shall be examined in extent measure of eternal "testing by fire" worthiness, and rewarded accordingly. The Saved faithful believers all Saved by God's Grace alone, yet as exampled here, one's works in service to the Lord do not go unnoticed, unrewarded.

The Jinn

In Arabic the Jinn means *hidden*, and they are also known as beings of smokeless fire. Just as the hierarchy in heaven of holy angels has many rankings and levels, so there is among demonic forces, and stated as such in the Bible. Native Americans describe them as tricksters. They seem to be in the lower and intermediate range (what you might call the lesser demons), but that's roughly the equivalent of saying one poisonous snake is less poisonous than another. If you think of smoke curling up in a tubular shape as it rises from a cigarette (as claimed by a pastor who said he had the ability to see them), it is much the same except invisible to most. Sightless smoke then, perhaps; more definitive than smokeless fire as commonly described.

They enter humans through head cavities (ear, nose, etc.) or in and out of the top of one's head. Have you ever experienced a dream where a group of people in the dream are carrying out, performing, or in some way doing or practicing something that seems like occult, demon favoring summoning, or witchcraft? I noticed once or twice a year I would get one of these unwelcome and uninvited dreams with a slightly different script.

Upon awakening and giving some thought to it, I decided it was some lesser demon, probing for a reaction; placing a dream in front of your subconscious film screen testing for spiritual weakness. I decided the next time it happened I would cast the demon out right then and there in my sleep without even waking up! It worked, and a tingling feeling almost like a mild seizure coursed my spine. The next morning, after getting up, I noticed I felt a vibrant revitalized, healthy energy that seemed to suggest my little in-my-sleep exorcism experiment had actually occurred! Try it yourself, should one of these lesser demons invade your psyche's sleep. Most people uncomfortably try to just ride the dream out until the next morning. Don't allow it! It isn't something you ate; it's an invisible Jinn invading your private mind space. The undesired dream will vanish once the Jinn is cast out. It amazed me, and Wildman is a bronco-riding cowboy at the nightmare rodeo from way back! Guess you can teach an old cowboy a new trick after all.

The problem with people who try to channel spirit entities is that they can easily dial into the wrong channel and unwittingly summon the Jinn, who will masquerade as whoever it is you want them to be. This is why I am a psychic who avoids reaching, since you can't always be sure of the source with which you are dealing.

Even in some cases where I feel pretty certain of angel involvement, I must have a subjective/objective viewpoint; not assume it. The Bible states that Satan can impersonate or masquerade as an angel of light, so one has to be cautious and be wary. While both the later chapter, Saints Covenant Prophecy, as well as my angel orb episode, could be questioned, I do think both are legitimate. The prophecy is sealed so I don't get accused of being a false prophet; and, if fulfilled, it will clearly serve God's purpose, which is why I think it is authentic. The angel orbs? Same thing. I sense the involvement of good rather than in any way evil perpetuity. It also all ties back to this book, which in turn serves God's purpose, so I'm not too concerned.

The Jinn are said to require a human host to enter our dimension, but can they manifest themselves, some believe, in a variety of forms, such as E.T.s, angels, loved ones departed, or other envisionments (This is why I make it clear to my readers that deceptions, even involving the holy subject, could have been manifested, even though I hope and think not.). There are those who construe the Jinn as looking half-human/half-reptile. My own opinion is that they are describing fallen angels or demons who are higher in rank (the Jinn's supervisors, in other words).

Beasts from the pit: demons, Reptilian E.T.s, and fallen angels, since the very beginning, are all one and the synonymous same entity. That is my take anyway, and I will show you why. For one thing, you can't describe Jinn as being trapped in that dimension like a jeanie in a bottle on one hand, and have Reptilian E.T.s engaging in frequent U.F.O. saucer, free-wheeling saucer flight which my lie detection verifies was witnessed. Yes, both are demonic entities, for certain; splitting hairs in a sense, perhaps. But how do you then square a description of invisible, smokeless beings with half-human/half-reptile, snake-skinned, split-eyed looking person (I never said a word about the tax collector)?

Since the book of Enoch, angels have been described as The Shining Ones and God's Watchers. The Rebel Watchers and the fallen angels (or demons) since those early times are one in the same. What is interesting is that just before God decided to inflict punishment upon the fallen angels, they are accused of having had intercourse with human women and of having delivered knowledge of astrology and astronomy to early civilization (They didn't become demonic E.T.s until later).

So God decided they had to be punished, had sent off his own watchers, including Gabriel, Raphael, and Uriel, to enforce His will, says the Bible. The Rebel Watchers then rounded up and imprisoned close to where they descended on Mt. Hermon. In one version, they are destroyed by fire, brimstone, and naphtha, but then God also decides to cleanse the Earth by a great flood (from which Noah is the only survivor).

From an obscure fragment of ancient text, Rebel Watchers are described as having a visage like a viper, meaning they look identical to Reptilian E.T.s, demons, and beasts (see also the E.T. depiction of Reptilian). So apparently, for whatever reason, they are still presensed. One then asks, if angels and demons never lived, and these E.T.s are really demons, then in a sense aren't they more like demons flying U.F.O.s than E.T.s? A matter of semantics, perhaps. What would we find on their home world (or is this actually their home world), since those other locations haven't exactly been verified?

It is no wonder they tried for so long to keep the deeper meaning of E.T.s and U.F.O.s a secret. As I have personally experienced, and other telepathic psychics have reported, as well, they make every attempt to block a clear view of their Reptilian selves. While not everyone believes in the Men in Black reports, they make perfect sense in this context.

Since they were likely, at one time, more human-looking than a human reptile cross, the transformation in appearance must have come around the period of ancient storied imprisonment and God's punishment, but yet surviving to torment humanity in varied ways today.

The transformation lending credence is that sense to imprisonment/punishment account itself. This, in turn, ties in with the Noah/world flood account, giving it some indirect credibility from unexpected sources, as well. Once God's watchers, then Rebel Watchers who became Rebel Watchers/fallen angels, and then demonic Reptilians/beasts as they remain even today.

In its own alternate way, proof of God's existence, as well, is exactly as ancient texts describe. You don't have enough fingers to count all the many ways this book will prove God's existence. One of God's greatest gifts to man are those good angels that we will explore next.

One last note: With bearing later, shape-shifting abilities are something these demons possess and use; they are usually animal manifestations, and then can simply vanish. The Sasquatch is a real ape, and that wolf is a real wolf. Maybe not!

Holy Angels

Saint Thomas Aquinas listed nine choirs or ranks. They are seraphim, cherubim, thrones, dominions, virtues, powers, principles, archangels, and angels. Paul, in Ephesians 3, uses the terms rulers and authorities to reference angels. Some difference of opinion comes about when the archangel classification is discussed. Many believe Michael to be the only archangel, or restating it, that there is only one archangel: Michael. The other viewpoint doesn't dispute that Michael is the clear leader, but that there are other archangels (plural) under his command, thus saying there are archangels in number, not just (one): Michael. Clearly, either way, Michael is the leader of all angel groups.

The seraphim, cherubim, and thrones are protectors to the throne of God (guardians of the Most High One). Dominions are next in authority to carry out the sovereign bidding of God through distinct domains (Not dissimilar to human organizational processes being departmentally divided).

Rulers are next in line of authority/dignity rank, and they are the enforcers of God's rules to make sure that the rulers are observed by the practice of the other angels. They are Inspectors of the Rules of God.

Authorities function is less certain, but believed to be what you could compare in human corporate terms to *middle management*. They manage the angels of lesser authority.

Somewhere here is a ranking structure of powers, virtues, and principles (not necessarily descending in rank), as perhaps split among their varied functions. Then archangels, and finally angels, who are majority in numbers. Angels are beings separate from humans who have never lived; they are a creation of God.

Numbers ten thousand multiplied by ten thousand or one million, since the beginning, and Colossians 1:16 stated that He is the one who created all things, including the angels. Angels are joyful, and they are exceedingly wise beings who are given the power of discretion.

Throughout history, certain names are prominent as eternal beings appear and reappear over centuries. The familiar names of Michael, Gabriel, Uzziel, Raguel, Camael, Raphael, and Uriel are just a few of them. Other names that are less known also appear. Besides Michael, many of these do not ever seem to reveal their ranking or titled position. In the scriptures, angels generally appear in human form. This statement is according to a description by Biblical appearances, including Jacob, Abraham, Moses, and Joshua. In that context, my own clergy-collared angel, a vision appearing out of thin air, would be consistent.

Coming immediately on the heels of a *yes* answer to a prayer question, that sounded like the deep, booming voice of God crashing down through my ceiling (It's a good thing I have a drywall ceiling and not old-fashioned plaster, or there might have been some on the floor.). It was a voice, not too dissimilar to the jolly green giants, to give you a comparison. Then, just to my left, and about half an arm's length away, an angel, I assume, appeared or represented himself with a clergy collar. He had darkly manicured, slightly curly hair and was in his late thirties or early forties. No wings were seen, so appearing in human form in this case does match these Biblical accounts (More on this again later in this book.)! The vision was a head and upper chest only and life-sized.

My guardian angel is likely different and is the one holding the highlights film reel of his many saves from my many close calls. I can't be sure about the waking dream of the four ladies and, in fact, the subject of both sexes as angels isn't even agreed upon; a bit like the archangel controversy. The four angel orbs, however, I do think likely were, as well. Does everyone have an assigned guardian angel? Likely so, but another questions without certainty. The angel orbs are discussed/accounted later in the book, as well. Furthermore, as you will learn in the Psychic section, I credit the angels as being the intermediaries in all my precognitive—and even intuitive—awareness experiences. So do angels exist? You already have my answer, not to mention the Bible telling you so. It is surprising the number of well-educated individuals who aren't sure, despite what the Bible says. They definitely do exist, evidencing God's existence in the process; a bit like leaves on the ground in autumn, around the base of a tree evidences the tree.

The angel Gabriel not only has ties to early Judeo-Christian accounts but to Islam, as well. In Islam, Iblis (the Devil), the Jinn, and other demons are comparable to the Christian concept of Satan, and fallen angel/demonic accounts. It is in contrast to the Sons of God, the angels, or the holy ones. It seems the angels themselves set about making man in early civilization aware of the nature and order of things in religious context, so as to develop man's understanding toward conditions of existence and the true nature of God. The name Gabriel literally means *Mighty One of God*.

He is distinguished (Daniel 9:21) as one who stands in the very presence of God and can fly very swiftly (Daniel 8:17). It was Gabriel who delivered the message of prophecy to both Daniel and Zechariah, giving wisdom of correct interpretation (Daniel 9:22). The average person without psychic ability likely does often receive angel messaging. But it is done so subtly that they aren't even aware their thoughts have had positive input influence. What I'm trying to say is that not all your inspirations are originated from you, but that is what is intended. Thanks to angels are welcome, but their worship is forbidden. Being helpful to humans is just part of their function.

In the Bible (Hebrews 2:6–8), God made man a little lower than the angels, but in Psalm 8:5 it is indicated that while man was made lower than angels while living, in the afterlife redeemed humans shall be made higher (heaven). In

Corinthians 6:2 it says we shall judge angels; this is further suggestive of this, as well as (the redeemed) the Saints shall judge the world.

Some people have wondered if the Bible includes any examples of angels appearing in female form, says Author Ron Rhodes. He goes on to say that, in reality, the angels are genderless beings. Suggesting that, in many cases, they are messengers and warriors of God. Perhaps these are more male traits, and thus the preferable representative image. Are there no Biblical examples of angels in female form? But does this not preclude automatic deduction (that must be the case), instead, leaving the door on that question still ajar, not concluded? Doing the same and asking the question: Do they all have wings? Certainly many do, but not necessarily all, and in the case of angel sightings, it doesn't mean they necessarily reveal them even if they did. Remember, too, that angels aren't restricted in as much as they have discretionary powers in conducting their business. This could be why genderless angels could choose to reveal themselves as female if they felt that form more appropriate fit to circumstance.

In further examination of my four ladies vision, I did not have the connection to the holy source that I did with the clergy-collared angel, yet I do feel I witnessed four actual female, miniature-sized spirit entities, and not just a mirage or an hallucination. There was just a little too much detail; I even noticed their smiles! Similar to the angel orbs, four is an angelic associative number, and it was as if in military fashion (shoulder to shoulder) they were announcing they were reporting for duty (assigned for my protection).

So then the question is: If not angels, what then? On the subject of redeemed human spirits, there are two schools of thought. One is that redeemed human souls remain in heaven and do not return to Earth in assistance of angels, and ghosts seen are Earthbound spirits only. No ladies auxiliary of redeemed human spirits, in other words, and no male angel assistants, either.

If it were possible, then this removes the gender possibility as a sticking point because redeemed souls could represent themselves in similar fashion as they looked while alive (As mentioned in the Ghost section, most choose to look as they did in middle age or in the prime of their life.). While this is not the majority viewpoint as to whether or not redeemed human souls might actually work in tandem in assisting angels, it has been a theory in existence for several centuries. This then gives the impression of angel helpers being somehow subordinate when, in fact, it may actually be lower-level angels assigned to assist them! There are a lot of possibilities and few certainties, but that pretty well sums up the entire supernatural realm. You get probabilities out of an experience, but definites are few and far between.

Why do I think my four ladies were angels besides the number four? Because it is angels who deliver intuitions and other psychic conveyance. As my initial impression, I had likely seen four female represented angels. Since angels often choose human-looking appearance in which to reveal themselves (but not limited to it), they might have later been the very same four, dancing orbs of white light. It is said we will one day learn in the afterlife all the interaction and influence angels had in our lives. When that time comes for me, I think I'm going have to make myself comfortable because I think that is going to be a long session (My guardian angel alone has more saves than most major league baseball relief pitchers on his highlights film reel.).

So, what spirit form are the four ladies? You are free to draw your own conclusions. Four, miniature angel bodyguards works just fine for me, and the clergy-collared angel could be anything. Did I get a look at the face of Gabriel? I can't say for sure, but perhaps so! If my prophecy vision fulfills as expected, it will prove in retrospect I perhaps did see a famous holy angel. I regard all of it as genuine, including the prayer answer and prophecy. This chapter then will take on special, profound meaning, within a book itself that fulfills destiny!

What convinces me the four ladies were in fact four holy angels? Here are several points to consider:

1. I'm not a person prone to waking dreams in my lifetime; in fact, I can't remember any prior, but if I ever did have any, it was when I was much younger, decades ago, if at all. This episode happened during a time period of other frequently occurring supernatural events, including angel sightings, parapsychic activity (both awake and asleep), not to mention other acts of God occurrences in general, with religious overtone connections.
2. The image lasted perhaps five to seven seconds, rather than just one or two seconds, because after detecting these four ladies in miniature I recall gazing upon them to recognize greater detail. I was able to discern what each was wearing (dressy, but semi-casual office or business attire would be an accurate description); perhaps symbolizing they mean business? Each was dressed separately (non-uniform) and the outfits were all of different heights, although in Lilliputian miniature.
3. They were *at attention* in military fashion, all facing from the right side (foot of my bed) toward my feet, but their heads were all turned toward my head as I opened my eyes. Each of these brunettes was smiling, looking right at my horizontal face, peering back in astonished amazement at their image.
4. I could see background items from my bedroom behind and around them in close proximity; meaning they were sharing reality space within this dimension.

5. I do think either I was viewing two dimensions at once, or that they were within another dimension and sharing visible space within this reality dimension of human existence; human consciousness maintains a basis within (not an illusion; in other words, even if only witnessed briefly).
6. Thus, my level of consciousness may have shut the viewing window as it elevated into a more awake state, rather than the four ladies vanishing on me. Possible they were still there, but I no longer was able to see them standing there, shoulder to shoulder, at attention, even though they were still there in their dimension.
7. When I started to speak the words out loud, *Good morning, ladies*, it may have also been the disappearance trigger. Reading my thoughts, they then knew I'd seen them, and their mission of achieving my awareness of their presence had now been achieved. Four angels God sent for my protection reported for duty. It was very reassuring. Never underestimate four holy women with confident smiles who mean business!
8. The only place in the Bible where potentially, but without certainty, there is mention of holy angels in female form is Zechariah 5: 8–11. Here it mentions two women in metaphor, of sin and wickedness, in ephah (basket), transported out of Israel with them inside, but the basket being removed to be emptied in Babylon, then transported by two winged women (clearly not human) doing the transporting. In essence, this analogy used female angel forms.
9. The *T. Nelson Bible Commentary* (2005 Edition) states: There is no reason why angels could not have the appearance of women, as well as men. Your honor, I believe I truly could be in the protective custody of four female angels (although seen in miniature, all brunettes, and quite pretty); and, whether true or not, I must confess I rather enjoy thinking that I am! Angels being genderless more often do choose male form to reveal themselves (my clergy-collared angel sighting, perhaps Gabriel), but with discretionary powers, even in the case of my orbs of brilliant white light, also four in number. What should be apparent is that they reveal themselves in a variety of forms and in multiple ways (more orbs details later).

Why would the author of a book, a psychic Christian prophet, require protection, you ask? For the same reason U.F.O.-logists who get too close to the truth of demonic E.T. involvement experiencing demonic forces threats to back off or else. Unfortunately, not all of them had angelic protection (not true Christian believers), and some ignored these warnings, only to encounter tragic consequences instead. Thanks, ladies (Philip Imbrogno's book, which I will repeatedly refer you to in this book, is just one source of some excellent examples.)! *Interdimensional Universe*, an absolute must read, complements statements made and opinions given in this book quite often. His book is much better than most realizing, which is why he will receive credit.

Well, what do you know, seven chapters in this book on U.F.O. subjects are, perhaps, the reason for the aforementioned protection. A rare E.T. demon mug shot from this author's dream sleep camera alone is enough to make the demons angry. You will see this depiction later, but these E.T. demons are not very photogenic, and any depiction at all is rare. Aren't you lucky! Although a great deal in this book is fictional sounding, very little is, and I point it out for the sake of humor. There is a later chapter's account of spilling hot Starbucks coffee in the demon's lap, as my sense of humor refuses to let go, but in more general terms it is an explanation as to why protection is required. They know where you live!

The most likely probability is that the four ladies were not the angels themselves, but representative manifestations used to give me awareness of an angelic presence and divine protection, as this is exactly what I sensed at that time. Four ladies standing at attention, shoulder to shoulder, sort of like letting me know they were reporting for duty, but in fact not answering to me, but as always to God. It is likely extra protection for me was required at that time for perhaps much greater threats and dangers exposure, but I was about to be subjected beyond my realization, which came up on God's radar screen for my immediate future. A wild guess from Wildman was the risk of my death being of central concern, stemming from a bounty the Devil recently placed on my head most likely for being a Christian prophet, staunch adversary, Christian witness author, and becoming a real thorn in the side, but, and in the business as a subversive disruptor of the master subversive disruptor, a thorn in God's side. Every demon on this side of the galaxy hopes to cash in on that bounty reward a legitimate potential explanation; in my mind, anyway. A metaphor here, of sorts, that all the demons on this side of the galaxy are no match for just four, angelic women under God's employ and command. It's hard to say, but ladies probably like the concept anyway, regardless!

Clergy likely afforded extra protection at times, perhaps without even being conscious of it. However, clergy who make serious transgressions against God could at some point lose protections unseen, and then leave themselves exposed and vulnerable. Once you fully commit to Christ, there is no turning back without consequence, even deadly ones.

So, although I enjoy thinking of them as being the angels themselves, the likelihood is, the four angels (larger) nearby simply used a pleasant image to reveal their presence and the message to be conveyed; it was an extra security squad protection for a Christian prophet and author. With a bounty on his head for sabotage and espionage, not to mention public disclosure of demonic state secrets, was there not a serious security breach? Probably on the bounty part; definitely culpable for the rest of it.

Angels can be actual representations or manifestation projected images, but by their discretion that is appropriate, according to the holy purpose. They can insert message information to humans so subtly we aren't even aware we did not source these ourselves (always helpful, useful, and benevolent). A medium can sense the holy angel presence occasionally, even when no other sign is obvious; having done so myself multiple times through life.

One thing that needs to be pointed out is that many feel that guardian angels and spirit guides are one in the same entity (including myself), but not all psychics and experts agree on this point. One clairvoyant/psychic author who works in the field of psychology, healings, and therapy wrote a book on angels and describes spirit guides as the deceased spirit of a family member, distinctly separate from angels (no response was made in my attempt at contacting her through her publisher). Whether combined or distinctly separate, they are helpful, benevolent, and protective of us living humans, so it's perhaps not a major issue, but one I wanted you to understand in this regard. In reviewing this other author's book, I was in agreement pretty much everywhere else and found her description relative to angel telepathic interactions consistently accurate with my own; and her book, in general, credible. To make comparatives to my own experiences was my goal objective in reading her book. Clearly she, too, correctly sees the Christian holy trinity model as what is, in fact, the spiritual hierarchy behind the holy angel.

By the end of this book, *New Realities*, I've investigated, examined, revealed, exposed, cross-reviewed, and dissected the supernatural spiritual realm to such depth and completeness that even the leaders of other non-Christian faiths will concede they've been struck a deep wound that undermines their own religion's validity and credibility to such an extent that it will never be the same again! I also hope they realize it is not done in disrespectful disregard for them in a hostile way, or for those people now practicing these other faiths, but rather in a manner of unity and friendship with people of other faiths. I'm demolishing the structural support columns of these other belief systems' spiritual ideology, and making sure every one of the people is out of the way of the building before it collapses, rather than having no disregard whether or not I bring this building (credibility) crashing right down on their heads because that is the Christian way. That is the spirit of soul-winning Christian Evangelism. By being in a position to provide spiritual truth so profound through direct act of God connections (charge wires and detonation caps), hopefully leaders of these other ideologies will be thankful, rather than angry that the Prophet Wildman led them safely away from these buildings of false sanctuary before the Tribulation arrived.

Christians need to be exceptionally warm and friendly and welcome to all people by encouraging them to become Christians and not acting like the Christian faith is an exclusive club for members only, requiring that all people desiring to join first be nominated for membership or something!

Just as guardian angels and spirit guide aspects are seeking the best outcome for their assigned living human, then so a prophet carrying out the will of God is in essence an extension of that angel purpose that reaches into the realm of the living. When God's purpose in the larger sense extends beyond individuals to all humanity, as it does here in this book and relative to the Tribulation (discussed in detail later in this book in Part II), then similar to the biblical prophets of old it becomes more expediently efficient to enlist the help of a psychic or prophet where the awareness task at hand needs to reach masses of humanity rather than individuals.

People of other faiths should recognize that the Christian God is a God of love and forgiveness, who demands worship and respect for his all-powerful nature. The timing of the awareness that came to me relative to the Tribulation in 2008, other than the specific message delivered to me, are directed toward just two groups. To Christians, he is saying, *Ready and prepare yourselves*. To all others not of Christian faith, he is proclaiming to them that a line in the sand is about to be drawn. Non-Christians, after reading my book, should then take stock of their own spiritual beliefs. Being on the wrong side of that line in the sand that is being drawn by God, as if to say, *I don't know how much more or what more can be provided that hasn't already been provided to bring you to acceptance of faith in Jesus Christ as your one and only spiritual salvation Savior of humanity in afterlife eternal outcome*. You must truly believe in order to truly receive.

Having been the prophet to receive this awareness, it is also my responsibility to fully explain them and then provide encouragement to all in acceptance of them. Christians need to strengthen their resolve in their faith, while non-Christians need to come to the Christian faith in full acceptance, even if they have to do it crawling on all fours to get there. In the brave new spiritual world their doubts try to prevent them from delivering themselves to that threshold doorway. I'm saying that, through this book, it is also my responsibility to assure all who reach that door that, to reassure them, it is both necessary and correct for their best possible spiritual outcome to pass through and enter. Salvation is not certain, yet if belief becomes deep and genuine, salvation does become certainty through faith. A prophet experiences God in some of the most incredible and profound ways a human is able to, and so what this book attempts to accomplish is to let all people of the world know of this coming, this line in the sand, and to side with God.

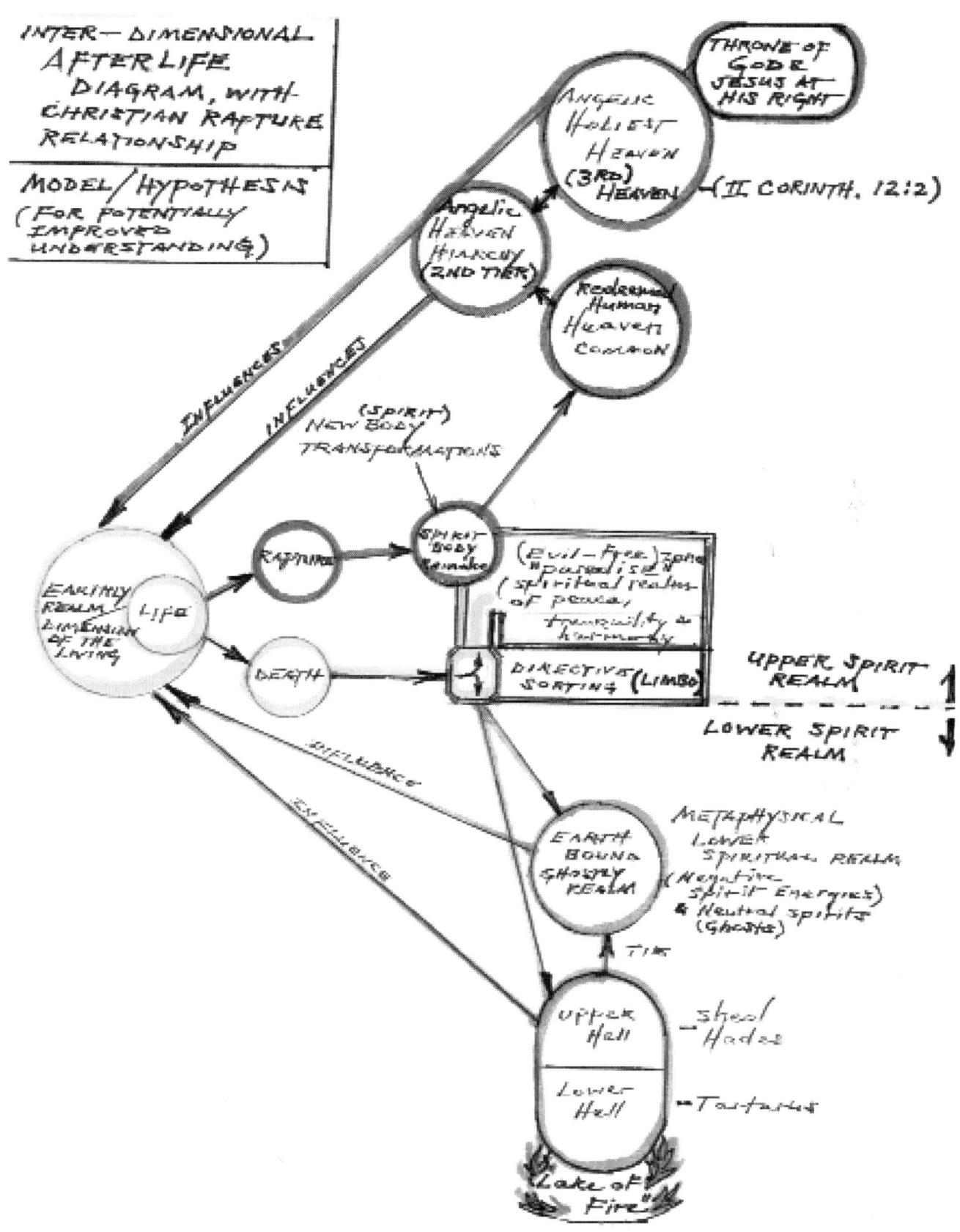

Chapter 3
Monsters

Small children often refer to and identify with anything when they become spooked by, as a monster. At the same time it is now known that there really is such a thing as shadow people, along with garden-variety ghosts. Because they are invisible, most adults are little aware of how common minor or lesser demons are, which are also referred to as the Jinn. In all, at least in some cases what small children see or sense can be quite actual.

Children often create imaginative monsters as justification for their fears, or non-certainty over what they are sensing; it can be simply hyper reaction and nothing more. Yet, in some cases, there is true justification, with parents often only having what a child tells them to go on. While most ghost spirits are harmless, especially to children, sometimes the child is the only one to have capability to see them. In most cases children have nothing to fear.

Going back into history, even adults did the same thing when something supernatural in nature or origin was perceived. A tale would be created to explain it, eventually turning into legends and mythology. It was explained a certain way with no evidence to confirm it, but a tale told repetitively eventually took on a level of truth. Land monsters and sea monsters were then sighted with legends preceding them. Werewolves, vampires, dragons, and more were legitimized. Was Moby Dick, the giant octopus, an enormous sea serpent, and other accounts all myth? Most would say yes, but at least, in some rare instances, even perhaps in a different era in time, some of this was actually observed! Which ones and when are impossible to say, but when I get to my category differentiations, you will see some of these could fit even in today's world. In fact, the last thirty years has seen some rather remarkable reports along these lines. There are too many, in too many geographically diverse places, to simply be dismissed as myth. You then realize if such could be true in these terms, it could have certainly been true in centuries past.

Science has only started to realize and take seriously what might be described as *Interdimensional* Transfer abilities among entities. The hosts and several monster categories I will get to, as well as E.T., angels, and all diplomats with immunity disappearance/appearance rights and capabilities.

Perhaps the best example in the monster category is Bigfoot. As humans we would probably prefer to believe it to be just a rare and oversized member of the ape family. A leftover from a more ancient time, and it's certainly not impossible that in at least a few cases, in very remote regions, that isn't true. There have been numerous sightings worldwide, and real footprint tracks have been found. Yet this giant, five-hundred to nine-hundred pound, seven-foot to ten-foot creature has never died or left behind a skeleton carcass. There are no buried remains of such, either, but why? The reason can only mean one thing: They are inter-dimensional.

Worldwide, the tall, hairy ape goes by an assortment of names, and here are some collected from several sources:

Northwest U.S.A. and Canada: Heyakehute or Sasquatch
New York State: Ape Man, Hairy Man, Bigfoot
Ohio: Grassman
Louisiana: Swamp Monster (Honey Island)
Florida: Skunk Ape
Australia: Yowie
Mongolia: Almas
Venezuela, Columbia: Mono Grande
China: Wildman
Indonesia: Orange-Pendak
Himalaya Mountains: Yeti, Abominable Snowman

This isn't even a complete listing, but it gives some idea as to the worldwide distribution of sightings. Yet, as previously stated, there are no fossilized remains, skeletons, or carcasses recovered. Sightings are almost exclusively adults, and why has one never been shot and killed? Sometimes they are seen eating berries or vegetation, and they often leave footprints, but they also often vanish just as mysteriously as their arrival. They do exhibit typical ape behavior in remote wilderness areas, but here are two case examples to further suspicions:

1. In the 1972 reported sighting case in Indiana, an ape ran from a farmer and, upon passing over ground soft enough to leave a track from such a heavy ape, left none. The ape then, in an open area, simply transitioned *Interdimensionally* and then vanished in thin air! It would run and jump, but somehow wasn't touching anything, and when it moved through weeds you couldn't hear any rustling sound, said the farmer. It seemed like you could look right through it.
2. In another case, a farmer who was losing numerous chickens, shot at it at close range with a shotgun (one hundred feet), but the hairy biped was not affected. It seemed the bullets passed right through it (In August of that year, there were more than forty sightings.).
3. In 1973 there was an incident where a Pennsylvania State trooper was summoned because both a burn circle on the ground (U.F.O. landing site) and several hairy, ape-like creatures were seen by three, young adults. One of the witnesses claimed to have fired a rifle at one of the apes just before the apes ran into the woods (no ape body was recovered).

Other accounts of hairy biped sightings, not to mention a whole gamut of strange creatures, weird flying humanoid, evil-looking entities, such as Springheel Jack, the Dover Demon, Ohio's Loveland Frogs (1952, 1972 reports) in the Miami River area, and the Jersey Devil can be found in *Unexplained* by Jerome Clark, an ideal source of reference for all sorts of entity phenomena that includes greater detail of the cases I summarized for you on Bigfoot. My conclusion on Bigfoot is that it not only definitely appears to be multi-dimensional, but the U.F.O./E.T. link is seen as related, too.

There is no correct category definition because it varies widely by personal discrepancy of opinion. The scientific category is the most conservative because it deals with a *proof first* approach. My view is much more liberal here since *Interdimensional* beings are in no mood to cooperate with scientists anytime soon, so it appears. So my classifications are on the controversial side, I admit, and my terminology is less formal and more casual (Maybe that's why the paranormal transacts its parapsychic business with me because there's nothing conventional about them, either!).

Monstrosities are categorized, so let's start with what I call throwbacks. Scientists commonly call these crypto, cryptids, cryptozoids, and cryptozoologicals. For example, if you think of the Lockness Monster, Nessie, the Lake Champlain Champ (a plesiosaur), British Columbia's Ogo-Pogo of Lake Okanagon (a zeuglodon), or a sea serpent (an enaliosaur), these would all be cryptozoids if shown to be scientifically factual. These throwbacks are only cryptozoids in theory. Until then, they are essentially creatures who definitely once lived, but may or may not still have surviving members.

A 1977 Japanese fishing boat allegedly caught a sea specimen of a dead plesiosaur off the coast of New Zealand. Color photos were taken, but the carcass was then dumped overboard so as not to contaminate the catch. It was determined the animal was neither a known mammal or fish, clearly evidencing that prehistoric animals can potentially still be found to exist.

From time to time, large, winged birds have been reported. Raptors, terratorns, pterosaurs, Indian thunderbirds, and giant condors sometimes are still claimed to have been seen; even occasionally from the air by pilots of light aircraft. Possible? Sure, all of these cryptids are at least possible, just not certain without strong evidence, and that's the problem. Cryptids are kind of old, and they don't get out much (just joking). They still habitat remote regions that are little explored, so while we seek evidence, the possibility is open.

My next category is giants. If they exist, we already know the common size of a particular species. But these are super-sized and rare. Squid or octopus, certain fish, birds, spiders (trachnids), and others fit this category (they are often found in remote regions).

Then comes a larger heading, under which I place a sub-category. I call these N.O.T.E. (Not of this Earth) Entities. Here you have to be open-minded enough to accept that not all answers are necessarily found in science (similar to Bigfoot), but in the spirit/supernatural realm. That includes religion, that even theologians concede to one-third of the share of hostile-to-human, dark-side, evil entities. The troublemakers! Quirks and anomalies of nature beyond human comprehension own a slice, and the holy Entity is the majority, thank God! So you have good, evil, and neutral forces at work, in varied degrees or shading.

Sub category: (of N.O.T.E. Entity):

(A) Demonic Rares – (C.F.H.s) Creatures from hell
Examples:

Dover Demon – (Massachusetts)
Jersey Devil
Wisconsin Dogman – (wolf legend, also possible)

    (B) Various shapeshifters – (this itself is generally a demonic sign as to origin orientation)

This group can include big cats and wolves, and often a telltale sign is that they only drink blood rather than eat their kill as a normal predator of the species would be expected to do. Another non-native vampire, the Chupacabra

    (C) Ultra or Extraterrestrial (suspected or related):

This category is very similar to the above, but potentially more weird than hostile to humans; perhaps with less killer instincts, but still certainly dangerous. (also demonic)

Examples:
Bigfoot
Reptoids
Ohio Loveland Frogs
Mothman
Owlman (It isn't clear if these should be in category A or B) and another reported worldwide demonic, flying humanoid

    Yes, categories A and B are a bit of hair splitting since the ET groups associative are demonically oriented also. Here I'm just attempting to form subcategories, those with possible E.T. links, and those N.O.T.E. entities who to date do not. The West Virginia Flatwoods Monster is noticeably absent because it may actually be a cousin of the Reptilian group of E.T.s, but of lime green color instead of beige/orange. They are very, very similar in appearance. So much so it makes classification hard. An E.T. or demonic N.O.T.E. entity? With all of the demonic entities who are, in most cases, shapeshifters and have the ability to move *Interdimensionally*, it's really easy for the classification lines to blur.

    What is interesting about Mothman is the *omen of death* aspect. In reading concepts and accounts surrounding the Jinn, it is said not a lot of them have the same level of hostility to human demeanor dispositions, and perhaps something of that is true here. Realize that God can't send a holy angel to represent something like this, and any act of omen mercy is not likely attributable to evil forces, even though the entity itself might have flown out of an evil dimension. I see this more as an act than derived from holy side sources (direct order directive). While it may not have saved any lives at Point Pleasant, the new sightings offer real opportunity. The appearance of Mothman should not be interpreted necessarily as a bridge location, but the greater location and the greater locale, in general. Bridges make a nice perch, but the forewarning tragic loss of human life death omen we now understand is the message being conveyed.

    Examining Chronicles 10:15, the devils mentioned here in Biblical times translated Satyrs, and this often means part-human, part-animal (as with the Reptilian E.T.s). But commentary in the *Nelson Bible Commentary* mentions, on page 419, hairy-like animal demons. Are sasquatch characteristics and descriptions a match? Are demon phyla/species the same as satyr-class demon or species like Sasquatch? A little Biblical biology mix?

    What about sightings and footprint tracks? They are always seen worldwide for short and limited timeframes, and it may be possible that, materializing in this dimension, they achieve corresponding weight that enables deep, large footprints. But existence in this dimension is never sustained very long. Native American and North American tribes, and other more ancient peoples, knew these were supernatural realm beings rather than natural realm animals, and they were aware of trickster, shapeshifting abilities, too. Devil entities were seen in the wilderness, even during the time of Christ. Demons by a different name are demons just the same.

Mythologicals

A cryptozoological would be an actual species of this Earth found still to exist. My third N.O.T.E. category would be an *Interdimensional* version. A flying dragon, perhaps, if you saw (similar to Bigfoot) an apparently real pterosaurus (flying reptile) in the Mesozoic period, but in flight it suddenly vanished if made out of smoke. Again, an *Interdimensional* being, but a crypto one! Perhaps this is where Bigfoot belongs in this category. For now, because of a possible E.T. link, he's listed under the B category. The pterodactyl during the Jurassic period is another possibility. During the Tribulation period, as discussed in later chapters (let's all hope not), some of these creatures will once again be seen, but in *Interdimensional* demonic duplicate form. With the lid of hell and the abyss rolled back, there's no telling what might fly out! As you will also read later, that day could be closer than you think (This book is giving ample warning.).

Now I am aware not everyone will agree with my assessment, and they are just as entitled to their own opinion. Sharing differences of opinion stimulates thinking and analysis, sometimes causing people to reevaluate their own line of thought. It's healthy, free, and can only be constructive.

Something else that is worthy of mention, but not that surprising, was when I did a charting of monster reports that occurred according to months, and an almost-perfect bell curve was formed. During the summer months, when humans spend more time in wilderness areas and creatures migrate in search for food, the charting indicated exactly that. From mid-May until mid-October, peaking during July and August, and then gradually declining in September, over 80 percent of all monster sightings are reported on a worldwide basis and going back over a century. Places where the summer months were adjusted, such as South America and Australia, summer is definitely monster-sighting season (human-sighting season for them).

Native American Indians understood subtle differences in nature, and they knew when the spirit world was delivering a message, just as I differentiate a psychic dream from a regular one. Their cultural heritage was very rich in keenness of interpretation, and they had a deeper knowledge and of the mechanisms by which elements of the Supernatural work. It has been retained in their tradition, but lost in the modern era. Cosmic understanding is more advanced than most realize.

Getting back to the discussion of Bigfoot: Did not enough conclusive evidence exist to make a claim with certainty in any theory line direction? Later in this book I mention something I dubbed as Isotope 6 material.

This is based on U.F.O.-delivered particle beams (from demonic E.T. sources). Without getting into all the details here (that will later be fully described), I'm referring to material that looks solid, heavy, and having both form and texture, as well as coloration, but is both visible and invisible in this dimension. I was able to walk around it and from all angles and side directions, and I saw the identical thing. It was something that had this description, yet was both visible and invisible. Further, I could control the appearance and disappearance simply by eye focus (the same from all sides and angles)! It was only there with undivided focus, but if you tried to split focus between something in this dimension and it (from another dimension?) it vanished in thin air, only to reappear as long as complete focus was given! While I can't state direct correlation to Bigfoot, it could be an investigative clue for comparative purpose in the future.

Some think these giant, ape-like creatures, possible giantipithicus remnants of the past, actually exist because of tracks. However, these tracks are often, when examined by experts, revealed to be a distorted bear or some other known species track (Bears can walk short distance; they are bi-pedals.). Seldom is there both a sighting and tracks. There are sightings, and there are tracks (authenticity inconclusive), but rarely are there sightings with tracks. Why?

I think there is a good chance these are actually *Interdimensional* creatures, and that should remain a viable possibility until shown otherwise. They come out of another dimension just as ghosts and angels to reveal their presence and then return. Perhaps if the process of materializing in this dimension continues beyond a certain threshold, they actually can then leave a foot imprint in damp sand or soil belonging to a six-hundred to eight-hundred-pound, ape-like being. The point is, they don't seem to remain for prolonged periods in this dimension, and yet potentially they have the ability to de-materialize, as well (Something that U.F.O.'s seem to be able to do.).

For more on the *Interdimensional* topic, once again I direct you to Philip Imbrogno's *Interdimensional Universe* (as I will do many times throughout this book). He likely will not get the recognition he justly deserves for his accomplishment that his book makes in the endeavor to get at the truth and get answers, but it takes someone like myself who has had similar types of experiences to fully appreciate the contribution to investigating these phenomena that Phil has made. A scientist who is saying he followed the trail until it led into the spiritual realm and could follow it no further, is huge in and of itself, wouldn't you agree? If you can't say for certain you agree, then read his book, and then you will understand what I mean. Regardless, read this book! In some ways, I've tried to pick up that same trail in this book where he left off and, in places (many places, actually), his findings and mine are in total agreement. His arrived at thorough scientific case study investigations, and I through psychic occurrence, which he notes often does play an involvement role. So on the subject of Bigfoot, both Phil and I are telling you that this very likely is an interdimensionial being. Like the

Isotope 6 particle beam material I witnessed, perhaps it is in a transitional state between dimensions. An ape-like creature could then appear solid without being solid at all, and this conforms to some eyewitness accounts already given in this chapter. While the demonic realm is known to possess shape-shifting capabilities, the origin or aspect can neither be confirmed nor denied relevant to Bigfoot, but the one eyewitness account did show U.F.O. correlation in the Pennsylvania case. We are closer to the truth, just not fully there yet.

There is one more disturbing note to bring you, as if this book isn't already well over the shock and awe weight limit in bulk. Later chapters will give you details of the Tribulation's seven-year collection of horrors (Part II). Not to leave any stone unturned, while we are still in this chapter I should point out that in a number of cities, because of widespread destruction, you can expect dangerous wild animals to escape; humans can then, in some circumstances, suddenly be attacked as prey. I did read one psychic clairvoyant's prediction of eventual human cannibalism, and underground shelter was advised in the Supplement section and not excluded this avoidance either (above ground was too dangerous). Animals escaped from the city zoos, while humans turned into wild animals, acting like they belonged in one!

The point that I'm getting to is that people not raptured can expect all the demonic Rares to come out of hiding in the late 2024 to 2026 period; deciding they, too, have been released to do so, and perhaps in much greater frequency! This is no certainty, but if anyone is unfortunate enough to still be scavenging around for food at night, struggling with survival, there may be supernatural unholy entities, as well as those natural wild animals in nocturnal hunting mode that view humans as food!

You will need to read Part II of my book, which provides complete timing and even breakdown forecasts for all major Tribulation events! Exactly how many other dimensional entities will be allowed to jailbreak into this dimension is not known (if at all), but entities that are already here and sighted worldwide on a regular basis. Perhaps the Bible's description of increased Earthquakes and geological upheavals immediately before, and leading up to, the Tribulation, like the birth pains of a woman in labor, might also apply to other dimensional entity. Also, suddenly one day, all crashing into this dimension to hunter/gatherers scavenging for food and sustenance in some locations, then only to find the wilderness areas of the world with other worldly hostile-to-human entities that reveal their presence with uncommon frequency. This is conjecture speculation, nothing more, but the Tribulation will earn its name, and this could be one of those hidden, yet-to-be-revealed, nasty surprises among others to look out for. In other words, don't assume conditions will necessarily continue to be the same in other dimensional realms where all the wood-knocker, go-bump-in-the-night, shape-shifting demons reside. It well could be ultra-high-definition Halloween all the time, every night, fright night! Run, Charlie Brown, run!

You know, people who didn't rapture would now be tracked and hunted down by all the demons of the world, like as if the humans were the jail breakers in this picture. Is that coyote howling really a coyote? Maybe so, but in the Tribulation timeframe, especially in more remote regions, I promise, at the very least, people's nerves will be very frayed, and knowing that they are living through the seven-year Tribulation, when many others succeeded in escaping through the Christian rapture, they will live aware that there is much more going on in the spirit realm, both good and evil, that is beyond their awareness, beyond their control, and most unsettling. The very passing of time will often seem to have slowed, and people will be under extreme assault upon their mental faculty to keep their wits, and mind braced against fear, and panic, and the challenge of not unraveling under so many pressures their minds are unaccustomed to dealing with on a continuous basis. Once a person's mind begins to slip, they simply succumb, no longer able to mount resistance or even function for their own extended survival. Strong faith is the antidote, but those people by now have departed in rapture. Clearly people without faith in Christ, and then under demon attack, both visible and invisible, will be driven madly insane. Tribulation insanities are the silent killer. Insanity before death, and perhaps insane in the afterlife, too.

There are some people who think that because Sasquatch are, on occasion, picked up on thermal imagining cameras that this suggests a warm-blooded mammalian gorilla-like entity, but not necessarily so. Similar to the large footprint left behind, even not necessarily so. It doesn't explain why sometimes when a large footprint should have been left behind it wasn't. As for the thermal imaging, even ghostly spirit entities, also other dimensional, clearly register both hot and cold heat signatures in various location. Thermal imaging heat signature proves nothing other than the location of an entity presenting itself, and nothing really more. U.F.O.s seems to seek EMP energy that is naturally occurring from our planet's core and then reside up and outward into the Earth's atmosphere, toward space. Ghosts are known to drain batteries. Clearly a spirit energy seeks electromagnetic energy, be it neutral, or demonic. Holy entities have their own holy energy from God in abundant and unlimited supply, and require no battery charge, so to speak; just the way God designed his system in order to keep upper-hand superiority advantages. Can you blame him? Only the Devil mutters about that.

The point being—assuming these are ultraterrestrial entities, affiliate demonic manifestations, which I feel certain they are—they likely draw energy naturally occurring. A Sasquatch out for a stroll is likely seeking energy recharge. Otherwise, he goes invisible; no footprints. Fully charged, then walking through moist ground, and footprints are left behind. But I shouldn't tell you that because T.V. networks are left behind. But I shouldn't tell you that, either, because T.V. networks rake in enormous commercial advertising revenues keeping the Sasquatch mystery alive! It is the demon manifestation of an ape! There, I ruined the ending, and the T.V. networks will go right on as if my explanation never happened. It's a lot more fun thinking a real, undiscovered member of the ape family is still a genuine ape. Track the mall Santa Claus to his car, and he'll leave footprints in the mud or in the sleigh, too, but it doesn't make him really Santa Claus!

When ghost hunters coax words from intelligent spirit ghosts, it's never lengthy. A word or two; no sentences or paragraphs. Energy is the reason (or lack thereof), when it is available to expend. Physical acts, a demon pushing, scratching, biting, or shoving a living human is a clear sign of a more powerful demon entity, usually associative to hauntings and an open spiritual portal into demonic dimensions. The Sasquatch entity, in cross-reference energy comparison, would not be a lesser demon spirit, but a much stronger one manifested in ape-like form. Remember, not all entities in the ghostly spirit realm are demons, and many are what could be described as non-harmful or neutral. However, just as the Reptilian E.T. demons are about the same (seven-and-a-half-foot height), this being a match for these Sasquatch creature suggests this demon theory of shape-shifted manifestation is correct. I believe it is exactly so, and their temperament toward humans seems to suggest so, as well.

Why move into this dimension, and how? The *how* part is unclear, but perhaps riding dark energy (see the chapter on Leys) could be one explanation. Riding energy up from the Earth's core to the Earth's surface, then manifesting as an ape, is not unreasonable. The *why* part has to do with the similarity to the jeanie in a bottle story. All the demon entities of the dead would much prefer to be let out of the bottle, so to speak, and spend time among the living. The veils between the dimensions are actually all around us, and wispy thin (You'll read about my metaphorical supernatural building, side door break-ins, looking for answers back in my college days, both in the U.S. and in London, studying abroad a little later on.)! Probably the most incredible aspect is many of those highly classified files containing answers I was seeking back then became available once I began writing this book, and I could not be more serious. It was like the supernatural world coming to me and saying, *You remember those supernatural files containing answers that you were looking for back in 1968 and 1969? Well, here they are!* That doesn't mean I have all supernatural secrets in total—far from it—but whether you want to call it act of God episodes, paranormal/parapsychic supernatural activities, or both, it was like suddenly holy angels were helping me with gathering supernatural information. Talk about high-level security clearance access to restricted information! The angels were even informing me, forty-four years in advance of this book's writing, that I would, and then teaching and instructing me through my mid-life years are all very incredible, but incredibly true.

Now remember, evidences on most supernatural stuff is scarce, but all I'm trying to do with my opinions, perspectives, and hypotheses is give others a reasonable comparative model. Little is proven, or likely with time remaining ever will be, but still I'm sure my contributions will assist with further understandings.

Remember that no skeleton, anywhere, ever, over centuries, has ever been uncovered. That is because of their true (nonliving) manifestation nature. I truly believe they are interdimensional shapeshifters. A shapeshifter, as far as we now know, is always of the demonic realm.

What I am suggesting is that the Flatwoods, West Virginia, monster seen as a lime green, seven-and-a-half-foot-tall Reptilian E.T. could just as easily, in shape-shifted form, take on Sasquatch's visual appearance identity. Both are known for brimstone, rotten egg, sulfurous smell, as well! The elevator up from hell that brought them to the Earth's surface is potentially known as a dark ley. I don't know that for sure, but my observations of this overall situation suggests this is one reasonable possibility. A demon by any name is a demon all the same, regardless of external appearances. Normal animals sometimes do exhibit ghosts, and they would be neutral spirit entities. They lived and then died. Demons never live, nor do they die; they merely seek to cause humans misery and death. Humans have souls, as well as spirit identities, whereas that animal as a ghost is merely a spirit entity. Believe Christians are the only ones who can receive salvation for their souls, thus attain heaven if God so wills it. Other people, as covered in Part II of my book, who practice any religion not following the Holy Bible (word of God) in similar exactness to K.J. version are practicing false religious beliefs, incomplete religious beliefs, flawed and invalid religious beliefs, or just plain cults, which are completely bogus. When people read Part II of my book, I think it pretty well bankrupts all other religious philosophies beyond Christian fundamentalism practiced by the majority of Christians. Not just rhetoric either; cold, hard evidence, prosecution case, strong enough to make even the Devil sweat! Part II of my book is certain to become a classic favorite among theologians, potentially at least.

When you read about my sighting of the act of God arranged, so it appears, Book of Revelation's scorpion-like stinger tail /U.F.O.-delivered particle beam, and what I dubbed Isotope six material, looks very solid, even at close range, yet is visible/invisible at the same time. You recognize a possible mechanism linkage here to demonic entity shapeshifter capabilities. Dracula himself might not be real, but that demonic visible/invisible Isotope 6 capability I saw firsthand is very much real. Is it shifting between dimensions, or is there that capacity/nature to it within this dimension? You see how it brings us a step closer to understanding as mortals. What in the heck the demonic realm has for operational devices? Yet then new questions emerge about them. Parapsychic heavy lifting to have holy angels tell you that nineteen and a half years later you will one day witness something no other human has ever witnessed, something only found in the Holy Bible, the New Testament, and the Book of Revelation. And then, nineteen and a half years later, fulfill exactly as the holy angel delivered premonition promised it would. I mean, this is just one of multiple Tribulation confirmations received. In Part I, I'm looking at it from the supernatural relationship side, but make no mistake; all the new evidence files, so to speak, that the supernatural realm just sort of dropped in my lap, all have very, very strong Christian spiritual linkages. Part II examines it all from the religious angle. Greater meanings take away you have to understand where I'm coming from in Part I, with U.F.O. particle beams coming down at me in my front yard, being holy angel directed/supervised apparently on direct order from God, I can only suppose. I'm sure the Devil is just thrilled to have some of his subordinate E.T.s give a Christian prophet a look at some of his top-security secret Tribulation particle beam advanced technology (Then disclose these secret details to the entire world through a book.)! This is why I am sure I'm under God's witness protection program. The Devil wants the Prophet Wildman dead in the worst way, which explains why I seem to have lost my appetite for Devil's food cake ever since!

While you can't say for certain the Sasquatch isn't some long lost zoological ape cousin of known apes, I think the likelihood of this being the truth of what is really happening (to the chagrin of the T.V. networks). There isn't evidenced enough either way to prove or disprove either theory, but as quaint as it might be to entertain the thought of the Sasquatch as living, I rather think it's a nonliving, sort of Isotope 6 (visible/non-visible existence spiritual entity). Ghosts exist, this thing surely does exist, but is not a living entity at this point. No bones have ever been found because spirit entities don't leave behind bones.

On the particle beam at the very tip are two, rectangular-like plates. They are sort of cobalt blue and everything else is black as pitch, and they actually look exactly like asphalt pitch, but with very fine granules on the surface. The Holy Bible says the color jacinth is only found in the bottomless pit, where this U.F.O./E.T. crew is from under direct order from God, to show a certain Christian prophet particle beam (or else!). Jesus described this particle beam almost two thousand years ago to St. John. You can doubt the Wildman's word if you want to, but you would be a lot wiser to believe every single thing I tell. I am hardly in a position to lie, and it's not what I'm about anyway. Yes, I will blow your mind, but you can always repaint the wall figuratively right over the brain splatter!

What about all the people who believe these are long lost branches of the hairy ape family, and in some sighting cases, human hairy man Neanderthal-like beings? Let's take this second situation first. A very rare, tiny percentage of the hairy entity sightings worldwide are in fact likely hairy men; ancient remnant uncivilized first cousins of modern homosapiens. In the Pacific Northwest, a tradition among a few native American Indian tribes among tribal Chamen of going off into the wilderness to commune with Spirits of the Forest, but never returning though still alive, accounts for wild men sightings of that region being repressed humans, rather than ancient men surviving forward, able to do so in remote backlands of the world. They likely do exist.

As for the seven- to eight-foot-tall Bigfoot/Sasquatches sighted, you must remain open- minded and not disqualify any and all possibilities at this stage, with so many unknowns and uncertainties. Respectable scientists and zoologists and cryptozoologists do investigational studies, but one must also realize their examinations are being conducted along conventional lines, hoping to verify a conventional, ape-like omnivorous entity of this dimension of living animals. Should in fact the correct answer solution lay beyond such parameters, then you have, in essence, sent plumbers in to locate an electrical problem. Perhaps by their very scientific approach/skill set training nature, they are likely to be very reluctant to openly make public statements confirming multidimensional, ultraterrestrial theories of any sort, even if in private among themselves they regarded it as credible strong possibility that indications of their evaluations kept directing them. If they made such confirming statements, their colleagues would ask them, *Are you guys crazy, gone mad, now on drugs, or something else?*

No, none of that, but that states as example of colleague reaction if they did publicly reach such unacceptable within their own field conclusion, then quickly asked based on what evidence proof? Actually, if they were on drugs they'd probably reach that conclusion faster, but it is better I leave those discussions for Chapter 16 before you start having hallucinatory Sasquatch sightings (Is that him, right behind you? I think I need to heavily sedate my sense of humor!)!

With so many sightings across diverse geographic expanses, and over considerable time expanse history, clearly such an entity is out there. The true nature of it is the million-dollar question. All the correct *how, who, what, why, when,* and *where* details.

We know other dimensions exist, and other sightings of other forms of creatures seemingly unknown entities not of this Earthly dimension occasionally and over many centuries have been witnessed. Even further back in time, dragons were no myth, were even mentioned in the Bible, and were demonically associated.

Those who choose to believe Bigfoot as a seven-to-eight-foot, six-hundred to eight-hundred-pound, living omnivorous specie of the ape/gorilla family and a distant, long-lost cousin, point to encounters of human-witnessed reports. There are things like car collisions with them damaging a car, broken large branches, hair sample snags, large stones, and boulders tossed, wood knocking, large tracks left in moist ground, sticks and grass, windbreak shelters crudely constructed, tree climbing, even humans being chased away, or even actual chases with similar wild animals yells/roars/vocalizations.

However, other evidences seem to run counter, like bullets that pass right through their body, not affecting this creature, more than one blaming of witnessing a spry, twenty-foot leap, followed by bounding into another. A pink elephant sort of move for a six-hundred to eight-hundred-pound Bigfoot? What about the *no footprint where there should have been*, or the *non- disturbance of vegetation that should have been, with no trampling*? If such an entity was *Interdimensional*, and could exist in solid form in this dimension, but with limited shelf life, and a transitional phase more ethereal, both upon entry and upon departure, you can now explain all of the witnessed conditions previously described. All of it then fits. Otherwise you are back to cryptozoologists smoking crypt bud to send their thinking into other dimensional awareness; sort of like plumbers going to night school to figure out that electrical problem solution (the excuse works for them). The problem, however, is not in a correct postulation. But then how to manage to get conclusive evidence proof of such? That is the challenge.

Animals are neutral spirit entities, but such as demonic rares are literally animals out of other dimensional realms that apparently can and do enter this dimension for a short shelf life periods. The late John Keel seemed to grasp and accept this multi-dimensional, ultra-terrestrial type theory concept because in no other way could such rare multi-dimension zoological entity sightings be explained. I think John Keel was way, way ahead of his time, and until he is disproven, consider his theory to be the most likely correct; even working with some E.T.s is quite likely. An ultraterrestrial is then an *Interdimensional* entity. It seems so many like Keel have to die first in order to have their theory accepted.

In my case, I am a little different as an apocalypse prophet. They come to the realization upon death, and my advanced prediction of it was correct (It sure weeds out the skeptics.)!

Chapter 4
Extraterrestrial Aliens and Ultraterrestrials

Information contained in this chapter is for the most part nothing new to U.F.O.-logists, but provided as a kind of primer for those readers with little background to get them acquainted. Some of this information becomes very relevant in later chapters. It is based on consensus from all books researched; many sources, as to defining characteristics of extraterrestrial root races known to exist (Bibliography is segmented between general contributions, and near, or direct quote.).

Perhaps what readers need to realize most is that these entities, as well as their spacecraft, are *Interdimensional*, and they possess the capability of moving in and out of our dimension at will. In other words, there are different planes of existence, including additionally subspace or mind space planes. Thus, describing these life form beings as multi-dimensional is, in fact, a very accurate characterization.

Most types or groups communicate among themselves telepathically, and this is well-documented. In most cases, they can intercept human thought, as well. What many people don't realize is that not only are ghosts and angels able to move close to humans without knowing it, but these guys can, too. Many have light sensitivity to their eyes, so an E.T seen or unseen is much more likely to be in human proximity at night and in dark space. In fact, bright light could be a deterrent to drive one away if that was the goal; however, many abductees reported body paralysis from the neck down upon encounter. Somehow, by sheer will, it instructs your conscious motor brain activity to shut down. These, of course, are the E.T. groups wishing to violate humans usually for the purpose of abduction in order to perform D.N.A. extraction. At that point the human is rendered unconscious, remembering little until afterwards. While most E.T. groups are favorably aspected in their regard for humans, some strongly resembling humans, but unfortunately not all.

Since there is not a total consensus or awareness on all points, I've expressed my own viewpoint in such areas open to personal interpretation.

In Chapter 25, further discussion of ancient visitation and interaction is made; usually the Samarian/Babylonian account of Annunaki is mentioned, as is the writing and depiction of star people. The problem here is that nothing can be verified, and more questions than answers get raised.

Were they solid in appearance or somewhat ethereal/semitransparent looking? What E.T. group? Clearly with evidence scattered all over the world; North America, Central America, Yucatan/Mayan, Peru, among several South American countries; Japan's legend of an ancient, egg-shaped saucer on the beach with a woman emerging. In Israel, Lebanon, Egypt, India, and Africa, as well as Lemuria and Atlantis lost civilizations, E.T. visitation goes way back. What E.T. group in what time period and exactly what interaction with humans did take place? The three most likely and believed sites for the Garden of Eden were the Holy Land, Lemuria, or Atlantis. Is there an E.T. connection there, too? Where was Noah's flood? Yet another question is often raised about early astrology and astronomy information transfer to humans by E.T. Did that occur also? There are many questions, with little verifiable certainty.

From a starting point like that, it is no wonder that exactly how many E.T. groups we are talking about cannot be determined or agreed upon. Some say as many as nine E.T. groups are visiting Earth; some not so recently. Part of it has to do with how you classify them; two of the groups have separate factions and really should only be counted once. In another case, it is not clear if there aren't actually several names for the same group, or if they are similar yet distinctly different. In any event, if you count the Nords, or Talls, and the Lyreans as being the same group, then you can come up with a total of eight. The person counting nine probably counted these as separate, but either way all known groups according to Good, Evil, or Neutral

Good, Holy, or Lightside Orientation

1) Nordics – Also called Talls and likely are Lyreans
2) Plaiedians – In legend, Atlas' seven daughter stars named after that Constellation
3) Martians – Decimated, but still existing?
4) Pryocyons – From the Pryocyon star system
5) Lemurians – Some say the origin of the Asian human race

Neutral - Orientation
The Moderate Greys (the Good Greys) are soul-less, but with an awareness of God the Creator; they aspire to a higher ethic.

Demonic – Evil Orientation

1) The Bad Greys – A breakaway faction of the Good Greys; likely now serving as agents of the Reptilian
2) Reptilian – Like the Greys, a moderate faction, and a breakaway Renegade faction. The Renegades being the worst of the worst you could say. They and demons, one and the same.
3) Albino – A separate group, but also agents of the Reptilian, probably the Renegades

---

Discussion of Each Group

Lemuria/Lemurians
Lemuria, similar to Atlantis, was said to have been a large land mass in the Pacific, southeast of Japan, that collapsed coupled with rising sea levels in the one-hundred-foot approximate range, in 40,000 B.C. to 50,000 B.C. timeframe. Inhabitants were said to be from the planet Aurora. Some believe this was the Garden of Eden location, but not all agree.

Some Asian legends say they migrated all across the Pacific and others say one group migrated to the interior of planet Earth, for reasons unknown. These are mythical stories of the Deros, but surprisingly such legend is widespread in India and Asia (not to mention similar stories found in Europe) of little people living underground. In Asian regions, the Nagas and Men Shan are spoken of; the Nagas meaning serpent people. It is possible that dragons actually did exist in ancient Lemurian times, so it could all fit.

The Reptilian symbol is the dragon, so prevalent in Asian culture, and some think Reptilian E.T.s have not only been around that long, but interaction with humans may have occurred, (in what ways is unclear). Descendants of virtually all Asian countries and regions could well have originated out of Lemuria. Migration as far as India appears to date that far back, and tablets that chronicled the Lemuria destruction were recovered. It would seem ancient Chinese history begins where Lemuria disappeared.

Procyons
The star system Procyon, is in the Canis Minor constellation (approximately 11.4 light years from Earth, contains the bright star Procyon. There are believed to be human and attractive looking appearance. They resemble the Nordics or Talls, but are shorter and not as thin (more like humans). It has been said there was an ancient war known as the Rigel-Procyon War, and it was said to have devastated their population; the Rigelians being the E.T. Greys. Not much has been heard from the Procyons, but they could well still exist.

Plaidians
The Seven Daughters of Atlas star system is in the constellation Plaiedies. Often spoken of as benevolent to humans, and being human looking themselves, they are referenced in Mayan and Atlantian record, as well as being the origin of the Crystal Skulls. They have not been seen or heard from recently, unless the channeled contact with spirit entities through the Skulls are included as contact. The Swiss Billy Meier alleged accounts most feel were hoaxed, claiming a modern day contact.

The Plaiedians were very similar to Lyreans or Lyrians, and they seem to have a connection with a holy dimension, or perhaps an angelic realm. The Crystal Skulls can be a channeling tool to positive dimensions, but they are also claimed to have mysterious healing powers. This further underscores the connection to a higher spiritual plane, as well as E.T. beings.

Martians

The little green men image that humans developed associated with Martians is said to be false. Like the E.T. groups mentioned above, they, too, are said to closely resemble humans! Then one wonders, Did they originate on Mars, or was Mars an ancient colony of one of a number of possible other E.T. groups? Yes, they are very human looking; better take another look at your mother-in-law. What's her name again: Marsha or Martha?

It is rumored, as some believe, to be a serious comet or asteroid event that devastated their civilization on the surface by natural means. The surviving population is relatively small and said to now be living underground, in temporary colonies.

With the help of the Greys' arrival, they worked out a covert cooperative agreement with the U.S. government and the C.I.A., and an agreement for a research colony beneath Santa Fe Baldy Mountain was reached (This was neither proven or disproven.). Considering secret E.T. bases at the Sandia, New Mexico, and Dulce, New Mexico, sites, it is at the very least a claim in the correct location. Frankly, while I'm not saying you should accept this, it is also not inconceivable. It is also fascinating that just coincidentally NASA has a great deal of renewed interest in exploring Mars (Could some inside information be prompting them? Could there be gold or diamonds there?).

A Martian colony already relocated to the U.S. (Are they eligible for citizenship?) is difficult to imagine. So, pour your imagination a double Martian martini and suddenly the concept of civilized Martians now starting to become plausible (Don't forget the organically grown underground little green olive or the government napkin.)! In his book, *Cosmic Explorers*, author Courtney Brown, PhD., obtained considerable remote viewing data, and I highly recommend his book for those who might desire additional detail on this subject. As far as the spacecraft being able to penetrate directly into the side of a mountain, remember what I told you at the beginning of this chapter about inter-dimensions; to me, that part is totally believable. His book will give great insights into E.T. psychology and was very valuable in forming correct consensus of opinion among all authors that I've tried to bring you.

Lyra/Lyrians (possibly also known as Nordics or the Talls)
Lyra is located on a corner of the Summer Triangle constellation, and the bright star, Vega, is actually in the corner, while four stars known as the harp of Lyra nearby as viewed from Earth.

Like the Plaiedians, there are reference ties to both Mayan and the Atlantian civilizations. The Nordics, or Talls, sound very similar to descriptions of the Lyrians, thus many feel they could be one and the same; it's just not clear. The Nordics are said to be tall and thin (seven to nine feet tall) and with blonde hair and blue eyes, red hair and green eyes, and later Atlantians developing from these said to have brown hair and green eyes. They are said to have pleasant disposition toward humans (more recent contact), an attractive, friendly expression, and have telepathic ability. Sometimes they are said to have angel-like qualities. It is believed by many that Atlantis was the site of the Garden of Eden, and that Atlantians were Caucasians from the Star System, Lyra, through Adam and Eve.

Edgar Cayce suggested in a trance state that these early Atlantians were not originally physical in form, rather sort of ethereal and semi-transparent. He said they became trapped in this dimension, as the vibration of their existence made them ever dense or solid. Cayce tied his own ancestry to Atlantis (as do I), so to accept this explanation is to suggest many of Caucasian or European descent (through Adam and Eve) actually trace further back to origin of Lyrian descent!

While my book makes a strong case on the side of Christian fundamentalist core beliefs, I think as long as you leave the presence of God in whatever provocative theory you choose to entertain, it is an acceptable, healthy way to examine creation. While this book presents a strong case for the existence of God, accepting the possibility that there could have been a little more going on than book of Genesis reveals, and that because God is not obligated to man, man is obligated to God. God doesn't have necessity to reveal all his secrets. In Biblical times, this may have been beyond early man's comprehension level. If you consider an E.T. Lyrian as higher on the spiritual plane than man, but a sort of lower-level angel whom God delivered and transformed in the case of Adam and Eve, from two prime candidate Lyrians into young adult humans, it becomes conceivable. In other words, this does not challenge Biblical description; it is merely an attempt to explain how God may have performed this act. Adam and Eve could not have arrived as infants, or there would have been no one here to raise and nurture them. In examining this concept, you also have to realize it only works with the existence of God exactly as the Bible stated it happened. Adam and Eve may have been pre-existing Lyrian form in another dimension, from which God created them as having human form, rather than being from which God created them as having human form, rather than being totally non-existent prior. It is a theory that has been around quite a while. I'm not the originator of it, but it is interesting because it doesn't conflict with account found in Genesis. Lyrians are already in God's image, but in a more ethereal dimension; Adam and Eve were formed by God from them.

This theory is only as credible as Edgar Cayce's account, but he had one of the most remarkable and incredible psychic careers. He proved successful looking both into the past and the future, usually only making error on timing, rather than even description. When you examine this theory in larger context, it interestingly can be seen to conform to several other disciplines, as well without conflict. Between the Bible and Greek mythology, there were the demi-gods that easily could have mistaken what was actually taking place in attempt to explain higher powers of the spiritual realm.

Spirits among God's angelic realm included Lyrian, if they were, in fact, at a lower-level within that realm, as well as higher-level angels mistakenly described as demi-gods.

Cayce's early Lyrian description was very close to this mythological explanation. If theologians would buy into this one possible, but potentially legitimate, concept; you now have Mythology, Parapsychology (Edgar Cayce), U.F.O.-logy (Lyrians), and Theology (Bible Book of Genesis) all on the same page!

Unfortunately, some agnostic scientists pushing for several varied versions of Big Bang Theory can't sign on. This Lyrian Adam and Eve hypothesis still involves God. They want God to go away and stop from being a stumbling block to their theory. To them, this Lyrian theory still involves Garden of Eden, and that involves God. The Garden of Eden they want to go away, too!

To Theologians my answer is, *Let's beat these agnostic scientists at their own game*. My Saints Covenant Prophecy (Chapter 24) can be converted into a mathematical equation. Each component of his equation predicates on the previous component and runs in a circle. I'm not so great at math, but God is; he invented it! This equation is going to be the God equation, where God will prove the existence of God with the help of his trusted psychic assistant: me, Wildman! As an extra bonus, the confirmation of two proclaimed saints will be shown in the process as in fact being crowned Saints in heaven!

Through a prayer question/affirmative answer, a prophecy was spawned. The mathematical probabilities of Wildman having awareness of information pertaining to a 2013-2014 timeframe, from any other source other than God about a billion to one. These agnostic scientists must agree in the existence of God if this prophecy fulfills as Wildman describes it, since there is virtually no other way he would have this knowledge than from divine source (Information was notarized, and date stamp documented, and is now being held in sealed envelopes by clergy.). In other words, in a formula rotating in a circular pattern, all components are predicated on the preceding one. With one component being a billion to one, if in January Wildman supplies the correct billion to one answer/integer into the formula, these agnostic scientists must abandon their Godless version of the Big Bang theory. It will have then become a billion to one in favor of the likelihood of God's existence, and therefore the Big Bang universe involvement of God Almighty. In other words, if they lose this challenge once accepting it, then they must concede once and for all it was an act of God Almighty, with no ifs, ands, or buts about it! The astrophysicists who don't currently accept God's responsibility for the universe creation must openly acknowledge acceptance if they lose (Like they should have in the first place.)! This will be mentioned in Chapter 24 (related) and God's Equation.

Theologians are, perhaps, a bit nervous, too. What if Wildman doesn't succeed in using mathematics to beat the astrophysicists on their home field and turn the tables on them? My answer is, Relax, God is running this show. I'm just his psychic assistant, and that domino is as good as already fallen, and that table is as good as already turned. They just don't realize it! It will take four years to get those odds, as no one could have received this information and documented it unless it was received from a holy source.

Mythologists might describe this as being like the sword of Damocles, pausing to allow history to catch up with legend destiny (How right they are! U.F.O.-logists say we told you so on the ancient E.T. presence of Lyreans.). Para-psychologists warn astro-physicists to watch out for a psychic with a Christian psychic sword in his hands that hasn't been seen since the Crusades, especially this one known as Wildman the Prophet.

After event fulfillment (of God's equation), 2014 timeframe, theologians will be saying, *Not bad!* One swing of the psychic sword and it proved existence of God in the holy trinity concept, two Vatican proclaimed saints now confirmed to be crowned saints in heaven, and the direct involvement of a holy angel. The renewal of holy prophecy; in doing so, turned the tables on the astro-physicists supporting a Godless Big Bang theory on the backswing! Thy Kingdom come, thou shall be believed on Earth as it is in heaven. Wildman is re-examining conventional academic theory throughout this book, and then rewriting it in Christian acceptable version!

The astro-physicists might want to consider conceding defeat, cut their losses, and save some face. It's bad enough to get beaten, but Wildman using mathematics to do it could be quite humiliating and embarrassing. They might want to check with the anthropologists expert in the Mayan civilization that Wildman did something similar to in Chapter 21 (Part II). See how precognitive psychics are, always referencing the future! The 2013/2014 event fulfillment of prophecy originated out of prayer/question answered by God (This was now verified by lie detection and all detailed later in the book in Part II.). This book is just chocked full of God/Holy Trinity, K.J. Bible, Book of Revelation and New Testament validations and verifications! Others will be fully described besides this event.

Any one in itself offering indisputable proof, but in total sum by the time you've completed this book, it should be virtual certainty to you, even though you may have already been quite strong in belief commitment to these Christian fundamentals already, through faith alone. Let this supporting evidence inspire, uplift, and bolster your faith to new heights. When you can verify Christianity through new evidence, even the scientists have a difficult time refuting it; it is time then they accept what Christians have been saying all along.

It isn't that Darwinist evolution isn't valid. It doesn't disprove itself as being only a small capsule within God's universe domain. E.T.s are aware of and recognize God's existence. Both E.T. and humans lower orders of God's creation.

Where I have mentioned the Lyren/Garden of Eden Theory, I am doing no more than that, mentioning an intriguing concept. I am not trying to promote this; I am trying to convince anyone not in acceptance of Christian Holy Trinity belief that they should be! The Holy Trinity is the concept of a supreme deity, ruler (and creator) of the universe; his crucified and resurrected Son, Jesus Christ, Lord and Savior of all humanity that accept Him and the Holy Spirit, obtained through faith in this very belief.

Realizing this is the starting point to understanding all that is within the supernatural realm. It can be examined or monitored scientifically, but is totally owned and operated under the auspices of God. The Holy Bible is totally accurate on account of the nature of God and Christ. The E.T. mention occurs in the Book of Revelation (9:5), and Wildman is the only person in human history that I know of to actually get a look and see at U.F.O./Particle Beam, scorpion like stinger/Taser tail (through lie-detection verification). What you could call a one-night-only appearance that no one less than God himself could likely have arranged, since these particular E.T. are loyal to the dark side you could say. Clarification is needed in this book apparently on this subject; decided by who I respectfully refer to in this book as my senior editor in his offices upstairs.

Now let's examine the remaining E.T. groups:

The Good Greys
To most people the image of a Grey is the first to come to mind when the word E.T. or alien is mentioned. Their home star is Zeta Reticuli II in the Draco Star System. It's about five light years away in the Dark Rift center area of the Milky Way. It is believed they first arrived at planet Earth around 25,800 years ago and have had a presence here ever since.

One thing convincing me that this probably is true is my own sighting in 2008 of the U.F.O. I dubbed Alpha. A double row of blinking colored lights, just below or along the saucer centerline, remarkable in similarity to a cave drawing depiction, although simplistic, considered by experts to be that of a U.F.O. on a cave wall in Southern France. A Cro-Magnon depiction of a U.F.O.! Complete with double row of round circles beneath a horizontal line (shown on History Channel-History of U.F.O.) Edgar Cayce confirmed the likelihood of U.F.O.s at Atlantis, as well, and there are other recorded B.C. time period sightings.

It has been stated that often including from conversation between Greys and human abductees that they move through both time and space, perhaps in some warpature manipulation *Interdimensional*ly. They hide their craft inside mountains, lakes, and sea bottoms, with believed bases. It is difficult for a person who has not ever experienced E.T.s or U.F.O.s before to conceive of this as reality, yet U.F.O.-logists, I am convinced, are absolutely correct in stating this is what is happening. Even though I haven't personally witnessed this aspect, based on my many sighting experiences, and weighing the total of evidence, I do think it is true.

At Roswell back in 1947, it was one of their craft that crashed, as well as in Northern Germany, Timmensdorfer Stand in the early 1960s. The government, of course, covered up other crashes, as well. The Timmensdorfer crash revealed twelve, small alien bodies, from forty to fifty-eight inches tall. They had no alimentary tract, no rectum, and no teeth. There was body fluid of a yellowish/green color, but no blood. They did have lungs and a heart, but no sex organs. The crash was investigated by British and American military intelligence. It was stated that such information has been kept secret from most U.S. governmental officials, military officials, and particularly the public.

It is also widely held that the U.S. government become involved in a secret agreement with the Greys during this time of the Eisenhower administration, and continuing forward since. It has been kept under a tight lid by the C.I.A. and treated as a national security issue.

It is said that the Greys really do have a triangular emblem, known as the Tri-Lateral insignia of the Betelgeuse. Guess we know where the idea of the Tri-Lateral commission came from, and whose purpose in those early years was to discuss relationships between humans and Greys relative to national security interest (The Greys were treated as any other foreign power, with a little added emphasis on foreign.).

The secret bases of joint co-operation in New Mexico, particularly Dolce, makes perfect sense if you think about it, since re-bio-engineering is the Greys priority concern and focus. Receiving assistance in doing this from humans serves both them and humans well (There is little doubt such facilities exist, with reports of certain activities leaking out from insiders periodically.). The concern of some is if you have a faceless oversight, except through small circle of individuals within the C.I.A. with high security privileged enlightenment, are there really any restrictions, or is this a morally oblivious Frankenstein's lab? Are the experts really expert enough when moving in potentially dangerous, uncharted Galactic Zoology? The thought is that it is well-contained, and perhaps so, and if humans can help the Greys with their quest for both biological D.N.A. improvement to the point where using the human fetus to carry an alien baby, but deliver before term method will no longer be necessary for their reproduction. Humans and abductions of humans are no longer required and are certainly beneficial to humans. I also think there is much more going on in the spiritual realm than the average human has any awareness. Perhaps the kingdom of heaven and the Galactic Federation both signed off on their approval of this.

In his book, *Cosmic Explorers*, Courtney Brown, PhD, states that this appears to be the case in regards to the Galactic Federation. He states that, apparently after serving the Galactic Federation as members in good standing for a long time, the Greys applied for permission to travel to Earth and obtain human genetic material to create a new race for their souls to inhabit. However, now being cold-blooded and emotionless, I am not convinced that the Greys actually have souls similar to humans. I am not convinced that they ever did, and I think part of their aspiration is to improve to that higher spiritual plane or level. For them, I believe, human hybridization possibly could be a way to achieve both goals. Thereby potentially having self-reproduction capability and be in possession of a soul, not to mention emotions. An ancient species within the galaxy (some say they have an average life span of one thousand years) that was on the brink of extinction brought back by human help. Animals, such as dogs, have spirits, but they are not equivalent to the soul of a human gifted from God, with many documented cases of dogs returning as ghosts. I would equate the Greys as being currently on a level, spirit wise, as that of an animal, since they lack emotion, almost like an android. Their intelligence level is high, their soul level is low, and they are due for complete overhaul. They are aware of all this better than humans can comprehend, and with human assistance (as being worked on at Dulce and elsewhere) we certainly can and should try to help them.

Why? Because although they are a race in decline, they are one of, if not possibly the most, prolific races in the entire galaxy. There is an equivalently large fleet of spacecraft, as well. It is better for humans to have them on friendly terms than hostile. When you read Chapter 27, and what I've predicted, it is quite possible in this scenario that the Greys could even become role reversed and help save humanity from itself. Humanity can even became role reversed. Humanity is under the rule of a new anti-Christ world government. Therefore, just go about your business as a (Chapter 13) uninformed mushroom and just pretend to be oblivious; realizing, however, that collectively, as humans, cooperation with the Greys is in fact likely critical to our own survival, as well (Realize, too, there is an identical breakaway faction of the Bad Greys who are associated with the demonic Reptilians.). I will discuss them in just a bit.

The Betty and Barney Hill abduction case, from September 19, 1961, is what you could call a U.F.O. classic case study, verified telepathic thought transfer communication, and an origin as Zeta 1 and Zeta 2 in a later study conducted at Northwestern University (1968), known as the Marjorie Fish study. Zeta II is said to have a double sun, with a planet circling them, 37.5 light years from Earth. It is quite clear from the study that the star pattern Betty Hill described, with little knowledge of astronomy was a near match for Zeta II, just as the Greys described it. To date, it remains one of the best verifications of the origin of the Greys. Although not fully confirmed, I personally consider it valid and accurate until such a time it can be shown otherwise.

It is my belief that the Greys E.T. race performs another important function. They are the diplomatic couriers; intermediaries between groups that can't get along. The communication bridge between good and evil oriented beings that can't and won't associate or communicate, except through a neutral third party. The Greys are that third party. Through the Bad Greys, vital information and messaging can be transferred when electronic transmission is not advisable. Thus through the neutral Good Greys, a link to the Bad Greys and a way for entities of light to be communicated by third party with entities of darkness (or vice-versa).

There seem to be two different sized Greys; one around four feet tall (give or take), and a taller one around five feet tall. The shorter ones are described as workers and are lower in rank or status than the taller ones. Sometimes an abductee has sensed differentiation between male and female, and sometimes a female appears to be in command. Where a tall insect looking entity often described as looking a lot like a seven or eight feet tall praying mantis-looking creature wearing a monk-like hooded robe, it is my belief this is a demonic entity associated with the Bad Greys and is not an associate of the Good Greys. Reinforcing the fact that the Good Greys really are good is the fact that the Reptilians are enemies of the Good Greys and the Galactic Federation. It is only the Bad Greys that align with the Reptilians and the Albinos (here on Earth). Elsewhere in the Galaxy, the Greys are said to be assisting the Albinos; the orientation of either is not clear in that situation. The mention of obelisks and pyramids is also interesting.

The Bad Greys
What are often descried as the evil Greys are similar in appearance, wearing the one-piece silver/gray jumpsuit and telepathically communicating among themselves by thought rather than voice. These are the moderate Greys gone bad; the bad bunch faction. They seem to be closely tied to the Reptilians, and are most likely the bad bunch; the renegade faction of Reptilian. They are the human abductors, animal and cattle mutilators, satanic ceremony rapists, D.N.A. extraction, or organ extracting Bad Greys; they have a hostile attitude toward humans.

Most Floridians aren't too aware of the volume of Florida U.F.O. activity. Since Florida was the twenty-seventh state admitted to the union, I named the North Florida U.F.O.s the 271st Alien Air Wing, and the South Florida the 391st Alien Air Wing. A bit tongue and cheek but, unfortunately, quite true in terms of total numbers I've seen on display. It is sort of a dirty little secret that the aliens control the late night skies over South Florida. They don't interfere with human commercial or private aircraft, but after midnight a lot of lights that aren't stars or helicopters in the sky are sometimes heavily presensed, to put it differently (as many as sixty). They normally number from zero in rain or heavy cloud conditions to between ten and thirty just within my reasonably small viewing circle.

It is my thinking that these must be the Bad Greys (although I can't be certain) because they are apparently based in the Deep Puerto Rican undersea trench as their base. My sighting records confirming storms/high wind conditions there that translate into suspended flights of U.F.O.s over South Florida. It can't be said with certainty, but my suspicions are these may be Bad Greys since they have been seen in the presence of Reptilian U.F.O. craft. Since it isn't clear which group is based where, this is far from conclusive. For decades U.F.O.-logists have felt the underwater deep trench area off Puerto Rico to be a USO base, and my own findings match with at least six or seven cases of high winds/no U.F.O. activity. Only the C.I.A. and the Greys know their correct home address, and neither one is talking.

The Bad Greys received the government memo about ceasing abduction activity in the Gulf of Mexico and the Caribbean, except it was written in English. It seems the government has been having some difficulty enforcing it. Bon voyage, yacht owners, and watch how suddenly the Bermuda Triangle turns into the Devil's Triangle when you have an encounter with the Bad Greys. Being an entrée for Bad Greys or hostile hungry sharks! Either way, you won't be needing your yacht anymore, and it likely wasn't what you had in mind saying you were going to go out for seafood, either! It's amazing how every year boats missing crews turn up, but it gets hushed up by the media. There was nothing valuable missing on board; just the human passengers.

The Reptilian
The worst of the alien groups, evil wise, and they are the Reptilian moderates, even worse than them a breakaway faction known as the Renegades (Our government does have dealings with the moderates.). The hostile to human Renegades are out of anyone's control, even their own moderates. The Renegades are, I believe, to be extremely demonic.

As if in human evaluative terms it wasn't bad enough to be demonic, these E.T.s are at the extreme end of that scale. Speaking of scales, they are said to have snake-like skin, and have beige/orange in color with some green scales, as well. The beige/orange skin tone was noticeably orange in both my 2004 sighting (even from five eighths of a mile distant) and in my 2008 dream premonition (consistent in both). While the Greys are not as adverse to human awareness as them, the Reptilians go to the extreme to not reveal themselves or their agenda (hostile to human). These are literally demon beings from across the galaxy that cannot be trusted. Fortunately they are fewer in total numbers than the greys, at least for now, here in Earth's vicinity.

Just listen to the list of adjectives various authors have used in their descriptions including phrases: manipulative; deceitful; untrustworthy; short-tempered; impatient; enjoy torturing humans; sly; cunning; sneaky like a snake; programmed mentality to conquer and consume; tricksters; aggressive; warlike; stealthy; destructive; shapeshifters; repulsive; obnoxious; and demonic.

Yes, and those probably their better qualities, certainly personality, behavioral, and anger management issues going on; not that some humans don't fit the profile (except shapeshifters are a little difficult for most true humans). Some think there are human/alien hybrids living amongst us (Hy-or Haybots?). They are more likely demonic/Reptilian spirit possessions. In different dimensions, spirits actually do move into and out of Earth. Usually they are minor animal spirits; human souls who have not moved on, and an assortment of mildly demonic to very demonic spirits (Include the Reptilian in this category.). Not only underground USO bases, but portals into other demonic dimensions are located around the globe. The Caucasus Mountains and the Himalayas (both India and China sides) are often mentioned as portal sites. It all sounds pretty thin proof-wise, but if it happened right under your nose, in some cases you would have no awareness of it at all. That is why proof is so thin. But when you see the larger picture, it does have merit; it's just beyond some people's ability to comprehend.

Now in later chapters in the Psychic section I explain some of my psychic experiences. I mention dream catch dreams. One that just before I awoke told me that one group of aliens is fluent in the tongue spoken in hell. I consider this class of dream to be a legitimate psychic message conveyance, and thus the message I feel certain is true. Sure it could be the Bad Greys but, much more likely, the Renegade Reptilian. These beings are apparently working a day job as corrections officers in hell! The brief look at the individual E.T. in the 2008 Dream Premonition was clearly a Reptilian, and accompanying cohorts were primarily Greys. The one who seemed to be delivering the dream was the Reptilian, and dialing up the torture voltage, you could say, as the Premonition progressed. I can totally accept someone else's claim that they enjoy torturing humans. Correction officers from hell means they must thoroughly enjoy their line of work. This, in turn, squares with my psychic message (discussed later) of the alien group being fluent in a tongue spoken in hell. It is the Reptilian. The Bible talks about dragons and serpents, and these guys are simply second cousin demons from across the galaxy. Or are they home grown? They are demons, regardless.

They are usually tall, in the six to eight foot. range, with a head something like Spiderman, lizard/snake like scaly skin, beige/orange and green, three- or four-fingered with long, claw-like nails, with dark gray webbing in between, cloven hooves (three-toed), and a human, snake-like face with drawn, oriental eyes shape, with vertical slit pupils, yellowish in coloration, and black vertical slits or dark, greenish slits.

In the 2008 dream premonition, this one was shorter, under six feet tall, yet what I saw in that fraction of a second glimpse matched all of these descriptions exactly. These E.T.s, by far, represent the greatest threat to humanity. Their spacecraft is highly advanced; likely their weaponry, as well. Like the Greys, it is the human gene pool that is coveted.

In a future time period (Chapter 26), it's been suggested they will:

1) Use human women to evolve their Reptilian species through further hybridization to evolve both generationally and genetically. Humans with lizard tails? No, God won't allow that to stand; it is a clear sign that Armageddon is right around the corner.
2) Other humans not used for the gene pool will be subjected to organ removal. You really didn't need your heart, did you?
3) Most humans, other than reproductive-age females, will be considered anti-Christ's expendable liabilities against a tight food supply.
4) Mass enslavement (remember they love torturing humans) and a mass annihilation program will likely take place. No one without Reptilian ties will be exempt (or 666 mark).
5) Their ultimate goal is to take complete and total control over planet Earth, betraying those humans who assisted them in the takeover, and saving their annihilation until last. They seek the emergence of a totally Reptilian planet. It is not clear the fate of the Bad Greys or the Albinos.

(2026–2030, Planet Earth becoming a very rough neighborhood)
It's claimed by several authors in mention of E.T./U.F.O. subjects that there are actually E.T./Reptilian hybrids living among us. Not something only recent, but dating back through history. Among such authors is British author David Icke. In his book, *Tales from the Time Loop* (chapters 9, 10, and 11), he commented on both Reptilians in general and in hybridization.

Not an easy subject to compile extensive witness accounts/comment on, but yet he offers accounts form several witnesses in varied location time and circumstance; all testify to pretty similar descriptive accounts. Humans, sometimes holding very respectable positions in society, suddenly shapeshift into reptilian-form appearance. Not humans demonically possessed in the normal sense, but humans genetically possessing an E.T./Reptilian side that exposes itself, generally for a short period, before that individual returns to human-looking form. Many of these eye witness accounts report the shapeshift producing a gain in height, growth of tail, or change to a reptile-like face, head, and snakeskin body!

The average person asks themself, *Could this really be true?* The question isn't so much could it be true, but exactly how much of what is claimed is true, and how widespread is it really, if so. Too much of it reads like disinformation, where truth is imbedded in a very sticky bundle of the absurd that they would like you to dismiss, then overlooking the truth contained in the center. governments are behind the disinformation because they don't want people picking up on the tie-in between the powerful rich, the powerful in government, and the criminal organizations; the new, so-called Illuminati. David Icke doesn't leave that stone unturned, either; in fact making a strong case of the Reptilian hybrid being *Interdimensional* power players directly involved in all these groups. The Illuminati is essentially controlled by the Reptilians. The Reptilians are demons, and thus Satan's interlocking directorate of world power brokers. So if this theory proceeds, Satan wants to control the world, and through this power base already does in one sense, albeit behind the scenes, below the surface.

Unfortunately, I can't substantiate that with evidence for you. David is taking the Reptilian hybrid thing to a whole different level. I'm well behind him there, still verifying that yes, Reptilian are E.T./demons with blood-drinking, shapeshifting characteristics who fly U.F.O.s. On that part, he's absolutely correct. My evidence on these E.T.s is not on anything hybridization wise; if you consider it, though, it's not such a wide gap or stretch to get to that aspect. I suggest you reserve judgment until later on this subject with brimstone, sulfurous smell to it. Consider that, at least by one account, the original fallen angels got in trouble with God for interbreeding with human women somehow back in Noah's day. Both they, and the wicked hearts of men in that Biblical time, are said to be the reason for purging the Earth by flood. It is said also a race of offspring giants were created, and there remains archeological evidence in support, not to leave out the Bible mentions. The question you are really asking is, have they since then, perhaps with the help of wicked evil minded humans, or simply humans who were duped, managed to perpetuate a stock of human/Reptilian hybrids among us? The numerous witness accounts suggest they have!

In this book, I point out emphatically that a new world flooding will take place on the heels of the comet wormwood appearance (see also World flood in supplement Section, Part II). This one is not covering the entire Earth; only temporary, and likely not as deep, with many places of the globe at higher altitudes being unaffected (about six months, in total). Could these Reptilian/human hybrids be on the list of reasons why, in Biblical times, such is necessary? Later in the book, two U.F.O. sightings, both of Reptilian registry, are discussed. Does Satan drive a Low Hat? More on that later.

When you add in the fact that the Bad Greys are under the command of the Reptilians, and many human abduction cases report definite sexual experimentation on human women, including inseminate impregnation, but later being re-abducted for purpose of extracting before full term, and alien/human fetuses, it's not like all the dots connecting aren't in place. It's more a case of how much evidence is required before it's overwhelmingly convincing. Some are already convinced Reptilian/human hybrids exist, and have been among us for centuries, continuing further these bloodlines. So, while no definite answer is evident, you seem to be right down that street. Like asking the question, *How dirty could the demons possibly be, dirty enough to slyly pull off such an act against humanity?* You don't need me to tell you the answer and remember stealth and deception is their trademark.

With the rise of the coming anti-Christ right around the next decade corner, perhaps the pertinent question is, What will he be? Simply a demon-possessed human, a human/Reptilian part-demon right in his D.N.A. (If such exists, we are speculating here or both). With the word demon involved in all three scenarios, we already know the end results.

Albinos

There are a group/race of E.T.s described as beings in hooded monks robes, sometimes appearing to have a face, sometimes not. Sometimes they have glowing, red coals for eyes on the faceless ones. Other accounts claim they have very pale, white skin (hence the name) with blue coals for eyes. Still other accounts have claimed they have brown skin or greenish skin and black eyes!

They are sometimes called Chitauri, or Children of the Serpent; the serpent being the Devil. So children of the Devil, and certainly no matter which version, demonic spirit orientation. They are also called the Children of the Python.

They are usually associated with or figured to be agents of the Reptilian. They might be presented in the company of Bad Greys, too. They are often called the Warlocks by some. Similar to the Greys, they are in the four- to five-foot height range, usually with their distinguishing, hooded robe. It is quite possible Albinos outside of Earth's vicinity are not demonic, but not enough is known about them to discuss.

If the Reptilians have associated with them elsewhere in the galaxy, then they would be demonic there, as well, but the Reptilian moderates less so. The Reptilians are from the constellation Orion and the bright star Sirius in the Rigel System. It is also said the Big Dipper includes the star Alpha Draconis, and it is the home of Reptilian royalty, the elite leadership known as the Draco (not to be confused with the Draco system home of the Greys). You will remember also the Canis Minor system and the bright star Procyon, home of the Procyons (well, Canis Major), the Constellation known as the Greater Dog, is the one tied to Orion and containing the star Sirius. They are close neighbors in a big galaxy; they only live a few thousand light years down the street (so it is believed).

The Unidentified

Most E.T.s seem to be *Interdimensional*; much more ethereal or wispy ghost like beings. With so many different, non-human piloted U.F.O.s seen around the world in so many varied shaped crafts, it is quite probable that there are other E.T. groups completely unknown to us. This then is a catch-all category for what might be. We know you're there, whoever and whatever you are.

In the back of Chapter 13, the government Conspiracy chapter, is a section examining the Illuminati conspiracy, as well; the two being possibly linked if this is in fact really true. Is David Icke's book and explanation of Illuminati belief written as disinformation? A secret Satanist boilerplate manifesto imbedded/contained right there in full description explanation within David's book? Yes, it appears so! Too lengthy to include even summary of here; you'll need to read his book if this is of interest to you. Whether the overall book is a disinformation attempt or not, either way some substantial evidence gets laid out before you there in broad ISIS moonlight; likely the genuine article for their belief doctrine core! It is evil idol worship on loan from the ancient Egyptians! Dumbness with compounded interest, you could say, but unfortunately evil ideology compounded, too.

Remember that the Bad Greys are subordinate to the Reptilians, and the human hybrid in theory is the link to the Reptilians as the Illuminati connection counterpart as human subordinate to the full-blooded E.T. Reptilians. All worldwide wealth is secretly linked in a diabolical web of influence among all the world's wealthiest; government key leaders and financial resources, with the end game goal of bringing all worldwide power and influence into the hands of a few controlling the shots of a One World, or World Order government (Wasn't that Hitler's, second anti-Christ's goal?). The Illuminati draw their manifesto from the ancient Egyptians, and the pyramids are in perfect alignment with the home stars of the Reptilians and the Greys, and the Bible's characterization of the coming anti-Christ being a like thinker to Hitler's One World conquest/domination iron-fisted rule. All of which turn in a pretty tight circle in the minds of many who recognize too much lining up here as supporting such theory. The Bible is clearly warning this third anti-Christ is the bloodiest and most cruel and inhume dictator of all, and is nothing more than Satan's puppet. Human/hybrid and part Reptilian puppet is the question that Illuminati conspiracy theorists ask. News media recently reported that the super wealthy now control more than $21 trillion in safe haven tax accounts.

Another E.T. group previously not mentioned is the Atlantians. So little is known, and they are seldom discussed. They sometimes are associated with Atlantis, but are they then simply a pseudonym for Lythians or the Plaiedians? It's hard to say. Did they only later receive that added moniker after settling or visiting Atlantis? I mention it only to make you aware that the name does come up periodically. All three groups have at least a potential tie to Atlantis. With no negative legacy association, all three names should be considered in good standing with the holy side as far as their affiliation, and all could be similarly human-like in appearance unless proven or shown to be otherwise. It does seem there is more evidence to support this belief than contradict. These other E.T. groups could explain some of the more exotic-shaped U.F.O. crafts occasionally witnessed; one should realize that the total number of E.T.s is open-ended. These groups are likely just a fraction of the total number of ones out there.

Atlas is often thought of as being among the demi-god names, but they could have been regarded at the time for the one true god, or God Almighty, as simply a different word for Jehovah, or the great Yahweh. There is evidence, in fact, of two religious factions in existence in Atlantis. One who did believe in one true God, or as they were known, Believers of the One Who Created Heaven and Earth. This the oldest belief system descended from the earliest Atlanteans. It is said to be very virtuous, righteous, and possessing great spiritual connectivity and wisdom to God and through God.

Depending on how far back you date Atlantis, somewhere in the more recent history of the total Atlantean existence, another faction of idol worshipers described by Edgar Cayce in trance as worshipping Bad Gods and idols, and were known as the Evil Sons of Belial, the exact same term found in Samuel, and the evil sons of Eli as comparative in the holy land. (Baal, False God worship, with false idols statuary)

So one account claims that the faction known as the Believers of the One migrated to Europe through the divine providence hand of God. This then explains how the record of this survived by coming with them. More on this as described by another author is mentioned in the epilogue. It is my belief that psychic prophecy was the mechanism God used to alert his faithful, instructing them to leave because he was about to destroy these islands (Not only do I feel certain this is true, but in the epilogue I will present evidence as to why I likely am, as was Edgar Cayce's ancestor from this Atlantean group!). It was 2,193 B.C.! (Epilogue the end of end of Part II)

We know from the Bible account relative to the oracle at Delphi that the Greco Roman demi-god Apollo is exposed to be demonic connected influence, and the Bible teaching essentially that all other such, are just false Gods, having no power whatsoever, except through influence and powers demonic in origin. Using the name Atlas as one of many gods would be false but, as I pointed out before, if Atlas was the name referencing the one force behind the entire universe, simply their term for God as we would describe him, then this would not be false. Perhaps that was the one true god, and why the believers were forewarned, enabling them to then migrate through prophecy received immediately prior as I believe was the case! God as we know him would not have spared these people unless they were faithful to him, and him alone. Think about it. They sailed to Europe with four hundred ships, leaving Atlantis home islands just in time as the account claims they did. My four-part destiny, which I'll later describe in much greater detail, is possibly linked.

I told you to consider wearing a motorcycle or bicycle crash helmet (metaphorically speaking) when reading this book. The truth absorbed suddenly will jolt you right over the imaginary handlebars of that off-road ride of yours, usually with little warning, and just that sudden. Wear one literally only for added protection (To reduce brain splatter on the walls of the room you're sitting in to reduce repainting area required. Just joking of course; or maybe not.)!

Anyway, don't say the Wildman never warned you of what to expect up ahead in a book just chocked with mental stress, soft brakes, and dead man's curves on steep inclined, and rutty bumps of shock and awe, and Twilight avalanche zones! You are pretty brave to tackle such a mental enduro course; to your credit you are up for this challenge of exploring the back roads and paths of the supernatural. Interesting and rather nice to see so many clergy have joined us along for the ride on this reading adventure journey. Nothing worthwhile comes easy. A pack of off-roading clergy bikers down trails of the supernatural led by Wildman as their guide! That's practically a Twilight Zone image photo op itself, as I bet you would agree.

If that sounds bizarre, telling you a bit later on that it was as if God enrolled me to take a crash course in E.T. and U.F.O.-logy to provide me with better awareness essential to be conveyed in this book, because it is an integral part of understanding Tribulation, and critical information a typical person wouldn't even accumulate knowledge of in an entire lifetime, I was going to need, and so he alone could bridge that gap; and then did! Nine verified definite U.F.O. sightings (among even more) does this have you thinking that Wildman might be better described as a madman? Hopefully not.

Hopefully those clergy along for this ride can defend me with some statement to exonerate me from such characterization. Maybe saying, *That sounds exactly like something God would engage participation in. a necessity if his purpose is to be served. An anointed prophet would be one to follow where ever God leads, and in revelation of his secrets, that He (God) wishes to make known.* Clergy are on your side is a good thing.

I'll fully grant you the bizarre part, but walks on water, or coming down from the Sinai mount to explain to people how God spoke through a burning bush of fire have already laid claim to bizarre where God is concerned going back to Biblical days you can't deny. Bizarre is consistent modus operandi of God occasionally, but on an as required, if needed, basis. We should all be endearingly thankful that God's holy angel provided the Tribulation awareness to me that he did, which is explained toward the end of this book. Sorry if that tossed you over those metaphorical handlebars, hitting the brakes too hard there maybe. Don't worry about that until later in the book, after the primrose path, then the Tribulation trail (I'm joking again!).

It does seem pretty extreme, even in the twenty-first century, to be discussing God and E.T.s and U.F.O.s in the same sentence; never mind the same book. Why the clergy are on this trip quite likely, wherever God has been they wish to follow to learn new insights of spiritual value. Getting out in the outdoors and getting some fresh air and exercise sure beats giving the funeral worship services some are shackled to give.

I'm no more a madman than the person who is overtaken by the Spirit of the holy Ghost who then starts babbling, speaking in tongues, or is released in expression of abundantly overflowing amounts of deeply felt joy and uncontrollable laughter. When God so touches you, you know it, and then you move in whatever direction God leads you. You are taken of the Holy Spirit, and irrelevant whatever direction it is, but knowing it is relevant to God obviously, and that is all that matters. Is it bizarre sometimes? Sure, it can be very much so, but welcome! Let God's will be done. Let God's word be heard. Rejoice and directly participate in anything of the Holy Kingdom.

A U.F.O. airshow was necessary to educate in the E.T./U.F.O. subject; not at all a random circumstance, but required to rapidly provide awareness to me, that could then be expressed to readers of this book. Ordinarily such subject would not have priority in relationship to religion, but it during Tribulation, a critical component to accurately understanding the Book of Revelation. I'm sure it really angered the demons to have to breach their high-level security and show me that stinger Taser, scorpion-like particle beam weapon as the grand finale to the air show. Bizarre? Yes, but completely true. Weird? Very, but still completely true. God asked me for ten to fourteen nights of observing the night skies, and I gave him fourteen months so as not to miss anything. What signs and wonders I did see!

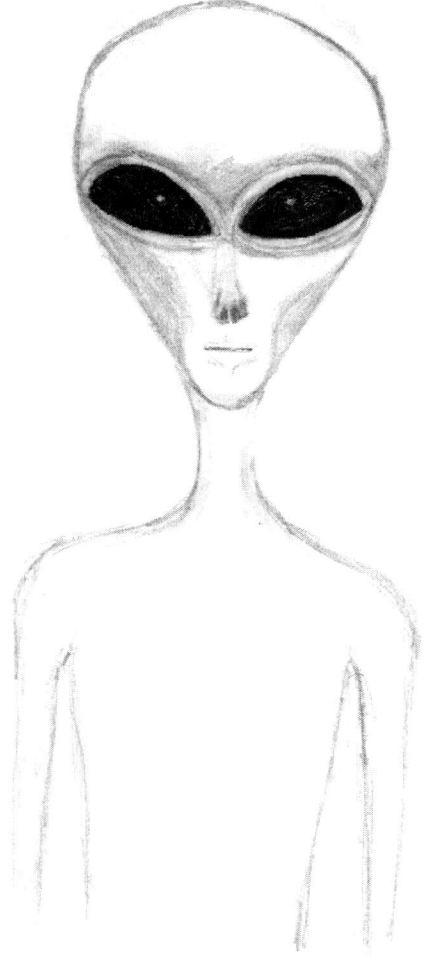

The Grey's Alien

New Realities of the Twenty-first Century, Part 1

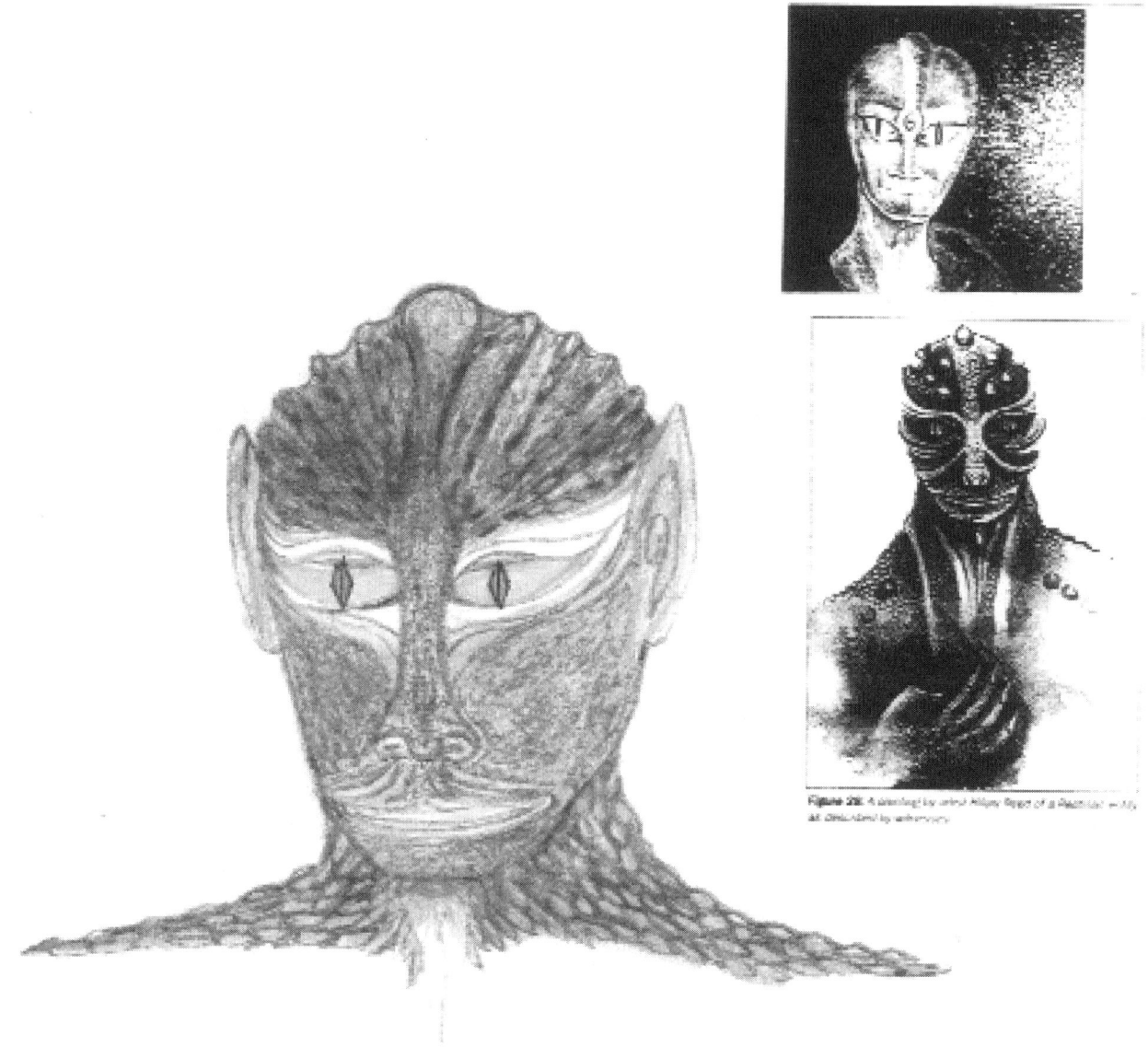

Note: the psychic vision I got only lasted a split second (from being telepathically blocked) but the orange beige/orange snake like neck/shoulder skin, and green/orange ridgey head more certain than other features. (either no ears, or if so, as depicted)

(spelled -ian) Reptilian Alien (demon) Bible "Beast From the Sea"?

Source: These comparatives courtesy David Icke,
"Tales From the Time Loop" - as Biblio. noted.

Chapter 5
Humans Possessed/Vampires
Vampires and Human Demonic Possession

Vampires. Have they ever existed? Author Angela Cybulski's book, *Vampires: Fact or Fiction?* covers that very question. She provides viewpoint arguments on both sides, and then leaves the unanswered question to the reader's own evaluation.

The most widely held and accepted view being no, they do not, and unlikely that they ever have. Mysticism of earlier centuries simply sought explanation to what was not readily understood by means of a supernatural one. She provides circumstances and evidence surrounding several of the most famous cases so labeled. I will not explore these here, but the cases she lists:

1) Vlad the Impaler, (Dracula) Fifteenth Century Prince of Moldovia (now part of Romania) Bram Stoker book published – (1897)
2) Gilles De Rais (France) 1440
3) Peter Plogajowitz 1725
4) Elizabeth of Bathory, The Bloody Countess of Hungary 1611
5) Peter Kurten, The Monster of Dusseldorf 1883–1931
6) Sergeant Bertrand (France) 1849
7) Fritz Harman and accomplice Hans Crans. 1879–1923

For over five centuries, it was a prevalent explanation for disappearances in Hungary, Romania, Transylvania, Serbia/Yugoslavia, France, Germany, and Russia, along with werewolves and other supernatural supposed causes.

Another case was that of Madame Blavatsky, noted mystic of her day. An account she entitled, Isis Unveiled, told of a Russian Provincial Governor of Tch, whom she claimed committed an act of vampirism. The story had some witnessed account to add a degree of believability.

Unfortunately, or fortunately, depending on your outlook, Madame Blavatsky was later (in India) exposed as a fraud. She had been caught rigging props to show mystic occurrences that matched her claims. This was described in what became known as the Kut-Humi letters of Emma Coulomb. This, in turn, discredited the earlier Russian Vampire claim.

What is my opinion? It has some conventional, as well as some unconventional, aspects to it, as if that surprises you. Most clergy will tell you that a demon/evil spirit in any form is not allowed by or according to God's rules to directly cause the death of a living human. This was Dr. Lancy's view, who you will read about in the Religion section later, and a view with which I would agree.

Evil can cause you death by fooling you, trickery, deceptions, or misconceptions. It can cause you to make false assumptions that might lead to actions where you cause your own death, or create a situation to have someone else or something else cause it. It doesn't mean they don't try, it means they aren't allowed to do it directly, and they must do it in some clever, indirect way. Since vampirism would represent death by direct cause, it is invalid on spiritual legal grounds, you could say. The neck- biting Bram Stoker vampire then is a fictional non-entity.

However, as one with a heavy accumulation of Twilight Zone frequent flyer miles, and having looked at the spiritual house from the side view, as well as the front (that view just described), you see something a little different if you look down in the basement. Let's just say that I have seen human-looking, evil-fanged entities (vampire-like) that do exist, but in another (likely demonic) dimension. Hallucination? Yes, but as you will read in that chapter, some things can be simply distortion of this dimension; while others are likely passing in and out of another dimension of which there are many. So, my answer is that there are no vampires in the musical octave of the living, but drop it down an octave or two or three in the Octave of The Dead, and if you should be so unfortunate as to be there, you might just find something looking very much like a fanged vampire. Yes, that's right, over in the Transylvania district of the supernatural city underground; you are now fair game!

In the Dracula book and later movies, he shifts from bat and other animal form back to human shape. E.T shift form and evil can shift form, and this aspect of the evil equation is legitimate. Many Native American Indians tell of demonic, shapeshifting animals. True? Although rare, yes, this is an entity from another dimension that is almost always demonic. It isn't that the powers of holiness can't do the same, it's just that it is even rarer that they do. Remember, too, demonic powers are limited, while holy energies are unlimited. Both the blood drinking and shape shifting should, perhaps, be seen in the larger symbolic sense.

Psychic vampires exist, sure, but that's a step from blood drinker. The well of evil is a bottomless pit, and summoning or even involuntarily drawing from it, or having it draw from you in any sense, is not without danger. Blood is life's energy, and spiritual energy is directly tied. The Christian sacrament is symbolic energy of Oneness and communion with Christ's Holy Spiritual energy. If psychic energy is drained, it can mean positive spiritual energy reduction, as well. That in turn creates a temporary vacuum that can allow negative energy to enter. Just like a magnet, the two are not compatible; they repel. Humans need to keep their spiritual batteries charged with positive energy, and negative will be repelled.

Draco means dragon, and Biblically speaking, dragon means the Devil. The Reptilian E.T. that I've categorized as definitely demonic are said to be blood drinkers. The Draco are also said to be the Royal Bloodline of the Reptilian.

Interestingly, Vlad the Impaler, son of Vlad Dracula, had a family emblem of a winged dragon. Since Vlad the father was in essence the family embodiment of the family symbol, it made Vlad the Impaler or the son of the Devil. A description his reputation lived up to, soaked in blood. Influences of the dragon symbol extend back to ancient Oriental, Babylonian, and Egyptian origins.

In Chapter 27, when I lay out my psychic prediction of the future for you, this should evoke an immediate, profound impact response from you. Why? Because during the Tribulation period that chapter will describe how these very same regions and country will compromise a newly formed Evil Empire. Out of the ashes of ancient evil, not unlike Vlad the son of Vlad, will come one, huge, evil dragon empire, far worse than the separate ancient empires; collectively making war on all who oppose it. The evil dragon is soon to be reborn and fly again; make no mistake, no one is secure, and this will happen soon for certain.

This Evil Empire will draw much blood, bring many deaths, and much of it, sadly, wouldn't you know it, will be the blood of Christians! The anti-Christ world government will be this re-born dragon. The E.T. Reptilian Air Force (saucer U.F.O.) assisting. The flying aspect of this winged threat. So, perhaps in this new sense, vampires have (will in the future) again shifted shape and are evil in different form. The world will watch in horror as this Devil's son (the anti-Christ) and his winged dragon Air Force draw blood through war. To the present day, the Dracula family mountaintop castle is said to be haunted by evil spirits. The spirits of murdered victims? Or Vlad the Impaler?

It would appear that a new cycle of intensified evil is not far off and not unlike the crusades of Vlad's day non-Christian armies from the mid-East will march West. While human vampires in this dimension might be fiction, the evil embodiment of the dragon is set to return and draw blood soon. The evil energy the vampire represents certainly does exist; you could say it is simply in shifting form.

Humans Possessed

The question isn't what possessed you to drive a Devil-le, it's what drove the Devil-le to possess you? No hot sauce for you!

In Han's Holzer's book, *The Supernatural*, he states that only a trained academic parapsychologist can distinguish between genuine schizophrenic illness and possession, and nearly all doctors will not even consider a diagnosis possibility of a case of possession. But can and do people really become possessed? The answer is most definitely yes, and with many documented cases by credible witness and professionals in this field to prove it. Much more of it going on than gets reported, often because of embarrassment or the desire to forget such episodes by those victimized. In the majority of cases the victim is freed of the evil spirit, but in some cases the victim is driven mad, and usually ends up in an asylum.

I can relate with some stories that might surprise you. A personal crusade you might call it; counseling people with drug or alcohol addictions. If you take this role as counselor, you can't be too overly optimistic or have expectations of success quickly. It is a process, and my unofficial and unsponsored, but with someone who at least has an open ear. I try to be a positive influence and put constructive ideas in people's heads. The hope being these ideas like seeds planted now will blossom forth later and be instrumental later in assisting that person when they are wrestling with their problem and need hope and inspiration to hang on to. It takes enormous determination and willpower to break addictions, and that in turn is arrived at through motivation. Encouraging is the fact that all I have counseled in this regard have later admitted that some of the things I spoke about did leave a lasting positive impression. Something of substance they can grab hold of later, and my efforts not completely wasted; that something said now would possibly be either a motivator or reinforcement. Only they can transform themselves, and only when they've attained sufficient determination. As you will read later, I did have one success, and that person credited me with not only turning their life around, but saving it, too.

Not to get sidetracked, but it was a husband and wife couple that I had invited to stay with me for a few days in order to counsel that this story involves. One evening, talking to the husband, I had to stop for a second and do a double take (His wife was sitting and he was standing not far from where I was standing.). The pupil, or center of the human eye, is round as you know, but not his! His was the vertical slit of a reptile! I got right up in his face and told him he was possessed, and that I was looking right at the Devil who he had inside him. I told him he needed to fix that pronto! It is clear what possessed the Devil to enter him; his addiction! Do you see where your addiction has led you? He was proving my point in a way I hadn't expected, but I wasn't surprised at. He would have to work on that more immediate problem before he worried about the monkey on his back. There is no coincidence that the demonic E.T. Reptilian have vertical slit pupils for eyes; true to their name and clearly proof of demonic affiliation, too. Dragon = Devil

Dragon = reptile

E.T. Reptilian = slit reptile-eyed demons

Vertical slit human pupil = demonic possession

Notice how this runs a pretty tight circle.

The story of the short-handed Jesus is not about possession it in or of itself, but rather the lead in to one. Back in 1980, a friend that I worked with named Martin (Marty) had told me he'd like to have a painting of Christ for his church. I thought he probably meant in a back room, office, or Sunday school classroom area; something along those lines. I told him I would try to help him out, even though I'm an abstract and landscape painting artist and not too experienced at figure and portraiture. I had an available canvas and went to work; it was to be a donation. As I completed the painting I was not happy with my hands clasped in prayer. The hands were slightly incorrect to scale. They should have been a little larger and the fingers a little longer. I was about to rework the hands when Marty came by for a look and said he truly liked the painting and was anxious to show it to his pastor. He was satisfied with the hands even though I wasn't. Oil paint dries slowly, and there was time to make the changes, but he insisted it was fine the way it was.

We arrived at the church to turn the painting over to the pastor and Marty, who was known for joking, began to embarrass me by pointing out the shorter hands. He told the pastor that when we pass the collection plate we can tell people to dig deep; can't you see Jesus is short-handed? He needs your help, so dig deep; he's very short-handed right now. I thought they would hang the painting in the back but, to my surprise, it was hung in the main sanctuary! In that church of Marty's, Jesus was always short-handed, as anyone could plainly see.

When we had met the pastor out in the parking lot to turn over the painting to him, he had just returned from the laying on of hands and exorcising demons from a person possessed. He said he had done many of these and, in fact, claimed to be able to actually see the demons exiting out through the tops of people's heads. He said they look like slinky and snake-like (reptile again), invisible to most but a bit like cigarette smoke as to outlining or defining their form, seen on many an occasion.

The 2006 best-seller by Bill Weise, *23 Minutes in Hell*, gives an account of what hell is really like. Is he correct? Yes, I suspect he is. I haven't read the book and don't need to. Why? Because I already believe there is such a place within a different dimension, and I don't require further convincing. The Bible makes mention of it and is valid, I am convinced.

It is the people who say, *I don't believe in heaven or hell,* or those who think that those are places all in other people's heads, but not real, who are really saying, *I don't believe in God* or want to say they accept God, but on their terms. No, they are the ones incorrect; you accept God on his terms, and heaven for obedience or hell for disobedience are his terms. Not accepting his terms constitutes disobedience, and they need desperately to read Bill Weise's book.

It is often proper behavior that would lead one away from a path toward punishment in the afterlife and that also leads one away from any behavioral proximity that might invite possession in this life. There are two different types of demonic possession. Perhaps variations rather than types is more descript. The first is from an evil ghost-spirit taking possession (usually evil while living; a murderer, perhaps), and the second is from an actual demon who has never lived as a human, but wants to possess the living. It can be a bit dangerous dislodging the evil entity in either form; although any clergy may have success, tougher cases should be left to a Catholic priest. Certain rituals in Latin seem to be effective, and the spiritual power within the Catholic church should not be underestimated. I will speak more on this in the Religion section.

What about a demon shapeshifting into animal form, when vampirizing not humans, but farm animals, you ask? There already are documented case example of farm animals being (The draining of their blood is the cause of their death.) killed. One example are large cats (often black), such as pumas, jaguars, or cougars/mountain lions. Clearly carnivorous, it would not be normal behavior for them not to devour their prey after killing it. So here one has to think this a demon shapeshifted into animal form.

If you shot it with a bullet would you have a carcass, or would it simply vanish in the air? Likely you would be left with a carcass as the demon inside vanished in thin air. Remember, a demon has never, in fact, lived in the first place, so you can't kill what isn't a living entity. This happened in similar Chupacabra cases that seemed not to be non-naturally occurring animals, but rather something out of a demonic dimension. What a coincidence that Chupacabra cases first occurred in Puerto Rico, with deep ocean abyss USO bases of demonic Reptilian E.T. right off shore!

When someone is possessed and/or there is a site that demonic spirits have laid claims to, an exorcism of these unHoly Spirits is required. Who is it that gets called? A Buddhist monk? No, it wouldn't work. Maybe a Japanese Shinto master? No, it wouldn't work. A Hindu Yogi priest? No, it wouldn't work. A Jewish Rabbi? No, only limited success. A Moslem/Islam Imom? No, it wouldn't work. Who then?

You call a Christian clergy, pastor, or minister, and in those extra difficult cases, a Catholic Father/Priest specially trained for such. In milder cases both awake and asleep you can exorcise demons yourself! This may or may not work for non-Christians, but will work for Christians.

You simply take charge and command those unHoly Spirits in the name of God the Father, the resurrected Spirit of Jesus Christ, Lord, and the archangel Michael's holy sword that they depart from you and your space. You must command them in Jesus' holy name to exit, leave, be gone from this dimension of the living, and your space. A sense of relaxed peace and calm will let you know they've departed. There is no stigma attached, since they look for spiritual weakness, and will invade the space of literally anyone and everyone, silently and invisibly. The higher your stature or position, level of wealth, or achievement, the more likely a target you are. Congressmen, pro-athletes, attorney generals, governors, even fallen clergy; I could put a name example next to each one of these. Satan the destroyer of careers, reputations, marriages, public trust, etc. In business, government, and religion; it happens everywhere, and it happens in life. As an individual in this life, you have a perpetual adversary, but also a perpetual deterrent. That deterrent is Christian faith, your shield. Let down your shield, and you get the picture.

Only Christian Holy Trinity succeeds in pushing back evil. It is only through acceptance and belief in Jesus Christ that the resurrected Spirit that has the power to do this. If that isn't true testament to the New Testament, I'd like to see a better one. This book will provide you with other New Testament validations, but none better. Even a scientist cannot dispute the results of successful exorcisms, and there are simply too many case studies to dismiss the role of Christian faith's spiritual power. Sort of leaves those other faiths a bit tepid in the proof department, validity-wise. Oh sure, they believe in one God, too, in most cases, but they can't acknowledge Christ; if so, only on limited terms. Too bad. A tool only has purpose when used to complete a task. This book will bring you many examples of New Testament validity. Use these examples to build Christian faith within yourself or strengthen it if already there. These examples are tools to build Christian faith. Wildman also invites the leaders of all these other faiths to convert to Christianity. Incorporate Christianity, accept Christianity. Christianity doesn't have closed membership; it is there for all people, those of all nations, and all the time. You must first reach out to it, but if you truly do, you will never be refused, for that is but one of many promises the Spirit of Christ will always keep.

Chapter 6
Other Phenomena

This is sort of a catch-all category for everything that doesn't necessarily have a descriptive category of its own, and thus comprises diverse, unrelated anomalies. Anomalous clouds, anomalous rain, ball lightning, and sky drops all seem to have a tie in with atmospheric conditions and weather. Does that in turn have ties with the spirit dimensions?

Through history around the world some very strange weather occurrences have happened in ways not the normal and clearly demonstrating what seems to be the involvement of some other factor. Could it be supernatural or simply strange twists in nature, to which it seems to have quite an adequate supply. Many among the American Indians tell us they feel (or believe as told by their ancestors and handed down over generations) there is, in fact, most definitely a definite connect between nature (the weather) and the spirit world. That nature and weather are spirit influenced. Is that true?

One could actually make the same argument from the Christian perspective along the very same lines with stories straight from the Bible that, in fact, the spirit world can and does influence the weather, and perhaps some anomalies included. With the spirit realm divided along good and evil lines, one could then realize anomalies could generate from an evil source. The Jinn are tricksters and pranksters who sometimes engage themselves in such activities that very much resemble some of these anomalies. E.T. with demonic ties are no exception, either, so either group could claim responsibility. It isn't that these things couldn't also come from a kingdom of heaven source, it's just that none of this serves their purpose, and other than extreme cases, is far more likely to generate from evil rather good. So, perhaps there is a lot more non-random acts of nature that go on than man realizes, within the natural boundaries, since the spirit world is part of nature, too. Or, expressing it a little differently, say that nature runs its course unless the spirit world decides to alter it. I'll have to remember to ask a ghost or spirit entity that question the next time I see one, but they usually aren't very talkative (Move their head specter up and down for yes, and side to side for no, I suppose.)!

Will you guys leave me alone? Since you're already up late night, go bother David Letterman for a while! They said they've already been there and done that, but couldn't bring nasty weather and sky anomalies into the studio with them, or they'd have put on an unscripted show. David Letterman with special guests: anomalous clouds and rain, ball lightning, and sky drops. As a precognitive psychic, I predict you'll never make it through the book without your imagination asking for a pay raise many, many times. Or that you enrolled it in an enduro iron man or woman triathlon workout/Pilates class with an instructor nick named Wildman, a question it frequently asks you. Your imagination is now questioning your judgment, in a book on the supernatural in a chapter, Other Phenomena. Now, isn't that ironic? You couldn't even wait until it got to the Psychic section to cause a rebellion. If it thinks this is bad in terms of imaginative ditches, better not inform it of the Grand Canyon in the dark; that lies ahead in later chapters.

Anomalous Clouds
Some clouds resembling U.F.O.s have been reported, including saucer and cigar shaped ones. Some people have even reported that contained U.F.O. inside emitting is a sort of steam fog that enveloped the craft form from view. In these cases, smaller elliptical and disk-shaped crafts with the ability to hover inside the smoke screen that they were, in fact, causing. Reported cases go back to the nineteenth century; even reports of this at sea from a sailing vessel, and some clouds with colorations have also been reported.

Anomalous Rain
Every day for three weeks between mid to late afternoon, whether the sky was cloudy or clear, water fell on a patch of land between two trees in Charlotte, North Carolina, according to the *Charlotte Chronicle*, October 21, 1886. In a

similar October rain occurrence in Aiken, South Carolina, it rained from morning until night on two graves in the town cemetery—and nowhere else (witnessed by hundreds of locals). Other strange occurrence extend worldwide and through several centuries.

Ball Lightning
Ball lightning seems to generate a concentrated electrically charged energy, forming a ball and glowing red. Similar to other lightning, it appears during disturbed weather/thunderstorm activity. There have been several documented cases through history, witnessed by many, and often, but not always, results in the balls explosion. This can occur when it strikes a solid wall or object, and when the explosion does not occur, it can still burst into multiple, smaller streaks of zig zag lightning streaks crackling out from the ball. It has caused serious material damage on several reported occasions. The witnessed accounts, as well as the caused damage, is evidence that it does exist and has happened in different centuries.

Sky Drops – Non-Organic Matter
Non-organic matter most often refers to stones or rocks falling on a localized area. Phil Imbrogno's *Interdimensional Universe* clearly makes a stone's sky fall to a U.F.O. link. As I had suggested earlier, E.T. and spirit entities are evil in character and are highly suspect in these cases, as well as linked to other dimensions not disconnected from involvement. If they are responsible in the non-organic matter cases, they are certainly then highly suspect in the organic matter cases to which there are far more, occurring worldwide and through centuries.

Sky Drops – Organic Matter
These, in turn, fall into two subcategories: animal and vegetable (zoological or botanical). The plant life dropped includes: straw, leaves, seeds, hazelnuts, slime, and grains such as corn or wheat. The animal drops include: both fresh and salt water species fish (normally all the same species), toads and frogs, mussels, worms, lizards, turtles, baby alligators, salamanders, blood and flesh, or organs of animals, animal hair/and or skin hair. Again they are worldwide occurrences and although sometimes during turbulent wind conditions, they are not always so, but through centuries, too.

Ringing Rocks
Southeastern Pennsylvania is home to several spots that have strange, musical rocks that sound different notes of the musical scale when struck; some are even said to contain an entire scale. Stoney Gardens (Haycock Bucks County), Devil's race course (Franklin County), South Mountain region at Pottsdown, and the most famous the Upper Black Eddy (Bucks County), a mile west of the Delaware River. Even geologists are stumped as to exactly why and how this is.

Crystal Skulls
Found among Mayan temple ruins, and elsewhere in Mexico, Central, and South America, they are believed to be ancient crystalline, imperfection-free skulls containing or channeling mystical powers; particularly psychic and healing interface connectivity. Some hoaxed ones are said to exist, but the real ones are said to each have spirit persona attached. The source is said to be ancient Plaiedian visitors to Earth who are E.T. of positive spiritual aspect. While there is mention of the ancient Plaiedian in several cultures, the skulls are beyond the capabilities of even current civilization to replicate, and certainly would never have the spirit connect. There are legends that additional skulls exist and will be mysteriously discovered in man's final end times, and that important secrets will then be revealed. As you will discover in Chapter 27, that day is not far in the future, if the legend is true.

There are certainly more phenomena; this chapter has been a summary of a few. These are not areas I have personally had contact experience with, so let's proceed on to the next section: U.F.O., where my experiences are many and, in fact, created many new realities for me that I was unaware of until then.

Before moving on, however, through this book I have shown linkages between different aspects of religion to the supernatural and aspects of the supernatural to religion. It is clear to me as I'll later explain in greater detail how U.F.O.s and E.T.s have strong, religious connections, it so appears; some are affiliated to the holy side, while other have demonic loyalties (not randomly by accident, but under God's auspices as with angels and fallen angels).

With extensive discussion later in this book regarding Tribulation, I should draw for you the comparison of the future Anti-Christ's false miracles, and what I outline as pretty conclusive evidence supporting the tie-in between himself and U.F.O.s/E.T.s Likely what is described here as simply *other phenomena* are actually quite possibly U.F.O./E.T. involvement occurrences, and the Anti-Christ's clever magician like miracles, are or speaking in future tense, will be, U.F.O./E.T. assisted deceptions done from the sky. These E.T./demon-orchestrated events assisting the Anti-Christ with actions designed to impress people he wishes to win the support of by seeming to have supernatural powers. He will claim them to be holy, when in fact they are unholy source derived, exactly as the Bible says they will be.

It seems strange that such a world leader rising to power within the Tribulation timeframe (discussed in detail later) would be able to succeed in getting away with fooling so many in such masterful deception, but then deception is the calling card of the Devil to begin with, and this play book already written long ago. The U.F.O./E.T. here are the equivalent stage hands orchestrating these props for the Anti-Christ's sales pitch. Convincing and impressive display, but behind the scenes completely demonic other phenomenon, yet strangely resembling holy side signs and wonders.

Death Phenomena

T.V. drama would be lost without something to capture our seemingly endless fascination to something that has been around as long as life itself. The phenomenon attached part is in our never knowing what unseen supernatural/unseen forces might have conspired behind the scenes in the invisible dimensions.

In this Morgue section of Chapter 6, no one gets mentally driven around the bend. The Entities section is just getting things started, this is sort of an autopsy of death itself. Topic here is inter-dimension forensics connective causes of death. Those suspected supernatural/paranormal force invisible properties known to exist, often having involvement, but rarely confirmed presence in proof. Aside from entities both visible and non-visible sometimes crime scene present, so are unseen properties like fate, destiny, and tragic/tragedy outcome showing up at random occurrence accidents also.

The point being death goes way beyond the obvious simple causes, like sickness/illness, diseases, old age natural, and accidents random. Excuse the pun, but you didn't think that was the end of it, did you?

My T.Z.U. (Twilight Zone University) alma mater degree/non degree qualify your forensics examiner in giving this lecture? That's for you to decide, but some of these outside forces, even natural can cause and effect non-human things like organizations, governments, and even such as institutions like college and University, so it's not limited to people only. I'm going to divert from the primary theme here a little, but it does tie-in.

At the end of my senior year, wondering if I should repeat a couple of courses I really didn't care for, and already having more than enough total credits to graduate, I was pondering, did I really want to push an extra year for the degree (One course only offered in the fall and the other only in the spring semester.). Just then a holy angel spirit guide chimed in telepathically. Saying almost word for word, *You can go for your diploma certificate/degree if you want to, but if you decide not to,* and then continuing the description of how my life will in my future turn out. Basically reassuring me I'd be fine without it (true story in 1970). I decided right then and there, I'd completed enough total degree credits, and with holy angel reassurances, I would be satisfied to get on with my life. What can you do with a liberal arts B.A. degree anymore in this world anyway, really.

Maybe write a book about your holy angel guidance counselor one day; that sounds more like his biography than yours! A little over a decade later, due to reduced enrollments nationwide, and coupled with increased costs and crushing debts, the college simply folded! Twilight Zone University simply packed its bags and returned to the Twilight Zone so to speak. Ironically, it was "Ten Years After", one of the rock bands I listened to back then; perhaps one of those ironic tassels on my invisible graduation cap. Had I gone that extra year, received an actual diploma/graduation certificate, it would now be from a now non-existent College. So instead I have a holy angel *you'll be just fine* diploma to T.Z.U. holy angel delivered! How cool is that. If I had actually received the diploma in fact, reading between the line it would have screamed. Man-o-man, anyone graduating in that year has a way-cool deep mind space astronautically exploration extra curriculum certified T.Z.U. credential. That's okay, I didn't get certified in this dimension so the supernatural just sort of certified me a genuine psychic chaman Spirit/prophet over there. Tough knowing you have full mind space certification in both dimensions but no proof in, either. The invisible realm is not known for material documentation generally anyway. So, I'm graduated in absentia, from a college itself now in absentia, but with an incredibly intellectual mind, with my college guidance counselor contributing additional future awareness throughout my life. Quite amazing, but all factually true.

Now that you know about my college's death, let's get back to that death dissection discussion of Interdimensional supernatural properties occasionally being role player, all be they unseen immortals suspected of contributing to the demise of mortals. Now I'm going to exhibit a case study of a death tragedy from my old college.

The college sat on a Vermont hillside with a steep, sharp curve on the narrow two lane road leading up from an old New England country town, Guardrails on both sides because of steep embankments, the road sitting higher, and on the outside of the curve, an old (more than two-hundred-year-old cemetery. The curve had nicknames like Cemetery Hill, Tombstone Curve, Deadman's Curve, and One Chance or No Chance Consequences Corner. You get the idea. Maybe haunted hill curve, as well; no telling what spirits lurking there. The cemetery in a low hollow about fifty feet below the curve.

Our tragic Shakespeare like characters, boyfriend/girlfriend. The year 1968/69 timeframe. They'd been drinking (beer or wine) and then decided to go for a motorcycle ride on a 650 c.c. motorcycle. But just before going for that fatal ride, taking hits of LSD. A four wheel auto is hard to operate on a flat straight road on LSD. A motorcycle ride on LSD, on a sharp downhill curve, to be taken serious on that curve even when not high. Well, I'll spare you the gruesome details that your imagination had better not look at unless you want to lose your lunch just contemplating it. Not only impairment from alcohol, but hallucinatory heavy drugs a deadly cocktail mix. They never did finish their ride or trip, as it only lasted about three-sixteenths of a mile. Was this intentional suicide or accident? Might there have been some demon/death Spirit on the curve, hallucination so horrific, it caused the accident by momentary loss of concentration/control? Sort of like death meet and greet on the curve, welcoming them to the cemetery? So much for those don't operate machinery warning labels. Was this an event fated to occur? What did the driver experience firsthand just seconds before the crash, was there a supernatural or parapsychic episode or awareness occurring simultaneously? The answers go to the grave, recorded for all eternity, seen or unseen, heard or unheard, told or untold, known or unknown. Dead men tell no tales, so they say, but sometimes they certainly hold secrets pertaining never to be revealed.

Complexity in these matters beyond our comprehension. Coroners can only observe cause of death even with supplemental lab work. Physical evidences, but here the emphasis I've placed on non-physical supernatural and paranormal evidences so seldom revealing themselves, yet we know are going on in cases behind the scenes. Other dimensions and forces, unseen, and all around you! Silently, invisibly, but even although without a trace, also without a doubt present. It's there interface, interactions, and presences so elusive to distinguish, but death circumstances involved on a regular basis.

Things happen on a regular basis in human medical conditions both positive and negative, every day. Unseen, undetectable. demonic principles and powers, but also holy angels and supernatural properties fully in God's control; fate is particularly stealthy, too. An airplane crashes in clear weather, no mechanical failure evident, and a highly experienced pilot, only leaves us in wonder and awe as to why? It is part of life, and part of death. The entire supernatural in God's all seeing, all knowing, and Almighty hands. God is in control. Disbelieve or forget that at you own peril. God is in control.

While we will never have full understandings of all the mechanisms and manner by which the workings of God are conducted, simply beyond that of human comprehension, he does tell us in scripture. My ways are not your ways, my thoughts are not your thoughts. We also know through the Bible that God favors those who favor God, and encourages us to win his favor in that manner. Romans 8:28 states, He causes all things to work together for good, to those who know God, and who trust in Jesus his Son as their personal Savior

In essence, to come into harmony with God through his Holy Spirit, as obedient followers of the teachings of Jesus Christ. This being a spiritual starting point with God, that God can then apply his Will to, for our lives that our lives develop in full potential according to his plan for our lives, that it might have a chance to be accomplished. I hope atheists and agnostics out there are paying attention to this. A human's full potential cannot ever be achieved otherwise. It doesn't mean you still might not have success in this world, but one's fullest potential which includes spiritual achievement, development and growth, simply cannot be accomplished without direct relationship with God. No exceptions. Extra helping of blessings? Not a chance. No favor from God, unless you are one to favor God, believe in God, and praise and worship God through relationship/partnership with God. You need God as faith is spiritual sustenance necessity. He can survive without you, but only agnostic and atheist fools see it differently than I'm describing it, and as the Bible describes it.

Just wait until I get my full Christian witness mentions cranked up in Part II! These atheists hunkered down in their metaphorical spiritual shoreline bunkers will think they are being pounded by figurative big navel guns of a Christian witness battleship parked just off shore. Not to mention holy angel air strikes in on their false and unsafe, incorrect philosophy positions (getting blown to bits without a shred of evidence leg to stand on in support of these positions). Clergy wearing life vest/flak jackets a sure sign of heavy enemy battle engagement. Figuratively, devout Christian and clergy on board with me. Those heavy theology and witness rounds being fired off cause some big message fragments upon impact explosion; about the size of an atheist! That battleship offshore aptly named the S.S. Prophet Wildman, and her sister ship the S.S. Christian Witness just pounding away at those atheist shore batteries! Figurative, humor coupled in imaginative character? Sure. But truthful analogy? Yes. Part II of this book packs some spiritual Christian witness wallop/punch. Part I is needed to convince you, and prove Wildman is a genuine psychic/Christian Prophet, and this is needed in order for you to recognize him as having the proper credentials to be a worthy Captain of such a battleship, even though not a clergyman, a Prophet/theologian equally masterful. In other places the analogy of a Christian army Intelligence Corps First Lieutenant is used, and the rank is irrelevant, it's about Jesus, who is Supreme Commander, in all cases, and witness to promote belief in existence of God, and faith in Christ as the Savior of all humanity. Recognition of the Bible (K.J. Version) as accurate, true, and correct, and the Christian concept of Holy Trinity therein, the same truth.

Now there were other examples beside the motorcycle accident that I could have chosen, but there is that direct personal correlation of its occurrence at Wildman's old college T.Z.U. alma mater. You see of the twenty or more close calls with death experienced in my life, perhaps just nine months earlier (summer of 1968), I had a near death experience auto accident close call myself. It was just four years after a psychic episode in church, telepathically messaged by holy angel foretelling of the writing of a book when I was sixty-one or sixty-two. Yes, this book, Part I, and II! Almost forty years later after that accident close call, then in 2008, as I began writing these books, the supernatural rain turned into the sky opening up (as in the heavens) with new supernatural, holy angel, para-psychic messaging. More on this later.

Driving a convertible sports car, with the top down (without seat belts), I nearly killed myself, a college upperclassman honor roll student, buddy, and God only knows potentially how many other cars and the people inside them. My friend Gary was Jewish, and a top tier psychology major. Psych major at paranormal/T.Z.U. college, in his/this case meant you don't just read about near death experience, you apparently are offered the chance to live through it firsthand by riding with the Wildman. Only a miracle from God could have prevented our deaths, and we both knew beyond doubt that is exactly what likely occurred. Divine interceding miracle of death preventative intervention. A task force of holy angels possibly involved!

You would not be reading this book right now if they hadn't, and I'm pretty sure this Book is why the intervention. God had already read the book at least forty-four years prior to my even writing the book, then deciding perhaps my book, and that Christian witness battleship were very much needed for his future spiritual warfare campaigns. So because the near tragedy auto accident was averted, Gary and I got to live, this book became authored and published, and some new rhetorical Christian witness battleships were commissioned to be built over in the T.Z. shipbuilding facilities of the holy side naval docks. Arc welding by Arc angels maybe, but talk about some advanced system technologies on board!

God never breaks a promise, or leaves a forth telling or prophecy unfulfilled. Keeping me alive kept the holy angel promise/forth telling relative to the writing of a book when I was sixty-one or sixty-two years old. That doesn't mean I was indestructible or death invincible, as death cancels contracts, but it was a preview of my own future, and first indication of pre-destiny involving God to become an intermediary, and Prophet. God had looked forward upon my life, and other times during my life, holy angel forthtellings I realize now was to train me toward one day receiving holy subject prophecy, little different that prophecy on general subject, only dealing with my own life in training example. Yes, Christian Army O.T.S. for Intelligence battleship naval officer when offshore. The psychic realm does explore the deep in parapsychic terms if you think about it. Heavy psychic guidance systems required to navigationally cut though deep spiritual fog sometimes. Sure, all figurative, but strangely pretty accurate.

With that auto accident, I'd hit a frost heave at the bottom of a steep hill (downhill like the motorcycle accident), traveling over one hundred miles per hour. Over corrected when the back end spun out then upon jumping the curb on my side of the road, missing a street sign, telephone pole, an electric pole maybe, I'm not sure, but a chain link fence a little further back, as we went into circular high G-force end to end spin, as we were being serenaded by the heavenly choir so to speak, crossing four lanes of traffic, and coming to rest parked tightly to the curb, having not hit even one of four or five cars in proximity, and coming to rest facing the opposite direction, all in just a few seconds of elapsed time Protestant Wildman had converted his Jewish buddy into a Catholic in what, less than ten seconds conversion time. Tears streaming down both our faces, I had him repeating, Hail Mary, full of grace mantra, and probably the record for converting a Jew into a Catholic (joking) the land speed record for that probably still holding to this day! Pretty fast convert skills for a Protestant spiritual rodeo calf roper you could say. More like a bull or bronco riding, with a big assist from God, that we both made it out alive. Are you kidding? We both knew we had just died back there a few seconds ago. Any children or grandchildren then, too, in essence, deprived of birth in collateral after effect result. I never made such reckless driving error again, realizing later just how many lives could have been negatively impacted. God realizing for me ahead of time, then preventing such tragedy from ever happening, performing a miracle to prevent it, through holy intervention. Not the last time to do so, either! True story.

My top down, convertible death debenture; that's God's protection for me, refused to cash in. My friend being unaware I had additional insurance coverage beyond the worldly kind. Additional B.I.P. (bodily injury protection) and accidental death and dismemberment insurance apparently a policy in force with God. It is proof Christian faith does have its hidden perks! They never pay claims, they just make sure the accident never happens in the first place! Not the first time that the supernatural took charge over the natural, and goes back to what I did state to you earlier, about those who favor God being favored by God. Being pre-destined to prophecy for God possibly coming with free insurance, too, I can't say, but God keeps all promises, and if he says he favors those Christians who favor him, well, I've given you example of that in actual practice, and happening more than once in my life with-out any doubt. I'm telling you not only to be a believer in Christ, but that God really does appreciate his Christians! Alleluia, praise His name, holy and sacred forever. Praise Him, He is a loving God.

God does intervene in death sometimes; God is in control. With the motorcycle accident Deadman's Curve reference it is, as well, a good metaphorical analogy of the entire world recklessly headed for that bad curve, traveling too fast, and not in recognition of the hazard/danger of death that awaits, upon Tribulation destructions commencing catching so many by surprise, despite the detail description for it more than a dozen years in advance of it. A Christian prophet named Wildman, with 2008 Tribulation awareness, received in apocalyptic fashion. Confirming the Book of Revelation, where billions worldwide will meet their deaths on that Deadman's Curve, they weren't expecting. Many not Christian, and with no idea, of Bible, Book of Revelation, or the Prophet Wildman. A cemetery on the hollow of the hillside, alongside the curve. Further metaphor as being ready to catch any unable to navigate the curve, and with a demon possessed Anti-Christ meeting them just before impact to escort them to death (Many afterlife spiritual deaths then, as well). Jesus was, is, and always will be the only Savior of any Deadman's Curve, regardless of which one. The seven-year Tribulation is unusually bad.

Chapter 7
U.F.O. Section
Main Theories

The Theories of U.F.O.s

Worldwide, there are approximately nineteen million people that have claimed to have seen U.F.O.'s. More than 80 percent of world population now think they do exist, with an even higher number in the U.S. Hardly rare or isolated incidents, and seen back in pre-history times in cave drawings depicting them, and passed down in accounts from Native American Indians. They were described by Psychic Edgar Cayce in readings taken during his trance hypnotic state statements, as present millennia ago in B.C. age time period in Atlantis, and although many don't realize it, let me confirm to you, when correctly interpreted, in Bible Book of Revelation relative to being described as locusts form the bottomless pit. By the time you have read both Part I and Part II of this book, you will understand a great deal more on that score, including a five-month sting period (when to expect it Part II explains).

This chapter explores some of the long standing theories. There are at least seven more conventional ones that have been around decades, as well as several less conventional ones. I'll examine and comment on each of these according to my own multi U.F.O. sightings opinion. Florida a U.F.O. hotspot, as other chapter to follow attest to, and especially prevalent in winter when the snowbirds tourists are here, so are the U.F.O..

Some of these theories we will examine are partially correct (again in my personal opinion), but none represents in total the likely complete answer/picture, and not everything is confirmable. I try with this book to contribute to what is known, and as Chapter 13 attests, our government knows a lot more than it is willing to reveal to us. We have come a long way toward better understanding, but at the same time, humans have only scratched the surface of all that is to know on this subject. E.T. and U.F.O. definitely do exist, emphasis on definitely and exist. When you combine correct elements of these theories together, a more accurate image of correct interpretation is seen. My opinion then to assist you in formation of your own opinion.

There appears to be some E.T./U.F.O. around most of the time, and other that may have used our planet as a stepping stone for deeper space explorations. Perhaps Earth is rated as a five-star first class stop over point on alien interplanetary travel maps, as one of the great wonders of the Milky Way galaxy system. Andromeda visitors? We never know where most are from, but lower atmosphere unusual shaped craft attest to some non-native U.F.O. occasionally passing through. This book confirms what some of the more common native ones look like in upcoming chapter. Likely our planet has been visited by a long list of Extraterrestrials over the billions of years of our existence. Ideal living condition for us perhaps not so for them, but our planet has gone through past metamorphosis changes to surface living condition, and is soon to go through another, according to God's pre-planned New Age soon to be (Christ's second coming is mentioned in this Supplement at the end, but his millennial reign is covered in Part II). If you go extinct like the dinosaur, it will be no one's fault but your own, and less than twenty years from now, most of the world's human population will do just that! Again covered extensively in Part II, but I can tell you that more than a billion people (Bible's forecast) will perish in a timeframe less than fifteen years from now (Non-Christians ineligible for rapture, and Christians who thought they could be Christians on their terms, rather than God's!)!

We were talking about aliens a minute ago and the theories on them, you are probably saying, so how did I get talking on Tribulation you are wondering. It is because it is all related subject. It is all God's control. If you learn nothing else from my books, realize that is the starting point to understanding, and figuring out all other mysteries. God does exist, and by the time you finish both my books, you will have had Christian Holy Trinity concept of God presented and evidenced so convincingly, and approached from so many different intersecting approaches, and I will have made a believer out of you if you aren't already, and if you are already so, then expect to be amazed by my presentations. I point out God's oversight control in many of these chapters discussing particular aspect of the supernatural, but it is in total also, and it typically is scientists who get lost in that aspect of the supernatural who lose sight of God's involvement role, but others also. In Math you have certain givens that are solid, proven, and unchanging. God is such a given, a certainty, in the spiritual/supernatural realm. If you don't use that given as a foundation it is then impossible to reach correct full understandings, because that base component that should have been in your formula calculation wasn't present. When some people see the vastness of the universe, and seemingly random creation life forms like these Extraterrestrials, it becomes easier for some to challenge one's concept of God and creation, find Book of Genesis statement which don't in fact square with Science, and net result culminating in weakened faith. However Science now recognizes multiple dimensions, and E.T./U.F.O., and equally other things which do square with the Bible. For now, until I explain how God has interacted in so many ways in my life to fully evidence for you the existence of God as Christians perceive him, just go along with me if you're not fully in acceptance, and maybe I'll make a Christian out of you by the time I'm done, or if you prefer, be one of the billions of humans of limited faith to experience what the Dinosaurs did with their extinction. It's not a matter of seeing it my way or hitting the extinction highway; it's seeing God so they realize the necessity of seeing it his way. No telling how many stars and planets in God's universe that once supported life, but no longer do. Is it possible God gave them explanations and directives they failed to pursue because they saw themselves as an advanced civilization, and in the process of getting to that point, had subsequently in inverse proportion diminished their esteem for God thinking themselves self-sufficient without God? No longer appreciating God, no longer worshiping God, even many no longer believing in God? Has this happened before among other of God's intelligent being creation elsewhere in the universe, in millions or billions years ago past? At some point we exceed the limit and tolerance point of one with the love and patience of God, and it's then lights out extinction time for those arrogant critters! Those little punk ass bastazoid, next to worthless, conceited, sinning, slime-morphous, crustaceous, Zugaladons! Dinosaurs no more! I make the point because understanding of humans who like babies must keep God up at all hours with our incessant whining and crying, and made a mess dirty diaper of our lives! We are little pee-ons, the E.T. are little pee-ons and what we have in common with them is our common creator God. They have full awareness of this same God, and at least some humans have the correct understanding, as well. It is in fact the God of I AM, the very same God of Moses; Jehovah God. If you think about it, Jesus further confirmed it, just as God had confirmed the coming of a Messiah/Savior to the Prophets, well prior to Jesus' birth in Bethlehem. E.T. fear the awesome power of God, and know better than to defy his will, but humans tend to push God's patience to the limit and beyond, thinking of themselves as God's little darlings. In a sense that is true, but he's also made it clear of his intolerance for disobedience and un-Godly behavior (God's breaking/boiling point is only a dozen years off!).

Think about this; to those E.T. we are in some cases the odd look E.T. in their perspective. Those funny-looking humans from Earth!

You have to realize then with E.T., as well, one size shoe in the description or explanations does not fit all. There could be virtually unlimited number of distinctly different E.T. groups scattered far wide across the universe, most of which we will never become aware of or ever see, or learn about. Some not so advanced intelligence wise, and perhaps others highly advanced technologically, and civilization wise. It also is not God's intention that we should ever know, at this time at least, right now. Basically the clock will expire before we could ever have that chance.

During Jesus' upcoming Millennial Reign, you'll be able as a redeemed one essentially meaning devoutly righteous enough in being saved by God's grace out of this current existence through rapture, to then receive extended existence in Jesus' New Reality. Most humans perished back in those Tribulation years (yet to come). A lot of permanent extinction, by people who did not comply with God's will in preventing it (Even with Prophet Wildman's warning of Deadman's Curve just right up the road.). It's not rocket science telling people that they need to get their spiritual house in order, and start taking Jesus way more seriously! Because that is what it comes down to. If you are one of the fortunate one's saved by Grave of God, redeemed through rapture, and to then experience Millennial Reign, you'll actually be able to ask question directly to Jesus and have them answered through his infinite wisdoms. All those E.T. questions, and none that cannot be answered, can you just imagine if it was made into a question and answer educational movie with Jesus narrating it how much you could learn? A lot less here with me, yet wise enough to explain that score to you.

I will deliver some seriously shocking acts-of-God episodes with no shortage of awe, and all true, non-fictional factual. How you handle in reaction is in your hands. Christians will for the most part receive these rather well, even smiling and chuckling. People of little or weak faith, then relating the example just made above to their personal status spirituality situation could find themselves shortly reaching for that bottle of extra strength migraine medication, or maybe just that bottle. Alcoholics just love an excuse to drink, and my books are just slammed full of them! Crime scene investigators saying something like: You know this is the third time this week, no entrance wound to the front of the head, the back of the head blown off, and empty or near empty liquor bottle beside the person's chair, and a book, the same book opened to the same page in the person's lap each time (Just joking, a bit exaggerated, I'll admit.)! But to make a point, that the person of faith who reads these accounts in my books can smile with a sense of joy in knowing their faith is true and correct as my testimony provides further added evidences of, while the person who's spiritual side is absent or an absolute shipwreck, will react completely differently, knowing that they have separated themselves from God, and realizing they need to now make repairs and change direction in their lives, but ultimately that can be a good thing. An eventual positive born out of the realization negative in despair. Both types can draw greater awareness leading to new resolve toward improved Christ faith relationship with God. It is even more profound when you realize I'm not a clergyman but Prophet, but called by God just the same to witness for Jesus. Those positive take aways are what Jesus is always hoping to deliver to people. Someone's reading chair won't really blast through the ceiling or roof, or they have my book blow their mind, back of their head off in the literal sense but in the figurative sense, people who read both Part I and Part II will have full comprehension of what I'm getting at here. Realize, too, before I could tell you about U.F.O./E.T. theories it was essential to explain to people who humans are! You are laughing probably, but most people don't quite understand conceptually our human relationship with God as our creator, or in many cases worldwide are in worship of a non-existent God, False God concept, who did not create them. Nine out of ten with no God, False God, or correct God but False religion interpretation of the creator. Look, Wildman pulls the supernatural veil back for you like it was a cheap flimsy shower curtain, then describes it for you, and in some cases even more shocking, even to me, God pulled it back for me so I could relate something to you! What a God, and he does love humans who love and respect him, a God most worthy of your love back. The God of Christian Holy Trinity, trust Wildman, believe in Jesus. It is important to explain humans first before we even get to E.T.'s! okay now we can do the long standing theories on U.F.O.'s.

The U.F.O. Theories:

1. Secret Weapons Theory: This one has been irrelevant for so long, it's entered an Age of relevance. From World War II era onward any anomaly aerial craft was explained away as a secret government project being tested. Back in those days seldom true, but increasingly so over decades. Now true worldwide, often military technology testing under secrecy. At least some sky phenomenon are human originated, not E.T./U.F.O. craft, but U.F.O. sightings also with greater worldwide awareness are on the increase. It remains a convenient dismissal explanation by military to claim U.F.O. as being human craft experimental in nature, knowing full well they aren't. it is convenient, as well to then conclude, and we cannot comment any further. The real purpose of Project Blue Book was simply a means to cover-up and dismiss using national security as an excuse to do so. Ever since Roswell, New Mexico, in 1947, our government in fact has known very little, only a select few in Air Force and National Intelligence Services maintain these highly classified files. The cover-up continues today, but with a far more knowledgeable public, not so easily fooled. The big difference at the same time, there really are some black ops secret projects on-going. Laser weaponry, saucer propulsion research and experiments, low Earth atmosphere orbit experimental craft, all of these. Hey, if I can pull the flimsy veil shower curtain back on the entire supernatural realm, you don't think Wildman's psychic radar can't penetrate classified government projects did you (Joking, but the E.T. are taking Wildman very seriously!)? Our government is fully aware of the U.F.O./E.T. situation, but don't want to admit that they have had on going contact and even cooperation with E.T. going on for some time (Chapter 13 further discussions)!

2. The Hollow Earth Theory: In the 1940s World War II era, Hitler not only believed in this, but dispatched search parties to search and seek out secret entrances (Someone neglected to mention it is in a different dimension, as is hell.). Living civilizations underground, is that even possible? It is when you realize some E.T. are of the spiritual ethereal body form. Little people, legends of them moving in and out of trees and rocks, or vanishing and reappearing in thin air. However this theory as it originally was conceived was talking about this dimension, thus the answer is no, it is untrue in that context. The molten magma depth depends on location, but Earth's mantle is twenty-six miles deep, often solid rock, and with little oxygen. No oxygen a good reason for nonexistence of human form similar to existence on Earth's surface. True there are caverns, shallow caverns, but temperatures in the South African gold and diamond mines at a depth of six miles deep produce temperatures in the 120 to 140 degree range; very hot!

Even today claims of underground bases inhabited by aliens are made. E.T. conceivably could have such underground centers of existence, but likely much closer to the surface. This is a far cry from those deep underground civilization claims, or the entire Earth's center being hollow which we know now definitely not to be true, but molten magma filled instead. So, under mountain and undersea USO bases are not only possible, but even likely, but these E.T. of undetermined exact dimensional characteristic nature, as are their craft not fully understood. Penetration of solid geology, mountainside above water, or in deep ocean underwater, more likely possible than not! I do personally believe under ocean USO bases actually exist. Their existence demands such technology U.F.O. capability, and explains the transition sightings from water to air, or air into water, worldwide too numerous and too geographically divergent by account witness not to be correct.

Psychic remote viewers seem to confirm this capability, as well. U.F.O. seem to be capable of cloaking, vanishing in clouds, etc. so cloaking in stealth technology is not Star Trek imagination, it is real, and as are other things these shows exhibited you might have thought was just Hollywood fiction.

In the section on Entities you completed, specifically the chapter on monsters, Chapter 3 where I spoke of a N.O.T.E. entity; it characterized, perhaps, an animal looking like an Earthly mammalian primate, but in any event image wise like an Earthly animal species, at least somewhat, no matter its creature features. Now if you apply this same reasoning to the general catch phrase U.F.O., but distinguish Flying objects not within this Dimension, you might term such as being Not OF This Dimension Flying Objects or, N.O.T.D., U.F.O.s. This separation then distinguish thus something with solid mass and weight, and entity inside the same versus other dimensional flying objects. You look at a movie screen in a theatre and everything appears solid and real, yet you know it's only a projected image. We know that a ghost seen in this dimension projecting an image of its former self to varying degree of intensity is still contained in another dimension. Likely then some U.F.O. are visible similarly in this dimension, yet actually existent within a different dimension. These other dimensions are thinly layered all around us, how many we don't know, likely somewhere between six to twelve total!

Thus a U.F.O. of such other dimensional characteristic would have no problem flying right into the side of a mountain and through it, into an inner base contained within in, similar to a Spirit, or ghost entity. Some believe the E.T., or at least certain ones have capability to shift form between dimensions, and back again at will. Some such entity such as the Reptilian are demonic in identity, thus one has to wonder is this technology, or simply some black magic stuff that is carry over from fallen angel/dark angel capabilities. The power side of evil powers and principalities that the Bible mentioned. This book repeatedly confirms the Reptilian being demonic E.T., whether from across the galaxy, or native, regardless of the higher hierarchy in demon rank. Satan's air force of U.F.O. locusts from the bottomless pit, day job as correction officer's from hell most likely and I wish it was a joke, but this is hard evidenced factual stuff, and added incentive to be among raptures of Christian faith.

Admittedly I sort of come back and harangue on this point in this book, but it's to get people to come to full awareness understanding that Reptilian are in fact, E.T. or not, definitely full demon status. The Bad Greys, as opposed to the Good Greys, are the subordinate of the Reptilian. Yet from the Roswell crash, we have proof of solid remains and wreckage from the crash site, as well as a similar one that I'll cover later from the 1960s in Germany. So the question is, if the Bad Greys have solid craft, and are tag along to Reptilian (notice Reptilian not spelled *ean*, by *ian* to distinguish the E.T. aspect), then is the Reptilian craft solid, as well, or other dimensional? Unfortunately my two Reptilian U.F.O. saucer sightings of High Hat, and Low Hat were too far away to get any insight into that answer.

Beside the concept of a U.F.O. flying through the side of mountains above sea or below, there is another concept theory that they can produce a sort of plasma enveloping field completely surrounding their craft that would allow occupants inside the craft to be in a different dimension, but protected by the plasma field surround (Think of a candy bar completely coated in an outer chocolate layer, and that layer what would allow the craft to penetrate the mountain!). No, not a U.F.O. covered in chocolate, don't be silly, we are speaking comparatively here. A little beyond human physics capability, but if Wildman can conceive of it and aliens may already be using something similar, then somewhere you can just about bet scientists are working on exactly such experimentation showing the aliens where the showers are to wash chocolate off themselves after crashing into the side of imagination mountain? Hope not. I think most readers understood my example.

These Bad Greys and Reptilian piloted U.F.O. are garden variety native to our planet E.T./U.F.O., but gaining better understanding of what is going on with them, well could be key to understanding some other shape U.F.O., other temporary stop-over visitor of the U.F.O. and E.T. Unfortunately, our government's limited sharing of information with civilian population, only slows this process (more in Chapter 13).

3. I went from Hollow Earth Theory directly into this *Interdimensional* traits theory. It is not clearly defined, or limited to just one hypothesis concerning it. However, I will tell you that it is definitely a component in some cases. The problem is this is as elusive as ghost chasing to evidence conclusively. We don't have any more but vague sketchy general concept to go on, at least the public at large, our Intelligence Services not talking on what, or how much they know, but it's pretty certain they do know a lot more than they are willing to divulge. National security is in multi-dimensions.
4. Space Animals: This is really old, probably outdated, and incorrect theory. That perhaps Amoeba like E.T., but having intelligence and much larger in scale as example might be piloting such U.F.O.. It isn't to say other life forms could be quite different, but this is sort of an archaic 1950s genre, sort of crude impression then postulated as maybe. Certainly other life forms could be non-Earthly looking, but from what we know, most at least have some human resemblance. Symmetry, one head centered, two arms extended from a single body and two legs. Differences more in details like toes, fingers, claws, hoofs, eye pupils, skin, and height weight/proportion, head shape etc. yet, the symmetry is a sign of one creator similarly common (God) which other people may suspect to be true, but I know

to be true (Jehovah God). Symmetry, which is balance, is actually a common signature trait of God, and in Part II, I will reveal other aspect of God's symmetry that the world is unfamiliar with. That's what happens with Christian Prophet in the research and development lab, formulating extended holy awareness extrapolations using Bible scripture and the periodic table of elements calculations! Even the thought of Wildman in a research lab delving deeper into uncharted, unexplored territory, then making some major discovery should perk my reader's curiosity/fascination over in Part II. I keep running out of ground breaking shovels, all through both books, but the shock and awe warehouse has them back ordered (joking).

5. The Extraterrestrial Theory: You can tell how old some of these are. That E.T. pilot U.F.O., having traveled across the galaxy to get here, across great distance expanse, perhaps using some Time/Space continuum to shortened the distance. We know this is likely true on that aspect, and definitely E.T. from across the galaxy is true, but how many different E.T., from what origin, of what description they and their craft, and what shape, size, and type of craft? It is true, but couples with the *Interdimensional* Theories likely also. In all still, many more questions than answers remain.

6. Time Travel Theory: Sort of a variation of the above theory, except this theory is a humans of the future coming back to revisit their past theory. It is incorrect for a couple of reasons. One I mentioned earlier. We are running out of time. That signpost up ahead doesn't say You are Now Entering the Twilight Zone (although it might, as well). It says a dozen years from now we will be entering the Tribulation Time Zone. In other words, we ran out of time to develop such technology, before we could employ time to use it.

There is another problem. Scientists and physics academics now believe that you could never go back further in the past than the time point at which such time machine was invented, in theory, which is all that they have currently anyway It is not God's will that man go back in time, anyway, and thus our efforts in this direction to do so, could be number 412 on a long list of reasons why Tribulation is required before this ever takes place. Theologian can supply many of the other reasons likely on God's list making Tribulation time intersection seven-year point where it currently is on God's schedule of events calendar (thanks to Wildman's holy angel messaging, on yours to, in Part II detailed). A good reason why special preparation training by reading Part I is required in mental mountain climbing, before you go on to shock-o-holic Mt. Everest Part II. Think about it, high altitude (spiritual subject/religion), steep mental slopes, and a crazy named Wildman as your guide. If you fall you become one of those people the CSI people find with no entrance wound to the front of their head, but the back completely blown away, or a shrunken head sitting on a big neck. (Figuratively speaking of course) One of my books open in your lap in your favorite reading chair just prior to brain explosion or implosion. People wanting to learn about the supernatural only to become full-fledged citizens of it, and time travel in mountain time. Maybe reliving the climb up, on the fall, on the way down. CSI noticing the anomaly of all the victims watches having stopped, too. You think Rod Sterling being Dean of Students at my old alma-mater T.Z.U. having anything to do with it? Sterling syndrome in its early stages, could mean you're in big trouble later! Another reason for this Time Travel of Humans back in Saucers to their past, is that humans are too fragile to withstand the enormous G-Force involved inside, and this obstacle would have to be technologically accomplished first, and since this is still not available now, it becomes another flaw in this theory, that coupled with those other flaws, makes this one quite improbable.

Now if you and human resembling E.T. of a much older civilization somewhere else in the galaxy arriving here somehow manipulating the past or future, then it is not inconceivable, because we don't know all their full circumstance, but it's not humans returning to the past through time travel, it's E.T. manipulating both Time and Space, and in that realm possibilities become as infinite as the universe itself. It's not explaining anything at that point, but purely unlimited conjecture with no basis in fact. Yet much of what is going on, starts out by conjecture on our part, what if, and contemplated.

7. Parallel Universe Theory: What this is really about is parallel dimensions. That is most certainly true. A space fabric of woven dimensions invisible to us humans generally seeing but the one we occupy, but with multiple other dimensions close at hand. Different vibrational frequency, plane of existence, Ultra-terrestrials we cannot see, but of high intelligence sharing close proximity space? holy angels and guardian angels certainly qualifying in that description. Telepathy which is silent transmission of thought expression in communication is the norm among most if not all Ultra Terrestrial, or Extraterrestrials it seems. The ones with shape shift or *Interdimensional* transfer ability, that ultra-aspect, as we can't say all Extraterrestrials have it. Both the holy-side and the demonic side having that ultra-capability feature.

There are certainly aspects of this parallel universe theory that are true dimensional in the universe we are aware of, but separate universe disconnected is not theory I would subscribe to. I think the one we are aware of is plenty big, and all inclusive of more strangeness than we can comprehend as it is.

One gets the sense that similar to the Bible stated two-thirds holy angel, one-third unHoly Spirit, this seems to carry through the universe also. Not just with angel, but across all intelligent E.T. life, the impression that I get is that two-thirds of them are friendly to human, not hostile. It is that one-third that is of concern. In fact if you think about it, angels do have the power to materialize from another dimension and good angels interacting with humans are proof in themselves of ultra-terrestrials who are non-demonic. It is said that angels have never lived before, but often described as spirit guides.

In any event, roughly two-thirds of extraterrestrials group category appear to be non-demonic, and the two-thirds split coincidentally a match with the percent described as good angel versus bad. By the very fact that these groupings have been shown to be non-hostile to human or are even disposed to trying to help humans clear indication they then are not hostile to human demonic alien. As I will point out elsewhere in this book, the Reptilians are not demonically leaning ET, but rather demons period! Yes, demons flying U.F.O., imagine that, I didn't think so at first myself, but in total and in firsthand eye witness, the *I would not have believed it had I not seen it for myself* rule applies here. In total in fact, I suspect in experiencing several of what could only be described as acts of God connected with this book, awareness of this for my understanding of E.T. was necessary, so it could be passed along to you. Think about it, Wildman with a senior editor who can command the demonic aliens to oblige, and they don't dare say no to. Demonic E.T. being more obedient to God than some humans choose to. No wonder the seven-year Tribulation is right up the road.

Perhaps when they were still good angels, once upon a time they had wings, but not anymore, and now need a U.F.O. propulsion vehicle for flight, that is unclear. However, both the dream premonition (2008) and the 2004 sighting from five-eighths of a mile distance, both confirm the beige orange color of scaly snake-like skin. Claw like fingers and three-toed cloven hoofs, looking half human, and half beast/reptile. That is a beast like head/somewhat human looking with two eyes. Day job listed as correction officers in hell? Meeting all qualifications wouldn't you say? With certainty. A faction of the Greys, known as the Bad Greys, are aligned to, and take orders from the Reptilian.

What are the unconventional theories? Too many to review them all, but most aren't worth the effort, including some already given you frankly I'll mention a few individuals in this regard who took positions instead.

Carl Sagan who passed away more than a decade ago, quite a noted astronomer/astro physicist dispelled both the church and existence of U.F.O.. Erik Von Daniken who will be discussed later, another deliverer of alternate theory. Sagan wrong on both counts, too brilliant in other disciplines, truly agnostic, did he also truly believe in the non-existence of U.F.O.? Remember this, at the time Sagan was making these U.F.O. non-existence remarks, he was also doing government contract research. A little arm twisting going on? This was at a time when the government was desperately trying to dispel U.F.O. existence. What better than to have a prominent scientist searching by powerful telescope the galaxy, say this for them? Sagan had a mortgage and bills to pay too, but it doesn't square with other comments he made.

Such as the possibilities for existence of intelligent life in our galaxy in terms of numbers quite high. If the intelligent life exists, then so does the intelligence necessary to busy seaport, then making statement that dismisses the existence of ocean going vessels. Sadly, like Carl Jung (discussed under agnostics Part II), an otherwise brilliant man of science completely lost in discovering and holding faith in God. Stating our Milky Way Galaxy alone one hundred thousand light years wide, and that there could be millions of places within capable of life, and sustaining civilization. As an advanced extraterrestrial civilizations. Read between the lines, and possibly he secretly recognized U.F.O., but because of his close ties to the government was forbidden to state his beliefs freely.

In some locals U.F.O. are about as common as a taxi cab in NYC., miss one and another will be along shortly. Guess that shows either Carl was not spending much time in any of the U.F.O. hotspots, or was looking so far into deep space for U.F.O. he neglected to look in Earth's atmosphere, perhaps similar true in lack of belief in existence of God, as faith begins within one's self, not millions of miles away.

We are not too far away from the day (year and months five given later), as described in Book of Revelation when, like the movie, *Independence Day*, the skies of the world will fill with U.F.O. locusts. Bad Greys and the Reptilian piloting these, their loyalty to the Anti-Christ. No one will not believe in U.F.O.s then. It will be difficult not to believe in the Bible's Book of Revelation, seven-year Tribulation, the Bible New Testament in total, or Wildman's psychic reliability for that matter, when that day comes, and all will become believers of God (Holy Trinity) as Christians know him because they will witness the antithesis right before their eyes. That is if they survive long enough to be there.

While Albert Einstein acknowledged God's existence, Carl Sagan preferred a more non-committed approach to religion, as he was already on board the Big Bang Theory without God's existence or involvement (all the time beholding the sheer majesty of God's creation; the universe).

Ancient astronaut theory of Von Daniken true? Visitation by E.T.s certainly is, with considerable evidence, but subject to discrepancy from critics. Sure, they were here thousands of years ago until the present, I fully agree. Others will change their minds when the Day of the Locust arrives, if still here to see it. Von Daniken deserves credit for all his worldwide research, but I cannot agree with conclusion representing ET as in any way shape or fashion Gods, especially God's (plural) How many U.F.O. or E.T.s has Von Daniken ever seen firsthand? My guess zero. Especially with certainty knowing the Reptilian E.T.s are not only not Gods, but in fact demons! So which group of E.T.s is he talking about? Are they all the same? You notice he always uses question mark such as I just did, never firm statement. That leaves the perfect defense to stand behind, but, I never said for certain, I just asked the question! Clearly some E.T. groups were here and left millennium ago, while some of the worst ones still here if in fact, that their true identity.

On T.V. commentary, Von Daniken claims to still hold claim to his belief in One God and Christian faith, but it is hard for me to square that using E.T.s and Gods plural in the same sentence. One wonders how much damage he has done to Christian faith and belief in One God, God the creator around the world, and likely not intentionally. Now in this book I raise the issue, also stating with uncertainty about what some have theorized might be an alternate version of Book of Genesis account for God's creation of man (the Lyrean connection some make). You will notice I am quick to point out I do not entertain any theory that tries to exclude God's involvement in creation. Many Christian fundamentalist will not budge an inch from literal interpretation. It is their interpretation to do with as they please. I think it healthy and curiously intriguing to examine alternate theories, but theories such as Panspermic Theory stating humans were seeded by ET who then left our planet, in a universe void of God, oh no, sorry, that automatically nullifies it right there. I refuse any theory, to even take the first look if it voids God. If it starts out wrong, how much is the rest of it worth?

The whole dynamic of understanding and being in acceptance of the Word of God, holy Bible, then believing to fullest measure changes when you have had profound direct involvement with the Holy Trinity, then to firsthand experience what the Bible refers to as an anointing gift. In my case after more than forty-five years as a precognitive psychic medium in receipt of holy angel sourced awareness transactions, then in 2008, having future awareness shift from general subject to holy subject/topic, is what I'm referring (covered further later in this book). Your author is a testimonial witness for and in the correctness of faith in Jesus Christ the Holy Spirit concept in Trinity, and true Holiness of the holy Bible as genuine and true, carrying through all supernatural dimensions. Also, I'm a genuine (holy source information) apocalypse prophet! Those awareness provided from God as of 2008, all relate to the coming seven-year Tribulation, and in doing so, confirms Christ's second coming, as well (Part II of this book will fully detail Tribulation for you, including some new event/timing match-ups predictively, all according to Revelation, exactly as written, new confirmations (some Part I intentional leaks, are provided on a few important future timings, but you still want Part II)! Old Testament Hebrew Prophets foretelling of both Christ's first advent, and soon, twenty-first century second advent, seventh trumpet, mighty angel return, prior to Armageddon as a spectacle in the sky above Jerusalem. With those Old Testament accounts, and Prophecies, Book of Revelation Prophecy, and other Prophet's prophecies including mine, all of it pertaining, none conflicting, derived from God, and spanning Millennium, it speaks confirmation well beyond these Prophecies themselves. It revalidates the entire K.J. Bible (for anyone in doubt), but in doing so, Christian faith, as the only correct religion, re-verified (It'll take clergy a bit of getting use to that God's holy angel and a Christian Prophet named Wildman were responsible, and not a chance in the world I would ever speak falsely on holy sacred subject, but don't need to, because it's the total truth). Jesus is Lord and Savior, no question.

That is unless your name is Eric Von Daniken who makes a living in peddling counter to the Word of God hypothesis theory often using factual but sometimes non confirmable evidences that can be neither fully disproven, nor proven independent of what God (Jehovah) or Jesus' own witnessed and written word is. The Bible warns against such false teachers and his like-minded friends. E.T. Gods (plural?) Demi-gods, or Gods? Which E.T. group, Eric, care to be specific? Cult leaders prey on the spiritual ignorance/curiosity of people, leading them further from God, instead of toward God from deception they are equally misdirected in themselves. You see the parallel here to a thirty-year theory hustler? I don't know which is worse, denying God's existence, or attempting to convince people to seriously entertain the thought of God singular instead with ET Demi-gods. Didn't the Babylonians, Egyptians, early Greeks, Baal worshipers, Pagans, and Mayans try this before, only to be proven this is not correct? So why would twentieth-century Erik Von Daniken want to have you believe what has already been shown obsolete spiritual belief; bankrupt, corrupt, and false? It isn't that these demi-gods didn't exist; they did! It's that they were exposed as Reptilian linked (demons). Even the Bible is providing evidence.

In later chapters I mention a 1988 T.V. show, *The Bible and U.F.O.* that brought up the Lyrean connection with the book of Genesis. This is not my theory I originated, I mention it in later chapter because it offers an intriguing figurative rather than literal interpretation of Book of Genesis. That is, God might have created man from an ethereal, but very human looking in appearance ET/angelic like being mixed with that handful of dirt, and instead of the handful of dirt alone. A woman created by D.N.A. gene alteration already existing in a Lyrean woman possibly rather than simply Adam's rib likely not meant literally. Ethereal E.T.-like beings also matching account given by Edgar Cayce, as his Atlantis description of earliest humans. Cayce stated that, over time, these ethereal ghost like beings took on greater and greater solid form. I don't try to tell you this is true, or promote this, I'm simply making mention of it. On the other hand, Chariot of the Gods is an affront to both God (singular), and the Christian Church/holy Bible, and although hiding behind question marks, seems to be promoting the Demi-gods/E.T., thought to be long extinct (concept/validity wise and mythical only).

This is the path leading to the overhead crossbeam. Here is a coil of rope. Here is a diagram of how to tie a slipknot, used by hangmen. Then when reader's follow this path, and some among them hang themselves spiritually by abandonment of Christian faith, or other Religion for that matter believing in (One) God, you might then expect Von Daniken to say something like, *Yes, but I never instructed these people to commit spiritual suicide, and hang themselves.* By abandonment of their true and correct spiritual footing- Christian faith, or at the least, belief in God singular in earlier era, something proclamation such as this would have been more than enough to get Von Daniken burned at the stake as a heretic. Freedom to express your views in this age, right or wrong is tolerated, even if the church is ideologically undermined in doing so, and the controversy reaps profits from doing so, even though principles and evidence it is based upon are clearly weak and misleadingly inconclusive. Religion, particularly Christian faith is very hallowed and sacred ground, and if you question its validity, you better come forth with much more conclusive evidence than Von Daniken's comments. In other words, you better be right if you do this. I'm telling you and vehemently, these hypothesis he makes are completely incorrect! In stating this, I would not do so if I was not certain of my words also. I am not incorrect, and have the evidence to both prove this ET Demi-god stuff a bunch of demonically linked baloney, but prove also in the process, the Christian church/holy Bible/Holy Trinity belief, New Testament, and Book of Revelation are quite correctly genuine. Jesus Christ equals the truth, and the truth equals Jesus Christ. The holy Catholic church is in fact holy, their proclaimed Saints, actually are now crowned saints in heaven, and heaven is property Titled to Christian ownership! These not just words, but truth. Jesus Christ really is Lord and Savior of mankind, and with certainty! While most of Wildman' psychic angelic future messaging was not holy related subject, a few recently were. As you will later read both in this book, and more extensively in discussion in Part-II, Holy subject Prophecy has been renewed from Holy Kingdom sourcing, and this author/Prophet in receipt of such.

Is Wildman a Christian Zealot? No, A Prophet who is Christian, and credits holy angel with all his future seeing awareness, whether of holy subject or not is of even greater spiritual intensity and awareness than even a zealot! It is the Christian Prophets from whom the zealots draw their energy/fuel supply (and Wildman has vast supply reserves!). You will never be able to accuse Wildman of being a False Prophet because I seal all holy in nature Prophecy until it fulfills my message; it is limited to what is contained between front and back cover of the holy Bible, or what comes from holy angel. The purpose of a Prophet is to exalt Christ, not one's self, and that is where I try to keep the focus, off of me, but on my message. Only the word of God is holy, no mortal except when Christ was in the flesh ever can be.

Examining alternative thinking is healthy, even the Catholic Church, long a bastion of conservative fundamentalist thinking, seems to have adapted a more liberal policy in recent years in inspecting and examining other thinking from scientific to spiritual. This is good, because it gives your own perspective a more informed viewpoint. Inspection does not require acceptance. Von Daniken demi-god theory is unacceptable, and incorrect, unless demon worship is your preference. As said before, I recognize all the positive contribution he has made, such as convincing the public of ET existence both now and in Earth's ancient past, and in research surrounding it. All excellent there, and deserving of credit. At least he and I agree on this much.

In the 1975 book, *Invisible College*, author Jacques Valles' theory claimed that U.F.O. put forth some kind of power which directs to a deep human subconscious level that can control human experience, thus situational outcome. Extraterrestrials/ultraterrestrials if you prefer, do use telepathy for communication among themselves, and can and do use it on humans. Certainly true (numerous abductee cases in confirmation of this); however, there is nothing to correlate this as tied to central purpose, or the majority of U.F.O. encounter.

High Strangeness and Oz factor mentioned more, later in the book are cases where invisible forces acting upon the human psyche do seem to be involved, and in manipulative ways. To mean a U.F.O. at a distance with no direct connect except some brain wave frequency humans operate on is somehow tapped into. Phantom cars mentioned later in this book points to mild demon/human possession internally altering perception for a brief period. Perhaps since some ET are in fact demonic demon, then there could be some sort of link. I consider this theory to be valid except perhaps not functioning precisely that way. Since it's not know for certain, for now, it's a concept that should be neither accepted or dismissed until more is discovered along these lines.

Another theory put forth by Jerome Clark and Loren Coleman decades ago, is known as the psychic projection theory. Based on Carl Jung's concept of collective consciousness, it bases this as grounds to debunk U.F.O. existence. Clearly they've never lived beneath an endangered species U.F.O./et preserve flight area like Wildman or observed entire South Florida. Alien Air Wings in flight (North Florida 271 St., and South Florida, 391st Alien Air Wing Squadrons; tongue in cheek), as Wildman has aptly named them. Sixty saucers in flight observed, in one night proof of that! That's a lot of collective consciousness in flight, wouldn't you say? Carl Jung think taxicabs in New York City's collective consciousness, too? These debunkers are hereby debunked, at least in my view.

It is only in the last sixty years we've slowly come to accept the very existence of E.T. and U.F.O., despite numerous sighting accounts, but then because of numerous sighting accounts. Later in this book (Part II) I'll mention when to expect by my projection, Bible mentioned locusts (U.F.O.); but even by then, humanity has only scratched the U.F.O. understanding surface.

Chapter 8
South Florida (1990s) U.F.O. Infestation and a 2004 Sighting

Before I give account of the 2004 sighting, there is background information required for a broader understanding in full comprehension. Some tie-ins with other chapters are noted also.

Back in the early 1990s a book was published that had South Florida U.F.O. infestation as part of its title if I remember correctly. I did not read the book, either then or now, but do remember some comments from a newspaper review of this book at that time. I don't recall the author, either, except they were reporting experiences that happened in the Ft. Lauderdale, Fla., Broward County area relative to night sky observances. Also on apparent media blanket of silence on the U.F.O. subject that they also experienced relative to reporting their claims to the public.

The only reason I am not reading this book now or seeking to do so, is that I've basically I am sure, re-verified everything they claimed to be true in 1990, and still true in 2008 timeframe, including reluctance by the media to report on this subject. Ironically also, housing market recession then as currently, an added reason not to bring up anything if construed to be detrimental. As in deterrent to mental stability when in contemplating the local real estate market. That's the excuse, or one of them used by media in bad times, but it continues to be a favorite topic to sweep aside even in better times, just to slightly lesser extent.

It also triggered a type of psychic episode (discussed again in the Psychic section) so rare, I had to come up with my own term for it! I've had four of these in my lifetime, and I call them intunitions. The very first one occurring in 1964, informing me through telepathic holy angel messaging I would one day write a book when sixty-one or sixty-two years of age. At that time instructed to remember detail of the church sermon that day. Three other times in life, very similarly holy angel telepathic instruction, *Remember this or that, you'll need it for the book!* An angel intuitively instructing me to remember something of future importance to a book, and the book important to serving God's purpose. angelic intunitions then a part of Wildman's parapsychic vocabulary nomenclature. By the early 1990s I already knew I'd be authoring a book exploring the supernatural that would include religious discussion, ghost mention, and now adding U.F.O. subject material according to my reliable holy angel source, my intuition provider. One can almost imagine God instructing this angel: *Every time the Wildman's life path intersects with something that has value for the book he will author, I want to bring his attention to it.* At least that is the way it seemed, and a rather convenient calling card for an angel to drop along with the message, that you are being watched over, as reminder (Holy angel protective agency is quite real; no question about it.).

It seems this other person from Broward County began keeping a sightings log, then wrote their book from notated log entries. I remember that and a few other things from the book review article. The primary premise being that U.F.O. routinely masquerade as pretending to be stationary stars, in observation of humans below, perhaps among other things. Well everything they postulated then hypothesis wise, I can now vouch for and then some. As if that wasn't enough, (as you'll later read, a 1988 T.V. Show, *The Bible and U.F.O.* sparked a premonition right while I was watching the T.V. in front of me regarding both a U.F.O. and Particle beam, but one mentioned in Book of Revelation was foretold I'd one day witness. The only thing even more remarkable was it fulfilling in 2008 exactly as foretold (more on that later).

I recall the other author mentioning different shaped U.F.O. types and names from that review article, like Pancake, High Hat, and Low Hat, etc. I recall, too, this other author felt in describing High Hats that they were the rarest to sight because they rarely came inland, and would be seen only along dark patches of coastline very late at night. That is perfect match for my 2004, first sighting of a U.F.O. at reasonably close range (five-eighths of a mile distance). At low altitude, exactly what myself and two others witnessed. Eat your heart out Orson Wells! at the time, I really had no idea what I had seen, and figured that the odds of ever seeing one again were pretty remote. Very wrong there, and in 2008 seeing so many more I, too, began keeping a log to record it all. I guess for someone who lives near Carlsbad Cavern, they shouldn't be surprised at cave bat sightings in number, and South Florida long known as a U.F.O. hotspot. Chapter 11 will discuss more about these Star Pretenders, and doesn't it just figure my 2004 sighting would be a rarely seen one. Only much later realizing what I'd seen understandings wise.

In tribute to this earlier author let me say this: You deserve to be recognized as having made accurate and truthful statement to the cause of furthering U.F.O. understandings and study, and I salute you for your effort. In Chapter 13, I'll discuss the continuing government cover-up conspiracy to keep the public from information which should not be concealed. I do my best with this book to reveal as much as I know, and better inform you.

Here's a Wildman quote:

U.F.O. move with impunity through South Florida. Late night skies, and sometimes in significant numbers. Particularly after midnight the way some endangered species move through wildlife preserves elsewhere. Unfortunately in this case humans are the species approaching the day of endangerment, while our government protects the U.F.O./E.T. aliens (They just don't want the public to know!).

Oh, but the public already had some idea anyway. That other author mentioning when high winds or Hurricanes pass in or around the deep trough/undersea trench off Puerto Rico, U.F.O. activity ceases completely in the entire South Florida region. My study (and that of others) concurs a similar conclusion. U.F.O. are also USO with undersea bases, and that deep Puerto Rican trench area is one Devil's Triangle base location. Out in the deep Marianna's trench of the Dragon's Triangle, the very same. Is it any wonder human aircraft or large sea vessels routinely vanish for no apparent reason, or smaller recreation boating craft for that matter.

One of the themes of this book is the interconnected vine tangle of the supernatural, but then how all of it then ties back to trees of the spiritual in God's forest of religion! Here I'm trying to get to further describe my 2004 U.F.O. sightings and before I can get to that, I need to first explain some of the incredible interconnection of supernatural vine along the way. No one questions that there are no limitations on the extent to which the supernatural can become strangely strange, weirdly weird, or bizarrely bizarre. Just heavier vine tangle! Later in the Psychic Section discussing the parapsychic and something referred to there as the psychic matrix is exampled here.

What I'm about to explain is going to sound like some cheap 1960s Mickey Spillane fictional murder mystery account. Except it's anything but fiction, but rather factual account of event which actually happened, just presented along with accompaniment of supernatural aspects that I've identified for you.

Now I'm sure you've heard of some families which seem to be fated or some say cursed or jinxed in the direction of perpetual bad outcome, and including untimely and unnatural deaths that become the rule rather than the exception within such family. Marry into it, and you could then be exposed to similar fate. Associate with family members, and ill aspects of the supernatural may have consequence for you, just from intersecting point association. You wouldn't at first think that second part to be true, but after what I relate from this story you might not be so sure. My intersection starting point seems to be one evening late June of 1980, introduction to a "generationally cursed" Family.

I'd decided to stop in a little bar on the north end to knock back a couple of cold ones, and age thirty-two at the time, and divorced. The bar maid was exceptionally pretty, and striking up a conversation (the place was not real busy), and she told me she was estranged but still married to her second husband. Her name was Jackie L, and her second husband was H.L. She mentioned two daughters by her first husband who she had divorced because he was a chronic, often unemployed alcoholic. The daughters initials J.S. and R.S. would years later intersect my life also, as well as their grandmother.

It was already clear as of 1964, I was one day when sixty-one or sixty-two destined to write a book (this book), but how much of what happened in my life leading up to this book was fate running its course as opposed to just random occurrence happening is something any of us have difficulty determining. Can you imagine if when Jackie L. served me that first beer and she said something like, "You realize I come from a family with a curse or negativity fate of some sort hanging over it, and by your life now in intersection contact connection with mine you have exposed yourself to untold vulnerabilities. "Your next thirty years will include a supernatural extravaganza of parapsychic event activity of future foreknowledge and fulfillments, including a U.F.O. sighting you'll have with my youngest daughter present, twenty-four years from now, who you'll meet twelve years from now, and much, much more!" Or, maybe someone like a bouncer at the entrance who said to me, "Realize if you enter, you'll be stepping into thirty years of Twilight Zone episodes you'll experience, with no one knows what could be headed your way." Are you sure you still want to enter?" No, nothing warnings wise, yet both of these statements would have been true!

Did my brand of beer change the formula or something? Now with the cat with the hat in the vat or something? You wonder if you are feeding the supernatural dog table scraps or dog biscuits, or is it the other way around and it's feeding you. Either way it's like you hear the crunch of supernatural Scooby snacks, Kennel ration bizzarro biscuits, and the weirdness wafers. Crunch, crunch, crunch! Of course, all in hindsight. At the time it all seems perfectly normal! Some normal! As in supernatural organic psychic soil or something. Getting high back in my old college days, a different type of vine. These were double shots of reality with the parapsychic already built in, with delayed reaction with Twilight

Zone residency included. Did this mean all my old Twilight Zone frequent flyer miles were now obsolete from my college days? It now coming to me? It seemed so anyway.

About ten days to two weeks later, returning to that little bar, to stop in and say Hi to Jackie L., it seemed my thirty-year supernatural rollercoaster ride had begun, and the first emotional hill was being climbed. Jackie L. had just died, perishing in a plane crash! That tragic family curse/fate claim her? It seemed so, although again not seeing it in that perspective until many years later. At work, our company had recently hired a yard worker who we'll call Jimmy D. He wasn't aboard the plane but something like 7 members of his family were. It devastated him for the rest of his life becoming a heroin addict, unable to cope with his grief. Of the twenty-four passengers and three or four crew members of the old DC-3 prop aircraft, it seemed I had tie and knowledge of several of these who were fated to be aboard this Fourth of July night flight gambling junket to the Bahamas.

The plane had taken off, but soon returned for inspection and repair as there seemed to be a malfunction with one of the engines. Several hours of delay were necessary, while meanwhile out over the open ocean offshore a violent thunderstorm had developed. After several hours, it was deemed the aircraft mechanics had fixed the problem, and the aircraft was now safe for flight. Now however, the aircraft would not only have to fly in to a violent thunderstorm with heavy lightning, but perhaps headwinds of fate blowing out of the supernatural, as well. Passengers had gotten a promotional discount for the flight, but clearly no bargain.

It is hard to imagine something more terrifying than being abroad a plane that perhaps had an engine stall out over ocean (shark-infested) waters at night in zero visibility during a violent thunderstorm and knowing your death was likely only seconds away, yet just enough time to become traumatized by shock in realization of your own impending expiration from this world by these terms. Subsequent investigation revealed the plane may have flipped over upside down as it hit the water, as well. All passengers had already gambled with their lives and lost before ever even arriving to gamble. The expression never gamble unless you can afford to lose comes to mind, but then we all gamble with our lives don't we! Bermuda Triangle claiming another victim, as well, to its fate tally. Swift Gulfstream current, five hundred to eight hundred feet in depth, and many bodies never recovered (Don't worry, I didn't forget the U.F.O. account of 2004, this is all background information stemming from 1980 origination.).

Now after investigations, it was deemed the old aircraft was simply no match for the thunderstorm, and it was ruled basically that the storm coupled with already exhibited mechanical malfunction had been the cause. Jackie's mother wasn't buying it. According to Irma H., Jackie L's estranged husband H.L. was a mid-level gangster with the crime family of a Ft. Lauderdale based mob, and H.L. was heavily involved in Columbian cocaine trafficking.

It seemed when I met Jackie at that bar, she had only recently hired on, coming out of witness protection over in Texas. Why? Because H.L. wasn't paying child support, Jackie L. had agreed to cooperate in Federal custody and testify against the second former husband now estranged from but not completely out of contact with. What brought her out of protective custody wasn't clear, probably naivety, and underestimating risk.

So after the initial newspaper headlines of the crash itself had died out, here was Irma H. (who passed away around 2002/2003 timeframe) reporting to the newspaper she was certain the aircraft was sabotaged by the mob, because of the threat her daughter's testimony represented to them. More investigation, and eventually no conclusion remained official cause of crash explanation.

Then there was a lesser known third theory. That theory involved corrupt politicians and judges from the County level all the way up to the Federal level who were corrupt and had received dirty money from the mob. Could it have influenced the plane crash investigation itself? Agencies of the Federal government? Mob/Govt. complicity in the lucrative drug trade during the Ollie North era, possibly have anything to do with a civilian aircraft crash with a Federal star witness aboard? In other words, according to this conspiracy theory, not only would Jackie L. have pulled the tablecloth fine linen of respectability off the dining table, to local crime family mobsters, but the heirloom china of state judges, and State and Federal Congressmen could have been implicated, not to mention the intelligence services place setting silverware possibly being abruptly knocked to the floor in the process of all this. In other words, the mob was threatening to expose the government's key players if Federal prosecutors pursued their case. Both theory 2 and theory 3 says the government was complicit in the cover-up because Jackie L represented a loose cannon for them, as well, under these conditions. Is it true? We'll never know. Those aircraft mechanics both turned up missing, vanishing without a trace, both now it seems having met with an accident shortly thereafter. Imagine that, stepping in front of a gun as it was being fired. No, I'm joking there, but one is definitely dead, the other is simply missing (for decades) and the presumption is, now 'permanently missing' also.

Jackie's youngest daughter J.S. was obsessed for some time in trying to learn more about her mother's death, but through some mafia channels she herself had, and pursued, she only succeeded in nearly getting herself killed sticking her nose into off limit discussion topic. Little more is known today than it was back in 1980. Mob involvement? government conspiracy and cover-up (more of that in Chapter 13)? One World Order and Illuminati theorist linking the rich and powerful including criminal, political policy secret agenda. Could even this be a fit? You tell me.

Now the psychic supernatural gave me explicit warning NOT to include the information I just provided you with, delivered to me through a dream Omen. Very clear warning! I endanger myself by even discussing what I've told you. So why tell it? Because, I really don't know anything more than this, but if you think about, the supernatural is also in a sense saying to me some guilty party will feel threatened by release of information like this supporting either theory two or three has some basis to it! Could Jackie L. still be out to indict the Mob from a watery grave! Talk about a women scorned, why don't you! Remember this all started with meeting Jackie one time and ordering a beer! The Omen didn't arrive until 2008. Wildman ignoring a death omen to relate the background to a U.F.O. story I am gradually getting you to. The name Wildman a perfect fit here also. However, it's only because I don't have any other incriminating evidence that I dare speak out in the face of a *to be taken seriously* omen. I have holy angel protection on my side as you'll read later besides!

Interestingly, Jackie's youngest daughter J.S. was not only one of the two other witnesses to the 2004 U.F.O. sighting, but one of two women of the (Psychic section) Parallel Premonition. A few months after all of the headlines of the plane crash, then Grandma's indictment of the Mob being directly involved, desperately sabotaging the aircraft in order to silence Jackie, now J.S. only a few weeks later was making headlines herself. A teenager with a driver learner's permit, she had gone to a bar, and upon leaving (she claims she was drugged, as well), was involved in a traffic accident fatality, killing a young man waiting for a turn lane signal (more tragedy). J.S. herself nearly died, and through subsequent blood transfusion, eventually contracted Hepatitis C.

Your still wondering about the U.F.O. tie-in, and this roller coaster car probably seems like it's slowing down in climbing this hill. This is all background information.

Now I'm driving along just directly West of where J.S.'s accident happened and I'm listening to the radio station talking about this accident, and whether State of Florida will charge her as an adult or not, etc. and as I'm driving north on State Psychic Road 809 (discussed later) here comes a telepathic message that I will one day meet this girl, who I already recognized was Jackie L's younger daughter! I sense only in a vague general intuitive way how far into the future this will be as of the time I'm psychically receiving the message. My radar saying roughly a decade or ten years, and it actually turned out to be twelve! Along with the silent messaging through conveyance telepathically received, was a vision of storm clouds very dark rolling in, a funnel spout starting to form beneath, and accompanying lightning likely! A female tornado that I was being foretold I'd one day meet, and my angel never wrong. Kind of like, you've got more than a ten year head start to avoid this Tornado. Storm chaser that Wildman is, God knew I'd be drawn to a pretty, sexy, and alluring tornado in moth to a flame fashion, and would learn the hard way never to ignore angelic warning! Why did I ignore the Omen previously mentioned then? That will be four years ago by the time you read this and hopefully no longer applies—hopefully (It might be the guardian angel telling me, that guarding the Wildman is hard enough for them without me inviting challenges for them, causing then to have to requisition more saves highlights reels or something!). Wildman already tying up a detachment of four angels instead of the normal one!

In 1993, I met J.S. as the premonition predicted, and she was still on probation from her fatality D.U.I. We became romantically involved, but briefly. She had an ankle monitor on her ankle, and I joked that she was not allowed 150 feet from the phone next to my bed. Restricted female tornado on house arrest at the Wildman's house/bedroom. That's what you call having the justice system work in your favor. Short lived, though, because she soon violated the terms of her probation, getting a little too frisky. She had violated a curfew on top of not notifying her probation officer, and visiting a bar serving alcohol she was restricted from entering. A violation in triplicate, at a cost of three and a half years in a women's state correction institution upstate. (storage facility for other female tornados!) Tornadoes are habitual offenders, so, too, the name seems to fit. Even in knowing neither of us figured we'd be an item together longer term afterwards, that didn't mean I didn't still have some feelings for her, and decided to at least send her a little money for her weekly canteen, no one else likely would unless I did. I'm not sure why, but I wanted to at least maintain a friendly relationship. On the supernatural/parapsychic side of things, there were a half dozen or so additional episodes involving or concerning her, as it later turned out (Psychic section discussing some others).

There isn't room here to discuss everything that occurred between 1996 when she was released from women's correctional, and mid-2004, but in that later end, virtually everyone was advising me to simply cut my losses (that were extensive) and say good-bye to her for good. She had been in a downward spiral of self-destruction increasingly over the past years, and I finally did reach the point of saying good-bye for good. A truly strange psychic awareness episode then occurred. I'm telepathically being told, *You can if you want to, but if you choose to do so then you will miss out experiencing something big!* What could that be, I wondered? I sensed it was only a few months into the future, and in fact my intuitions as usual were correct. I just never expected it to be a sighting of a big U.F.O. about four months later!

J.S. was a night owl, and I was not, and definitely had I not been in her company, and assisting her with a ride across town, there is no question my angel was right, I definitely would have missed this U.F.O. sighting five miles away on the other side of town, and fast asleep instead like most normal people would be. In retrospect later, tracing this vine tangle back to its origin, I realized everything seemed to stem from meeting J.S.'s mother, Jackie L. twenty-four years earlier. Then later meeting JS.'s grandparents and sister (different vines).

It somehow all seems to tie back to my walking into that Twilight Zonesque bar back in 1980. Jackie L. had only just begun working there then, and it wasn't too long after her death that the place just closed up and vanished itself, as if never being there at all. It would seem there might already have been a tragedy vine in place even then to account for all the tragic deaths. Jackie had an older sister and cousin who had died in a car accident in N. Florida in the 1970s. Vines of tragedy seemingly interwoven strangely everywhere throughout this family. Jack H., Irma's husband had died from a brain aneurism, going into a coma he never recovered from. It stemmed from a severe head injury sustained when he was much younger that made that part of his brain vulnerable. Jackie's sister's husband had fallen down a flight of stairs and broken his neck even prior to her sister's death in the car crash. Was there a possible tragedy vine link somewhere?

When Irma's husband Jack passed away I continued to help granny with rides to the pharmacy or supermarket generally, even though there was no longer a relationship with J.S. (My Christian conscience telling me it wouldn't be right to leave a widow in need of something that I could supply and help with.). I even mowed the grass in her small yard in the summer, expecting nothing in return. I was living up to standards that I held myself to, or 'living the faith', rather than just talking the faith.

Had I not continued to maintain company with J.S. in 2004, then I'd have missed the U.F.O. sighting, and in similar fashion had I not maintained contact with her grandmother, I'd have missed a rather shocking confession revelation just before Irma passed away from throat cancer around 2002/2003 timeframe. Something that although not conclusive, might be a link to the seemingly tragic curse of death this family seemed to have hanging over it. Even someone as remotely linked as J.S.'s sister R.R.'s husband's first wife died tragically prior to Irma's death. Was Irma the key?

Irma was Miss Tampa 1920 something, all of about five feet tall. When ballroom dancing became big during the 1930s, 40s, and 50s, she had become a top tier instructor with Arthur Murray's, and taught other instructors the more complicated steps.

Accusing Jackie's sister of flirting with another man, her husband had given her a severe beating sending her to the hospital. Irma and Jack lived in a two-story at the time (early 1970s). Irma generally had a smiling pleasant disposition, but it seems was angered to the point of rage that her son in law had inflicted such a beating on her daughter. It seems allowing her son-in-law to lead in descending the staircase, she impulsively decided to give a dance lesson he'd neither ever forget, or ever remember. The tall staircase two-step! She took one step back, then turned her foot sideways to push off with a karate like mule kick. Impromptu dance lesson or maybe just teaching him a lesson/retribution for beating up on her daughter! Lying at the bottom of the staircase with a broken neck, it was ruled an accidental death and covered up all these years! Irma confessed this to me before she died. Murder! A Ten Commandments violation and possible evil soil the tragic death curse was rooted in?

Hard to say, and neither Mafia long extension tentacles, or long extension vine tentacles of the supernatural are known for answering questions, giving up secrets, or making confirmation as to profiling exactly how they conduct their business, but here was an 89 year old grandmother who back in 1980 accusing the mob of sabotaging her daughter from testifying as Federal State's evidence, and further accusing of a cover-up to conceal it, herself already covering up the murder of her other son-in-law! No wonder the whole family seemed to be living under a dark tragic curse of death cloud!

Well it seems so, even if not actually so, and ironic that the 1980 premonition of my meeting J.S. twelve years later actually came with a visual of a dark storm cloud, or in angelic symbolic speak: this girl you will one day meet comes with a lot of supernatural baggage, she is bad news, and you may want to think about moving to New Zealand. No, Wildman is a storm chaser, or until he learned his lessons the hard way. Years later, there is still wreckage from my life dangling from the tree branches, but I've improved my angelic symbolism interpretational skills a great deal since those early days.

In 2008 I had an Omen not to mention any of this account in this book and it is only because I feel the danger has passed that I now do. If you analyze it, it means there is still a person or persons who might feel endangered or threatened by the release of this information to the general public. The aircraft crash has been a closed cold case since 1980, and many people who might have known but weren't telling, are now likely in their grave by this time, as well. It is highly unlikely what happened will ever be known for certain one way or another. When the U.F.O. took off at near instantaneous speed from a total hover standstill around 4 A.M. early on the morning of December 8, 2004, twenty three and a half years after meeting Jackie L. it passed across the very ocean waters where on July Fourth weekend 1980, Jackie L.'s plane had crashed.

Now I don't put much credence in numerology, but just for a moment consider the thirty-one days as years in the month of December, drop the half, and you have twenty-three years separation. Subtract twenty-three from thirty-one and you have the eighth. It isn't that there isn't numerology involved, it's just not anything confirmable usually beyond saying it's merely coincidence. It's no big deal even if it is imbedded the way I look at it. The supernatural already has enough vine tangle and psychic web matrix (Psychic section) to worry about, without examining vine casing texture so to speak. Gad zooks, Charlie Brown, gad zooks!

Oh Granny, you shouldn't have!

Now I could have taken you straight to the 2004 U.F.O. sighting with this Chapter account, but then you'd have missed all of this background, and a 1980 time portal window chance to have a drink in a Twilight Zonian bar with pretty

Jackie L. as your bar maid!! You'd have missed Mickey Spillane sitting on one side of you, or Paul Harvey sitting on the other, with the rest of the story, and passing you the bowl of Scooby snacks pretzel, while you and Irma were waiting for your roller coaster car to climb the hill of that story. Even you have to admit the view from that hill, and the surrounding scenery were quite surreal! Rod Sterling sitting next to Paul Harvey reminding all of us that the truth is much, much, stranger than fiction. The supernatural with truths uniquely its own.

Sure, these metaphorical characters for figurative analogy purposes are fictional, but they all have factual identity none the less, living or not. Every lick of the story I told you was factual, whether some believe or disbelieve is up to them, which pretty well can be said for this entire book. I'll deliver the incredible story or account that sounds more fictional than non-fiction I realize, yet this book and all accounts delivered both in Part I, and Part II, are all one hundred percent factual. Everything described, the Wildman actually lived and witnessed firsthand.

Part II of this book is devoted exclusively to religious/spiritual aspects of the supernatural in a similar, first-hand review. Meaning I did actually experience religious prophecy forth telling and foretelling, no different than the Biblical Prophets did. I won't hold it against anyone now, prior to reading Part II, who chooses not to believe so, but I can tell you this: Wildman will amaze and astonish virtually everyone in the religious community when my foretold prophecy begin fulfilling, not to mention worldwide public at large. Especially non-Christian theologian when Prophet Wildman proves convincingly the validity of Christianity, and causing the legitimacy bankruptcy of many of them in the process. Part I gives background for Part II, but equally so, after reading Part II, if you return here to Part I, I think you might gain a few insights that can be applied here from what you derive there. Yes, I always keep one foot into the future for you so to speak. Lucky you!

December 8, 2004, U.F.O. Sighting: The Account

Age 56 at that time, I was set at that time, and would have been considered a credible witness in a court of law. At that time, J.S. with me, as also, a younger male friend of hers. She somewhere around forty-five and her friend somewhere around thirty-five or perhaps even younger. Unfortunately by legal standards it is questionable if either would be credible witness in a courtroom, but for a U.F.O. sighting, either they saw what I saw, or didn't, but having two other breathing humans witness the same U.F.O. sighting circumstance is credibility enough for me, and hopefully you, as well. While this particular type of craft is a more rare sighting I was to learn from later research, having a U.F.O. sighting in South Florida not nearly as uncommon as I thought at that time (never expecting to have many more sightings).

Extensive Truth Verification/Lie Detection exams backs up all of the statements I present you with here, and full transparency of the questions is presented in that Section. It is important to note I was totally sober having no alcoholic consumption prior, no drugs legal or medication, and no illegal drugs consumed either then or prior. I was one hundred percent clean, and one hundred percent credible. A designated driver, now a designated U.F.O. witness.

A lot of fictional movies, and T.V. subject focus on E.T. and U.F.O., but often conveying fictional content, because the producers don't know too much about what really is true, but also know most people don't, either. That is one of the goals of this book to present the factual side, and it has much more important bearing than most might recognize at first. Even U.F.O. experts have only scratched the surface of all there is to be knowledgeable of on the subject, and while much of what I bring to this examination table is confirmation furthering existing hypothesis as re-evidenced to be factually true. Still, valuable cutting edge contribution to the cause of better understanding on a very elusive subject

For some unexplained reason that night, I'd decided to travel an indirect route heading south, going a few more blocks Easterly first. Had I not been in the company of my passengers providing them this ride (as stated previously) I would not have been present over on that side of town at that hour at all (the sighting occurrence between 3 and 4 A.M.). This was a route rarely taken, and have no idea why I did that on that night. Dark night, dark intercostal waterway, nothing to see, right? I turned Southward traveling along the western shore of the intercostal waterway. Travel straight East, and a bridge will take you on the South end of Palm Beach Island, and Billionaire's Row of expensive property and luxury mansions.

Crossing two bridges with an island in the middle of the intercostal, the elongated island is a mangrove enclave and bird sanctuary for water fowl, stretching for hundreds of yards southward. Turning South then, before crossing the bridge, there was the mangrove island off to my left but hard to see because it was a dark night, yet some mangrove treetop silhouette were visible, but why? At first noticing something hovering about three hundred feet off the ground, I remember asking myself what in the heck is that, it was much too big to be a helicopter, and rolling my window down, there was no prop noise, only silence! Then as I was past the end of the Mangrove island, I suddenly realized this was one huge U.F.O. I was witnessing (we were all witnessing), and that realization just stuns you like a truck load of Twilight Zone bricks being delivered and dumped off the top of your head! Is that where that lump came from? It is a feeling I am all too familiar with.

This thing is about eighty to one hundred feet in diameter, but you couldn't get an exact feel for where the edges were because it was a moonless night. It had running lights on the western side of it (closest to us) that at first had given me the impression of large helicopter, but by now there was no doubt from the likely (though not clearly visible) saucer shape that this thing was a big U.F.O. Lit windows on the South facing side, but dark around 70 percent of the other edge (above the middle rim edge).

I realized I have to pass the position of the craft in order to get the best viewing angel, and the Intercostal about five-eighths of a mile wide, and the craft above the shore on the opposite side. In order to do that I'd have to run on low beams in order to kill my taillights, otherwise the taillights might draw added attention. With a locking steering wheel, I anticipated also, I'd have to swerve diagonally at the last minute in the road before killing the engine, otherwise I'd be unable to turn the steering wheel later. I executed all maneuvers perfectly and although blocking the entire road, there was no traffic on that road at that hour anyway, except us three. We now had achieved an ideal viewing angle without spooking the saucer, and were in total darkness camouflage.

I recall trying to get as much accurate detail information through observation as possible from this rare opportunity. You know to start with it has its limitations, but you want to absorb as much as you can because you know you are observing aliens! Although the craft seemed like it could have been manufactured from a human aircraft factory, as far as those running lights, and the fact that the horizontal string of cabin windows had little curves in the corners, and rectangular shape resembled something similar to what humans might produce, there was no doubt in my mind really that this was an alien spacecraft we were enjoying limited engagement viewing privileges upon. The outer running lights were white blue and red, and evenly spaced, and some would blink on then off, but more off than on. From the distance we were at, scaling reliability is approximate at best, but I'd have to say the horizontal string of windows were roughly twenty to twenty-four inches wide, and forty to forty-eight inches in height. So maybe twenty-two by forty-four, or something like that. The height off the ground estimate approximate also at three hundred feet, but give or take, for the U.F.O. itself.

At different times beings were seen in the windows almost human like biped forms, but seemed beige orange in color rather than beige. I believed a total of three were witnessed, and moved similar to humans walking even though you pretty much could tell they weren't humans! Another strange observance, yet quite clearly happening, not unlike Star Trek where people get beamed down and vanish in-between, here it was almost like entity beings sliding down invisible ropes except a bit more slowly, and what seemed like groups of half a dozen or so at a time. Again, some human background street lighting giving the beings orangish color cast, or almost orangish gold appearance from a distance. Definitely there was ongoing downloading of beings when we first arrived, and after twenty minutes to a half hour later, uploading in reverse fashion. About fifteen minutes down, fifteen minutes uploading, and twenty minutes in between would be close, although it could have been slightly faster at around forty-five minutes all together. Some sort of meeting on the ground? That part is a real puzzle. What were they up to?

I waited until all the aliens had completed their upload, then giving them a return the favor surprise, I hit my headlight hi-beams! It was Bang-Zoom gone! Instantly from stationary hover, to 5 miles gone from sight over the horizon of the ocean in a fraction of a millisecond! So fast if you blinked you missed it, and even if you didn't blink, it was as close to instant as almost instantly gets. The G-Force inside of this saucer, must have been off the chart, and something no human could have withstood. The Star Trek warp speed light streaks you see of color trails were there, too, but lasting only millisecond wise also. I didn't just drive away though, I continued to observe. Both the empty sky where it had been, and calculation in my mind the angle of trajectory direction of departure from the coastline. It didn't really ascend much if at all, because of the speed of departure, so the angle was pretty straight if I could make an accurate assessment. It had traveled in a Northeasterly direction slightly more than thirty degrees, but less than thirty-five was my conclusion. However, you have to allow for the coastline not being in true square with Long./Lat. Lines. A few degrees difference. So if it was say thirty-two degrees, but two and a half degrees out of square (which is pretty close to actual), and then you arrive at thirty degrees northeast heading. I do think this accurate for in my head calculation. If you extend my calculation into open ocean, and draw an intersect line due East of Cape Kennedy, perhaps there is a USO base out there somewhere more than five hundred miles off shore?

The deep-water trench off Puerto Rico unquestionably is a USO base area of interest, but could there also be something directly East of the Kennedy Space Center? The Old Poseidon City Air Terminal location? My psychic sonar going ping to a U.F.O./USO underwater base? Oh, I don't know, maybe something like 27.8 degrees Longitude, (directly west Merritt Island Fla., and 68.6 degrees N. Longitude or something? Has your imagination ever gone deep sea diving seeking an underwater U.F.O./USO base or staging area? Columbus had a sighting in record of the 1490's log entry of strange lights in the general Sargasso Sea area. Part of the Devil's Triangle, as well. All I'm saying is these guys were last seen heading in that straight shot direction, and if they arrived any faster, it would have been ahead of their departure, and that is traveling even in the N.B.A., not even stopping to dribble.

Highly advanced propulsion system, or just Black magic? Exactly what the craft was comprised of, how it operated, in what dimension it operated, or what material/s it was made of is all unclear, but this is the profile fit for the Reptilian alien, and while many U.F.O.-logists have stopped short of calling them demons, but rather demonically affiliated or demonically leaning E.T., I do these guys no such favor. Clergy, are you listening? These are demons, pure and simple. What those fallen angel are driving around in these days. (beasts from the Sea, demon specie phyla for the Zoologist inclined clergy, and forget polite affiliated or leaning adjectives. What, you think you're going to offend the demons feelings by addressing a Reptilian E.T. as a demon? E.T. or not, these Orange/beige snake like skinned demons, that got caught in my headlight both literally, and here figuratively, as in mystery solved. Reptilian E.T. are full blooded demons. End of that story. A boatload of demons.

Whether originating from across the Milky Way Galaxy/Dark Rift center or not, it is time people recognize them for what they are. It's pretty hard to character assassinate a demon because every derogatory remark you could possibly throw at them they likely take as a compliment from their dyslexic viewpoint. I'm saying it's time to label them as demon first, and Extraterrestrial second, since demon are by definition Extraterrestrial anyway in the other dimensional sense of state of existence. It is only the from across the Galaxy part that is unconfirmed. I don't use the word definite except sparingly in this book because I'm seeking a very high level of authentic truthfulness and credibility to my word. I will use the word definite here though, and try to drive this point home in several places of this book. They are enemies of humans, and in Part II of this book in discussion of the coming 7-year Tribulation, return of Christ, and a World Leader Anti-Christ, I'll explain when and how they will factor in most likely! For some it might be difficult to fathom 7 foot tall, orangish snake-skin demons piloting seemingly advanced technology U.F.O. saucers, but possessing advanced characteristics and capabilities, as well, might be difficult for some to accept. Yet, not if you first come to the realization that there really is a lot more truth imbedded in Star-Trek conceptions than most are willing to accept. I'm not saying those T.V. shows didn't contain healthy quantity of fiction, but what I'm saying is, there is far more fact, or close to fact reality going on in E.T./U.F.O. terms than most people are willing to believe.

Now for the unofficial version for human purpose of the 2004 sighting..(Later in the book in a few places I reference back to this version of the U.F.O. sighting. An Illuminati eye witness smoking gun link to the Dark side along Billionaire's Row? A clandestine meeting of highly classified C.I.A. and other Black Box operatives attempting negotiations between our government' innermost secrets, and the Reptilian Ambassador from the Orion Constellation? Who's estate did it take place at? Were there humans involved, and was this some sort of Black blood ritual or was this strictly a business meeting conducting diplomacy? From well five eighths of a mile distance where we were observing from, these are all unanswered questions, offering several scenario possibilities, and I don't think a Real Estate agent showing the E.T. a listing at 4 A.M. is among them. Either is a poker game, or hot tub party!

It would have had to have been some pretty serious business of some sort, and likely invited guests to a planned in advance rendezvous meeting, which suggests human involvement. Back to the Illuminati smoking gun theory, or Intelligence Service secret operatives conducting some inter-Galactic official business. I decided to label the craft *eight-ball* since it was mostly black with a little white. Maybe the C.I.A. did, too, as in operation eight-ball. If not before we arrived, then maybe after as we become the million to one odds of showing up in that location at that hour, and on that night. Some computer programmer at the C.I.A. mathematics dept. having to recalibrate their algorithm model thereafter as a result (the Wildman factor was never taken into account).

My misconsideration from this event in thinking it was a rare occurrence, and I'd experienced my first and only lifelong U.F.O. encounter. In this humor version, the commander of the Alien Air Wing was captaining his flagship, and delivering the Reptilian Ambassador to this high level meeting with U.S. government Intelligence Service officials. This version a mix of fact with humor allows me a chuckle to think of it in this way, but the fact that there are so many unanswered questions allows for imagining in conjecture fashion, perhaps there could even be some further truth imbedded here somewhere (the Lie-Detection/Truth Verification is confirmation of the other version's observations seen by three people that night/early A.M.).

About a month after the sighting I experienced a Worker's Comp. injury, and the taking of the truth verification exams had to be put on hold. By 2008, I went ahead and conducted those exams, through a former Army Intelligence Captain, retired. Undoubtedly the information then made its way back to the Reptilian? Here is where that guy lives that spooked your saucer after that 2004 meeting with us? Well, it seemed like that anyway, because it was then shortly after that it seemed like the E.T. had my house under a stake out surveillance wise. Fact or imagination is unconfirmable, but my suspicions are over observations over an extended period. Kind of like me verifying them watching me, or so it seemed.

It was once they knew who the guy with the headlights who had them spooked back in 2004 was, then I got a dream delivered to me in my sleep being cordially invited to attend an upcoming air show, and E.T./saucer air show. Payback time! My theory for this version is this:

The U.F.O. Air Wing Captain had just put his hot cup of C.I.A. complimentary coffee up on the dash above the control panel to let it cool down a little as it was still scalding hot. Double latte mocha with steam coming off of it, and when I startled the crew (nothing they dislike more than bright light) they panicked and in departing so rapidly, I caused the scalding hot coffee to scorch the Captain's lizard tail, and all over himself, and neatly polished cloven hoofs. All this as he was pinned back in his chair speeding off at more than 1,500 m.p.h. departure over the horizon. To make up for this embarrassing incident, the C.I.A. had offered him a Starbucks franchise back on his home star in the Orion belt at no cost, and agreed to release the information as to who did that to him. The human who made him a Reptilian laughing stock. How embarrassing being the first demon being scorched, and caused by a human. Not just any demon, the Air Wing commander no less! It certainly goes a long ways in explaining why the skies in the immediate vicinity of Wildman's home were selected for their 2008 alien Air Show. Or that the invitation included being jolted out of my sleep by psychic dream conveyance. holy angel delivering the dream as usual, but the message clearly from a Reptilian U.F.O. captain. Yes, pay back motive.

My neighbors oblivious to the heavy star concentrations around my home. How would I explain it? Pretend I don't know? Simply say I'm a star hog? Or, those aren't stars, those are U.F.O., but it's okay, they know me, I attended a party over in Palm Beach with them back in 2004! That air show like an invitation to receive free alien rules tennis lessons using my brain as the tennis ball. Teach me a lesson or two; in other words, served on hard surface reality court intentionally trying to fray the seams of that tennis ball brain of mine. Wicked serve and backhand those demons have! Realizing just how totally insane it would sound to tell your neighbors, "The demons are out to get me" or "I'm being chased by a demon E.T." is not an option. Ironic also, that my front yard some eighteen to twenty years ago was where the psychic intunition was received regarding that other authors just then released book with South Florida U.F.O. infestation part of the title. Basically knowing then that this book would be confirmation for that book, even twenty years or so before writing this book! How profound is that. Funny my front yard doesn't look like a reality hard surface tennis court to look at it. Cause the demon Air Wing Commander to spill his C.I.A. scorching hot Starbucks double mocha latte' all over himself, then ridiculed by other demons, and watch how fast payback time arrives for you once he learns where you live!

Clearly the Reptilian back on the Star Sirius (constellation Orion) in the Rigel System have a dossier on file in their intelligence system on the Wildman. Human who knows about them, knows some of their classified secrets, and has spilled many secrets to other humans through a book. Including description of their Particle beam laser/taser (Chapter 12). Wildman just working his way up the demons most dangerous humans list. A particularly dangerous anti-Reptilian activist/terrorist group known as Christians they've had numerous run-ins with before. Wildman with Chamen spirit and Christian psychic/Prophet capabilities posing a really genuine threat to their empire (why my name is rocketing up their enemies list). They've already heard rumors about Part II of Wildman's book, heavily promoting and advocating Christian faith, and providing evidence after influencing evidence of Christian faith validity. Very damaging to their cause of unrighteousness. This could undermine their efforts to undermine! Why the order came down to keep an eye on him, a Godly activist Christian saboteur, and an extreme threat to their entire operation here on Earth. Maybe they should file a formal diplomatic complaint with the N.S.A. Out of nowhere comes this Christian renegade Wildman guy intentionally conducting guerilla warfare against them. Why couldn't he just be sedate and well behaved like the clergy. Most of them pretty benign problem causing wise.

The Wildman with known ties to evangelicals and Pentecostals and Charismatics organizations. These groups are really troublemakers, too. A whole strata layer of holy side vitality and non-iniquitous behavior. How dare they challenge demon authority like that. How un-Pagan of them exhibiting so much heart felt love in worship of the Almighty, and in such spontaneous fashion! Just terrible all the positive influence that these Christian splinter churches are having in spreading that six-letter word (the Gospel). Just undoing all the damage that the demons work so hard to achieve in destroying morality. Yes, Wildman is definitely one dangerous to the demons hombre, and they are well aware of it.

Most places in this book, mention of the C.I.A., or NASA, or the N.S.A. or other real government organization is not to be taken too serious as was done here it is in the tongue-in-cheek vein of humor, or as in Chapter 13, to cause people to examine something perspective wise in terms of government policy perhaps overlooked. America might have a few flaws, but you can't find any other nation on Earth to compare with all of its attributes, well intentioned good will, or commitment to preserving freedom and democracy, and economic prosperity worldwide. There is no actual linkage to any of these Federal agencies in fact, but conjecture in their direction is useful tool in examination of possibilities whether fact or not achieve the desired result of your consideration of what might be, rather than what necessarily is definitely proven to be so.

Scorching the lizard tail of the Air Wing commander's with hot complimentary C.I.A. coffee from a 2004 diplomatic meeting when I spooked them with my headlights makes me chuckle just to think about it, and why, although spiritually imaginary, it is also based primarily upon factual/actual occurrence which really did take place in 2004. I suppose anytime we humans can turn the tables, and be the undoing of a demon, whether garden variety, or E.T. from across the galaxy, it feels like a victory deserving of a chuckle, and one I hope and expect to have more of.

Likely none of us will ever know what really went on that early December 8, 2004, as to the reason demonic E.T. descended to the ground from a saucer hovering for almost an hour, then returned. Billionaire's Row on Palm Beach's South End mind you! Some sort of blood drinking human sacrifice Satanic ritual? That would definitely attract the demons, or were in attendance? C.I.A., N.S.A., both? Is there at least some sort of smoking gun here, connected to this deeper mystery. You tell me. I think I've done more than my share of controversy stirring, and even the demons would probably agree with that.

For reader's still scratching their heads after my earlier background linkage explanation, not sure they follow the tie-in, two more upcoming explanations, one in the Psychic Section –Web Matrix, and still additionally one perhaps equally relevant, as well as helpful for those struggling to relate. Realizing, too, sometimes the supernatural seems to cue your thought toward or in the direction of clearer perception when you are the one experiencing it firsthand as a psychic (most likely angel influence done very subtly). What I'm getting at is that occasionally I pick up on things regarding mechanisms of the supernatural that the average person likely would not, and only become adept at once you have years of accumulated comparative references to draw from. I certainly don't have all the answers, but I've scratched the surface deep enough over enough years to at least deliver to you some understandings. Cosmic Model in the Metaphysical section discusses interconnections within one's personal life. This material in these other chapters coming a little later or will perhaps clarify what I'm trying to explain here, and better elaborated upon, hopefully it will then make perfect sense.

The 1988 U.F.O./Particle Beam Premonition

In 2004, after the U.F.O. 'High-hat' sighting, it did not bring any memory recall of the 1988 U.F.O./Particle Beam premonition. Apparently now covered in dust in my memory, and like a box in storage with others more recent placed over, in front of, and on top and around it. This extremely significant occurrence temporarily overlooked, but not completely forgotten. It is unrelated to the 2004 sighting other than U.F.O. subject. Rather than discuss it here any further, I thought I'd simply index for you several other places different aspects of it are discussed.

Part I (this book)
    Chapter 10-U.F.O. subject
    Chapter 19-Psychic subject

Part II
    Chapter 25-Other aspect of Religion & the 1988 T.V. Show
    Chapter 26-Topic: Trusting in God
    Chapter 27-Tribulation Period indicators, both timeline and event, as well as other
T.V. Show connects

Even after Lie Detection, some might still try to convince themselves this is some kind of hoax. In reading through the Section on Religion (a subject I take very seriously) at the end of the book, I hope it will become clear to you, I am not one to create a hoax at all, but especially on the subject of Religion. It is not a hoax, it really did happen exactly as described, and no one more awed by it then I am.

Not only is this what I can only explain as being an act of God, but not the only one! Indication given to me this book was known to God 45 years ago! A focal point, I can only think he read it and liked it! It seems I have both a contributing, and senior editor. There is just no other explanation. A coincidence?

A book where the author is making a strong case in defense of the existence of God, while at the same time giving a timeline to the start of Tribulation Period. Then in pops a particular U.F.O. and particle Beam being straight out of a Bible Book of Revelation almost two thousand-year-old account. (Just one of many future 'locusts' mentioned there, and confirm of the authors existing timetable for Tribulation as being correct! Only with God as a senior editor, do those kind of things happen, and so I really do mean act of God here. No need for a hoax when you have that kind of wind in your sails, and this is a book, *New Realities*. Still, no one more in Awe than I, and you should be as well; awesome!

I think it's pretty hilarious to imagine the C.I.A./N.S.A. (ex-trilateral) offering the Reptilian/Rigelian Ambassador a Starbucks franchise back on Sirius to apologize and make up for my spooking them, and the saucer captain/Air Wing commander into spilling hot complimentary C.I.A. coffee all over himself in rapid departure. Or instead of hilariously Sirius, at least serious hilarious.

Being pinned back in his chair from 1,500 m.p.h. G-force while being scalded, and his demon lizard tail scorched while being helpless to do anything about it, resulting from reaction to human caused incident is poetic justice somehow. If true, it certainly would've been quite an unforgettable impression made.

Why do I get joy out of believing it's true, even knowing it's just imagined explanation? Why does seeing a Starbucks logo put a grin on my face in reminder, as well?

Did the C.I.A./N.S.A. operatives ever get that advanced technology weaponry information they were negotiating for at that meeting? If so, did it come with a big coffee spill blot right on top of the most critical details? Meanwhile, does this mean they now have human gourmet coffee shops back on Sirius, with Devilish pricing (a lot of people think that about their shops here)? More unanswered questions.

Knowing it's unlikely I'll ever have the answers, and know the real truth behind that early A.M. sighting that we three witnessed, it's easiest to imagine/mix some fantasy that provides a laugh, but also an explanation reason for necessity urgency of aliens wanting to teach me alien rules tennis lessons at 3 A.M. in my front yard in pay back for (the Air Wing commander's dry cleaning bill for his uniform, except they don't wear uniforms!). Something similar though I'd imagine. They just needed to know who I was, and where I lived, and as of 2008, they know.

What they don't know is that Wildman doesn't care how many cloven hoofs he steps on, the more the better, because it's game on. I'd be striking fear in their hearts except they are heartless, so I'll just go after Reptilian vulnerabilities. You guys may as well just move my name even higher up your enemies list, why wait until later when a lot of lizard tail gets chopped off! That razor sharp psychic sword that I carry with me at all times can cut lizard tail like it was butter. Touché, game on. Anyway, it's a rare documented case of humans spooking the demons. You've gotta love it; those subversive Christians.

Representative Likeness of The 2004 Sighting 5/8 Mile Distance

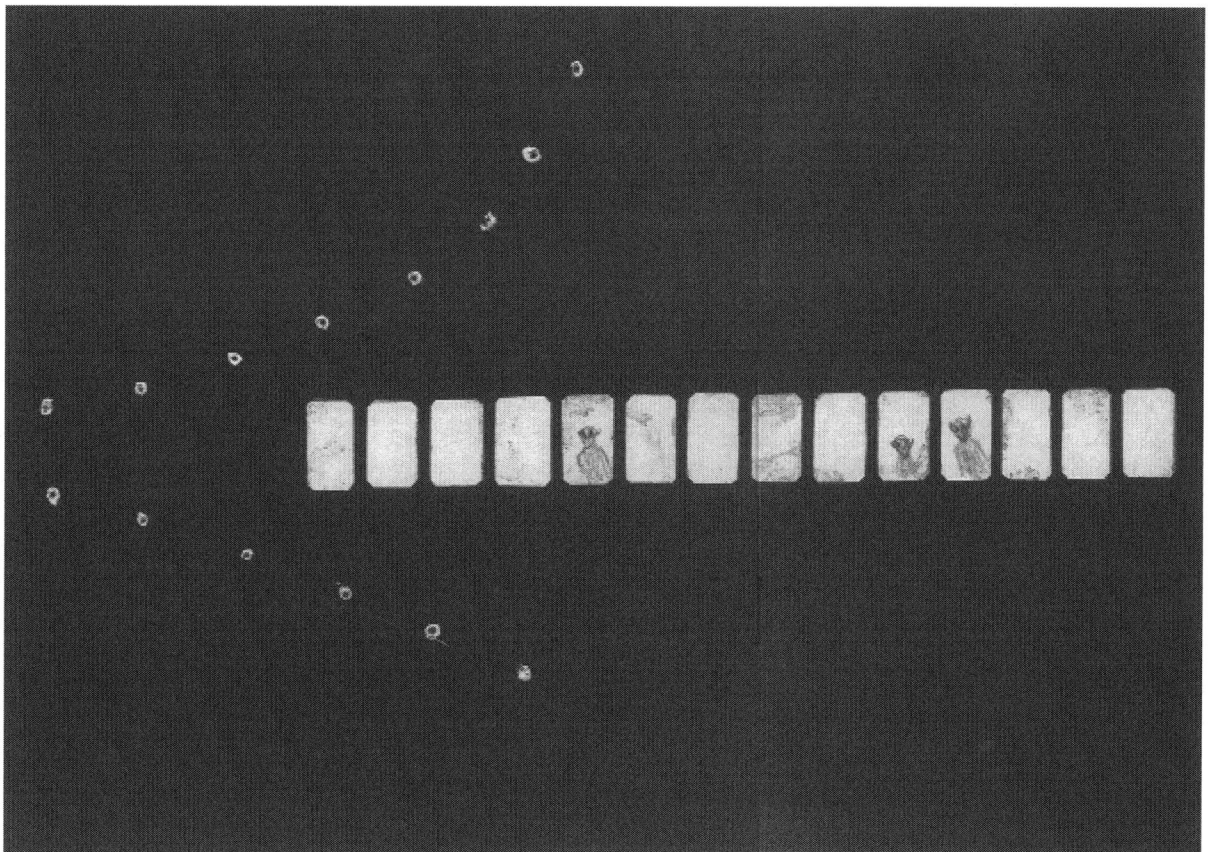

Author's front patio - 2008 UFO sightings that fulfilled psychic dream fortelling of it
(Sighting of 15 Fortold / 6 Definate)

The Dream A Night View of Same Patio 15 E.T. Positioned on it, Corrolated to the Eventual Actual Sightings

Chapter 9
A U.F.O. Psychic Dream: 2008 U.F.O. Premonition

Before I even begin explaining this U.F.O. premonition, I want you to know if this had happened to you, and you explained the very same thing to me. I'm not at all sure it would be easy for me to believe you. So for now if you don't that's okay, because by the end of the book I think you will. Realize, too, there is no filter for a psychic, there is no picking and choosing, we catch whatever fish are caught in our psychic net. It certainly isn't typical for me to dream about fifteen extraterrestrials on my front patio surrounding me at 3 A.M. in the dark. Dark enough that I thought it must be the dimly lit inside of and alien saucer my dream had taken me to, only realizing later it was my own front patio.

There are numerous Lie-Detection questions in that section on this but even then a tough pill to swallow, not simple to comprehend. It is something my mind is still grappling with months later, so take your time trying to mentally accept this because no one is more awed by this than I am, especially when examining some of the finer details. There are questions to certain aspects of this that likely never will be known for sure. In the dream the aliens were putting me through stress and anguish, mentally torturing a human who just happened to be me. As the dream progressed, it was like higher and higher voltage electro-shock. They were destroying old reality parameters, New Realities (source of title for this book) were soon to be shown me, their message. The voltage/shock level steadily increasing as I was watching my own face grimacing in anguish, then jolted right out of my sleep. Yes, to most people this would have been a nightmare and nothing more. But in the case of a psychic like myself, it could be and was something more; a premonition.

The only problem was, I wasn't totally sure it was a premonition and not a nightmare. That would require convincing myself that in fact Extraterrestrials really were giving me scholarship enrollment in the Twilight Zones University, as an advanced applied Psychology student majoring in a shocking new course offered by that department known as New Realities; an alien air force air show the highlight of this study.

No, it wasn't clear what I had experienced, but if it was in fact premonition, I would need to start observing night skies. With a cold front perhaps the last of the year moving in, I sensed this was likely to produce results if in fact there were results waiting to be discovered. I was not wrong!

So here am I keeping a vigil of night skies from my front patio because aliens might have suggested that I do so. Try explaining that to your neighbors (Who, fortunately for me, retire early.). God knows my brain is equipped with heavy duty Twilight Zone Off Road Shock absorbers, notice Shock with a capital *S*. That is the explanation that makes the most sense as to why Wildman's straw was drawn from God's psychic pool. Great bounce back sense of humor to wash it all down with, as well. So this is Twilight Zone University (I seem to remember some night classes here a long time ago.)! Close by home, too, I just walk out my front door and I'm in class!

It's about 11:30 P.M., I'm in class, and what do I do now, throw my brain up in the Air like it was a tennis ball and let the aliens begin volleying it? Yes! The very first night, 4/14/08 and the 'game' is underway. I'm observing over to the Northeast, above what is the north end of downtown West Palm at a star about 40 degrees up from the ground at my observation point.

To keep track of the stars in the sky I found it easier to keep charts, and assign names to various stars. This one became known as Alpha. Alpha was experiencing upper air turbulence in strong wind currents and having difficulty holding position. It was getting knocked around up there! I saw it get knocked sideways then return to its previous position more than once (Like stars millions of miles away are going to be affected by Earth's upper air currents.).

Then the first of many, many more shocks to come. Apparently Alpha could not hold its position without starting up its main turbine engine. As it did so, it lit up like a Christmas tree (as if stars millions of miles away had rings of colored lights as typical display). This U.F.O. had totally blown its star pretender cover, and a student down on the

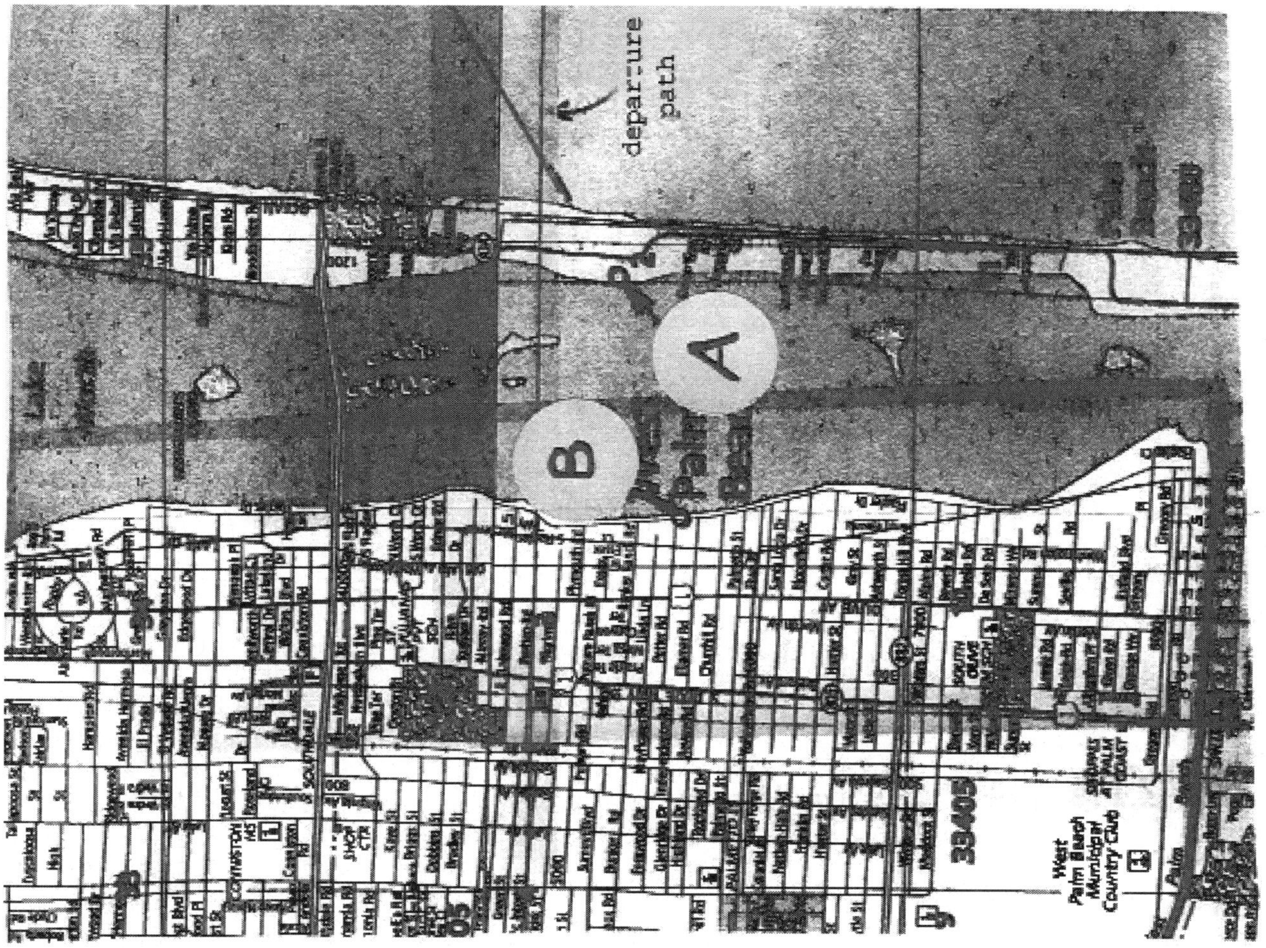

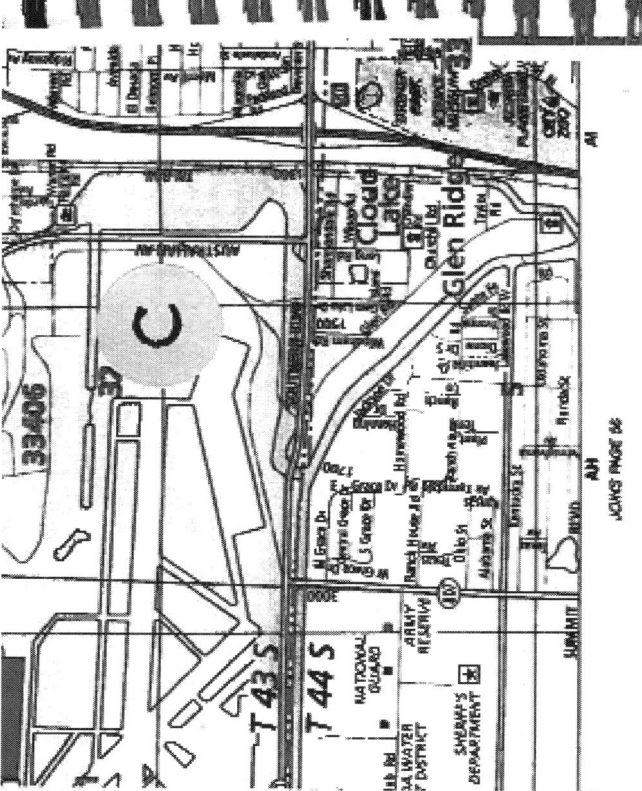

A) Position of UFO Sighting, Dec. 2004, 4:10 AM
B) Position of small Van with 3 observers
C) Proximity of local Commercial Airport

ground was observing it all! A description page to sighting to try and explain the double row of diagonally moving colored lights observed to you.

As a light came on and then blinked off in the upper row, one immediately below and to the right would come on then blink off in the lower, then upper row, around and around from right to left. Red, green blue, white, yellow/orange amber, never two the same in this diagonal up down sequence.

When it seemed like it had stabilized itself, the engines must have stopped and the colored lights went out. There were about twenty or so lights going on and off at a time when it lit up. Now it's back to trying to play star in the sky. It had only lasted a couple of minutes, or perhaps only a minute and a half, I'm not sure, I wasn't wearing a watch. The distance perhaps 5 miles land distance was likely 6 miles diagonally in the air. The lights were each about the size of pin heads, yet unmistakable colored lights against the night sky.

It was only perhaps not even five minutes later and the wind currents kicked up again and I observed everything all over again! It was virtually and almost identical replay. The U.F.O. regained stability holding position, and the lights stopped! Then a third time! I am wondering if I am the only one seeing this stuff. No telling, it stopped, I'd seen enough for one night. I got the ball back from the aliens (my brain) and went inside (Remember, I did pass lie-detection).

In the book, *Silent Invasion* (Chapter 3, page 34), listen to this quote: "Some lights were steady, others blinked in multiple colors." U.F.O. sightings in lower NY state are being described. Watching a History Channel show to do with U.F.O. back through centuries, it noted a prehistoric cave drawing in southern France, Cro-Magnon maybe, but what caught my attention all you anthropologists out there was the double row of circles below the rim of this U.F.O. in the depiction. Had this same type U.F.O. been seen by them Millennium ago? I do think so. Humans have been sharing this planet much longer than they realize with extraterrestrials I am quite convinced. My applied Psych. Class throwing in a dab of history/anthropology I see. Whatever it takes, the aliens sparing no expense to dissolve my old realities, teaching me tennis from the ball's perspective. Ouch!

I was to see Alpha again so many more times. It seemed like it had been assigned a certain territory, it's being the downtown area. Often but not always in the same sky location, yet my notes often showed the presence of Alpha, with quite possibly the same crew of aliens. It's certainly refreshing to find out from the aliens rather than humans because of a massive human cover-up, that the skies over our home are a kind of wildlife preserve for alien saucers that move about up there pretending to be stars! Once I became skilled at the art of distinguishing U.F.O. from real stars, I can't even being to tell you how many nights I realized nearly all, if not all, were U.F.O.!

Now the Grey's may be more innocent and tame than the Reptilian extraterrestrials, but it's still wrong that the public is not informed by our own government and media. It is my sincere belief that some of the Reptilian (another author describes as the Renegade faction) are not slightly demonic, but very much so, with an agenda not exactly in the best interest of humans. Yes for more than 50 years our government has known what is going on while treating the public like it was a mushroom farm (well fertilizing with bull**** and kept in the dark).

Sighting 2

Psychics are also sometimes called sensitives. They can also pick up vibes of good and evil, even from a distance. From about a mile and a half estimated distance, had the sensation of evil been the same as raw, fresh garbage, this next sighting smell would have knocked me over (evil vibe). Only one other time in my life had I sensed Evil to this overpowering level. (that other time described in the Psychic section- Hallucinations Chapter. Because of clouds, rain, haziness, and generally poor sky condition, the next (of the six definite sightings) didn't take place until April 19, 2008.

On this night the sky seemed partly cloudy, but after midnight, my vigil was again underway. I thought I saw Alpha again to the Northeast and headed into a cloud bank. I went out to the street to change my viewing angle. It went into a cloud. As I was walking up my front sidewalk, I thought I'd check the time by a clock in the kitchen. It was just then out of the corner of my eye, I thought I'd seen something pulse cherry red. I looked to the west and I couldn't believe my eyes. Definitely a U.F.O., reasonable low altitude (perhaps under ten thousand feet), and bathed in red! Close enough I could even see clearly the silhouetted outline and features apparent! I could plainly see a row of horizontal tightly spaced together individual windows. A perfect match to my 2004 sighting. I have since come to the conclusion the 2004 sighting a Reptilian High Hat type, and the one I'm observing here, I later concluded was a Reptilian Low Hat. Different shaped saucers but apparently windows from the same Reptilian window mfg. company! alien lizard looking bipeds in the window and aircraft business, now that's certainly full capacity for anyone's imagination, yet somewhere over by the Florida Turnpike to the west, that's exactly what I was seeing!

I ran up the road to the west then a little to the North where there is a small lake/open air space. It didn't move for about 45 minutes and I finally left because of the evil vibe it was giving me. About as inviting as an immense oil storage tank on fire, billowing black smoke and ready to explode any moment. Something ominous, nefarious, overwhelming sense of evil and danger! Almost like death itself. I wasn't about to try to get closer for another look, no thanks, I'll pass on that. If I went chasing after this thing in my truck, it looked like it could suck my whole truck up inside, suck me out of the truck, then spit the truck back out like a wad of chewing tobacco! No, I think I'll pass on that. Tongue in cheek I named this one Romeo, total misnomer, but red like in Valentine's Day. Satanic valentine!

Yes, the Grim Reaper captain of this thing (Captain Reaper to you) with his crew, the four horsemen of the Apocalypse. For your non entertainment displeasure, the Macabre orchestra, with guest stars Jason and the Friday the Thirteenth chainsaw massacre comedians, Vlad the Impaler, Freddie Kruger, the entire homicide ward from State Mental Hospital, plus and including a convention of morticians and undertakers to keep things lively! Welcome Aboard. They are sure to enjoy you, fresh blood is on the menu.

Actually that's a very disturbing side to this. Over the next few days a rash of unnatural deaths. A boy, fourteen years old killed on bicycle only about a 1/4 mile south of the sighting location around noon at a busy traffic intersection crossing it. A truck crash on the Turnpike two more dead. Other unnatural deaths also. This spike in the death toll coincidence? I'll let you decide that. Let's just say that if this thing had a license tag, you would expect Romeo's plate to read more like Evil One, Death star, or Soul taker, or maybe Grim Reaper. Now I think back to the premonition with a nasty Reptilian day job in hell, turning up the volume on the electro shock on me. Mental torture at the hand of a demonic alien, and now fulfilling! Sighting two was definitely a rough outing. Taking a mental whipping from extraterrestrials. Oh what the heck, I'm on a free scholarship, if the C.I.A. hadn't told them who the Earthling was that spooked the Reptilian Ambassador's saucer, causing the captain of that craft, who just happened to be Air Commander of the 391st Alien Air Wing to spill his scalding hot cup of complimentary Starbucks coffee, double Mocha Latte all over himself when I startled him, none of this would be happening? It kind of gives a double meaning to the word counterintelligence. See where paying taxes to the Federal government gets you!

Aliens moving through the South Florida night skies with impunity. Or is it diplomatic immunity. Why don't you just go and seat them at the United Nations while you're at it! A delegation of demonic aliens sure to do wonders for world peace, but then humans don't need any help making a mess of things do we.

Superior aircraft, superior weaponry, how do you tell a family with small children, oh, don't worry about the flying lizard like demonic aliens who control the skies at night. They won't hurt you? Romeo leaves me wondering about that, as well as how much the government knows about all this they won't talk about.

Well enough about sighting number two. I'm on an alien scholarship to be mentally tortured and given New Realities classes, while playing tennis by alien rules, my brain the tennis ball. I'm learning they serve very hard on to a very hard surfaced court.

The third sighting occurred April 20, 2008, seven or eight miles to the southwest. This was the very next night after Romeo's jolt, and with a full or nearly full moon. At about a fifty-degree angle from ground or more, I'm looking at this star? It had been motionless, and was in this sort of open space, like a big room, with clouds on three sides except the side I'm viewing from. Then I noticed a saucer/disk shape to is as it began moving sideways. Then in a series of almost perfectly measured moves, and without change of incline, it began to execute moves like a child climbing steps or stairs. I think I counted about five. It moved sideways, then up, sideways, then up, five times. Each sideways move the same distance, each upward move like the riser on a stairs the same measured distance. When it reached the top it was like watching a child slide down a slide. The disk never tilting the whole time! At the bottom of its imaginary slide, a little clockwise circular turn. Then stopped. Show off (take a bow for the audience)! I named this one Ranger because of the full range of maneuvers it displayed. So let's review, I'm at Twilight Zone University, on full alien scholarship, taking a course in alien tennis applied Psychology, and my professors have just demonstrated what a pancake type saucer flown by a crew of Grey aliens are capable of in sharp angle turn aeronautics. It's about now that I realize the significance as to the positions the aliens were standing in surrounding me in my premonition dream. These sightings are matching up! That's another shocker, as well to realize it's playing out as described in the dream! This much payback must mean that alien commander back in 2004 must have really scorched his tail (excuse the pun) on hot coffee. His saucer lurched away at such high speed, he was pinned back in his chair having to endure the scorch, muttering I'll get that Earthling if it's the last thing I do. Hence my full scholarship, at alien mental whipping academy.

By now they figure they have me on the ropes, my tennis ball brain getting crushed almost like a tomato they think, but I'm much tougher than they figured me for. This time they think a combination punch is going to put me down for the count. Not so.

First, standing in the very spot of the number four alien in the dream and here is another pancake saucer with a crew of Greys, and I'm looking straight up as I see a perfectly circular disk moving in an East to West jig-zag pattern. Like a speed skater would. First pushing off one leg, then the other. Forty-five degrees left, then forty-five right, forty-five left, but moving forward rather rapidly. Another show off. I named this guy Jitterbug. Now that wasn't too bad, and four of the six U.F.O. indicated in the dream already having performed. In the dream that left the two in the background. That meant just as all of the other U.F.O. had appeared according to their position in the dream, it meant I should look to the West. Now the only thing to the west are what look to be a couple of century real stars.

It's getting later and later, now around 3 A.M. Then I see something happening to the star upper and slightly to the left (south) of the lower one. In incremental movements a beam of some type is now being extended downward, and slightly angled not straight down. It came down say in five increments of five hundred feet each increment, a slight pause between each increment, five times twenty-five hundred feet total, perhaps. Then it was like the beam attached itself to the lower star, and I'm watching the upper star tow the lower star sideways! Now I'm totally sober, and not so tired I'm imagining one star pull another star sideways. No this was really happening, and these weren't stars.

I'd always thought tractor beams were Star Trek, Hollywood, and Buck Rogers made up stuff. No it wasn't! When the beam released it was just like turning off a flashlight it just went off. Apparently did disconnect from the lower craft, but not much later, here's the beam coming down from the upper craft again, just like the first time, in even increments. Identical to the first time, too, it attached and they both began moving sideways again. Roughly same distance the second time. Must be older model U.F.O.! I named these two The Tractor Beam Pair. I calculate the distance was about seven or eight miles but the sky condition clear enough to see the beam no bigger than the sewing thread thickness at that distance, but I have excellent distance vision, and am totally certain of what I saw. The repeat performance helping to confirm this as well. Then they just remained stationary.

That was enough brain abuse for one night, and the six sightings now fulfilled, can I get my diploma now? No. The aliens showed me a wicked backhand tennis shot, but couldn't put me away. They wanted one more chance! How could they do that, the six sightings and premonition had fulfilled right? Yes, but I had forgotten all about my 1988 premonition, the aliens still had one last chance to beat me. I had this so buried in the archives of my memory that even after the aliens showed me this, it took some time to figure out what it actually was. It caught me off guard, a sucker punch, I never saw this one coming. Right near the end of the month, I'd been watching the 2008 NFL college football draft. That means Saturday or Sunday. I think it was Sunday. It's late and I see this U.F.O. circling around behind some tall trees on the other side of a drainage canal. Just at an angle and below the top of the tree where I can't get a good look. It is of the bright classification, and at night when you try to look directly at it even from a distance the bright light obscures the disk shape. At closer range, the same only worse.

So, I'm standing there at my Twilight Zone University front patio with an alien Air commander jockeying for that final chance to see if he can crack my sanity. I see what looks like two blue eyes coming down at me. Something sort of round behind it but it's black! I am standing perfectly still, and slowly but steadily it's descending. It looks like a black snake with two blue eyes!

It lowered down to within ten feet of my head, then even closer, now 8 feet from my head. The blue eyes weren't round at all, rather two rectangular plates I'll call them, that seemed to be about four inches long and imbedded in what I can only describe as looking like the black foam insulation air-conditioning men use to wrap copper pipe in. Or a black pipe about two-and-a-half inches in diameter, blunt end, and these two blue rectangular plates, kind of cobalt blue,-side by side, parallel imbed on the end

If you think of a crankshaft, this center black pipe seemed to on the end extend who knows how many feet back up to the U.F.O. Yet there were these donut like rings completely encompassing this pipe running up through the holes of these donuts. The donuts were staggered in somewhat random pattern one atop the other. the thickness of each donut about three to five inches wide with total diameter wide about eight to ten inches.

In trying to examine the consistency of these black donut like, alternately staggered rings was what looked like extremely black (as pitch) color, darker than the night sky! If you bought a bag of asphalt patch it was that same black tar color, and with granule texture rather than stone, perhaps one quarter or three-sixteenths granules. It looked very dense, very solid, and quite heavy. It wasn't. It was a black particle beam! Focus your eyes away, with one eye on the beam and your other eye on any close by object and it would vanish! invisible! Sight up the beam and it would totally reappear just as before! I did this perhaps twenty times or more. The beam remaining perfectly still, disappearing and reappearing according to how I focused my eyes!

I finally had enough and simply walked away and went indoors! Now can I have my diploma? Yes, they would have to award my diploma now. They had thrown everything at me and couldn't crack me. My diploma trophy for all this New Reality in my face; I got to hang on to my sanity! They didn't know about the heavy duty off road Twilight Zone Shock absorbers cushioning my brain through all this madness. The tennis ball stitching on the casing a little frayed from all the hard surface slams, but it's fine.

This particle beam bugged me for quite a while, then that ton of bricks on your head moment when the pieces fit together and you come to this New Reality. Since the Bible was written almost two thousand years ago, likely no one has seen the scorpion Taser tail mentioned in the Book of Revelation. Until now. I've described to you what I honestly believe God allowed or wanted me to see to witness in this book to others and it cracks the Bible Tribulation time code, as well!

WOW! It did have that black, demonic dark feel to this thing. Now when you figure how all my other U.F.O. premonitions fulfilled, and then realize how the 1988 premonition began, with the T.V. program dealing with exactly such a beam, Yes, I'm absolutely convinced that is what this was right down to the rectangular plates on the blunt tip.

This is the Scorpion stinger, scorpion, Taser tail from book of Revelation and I kid you not! Black Evil demonic Magic! demonic aliens!

In the Bible God and all things holy often described as the Light. Many references to Jesus in this manner. Many references to Darkness as Evil conversely. These are the aliens so mentioned (inferred) in verse in Revelation there also. Evil Reptilian aliens? This U.F.O. Bright with the black particle beam I had named Illustra. An ill luster, as well to this beam. Want proof the End Times are here? This is it. Do not, take this lightly. I'm quite solemnly serious about this.

A brief chapter in the Psychic Section of the book will discuss this whole Particle Beam premonition further in greater detail. You may as well leave that crash helmet on that your wearing through this whole book. It doesn't even get easy in the Religion section! Show me any other book where you need a crash helmet for five chapters on Religion. Off-roading through the Twilight Zone with Wildman is apt to do that to you!

Dark cover Ups and Bright Street Lights

In the book that came out in the 1990s relating to U.F.O. sightings in the Ft. Lauderdale, Broward County, Florida, area, and this author talked about the South Florida U.F.O. infestation. The other aspect being that the media would not cover stories on this topic. T.V. magazine, newspapers, all considered U.F.O. a taboo topic this author claimed. He was correct and the silence continues even today. Sure it would hurt an already damaged Real Estate market; construction and housing traditionally a large part of the local economy in a bad national economy. But when times are good and business booming it is no different.

After sighting Alpha and not receiving any interest from local newspapers in a story, I decided to write a letter to a local T.V. station. I had waited forty-five minutes in the lobby of the newspaper, but knowing my story had to do with U.F.O., no one would even speak with me! I finally walked out having been ignored, and having spoken to no one! Of course when I returned home someone called to offer a newspaper subscription. I think you know what my response was. The T.V. station never did respond, either. Media subject suppression at its finest!

Then something strange occurred. The condominium park where I live typically maintenance wise, very slow to change a burned out light bulb in a street lamp. Suddenly now wants to replace the lampposts themselves with taller ones, and of the several hundred in this park, for some reason, those in front of and around my house a priority! I joked to several people that since the Condo association didn't have money in its current budget to do this, it must mean they were sending receipts to the C.I.A. for re-imbursements. The lamps about three times taller (around twenty feet high) made me laugh also because the top covers kind of reminded you of a U.F.O.!

Was it to make sightings/sky observations more difficult? It most certainly did accomplish that. Too much ground light especially bright in your eyes light, makes sky search much less conducive conditions wise.

Or, was it to give you better lighting when the aliens shred your brain to confetti, and at 3 A.M. when your down on your hands and knees crawling in wet grass picking up confetti before it gets too wet to glue back together, and before the winds pick up. No, it was the latter.

Make sighting more difficult. Too many sightings, someone might write a book about U.F.O.. Like me maybe?

You know, how the C.I.A. has clandestine meetings with Reptilian alien over in Palm Beach at 4 AM. Or that they hand out scalding hot complimentary Starbucks coffee to the Reptilian Ambassador, the other delegates, saucer captain and crew, as well.

We don't know that part for sure, or if the C.I.A. gave the Reptilian GPS turn by turn directions as to where that Earthling lives who was the one that spooked them with his headlights after the December 2004 meeting. It is kind of (coincidental?) funny that once human intelligence service knew who that individual was, who I was, only then four years later, did I receive a cordial invitation from a Reptilian alien in my sleep to attend an upcoming Air Show, and receive mental anguish and torture the boundaries of my existing realities! Apparently the leader of a commando squad of fifteen other aliens delivering this premonition to me, jolting me awake at 3:30 A.M. Seeing all these aliens surrounding me in the vision, I thought I was inside a dimly lit U.F.O. interior, instead of my own Twilight Zone front patio at night.

Does it prove the 2004 saucer Captain held a grudge all that time, swearing payback upon that Earthling if ever given the chance? Hey, it wasn't me who put the scalding hot coffee up on the control panel above your captain's seat. Multi-dimensional aliens immune to intense heat as they punish humans in the afterlife in that dimension, apparently lose their heat immunity in this dimension. A living human putting a scorch on a demon from hell, now that's an ironic twist (something the other demons won't let him live down). No wonder the intense desire for payback even after four years!

Receiving a Doctorate degree from T.Z.U., a new tall street lamp immediately in front of my home with a lamp lid that looks like a U.F.O. paid for by the C.I.A., and a brain that now doubles as an alien tennis ball.

Something else, too. Ever since all this, an unusually heavy concentration of stars in the immediate area of my home. Like some chocolate chip cookie with all the chips loaded to one side. Just three quarters of a mile north driving to the Post Office, the sky usually almost totally devoid of stars, and nearly all the time! Yet around my home, twenty-five to fifty stars! Wonder what they are saying? *He's cool, he already knows about us* or, *That is one dangerous Earthling down there* (the one who lives just south of that bright street lamp). The air wing commander said to observe and record his every move.

Will the neighbors start asking why all the stars in the sky seem to be concentrated above and in the vicinity of my house? I guess that's when I'll just hand them a bag of lopsided chocolate chip cookies, and say something like, Isn't that strange, maybe you folks can figure out why! You don't suppose there could be anything strange going on here in District Nine, do you? I can't bring myself to tell them that one night during the period of the ET alien, 391st Air wing Air show, I counted more than sixty-five other saucers, I mean moving stars in the immediate sky overhead! No, that would be both figuratively and literally, over their heads! Those flat disk shaped stars moving laterally in heavy traffic beneath and through the clouds! Yes, that's right, those aliens up there looking down at me and the entire city's lights maybe munching on lopsided chocolate chip cookies for all my neighbors are aware.

What exactly are they doing up there besides doing a poor job of star pretending? Absorbing electromagnetic pulse a possibility among many. Honing their surveillance /reconnaissance skills another along with navigation and coordinates handling experience another. demonic spiritual negative activity hostile to humans below is not to be discounted, although little understanding as to how and what specifically might be going on.

Vultures will circle dying prey on the ground, even while an animal below has not yet expired, but is about to. Unfortunately in this case, I don't need to tell you who that prey will be! As you will read in the later Chapter and Supplement Section, not only as alerting you to when to expect Tribulation start, but cataclysm will accompany. Florida in my opinion will experience total submersion (hence the U.F.O./demonic E.T. saucer vultures). Possibly a Tsunami tidal wave effecting the entire U.S. east coast, followed by a minimum of fifty feet (or likely more) of rapid sea level rise at some point within the May 2023 to August 2024 timeframe. After May 2023 Florida is extremely dangerous, even though as I will later describe, out of several possible scenario within that larger time frame July/August 2024 is where I suspect the danger might actually turn out to be. How serious do I take this? I've lived here over thirty years, and for a Floridian now retired to pick up roots, and head for higher altitude ground whether I rapture or not, pretty well tells you I believe fully what I'm stating for you. actually this whole book, no matter how shocking at face value it seems, I genuinely believe myself, and am speaking truthfully. You still want to retire to Florida? You can, just evacuate prior to this danger/hazard period, and you will be fine other than the periodic hurricane or two!

Above: Same View (but at night) of 2008 Premonition UFO Sighting Predictive Dream

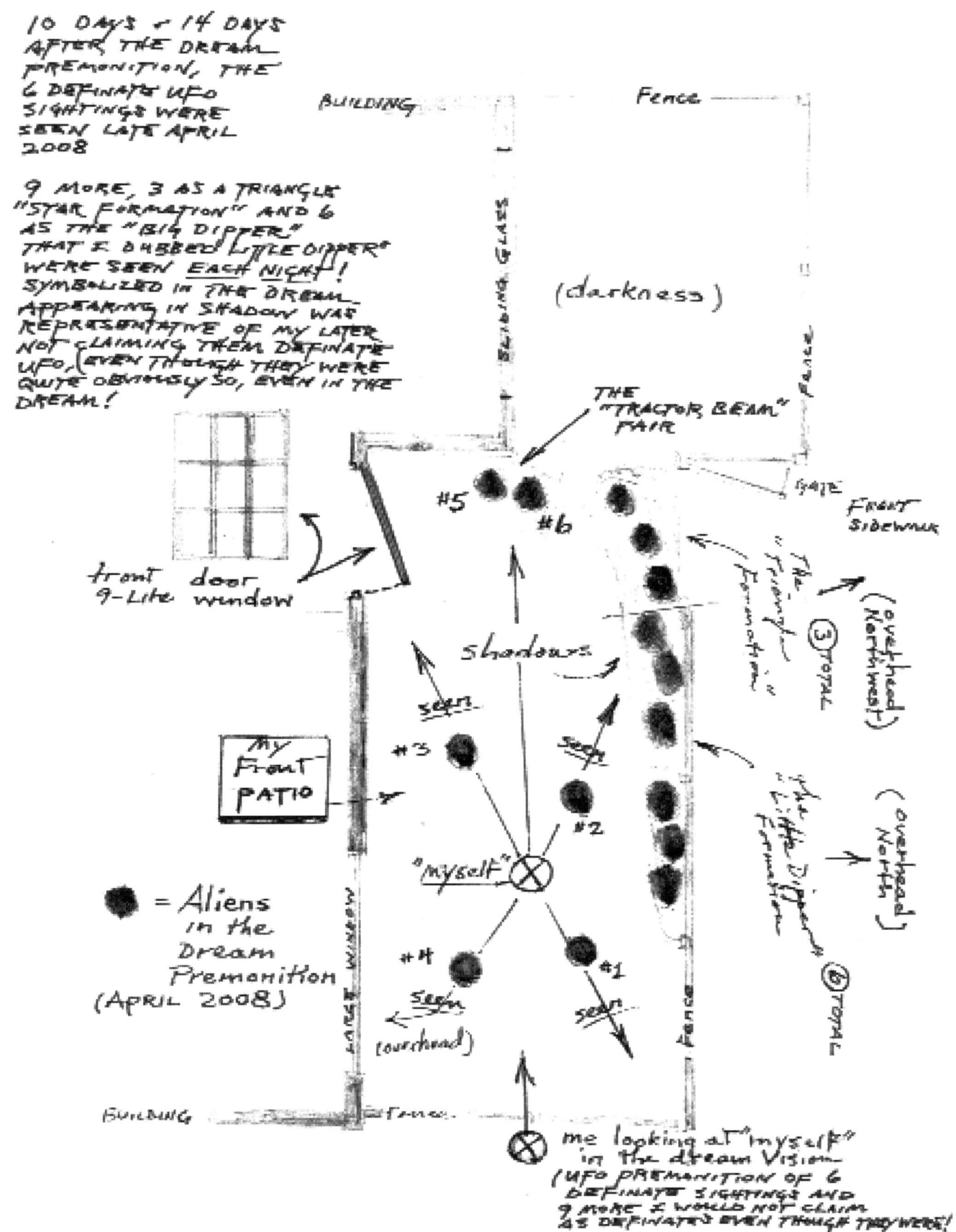

LIST OF "DEFINATES" SIGHTED

Sighting Date	Direction Sighted	Saucer Name	Saucer Type	Characteristi[c]
① 4/14 2008	Northeast Downtown W.P.B.	"ALFA" "-r Alpha"	Pancake (or) Lowhat (probably)	Double diagonal of colored ligh[t]
② 4/19 2008	West slightly N.W.	"ROMEO"	Lowhat – Reptilian	Red pulse
③ 4/22 2008	Overhead	"JITTERBUG"	(Smaller) Pancake – Greys	Movement ∿○
④ 4/20 2008	S.W.	"RANGER"	Pancake – Greys	Aerial Maneuvers!
⑤ 4/22 2008	West	⎧ Tractor Beam Pair	Uncertain (Undetermined)	Towing!
⑥ 4/22 2008	"	"	Likely – Greys	"
⑦ (Aprox.) 4/27 2008	Overhead slightly S.E.	"ILLUSTRA"	Bright Undetermined	P-Beam 1988 Premonition
⑧ 5/19 5/29 2008	South (nearby)	"ILLUMUS"	Bright Undetermined	Revealed itself & Am (Twice) on Different date
	NOTE: #'s 1 through 6 were premonition predicted. #'s 7 & 8 were seen later and NOT pre-predict[ed] along with 1 through 6, however #7 was pre-predicted by the 1988 premonition			
⑨ 2004 (Dec 8th)	S. Palm Beach Island	"8-BALL"	Highhat – Reptilian	BIG! (& Fast)

Chapter 10
1988 Particle Beam Premonition: 2008 Fulfillment Sighting

First of all, it wasn't until months later did I realize another U.F.O. premonition had occurred back in 1988, this was not my first U.F.O. premonition! The other was moved to the back archives of my memory, and with a layer of dust atop, it was not recalled at first. That one while involving a U.F.O., was more about a particle beam being emitted from a U.F.O.. More specifically the scorpion like stinger/Taser tail as mentioned in the Book of Revelation 9:vs.5 that would in the days of Final judgment inflict pain and torture. Since this spans several Topic Sections of this book I've moved further discussion to the Psychic Section, Chapter 19. The Religious aspects quite clear.

So the 2008 U.F.O. Premonition was not my first U.F.O. Premonition, but rather my second. Two scoops of Twilight Zone raisin bran instead of one. See what happens when you sprinkle too much peyote on your breakfast cereal! Don't worry God is a loving God, and he has a sense of humor, too, we are after all created in his image, our mistake not being obedient to his word, many not realizing just how valid the Christian faith/Bible is. If the Bible is not accurate, how then is the description and drawings supplied in this book a match with description offered by John of Patmos nearly two thousand years ago? The fact I was even witness to this particle beam I believe in fact likely was an act of God, his purpose likely so that I might warn the present day world of impending disaster just over the horizon.

There is a great deal more to talk about regarding this 1988 Premonition, but I'll detail further in Chapter 19, this is mentioned here to make readers aware the 2008 Premonition involving U.F.O., was not the first.

In the average person's night sleep they can experience more than one deep or R.E.M. sleep period, the length of which varies from person to person. People with precognitive ability can receive psychic messages both while fully awake in the middle of the day, or by dream visions in their sleep. What I've noticed with my dream visions at night is that they are almost always received between 2 A.M. and 6 A.M.

In other words, when at least one or more deep sleep R.E.M. periods has already been completed, and while still in need of further rest, the brain is clearly in a more refreshed state of strengthened capacity while involved in Psychic message transferal, even though the night's sleep is not over.

There are a couple of things that intrigue me about what occurred with this particular Premonition. One is that time of heaviest U.F.O concentration is the same time frame – 2 A.M. to 6 A.M. From a sighting log I began keeping, it is likely, even very likely heavy U.F.O. presence was both directly above my home, as well as very close to my home at the time of occurrence of this late April 2008 premonition. While I feel quite certain my guardian angel is involved in all of my other premonitions, this one leaves me asking the question: Could U.F.O. and extraterrestrials played a similar role this time? The serial # or no. their U.F.O. being the return address for just this particular premonition? In his book, *Cosmic Explorers*, author Courtney Brown states that the attempts through remote viewing technique to physically spy on the extraterrestrial group known as the Reptilians. Attempts are quite routinely psychically blocked somehow. This group he states, particularly one faction of this group he calls the Renegade Reptilians have an agenda quite hostile to humans, thus the reason for secrecy. Just before awakening from this premonition, I did experience what could be considered possible blocking. My conscious although still sleeping in a state of interpretive awareness to the vision was asking my subconscious to go back and try and get a clear view for what the faces of these alien looked like. It came back with confirmation that a look at their faces was not possible, but did supply a shoulder, neck, and head-side view. Reptilian! Something more. Just before awakening sort of like if you saw shadows of a group of people in a room with the lights out, but then the lights just for a second or split second were flashed on, then immediately back off again, yet just long enough to get a fast glimpse. The one standing in the 2 spot was definitely Reptilian, and the one ratcheting up psychic torture on me. (torture of all types a favorite Reptilian pastime- since they are demonic.

I give you this prior to the actual explanation of the occurrence – so you have some idea of what could be alternate possibility as I view it. Did God/Kingdom of heaven sign off on this one, or were the Reptilian Renegade faction responsible? Essentially it was like these aliens had sent me a psychic message in my sleep telling me I was cordially invited (tongue in cheek) to attend an alien Air Show in order to crush and replace my old realities with new ones. This is where the title of this book comes from. My research shows that April 30 and prior is kind of an ancient pagan demonic high Evil black Unholy Day. An alien Air Show to celebrate Satan's birthday, maybe? And I had received telepathic invitation by the commander of the 391st Alien Air Wing (Satan probably holding the lease to their USO air base)! The premonition around April 2 (I didn't notate the exact date, but is close and not as significant as what eventually occurred) was that my conclusion that my 2004 U.F.O. sighting was a once in a lifetime event about to be shown totally incorrect perception. U.F.O. in Florida I now realize to be more common than mosquito, with much more powerful stingers!

In the dream vision, surrounded by aliens, I thought I was aboard a saucer, it was quite dark, and I didn't seem to recognize my own front patio as the location, which wouldn't you know was the location where the sightings took place a little over ten days later the alien Air show underway as advertised. Premonitions often are accurate and detailed, but symbolism not always correctly interpreted until after the fact. When you compare the dream to what occurred it's just amazing.

Now my patio is surrounded by a wooden shadow-box fence, and in the perspective in the vision, I am standing outside the fence on the East looking West (at night) and I am looking at myself sitting on a stool (which I actually did use at times during the sightings). Around me are four aliens, each about three or four feet away, spaced like four corners of a box, with myself in the center of the box. There is a wall in the background with two more aliens there. I believe all aliens on the left in this vision were just slightly taller than those on the right. All along the right side of the vision were many more aliens but I couldn't get a definite count of heads, a mass of shadow with aliens within it! Along the front of this fence in reality it measures fifty-two inches in height. (This corresponds with the shorter of two size aliens of the group of aliens known as Greys) They were about the same height as the fence, yes an accurate measurement of the aliens in my dream!

In this dream vision the alien standing in the two-spot according to this vision (Reptilian) seemed to be administering something like electro-shock therapy, and intentionally ratcheting up the shock level as the dream vision progressed. You recall what I mentioned about Reptilians enjoying torture of humans. This was definitely intentional on this aliens part, the greater the voltage of new reality the more it was clear I was in for one mind blowing alien Air Show. If they could drive me crazy in the process, all the better. Clear hostility toward humans, and me in particular. Could it be I really did cause the commander of that Reptilian high-hat saucer to spill his Starbucks double mocha latte (given him by the C.I.A. at their clandestine meeting back in 2004? Don't they appreciate I waited until all delegates and the Reptilian ambassador were safely back on board the craft before I hit my headlights spooking them? Apparently not.

I will return to this payback theory in a bit, but first I need to describe how accurate the symbolism contained in the vision truly was. The fulfillment didn't occur all in one day as most premonitions do, but over about a ten day period. Could that be yet further indication this was in fact alien delivered dream vision telepathically? They definitely are known to communicate telepathically. I will likely never know this for certain, or if spilled coffee is involved, either.

Comparing what actually occurred in reality back to the vision, it is clear several things were foretold. Each extraterrestrial in the vision represented a U.F.O. saucer in reality. The position each of these extraterrestrials was standing in the vision, indicated in reality what direction each of the saucers would be seen in. the height of the aliens (ones to the left taller) indicated the saucers to the left correspondingly would be seen higher in the sky! They were! The two aliens in the background side by side, were seen together that way in reality. The left alien being taller was seen exactly that way in the sky (I call these the tractor beam pair). The ambiguous aliens along the fence in shadows that would not be definite sightings were in fact two star formations (actually U.F.O.), nine in all.

So in this dream vision in my sleep, my current subconscious, and relaxed state conscious are looking over my front patio fence at around three-thirty in the morning, thinking they are viewing inside a saucer, with my future self-sitting on a stool facing northeast/East the direction of the first sighting. As the shock was ratcheted up from overexposure to new realities I awoke practically lurched out of this dream seeing my own face grimacing under the shock therapy!

Knowing an old theory that cold water temps mean increased U.F.O. activity, when a week later I knew a cold front was coming, I began my sighting vigil that was not to be unproductive. The theory is that USO don't like the extreme cold temps that penetrate the skin of their saucer aircraft (think of an aluminum beverage can in an ice chest). Now those familiar with northern winters know it doesn't take long to get cold inside your auto without the heat on, and the engine must be running to do that. The theory is the USO/U.F.O. are in the skies using their propulsion system for heat just like a car would. My observations seem to support some possible basis in fact for this theory. Clear cold skies/cold ocean waters, do seem to indicate heavier U.F.O. concentration.

After the premonition and sightings had completed (the next chapter will describe each sighting), at that point you want to tell somebody until you realize how ridiculous you sound. It would come out something like: "You're not going to believe this but I've been contacted by aliens that are out to get me. They want to inflict mental anguish and mess with my head." Then you realize you only have two choices. Either totally shut up and not tell anyone, even though you have a pressing need to or get yourself committed, Involuntarily of course.

Endless filling out of admission forms going into the Koo-Koo bin. Lousy food, more nuts than a Planter's factory, and medication that makes you think aliens are out to get you, except this time the aliens aren't real, your just paranoid delusional from the medication. Then you get a text message from the aliens, gotcha, we were just kidding! Their goal to drive you to check into the Koo-Koo bin (sweet revenge). Advanced intelligence torture-mental soccer, with your brain the ball.

Try explaining that to the doctors, they're sure to understand (increase your dosage), especially the part about the text message form aliens. The Koo-Koo bin doesn't allow cell phones!

No, that isn't an option, only silence. At some point you wonder.

It would appear somehow you've managed to do some serious stepping on of alien toes. You wonder how you've managed to accomplish this, and worse now must face the entire alien 391st Alien Air Wing single handedly since you could risk the Koo-Koo bin if you tell anyone. With my David and Goliath autographed model sling shot, and my pea-shooter my weaponry certainly technologically superior to the entire Alien Air Wing? As if I would be heavily favored with a handicap on wagering for sure, Not!

The U.F.O. were so prevalent I had to assign names to them in order to keep track of everything in the night sky. The U.F.O. that emitted a particle beam down on me occurred five days after this premonition fulfillment was complete. It was the fulfillment in fact of the 1988 sighting premonition. I had named it Illustra, but is in fact what some U.F.O.-logists refer to as a bright. In fact being a Lucifer's Morningstar as mentioned in the Bible. Reptilian registry! So, in a later dream message when my subconscious planted a message in what I refer to as a wild dream. Everyone has these, except psychics, so I've discovered, can have an enclosed message within it. Like peanuts inside the shell. The trick is to retrieve the message before you awake, or recollection is lost. These are not the same as psychic visions. This one told me a group of aliens is fluent in a language spoken in hell! I had heard of speaking in holy tongues, but a demonic tongue spoken in hell! I consulted with a clergyman who said many believe so, although no one knows with certainty, but that occasionally a demonically possessed human speaks in some such tongue. Well, this is a no brainer to figure out it's the Reptilians.

Another Morningstar I had named Illumus' but impossible to detect as a saucer at night often descend to lower altitude by this light in your eyes screening trick. However catch them around 6 A.M. as I did twice with Illumus, with dark background gone, sun not up, but getting light, the saucer reveals it's disk shape (what many might mistake for Venus or Mercury) really a low-level U.F.O. I caught Illumus twice in this manner. Definite U.F.O.. hell birds! Lucifer is actually a Roman word designing the Morning Star. In Hebrew it means The Bright One.

The Bible, Ephesians 2:2 "The Prince of the power of the air." Because Illustra was a bright, the shape identity could not be confirmed. Only later did I realize this was a Bad Greys craft, having to replay the original premonition vision in my mind from 1988! It was definitely a Greys U.F.O. in the premonition/vision.

Undoubtedly you are wondering if this psychic dream in prediction of an Alien Air Wing Airs Show involving scores of U.F.O. was holy angel delivered like all my other psychic dreams, I feel certain are, or is this one time where the demons delivered a psychic phone call invitation to attend this Air Show?

When you fit this psychic episode into my holy angel's lifetime portfolio of messaging it does fit the apparent program. What had sort of spooked me was what seemed like the demon controlling the dream ratcheting up the mental anguish as the air show progressed. It was that grand finale that I wasn't expecting that really did deliver a brain pounding, didn't see it coming blow. I'd completely forgotten, and thus overlooked that 1988 premonition. You add a psychic fulfillment like that to a skies surround of your front yard, and it really did fray the seams, as well as the seams of my supernatural bouncing tennis lessons at 3 A.M. brain a bit, especially when you reason God is behind it all, providing a crash course to get me up to speed on these U.F.O./E.T. Yes, try telling your neighbors that one! That God arranged the E.T. to throw a saucer Air Show just for me to teach my brain E.T. rules tennis at 3 A.M. Then before they left, they showed me a particle beam of theirs known in Book of Revelation as a scorpion stinger-like tail. Of course this actually really did happen, and yes, it was God who (insisted a nice word for forced them into) showing that Particle beam. So, it really was a holy angel delivering the dream after all.

Basically forewarning me the events about to be witnessed would be stressful, and increasingly so as they progressed, which they were. Since the E.T. types in the dream represented them days later at night in reality, it was necessary to portray the one saucer (Low Hat Reptilian) positively identified, to then be able to pass this information along in this book. This was God wanting this U.F.O./E.T. subject discussed in order to inform others through this book. The dream then was holy angel delivered like all my others, but it had me wondering analytically for some time, dissecting this from different perspective angles but I decided it was correctly interpreted as holy angel delivered.

The fact of the tie in with Book of Revelation in others ways that generated positive benefit in awareness understanding further confirms, since that is about the last thing demonic entity want to accomplish in humans. So yes, it was God and holy angel source, but man, about as far out on the weird end of the holy spectrum as it gets. Yeah, this looks like a job for the Wildman!

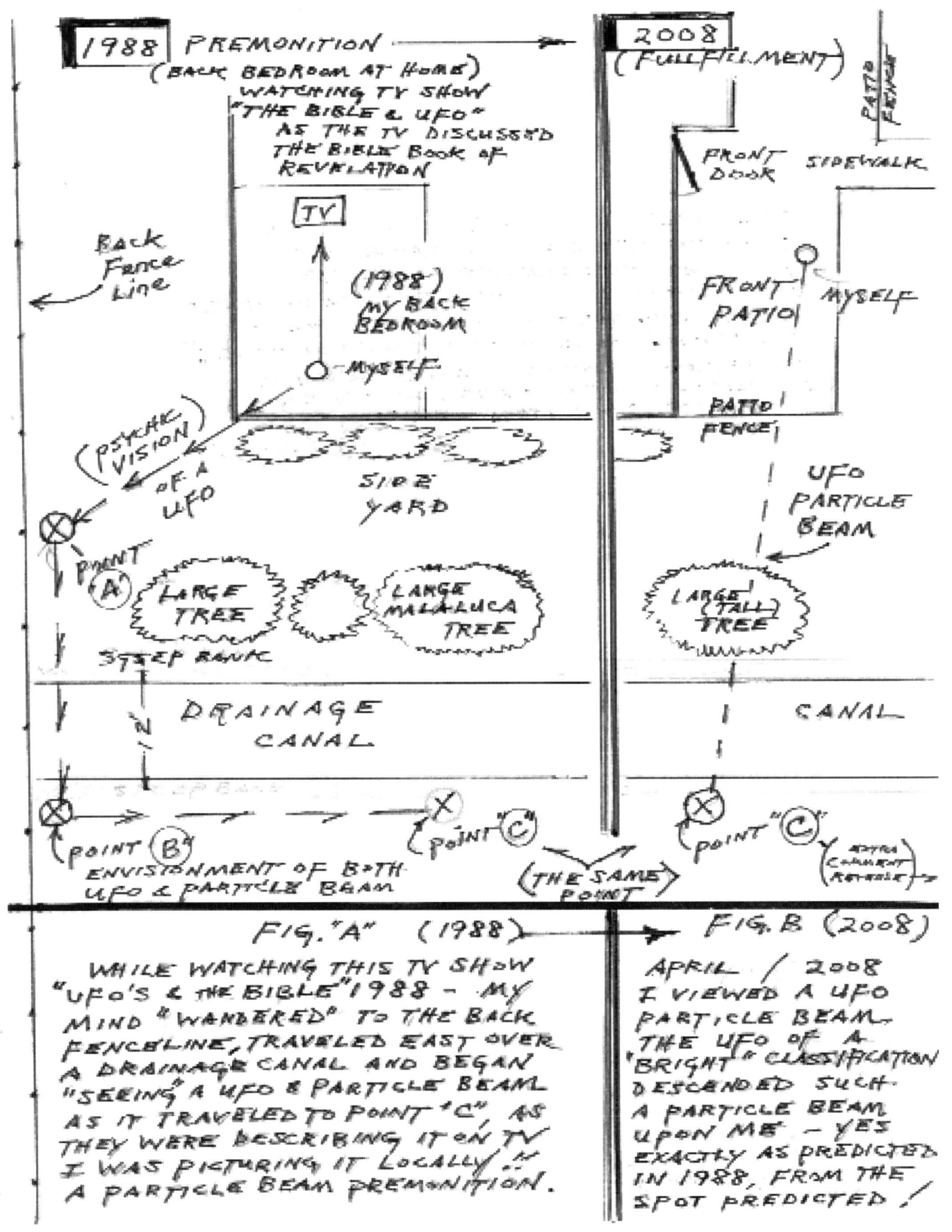

WHEN THE UFO SAUCER "SWEPT IN" IN 2008 FOR THIS EVENT OCCURANCE — IT FOLLOWED THE SAME PATH AS THE 1988 PREMONITION, APPROACHING FROM THE SOUTHWEST THEN MOVING NORTH ON THE OPPOSITE SIDE OF THE DRAINAGE CANAL UNTIL IT REACHED POINT-C !!

THE PREMONITION NOT ONLY PREDICTED THE EVENT, BUT APPROACH PATH OF THE UFO, AND THE VERY SPOT THE UFO WOULD DESCEND THE BEAM FROM.
— AMAZING!

WHAT WAS WITNESSED:

THIS PAGE DIAGRAM TB (TAZOR BEAM)

FUTURE (2027) PUNISHMENT FOR THOSE WITH NON-SPIRITUAL AURAS...?

EYE FOCUS DETERMINES VISIBILITY (OR NON VISIBILITY)

NOTICE RINGS → OUTSIDE EDGE ARE STAGGERED

SEE "TT" DIAGRAM

THOUSANDS OF FEET BACK TO UFO SAUCER ON UPPER "OTHER" END!!

THIS IS WHAT THE BIBLE'S LOCUST/SCORPION STINGER TAIL LOOKS LIKE!!

ALL BLACK PARTICLE BEAM SHAPE DESCRIPTION

TWO "JACINTH BLUE" RECTANGULAR PLATES EMBEDDED IN BLUNT ENDED CENTER TUBE SHAPE

DIAGRAM "TT" ENLARGEMENT DETAIL OF TAZOR TIP

AS THE BEAM DESCENDS, YOU SEE WHAT LOOK LIKE TWO BLUE EYES COMING DOWN TOWARD YOU AND A VERY BLACK "CHANNEL", TUBULAR IN SHAPE BEHIND THEM. (FROM A UFO SAUCER) THE BEAM HAS DONUT SHAPED RINGS 3 OR 4 INCHES WIDE AND 9 OR 10 INCHES DIAMETER ACROSS. THE CENTER PIPE LIKE TUBE (ALSO BLACK) ABOUT 3 INCHES DIAMETER, AND THE OUTSIDE EDGE OF THE RINGS WERE STAGGERED NOT IN LINE.

THE TWO BLUE EYES AS THEY GET CLOSER ARE ACTUALLY WHAT LOOK TO BE TWO DARK BLUE PLATES (RECTANGULAR) EMBEDDED IN THE BLUNT END. (POSITIVE & NEGATIVE? MAYBE) THIS BEAM IS AS BLACK AS PITCH, AND ACTUALLY RESEMBLES ASPHALT WITH HEAVY APPEARANCE TO THE RINGS EXCEPT THE GRANULAR TEXTURE 1/8" OR LESS NOT 3/8" OR LGR GRANULES. BLACKER THAN THE NIGHT AIR AROUND IT, IT APPEARS VERY DENSE AND HEAVY, YET IN FACT, IT IS BOTH VISIBLE/INVISIBLE DEPENDING ON EYE FOCUS!

BOTH EYES FOCUSED DIRECTLY ON IT AND UP A SIGNIFICANT PART OF THE BEAM MADE IT VISIBLE, FOCUS INSTEAD ON IT, BUT WITH ONE EYE ON ANY OTHER NEAR-BY OBJECT MADE IT INVISIBLE! WHEN YOU WANT TO SEE IT AGAIN FOCUS COMPLETELY BACK ON IT, AND IT RE-APPEARED IN THE SAME LOCATION. A DEMONIC BLACK, EXTRATERRESTRIAL TAZER BEAM, AND THE SAME ONE MENTIONED IN THE BIBLE BOOK OF REVELATION (CHAPTER 9) - SCORPION STINGER TAIL - AUDITIONING FOR INCLUSION IN THIS BOOK ABOUT THE SUPERNATURAL & RELIGION UP CLOSE AND PERSONAL WITH THE AUTHOR. (LIE DETECTION VERIFIED) ANY DOUBTS ABOUT THE BIBLE'S ACCURACY NOW?

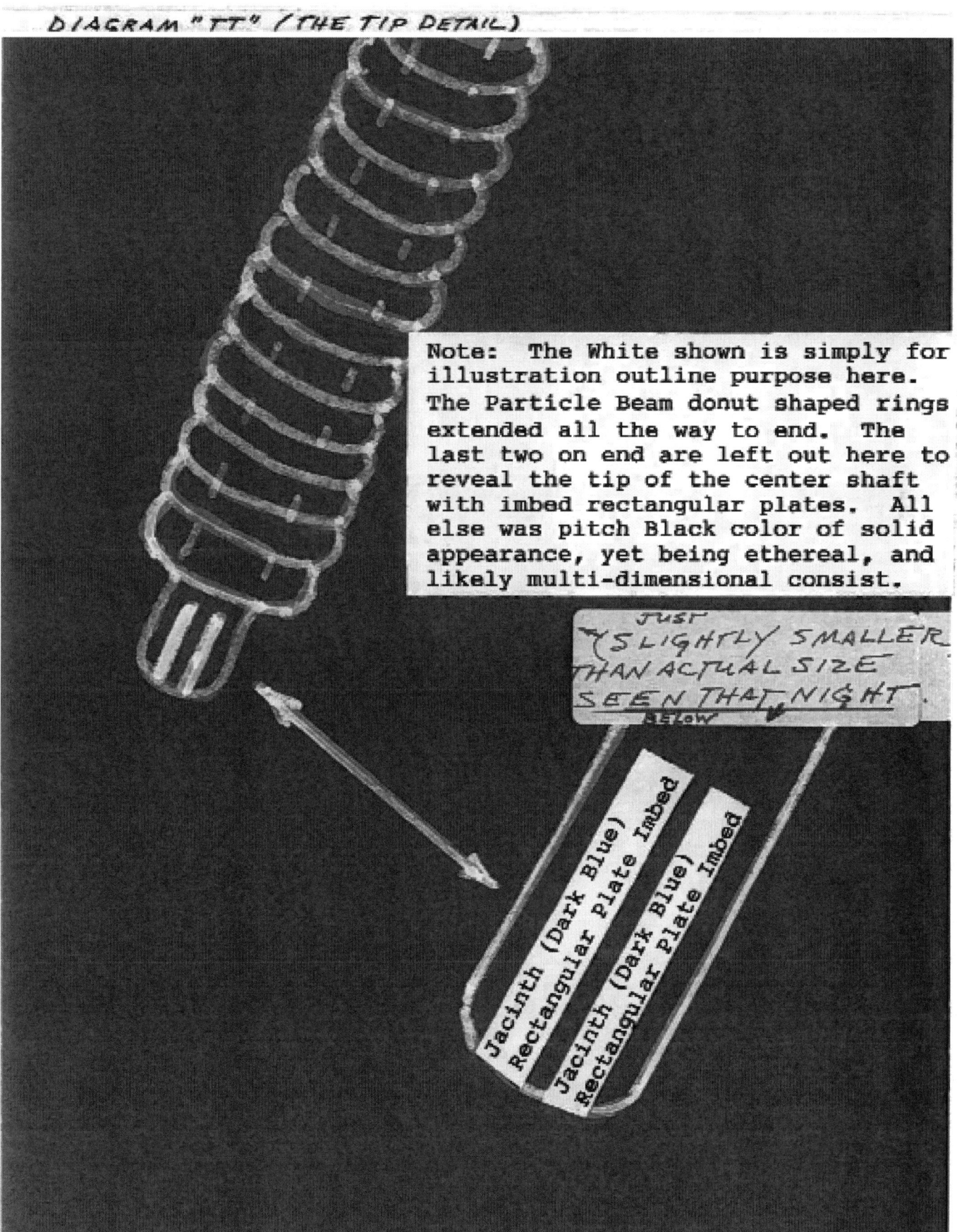

Chapter 11
Busting the Star Pretenders

What I'm referring to here is confirming that a star in the night sky is actually a U.F.O. hanging up there pretending to be a Star. This a favorite pastime of Florida variety U.F.O..

It doesn't seem to dawn on most people, that if you actually could see millions of miles distant in the night sky, why night after night, within a ten mile viewing radius, star count seldom rises above fifty or sixty. Having grown up and lived in several different parts of the U.S. other than Florida, I know it is not untypical to see one hundred thousand stars in the night sky. Real Stars! It's not that there aren't some real stars visible in South Florida, sometimes, it's that what most people don't realize is that of the forty visible lights in the sky, U.F.O. generally comprise the majority.

In total that is the conclusion based on a one year observation period, and sighting log maintained. This log noted moon phase, rain and cloud condition, total lights in the night sky numbers, times of observation (often several times in one night) and what direction and height in the sky the stars were, as well as configurations. (Single, Paired, Triangle, or multi-configured such as the Big Dipper. As you will read, this South Florida-variety Big Dipper busted numerous times, too! E.T. being big scam perpetrators on unsuspecting humans below.

It's tough viewing with the naked eye, but if you use any optical device for assistance, debunkers want to immediately point to some undetermined variable or flaw in the findings blamed on whatever instrument you use. Good binoculars in the $900 a pair range have distance accuracy of focus limitation usually several hundred yards, not several thousands of feet altitude. Telescopes, even cheaper ones often better for clarity, but a photo telescope with zoom adjustable lens is really a more professional approach. A photo speaks volumes. Movie type cam—eras often have the distance focus problem similar to binoculars. So, deciding I had enough evidence, and definite sightings already, I decided it wasn't necessary, and I already have additional Lie Detection expense yet to incur. I've already witnessed far more definite U.F.O. sightings than I thought I'd ever see in my lifetime. My claim of (9) nine definite sightings extremely low and conservative. I could claim ninety and even that would be low, but these are less definite. Oh they are U.F.O., and I know it, but I have a very tough standard I comply with as far as what I term definite, and I stick to it. I already know there are a lot more there, and it really serves no purpose to claim a much higher count.

In the 2008 premonition, the dream indicated along the back and right side were two groupings of E.T. huddled together in the shadows, of which definite count could not be made. However, upon fulfillment of this dream premonition when it became clear that the dream actually described what would be seen in the sky and where, both in terms of height and direction. I then realized the dream had confirmed that the ET location in the dream must also match the sky in reality terms. It meant the three stars to the Northwest were really U.F.O., and the six to the North in Big Dipper formation were really U.F.O. also!

I don't even count these nine more as definite, even though clearly as you will read, I busted them in several other ways, as well. First this Triangle formation could not hold a consistent pattern. My log confirms a continual pattern of adjustments to the shape of the triangle, a clear pattern of inconsistency over a months' time. That wasn't all to provide evidence in order to bust them. On more than one occasion multiple flickering colored lights, likely in the window area of one of the craft in the triangle was observed. A little jiggle, and circular mini-rotation is a typical U.F.O. hover trait that reveals their true identity, and it too was seen. Add this together and the Triangle Formation is busted on multiple counts.

The Big Dipper a bit sloppy in its impersonation also. Three stars forming the cup, and three more forming the ladle handle. One hundred humans looking up and seeing it would pronounce it to be in fact the Big Dipper, and one hundred humans would be wrong, having been fooled! If you live in this area I guess that means you're stuck with a Big Dipper knock off! They have gotten away with sliding this by you for, how long have you lived there? Sure, a long time. Cheap

Zeta Reticuli II import, and you've been duped. Florida's South region doesn't have many real stars or snow, but you've been snowed by E.T.s! This is sure to boost property values to your home, living under an artificial alien owned and operated sky. These fake stars over your home at night in control of Alien Air Wing Central Command. How reassuring to know that there is demonic Reptilian alien presence in these very same South Florida skies also, that you and your family just happen to live beneath (At least two of my nine definite sighting were definitely Reptilian saucers.)!

For now (some additional later chapter discussion, as well as in Part II, Chapter 27) there seems to be nothing beyond the ordinary threat, God having told the E.T. to leave his humans be? The question of threat to humans from hostile E.T. reemerges during the Tribulation period. Will God's rules change, some restrictions be lifted for the E.T., and humans never getting that notice in a time period after first Rapture? Will demonic E.T., loyal to the Radical Islamic Confederacy Anti-Christ Leader become extra boots on the ground helping to round-up, capture, imprison, and torture remnant Christians and Jews? Dr. Courtney Brown's book: cosmic explorers seems to indicate a future time period when such is the case. This is but one reason I lobby hard in Chapter 13 that our government's Intelligence Agencies responsible for withholding extensive U.F.O./ E.T. files of information, change policy, de-classify a great deal more. It is possible some people's lives could depend on whether they do or not, as this matter is much more serious than the average person has any understanding of. Has your government signed a pact of silence with demonic extraterrestrials? If they sign pacts with Evil humans, what makes you think they wouldn't with demon loyal E.T.? In your best interest supposedly, if so, but with what authorization or oversight? What exact dealings with Reptilian have they had, virtually you can fingers on one hand probably count how many humans know the correct and exact details within government intelligence of this highly sensitive, highly classified matter. You might call this: What they won't do to get their hands on cutting edge advanced military technology from co-operation with the E.T.!

There is no question that the E.T. are engaged in various aerial exercises, and reconnaissance of humans on the ground at least a part of their overall maneuvers objectives. Peacetime tactical training for the big Tribulation war game that is just a dozen years off? Do their saucers act like school buses to drop off invisible to human, dark mist like slinky coil like demons of lesser rank, to go infiltrate the human population's minds, then report back later? There is just so much humans do not know going on here, and again, why in Chapter 13, there is a lot of information the public would be well served to know that our government sees fit not to release, when in fact, releasing it would not compromise National Security, it would improve it!

In busting these U.F.O. star pretenders such as the Big Dipper, they clearly like visual down to the ground, so when rainclouds, rain, or just even heavy cloud cover set in, they vacate! I'm totally serious, and imagine the Big Dipper saying it forgot to bring an umbrella, and they can't see anything down below anyway, so the mission gets called off, they pack it in, the Big Dipper sort of punches his time card and six saucers just head off for the coast after breaking their Big Dipper best impersonation performance! They got bored. More than once this happened no less, they just figured no humans below were observing their charade anyway, what the heck, mission cancelled. Pack it in for the night early, head for the coast and back to their base.

Several nights in a row, doing all night sky vigils for my log, I'd first observe the Dipper around 10:30 P.M. and the Dipper would be high in the sky directly north of my home. The handle of the Dipper would be pointing to roughly 4 o'clock.. Gradually the entire formation would rotate as the night progressed. By around 2:30 or 3 A.M. going outside for my period check, the handle would have rotated to a vertical high noon position. Clearly, the Dipper is not supposed to rotate that much in the matter of just a few hours. It did this night, after night, but sometimes completing the rotation more quickly than on other nights! Furthermore, I had been tipped off from the psychic dream/ sighting premonition that these were in fact E.T. The dream like all my psychic dream conveyance by either God or holy angel. In the dream these six were in shadows along my patio fence. Three (triangle formation to the northwest) and these six directly to the north, then giving me exact count of how many were in the shadows. Shadows in the dream symbolic of not counting these as definite sighting! Nine E.T. in the dream about ten days prior, now in reality nine U.F.O. I don't claim as definite, but I think you agree, clearly are. Enough evidence here to practically get them convicted on charges of star pretending in the first degree. A bogus Big Dipper, only in Florida, and a triangle formation busted in star faker sting of Wildman's also. A little hard to handcuff the Big Dipper, but these guys are sloppy impersonators. One night one of their team's saucers must have been in the shop with engine trouble or something, and the Big Dipper never showed up for work that night! It was back the next night, same place, same time, but called in sick that one night, what I mean by sloppy, and this sort of sloppy sky pretending became more and more evident the more you observed. That was one reason I kept the log going, and kept on observing. It gets a bit humorous, too, at times like a strange episode I sometimes refer to as the Hallway Shift.

I think after a while, they were wise to my perpetual observation, so one night I went outside at my usual time around 10:30 give or take, and with a relatively clear sky, there should have been the normal thirty to fifty stars viewable from my front patio viewing station. Nothing! Not a one, completely void sky! There should have been at least some present. Taking my garbage to a dumpster a couple of hundred yards to my west I was suddenly amazed. My sky, in exact star positions kept, had merely reassembled a mile or so further west. A different navigator that night, an ET. apprentice, or was it intentional to avoid me? An E.T. Air Wing, once again for Wildman, and the whole sky getting busted on that nice try attempt. Everything set up identically as far as the positioning of these stars, except all slid down the sky hallway, so to speak (one half of a mile to a mile west). Did they mis-coordinate? Big sky pretender Bust that night. I busted these guys so many times, in so many ways, it starts to get comical after a while.

Dr. Courtney Brown's remote viewers identifying two factions of the Reptilian, the moderates, and the Renegades. Clearly from my dream it was the Renegade variety, full demon status E.T. involved, with the subordinate Bad Greys comprising most of the Air Wing's saucer craft. But that returns us to technicalities of Divine Law. demons have never lived, cannot cause human death directly it is believed (or we'd all be humans gone extinct already) and must abide by strictly enforced holy laws applying to E.T.s and ultraterrestrials. However, considering E.T. to include solid beings that do live, all be it source of origin from the dark rift zone, center of the Milky Way/Orion belt. then it is not clear exactly what God's Divine Law rules are for them, since they in theory could have a variant set of rules (and likely do) from the nonliving ex-fallen angel, now full demon. Are these Renegade Reptilian totally in disobedience of God's dictates and mandates? In other words, not knowing what exactly God's stipulations for them are with certainty, one and then two, not knowing if these demonic E.T. are even going to be in compliance come Tribulation time, or if the rules could change slightly along with a permissible five-month Taser Particle Beam sting period. Are they in essence living demons compared to nonliving? Quite possibly so. You have to realize also that E.T. can be living entity not as we would categorize living as being in as solid a form, but yet at least potentially with a set term of existence life which expires. There is nothing to show that all ethereal entity like ghosts, E.T. and angels and demons, must all be non-living. I'm not stating that it is definitely possible to be in ethereal form and living at the same time, except that the concept of living we as humans always relate to ourselves, and we have to leave the possibility door open to the fact that our definition of life in this dimension might not be all that is inclusive, just as theology suggests that a righteous person alive, if through grace of God salvation can transcend life as a spirit perhaps for an additional one thousand years as of Christ's Millennial Reign. A spirit in that sense maintaining the identity of the individual person. The life eventually ending, the person not immortal, but in spirit ethereal form, continuing as a living being. My point is if such can be true with humans, then non-visible, non-immortal E.T. can potentially exist; both holy side/loyal and non-holy/neutral. An extremely complex issue, and one where our government chooses to withhold information is extremely hazardous to human health, when it involves several seriously demonic entity groups.

Often the only way to recognize which E.T. group you are dealing with is by the distinguishing shape of their craft. I'm not trying to say our government knows every last detail, about every last E.T. group, but their wealth of information certainly far exceeds what private citizenry have managed to cull, observe, and collect on their own.

Since very little is known about the Reptilian, most authors on the U.F.O. subject focus on the Greys. Apparently the government's concern in releasing information about the demonic characteristic of Reptilian is what prevents them from going public, but my book will hopefully remove some of that dilemma from them as to correct action, release of information wise, and they'd find that I've essentially let this nasty cat out of the public awareness bag for them, where all they have to do is sort of say, "Yep, that's that nasty Reptilian E.T. cat alright; we'd recognize it anywhere." We weren't sure the public could handle such provocatively controversial information, so we simply kept quiet.

Yes, South Florida is a U.F.O. wildlife preserve, Wildman is right about that too, we didn't know how to bring that to the public's awareness, or those entire U.F.O./E.T. Air Squadrons/Air wings he mentions. No big deal right? How many nasty cats does Wildman have in his let loose bag anyway? I'm keeping that one secret from the government! Better that way. Like these stars being on the ceiling of a long hallway, and re-setting identical to the night before, but all of them doing a big sky shift coordinated effort. Big Dipper busted yet again in this new one night only performance down the Hallway. I literally busted about thirty-five U.F.O.s all in one shot that night. Clearly Central alien Command overlooked my taking the garbage out that night!

Gotcha! The entire sky busted! Providing additional confirmation, the next night they shifted back to their normal co-ordinates. When I see a star in rapid East -West motion, my overhang roof soffit has grooves evenly spaced that run perpendicular to the wall. By standing underneath and sighting up past it, it eliminates virtually all optic illusion or distortion relative to elapsed distance time measurement. The movement of a nearby cloud becomes a non-factor. This methodology making Fred Flintstone proud of his patented U.F.O. buster, but it works surprisingly well (although limited to east-west movement only).

Another night I had been observing a stationary star to the South-West, then leaving for about a fifteen-minute run to the Post Office, this guy wasn't there when I got back, punched his time card and disappeared. Quite often they will do something to give themselves away, but it can take a lot of patience, and often occurs at an hour when sleep is much more preferable than star observations.

An object in the sky from a single vantage point could be almost any distance, and beyond a certain point hard to determine. However a true star should be millions of miles distant, not fifty thousand feet. There is a method I call plumb/radius, which employs Geometry as it's principle, but no calculation required.

You figure if it is a U.F.O. at fifty thousand feet and can plumb down to an approximate point it is directly above, five or ten miles away whatever you determine, then if you know the area, picture where that is on the ground. Next imagine a giant compass swinging an arc, a radius that intersects with where you are standing. Now swing the compass on this radius line, and determine a point along that line, and where that point might be. Next is going to that point and re-observing the particular star of interest. If it is a U.F.O. it will still be at the same height approximately as before, still above the same plumb point. This method does not work well with a sky heavy with stars, or if you transit yourself to another point of observation along the calculated arc approximated is too far off the true arc's position, thus distorting end observation accuracy. A little bit off won't be difference making, but way off will. Transiting to other points on your conceived arc as added proof should all indicate the star being at the same height in the sky if accurate geometry wise.

In a more urban environment, more roads availability might make arriving at a prescribed arc point easier, you also have to make sure you are still looking at the same 'star,' and tall buildings can obstruct you view, as well as tall trees, etc. Consulting a map of local roads and actually using a compass to determine your arc might be necessary using this method rather than doing it in your head.

In April of 2008, as I became adept at distinguishing U.F.O.s from real stars, since they look so similar from the ground, I no longer employed this method any longer, and the number of 'likely' sightings over and above the definite count had exploded to the point that seeing or identifying more was a moot point.

Instead I simply looked for stars flinching (or sideways movement) or the little circular rotation jiggle dance they often do. This an instant give away, as something a real star would never do. Interior tiny colored light fleck (that takes a sharp eye to see) sometimes will flicker just enough to detect (your looking from the outside of saucer window to the inside) other lighting is external on the outside of the craft sometimes visible, as well, on certain occasions. The fourth way commonly used is observing noticeable discrepancy changes in star formations such as pairs, triangles, or larger imitation of constellation they routinely perpetrate masquerade of! Cheap knock-offs of stars!

Here in South Florida., the grey's craft will routinely in condition where mixed cloud condition in an otherwise clear sky exists, flood or bathe their saucer shape in bright light that looking up at one of these very bright crafts will disguise it's silhouette profile shape. It allows them to descend just below cloud level for unobstructed observations. Humans quickly dismiss what they see as a distant bright star or the planet Mercury, or Venus, when in fact it is within Earth's atmosphere, often in the forty to sixty thousand altitude range. Two saucers that I identified as definite Bright were named Illustra and Illumus. To bust a bright, if it is still maintaining position at about 5 A.M., keep observing until just at dawns first light just before sunrise. It will vacate, and when it does, ascend and move, and the disc shape will become quite visible, as the E.T.'s have already turned off the bathe of light on their external surface because they've lost the dark night sky backdrop needed. The star now a Luciferian Morningstar will be quite visibly a disk saucer you'll watch ascend and disappear! A star that many might have believed to be real, now exposed as a hoaxer of E.T. origin. Low level night sky human reconnaissance perpetrator of star impersonation hoax. demonic E.T., along with all other order from the demonic realm have eyes sensitive to sunlight. The Bad Greys are relatively benign compared to the pure demon spirited Reptilian, who are their superior officers in that Satanic saucer Air Force.

The Good Greys more neutral than actually good, are at least a separate faction not aligned to the dark side, and one has to suspect such is not random, but by God's design. I'm convinced they could be the communication bridge as diplomatic couriers between Holy side and Dark side. Two sides that want no direct contact with one another what-so-ever, but still need communication linkage, both sides being under the Omnipotent power of God the Father Almighty. As evil, vile, and detestable as the dark side is, it cannot operate independent from God entirely, and must obey God's rules. God has them on a very short, and tight leash, and though that day of rebellion is coming, the Bible has already claimed victory in that final Armageddon battle, pronouncing it so almost two thousand years ago, and as God has the ability to see the future (which I as a psychic Christian prophet can attest to firsthand). If God says he will be victorious in the final battle, then rest assured, thus will be so, because he has given his word it will be so! Even confirming to me the year in which that battle will take place, as you will read later in this book! Praise God, believe in the word of Jesus. If you take my 9 definite sightings as a representative cross-section, then you then have two Reptilian to seven Greys. Is that the percentage mix in total, in fact? Not necessarily exactly, but it gives very definite confirmation of the greys having U.F.O. craft in greater numbers.

As I would conduct sky observation during the first fourteen days of the U.F.O. sightings foretold by an in my sleep dream vision you will read more about in later Chapter, I notated 'star' positions, and broke the sky into eight quadrants each night if the sky was 'well stocked' with stars, to keep accurate monitoring. On nights with less than about twenty-five stars I'd simply make notation with sky direction like southwest, east, northwest, etc. next to an assigned name that helped keep tighter inventory control. A log was also kept to make additional comments relevant if deemed as being appropriate memory refresher later to equate any unusual behavior to a particular 'star' or star formation identity when reviewing later. The system worked pretty well. The charting only necessary when nights of heavier appearance concentrations were present to keep everything accurately defined in observation. Eventually, continuing the log on for fourteen months, even though God only asked for fourteen days, because I wanted to make sure nothing of value was missed. Here are some example of a whole long list 'star names' I'd just spontaneously assign as this process proceeded:

Star or Formation Name	Direction Seen	Description
Bowstring Pair	Overhead	pair
Alpha Surrogate	N.E.	single
Ruler Pair	Overhead	pair
Compass Pair	Overhead	pair
Diamond Girl	S.W.	single (bright)
Seattle Sigma	N.W.	small triangle
Beta	West	single
Zulu	N.E.	single
Bravo	South	single
Delta	N.E.	single
Riviera Rogue	N /N.E.	single
Omega	S.W.	single
Sigma	N.W.	single
Sigma Surrogate	N.W.	single

Without a doubt in my mind, a high percentage of these were likely, but not definitely U.F.O.. If I claim a U.F.O. as a definite it has to be exactly that. Definitely. My nine definite are definite and including the 2004 sighting in that count. In the larger picture, the how many and the what was seen less important than the why. There is absolutely no question at all that all of this occurred by God's design, occurred because of a book God foretold to me through a holy angel 45 years ago I would one day write, and for the purpose of confirming God in this most unique way, while at the same time confirming Tribulation timing, but combining this with greater understanding of the U.F.O./E.T. involvement role.

Only New Testament mentions a scorpion like intelligently guided Taser stinger tail, and as Tribulation approaches this needed clarification for both clergy and average citizenry alike. By confirming (allowing me a sneak peak preview) I can witness through this book having actually seen it and what it looks like, this confirms both Tribulation, and Book of Revelation as authentically accurate! Book of Revelation being accurate, it confirms New Testament, and thus Christianity in total.

But knowing how God operates, and what holy angel specialize in, you must also realize God has extended multiple layered purpose going on here at the same time, just like his multi- layered *Interdimensional Universe* fabric construct. Psychic visions and messages often have multiple message, and multiple purpose.

You then see this additional purpose side. He's explaining about the U.F.O./E.T. subject, in know your enemy the Devil fashion. This like all his messaging for me to report to humanity through the information distribution platform of a book, which clergy can then utilize in their better understanding of the enemy. Wildman on a special Ops recon mission for God, but for God's purpose of making this known, my book the vehicle God is using to accomplish this. Wildman a special agent for God, but so too, the Biblical Prophets, as well, just living in a different earlier age. God's gift of prophecy and forth telling, and foretelling as the Bible states it, are always to witness Jesus Christ, purpose one, but purpose two, to ultimately accomplish God's greater goal. Look at all who have ever received prophecy holy in nature or connection, and I promise you it is invariably purpose of God driven, and for particular circumstance accomplishment important to God.

Frankly I don't care if people think I'm crazy talking about E.T., U.F.O., and God, all in the same sentence along with holy Prophecy. When a psychic/Prophet suddenly begins receiving messaging from God, trust one thing, that person is fully aware of that, and I am fully aware of that. Tribulation is approaching, exactly as Book of Revelation describes it, and He (God) our loving heavenly father wants to give his faithful a heads-up so they aren't caught by surprise. He also wants to provide the non-believer, and Christian of weak faith a wake up warning. It is the last decade before the Tribulation decade. This other multi-layer purpose is to box those non and weak faith believers into a corner, as this book traumatizes them in new realty shock a bit perhaps! A last chance merciful opportunity to get into spiritual faith shape (before the alternative eternal death subdues them). He wants humanity to have awakening opportunity to surrender themselves to Jesus before they have to pay the price extreme for neglecting to do so. That showing God is a loving God (salvation through grace, and grace anointed through faith). Cutting edge U.F.O.-logy, Para Psychology, and Christian Religion all at a cosmic/spiritual intersecting point in a book written by a prophet who should have died several times over already, but is writing this book for you in witness to Jesus for you because God so destined me to do so!

World War III Implications
The Endangerment of Christian Nation Forces

As you will later read in Chapter 27, where I lay out and detail timing and events of World War III as I interpret it from all data, psychic and otherwise, this becomes a critical point. With limited time left to make effective statement, I sincerely hope that Theology professors and Bible scholars will close an extremely dangerous interpretations loophole. Sort of like a tax break for demons, except this is an identification safe harbor they've simply ignored for a very long time, giving the demons exactly what they desire most: secrecy!

Oh it isn't that in the last sixty years there hasn't been growing evidence to support at least the theory that factions from at least two or more ET groups had demonic leanings or loyalties, but just not the adequate proof these conservative scholars would need to mix U.F.O./E.T. subject as certainty consideration/interpretation. To them, this had to wait until the day there was further evidence. U.F.O.-ologists from the mid-1980s on had compiled much more extensive evidence to support such claims, but even they couldn't state such with certainty, but with highly likely instead. U.F.O.-ologists saw the Biblical ties possibility too, as the locusts mentioned in Book of Revelation to them were in fact U.F.O. flown by ET with demonic loyalties. Several studies done in U.F.O. hot spot South Florida. from the 1980s to present all showed similar result. The fact that when winds exceed forty miles per hour in the deep (six miles) ocean trench off Puerto Rico, all U.F.O. activity above South Florida ceases at night.

Wildman feels he now has sufficient evidence to indict two ET groups on crimes against humanity criminal charges dating back centuries. With no one yet figuring out how to build an interdimensional holding cell, or how to arrest them to bring them to trial, we'll have to settle for prosecution conviction in absentia. A demon by any other name is a demon just the same. Wildman has the evidence on these guys, but it requires the judges (Bible scholars/professors) to bring this to trial and to convict them in the interest of justice and humanity long victimized (cattle and human abductions only a fraction of the crimes). Those original fallen angels, demons, Reptilian ET., and 'the beast from the sea' all being one and the same.

Why is it so important to win this conviction, and urgent that such be done soon? The answer is this, if Bible scholars fail to accomplish taking a firm stand, airing this out, and blow this sewer lid cover off of darkness secrecy identity ambiguity away, then it will just a decade and a half from now cause deaths to soldiers under the Christian banner against the Anti-Christ forces in all likelihood. Those un-raptured Christians in the northern rim of the Mediterranean who are engaged in battles against the Anti-Christ forces, could be at greatly increased risk if they don't know the score on this U.F.O./E.T. situation.

The U.S. will be the giant that fell face first in the mud by this time, almost entirely a non-factor for two years, as it tries to pick itself up and make it to intensive care so to speak. When it comes to Tribulation, no nation on Earth can afford the luxury of simply being reactive, it is an absolute must that they take this threat/timing with certainty seriousness, and take drastic pro-active steps beforehand. For I told you so, posterity sake; Wildman's quote in 2010 referring to mid-2024 onward time period- for those still left alive then, it will seem quite prophetically profound, but worse true!

Christian forces, both on land and at sea will be at great risk from these U.F.O. -forward observation platforms. As early as World War I hot air balloons were used as observation decks to direct and re-direct artillery fire on the enemy. The Bad Greys who are subordinates of the Reptilian will have the locust numbers to cover a wide geographic (including sea area) and possess exceptional night vision even without instruments. In other words, if you were a commander for the Christian armies, and you were oblivious to the fact that that star overhead probably wasn't a star but an enemy U.F.O. loyal to the anti-Christ, you might mass forces to make an advance under cover of darkness. Bad move then, as you've just assisted the enemy in removing that chess piece from the chess board. The greater the numbers, the easier to spot movement from the air. It isn't even clear if these U.F.O. can always be picked up by radar. Rule of thumb, if it looks like a star, try to shoot it down. If it's a real star you know it's out of reach. If it's a U.F.O., it'll flinch when it detects a missile fired at it, and step back with a little circular move. Once they realize their cover is no longer adequate star camouflage, they'll at least have to keep greater distance away.

demons by God's rules cannot directly cause the death of humans in direct action, but radioing GPS co-ordinates to the Anti-Christ forces for missile fire as described here is not direct, thus well within the rules. I truly hope Christian clergy will make an effort before they depart in Rapture, to lobby for removal of this demon identity shelter.

U.F.O. Presence, West Palm Beach, Florida
Weekly and Monthly Log, 2008/2009

BUSTING THE "STAR PRETENDERS"
"THE TRIANGLE FORMATION"

FG #1 ↑	AS SEEN ON 4/24	FG #5 ↑	AS SEEN ON 4/30	FG #9 ↑	AS SEEN ON 5/10
FG #2 ↑	AS SEEN ON 4/26	FG #6 ↑	AS SEEN ON 5/1	FG #10 ↑	AS SEEN ON 5/23
FG #3 ↑	AS SEEN ON 4/27	FG #7 ↑	AS SEEN ON 5/4	FG #11 ↑	AS SEEN ON 5/26
FG #4 ↑	AS SEEN ON 4/29	FG #8 ↑	AS SEEN ON 5/9	FG #12 ↑	AS SEEN ON 5/29

New Realities of the Twenty-first Century, Part 1

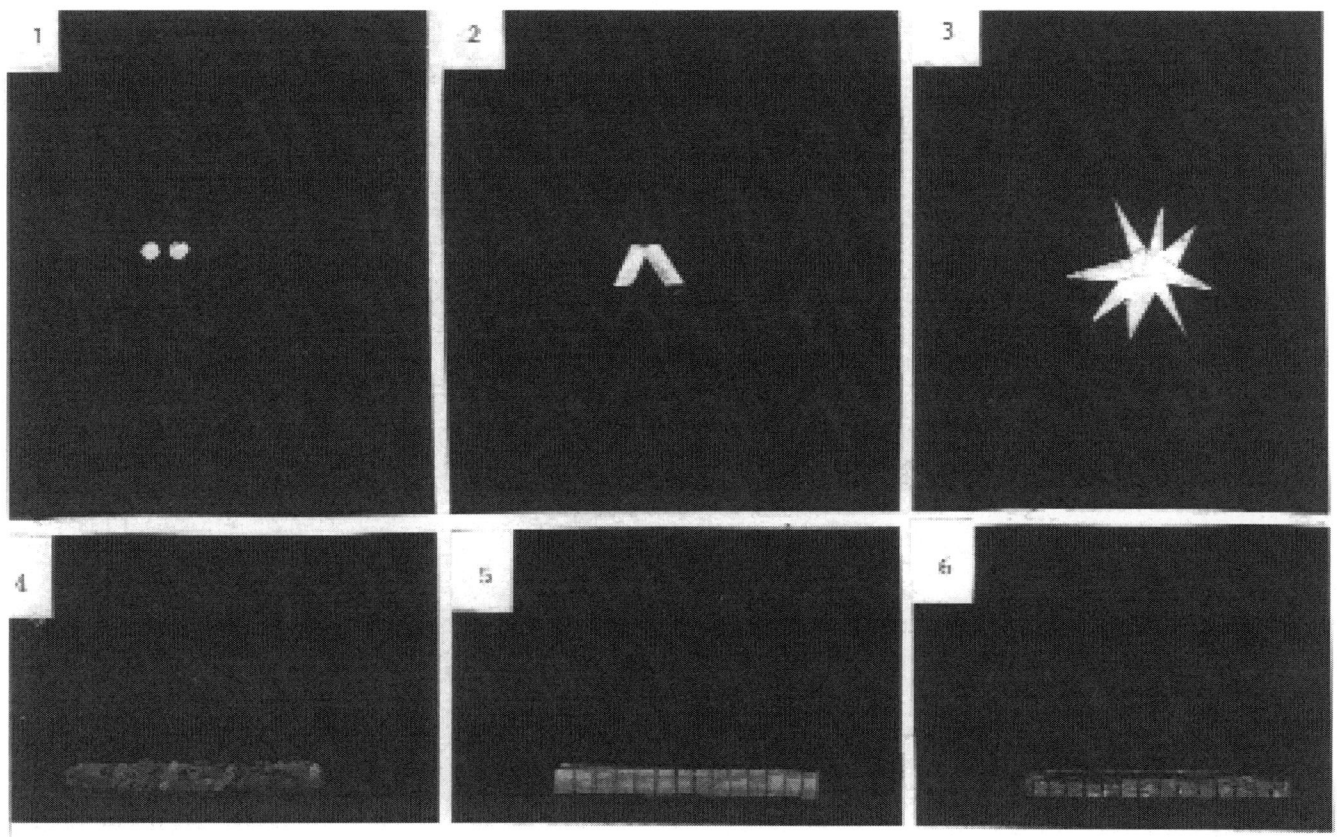

PLEASE NOTE: ALL DEPICTIONS ENLARGED SEVERAL TIMES LARGER THAN THEY WOULD ACTUALLY APPEAR IN THE NIGHT SKY.

DISTINGUISHABLE "SUSPECT" UFO LOOKS - SOUTH FLORIDA VARIETY UFO

Top Row: (white light only seen)

1. Two white dots close but not touching
2. (single dot can be UFO also)
   Two leaning rectangles
3. A very "Bright" object usually below 40,000 ft. altitude
   At daybreak (first light) this cloak evaporates, and their disk profile becomes visible upon departure that is typically ascent.

Bottom Row: (Colored light only seen - UFO window area)

4) 1. Balls of various colored light, sometimes stationary, other times appear to flicker or flash
5) 2. "Ambers", or what some call Fla. Oranges (rare)
6) 3. Very similar to #1, except the vertical window posts may be more apparent, instead of seeing colored balls of light only.

Typically UFO craft are likely in the 18,000 to 50,000 ft. alt. range

Chapter 12
U.F.O. Craft Characteristics

In the Entities section: Aliens (Chapter 4), I showed listing of known alien groups visiting or believed having previously visited planet Earth, some likely in our ancient pre-history past. It is quite possible from time to time, Earth is a stopover point to an even yet larger spectrum array of alien groups. Likely at times, going totally undetected, unrecognized, and completely unnoticed by humans, especially in sparsely populated areas and sub polar regions. Examples: Canadian and Siberian wilderness, as well as parts of South America, Africa, Australia, and Malaysia. The craft are not always detectable on radar or satellite.

That the Grey's and Reptilian have colonized our planet with their undersea USO bases in Atlantic and Pacific deep trench areas is likely. Other bases and staging areas could exist also, with one in the Indian ocean perhaps. The Bermuda Triangle deep trench off Puerto Rico seems to be one, deep trench off Catalina Island, California a staging area at the least. I also believe in the Sargasso Sea region, about one thousand miles or more due East of Cape Kennedy is another staging area that is frequented, and they've been doing this for thousands of years! These beings didn't originate here, they colonized Earth as an outpost. The drawings page depict what craft they fly, at least here in the Florida region.

By knowing their spacecraft, anything else points to the likelihood of the presence of a different alien group. Reconnaissance, mapping, charting, scientific experiment and fact gathering, in short, everything humans do when they go space exploring.

Aside from saucer shape, many other different shapes are also seen from time to time, evidencing the wide diversity and multiplicity of potential alien groups involved. Boomerang, wide V wing, triangles and trapezoids of varied descriptions, barrel and cylindrical, very long elliptical and cigar shaped, space capsule shaped, pyramid, spherical (solid and vaporous orb), sometimes exhibiting a color, multi-color, or hue, and even larger than a football field described craft, or flying platforms reported also. These reports are worldwide, over many centuries, and with more than one hundred thousand witnesses and growing. It would appear aliens have planet Earth listed in their interstellar galactic road map as a tourist attraction. It's only a matter of time before Disneyland taps into that market (just joking).

In Charles Berlitz's, *World of Strange Phenomena*, he mentions scientists relatively recent discovery of a black hole in star constellation Cygnus, star Cygnus X-1. He points out ancient Sumerians had knowledge of it five thousand years ago, as they described a danger star. They call it the demon bird of Negril. Negril the Lord of the Underworld to them, and described its location on clay tablets. When it is charted, it is Cygnus X-1. Some type of alien contact must have occurred as some like Eric Von Daniken would agree. That leads one to question are some of these alien groups re-visiting Earth, but not making human contact, having been here thousands of years earlier?

Many authors coming at this subject from divergent directions have mentioned the existence of something known as the Galactic Federation. It sounds like something straight out of Star-Trek, but then they probably got the idea from one of these authors. Galactic Federation outposts or headquarters they are termed. A kind of united alien nations peacekeeping organization, an alien U.N. Does it actually exist? The C.I.A./N.S.A. will never tell. It is actually a strong possibility it does. Depending on what version you believe, they have between 5 and 9 headquarter branches scattered across the galaxy. Seven is the most commonly stated number.

It has been mentioned by those who channel spirit entities, it has been mentioned by abductees who have engaged in telepathic communication directly with aliens (usually Greys), and spoken of even by remote viewers who are professional. It is interesting, too, that in some abductee cases, they were unaware others had reported the same. Indicating they were not influenced from prior knowledge. It has also been reported there is an underground Martian sub-station, but in what dimension should perhaps be the question. A Reptilian space sub-station based half way between

Earth and the Moon but in cloaked dimension? Possibly so, according to Courtney Brown's book, *Cosmic Explorers*. Aliens knocking human satellites out of the sky? Read Phil Imbrogno's *Interdimensional Universe*.

With the Florida U.F.O., Greys and Reptilian, the saucer shape is the distinguishing factor in determining registry. The Greys have I believe, two sizes of pancake flat saucers. The smaller size probably with a four- to six-man crew, with thirty to fifty feet in approximate diameter. Their larger disk in the fifty to seventy-five feet diameter range, with likely double the crew or more. It has generally speaking been the smaller, lighter craft that have crashed, but consistent with what I've stated here.

The Reptilian have Low Hats, and High Hats. The High Hats are far less frequently seen, and usually close to or hugging dark shore line stretches very late at night (my sighting typical). Because of darkness it was difficult to get an accurate estimate of the High-hat, but between seventy-five and one hundred feet in diameter. The Low Hat I witnessed four years later about the same size, and an identical window array. It was clear in the 2004 sighting that only windows along the South side of the craft were lit, and the windows along the north side (certainly there), were either covered or unlit.

The distinctive flatness of the Greys craft (hence the Pancake name) distinguishes it from the Reptilian craft. However, one or both of these groups using bright exterior craft lighting, causes the human viewer to be blinded by the light, thus kept from detecting shape. By using this technique, the aliens can then descend to lower altitude without human detection. A typical person would think they might be looking at Venus or Mercury which can also appear bright. They are also smart enough only to do this with one or two of their craft at one time. Seeing two bright at one time, but in different directions is not uncommon. Meanwhile (at least here in the U.F.O. wildlife preserve), what would appear to be star clusters in the night sky around them are in fact, as described in previous chapter, U.F.O. formations. Hundreds of thousands are going to feel cheated, to learn that their night sky is void of real stars most of the time, and filled with alien impersonators instead. Since when is a star equipped with dimmer switches it was clearly witnessed on one occasion. If you want real stars, Tallahassee will have to raise taxes, enact a star tax or something, maybe U.F.O.'s aren't so bad after all, they've been fooling humans for decades anyway.

Especially these Brights, referred to in the Bible as Lucifer Morningstar. The particle beam I witnessed that I feel is in fact the same scorpion stinger tail mentioned in the Bible book of Revelation was delivered from the Bright that I had dubbed Illustra. Was it a Greys craft or Reptilian? I can't say with certainty, but whereas my original thinking was leaning toward Reptilian, my thinking is now leaning toward a Greys craft of the larger diameter. The larger Greys craft is only slightly smaller than the Reptilian's Low Hat, and both likely with bright capability, but do both also have these Taser tail particle beams? Possibly so.

Some people have theorized that alien's use colored lights to signal in code from one craft to another. This is real possibility, as I've witnessed external colored light variation blinking (my 2008 alpha sighting) and, at times, colored light variations from inside the window areas of a saucer craft, perhaps signaling. But why with electronics available would they use colored light signal? It is anyone's guess.

Beside the normal star like look, and Brights, on a few occasions an amber or deep yellow orange glow would describe the look of some craft seen, and these only rarely, but on a few separate night occasions. I simply call these Ambers. The significance, again anyone's guess. A craft holding high ranking officers of the 391st Alien Air Wing perhaps. It is certainly reassuring to go to bed every night knowing the skies are firmly in the grasp of spindly fingered alien hands, and hovering over or near your home. Twenty-first century home security system I guess you could say, but who did you say the intruders were?

It is no wonder the government and Air Force would prefer to pretend U.F.O. and aliens don't exist. Craft speeds in the fifty thousand mile-per-hour range, possibly not even top speed. Zero to five thousand miles per hour instantly from hover position (my 2004 sighting) and highly maneuverable. To say astonishing is no overstatement. In the past, human aircraft have when engaged in pursuit, had their entire electronics system rendered immobilized, and likely only one in a wide arsenal of both defensive and offensive weaponry the aliens likely possess. Our most advanced aircraft and systems antiquated badly in comparison. This a sobering thought when weighed against what I will tell you in Chapter 27, and even earlier in Chapter 21 (Part II) where alien invasion possibilities are discussed. No need to panic, I wrote this book so as to prepare you with information that needs to be shared, so that you can evaluate your own circumstance in advance. An educated American or other human rather than a dead mushroom, a term I will elaborate on in Chapter 13.

In 1948 a scientist and Navy missile trackers group tracked an oval U.F.O. through a nine thousand miles per hour, ascent, and eighteen thousand miles per hour, departure.

In 1952, three civil aeronautical engineers calculated the speed of a U.F.O. over Terre Haute, Indiana, airport at 42,000 miles per hour.

Observers frequently describe U.F.O.s as moving so fast that their lights appear to leave a trail., or streaking away as fast as a meteor, or shrinking out of sight over the horizon in the blink of an eye.

This published 1994 statement matching my own 2004 witnessed account exactly (two others with me witnessing the same thing).

There are many reports of U.F.O. extremely high speed flight in our atmosphere, coupled with the ability to stop and start abruptly.

The now classic sighting in Redlands Calif. February 4, 1968, that was witnessed by over two hundred residents, all saw a disk-shaped object (estimated to be fifty feet in diameter) said to have hovered at an altitude of approximately three hundred feet off the ground (exactly the same approximate height as my 2004 sighting).

When the craft do touch down it is likely to be in an open area, free of obstructions. Burn rings, radiation, and other non-naturally occurring anomalies are typically reported at the site in the aftermath of departure. While the 2004 sighting I and two others witnessed at night, never descended lower than three hundred feet altitude, movement was clearly seen between the craft and the ground early in the observations. Later, after twenty minutes to a half hour, movement from the ground back up to craft was observed. Beings (at least three or four) seen behind the windows that appeared to be in control of the craft had noticeably beige orange skin tone. Forget little green men, try tall orange men! No they didn't play basketball for, or graduate from Syracuse University; their application turned down for lacking credits in the humanities they thought was a menu item (joking, of course, about Syracuse, but not the sighting).

Reptilian aliens visiting South Palm Beach Billionaires Row at 4 A.M, what were they doing on the island? Dip in the heated pool or hot tub? Not likely. Poker game with Illuminati? Not Likely, they weren't there long enough. C.I.A./N.S.A. quarterly meeting on a tight one hour schedule? Maybe so. Statistical analysis offered favorable odds that no human would travel that route at that hour to witness the event. It would seem Wildman never got that memo, then did! Here's one for your imagination: C.I.A. offering expensive French wine and Beluga Russian caviar (that the Russians got the aliens addicted to at their own trading post sessions) in exchange for technology tips, and recent abductee listing. Who would ever believe this taking place on the South end of Palm Beach island at 4 A.M.? Nobody but a lie detection test placing that craft there at that hour, on that day. Reptilian aliens definitely there, the C.I.A./N.S.A. guys with caviar stains on their hands simply won't fess-up. I often wondered why the Intercostal Waterway smelled like alien piss at low tide, it seems yet another mystery solved! Can't imagine why the C.I.A./N.S.A. wouldn't want you to know they are arranging clandestine secret meetings with a group of aliens known to be both demonic and hostile to humans can you? Worse has been said about North Korea and Iran, so that makes it okay?

Meanwhile NASA spending millions to learn about alien life, learns little and keeps spending. I spend nothing and learn everything. I can even see NASA launches from my front patio. My front patio kind of like a Twilight Zone space platform, having such a participatory role in so much of what I've encountered. My front door like some dimensional portal. You have to walk through the Twilight Zone to get to Wildman's front door, call it poetic justice. Think I ought to rent out my front patio to NASA? Charge more for my book? They make big bucks, read my book to learn what's going on, and then pocket the difference. I've already installed an outside, don't bother to attend memo drop box for the C.I.A./N.S.A., so they can leave message when not to witness their next alien trading post session (joking, of course).

In addition to tractor beam already described in another chapter, the ET also have, or at least I think they have something that I call a Horizontal Hitch. On a couple of different occasions I've witnessed what is the equivalent of a horizontal stiff hitch, except it is a particle beam connect of some type. Pairs are a common U.F.O. formation, and with two craft at similar altitude (one thousand to two thousand feet apart) one can lock on to the other, and if the first craft executes a say, thirty degree turn, they move in tandem keeping equal distance apart. This apparently to eliminate chance of bumping or collision when in tight formation proximity. How much did you say these guys at C.I.A./N.S.A./ & NASA are paid to learn about this stuff? Wildman now a credible information source for them at bargain book price? Pretty hard to discredit him with the E.T.s, holy angel, and God directly involved in this book. That's what happens when you give the E.T. coordinates and turn by turn directions to my home. No? you didn't? It seems like this book has the entire other side of the veil supernatural realm stirred up. They all want mention in Wildman's book. What a cast of characters!

Most of them multi, or interdimensional, and usually invisible in this dimension of the human living. not to mention interdimensional spacecraft. An equal mystery.

While the Greys U.F.O. craft we know from crash sites did generate a debris field of physical matter, as well as alien dead bodies, what about the Reptilian craft? Here the mystery plot thickens, or perhaps thins a more appropriate word. Never a crash, debris, or bodies? The answer is these are thought of as demonically oriented E.T., when in fact they are demons, period. Just as angels have never lived, these fallen angels, better known as demons have never lived. That is why no dead bodies, because they aren't living to start with. ET in the sense of fallen angel or demon spread across the universe, just like holy angel. If they aren't living, then unlikely there spacecraft is of solid matter material (although not impossible), but rather call it Isotope 6 matter. Apparition matter. Visible sometimes in another dimension, appearing solid, but really not (like the particle visible/invisible beam). Like Sasquatch sightings even, more Isotope 6 material, oh it looks very solid, and I observed the particle beam from about six or seven feet from the end of the thing. It looked deceptively solid. Who is the master of deception, Satan? His spacecraft and demonic employees, demons all, deceptively there but not there. Call it illusionary Isotope 6 matter, call it what you like.

A spacecraft appearing to disappear out of this dimension into a different cloaked one, in fact never left that dimension to begin with, deceptively, it briefly appeared transparent in this dimension to provide the illusion of visibly being in this dimension? demonic trickery from demonic tricksters of a U.F.O. actually in parallel dimension I truly think is the answer. A demon by any other name, a demon just the same. A lot of groundbreaking shovels dirtied before this book completes, and you have my senior editor's word on it! Mine, too.

Now what I think may be happening is that the 2004 sighting for example was solid, as were the beings inside, but under the cover of darkness as the U.F.O. vanished from a standstill disappearing out over the ocean night horizon at incredible speed, the brief light streak fraction of a second trails confirm I believe, solid object form.

Comparing that with Sasquatch tracks that do equate to a large foot imprint that actually would take six hundred- to eight hundred-pound, ape-like creature to make. This suggests that assuming it is comprised of some type of demonic matter such as what I termed Isotope 6, perhaps it can cover the full range of solidness in this dimension, from thin, partially ethereal, to so solid that it takes on accompanying weight characteristic. Only one drawback, limited time shelf life in complete solid state. It would explain why so many unexplained demonic Rares beings and creatures never stick around for very long; the solidness in this dimension fades! The Spring Heel Jacks, Owl Man, Jersey Devil, Ohio's Loveland frogs, flying humanoids, Dover demon, etc. etc. All of demonic source, but perhaps with Bad Greys or Reptilian assistance.

To comprehend this you must realize that other dimensions share the same space as the dimension of reality or dimension of human living. It is this stacked or layered dimensional fabric of Earth's atmosphere that allows for, or contains this existing dimensional condition. Quite likely it extends throughout God's entire universe. Complexity humans don't need to know about, yet does exist.

Coining the term ultraterrestrials, the late John Keel was pointing to exactly such condition of demonic source interdimensional goings on, both in terms of unexplained creatures, and E.T./U.F.O.. He was not wrong. Of course anything Evil prefers darkness, which is why most such sightings occur at night, but not all.

In conclusion on the U.F.O./E.T. craft topic, it simply can't be confirmed as to whether the craft are permanently solid, limited time solid, or whether they are actually in this dimension, or whether we might actually be seeing through a window into different dimension when sighting one. The only thing regarding Reptilian that I am thoroughly and completely convinced of is that the Reptilian ET are of the demon realm. No chance of maybe, not on that one, and demons being able to shapeshift form, well that's John Keel's ultra-terrestrial using that visible/invisible demonic Isotope 6. From premonition fulfillment, there is no question that the particle beam I witnessed was straight out of Bible Book of Revelation. The strangest thing of all then, ET revealing it, and in doing so, making verification of statement describing it in Bible Book of Revelation.

Among U.F.O. - logists, for years the prevailing theory (not proven) is that the Reptilian E.T. are in fact demons or once upon a time Fallen angels, but perhaps from locale from the Dark Rift Zone of the Milky Way. The deep Devil's Triangle in the Atlantic off Puerto Rico with a trench 6 miles deep, and the Dragon's Triangle in the Pacific Marianas Island region 8 miles deep, their bases (Biblically the Bottomless Pit and Abyss). Likely interdimensional gateways to hell or Hades. Does Wildman subscribe to this hypothesis? Yes, absolutely, and then some!

Take a look at my own confirms:

1.) Extensive research turned up confirm after confirm rather than one thing even remotely conflicting. Even going back in human civilization Thousands of years, this archival ancient evidence supports such claim.
2.) The 2008 premonition, during asleep dream psychic vision, the ET clearly influencing the vision and ratcheting up the level of torture was identified as a Reptilian E.T., caught in the act of inflicting psychological torture, until it jolted-high-volted me conscious/awake (human torture a favorite demon pastime).
3.) The psychic dream message, discussed in later chapters, with holy angel assist? Informing that one ET group is fluent in a demonic tongue spoken in hell.
4.) The intensity of the Evil Vibe accompanying the Reptilian April 2008 Low Hat U.F.O. sighting. As well as human deaths that followed in close proximity of both time and sighting location.
5.) Hostile to Human descriptive characterization by all other authors relating Reptilian ET also as demons.
6.) When high winds above 40 mph. in the Puerto Rico trench area is prevailing condition for sustained period near sunset into early evening, into late evening such as with a lingering storm, it results in suspension of South Florida. U.F.O. activity in total.
7.) Orange/Beige snake skin on half/human like beings, matches both the 2004 awake sighting, and the in my sleep vision glimpse in the 2008 dream premonition. Identical match.

8.) What my psychic glimpse vision appearance of a Reptilian was, and what other multiple source descriptions are is virtually an identical match (likely unseen leaving many a crime, accident, or death occurrence by shifting to interdimensional invisibility).

In order to understand their craft/U.F.O.'s characteristic, confirming the pilot and crew here is essential. Unfortunately I can't give you as definitive an explanation of the craft, but here I think it can be reduced to four possibilities. The fact that the Greys exhibited wreckage from a solid craft and alien bodies of solid matter doesn't help. Those were apples and these are snake skinned oranges by comparison. You can't assume anything is same or similar, evaluations must be derived independently (also Bible Revelation's beasts from the sea mention).

So, what four possibilities do I offer? After completing the book and reading about the year of the Biblical locust (five month open Taser hunt sting season on humans allowed) you might want to ponder these possibilities further. They are:

1.) Like the Greys their craft is of solid matter, in this dimension all the time, or at least in flight.
2.) It is solid matter, or some sort of quasi/semi-solid matter (or plasma matter) in this dimension some of the time, but in interdimensional mode, out of this dimension other times (these other dimension like layers not far from this one).
3.) It only appears solid and in this dimension, but never actually exits except in the other dimension. It doesn't appear so as to give us better visibility of them, it appears to enable them much better visibility of us. A mirage in essence, and perhaps in plasma form in that other dimension, as well.
4.) It actually appears solid in this dimension, because it does exit some other dimension into ours when visible. Later it returns to another dimension, thus appearing to vanish to us. In some type of Isotope 6 visible/invisible solid in appearance (similar to the Particle beam) material, but really no solid matter in this dimension, just appearance of such even though brief time/space and Isotope 6 matter space actually does occur within our reality dimension. Sasquatch made of Isotope 6 is of similar E.T. orchestration also. Interdimensional transfers.

The fact that the 2004 High-hat sighting upon departure covered an approximate distance of five miles from a standstill hover about three hundred feet in altitude off the ground in instantaneous sideways motion so swift it was about as close as you could come to vanishing instantly, without being instant. No human or any other advanced vertebrate could endure such enormous G-force and survive. No living being, but then these were non-living beings, exactly as previously described. The Bible mentioned beasts, the fallen angels. demons showing that the term "speed demons" not so contrived after all, or "bat out of hell," either. Not demonic ET or ET of demonic persuasion, but demons period, end of story!

Cigar-shaped craft/U.F.O., even greys craft at times have seemed to make vanishing acts into clouds, not to reappear. Cloaking devise? Some sort of plasma/matter interdimensional shape shift maneuver? I don't know, so I can't tell you, and only tell you what I do know. Perhaps a few humans in intelligence services know, but then they are professional secret keepers. The rest of us need to share information while there is still a humanity around to be saved!

Saucer "classes" Shapes/types

side view

(Grey's Craft) →

① thin disk or "pancake"
example: "Ranger"
diameter 50 - 60 ft (aprox.) larger, 30-40 ft smaller version

(Reptilian Craft) →

② "Low hat"
example: "Romeo"
diameter 75 - 100 ft (aprox.) (length)

(drawn from what was actually seen this depiction is very accurate of a "low hat")

(Reptilian Craft) →

③ "High hat"
example: "Bermuda Triangle" class
diameter 70 - 80 ft (aprox.)
nickname one that sighting as "starfleet #8" or "8 ball"
"coastline clam diggers"

this effect can be Greys or Reptilian →

④ "BRIGHTS" MOST LIKELY A LARGE PANCAKE OR A LOW HAT WITH BRIGHT LIGHTS. SOMETIMES "V" SHAPED BENEATH (UNDERSIDE) example: "DIAMOND GIRL", "ILLUSTRA" & "ILLUMUS"

(LIGHT)

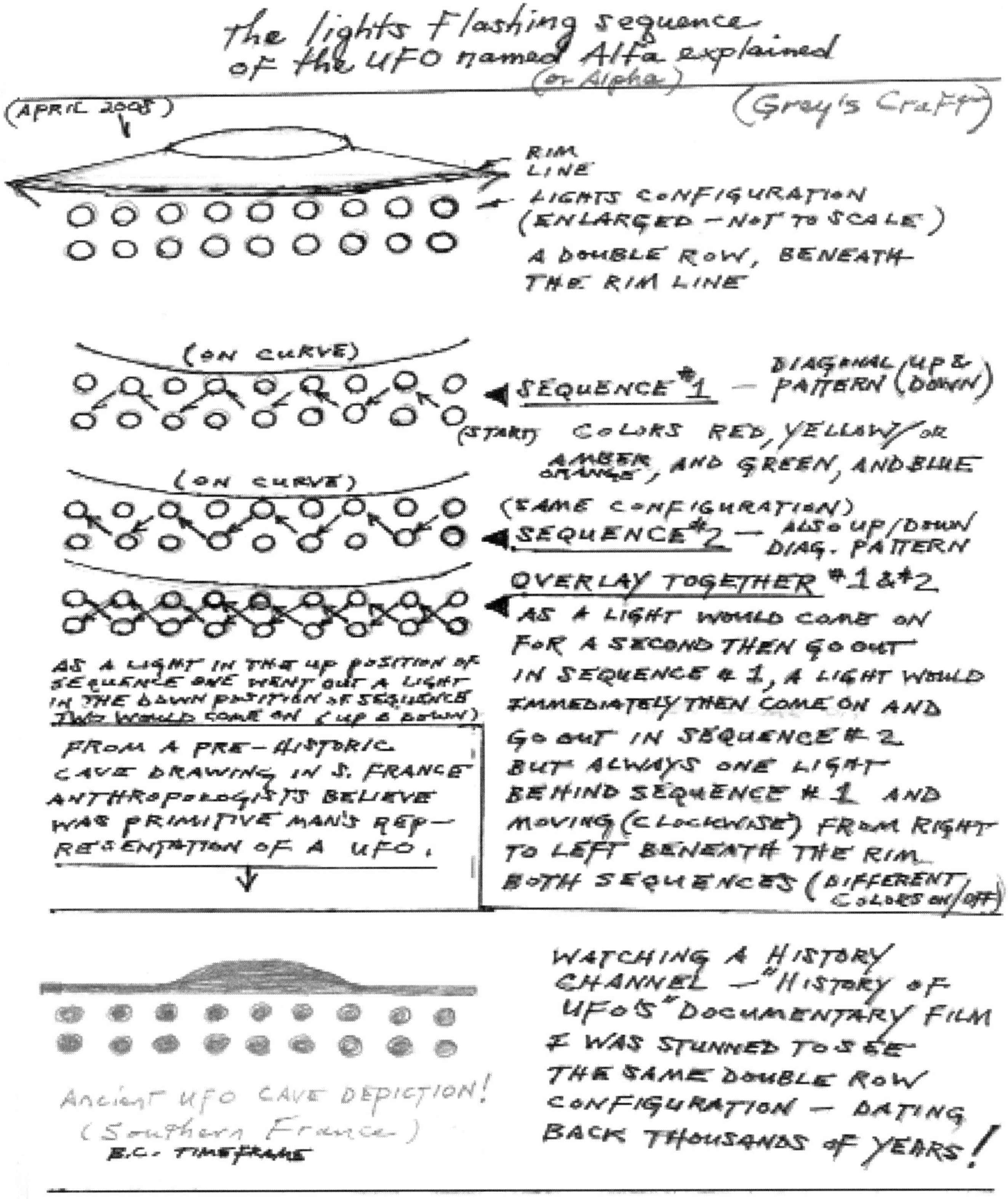

the lights flashing sequence of the UFO named Alfa explained (or Alpha)

(APRIL 2008) (Gray's Craft)

RIM LINE
LIGHTS CONFIGURATION (ENLARGED — NOT TO SCALE)
A DOUBLE ROW, BENEATH THE RIM LINE

(ON CURVE) SEQUENCE #1 — DIAGONAL (UP & DOWN) PATTERN
(START) COLORS RED, YELLOW/OR AMBER/ORANGE, AND GREEN, AND BLUE

(ON CURVE) (SAME CONFIGURATION) SEQUENCE #2 — ALSO UP/DOWN DIAG. PATTERN

OVERLAY TOGETHER #1 & #2
AS A LIGHT WOULD COME ON FOR A SECOND THEN GO OUT IN SEQUENCE #1, A LIGHT WOULD IMMEDIATELY THEN COME ON AND GO OUT IN SEQUENCE #2. BUT ALWAYS ONE LIGHT BEHIND SEQUENCE #1 AND MOVING (CLOCKWISE) FROM RIGHT TO LEFT BENEATH THE RIM. BOTH SEQUENCES (DIFFERENT COLORS ON/OFF)

AS A LIGHT IN THE UP POSITION OF SEQUENCE ONE WENT OUT A LIGHT IN THE DOWN POSITION OF SEQUENCE TWO WOULD COME ON (UP & DOWN)

FROM A PRE-HISTORIC CAVE DRAWING IN S. FRANCE ANTHROPOLOGISTS BELIEVE WAS PRIMITIVE MAN'S REPRESENTATION OF A UFO.

Ancient UFO CAVE DEPICTION! (Southern France) B.C. TIMEFRAME

WATCHING A HISTORY CHANNEL — "HISTORY OF UFOs" DOCUMENTARY FILM I WAS STUNNED TO SEE THE SAME DOUBLE ROW CONFIGURATION — DATING BACK THOUSANDS OF YEARS!

Chapter 13

U.F.O.s and E.T.s
Government Cover-Up

The History of
Ongoing Cover Up
Cattle Mutilation, Discussion of
Human Abductions by E.T.s discussion
Is Government Policy the Correct One?
The National Security Threat and Your Survival Discussed
The Illuminati/Conspiracy Controversy Re-Examined: E.Ts Again

In this scenario the little guy (public) doesn't even get to be the mushroom farmer; they get to be the mushroom. Kept in the dark, fed lots of bull pucky, and perhaps the very same mushroom to get stepped on not too distantly in the future accidentally? It's a funny thing about information, what you don't know can be lethal.

The government's cover up conspiracy begins with (1947) Roswell, and continues to this very day, few would argue. The evidence piles up increasingly that not only is the extent of withheld information on the subject vast, but an ever expanding covert circle is widening. In attempts to classify, hide, research and investigate or analyze this ever burgeoning and increasingly cumbersome volume of data. While at the very same time the public is further distanced, and with never any conclusive update. Saucers and ET still don't exist? What about those people with multiple sightings and encounters such as myself? Aren't we entitled to better explanation? No, I suppose mushrooms aren't supposed to ask questions, but not all mushrooms enjoy darkness, some do quite well in light, and I must be one of those.

This book will shed some light, even into areas this mushroom (government) farmer isn't aware of most likely. Psychically obtained information the mushroom farmer only learns from a book published by one of his mushrooms, now that is an interesting twist wouldn't you say! A mushroom with awareness of the future, which the farmer didn't have. And who is the farmer? Air Force and Army Special Intelligence, OSI, N.S.A., C.I.A., and involving extending groups and Projects encompassing Project Blue Book, Aquarius, Sigma, Special Studies projects, from the Trilateral Commission/50 Committee, PI-40, Council on Foreign Relations, The Jason Society, Quantico Meetings, Area 51 facilities, Dulce, Sandia, and many more Air Force Bases, Eisenhower, Nixon, Ford, Carter, Reagan, Bush, Clinton, and Bush, and now Obama. All of these wonderful groups, places, and Presidents farming mushrooms. Now they are getting a briefing from a mushroom! Unprecedented, a new strain, too, one that prefers daylight (Something tells me it'll be code named Wildman variety.).

Probably be sold in supermarkets under the MJ-12 Brand label, or bookstores that is. Not this information, the disinformation they'll now have to think up to try and dispel all this nasty truth! Well with that much firepower, we knew you guys weren't simply planning security for granny's bingo night (protection from U.F.O.s overhead).

Rather than get into full historical perspective mode on the full history of U.F.O. cover up and conspiracy, author Jerome Clark (1990) in U.F.O. in the 1980s VOL.I gives an accurate and complete compilation (twenty-two large pages) of detail (available at many libraries).

In business, the term tacit collusion refers generally to illegal practice in most instances. Most often it has to do with companies within one industry secretly reaching agreement to artificially fix or stabilize prices for their products above or higher than natural market forces would create, without buyer awareness of this practice.

If you were to apply this term to U.F.O.-logy, the term might mean you conjure up the image of the Federal government and secret military agency collectively giving covert approval to undisclosed activities on the part of E.T.s. Issuance of a secret hunting license to hunt cattle and even human prey? That was the claim for many years, and the government claimed it was too busy watching companies not fix prices to notice any such thing as that occurring. Was that happening? You don't really expect the government to admit to that do you? About now you expect someone among the public (mushrooms) to say something in Yogi Berra-esque fashion, like, we may be dumb, but we're not stupid.

Rumors on the other side of that coin were that the government receives valuable intelligence, some science and technology information, and possible even some weapons technology information in return. One has to wonder, how can much of this information from alien source be verified?

Are we secretly doing research in highly classified labs to aid them in their quest for survival? Leaked information would suggest that we are, if in fact those claims are true. If that is so, then it would also mean that the claims of presidential awareness from Eisenhower onward and all those secret committees for discussion on this topic are true also. It is known that these committees did in fact exist, but were ET and U.F.O. the focus? All the various tie ins while not proving this conclusively suggests it is.

We know also that the government has retrieved aliens from some crash sites, and that for decades the government has worked on projects to reverse engineer U.F.O. Since the Soviet era, the Russians certainly have been doing the same from crash sites of their own that they never disclosed most likely. The current status known only to a few.

It is not likely that aliens would give us too much knowledge in the area of advanced weapons technology since they would have concerns we might later use it against them. They would also have no control from that point on which human hands it fell into, or how it's use even among humans might impact their own security.

To distract the public from growing awareness of what was really going on, it would seem regardless of who sponsored it, a campaign of misinformation and a conspiracy disinformation hoax was launched. A sticky ball of yarn (fiction) was spun involving a whole new cast of conspiracy characters; namely Bilderbergers, Rothschild's, Freemasons, Yale secret order skull and bones club, Satanic Ritual groups, a newly reborn version of Illuminati, European royalty and political figures, maybe even granny's Bingo group and the kid's ice cream man. Yes, all co-conspirators in a world-wide plot. To that the mushrooms say, "We may be dumb, but we are not stupid," and not fooled, either.

Perhaps the greatest evidence that a treaty or agreement exists between the government and at the very least the Greys, but likely the Reptilian, as well, is what happens at night over South Florida skies. Something that dates all the way back decades, further suggesting the existence of ET/Human regular communication and some form of agreement.

There is no doubt that (see sighting log, Chapter 12) South Florida night skies, especially late night, are a Safe Haven for U.F.O., and a sort of saucer Wildlife Preserve. It is only within the last couple of years, with my definite sightings that this became totally evident to me. I guarantee you the vast majority of residents are totally oblivious to this presence, and even those who know U.F.O. do frequent Florida skies, are not aware of how massive the presence is on certain nights (World War II, picture Allied bombers over Dresden). No it's not quite that bad, and they are not dropping any explosive incendiary bombs, but since some of these E.T.s are most definitely demonically oriented and thus hostile to humans, perhaps their bombs are of the spiritual incendiary kind? To many that sounds like comic book fiction I know, and all I can say is that in the spirit realm all of this would be invisible to humans who cannot prove or disprove anything like this. demons are real, and they are invisible, The demonic E.T.s have shown (documented) ability to shape shift and move from visible in this dimension, into invisible in another. Remember, too, the Reptilian agenda is hostile to humans, and although the Greys at times have been less offensive, have none-the-less a long litany of invasive practice against both cattle and humans alike. They seem to be at their worst when Reptilian entities are in their presence.

Stars twitching restlessly, flashing colored lights, changing positions, moving, hovering, rotating for hours almost stationery late at night. There aren't even enough helicopters in the entire County to put on such a show, and what would they be doing at very high altitude for a helicopter (twenty to fifty-thousand feet) hovering in mass at 3 A.M. anyway. Many a night, I watched History Channel's show U.F.O. hunters, then went outside to see more U.F.O. in the air around my home than I'd seen in the hour long show, on T.V.

My home happens to be on the airport runway flight path for one of two runways. It is a shorter secondary one used by private planes while the longer one is used by larger commercial airline passenger jets. Having lived here decades I certainly know flight pattern for approach of these smaller aircraft coming in from a northerly and a few degrees slightly west direction. On several nights in 2008, what I observed was on several occasions when U.F.O. were particularly thick that these smaller planes not only came in at much lower altitude not typical, but seem to have been at extremely low approach altitude for many miles already! I'm talking about planes coming in at or even below two thousand feet altitude (approximately 1,700 ft.), moving tree tops in sway, and with another three miles of approach to runway still to go

(Must be allergic to bees, which is what some air controllers are said to reference U.F.O. craft). It must be a bit unsettling to make a runway approach at night, perhaps low on fuel, to hear that the bees are swarming.

The bottom line is that all this could not be happening without full government awareness and cover up (meaning our government and these aliens are on the same page). This could not occur otherwise. It requires pilot silence, control tower employee silence, and most importantly that same tacit collusion among all parties to keep this secrecy ongoing, especially concerning the media. Is this happening? Yes it is, exactly as described, and was first brought to light by another book and author in the early 1990s. It was going on then, and it is still going on now. That book was something about the South Florida U.F.O. infestation. As far as I am aware, other subject matter that book contained true, as well. Licensing is required of pilots, control tower employees, T.V. stations, radio, and even the newsprint media coalesces with the policy of not talking about U.F.O. because they must interact with the government constantly for news.

Interestingly I mentioned previously that at that time (1990s) an awareness psychically came to me that there would be a connection I would later have to that book. As I described in the Psychic section, it was different than a normal premonition, although similar, and most certainly correct precognition. It appears from all this that there is a mushroom growing at the intersection of ghost, U.F.O., psychic, and spiritual energy forces who has now decided to write a book about it (Mushrooms are exempt from Federal government Licensing, and can speak to other mushrooms openly.). Yes, add runway approach to that intersection point also. The supernatural realm converging on this book and mushroom author like it was the event horizon of a black hole on a mushroom farm. Bees, angels, Oz orbs, ghosts, and low flying air craft all competing for the same air space. above a psychic mushroom. Imagine that! Your imagination now wanting a pay raise.

Yes, I'm sure the Florida legislature could save money in the fiscal budget during a revenue shortfall year if instead of paying for real stars to hang up there all night and shine down, they just went and dropped that from the budget. E.T.s in saucers would be up there anyway and similar in appearance from the ground, most people can't even tell the difference.

Put the money into education for school children instead. Maybe teach them the difference between a star and a U.F.O. The only problem there, is that there aren't enough stars for comparative purposes to go around!

Everything swept under the rug of secrecy maintained by the government. The public with the wool over its eyes, with a manufacturers label on that wool item from the Draco star system, Zeta Reticuli wool mills, plant II, about 37.5 light years from Earth. Was that a Bush corporate tax credit for exporting textile worker jobs off the planet or something? Mushrooms may be dumb, but they're not stupid. It could even mean that E.T.s have figured out how the Washington lobbyist thing works (just kidding, of course).

In author William Dudley's book UFOs, he mentions comments about E.T.s and U.F.O., by then (1964) Sargent Major, Army Intelligence analyst Robert Dean. Dean stated, "The U.S. Gov't. knows of ongoing human contact with alien multi-dimensional beings. Such information has been kept secret from most U.S. government officials, military officials, and the public." Dean further comments, "Multi-dimensional travel is apparent common to them. The only people I know that can really deal with this are theologians, and quantum physicists. It's interesting to me to see these groups talk to each other." Yet another exhibit your honor, of how what was going on then, is still going on now, and those statements from within the military.

Other sightings occurred and are well documented within the military, and in all branches. Dudley's book names the 1965 sightings of sailors aboard the USS. FDR, a wave of sightings at various air bases including Edwards, and others. He also posts a figure of nineteen million sightings, and four million abductions. Cattle mutilation cases possibly attributable to U.F.O. exceed ten thousand worldwide, and many more never get reported.

There are many incidents the public simply never hears about—but isn't that the whole idea. Keep the mushrooms in the dark. Commercial and military aircraft sightings are far more numerous than the public realizes, almost common place. Much goes totally unreported.

You might read in the back pages of a newspaper how a small private boat turned up adrift with husband and wife strangely missing despite calm seas and clear weather (This actually happens more than you might expect.). Two Pensacola Navy jets don't return, (2006–07 timeframe) from a training exercise? Midair collision, or was it a U.F.O. takedown episode? These stories all seem to have one similarity, and that is little to no follow up reporting. When literally thousands of witnesses across several states report U.F.O. sightings, a typical military response is, "We didn't pick up anything unusual on radar that night, at that location and time." It is also funny how government account continually changes, even reversing itself in these matters. They just want the episode and attention to go away. So, are they up to their elbows in aliens and alligators?

Actually alligators are reptiles, so it would be more accurate to say yes, the government is up to its elbows in Greys and Reptilian. Evidence is conclusive, to which this book has contributed in further exhibiting. Don't expect the government to leap at the chance to make a disclosure anytime soon that these aliens are in direct communication, agreement, and to some extent involvement with our government. Why? Because that moves one step closer to the dirty little secret about their evil dark side, and in at least the case of some ET group, very demonic leaning/loyalty. Does the government understand it is literally dealing with the Devil in some cases? Yes, I think so, but that is at least part of the reason for the wool over the public's eyes, mushrooms grow well in the dark. Of course there are many people, that if you asked them if they know their government was dealing with the Devil, would probably quip back with something like, "Tell me something I don't already know," or "and have been for years." Then there are some very wealthy people who are convinced that the IRS is the Devil.

In spite of its efforts, the government is losing ground in its overall attempts to keep the mushrooms in the dark. Some information such as my own actually originates from the private sector, thus it is out of their control. While some think Men in Black are agents of the government, in truth, although these instances are somewhat rare there have been documented cases of ET hybrid or human resembling, or almost human looking entities dressed in black suits sometimes with black hats approaching U.F.O. sighting witnesses. They usually want the witness to keep quiet about the sighting. Sometimes there are outright threats or intimidations. On a few of these instances these entities upon walking away merely vanished into thin air. In fact, ironically, what they don't want known is the link, to become known among humans between ET and demonic forces.

Sorry guys, and are your efforts ever foiled, and by a mushroom! Humans are on to you, and now if we could just do something about our government's role in all this.

Is there an invasion threat, something that looks like a scene from the movie Independence Day, with the skies thick with millions of U.F.O. (Some theory on this will be discussed at large in Chapter 21.)?

We should be thankful to those privately run organizations such as M.U.F.O.N (Mutual U.F.O. Network) and C.U.F.O.S (J. Allen Hynek Center for U.F.O. Studies). These the two largest, but not the only groups who look to try and unravel U.F.O. mysteries, and work diligently toward the truth. There's is objective and scientifically subjective approach to conclusively prove elements along this path to the truth. They are the public watchdog groups in that regard. Like many private organizations they can use your financial help if you are able to donate. Do not rely on the government for anything regarding this subject, it should be apparent to you. by now that they regard you as just another mushroom also.

Cattle Mutilation

Exactly how much cattle mutilation is U.F.O. caused varies depending on who's estimate you choose to take. Natural predator, and disease caused deaths then leading to attack from scavengers is still by far the leading cause. Of the U.F.O. caused cases it cannot be determined which alien group is responsible since it is always an awareness that comes after the fact. It has been a worldwide occurrence showing a familiar set of circumstances no matter in what country it happens. Animal are sometimes lifted up to or inside an alien spacecraft, and many cases after scrutiny show the animal was dropped afterwards from considerable height. In these cases it is observed that neck/legs were twisted, broken, and contorted into odd configuration consistent with the animal carcass having been dropped from a U.F.O.. Here is a list of features common to these cases:

A) The incisions
   1. Angular cut, or even straight cut
   2. Intelligently guided, expert, precise, as to both depth and location
   3. Clearly high quality surgical instruments used
B) Near the site of the dead animal
   1. A circular ring impression is found on the ground. Radiation or chemical anomalies are present at the immediate area.
   2. Other strange occurrences or changes noticed within close of the site
   3. No human tracks at the site
   4. No animal tracks observed
   5. No motor vehicle tire tracks seen
C) Common anatomy body parts missing/removed
   1. Sex organs and utter missing
   2. Eyes, soft tissue gone, ears tongue, gone
   3. Anal rectal tract removed
   4. Blood drain is usually total

A telltale sign in the aftermath is that scavengers sometimes pick up a non-natural scent perhaps, or detect radiation, and will not go near.

Human Abductions

Some excellent books on human abductions are by David M. Jacobs PhD. *The Threat* (1998) and *U.F.O., and Abductions Among Us*, plus many other books that discuss the topic. Dr. Jacobs from the case study research perspective. He does feel that their (alien) agenda is to eventually merge with the human population, in sufficient numbers to eventually gain control. It is the most prevalent theory, and in various version.

Probably the second most widely held theory beyond all the variations of this one, is that hybrids are not being assimilated back into human society, the aliens are well aware of this coming World War III event, and are saving their hybrids until the appropriate time in the aftermath to then repopulate planet Earth with their hybrids integrating into the surviving general human population, and creating further hybridization. There is no correct hypothesis here, perhaps the situation is still evolving, there is some validity to both, and in fact might actually be some combination of these. The delineation Dr. Jacobs uses is:

1. Abduction
2. Breeding
3. Hybridization
4. Integration

The conclusion most widely reached, the consensus you could say, is that these E.T.s covet the human gene pool, even beyond our planet itself, a close second. Expressed by the Greys themselves to an abductee in Phil Imbrogno's book, *Interdimensional Universe* (Chapter 7, page 194) Statement from the abductee: He said that a long time ago his race searched this section of the galaxy, looking for life forms that were compatible to them that would not be rejected when the D.N.A. from both races was combined. He said we (humans) are the only beings in the galaxy that they have found that can combine with them to save their race. He told me they were from a star system thirty light years from Earth and that they travel through tunnels in space to get to here in a short time.

Since cross breeding here on Earth is difficult among species in most cases, often impossible, it was widely suspected then that these E.T.s were performing some type of D.N.A. gene manipulation process in order to achieve their desired result. That may well be, but obviously they can have compatibility by whatever technique or method with human D.N.A.. Similarly the Reptilian are said to covet the human gene pool also.

Very disturbing are some abduction accounts where alien induced human pregnancies occurred, where the embryo is taken for further development, but in some cases something much darker reported. Satanic Ritual abuse.

Forced sex, sex with an alien performed on a Satanic alter, Black Mass celebrated, human/alien fetuses sacrificed, and even hybrid babies sacrificed. The Reptilian alien group some are said to enjoy drinking fresh human blood, especially female menstrual or placenta. The book. *The Truth About alien Abductions*, by authors Peter Hough and Moyshe Kalman ("The Devil in Our Midst"), while Greys may be present, and even have such occur aboard a Grey craft; it is more the likely that such behavior is Reptilian sponsored and directed. The Greys are said to be terrified of the Reptilian, and clearly this is only the tip of that flame. Are the praying mantis looking, tall insect looking high priests as they are sometimes described, actually part of the Greys, or some demonic figure of the Reptilian one might wonder. It is pretty clear that the Greys act subordinate to the Reptilian.

It is likely that they share the same abyss deep sea USO air base, as the Grey seem to fly the smaller pancake style saucer, while the taller Reptilian have larger diameter saucer. However, my own impression is that from other authors accounts by statements from abductees that it is quite possible mixed crews of Greys and Reptilian are not so uncommon. It is also my impression that wherever a Reptilian is present, the chances for human abuse, or extent of abuse is increased.

The After Effects of Human Abductions

1. Something similar to Post Traumatic Amnesia generally occurs resulting in (A) Memory loss or (B) False Memory insertion. In all cases a sense that recall of the abduction incident has been blocked
2. Missing Time (Incident time period due to amnesia)
3. Upon recovery, some report a continuing feeling of flying, or seeing balls of light in the room upon awakening, or an unexplained feeling of illness which lingers
4. Feeling of paralysis lingering, or flashback of some (entity) standing over them while they lay horizontal
5. Migraines, headaches, (occurring and reoccurring, especially when recall is attempted, body aches in some cases
6. In most cases electronic chip implant is suspected. Body scars, scratches, puncture marks, bruises, bleeding, or any similar injuries

7. Sometimes recall of enduring painful procedures these most often include sexual organ, ear, nose, surface skin, and anal rectal canal (places very similar to cattle mutilations)
8. Occasionally victims are not returned to the same site as where the abduction happened.
9. Once tagged, humans can then be tracked, and are! Re- Visitations occur in varied frequency, often weekly to begin with. Then eventually bi-weekly, then monthly (From documented cases, this the typical pattern). In some cases it started approximately monthly and remained the same. One would suppose E.T.s think humans make great pets!

Hybrids are said to have in later development stages, increased mental telepathy, improved eye stare minds can procedure (similar to what ET use to communicate among themselves), as well as increased capability of visualizations within their own brain capacity. What has not been determined, is how much alien programming is automatically accompanying, as well. A certain androidization danger would seem to be an inherent danger possibility, especially if gene manipulation to a greater rather than lesser extent was occurring.

Android hybrid aliens with an attitude problem released in large numbers into the human population in order to trigger certain response at the correct time, once the topic of Science fiction, perhaps not as improbable as we might have previously thought. When you overlay this concept with what I describe in later Chapter for year 2027, it's an imaginary epileptic episode for ones imagination in a bad way. When you equate the Anti-Christ hypothetically in power, as well by then, you might as well add a studder to the imagination with epileptic seizure, but definitely a rocky uphill go of it.

Once our world economy becomes politically, economically, and most definitely militarily de-stabilized, count on the unthinkable to become prevailing conditions. A de-stabilized human world environment will make us increasingly vulnerable to interference from these aliens.

Even our atmospheric satellites, as *Interdimensional Universe* points out have not been immune from interference from E.T.s. The U.S. Russia, and China, as well, losing satellites mysteriously, but suspect of E.T. cause (and this prior to civilizations demise).

In spite of all this, if our government is clandestinely working with the ET, like them or not, it actually is the smartest path forward, rather than complete hostilities. Our government simply needs to inform and alert their mushroom citizenry better, otherwise it could become a very real National Security Threat, the next topic for discussion.

Government Cover-Up and the Threat to National Security

All of what I get into here will make far more sense, once you have read Chapter 27, perhaps the final chapter to more than just this book, let's hope not. Hopefully you'll realize it makes a lot of sense, and is far more than just whistling Dixie, so to speak. So it is probably better if you skip over this for now, and come back later to read it (however some delay in publishing Part II is likely to be expected).

Probably a good correlation is to equate this to the Cold War threat of Communism in the 1950s, 60s, 70s, and even 80s. Try to imagine if our government had adapted the policy of simply ignoring it, as if it didn't even exist. Few would deny that such would have been against the best National Security interest. Americans were kept informed at all times, and as the situation evolved over time, they had awareness.

Nuclear warheads are still poised at the United States, but the numbers (still too high) have at least been reduced. Even after sixty years these threats have not been totally eliminated, but at least the American people have been kept informed of what both sides were doing. Their own lives in the cross hairs so to speak.

Unfortunately, this has not been the case with Extraterrestrials, and U.F.O. Virtually all knowledge that the public has any awareness of any events, any facts, are all delivered by way of reports from the private sector, and what the media has been able to obtain.

Not keeping the public informed, withholding vast amounts of information it regards as classified, and continually failing to disclose information even years later, is not in the best National Security interest of our country as a whole, or to Americans as individuals, any more than it would have been to withhold information regarding developments within the former Soviet Union back in those days. E.T. and U.F.O. are a national security risk. Not so much at the present, but you can count on it in the future.

How will the government later be able to put its citizens on high alert to later, when they fail to acknowledge even their mere existence now. It does nothing to boost trust in the government, and the public is left to find out what they can on their own. Not a very wise policy, and if it doesn't change, eventually could cause some American citizens to become captured, imprisoned, and even to die needlessly all because they were not informed of potential threat from an E.T. source.

Yes, it's a public relations nightmare for the government, but the longer, and greater amount of water (information) that is allowed to accumulate, the greater the risk of a dam break later. What the government needs to do is slowly begin in stages to release documents and files previously kept from the public. The U.K. Great Britain, wisely has already begun doing this, and the U.S. needs to also.

There is no need for the public to panic, because there is no immediate threat, and that is certainly part of the reason for all the secrecy, not wanting to create apprehension or hysteria, but what happens to all these people downstream when the dam breaks completely. They need to initiate a program of slowly but steadily making some previously withheld information available to both journalists/media interests, and the public at large.

This is what the government should do, for starters:

1. Acknowledge in a formal statement the existence of E.T./U.F.O. and that a new policy of offering the public will be initiated immediately, but in stages, to release (oldest first) previously withheld documents and files for scrutiny and public availability; de-classify and release a great deal more files
2. Establish a person expert in the field for media and journalists to contact with questions. If something information wise is not yet de-classified, questions as to when it might be, or to clarify points on information that has been released.
3. A broad and vague statement, simply acknowledging to the public that while there doesn't appear to be an immediate threat from an ET source, it is a valid longer term concern. Simply making this one statement of admission releases a lot of water from behind that dam, and allows the public time to psychologically make adjustment gradually, rather than be told later to "Run for your life, the Dam just broke, and there is an alien invasion force headed your way!" What a coincidence, some discussion on the possibility of alien invasion is covered for you in Chapter 21. Somebody needs to look out for you in case the government doesn't.

What our government will never likely tell you or admit to, but is none the less apparently true, and relevant you know for survival should you not be participant in Christian Rapture at Tribulation:

1. Government alien (E.T.) contact communication has been ongoing since the 1950's Eisenhower era.
2. It is pretty certain the group they have had primary dealings with are the Greys. Mutual co-operation with the Greys likely ongoing at highly classified security base installations, actually bodes well for both humans and E.T. longer term if true, but civilians left out of the awareness loop is dangerous heading into Tribulation, since this situation only applies to the Good Greys faction.
3. The Bad Greys and Reptilian E.T. are hostile to human, and one faction of Reptilian clearly are operatives of the demonic realm. Humans cannot be sure if God will allow 'boots on the ground' assisting the Anti-Christ Armies or not, relevant to round up and imprisonment during Tribulation. Dr. Brown's book describing a time period in the future when such will be the case, can't really logically be any other timeframe except the Tribulation. The Bad Greys conducting the five-month sting period from U.F.O. delivered Particle Beam Taser as this book describes for you (timing described in Part II discussion).
4. The Reptilian saucer Air Force is superior to anything humans have. More maneuverable, instant acceleration, high top speeds, and very likely more advanced superior weaponry with faster delivery, and more sophisticated defensive technology, as well.
5. The demonic E.T. will use their saucers, from higher altitude pretending to be stars at night for reconnaissance spying and World War III forces battling the Anti-Christ.
6. The United States, Canada, and U.K., severely degraded from natural cataclysmic destructions at the start in all economic, military, government, and civilian infrastructure platforms and categories (unless extreme pro-active measures are undertaken well in advance and with commitment to), and then will sever links communication wise with civilians permanently without electric. Information not released instructively to civilian population prior to destruction onset will likely become undeliverable at post-destructions aftermath. Leadership failure now, will be end of United States/Western Nations superpower status!

Part II will provide readers with additional survival tips, whether you actually Rapture or not, it's advisable to play it safe in advance, rather than sorry upon Tribulation arrival, as quite a large cross-section of population are rapture questionable. Don't expect your government to provide any information on either subject.

More About Government Mushroom Farming

Not only are Intelligence Services stingy about releasing information, but in taking it from the public, as well. Are better protocols now in place for sharing info. between various agencies? Various agencies and private sector? Well, I can't comment on the information sharing part (most likely changes were implemented) because only insiders would know, but I can comment on the input from the public part. Try to imagine a well-recognized psychic like Edgar Cayce or Nostradamus attempting to input vital information to Intelligence services, but not succeeding getting it through. Then notifying a U.S. congressman, and a T.V. station, who by now figure this guy for a nut. No documented pre-cognitive (future seeing) psychic should ever be ignored—ever. Why? Because this is given through holy angels. You aren't blocking the individual who received it, you are blocking information from God! Is that what happened with September 11; valid, but previously unknown psychics sounding warnings but going unheeded? There are many virtually unknown psychics, and even if their ability is not proven or recorded, or in some way documented, they should as citizens be taken seriously enough that their information be inputted. This is a huge red flag that can wind up costing American lives if it is not corrected. If it came down to whether you lived or died on whether or not I succeeded in inputting that information, you would likely be dead. As you will read later, I feel the very fate of our nation is at stake.

Not getting through to the Intelligence agencies, I then wrote a very cynical and sarcastic letter to the congressman. That'll get his attention The letter taking verbal abuse to a new level art form, unfortunately I happen to like this particular congressman, so it was painful in that sense to write and send. This letter a real classic similar to certain antique model cars, Coca Cola original formula, etc. Not only did one of his constituents blast him with double barrel buckshot on this input thing but then re-loaded, and advised him what year Florida in the not so distant future would one day experience (salt water) flooding. In other words, had the Intelligence services inputted my information, they could have then briefed him. No briefing, $500 million in Everglades restoration money passes Congress just a few weeks later. Yes, your taxpayer money that the letter had stated would be wasted, and may as well have been tossed in the ocean! Then going on to mention, Oh, by the way, not only is your district but the entire State of Florida due to drown by such and such timeframe, and congressman; have a nice day! Ten percent unemployment and $500 million dumped into everglades restoration/fresh water purification. Alligators barking so loud they've got Congress' attention? What about the 10 percent unemployed, oh I see, they don't live in the Everglades. In fact, the State owns the coastal land offshore out a distance of a one hundred miles.

In other words any freshwater restoration accomplished will only have short term effect (Normally I would favor anything environmentally friendly, but not in this case.). I advised the Congressman against this, but the legislation passed regardless. Ten years to implement, then in the results only good for a span of a few years before Florida suffers not one but two different flood events, the second putting the entire State under salt water for good, and including Everglades restoration project. The land they spent $500 million on and for, now totally wasted, that they would own for free at that time as coastal land seafloor. Your tax dollars hard at work, all benefit now completely erased. Did my letter expose a classic taxpayer hornswoggle/boondoggle, as well?

One of the sarcastic remarks made to the Congressman was that the American people were tired of being treated like mushrooms on a government mushroom farm, and did this situation go or carry all the way up to the U.S. Senate level? Well, coincidentally, the following week, there is Madame Speaker of the House Nancy Pelosi, in heated controversy with the C.I.A. over being duped, mislead, and lied to, even accusation of being intentionally mislead for (during Vice President Cheney) years by the C.I.A.. Did the senator I contacted happen to discuss my comments with Madame Speaker Pelosi (they the same party) regarding Intelligence Services? Well we will never know about that, all I received back was a three sentence statement that he respectfully disagreed with my comment. A bale of $500 million now en-route to the Everglades. It seems the government mushroom farmers (Intelligence Services) really are growing big portabellas under the rotunda after all!

But let's be fair, although like the K.G.B. in the former Soviet Union, they wield enormous power (often unchecked) no one doubts the enormous task globally of countering threats from multiple sources and types to National Security. Cybercrimes and viruses, terrorist groups, criminal organizations internationally, and hostile adversaries and governments constantly working toward our nation's undermining and demise. Necessity to be involved in the wars in Iraq, and Afghanistan, and fighting in all related areas (Pakistan and others) are a clear sign the Al-Qaeda threat (Yeman, just one of many) represent substantial combined threat. Add in N. Korea Iran, and others, and no one questions their task is both enormous and daunting. Formidable, serious, and dangers very real. So while I make issue of U.F.O. secrecy, this is minor in comparison, as is perhaps the need to re-evaluate input protocols by comparison to everything else. My point is eventually both the U.F.O. subject and ignoring the input from private psychic citizenry will become critical issue if neglected or overlooked. By the end of this book (Part II) you should have a real good awareness as to why. Chess players make strategy decisions for moves based six to ten moves ahead. Most people aren't visionary in the least except for what is obvious. Precognitive, Clairvoyant and Telepathic psychics have been under the employ of the Intel. Services before, so they are fully aware of potential value on future pertaining information, the problem being confirmation is not possible until after predicted events occur, then too late to avoid consequences.

Do they already know Tribulation Period, and Armageddon? It appears so, yet it also appears most even in government not informed so as to avoid leaked information (My government mushroom farm hypothesis exactly, and like U.F.O./E.T. topics so as not to create public alarm or unfounded panic.). Keep working and paying taxes until the roof caves in on your head, and that will confirm for you Tribulation Period is in fact now underway! The problem there is too many crushed mushrooms, and I know you would agree, especially if you were one of them!

As the time draws closer, likely God will increase awareness among others with psychic messaging, you won't need to rely on my prediction alone, as to time horizon. In Chapter 27 (Part II), I've tried to piece together a patchwork quilt you might call it of all psychic awareness over the course of centuries on the Tribulation, a puzzle with many psychic pieces of which I entered my own, with no conflicting pieces if you get it right! Held together with scotch tape and safety pins, bailing wire and duct tape, etc. most motley and tattered looking, yet with leaks in the thatch of the certainty roof, and after all is said and done, if I help you to save your life, does that really matter? While most had concept of what was going to happen, even panoramic view, timeframe eluded them. The answer lies in combining all such future awareness together, and that is what I present you with in this book (Part II) according to my own interpretation Nostradamus, Edgar Cayce, and several other psychics including myself, believe where as there is the larger fate event, given pre-awareness we can avoid worst outcome by taking steps in advance to do so. The biggest misconception is that because God is bringing destructions about that you should simply accept it, take no action to avoid death because somehow it must be God's will that you be overcome. Not at all, God is saying fear the Almighty and my awesome power, and if I give those who believe in me advanced warning (through prophecy) take that knowledge, respect it as genuine, and use it to save your life. If the non-believers perish when these judgments come that is one thing, but he is making allowance for his faithful, so that they might not perish, but by their own hand be spared through preparedness. This is both my interpretation and numerous Bible passages in close correlation. Both as individuals and as a nation, we are allowed to take steps to survive. Much more on the nation part later. Your death only becomes automatic if you allow it to (or the ceiling on all the kept in the dark mushrooms crashes down catching them all by surprise crushing and squashing millions of them - actually more like scorching and flooding). Military bases, assets, and personnel were not moved to higher ground, Washington D.C., as well as many other lower elevation locations become flooded out, and resources of vital commodities. Food, drinking water, gasoline, heating fuels, etc. were not stockpiled at higher (underground) elevation and are summarily destroyed. Special power and telecommunication systems appropriate were not installed in advance. Navy and Air Force assets are also unprotected and destroyed. In a timeframe of just under three years, after Tribulation Cataclysms start (perhaps as little as two) the collapse of the U.S. is complete. Can't happen? That is the fate if nothing is done, I very strongly suspect. How's that fresh-water-revitalization look now, with Florida completely underwater (salt water)? The point also, understanding what is on the way later, can avoid wasting taxpayer money in current timeframe. If you don't believe these destructions are even coming, you don't take the steps necessary to mitigate losses. Death of an entire nation now on auto-pilot because your government isn't paying heed to God and the Bible? Being unable to input information, I'd say, unfortunately—yes!

My classic letter to F.B.I. for proper forwarding, congressman, and T.V. station/network having become waste basket liners in those respective waste baskets, and now at local landfill, sent by some nut case. Like they went right to work on a National Security plan for Cataclysmic disaster recovery and loss mitigation? Yeah, right. No, fate still on auto-pilot I see. What did I state in my classic letter? How about Information of National Security interest, Military preparedness implications, and future U.S. citizen safety issues down the road; possible high value data available for the C.I.A..

I don't have a key on my keyboard for flashing neon light surround or fireworks attention grabber, or even buy one get one. So, I guess eventually someone might take an interest in the intelligence community, but then again more likely not. They now taking language instruction in Arabic or Chinese for their next potential employer after Uncle Sam doesn't make it in the O.R.? No more Sam, no more paychecks. Yes, let's all hope it doesn't happen, but keep an eye on that ceiling if I were you.

What else in the way of heavy millimeter rounds was fired off in sarcastic abuse of the Congressman? How about where I told him he was not only endangering the lives of adults but children alike if this informatics was not inputted, but including and notwithstanding the President's two children. That this felt like radioing the Captain of the Titanic, with not only iceberg warnings, iceberg ahead, but exact time and co-ordinates the ship was due to make contact! No response, steady as she goes, full speed ahead. Frigid water, not enough life boats, but the good ship S.S. United States is unsinkable? Is September 11 already forgotten? No lessons learned (my exact words, all of it)? Additionally upon request, I even offered to prepare a special briefing in advance of publication of this book (Part II included)! Any interest? No! That voyage won't take place for several years yet, perhaps the reason, all I know is he disagrees, but with me or God, perhaps the greater question (Only one is right, and we both know which one.). It's not the one who dumped $500 million into the Everglades.

The thing is, I wasn't taking aim at the Congressman personally, as I did end the letter with favorable comment toward his service to the country to try and make it clear I was sounding off to him, but not at him With delays in publication of my book, this information still of too much importance not to be inputted, but with no interest? How are those families who lost loved ones during September 11 going to feel and respond when they read this? With outrage?

Or how about Christians and Jews on the subject of future religious persecutions in the same bear trap of fate (My Lie-Detection passed tests back up my conviction that these will become future truths)?

Yes, there still is over a decade of time left, and they will be much wiser not to waste one more minute of it. In Chapter 24, same problem. Churches uninterested in holy prophecy. Churches not interested in holy prophecy of religious subject, from holy angel source! Intelligence services not interested in vital National Security intelligence, and next I suppose dry cleaners will no longer be interested in taking in dry cleaning. If all this isn't proof the world is on final Tribulation period runway approach, I don't know what is.

From Jayson Q. Rand's Book, *The Return of Planet X*, he does a comprehensive and masterful job of collecting information resource on the subject, and while I don't (for psychic reasons) agree with his doomsday match of Mayan calendar/2012, timeframe, in all other regards it is worth the thirty dollar price, and getting input from several sources is always a good idea, if only the Intelligence community subscribed to that philosophy! Here are some quotes from his book:

Nineteenth Century, Father Jahenny: "No one outside a subterranean shelter will survive. Red Clouds like blood will move across the sky (Armageddon? Wormwood the passing Brown dwarf star?). The crash of thunder will shake the Earth, and sinister lightning will streak the heavens out of season. The Earth will be shaken to its foundation. (many Earthquakes). The sea will rise, it's roaring waves spread over the continent. The bodies of the wicked and the just will cover the ground. Three quarters of the globes population will disappear. Half the population of France will be destroyed." A Catholic father almost two hundred years ago making these comments. True? Yes, absolutely so, meshing with other psychic's statement, as well. My own predictions give timeframe, and that is something eluding many of these other predictions.

Another quote, this time, Mormon Joseph Smith: "The time will come when gold will hold no comparison in value to a bushel of wheat." Both these men are speaking of the same time period in which Edgar Cayce talks about coastal inundations early in the twenty-first century, with "the sea heaving beyond its bounds engulfing many countries." That in turn corresponding to Edgar Cayce's comment, "What is the coastline now of many a land will be the bed of an ocean" (that five hundred million dollar federal taxpayer money now doubling as coral reef restoration I see). What about mushroom rights? Oh, you mean the right to remain silent, and keep an eye on the ceiling when those Earthquakes arrive, that the mushroom farmers overlooked warning you about, as well as scorch, then flood, and in that order (Chapter 27 and Supplement Section will detail more.)!

They were also warned that when my book is published, and the public finds out about this, Wormwood might not be the only scorch event about to take place, or is your only right as a mushroom to remain silent?

For some, the cynicism, and criticism expressed toward the Federal government in this discussion might seem almost unpatriotic but I assure everyone, that is not the intention at all. Sometimes unless claims are aired out in public in order to make a point, no one is any the wiser that a problem even exists. Well, let me assure you that a very big problem exists, covers many fronts besides this U.F.O. non-disclosure stuff, that is only one aspect, and the larger picture relates to Tribulation itself.

This next subsection entitled Homeland Security hopefully will restore your confidence in Wildman's outlook not only being patriotic, but very much one of a private citizen with deep concerns that our non-psychic leaders really don't have the greater forest for the trees concept of where America is headed! Not that Congress has never been accused of that before, or been told the nation is headed right over the edge of a great precipice cliff they don't seem to have any awareness is being approached, and in the not too distant future. What would a precognitive psychic like me know about the future that congress doesn't know? The answer is plenty. Enough to write this book in discussion of. My deep concerns are for the safety and wellbeing of the American people, and in a sense an end run by pass of the Federal government to directly deliver awareness to the forum of the American people themselves. Greater understandings <u>all</u> Americans need to be aware of. Even if someone doesn't fully agree, they can hardly fault me for delivering a collection of information designed to save lives, souls, and maybe even our nation! Forgive then if I have to raise a little hell to explain what is happening with heaven, but with undeniable holy angel input being delivered to me, and other people's lives in jeopardy, then I am going to speak my piece, and if anyone's toes are stepped on, or anyone somehow offended by anything I say in my own book, well that's just going to be too bad then. Patriotic stepping on of toes, and offended reaction in whatever direction mind you is worth it if I save those very same people's lives, and many more because of it. They can thank me later (still alive to do it, perhaps).

It's rough when every time you say or explain something you have to plead with people's better judgment to believe you. Yet, the stakes are literally life or death, and rapture through faith or non-rapture. The back half of this book (Part II) delivers heavy Christian witness message as strong as a non-clergy could possibly deliver, so prepare for that also. God foretold me through holy angel over forty-five years ago this would be a book I'd one day author, then kept me alive to do it, so maybe deserves a look at it.

In summary conclusion, I don't claim to have anywhere close to all the information or answers on vital E.T./U.F.O. questions, just some of these. It's a national shame that our own government, We the People, By the

People, and For the People insists on withholding information from the public on the U.F.O./E.T. subject. Your government needs to de-classify a much greater volume of information on this subject. They could even raise money by accepting sealed bids, and selling it off at auction so to speak, to the T.V. network or movie company, or whomever was willing to pay the most for this information, but then required to release it to the public. Even that would be better than no release of documents at all.

The Congress and the Presidents aren't even privileged to it. It's only released on need to know national emergency basis. Meaning until we came under U.F.O. attack, this information withheld need not be de-classified/divulged.

This is information held by our government, but in fact the property of the American people, and needs further de-classification, and release to the public, no matter how it is done. It is absolute certainty that the Bad Greys are subordinates of the Reptilian E.T., who are in fact, whether originally from across the galaxy as believed or not, are without question, flying saucers of demonic registry. There's no maybe about it. Why does it take a civilian mushroom (psychic one at that) to inform all of the other mushrooms on the mushroom farm of this? Our government saying we grow better if kept in the dark. Yes, and let that demonic E.T. group that thrives better in the dark have their secret identity protected (hostile to humans) by our government; your government! How many more Extra-Terrestrial secrets are they keeping from us like that? The answer is a whole warehouse of documents full!

What is even more disturbing is all the Illuminati conspiracy theorists claims, of something along the lines of all the ultra-rich and all the ultra-powerful being linked to the most powerful governments all over the world (behind the scenes), criminal cartels etc., working together to control- fast and furious, as much of the world's wealth, and thus political and military power in order to achieve the ultimate goal of an Illuminati (secret Satanist) total domination rule and control One World Order Totalitarian government eventually. Radicalized Iranian Sharia-law aspiration of world domination eventually, coming through this same philosophy tunnel from the other end. No matter which way you slice it, it seems words like nefarious, clandestine, corruption in government, Illuminati -secret society, One World order, and demonic E.T. are all suspiciously seeming to show increased signs of linkage, whether or not actually any truth to all the rumors, theories, and conspiracy allegations. Personally, I think I, and most people would much prefer none of it be factually true, yet claims to such keep on surfacing, and my December 8, 2004. Reptilian high-hat U.F.O. sighting in South Palm Beach island, with E.T. (demons) actually seen downloading to the ground could have been an Illuminati theorist literal smoking gun witnessed account.. C.I.A./N.S.A. high level, E.T./human meeting? G.O.P./E.T. fundraiser? Or, an Illuminati conducting a secret Satanist sacrifice blood ritual? No one's likely to come forward on that one, and all that we know is that a U.F.O. of demonic registry was in attendance at a swank party at a private residence in an ultra-wealthy (Illuminati stronghold/bastion?) neighborhood. Democrats convinced this was an Illuminati/G.O.P. fundraiser, with both N.S.A. and E.T. blood drinking demons in attendance no doubt. Funny they had the same theory about it being the home of an Illuminati wealthy Democrat doing a secret 4 A.M. fundraiser, since they consider all Democrats to be tax imposing blood-suckers anyway! demon loyalists showing up only proving what they'd been saying all along! You can have a lot of fun with this joking around, but regardless of what it was, it did happen, that part is no joke, and the who and why of it all, what went on, on the ground remains unknown, except perhaps for a document lost in the government's archives, if in fact they had any prior knowledge of such a clandestine meeting on that night.

I neither accept nor reject such Illuminati conspiracy theories myself, but that episode described certainly an eye opener smoking gun for something, whatever it was, and I'm not buying that the demons/E.T have now gone into the mobile party catering business, either. High ranking E.T demons definitely up to something no good, possibly with some high ranking, up to no good humans! With stuff like this going on prior to Tribulation, one can only imagine what it might be like during! Hostile to human E.T./ demons pretty much tells you everything you need to know right there, and some further elaborations in Part II of this book are offered.

Our government needs to do more in the way of releasing and de-classifying files on U.F.O. E.T. subjects. Part of the Illuminati theory is that a few high ranking plants within the intelligence agencies secretly do not want a high survival rate among America's general population upon outcome of Tribulation natural cataclysm's after rapture, and the best way to insure non-survival is to keep the American people continued to be uninformed on the U.F.O./ E.T subject. Mushrooms suspicious of that mushroom farmer all along.

Examining the Illuminati Conspiracy Controversy (Again!)

It has become the center target of many authors scrutiny, and the subject of Television show topic, as well. What really is going on here? It always starts with a detailed description on the history of the Freemasons, and there is clearly linkage, but only a small inner circle within the top inner circle are said to be Illuminati, and the majority of Freemasons have only heard the same rumors, but don't know much more if anything than the general public, but certainly depending on which individual you are talking. Some having suspicions and have seen indications pointing toward circumstances they are sworn to secrecy to never discuss openly in public. The first thing that comes to most people's mind is why the secrecy rather than transparency, what are they so secretive about that must be withheld from public examination at all cost? So at least 95 percent of all Freemasons are lower degree Freemasons with who in many instances would quit the organization if they truly did understand what even those in the elite thirty-three degree rank even higher than they are not aware in most cases of knowledge privy to. It is only a tiny few who are chosen from recognized bloodlines and off shoot branching of the central bloodlines the Illuminati recognize as royal.' What few ordinary citizenry recognize is that these bloodlines are Extraterrestrial E.T. human hybrid bloodlines dating back to the time of Egypt and Samaria or ancient Babylonia (So claimed, but is this true?).

When an Illuminati explanation version of this story is told by them, they always conveniently neglect to tell you that these are not E.T. of credential in good standing with the holy side, but in fact are human/hybrid E.T. demonic cross breeding between Reptilian E.T. (i.e., fallen angel) and human dating all the way back to these ancient times. I should also caution you they have weaved a story to try to give legitimacy to themselves, when in fact what they are hiding is that this 'royalty' is of demonic variety. This I can tell you with certainty, because I get my information (all of it) from holy angel as a Christian psychic/prophet. The Illuminati are definitely a Luciferian, Secret Satanist organization with the real Supreme Grand Wizard being Satan himself in control of all evil worldwide. Illuminati are Baal worshipping Anti-Christians who have their own entirely different take on ancient history that contradicts the Christian Bible's version in instance after instance, and are although not to my knowledge openly anti-Semitic (that because at least one bloodline is in fact Jewish), yet deny much of Old Testament writing also.

What was it that back in the 1880s and 1890s their leader Albert Pike was accused of being? Here we are talking about the Freemasons leader who obviously was up to his Illuminati eyeballs in controversy way back then. They claimed back then he was an occultist, Baal worshipping, Sun God believing black magic occultist, Secret Satanist who was obviously also anti-Christian. An organization rich in symbols and rituals, and a completely bankrupt morality belief system totally false to anyone but Satan himself. So what sort of tradition do Illuminati have going for them today, you tell me. Certainly one validity challenged by the angel of Truth and Light and Life itself: Jesus Christ. It is clearly Satan who perpetuates this Illuminati doctrine of false belief continuing into the twenty-first century, perpetuated by the wealthy, politically powerful, and those of this inner circle drawing power from Satan as to promote these controlling agenda beliefs. Realize materialist wealth, and stature, and power of this plane of existence is poverty in the Christian spiritual sense unless it is put to useful purpose to benefit others. It is the agenda of the Illuminati to control the masses rather than to show benefit or charity to them. Just as the fallen angel rebelled against Yahweh the One true God, who's Bible makes it abundantly clear that these super wealthy cannot attain the Kingdom of heaven or pass through the eye of a needle in analogy terms, they then chose to reject Yahweh in favor of keeping their wealth and worshiping Satan instead. (having part demon D.N.A.) perhaps they feel damned for that reason, as well, hard to say what their reasoning is like (If the hybrid rumors are true.).

Here is what I feel is certainty. The E.T. group known as Reptilian those original fallen angels, and what the Bible describes as the 'Beast from the Sea' in book of Revelation are all one in the same, and do have U.F.O. craft penetrable through Earth, air, and water to great depths. Do they and their U.F.O. craft exist on a higher vibrational frequency than us humans but much less than holy angels? Possibly so. Meaning not quite as solid as humans possibly, but more dense than some other E.T. possibly.

The first interbreeding with humans created the 'Anunnaki' offspring race of giants offspring, to which there is great worldwide evidence once did in fact exist, and were linked to many pyramid, obalysk, tumuli, and other heavy lifting feats archeologically and architecturally speaking. These the so called 'Nefilmi.' In both the Bible and these ancient accounts, (The heavier density now as opposed to their previous more ethereal angelic state resulting after subsequent disobedience to God.). The great flood was necessitated by this E.T. now demon infusion intermix with human women was an abomination in the eyes of God, and this rebellion of 'Watcher angels' led by none other than Satan himself. So then if Noah's flood purged these 'morally defective' humans from the planet in total then you have to ask: How do these present day Illuminati have Reptilian (demon D.N.A.) also similarly hybrid to the ancient Egyptians and ancient Sumerians whose royal bloodlines then had it. (No surprise both of these cultures skewed toward sorcery, witchcraft, and worship of false Demi-god Idols., as did Mayan, druidic/Celtic, Greco-Roman, and Atlantean (Faction) cultures, all in different centuries, yet all somehow managing nearly identical belief, including human blood sacrifice of infants and young adolescent children (hence the sacrificial young virgin). In all of these cultures, literally the Devil did make them do it.

The annual Bohemian Garden blood ritual done in secret, or the ashes ritual done in the open before an altar, and forty-foot (high) stone owl, pretty much confirms where these Illuminati Luciferian's head screwed on backward is at. It is said Reptilian's will actually eat a human the way you or I might eat a piece of chicken. Isn't it convenient how someone on T.V. talking ancient alien/E.T. always conveniently leaves out the demonic reference which is virtual certainty. That's because the T.V. network is itself Illuminati controlled, what the conspiracy theorists are stating exactly. Disinformation is always the objective. Put the truth of the claims out in plain view, open air daylight, then have some 'expert' give an opinion dismissing everything as rumor, hear-say, and factless conjecture blown out of proportion so as to cause one to dismiss everything as non-sense. The less Godly the audience, the easier it becomes to get away with this. The fact is, the truth hurts these Illuminati. It is not exactly an image builder for the world at large to suspect some of these people of being of part demon, Reptilian E.T. D.N.A. blood which is increasingly making more and more wealthy and powerful persons suspect. It highly likely the coming Anti-Christ will be Illuminati, don't you agree?

More and more people are coming forward stating they have been witnessed to a human shapeshifting into a taller Reptile/lizard like human/cross breed, then morphing back into a totally normal looking human. It is said there are both male and females of this Reptilian/hybrid bloodline who routinely can do this, often at will, but sometimes unexpectedly even to them. Totally plausible though not completely proven, at least not yet.

But then you are going to say, wait a minute, didn't Noah's flood kill all of these hybrid humans who were an abomination to God? Yes, but it doesn't mean it didn't continue to happen through U.F.O. abduction, and D.N.A. gene splice, and/or human woman/Reptilian male E.T. egg fertilization, then through the demonic realm a hierarchy of the wealthy and powerful nobility could be cultivated through dark powers which nobody doubts Satan still possesses to this day. Remember Satan was bound for a thousand years, then loosed for a thousand according to your K.J. Bible, so he's had plenty of time to perfect hybridization of humans among a select group of humans of his choosing. Exactly which method is not clear, but it really doesn't matter if it is in fact going on (as it appears to be).

If you think about it the term 'Secret Satanist' and 'Illuminati' are interchangeable, except not all Secret Satanists are Illuminati, but all Illuminati it appears are Secret Satanists. The full blooded Reptilian have a thirst for human blood, and that is a fact. They will drink it out of a vessel such as a glass, but will resort to classic vampire style no doubt if the opportunity presents itself. These are not the human hybrid part demon, these are the seven to nine foot tall full demons described here. Remember, too, much Reptilian D.N.A. turned the offspring into a class of giant beings said to be all males, who could then not reproduce. So these E.T. apparently adjusted their hybridization to get to just the right percentage mix combination apparently, so that the hybrids would seem normal humans even though being far from it, and could reproduce in new generation of similar Reptilian/human D.N.A. strain. The hybrids have normal human looking skin, the Reptilian E.T. have orangish/beige or a lime green snake like outer skin, and vertical slit snake like eyes. Nothing like tracing your family tree back to royal demon bloodlines of E.T. Talk about inter-racial couplings. Just better not invite great grandpa over for dinner, or you could be what's for dinner!

Now all through this book I've brought your attention to some of the most incredible circumstance descriptions imaginable, but unlike some other authors who try to pass postulated theory conjecture off as fact for certain, I am committed practically to the point of obsession with strict honesty, accuracy and articulate defining to avoid misconceptions. Here is an example of where other author are presenting multiple witness testimony evidences of support for the human/hybrid theory, who claim to have seen shapeshift from human to tall Reptilian lizard like, snake skinned beings, then back to normal looking human form. While this is consistent with ancient Sumerian, Egyptian, and the fallen angel accounts of Enoch (of the Bible mention), I want my readers to realize it is still unproven circumstantial peripheral testimony that has not as far as I know been cross evaluated by several independent examiners as to the merit of these claims. They might be true, or have some partial measure of truth included, but until more fully evaluated in objective, impartial evaluation, it cannot be conclusively seen that human/hybrid shape-shifting condition capabilities either do or do not exist. Having seen a human demonically possessed whose eye pupil had actually been transformed from round into a vertical, reptile like slit, leaves my receptivity to such claims with a whole new liberal latitude, especially now having firsthand Reptilian E.T./U.F.O. knowledge and sightings. On one hand, I'm saying don't go and accept this human/hybrid shapeshifting thing as true just yet, but by no means should you dismiss it just yet, either.

Illuminati/Secret Satanist magnet of dark, evil powers vortex, and agenda/goal of a One World Control government, as well in match for the Bible's description account of the Anti—Christ's rise to position of such power in any way having linkage? Certainly on some levels of raw demonic forces evil, but all of the back door hidden connectivity of all parties with direct rotten wood involvement a bit like examining swarming termites on that rotten wood and pick out the ones most responsible! It won't be possible later, with so many now in negative contribution to ward final bad outcome. Only briefly, but the bad guys do get to win for a brief season during Tribulation, so the Bible tells us. While no one can say with certainty the country of origin of the Anti-Christ, as leader of a future Muslim/Arab States Confederacy of countries, it is a not unreasonable conclusion to draw he will be of Arabic descent, but in no way a forgone certainty. He could be a European of Arabic descent perhaps also, for example, but an Arabic link is likely. What if that Reptilian human/hybrid shapeshifting condition is fact, and true, might the Anti-Christ then be prime demon prototype poster boy? Instead of a human being demonically possessed, having instead some part Reptilian D.N.A. demon factor genes with excessive compulsive control through aggressive behavior compunctions (as in World War III). A human/E.T. demon trait hybrid in effort to control the whole world possibly what the Bible is describing? Like a python getting a stranglehold on its prey, to then devour it whole, as in the whole world?

With the United States, Canada, and U.K. all heavily damaged, as are Scandinavia/ Baltic region/Russia, and many other countries also, the Anti-Christ aggressions will be underway. So neighborly of him to take advantage of other countries vulnerabilities, striking them while in recovery. No longer receiving U.S. foreign aid prop up, it will become a string of moderate Islamic governments, then replaced from the power vacuum created by Radical Islamic regimes now conceding their loyalties to a centrist Confederacy union of Islamic states. Satan taking the role Allah, Satan who thirsts to be worshipped as a God, will succeed in pulling millions of souls into hell through this snare. The return of Jesus Christ which I predict (Part II) for this seventh angel event will rock the entire Muslim world. Christians should realize that these are good, hardworking decent people, often very good people who were misled into a false teaching theocracy/fascist state, that they cannot escape from any easier than Iranians can currently, but now by 2024/2025 timeframe encompassing the entire middle east and North Africa region, with sympathy in the far east and Malaysian areas, as well. The failings of the Christian Church to convert them, now coming back to be the haunting ghost of lost opportunity to have done so. Just as in the second anti-Christ's regime (Hitler's Third Reich) to attempt to escape or to refuse loyalty will be considered an act of treason punishable by death. After the return of Christ, and additional Christian and converts then are witnessed rapturing into the sky, the Anti-Christ's support within his own power base will severely erode and go into full crumble mode. I hope all Islamic will trust in what I tell them here, and convert themselves to Christians for the sake of their own soul before it becomes too late. I hope they will realize I would never tell them this, never even consider telling this to them on the very sacred subject of religion unless I was absolutely beyond certainty certain of what actually constitutes the truth, having been given information directly by God and his holy angel in prophecy forth telling, and foretelling, consistent with anointing gift of prophecy (fully described in Rapture supplement Part II Section under Saved/Anointed). Romans 12: 6-8, Ephesians 4:11, and I Corinthians 12: 3-10 as God has so blessed me to receive. For the rest of you, just keep in mind I have never made a wrong prediction for this reason, and when God provides a prophet with awareness, regardless of the subject specifically, it is in verification of the Holy Spirit, Jesus Christ as the Lord and Savior of all humanity whether they choose to believe so or not, and as a wakeup call to humanity as a whole, not just Christians. The prophet himself being a Christian, only serves as added proof. So this is why I say to the world: Turn to Jesus, people of the world, while there is still time to rescue your soul, and if you already worship and believe, then make resolve in your faith deeper and stronger yet.

Getting back on track with our Illuminati World government Control and domination discussion, it is central to the conspiracy theorists that the Reptilian human hybrid, wealthy and powerful have managed to insert and infiltrate moles within the highest levels of most of the world's intelligence services through their own 'handpicked' appointments to top level posts, who then open doors for others who have Illuminati loyalties. C.I.A., F.B.I., N.S.A., Homeland Security, and other top government departments they claim have already been compromised, and in many other governments worldwide, as well. Is this truth, or theorist propaganda paranoia? Again, I will never tell you something is true unless I'm absolutely certain it is, and can provide evidence to back it up. I know of no one who has any evidence, yet it does fit the broader scheme, so you have to just sort of shelve this for the time being on the claimed but unproven shelf in your mind.

For the fullest most detailed account, and exceptionally well written almost academic text book like style there is British author David Icke's book, *Tales From The Time Loop* and David Icke's books, *Isle of Wight* in the U.K. While it might be nice to have the luxury of being writer, editor with final say (always in agreement) and publisher (always in agreement). Now while David clearly is a talented writer, and both well academically educated, and intellectually and philosophically unique and decidedly brilliant, he could be accused of writing a book of 'Illuminati disinformation' just as easily as authoring a book to expose Illuminati secrets. Either way, whatever your personal take, his depth of description on the Illuminati philosophy sounds like it came directly from the Illuminati's own historical/philosophy manifesto! No details missing full explanation, which is why this could be seen as a book commissioned expressly for disinformation purpose. No, I'm not saying for certain it is, but the format is suspicious.

There is a set formula for writing disinformation, and this book is consistent with such format, no matter what the truth subject is that you need the public to dismiss, which is the end goal. You take 70 percent truth, in this case Illuminati truths, mix it with a binding agent of heavy syrup conjecture delivered as facts, stir in another 10 percent mistruths, lies (all be they disguised), distortions, half-truths, and hear-say, then mix in the final 10 percent personal opinion totally out there space commander new age drug induced religious philosophy postulated theory also delivered as truth with certainty. You wind up with a (excuse the pun) sticky icky gumball that the reader then desperately desires to discard in total. Is that what happened here? Disinformation or not, it is still a great book, and that 70 percent Illuminati truths in detailed accurate description imbedded once you wash away all the gummy-goo. A genius is seldom wrong, and I caught one too many places where he is incorrect to be deserving the genius label, but deservingly brilliant, even if in his own words some people question if that bloke Icke isn't a nutter or something (Somebody pay you a generous stack of quid to write this David?). Attacking the British royal family (and others) with such vicious abandon as hybrid shapeshifters sure smacks of disinformation, and that aforementioned generous stack of quid. Is it true? Something else for that shelf in your mind to place articles of the claimed but yet unproven.

Now if someone accused me of being a Christian zealot, I'd say why Thank You, I take that as a compliment, flattered you think so. Or if they said my mind is like a deep space satellite capsule, again; Thanks!

Some of the stuff being cooked up by David (Although I'm not to be mistaken as criticizing free thinking here, which is always wonderful.) seems like he has the Quinn Yin, Buddha, and the Yogananda working in the hypothesis kitchen using the rings of Saturn (on the far side) as their cooktop griddle, flipping conceptual postulation pancakes for your order of reading stimulus breakfast. Cooking up a Breakfast Surprise of blueberry Illuminati pancakes with breakthrough informational side dish. David seated at his imaginary table deeper out back by Pluto or Neptune. My deep space mind satellite capsule in RV-mode snapping photos of all this as it flies past powered off of psychic photo voltaic solar panel Translation: No matter how far out in deep mind space you go, you will not outdistance someone from the Twilight survey team, and bullshit no matter how professionally written, even if taken into postulation and imaginary deep space is still bullshit simply having logged a lot more miles or light-years as the case may be. I'm not fooled, and if it's disinformation here, it's still disinformation way out there. He presents too much as hard fact of what is actually thin and flimsy absurdity, and this smacks of disinformation.

Readers, even a dog will tell you that a bone that still has 70 percent meat left on it, (truth) is one tasty bone. David's bone, err, book is thus an excellent source of Illuminati truth, as long as you watch for that fat alongside. A meteor shower of cosmic debris, on your Breakfast Special, Illuminati plate, but those Illuminati blueberry truth syrup pancakes are fat free! The Illuminati commission the best writer author they could find? We'll never know, but I promise you, they never counted on the deep space brain capsule of a Christian prophet with psychic radar capabilities passing by David's imagination breakfast kitchen on the backside rings of Saturn Griddle catching his breakfast chefs Quinn Yin, Buddha, and Yogananda flipping those Illuminati/blueberry postulation pancakes, either. Was David sitting back there at his Pluto/Neptune table of his imagination with tongue in cheek as this was happening? Novelistic crime scene credibility heist perpetrated in the name of unbelievability? He didn't bother to wear gloves to eliminate finger prints, because his name was already on the book's front cover. Was this a truth boundary voyeuristic imagination expansionism crime scene? Despite all this haranguing of David, I still recommend the book, just be alert constantly to trim away the fat in places, if truth is your mission on Illuminati subject, there is 70 percent truth in there - somewhere! I'd have Sargent Dano of the literary police cuff him and book him, except like much of what is claimed in his book, there just isn't hard conclusive evidence on which to make a conviction. Illuminati with a big budget of fertilizer to dumb down the public mushrooms with. They can afford a writer who is top notch, and David is top notch to be sure, so is that what happened here? Just remember what I said: Wash off all the gummy goo and seek out the 70 percent, gold miner sifting for the gold.

One of those gold nuggets is David's remarks about Illuminati stronghold bastions, such as right here in the wealthy South Florida retreats such as Billionaires Row, on the south end of Palm Beach Island. Was my first December 8, 2004, U.F.O. sighting there, a virtual smoking gun for Illuminati conspiracy theorists? I think at least possibly so. It wasn't until years later after much research, I realized that it could have been just that. Just not with certainty. What was witnessed was roughly between twenty to thirty Reptilian E.T. descend from the U.F.O. to a home on the intercostal waterway, observed by myself and two passengers from across the waterway (approximately five eighths of a mile distance. This typically servants quarters for larger mansion up on the oceanfront, but not in all cases as there are guest houses also, as well as a few primary homes in the vicinity, as well. The entire descend and ascent back to the U.F.O. lasting a little less than forty-five minutes.

What do black rituals, black alters do? Summon demons. What would attract a whole boatload (U.F.O.) of demons? Human sacrifice, human blood! This location about an one eighth mile south of the estate of a billionaire who has been considering a bid for the presidency of the United States. Care for a hot cup of N.S.A/C.I.A. complimentary coffee Donald? Now you really can't hold anyone no matter who they are responsible for not knowing what is going on in their neighborhood at 4 A.M. Even though most Illuminati are Republican, not all are, and certainly only a tiny sliver of Republicans in total. Nobody is claiming that, and this again, is only the possibility of somebody performing Satanic ritual and only speculation of human blood sacrifice taking place at that location. Still, I'm not sure I'd feel comfortable voting for a billionaire, and one with a U.F.O. boatload of demons attending a party at another mansion within walking distance from the (now non-candidate's) home, especially when you are talking about the office of U.S. President. Your imagination might start having a nightmare of a U.F.O. descending on the back lawn of the White House at 4 A.M. here or something, never mind a Godless Illuminati president if that actually were the case (Some thinking individuals just as nefarious have come through the front of the White House during busy hours.).

The conspiracy theorist point to the cover-up of U.F.O. sighting by the press as part and parcel also. So, what happened when I went to the local newspaper(s) to report the sighting? A giant muzzle was very, very evident as being in place exactly as both U.F.O.-ologists and Illuminati theorist claim it is. I waited an hour, and no one would come down from their offices to even discuss it. Like being stood up by a prom date or something, and this imposed by the Federal government no question, so this is still going on, and any airplane pilot who holds Federal licensing will confirm the same. A muzzle on U.F.O. sightings and subject as far as going public, but okay to mention to traffic controllers as they, too, have to be Federally licensed.

Talk about missing and exploited children. Worldwide the numbers are staggering each year. One has to wonder how many become victims of this type of demented person with such mentally distorted mindset. If such human/Reptilian demon hybrid does exist, then it would at least explain consistency among the thinking of those who might even consider such behavior. Rough neighborhood that Billionaire's Row at 4 A.M., most people would have to be pretty inebriated to start seeing invited guests as tall beige/orange snake skinned demons, but not if you invited them to a freshly sacrificed human's blood! What say we elect a presidential candidate who has no idea what is going on just down the street in his own affluent neighborhood, to highest office? He would probably (excuse the pun) have to wage a bloody political fight in order to get elected. But then you could say, stranger things have occurred. It's 10 P.M., do you know where your children are? Yes, out campaigning for his Democratic Party rival political opponent you say? Well aren't you the savvy one, with savvy kids no doubt still on the campaign trail at 10 P.M.! The younger ones won't even go trick or treating at mansions down the street from Count Dracula's estate, lest they are the ones to get to be a 'missing and abused' poster child, tricked instead of treated (If only there wasn't some truth to this kind of behavior from deranged adults).

Now let's return to that Illuminati Bohemian Garden campground in Northern California situation, with a forty-foot-tall giant stone Owl demonic idol, that members ceremoniously perform the 'ashes of cares' yearly ritual before (Clearly counter to God's commandment not to have any False Idols, or to pay them greater respect than God Almighty particularly worship.). Now some might say it's all kind of innocent like a college mascot deified as part of a fraternity hijinks party celebration, and I only go to these meetings for purpose of making valuable business contacts through accessing this network of powerfully connected. Innocent? Not the way God sees it. It's guilt by association you could say, and if you enjoy rubbing elbows with many who have a very dark destiny in afterlife, if you're not careful you could be among them then, as well. Beware oh innocent ones, for your peril is great in the eyes of the Lord! God is watching you, observing everything, and you will one day be held accountable.

Probably true that the black alter, blood drinking, demon summoning activity that goes on late at night in much smaller group conclave is participated in by a much smaller group of attendees, only a small fraction splinter of total attendees so it is claimed, but likely quite true! Nelson Rockefeller and many more openly boasted Anti-God sentiment, Illuminati membership, but I think David Icke's list of dignitary is overblown to absurdity level since he includes shapeshifting being accompaniment to virtually most on his list, and why his book smacks of disinformation, not to mention several other points I don't have space to describe. What I'm saying whether unintentional, or paid for by the Illuminati intentional to construct a classic piece of disinformation pinnacle high art form writing on the subject, then his book succeeded! My guess is it was unintentional, and therefore David missed out on the stack of quid he could have been paid, simply letting the tabloid side of his journalistic nature get the best of his sense of control. What is hard to prove is equally hard to disprove. Being his own Editor Publisher; what controls?

An interesting attribute about the Reptilian E.T., that I am quite convinced are one in the same with the Bible mentioned Beast From the Sea, is relating to something Dr. Courtney Brown relates in his book *Cosmic Explorers*. Interesting, too, because his Farsight Institute actually obviously had done Remote psychic Viewing contracted by our National Intelligence Services.

His statements from his book describing two factions of Reptilian, both hostile to humans. One Moderate, but the other labeled as Renegade. Now the 2004 High-hat sighting possibly suggests being flown by the moderates, and this could account for a possible (but unsubstantiated) clandestine rendezvous at that SouthPalm Beach Intercoastal Waterway location, December 8 at 3:30 A.M., and reason to potentially drop suspicions of necessity for a blood sacrifice/black ritual happening associatively, as human fresh blood is a favorite beverage of Reptilian.

Taking Dr. Brown's comments further in applying them to my sightings, the other side of that Reptilian coin being the Renegade faction, the 2008 Low Hat sighting predicted by psychic in my sleep dream, then in fulfillment about ten days later in night sky observance from my front patio, would be a match for the Low Hat being a Renegade Reptilian one. Both the Reptilian seen in the dream, from which my depiction is taken, and the Low Hat sighting, again from which my accurate depiction is made. Being a medium that can sense the presence of Evil, and to sense it at a mile or so distant is essentially Evil at off the charts level. In 2004, with the high-hat sighting at only five-eighth of a mile distant, while I certainly didn't have a good vibe from it, it wasn't radiating Evil as was the case with the Low Hat in 2008. demonic registry affiliation to the hilt, as well as being the commanders of the 391st demonic Alien Air Wing (subordinate Bad Greys E.T.)? Can't imagine our government omitting to tell you who controls South Florida. night skies (weather balloon).

Wildman letting the contents of that 391st secrets bag spill out on the floor for the public to examine, won't in the least shock the public, but will shock the National Intelligence Agency responsible for withholding all this information from the public in secrecy! You've gotta love it. A Renegade Christian psychic sniffing out renegade demons like a bloodhound on the trail of blood drinking E.T., then exposing a Smoking Gun of government secrecy cover-up conspiracy! That smell sort of like a cross between spent gunpowder, burnt lizard's tail, and smoke exiting from the ears of a National Intelligence Czar. Quite pungently aromatic. The supernatural, parapsychic, Theological, and demon U.F.O./E.T. all at government cover-up conspiracy intersection point! Never underestimate a Christian.

That Bohemian Garden yearly campground meeting is held in July, and since none of Illuminati membership have a snowball's chance in hell of rapture, (unless some extreme repentance goes on before now and Tribulation) it means they will be in attendance at that annual meeting in defiance to God as usual. With that fort-foot (high) owl deity, continuing the tradition of literally giving God the bird, accepting the ancient pagan belief of the Egyptian instead. Taught to the ancient Egyptian by the original fallen angel Reptilian demon, hailing Satan their Serpent God. What a bunch of idiots these Illuminati are, and forget the wealth, power, and influence many command.

Here is a prediction for the Illuminati that I cannot describe as definite without knowing it is definite since it touches on religious topic/subject. However, I expect the very first stop on the Comet Wormwood's scorching itinerary is the entire area between Sacramento and this Russian River/Redwoods campground of the demonically oriented ultra-rich. That would mean in order to catch the members there, it would have to rapidly come in from the skies above the Pacific toward descent allowing scorch once over land, and do so corresponding to the July meet. My prediction forecast is that it is no coincidence that it will!

The word Illuminati means *Enlightened Ones*, and the symbol of fire and the torch bearer (such as the Statue of Liberty, Pagan Goddess Liberty, and the Whore of Babylon. Queen Semiramis also. David Icke's full Illuminati manifesto account (as described from their viewpoint) is a full forty-five pages of very twisted pagan/roman/pagan Egyptian/pagan Babylonian baloney thinking played out in full (accurate truth, all be it misguided) accurate detail there in Chapter 9 of his book.

Kind of ironic that an iron-oxide gaseous fireball brown dwarf star Comet will come out of the skies above the Pacific Ocean to melt the very flesh right to the bone of those Satanists with Fire as their symbol, now being consumed by fire in this future timeframe, at the very hand of the true God Almighty they refused worship and belief in. The serpent God Satan worshipers getting lit-up then, and going to a fitting fiery death! Your imagination can handle what a 2,500 plus degree Fahrenheit fireball scorch from the sky can due to a group of people in a redwood canopy forest. An abundant harvest of ash at the alter base of the giant Owl that year. Death by Fire their fate should they be there that year. A Christian prophet never wrong in fifty years giving this prediction more than ten years in advance, a warning! The Christian faith is the only correct and true faith, as God has so confirmed to me, they who hear my words of witness might then receive with conviction of faith therein. Holy Trinity Christian faith, no if, ands, or buts about it is the truth of Holiness characteristic of the metaphysical universe, and supernatural Spiritual realms, and I have the undisputable personal proof, as described elsewhere in this book, and I say with absolute total certainty is unquestionably what the truth is. Period!

What about the Northern California cottage industry of cultivating premium grade marijuana in that very same bohemian garden region owned by the Illuminati? An area often referred to as the Emerald Triangle. Let's just say they won't be harvesting anything that year, as the title of an old Cheech and Chong movie, *Up in Smoke* will pretty well describe outcome just before another movie title, *Gone with the Wind* (blowing east, slightly northeast) takes over. I would say the entire region from just north of Sacramento for 150 miles northward (into Oregon), and 150 miles southward into central California is all at great danger risk of intense scorch. That is in description of the blow torch like heat descending from the sky directly. Forests once ignited will create such a huge mega inferno, that even if a person was beyond the range of initial scorch, the subsequent mega inferno will engulf the entire Pacific coast. Forests and fault lines not prime underground shelter location, discussed further in the Supplement Section (Part II).

Put that Wildman delivered fate encrypted crypt-bud prediction in your bong and smoke it Mr. Humbolt/Shasta County farmer man. The supernatural is conspiring to send the Grim Reaper to (flash scorch) harvest both you and your crop that year. Filming a new tale from crypt episode entitled "The Ungrateful Dead" that they want you to star in post-mortem, where you go out in a blaze of "gory!" You interested? No, not even allegorically? Too stoned to speak, but from the head nod, I'll take that as a No!

San Francisco residents taking note of my fourteen years in advance weather forecast for record setting heat that day, plus two thousand degrees even! For them, the price of this book suddenly seeming a lot less expensive. Some advance warning will happen when the time arrives, but people need to consider now, well ahead of time, what they would do, where they will go, if they don't rapture, and instead are in direct path harm's way. This really applies to everyone, and this book a consciousness raising effort toward saving lives, and souls.

When you examine all the insane, deranged doctrines, and extremist ideology beliefs of lunatics, sick-o's, and utopian political farfetched foolishness, you notice it often begins from a maniac's world view. Godless Totalitarian State, or False

God Theocratic State not much different, and be these far left, or extreme far right neo-Nazi Fourth Reich hopeful secret militia para-military type home grown organization zeal, ultra nut, or Iranian Sharia-law. False God/Theocracy State sponsored terrorism, it's still little different than Ameri-European Illuminati, secret Satanist, corrupt ultra-criminal/ultra-wealthy thirsting for power and wealth. When you see the word of God, the Christian Bible being not in agreement but instead in contradiction, that's an infallible litmus test. Common factor feature being they can never grasp just how demented they are because they can't seem to comprehend the Bible actually being true to the fullest measure. A Christian Prophet, be they in Biblical days, or in this current timeframe, having received repeated firsthand confirmations, is one knowing then the Bible's correctness and accuracy, which I assure you, and every nut case under every rock out there, it truly is genuine. These False ideology, promoting false, arrived at from faulty perspectives based on flawed logic, irrespective of God (cancerous at the core).

Wake up America! Even prior to the 2024, November presidential elections, America will have felt massive destruction from the front end loaded Tribulation natural disaster cataclysms. This is definite, and Part II of this book will detail more extensively and informatively than The Book of Revelation ever has been to date. You need to read Part I, in order to accept me as one receiving 2008 holy prophecy forth telling, otherwise there is no point in reading Part II, unless you first come to accept me as authentically credible. The fact that I am, does you not the least bit of benefit until that recognition level of realization is reached. Hopefully you will also see that that is my goal, to benefit people, and you can only do that if you are one hundred percent truthful. I am, but I also know how act of God incredibles. can overwhelm, because I've already been there, experienced it, and it overwhelmed me, and I'm sort of familiar with holy angel interactions as a medium. My motivation is simply in fulfilling God's purpose of passing the information on to the public. Sorry, but in fact God can be pretty overpowering even in such an informational way, and the Bible backing me up there (usually it's me backing up the Bible).

It's a shame the super committee couldn't even come to agree on the compromises necessary to reduce the national deficit. Wealthy Americans and Republicans not fitting through the eye of the needle at the end of the line, still believing they can take it with them apparently, and that Biblical Camel metaphor for greed, as well as wealth, they now have saddle bagged with tax savings. (For their camel ride to hell?) Many wealthy like Bill Gates, Warren Buffett, and others realized philanthropy could bring them more joy and happiness in helping others, than the money itself ever could, and they still have plenty. Others seem to be drowning in their own greed. Some of these wealthy Republicans shouldn't be surprised when they get to hell to see that if they should bump into Grover Norquist, he's collecting signature commitment from the demons not to raise the furnace thermostat temperature ever in the future. It's a shame our national defense budget must be compromised by reason of wealthy wanting extra camel saddlebags! In hell, paper money quickly incinerated. Where's your wealth now, Mr. and Mrs. wealthy marshmallow? Think hell isn't real? The Devil has a marshmallow stick already waiting, and I won't let anyone disturb your imagination from cluing you where the stick gets inserted! Democrats say Grover Norquist already has Republicans by that stick, but I suppose your opinion breaks according to party affiliation. I'm an Independent whose vote is feared because it can never be taken for hip pocket granted. The American people are fed up enough this time to kick anyone even remotely conceived of as an uncompromising rascal out of office, and it appears there is a bumper crop.

It's time for our government to start informing the mushrooms on all the U.F.O. secrecy. They shouldn't have to learn from a psychic mushroom named Wildman that at least one third of E.T. similar to fallen angels are demonic, or that the Reptilian E.T. may actually be those demons, now commanding an air force of saucer U.F.O.. What about those other shape craft? Us mushrooms would appreciate it if the government mushroom farmers would kindly fill us in on those. Let's not make it a case where upon Tribulation arrival, the farmer was fat, the mushrooms were dumb, and upon devastations arrival, no one was happy. So sayeth a Christian psychic mushroom. While congress in Washington fiddles, the flames of our nation on the grill, could cause our country like meat on the barbeque to fall or roll off into the dirt and ashes. High unemployment, weak economy, and Congress fiddling, while our country gets burned. No proper perspective. Try turning the oven to broil and stick their hand in, and my guess they can't keep it there long, not for eternity. Something clergy have been pointing out, it seems for an eternity!

Democrats thinking Republicans have already sold their souls to Grover Norquist, now actively demonizing the legislature. While on the Republican side, they view Dems as tax and spend liberals likewise set on perpetuating entitlements at unsustainable levels. As it turns out, all those twenty to thirty years out, and fifty years out, projections are completely off the mark anyway.

Our country will not go broke trying to sustain these programs, instead, in less than fifteen years, our economy (and world economy, as well) will have collapsed with the on-set of Tribulation. Thus these programs will have adequate funding potentially to that Tribulation destructions start point. If Washington D.C. and Philadelphia/ NYC. all become flooded out under salt water permanently, it puts a real dampening on both tax revenues incoming, but with 25 percent citizens say in rapture, and 40 percent perishing, then a sharp drop off in pay-outs as of that time, as well A sharp recipient decline, reducing the entitlements from natural causes another way to phrase it. (a lot of early retirements, another)

Hopefully our Federal government will take Part II of my book with seriousness in explanation of cataclysmic events to come for our nation, before the catastrophic events to come explain themselves in serious actual outcomes of future timeframe. If they dare doubt the Wildman, it comes with consequence of licking severe wounds later on. Two thirds of a 307 million population gone through rapture and death? That does not have to be, my point, if I am taken seriously, lives and souls can be saved, but if not, then this is a likely relatively accurate assessment of future negative population resulting outcome numbers.

It's about correct awareness driving correct perspective. Knowing where this nation and decade is in relationship to what lies ahead with Tribulation arriving in the next decade is essential. Without these awareness, proper perspective is not achieved, not possible. If our government fails to heed warnings, then all the think tanks, and all of the president's men, in aftermath, will not be able to put our nation back together again! Voter Citizenry always knew there was a wild psychic mushroom out there somewhere among them that was far more future awareness knowledgeable than our dysfunctional government. But if these legislators in congress can't even work among themselves, what chance does the fate of a nation have resting on them taking a wild mushroom seriously? Your money on Washington going underwater, and the meaning of those think tanks now more like fish tanks? Politicians drowning in figurative greed before they drown literally? fate of our nation literally teetering on the brink as Rome burns so to speak, while Nero (congress) fiddles? They could learn a lot from a psychic mushroom, and being a figurative little guy yourself, mushroom citizen, you probably always knew in the back of your mind it would one day come down to this. Well, that someday is about to arrive, along with Tribulation itself. If congress wants to refer to me as a fungus instead, that's okay, because they then have to concede that even a fungus knows more about the future than they do, (what some have been saying all along) but, I think they just decided they prefer the term mushroom much better!

Better they release those classified U.F.O. files sooner, lest they come under a fungus attack. Mushrooms holding the power of the vote, and tired of being kept in the dark by our own government. All the other citizen mushrooms learning more from one of their own than from their government. With legislators seemingly pretty much in the dark themselves, and president's not fully E.T./U.F.O. aware, isn't it time to reign in the Intelligence services on this subject before Millennial Reign, reins the world in? Part II of my book with additional detail there, as well.

It would be a huge informational help if the American people not only had all the information from Prophet Wildman's books, but all the E.T./U.F.O. information our government is currently withholding which is quite sizeable. Otherwise, it only makes all these conspiracy theories of the Ultra wealthy in sinister secret alliance neo-Nazi Illuminati corrupt government demonic E.T. involvement nefarious agenda, policy, seem credibly correct!

A lot of mushrooms getting perpetually dumbed down, instead of being smartened up. A lot of mushrooms becoming increasingly intolerant of corruption (as Wall Street occupiers attest, activist wise) but many Americans reaching slow boil with across the board injustices and imbalances, and mismanagement of both government and corporate action.

Government by the government for the government, and special interests within government, is now what America stands for! The American mushroom public is up to its toad stools, and our patience and frustration saying: Enough!

For way too many Americans, it seems like Tribulation has already arrived, instead of into the next decade. The majority of Americans want the America back we all know, and love, and respect with loyalty. God has a history/track record precedence of drowning corruption, and America no Babylon exception (My book Part II provides details!).

This book confirming to the world that the Reptilian E.T. are demonic, and likely a match for Bible Book of Revelation's beast from the sea, then confirms correctness of New Testament, and the Judeo-Christian faith, the reason these Elite Intelligence czars don't wish to get on this subject? Because it opens up wider E.T. discussions, and religious controversy? Well if all goes according to Wildman's Prophecy fulfillment expectations, (covered in part II) all religions will have their validity cords disconnected from the wall sockets of spiritual credibility except the Judeo-Christian faith, and with God in direct involvement behind the scenes helping me cut off power to those other ones so to speak! God doesn't want to know anything about those other misguided religious incorrect ideological philosophy theology. The other religions will have a rude awakening when they can't get power restored! With removal of flawed and false religion, away goes the controversy excuse for the Intel czars to use as excuse not to release info about E.T. Such as are these solid humanoid bodied E.T., or are these ethereal multi-dimensional ultraterrestrials? What about their saucer craft? What else have they known, and how many years have they been hiding this stuff from Presidents, Congress, and the American people? These are demonic, hostile to human E.T. or ultraterrestrial; with Tribulation only a dozen years off, and Wildman about to detail it for readers in Part II like it was an expensive limo that just emerged from a very expensive car wash.

These Intel czars need to realize that the lives of all the mushrooms they've been withholding information from live downstream from the informational dam (or you might prefer the four-letter spelling version of the word). A patch of smolderingly angry mushrooms as far as the eye can see not a pretty sight. That's right, an Obama-nation since the presidents don't get briefed, either. You have grid locked portabellas under the rotunda (Illuminati?) Intelligence Elite covering up for the E.T. demons, high unemployment, National Deficit, Fannie & Freddie, and the E.U. banking meltdown resembling a Fukashima reactor, but the world has gotten too big to fail? The failure is loss of confidence in our privy Intelligence services playing God with human life downstream from this metaphorical Dam. A human Intelligence Agency covering up for E.T. demons! What are they threatening to blackmail you for something? I've got news, your wife probably already suspected as much from her mushroom farmer husband spreading manure on both the Legislative and executive branches of government no less. (lampooning here, but only they know how much is truth!)

I have to insert a little light parody in with all the serious subject once in a while so my reader's don't get lock jaw, or rigamortis setting in early before the shock that eventually slays them. If someone else were claiming a holy angel foretold U.F.O. 2008 Air Show, an entire air squadron (my 391st as I named them Alien Air Wing) or a tractor beam pair, or sixty or so U.F.O. seen all in one night, or a U.F.O. delivered Particle Beam direct match for one Book of Revelation described, this certainly could appear delusional, hoaxed, or maybe some high weirdness Oz Factor stuff. If I didn't know the guy who was making these claims better than anybody, I might think the same. In this case however, I am in realization that none of this is the case, but as an anointed, pre-destined to prophecy Christian, I'm just sort of riding shotgun, with God doing the driving. Whether you believe me or not, this is all act of God activity I'm relating. Now when God is involved, you always look to his purpose, his desired end result. It may actually be God doing an end around to pass on certain information that the American public is having withheld from it. Trust me I didn't know some of this U.F.O. stuff myself until it became clear in 2008 what information topic the holy side was desiring to message.

My making a bit of a stink about this is because I can only surmise something nefarious is going on behind the backs of the American people on this U.F.O. topic related area. Also receiving timing confirms for Tribulation, both areas clergy could use additional clarity upon, as well as the rest of us. Now I'm not stating something definitely is going on nefarious behind the scenes amidst all the conspiracy rumors and speculations. What I am saying is if the elite Intelligence czars had released more on the E.T. subject all along, perhaps God would not have felt the need to message one of his loyal mediums. Why isn't the government providing you with more information on this, because I suspect they know a great deal more they are unwilling to released details upon. It is not that there is any greater dangers for the next dozen years prior to Tribulation than there are now, the point is, once the Tribulation cataclysmic natural destructions begin, there goes all the those government secrets, as well, perhaps (I strongly suspect so).

No, not everything can be divulged for National Security reasons, but on E.T. subject, they can do better. Maybe if they stop playing God with people's lives, God will stop delivering releases of Intelligence in end around fashion. Wildman and God on your side, that's two *out* of three parties knowledgeable, you're still in pretty good shape!

Of course National Intelligence has warned you the American public of the coming Tribulation, right? No? Are they saying that is not their job, or that if you care to believe the Bible's foretelling in both Book of Matthew and Luke essentially that the baby boom generation born in the same birth of Israel/Post W.W.II time period of 1948 (1944 to 1954) would not pass away in death (or rapture) until Tribulation got under way, that's fine, your business, but as an Intelligence agency of a government representing diverse religious beliefs, they could not openly proclaimate such Tribulation start confirmation to the public, because it might offend certain religious factions without total proof? Apparently so! Oh, they know all right, but it's perfectly okay to protect the secrecy of weasely demonic E.T.? No oversight of these Intelligence czars the reason. The American public does not require confirmation as to exact Tribulation start? Remind me again, who is it they are supposed to be protecting with your Federal Tax dollars? Just a wild guess from Wildman; the American citizens maybe?

Well, I'll save them the trouble. A future awareness psychic never wrong in his lifetime who interacts with holy angel will drop a bombshell on you here. A Prophet who witnesses for Christ's second coming, an advocate of faith in Jesus providing this little certainty for you, and I rarely use that word, or describe prediction in this manner. Look to 2023/2024 as Tribulation start. I already stated, I'm convinced that there will be no presidential election in 2024 for that very reason. It might have been nice if they'd at least informed the Executive and Legislative branches of government. If they say they didn't know, then they are admitting that a mushroom knows more about this than the farmer. If they say they did know, but were withholding this information, could they please explain to the American people how withholding information on Tribulation cataclysmic destructions start timing could be in the best interest of America, and maybe do it on the Jay Leno, or David Letterman show so the American people can get a laugh out of their explanation. The Executive and Legislative branches of government have been victimized here just as you have. It's time for Intelligence service Congressional oversight with Pentagon participation. The American citizen assumes the Pentagon is privy to all Intelligence, but is even that necessarily true? Or, has little changed since September 11 as to Inter Intelligence Service co-operation? President and Congress left out of the Intelligence loop, and not what are forefathers envisioned for America. Your bookstore is not the way American citizenry should come into awareness on such vitally critical information for their own survival. If you read my book before the Intelligence Services do, does that mean then somebody's Grand-dad in Peoria then knows more about future National Security relative to Tribulation event than they do? Than Congressional leaders and the President do? You see anything wrong with this picture?

File it in that enormous informational storage warehouse behind that enormous informational government dam of publicly withheld information. The lives in jeopardy of several Hundred million Americans is a big deal to each and every one of those individual people. Yes, the most devout Christians will Rapture prior to destruction start, I firmly believe, but that still leaves behind the majority of Americans, just not up to spiritual snuff come muster time at Rapture, occurring just before destructions do. Unfortunately the dam break isn't just figurative but literal. Although secondary effect, the deadliest casualty cause in America, even ahead of Comet Wormwood is likely coastal and low lying inland flooding/inundations of sea, salt water (Hence my angry letter to the Congressman in denial of any problem, appropriating $500 million in taxpayer money to Everglades restoration of freshwater!).

My polygraph exams verifying a U.F.O. delivered Particle Beam, mentioned nowhere else than in Bible Book of Revelation, (exhibited in this book) in essence verify Tribulation, and New Testament Christian faith all in one neat bundle, do they not? Just remember who my senior editor, and his contributing staff of holy angels heavy involvement is here.

Part II of this book is devoted exclusively to all of the varied associative aspect topics connected, but where I was talking about the necessity of God to do an end around flanking maneuver, to raise the consciousness level of not only Americans, but millions of people worldwide on the Tribulation seven-year period approaching. At the same time it draws a line in the sand. Are you personally on Jesus' side of that line? You might want to reflect on that. You shouldn't require that a modern day Christian Prophet confirm to you Jesus really is the holy resurrected Son of the Almighty, truly King of Kings, Lord of Lords.

Another informational bombshell gift wrapped from Part II, and then brought here to Part I, can be found in the Supplement Section. An abundance of other bombshells over in Part II allowing me to do that. Just too important to withhold from the public. Who do you think I am, a National Intelligence czar or something, I'd never do that to you, and obviously God does have something to say about it!

In concluding this U.F.O. Section, and this government Intelligence community cover-up conspiracy, I've stirred the stew pot here for you not with any real expectation of change, but perhaps to draw attention of the American people to it in regard to information withheld from them relative to Tribulation and U.F.O. situation, not necessarily in the best interest of their own survival. The 7-year Tribulation is unique to Christian faith, yet a Christian psychic medium/Prophet in receipt of confirmations of its approach needs to be taken seriously. The very survival of the United States is at stake here, and what projects to be possibly between a third to a half of a future 307 million person population, neither rapturing or perishing, but instead fighting for their survival (2023/2024 timeframe, most likely beyond mid-year 2024).

A Christian Prophet is one who conveys holy informational message. All my 2008 holy messages (you'll read more about in the next Section) provide further details in exact match of the Book of Revelation. That should speak volumes to anyone doubting the validity of Jesus as the second holy component in the Holy Trinity, or Christian faith, holy Bible belief in general, and in total. The very people who are weak in faith, or no faith, or wrong faith, are these very same population group that will not rapture, but may survive Tribulation cataclysmic onset.

Severe population reduction coupled with severe shortages increases the level of the nation's dysfunctionality, and with no more electricity or telecommunications, collapse of the economy in chaos is practically assured. Law of the jungle kicking in, survival of the fittest, and with wild animals escaping from zoos it will be a literal jungle. No more fuels for heat, or transportation? No more businesses? Will there even be martial law, any law except God's laws? All resources will be scarce, and even gold and silver of little value of no function. Only useable commodity will be in high demand.

Government action or inactions now will be the difference maker in this future Tribulation timeframe. Will the Grim Reaper come looking to find you? Collect those lives that need to be paid as the debt for government inaction consequence? Nothing like dealing with the Reaper firsthand the hard way, when you could have come to Rapture with God doing this the easy way. Last time I sensed the Reaper, he was aboard a U.F.O. Low Hat, you know, government weather balloon. The Bible's weather forecast for seven years of extremely bad weather! With our government in denial driving this bus, viewing from ten years plus into the future, I can't tell if you are on the bus or under it, can you? Correct faith is Christian faith (and you are going to really need it!).

Perhaps I should apologize in advance to the Intelligence Services in speaking so harshly, and express appreciation to them for being good sports in tolerating such a cynical verbal assault tirade, of criticism, but that is what makes our country great and better than most is our right to Freedom of Speech. Like the Congressman I verbally chewed to shreds a few years back, I hope they see it is out of necessity to draw attention to an important pressing issue of epic proportion. Potentially over one hundred million American lives vulnerability of perishing just a dozen years from now. That only being one aspect component. If your life is among these, shouldn't you be concerned? Your larger family at great risk not an important enough issue?

What the World War II sneak attack on Pearl Harbor and Philippines, as well as the Titanic, and September 11 all had in common was warning indications were ignored, then tragically large loss of life numbers resulted. In each case it was thought the disaster couldn't or wouldn't happen. Precaution not taken representing lost opportunity to avert each of these. This has been Bible foretold for two thousand years. I received my fourth confirm from God in 2008, relative to confirmation of the correct time placement of seven-year Tribulation. I ask you, what is more genuine and reliable than a documented psychic medium, Christian Prophet with direct word of God information?

America as a nation is unprepared! The giant has rolled over and gone back to sleep. If it doesn't wake up, it will miss a golden opportunity to mitigate the ultimate mega tragedy!

So far I've got the attention of somebody's Grand Dad in Peoria, and a handful of common citizen mushrooms. Will the American people please wake up Congress, and tell them to put down the saddlebags they are trying to strap onto those camels for a minute, and convince the Intelligence Services that after Armageddon all the behind the dam Intelligence will be worthless, so how about they start sharing more, stop with the excess secrecy. Attempting to strap extra saddlebags, be they cash or in Intelligence, if the Camel can't get through the needle's eye, then what is the use. On the contrary, effort toward saving American lives is not effort in futility. The focus should be on the eye of the seven-year storm headed this way, due to make landfall in the summer of 2024. You have God's word on its approach, in confirmation of this seven-year period. If that isn't good enough for you, maybe not believing God is the real problem here. People now serving long prison sentence for failing polygraph exam, and my fully passing polygraph in witness of a particular Book of Revelation Particle Beam in my front yard sure convinced me!

Forget about government release of information to the public, you aren't likely to get much more than a nuclear war reprint from the 1960s, entitled, "Duck and Cover." Thanks a bunch! Is that the same manual congressmen use when dealing with disgruntled constituents?

The world being as unsettled as it is, with instabilities constantly present, unfortunately, I can't give you greater Specific awareness of the next dozen years leading up to the seven-year period. The Bible in mention of a peace treaty signed with Israel at close time proximity to the technical seven-year period start (May 2023) clearly means a military conflict/war was ongoing prior, but months prior or years ongoing prior I can't say. It appears to be non-nuclear damage, at least where Israel is concerned, the good news, but who the opposition is exactly is undetermined. Clearly Iran is undamaged enough to launch W.W.III conquest battles by the third and fourth quarter timeframe of 2024 by Nostradamus account, with further fine tuning prophetic analysis for you courtesy of yours truly, and quite accurately correct, as Part II will provide additional explanations.

It is not too early for the United Nations to begin developing an evacuation/refugee/relocation worldwide humanitarian master plan to avert the largest single human death by drowning death toll number the world has ever witnessed (more than One billion lives!). Without an intermediary organization such as the U.N. it will be difficult to have co-ordination finding host countries for all the island nations, and low lying coastal countries populations. You cannot be reactive where Tribulation cataclysms are involved, you must be pro-active, or this God given opportunity will be squandered. Unfortunately, the non-Christian demographic of many of these countries would not facilitate easy accomplishment of such large scale task required. It doesn't look very promising, especially since the Bible itself ironically is suggesting only mitigation success achieved turned out to be minimal. Yet we know that to God, every single human life and soul spiritually are precious to him, and why the likely forewarnings for Tribulation timing was provided in multiple 2008 psychic confirmation to a Christian Prophet medium, in match for prior holy angel involved awareness on Tribulation timing.

These life/soul preservers of Tribulation information awareness from Jesus to simply go ignored, unheeded, and discarded? Jesus' holy name, never wrong, right on these preservers very dependably reliable as is the holy Bible and Christian faith. Never more vitally important to have in a critical condition world.

Remote viewers are clairvoyants practiced at focused informational retrieval toward a subject target. Focus placement toward an event circumstance, either past or future, often can lead to accurate account awareness, however, completeness of exactness to timing/location details of such intersection point, vague at best. Timing usually the most difficult for all psychic mediums.

In Part II, Chapter 27 of this book, I quote several pertinent passages based on RV retrieval of Reptilian E.T. subject info., from Dr. C. Brown's book, *Cosmic Explorers*. Combining his Reptilian E.T. statement with his hostile to humans characterizations, and my Tribulation event timing confirmations, it paints a disturbing back drop condition picture, most likely occurring during the second three-and-a-half-year Great Tribulation period. The latter half of this timeframe will consist mainly (but not entirely) of humans with a very short remaining existence, and bad afterlife outcome awaiting them. actually you can't rule out E.T. related unfavorable to humans situations arriving earlier, since I place the five-month U.F.O. Particle beam stings on the back end of the first 3½ year Tribulation period. If the Christian faith isn't one hundred million percent valid, accurate, truthful, authentic, genuine, and correct, not to mention eternally Sacred and holy to fullest measure, then somebody please explain to me holy angel delivery of prophetic Tribulation timing forth telling messages received in match for other Tribulation awareness confirmed, and all of it in match for Bible account nearly two thousand years old! The explanation is exactly as already act of God described.

In Part II, it's a bit like having a set of God's Tribulation architectural blueprints with some timing clarifications/specifications additionally revealed. (five-month sting period included) What a coincidence the Prophet receiving those awareness has a strong background in architectural design drafting blueprints! Imagine that. About as random as a certain holy child, born of Mary and Joseph in a manger in the town of Bethlehem visited by local shepherds, holy angels, and three wise men from afar. I would never claim any Holiness myself, I'm ordinary like you, so don't misunderstand what's being said. I'm simply stating I'm conscious of God's planning and design both in my role as message conveyor, but as well, an interpretive reader of message conveyance as it relates to those Tribulation blueprints of Divine architecture.

Our government needs to start spilling information on these demonic E.T. Reptilian Extra or Ultraterrestrials while there are still citizen and time left to do it. Everglades reptiles with $500 million in Federal taxpayer money, but Federal Intelligence won't inform taxpayers about E.T.

While "Saints Covenant Prophecy" the last remaining unfulfilled prophecy on Holy subject is likely to fulfill soon, it is also contingent on promotion of new Cardinals from the ranks of Bishop by the Catholic Church. Without any doubt, all of my other Holy subject prophecy is genuine, relating to 2008 Holy source information received, that not only confirm Tribulation timings, but are identical match of statements that were given in a 1964 Ordained Minister's sermon that an Angel of the Lord I believe, instructed that I pay close attention of and remember back the during church services. Holy source both times, message wise. Part II includes full transparency Truth Verification/Lie Detection tests Passed.

It's not the nature generally for Christians to intentionally speak in sarcastic, cynical commentary tone as I had to do with this Chapter. However, this is extremely important, urgent, dire, and most serious as situations get. It's time to break the glass and sound the Tribulation alarm, but that doesn't mean panic. Still plenty of time for America to rally, and by doing so now, make necessary adjustment, avoid panic late through pro-active actions taken in advance. God has confirmed that the Tribulation in fact will run from 2023 to 2030.

In my lifetime, four separate confirms, all pointing to the same 2030 Armageddon. In terms of a psychic medium prophet, this is like God has chiseled it in granite, with numerals one hundred feet high on the side of a mountain just to get people's attention. No excuses later!

The U.S. should be stockpiling basic commodity resources of every description for those Americans left behind unraptured, yet trying to defend American shores while holding everything together, as best they can. Higher above sea level (2,800 ft. min.) underground warehouses and shelters should be prioritized, the only safe plan. Yet nothing is now going forward, and America's enemies will capitalize on this later if it isn't central to National strategic objectives. Forget the Gov't. assisting you as an individual, you need to consider personal survival as well. Christian rapture I project to occur in July, 2024, only then the severe cataclysmic destructions to follow. Your priority should be to Rapture, but a back-up survivalist plan in case you don't, not a bad decision. Much more on this in Part II, but I've just given you the key essentials of need to know, including that if Tribulation's approach is real, so is the correctness and validity of Christian Faith.

Chapter 14
Psychic Section

The Majors

"All the great psychics (precognitive) have excellent (better than twenty-twenty) long distance vision. They can see further than twenty miles away, and more than twenty years into the future" (both at the same time).
Prophet Wildman, 2009

In the Religion Section II will discuss my own predictions, but here, from the perspective of a psychic himself, let's talk about some of the major psychics. There are many ways to measure them. The total prediction success rate, number of total statements, distance into the future, and importance of prediction certainly all figure in. The timing is often elusive for a psychic. They know what will happen, and perhaps even see an event from the future clearly, but timing not as clearly. Methodology varies from psychic to psychic. Cayce was known as the sleeping prophet, while Nostradamus was almost always awake. I will speak more on these gentlemen in a moment, but first some basics.

I am of the opinion that all positive psychic information is accomplished through an intermediary angel (spirit guide). The angel or guide obtains this information through that dimension. Contrary to what some think, that a psychic just all on his own dips a ladle in, and returns with information through psychic magic. That's not how it works, I believe even if a psychic doesn't realize it, they are being assisted! They are silently present, likely your guardian angel.

So allow me to dispel another common misconception. Some think a more noted psychic somehow delivers information of higher quality. Not true, all psychics go through a learning process of handling their gift, understanding the psychic experience, and interpretation that can often involve symbolism. There are several different ways information is delivered, both awake and in ones sleep, and these can and do vary, as well. However, all information is equally genuine if in fact it is sourced through the Kingdom of heaven. A psychic in California will get identical quality as one in Pennsylvania. Any errors are due to the psychic's misinterpretation, but not with the quality of the information. It's all triple AAA quality Kingdom of heaven same source! Sometimes dates or timing aren't part of the package, maybe there is a reason why it isn't given. For example, perhaps the event is certain, but not the timing, so that may be a clue in fact that timing is still in a state of flux.

It is said that the subconscious is connected to the soul, and thus from out of a spiritual dimension, through the soul, it enters your subconscious. If you are sleeping the subconscious then devises a dream for your sleeping, but semi-conscious conscious to then interpret, or at least that is what I am convinced happens with me. When a premonition is delivered when you are awake, it is now the subconscious that is semi-dormant, and it can go straight to the conscious brain as any other thought, except this one is conveyed by the angel guide. I have experienced both many times.

Interestingly enough, sometimes when premonitions are received, even as conscious thoughts they can sometimes make not full sense when you receive them, but when they fulfill years later, you think to yourself: okay, now I see, so that's what my angel was talking about! The ones that make only slight sense at first, always make perfect sense later! The initial premonition is always followed by a profound feeling. It's like that's the receipt your angel is giving you. On that invisible back side it probably says backed by the Bank of heavenly clouds, with full faith and credit of the Kingdom of Heaven Bonding Agency, and is backed with Sainted Re-insurance. In other words, it is definite, and can't be stopped from happening with that much momentum behind it! Now only a matter of when and not if.

Clairvoyance a form of the same pre-cognitive psychic aspect. In this case although still spirit guide assisted, the psychic, either awake or asleep, directs focus into a particular spot the way you might narrow sunlight through a magnifying glass, except subject concentration is what is being focused upon, and the psychic a degree of control in doing so. In my case I don't reach out, it comes to me. In the case of Nostradamus and Edgar Cayce both, they had mastered a technique of Clairvoyant retrieval. This allows a psychic to have a prolific quantity of prediction. They both had enormous quantity of prophecy, but more interpretation on their part involved, thus more chance for error. Both did have some misinterpretations. In my case by comparison, only taking what is given to me, less chance for error, and one hundred percent success and correctness rating (That is sure to give some people pause for horror at reading my End Times predictions, not to scare you.).

Getting back to Nostradamus, we know he was an astrologer first and an astronomer's distant second. A medical Doctor with some formal education in this field who sought herbal remedies, as well.

When the great plague hit Europe in the seventeenth century, many doctors not having much treatment success, fled for their own safety. Not Nostradamus. He had conviction to his role as a doctor and a healer, much the same as Edgar Cayce's desire to help and heel others. What I feel certain of was that humanitarian spirit was intertwined with their own faith. In the case of Nostradamus, I think his efforts not only earned him respect and appreciation of the towns people of Solon where he lived, but from above, as well. Perhaps more was revealed to him than had he not performed so selflessly.

Although his mother's side of Jewish descent, he was brought up piously Catholic. Yes, he also had to hide his prophecy in quatrains, to avoid accusations of heretical mysticism, yet still devotedly Christian in his personal beliefs. It is not by accident that so many who have psychic gift are also strong in Christian conviction of faith. Remember who I told you the intermediaries are, and that is why. You need to be on their team.

Edgar Cayce was also a devote Christian. After attending church with his mother at age fifteen it is said he decided to go into the woods to absorb the peace as he meditated and prayed. He asked to be given a special gift to heal. A radiance as he described it then appeared and he was told that if he stayed true to his faith such a gift would be given him. This the beginning.

Next he found he could absorb all the information contained in a book just by resting his head on top of it. His grades in school and general knowledge improved dramatically. Then even with no formal medical training, he began to successfully diagnose others ailments, illnesses, and cures. His reputation growing. While he continued medical diagnosis of many, he also began taking readings of the future under self-imposed hypnosis. His prophecies and predictions quite remarkable and prolific beyond even Nostradamus.

The key to understanding the supernatural realm is to first understand that it all comes back to Religion, the Bible, your own faith, and the relationship you have with God. It's about multi-dimensions of Good and Evil. It's about aligning yourself both externally and in the internal spiritual sense, as well. From there your perspectives as you live in this dimension, but aware it is not the only one.

The orthodox Christian Church has always, and even today still often does equate those who are mystics and psychics as dangerous fringe element that also on its other border touches on the occult. The perception here that occult is automatically demonic or satanic. Not true, but not to say that it never does.

The Biblical prophets of old were for the most part psychics first so does that mean they are occult and to be avoided? Let's hope not. Here is the litmus test churches should use:

1. Is the psychic one who is of strong Christian faith?
2. Are the messages of positive nature that is helpful to an individual or greater good of humanity?
3. Is there a message of Religious/spiritual value received?
4. Is the message to help or warn an individual or group about impending harm or danger, even possible death?

Demonic spirits avoid strong Christian spirit, will never deliver anything in terms of helpful message, to warn of harm, or death, and certainly won't be the source of a message of spiritual value.

Psychics should be respected by their church, not seen as outcasts. They can be a direct link to the Kingdom of heaven by way of angels. Otherwise when God calls the church might not pick up the phone. They thought it was Satan trying to deceive them and they were right, he just did! They missed God's call. Churches if you have gifted psychics listen to them. Do not diminish those who God upholds, (because they uphold God) It is by God that they have this gift to begin with.

But what about the dark evil side of the occult, and possibility of negative source information? It does and can occur/exist especially when not cautious of the source you are drawing from. Personally, it is for this reason I stay away from all physical props such as regular playing cards or Tarot cards for reading. Gypsy methods like palmistry are innocent, and crystal prism and balls seem to draw positive light frequency and energy, rather than dark, and therefore I feel these are safe, as long as the person using it is of strong Christian faith (Christian faith = positive energy and dispels dark).

Wiccan in similar fashion I think although rooted in paganism, is a convenient way for an ethereal spirit to communicate by a whole array of means, all words ending in *-mancy*. I have experienced Bibliomancy and feel it was delivered by positive spirit rather than a negative one. However, there is little to confirm either information received by these means or its source. You never want to do anything that might attract a negative spirit (remember they want to do you harm not benefit); therefore, I avoid all of these unconventional aspects, even at expense of missing out on some valuable information. My philosophy being, my guardian angel will make me aware of anything that is essential I should know, and I just go with that.

It appears several alien/extraterrestrial groups communicate by telepathic means and thus can also be categorized as an additional source of demonic/dark side information. While the allegiance of the group that is known as the Greys is debatable, the Reptilian I am convinced are demons. By abductions and perhaps even other means, thoughts can be implanted in the human brain even without our awareness. Almost all abductees report time and memory loss, with some people receiving under skin chip implants that could potentially involve subtle messaging to the brain, as well as being a tracking devise. Re-visitation from aliens is very common, and such abductees often report other body invasions, as well.

Regular demonic spirits are ones who have never lived, enter the human head, (said to enter through, and leave through the top of ones skull) and do invisible harm) as slinky invisible, snakelike non-forms. Their interference is more like messaging than misgiven psychic knowledge. Example: You need to hurt this person, kill that one, steal this item or auto, deceive, cheat, disobey God's laws, give false testimony, set fire to this or that, burglarize this store, break into that house, beat your spouse or children, curse God, have extra-marital affairs, then run for political office!

Isaiah 2: 6–9, The false idea of Soothsayers

The term soothsayer in the Bible given negative connotation, and could be taken to not only mean false prophecy, but false and misleading information in general derived from disingenuous source. In Hebrew it means to cloud or cover over the truth rather than to shed genuine light upon it.

Ask this question also: Is the intended outcome positive or negative? A demonic source will never work toward human well-being or improvement. False prophecy more likely to generate directly from an individual who knowingly is committing deception for whatever the reason. Keep in mind, too, that with such a wide range of means used to receive information, and seldom without any way of confirmation from many of these, psychics, often do make unintentional errors, perhaps in interpretation. No prediction is one hundred percent certain until it fulfills, no matter who delivers prediction. Because of my conservative approach of letting information come to me, rather than delving for it, my success rate of accuracy is still perfect. The best prediction is when a consensus develops among two or more psychics both stating the same identical thing. This does happen more frequently than you might expect.

The Book of Revelation and John of Patmos its author, will be discussed in the Religion section of the Book later. In my view, even though his detailed predictions have not yet fulfilled, a major theme within this book is that they soon are about to. Thus the award for greatest prophet goes to him. He then, the Major of all majors. I say this with certainty because so much other prediction overlaps and confirms with his, including my own.

Beside Major, how would I classify other psychics? I would break it down into minor and intermediate levels. A minor psychic primarily receives information only concerning that person's individual self. The total number of predictions limited. I feel like this was a sort of learning or training phase I went through. Now, in my case, I feel I've moved up to the intermediate level. More prediction and fulfillment occurrences, and happenings and prediction now of importance to the general public. Important information that needs to be made known now occurring.

Of course much prediction that won't confirm until the Tribulation period that I'm putting forward, when people will be far more worried about their very survival. Yet, it is my hope that putting this information forward now can be a difference maker in that very survival. Don't thank me if that is the case, I'm not seeking glory, all glory goes to God, Thank God, and praise Jesus name that at least what is coming didn't catch you by total surprise. He is the salvation of mankind in so many different ways. Clearly his hand at work in both my prophecy and this book. So please take what is told to you with seriousness and prepare yourself for what is coming. You may not see the train, but he is sounding the whistle. It is his faithful who are receiving warning.

It is the non-believer who will complacently not take action. There are several places in the Bible that tell us to Fear God, in the sense that he is the Almighty, and his power as vast as the universe. In essence show respect, and yet in other places the Bible tells us to Fear Not, the essence being that once your spirit is one with God, and obedient to his word, faithful in spirit, and steadfastly loyal, then the spiritual side of your being (soul) is now in his care.

As in Biblical days God used prophets to spread his word, and in the Religion section there are many Biblical quotes. One I would like to state here is Daniel 12:9 where Daniel is told The words of prophecy are shut up and sealed until the time of the end. There aren't too many that doubt we are living in the End Times, but what I have to announce is that the seal spoken of here has now been lifted. It is only a matter a time before other psychics realize this, as well. The seal now lifted, End Times prophecy is now being dispensed! I'm stating this to bring it to the attention of religious leaders everywhere. Other than the Miracle at Fatima, and the Marion apparition as it is called near Medjugorje, and Mt.

Podbrdo, in more recent times, (both of which I personally view as authentic) prophecy of religious focus it would seem has not been evident. I feel it is in a now nascent budding stage. Religious leaders must be aware of this, and not be too quick to dismiss information from this time forward obtained through psychic means. I feel the budding I've described will blossom in the decade between 2014 and 2024, when the flowers of religious prophecy will once again bloom. True psychics delivering message of spiritual nature, should from this time forward, in my opinion be taken seriously.

Another Major psychic during the 1960s was Jean Dixon. She was a devout Catholic, and like Nostradamus, an astrologer. She often performed various types of readings that included crystal ball, as well. She definitely had clairvoyant skills. She warned both of the Kennedy brothers of the danger of assassination in advance, to no avail, but was known as an astrologer and adviser to presidents. She missed on a few predictions of her many, but to her credit successfully gave many of great significance.

Still uncertain as to accuracy, one of her greatest predictions could yet fulfill. One morning in Washington, D.C. in a vision that came to her, she interpreted it to mean the possible birth of the Anti-Christ on that very day, February 5, 1962, at 7 A.M. She felt in some way, even if symbolically, this could be a descendant out of Egypt from the royal line of Nefertiti. I would certainly check the birth date for someone rising to power from anywhere in the middle East, especially toward the end of this decade.

Some interpret the False prophet and the Anti-Christ to be one and the same, others think no we are talking about two different villains here. Certainly they will both be non-Christian as would be expected if they rise from an Arab country of origin. Jean Dixon could yet have her prediction fulfill, be watchful (I view it as two separate men.) Malachi O' Morgan A catholic Father from Ireland gave some predictions that were major, but few predictions in total. Both he and Nostradamus said virtually the same thing. That the final procession of Popes would end with one named Peter. This would be done just prior to the Tribulation period, and be a sure sign for the seven-year period to look for. He is interesting from another perspective, as well.

Take a look at all major and intermediate psychics going back centuries yet looking at a cross-section, something very apparent becomes obvious. They all have Christian faith in common. Not a cross-section of any other faith even involved. That should speak volumes as to the validity of the Christian Faith, the King James Bible, and most importantly Jesus Christ.

Examine:

The Old Testament Prophets (Faith in God)
The New Testament Prophets (Faith in Jesus), including John of Patmos
Nostradamus (Catholic)
Edgar Cayce (Protestant)
Malachi O'Morgan (Catholic father)
John Cornelius Vander Heide (Protestant)
Brazilian Spiritualist, Ramatis (Catholic)
Catholic Capuchin monk, Padre Pio
Mother Superior Hildegard of Bingen (1,098 A.D.)
Jean Dixon (Catholic)
Father Martin (Catholic)
Native American Psychic Prophets (Christian)

Plus many more unknown or little known, such as myself all sharing Christian faith, both Catholic and Protestant. Make no mistake, Christian faith is the key.

Over many centuries the coming disasters, what the Hopi Indian call the great cleansing and the arrival of the fifth world, have been seen in prophetic psychic visions and foretold. Some see visions of disasters through Remote Viewing technique targeting, some through Clairvoyant visions, and some such as myself through dream visions and premonitions. All are pre-cognitive, future awareness. Chapters 25 and 26 will discuss more about actual predicted events. Not all had clear time-frame indication of what they were seeing.

Overlaying their predictions with my own, plus the time template mentioned in later chapter (Dr. Lancy's), comparing this all to the Bible Book of Revelation, and a much clearer picture emerges. Then in later chapters this will all be laid out for you to look at. Not a pretty picture with virtually all psychics mentioned in agreement.

For those readers not familiar with basic existing para-psychic vocabulary/terminology, a Glossary of terms involving the psychic aspect is provided here. Some additional information mentioned also. Some of this may be useful for comparative purposes in the next chapter.

Glossary of Terms

Instinct - Knowledge by natural innate means, also said to be comprised or deriving from harmony of the five senses: seeing, hearing, feeling, tasting, and smell.

Intuition - Advanced knowing through sensing that something is so in the absence of objective evidence

Insight - Through prior wisdom, seeing truth intuitively gaining new understanding, additional wisdom

E.S.P. - Extra Sensory Perception (also referred to as ESP) First so named by J.B. Rhine, (1930s) initially referring to all psychic ability, often said to be one's sixth sense. Some say insight and intuition merged to a higher state of awareness. It is said to be classified into three primary categories. They are:

Telepathy - (The word first coined in 1882) Intuiting the mind of another person, or reading their mind.

Clairvoyance - means clear view. The ability to visualize a truth either in material form (space in time) or grasp intangible characteristics and aspects of a particular focal point, or realize truth through a visualized intuition (object, event, or influence)

Precognition - Seeing into the future, the opposite of retro-cognition, or Deja-Vu, which is French for already seen a return to familiarity from the past.

Psychokinesis - The ability to move or bend objects by strong psychic will.

R.V.r's - Yes, that's right a psychic driving a recreation vehicle. No! This stands for Remote Viewing, also known as Telesthesiaor Traveling Clairvoyance, or distance focused Clairvoyance (can be current, retro-cognitive or precognitive)

Depending on who is doing the classification, here are two very similar versions as to Types of Dreams:

Version 1
Anxiety
Nightmare
Prophetic
Past life
Astral projection, also known as out of body experiences.

Version 2
Dream caused by physical condition
Dreams of prophetic nature
Dreams in which the dreamer travels
Psychoanalytical dreams

Injecting my own opinion here, although certainly not a trained professional psychologist, most of these experiences can and sometimes do occur while awake, as well as during sleep, if only in our subconscious, yet many can occur in awake conscious state, too. Some examples will be shown in other chapters, although sleep state the most common.

High Strangeness - (U.F.O.-logist term)
Although rare, there have been a number of incidences that qualify for this psychic categorization. Reports are worldwide, and U.F.O., Extraterrestrial are believed to be responsible. Each case will vary, but all involve unexplained altered states of perception. Both time alteration and surrounding environment alteration can occur, often both happening simultaneously. More will be said in Chapter 18.

In the 1940s, S.D. Kirlian invented what became known as a process that could photograph a person's Aura, the silhouette of the soul. This Auromantic photography still known as Kirlian Photography. The Aura colors are believed to have varied meanings that I've included for you here.

Why is aura important? For those of you fortunate (or unfortunate, depending on your perspective) to live to the middle of the coming Tribulation period, alien U.F.O. (saucer) will rule the night skies. Humans out scavenging will be target for these U.F.O.'s Taser beam. Even these demonic alien will be required to play by God's rules! They are according to the Bible book of Revelation allowed to torture, but not kill. The Bible even stating the pain of one of these stings excruciatingly painful. However, only the ungodly non-believers to be stung, so how will the aliens know who is fair human game and who is not? That is because they will be able to see and distinguish between human aura. A bright aura means you avoid sting, but someone with no aura or a dark one is subject to being painfully zapped. (Picture a police Taser, but stronger Zap!) Many eligible for Zap won't make it until then anyway, but here are the color meanings:

- White – (could be slightly golden, as well) indicates an individual highly evolved spiritually, a bright soul, perhaps having lived many lifetimes, now on its final incarnation on this plane of existence
- Yellow - An indication of strong imagination/positive energy (psychic spiritual connection in my case!)
- Red - Negative aura color, disease, deteriorating health
- Gray - The worst low spiritually other than black, and sometimes the final stage of terminal illness
- Green or Blue/Green - Health normal, can be in combination with a lighter color, some aura, and multi-colored
- Brown - Seen as down to Earth dependable
- Violet -Healing taking place within the body or spirit. A lighter lavender shade is said to indicate ability to heal others.
- Black - Absence of Aura; Bad, Evil, possible demonic presence; a Dark shadow where the aura should be

True Prophets vs. False Teachers and Prophets

The Bible makes mention of false teachers and prophets to beware of who are out to deceive, and lead you astray, both in the former Biblical Age, as well as prior and during the approaching Tribulation. For the ordinary person it can be difficult to discern between the two, so I thought I would try to further elaborate on indicators to look for when trying to discern the difference. It's not easy, and when you are a true prophet you feel constantly on the defensive, with a legitimate skepticism concern, that pervades the climate of message delivery discussion. You feel half convicted guilty even before you've begun an uphill battle to win people over. You are the only one (and God), who is certain you are genuine. Most clergy are cautiously optimistic I'm not some sort of hoaxer, awaiting further proof they should believe me, and fulfillment of prediction with meaningful Christian value is the best way of accomplishing that (Chapter 24 further discusses).

Here I'm talking of future prediction connecting to religious subject, not general future psychic prediction. Prophecy is a promise from God, relative to fulfillment, and since all my scores of other holy angel delivered prophecy on future prediction related to general subject has always fulfilled, I have no doubt of my 2008 forthtellings and foretelling on the Tribulation subject, either, as to certainty of fulfillment. I will have my honor vindicated by God literally (yet fulfillment is by his timing)!

In the Christian spiritual sense, false teachers and false prophets will not only contradict the Bible from outside of Christianity, but within Christianity itself. So even though it's no fun being on the receiving end of skepticism, it is healthy that people are informed and on their guard not to be quickly or easily swayed under these circumstances. The single most obvious indication is something you can pose to yourself as a question. Does the message contradict or agree with the Bible & New Testament Gospel message? If it disagrees or alters significantly anything doctrine wise away from the word of God/Holy (K.J.) Bible, then that disparity is definitely legitimate reason for concern. Freedom of speech and First Amendment Rights allow people to offer alternate interpretation even of Bible interpretation, but you are also not obligated to accept or agree with what is being offered statement wise. One reason I feel secure in my New Testament/Book of Revelation interpretational viewpoints is that after my own unbiased investigation and examinations, the conclusions reached were little different than an ordained Dr. of Div. Minister's interpretations dating from the 1960s. Dr. Lancy a center of much discussion later in the book.

In this book I give Tribulation timing specifics, but only because it was God given information that I know God wants passed on. Dr. Lancy having given matching timeframe dates in a 1964 sermon is my reassurance over and above, which in fact these are both accurately correct, but are delivered from genuine holy source exactly as I regard them to be. My assurance level is extremely high; in other words, that of correctness. At least 25 percent or more of the Bible deals with prophecy, which is a psychic human/holy intermediary interaction, and a great deal more of the Bible is direct communication between either God the Father/Creator, and/or Jesus Christ in message delivery to someone such as the disciple Paul, or 'John the Revelator.' What I'm getting at to make a point, is that without the holy source connection on the receiving end participatory, where is the authenticity? In order to be quality information relating to the future, it must have holy intermediary involvement on the source side. Human calculation and interpretation are fallible, thus far less reliable. A false prophet or teacher may claim to have this, but in fact if deceptive to begin with, might be lying/hoaxing that aspect in order to gain respectability. My own taking of truth verification exams was to show I am not only not fazed by them, but sought them out because it is extremely important people take what information I offer them seriously. Verifying a lifetime of holy angel interaction and psychic for-telling fulfillments lays the foundational groundwork for being believed in receipt of the 2008 holy subject information. It came in a flurry as I began writing this book, (clearly intended for this book) and nothing more activity wise since.

In the fall of 2010, I contacted *U.S. News and World Report* magazine regarding an advertisement by family radio of Oakland, California. It appears a Mr. Harold Camping, who once before unsuccessfully had made attempt to predict the start of Tribulation, was at it again. This time it is May 21, 2011, when the Tribulation starts (by his interpretation) without holy source information to back it up.

I told the magazine that with certainty the Tribulation start was more than a full decade off, and Mr. Camping was likely incorrect/false. Of course Mr. Camping was using the adjective certainty also. While if you give him the benefit of the doubt you then say, he meant well, in his own mind he truly felt this was what the Bible was predicting, and it is yet another caveat emptor (let the buyer beware) application, he was in fact selling information to the public in this regard. At the time I wasn't aware 'Family Radio' was Mr. Camping's radio station under his ownership. That explains why they refused to discuss the matter that I made heated contention over, and accused them of scamming the public on this matter. Wildman was ready to unload an earful on them, but the woman who answered cut the conversation short with a 'gotta go,' can't tie up this eight-hundred-line excuse, from verbal grenades barrage I was launching upon them. Carpet bagging; Christian radio, my ass! When they refuse to handle rejection and confrontation to their message that is a serious red flag.

I'm trying to tell them I have the real message from God truth, and they needed to cease and desist immediately, but it gave me the impression I had exposed the fact that for them it wasn't about message, it was only and all about the money. Perpetrator inside the law, slipping in-between the cracks alongside the criminal minded, and little I could do to put a stop to their scam (intentional or unintentional) and halt them from it. Consequence will be paid to the 89 year old Mr. Camping in afterlife. This type of offense is especially despicable in the eyes of God as explained by Dr. Lancy who you'll read about later in the book. According to Dr. Lancy, this is one of those go directly to hell, do not pass go, and there are no forgiveness get out of hell free cards issued. By Dr. Lancy's standards and interpretation, Mr. Camping is literally now as good as toast, having committed the same crime twice no less. Mr. Camping should have known better, perhaps not understanding or agreeing with Dr. Lancy on consequence, likely to find out firsthand just how excellent an Ordained Minister Dr. Lancy.

My anger with Mr. Camping is that he arrived at his conclusion by interpretation based then on mathematical calculation (from scripture). Who checked your math Harold? Oh, I see, no one, but you were only interested in the monetary return? They would not even accept challenge, and considering how angry I was, I actually kept my cool pretty well over the phone considering. You use that same math back when you were wrong in 1994, Harold? Why am I so angry? Because this sort of thing can cost American lives when the Tribulation does come. When I try to convince people of the danger, and they pass it off as my being just another Harold Camping/False predictor prophet, but then ignore my information, the loss of life could be quite extreme.

Yes, I have to charge for printing and distribution expense of this book, but am seeking neither the monetary return, or fame. I've already committed to many ministries and charities, and prefer to conceal my real life identity as much as possible, even though I have to tell my story much of the time in first person, I want my readers to place focus on Jesus Christ, and not on me. Don't focus on me, focus on my message which is focus on Christ! I am just an ordinary person like you, but one with some rare and extraordinary, spiritually relevant experiences to relate. I come back repetitively it might seem to some on certain points, but only because they are important points, deserving emphasis.

Defending my legitimacy and truthfulness/honesty of purpose, as well as the Christian theme, but it always relates back to serving what I perceive as God's purpose, and the winning of souls for faith in Jesus Christ, and the saving of lives through informative passing along of my Tribulation perceptions. There is no absolute certainty until afterwards, but no one can be reactive to Tribulation. You must be pro-active, and take advance evaluation measures regarding yourself. Not everyone will rapture with the rapture prior to Tribulation destructions. I believe (as explained later in the book) potentially a second rapture opportunity will be available some three and three quarters years later. The catch being, if you are already dead, you won't be around to receive a second chance opportunity. A mercy rapture of sorts. No-way a certainty, more like a strong probability possibility. Yet, for millions of people who do not rapture in the first rapture, it provides one precious commodity during Tribulation. The hope for a second rapture chance for spiritual salvation.

The point here being unless people take my advice seriously, then act upon it, then I'll have been unsuccessful at helping them first extend life by survival, to even have this second chance rapture eligibility, if in fact I am correct in evaluating scripture. (in match with the view Dr. Lancy gave in a sermon discussing rapture) My anger with Harold is that he is doing credibility damage to true prophets like myself. It is possible, perhaps likely there will be others who are genuine in the time remaining to emerge, or I might be alone. The scripture relating to sons and daughters prophesying may now be completed, as well; I have no indications specifically on that.

The profile of a true prophet:

1. Should have a background in experiencing one or more of the E.S.P. psychic gifts (from God)

2. Clearly of strong Christian faith Conviction/commitment
3. True prophecy will clarify or verify (or both) existing Book of Revelation information, other Bible books are closed to re-examination except for Book of Revelation tie-ins
4. Nothing new message delivery wise should contradict with pre-existing scripture, rather it should help to clarify it further if authentic
5. God's purpose for the prophet's receipt of the message delivery should be easily recognizable and apparent. Typically something to assist with bringing one to repentance through greater faith understandings, conversion to Christianity, or, deeper personal measure of understanding concerning Tribulation to then cause people to evaluate or re-evaluate their personal spiritual condition relative to their rapture situation. The timings presented by this book to allow people to put this then in perspective of time remaining in order to allow them the opportunity to get their spiritual relationship in order and in tune with God. They cannot be caught completely by surprise.
6. If you ask the question in application to prophecy said to be of holy source, newly received. Does it promote Christian values or faith in Christ? Is it a Christian relevant message? The answer would/should always be a clear, *Yes*. The Kingdom of heaven does not engage in unnecessary frivolous announcement or pronouncements. It must be something relevant and of importance to all humanity, not one segment generally speaking.
7. The saving of lives can be an indication of genuineness. Message does not necessarily require being related, but when it is, can be indication of genuine prophecy from holy source.

Typically non-genuine, but claimed False Prophet message will turn up a red flag indication of more than one of these upon examination. Motivation is not easily recognizable, but if fame or monetary gain seems primary, but the person is attempting to disguise such this can be an indicator. If you evaluate the message, is there anything separating it that puts it in contrast to Gospel/New Testament message? Definite red flag there. God never contradicts his own word already given.

For psychics, timing is the rare air, hardest to come by, most desired piece of awareness to present itself, but seldom issued beyond year only or year/month at most, unless it is exception to the rule and required for a specific perhaps personal revelation. For example, if the holy angel for some reason doesn't reveal a specific day/hour then it might then jeopardize a human life that could be an acceptable exception to the rule. In general timing information when received is not in week/ or day/ or hour terms. Often month not revealed even (unless need to know required) so when the Bible speaks of only God knowing the exact start timing of the Tribulation, this is in fact true. Awareness postulations made in this book are not presented as certainty, rather as discussion of factors and other relevant scripture. Same with Christ coming as a thief in the night, no one knowing the day or hour. True, because day/hour is rare even in psychic awareness terms as just described. My Armageddon confirm received, discussed later in this book as example: was year only. Both month of Armageddon, and month/year of the Rapture of the 144,000 were inclusive in this psychic dream also, but interpretation of symbolism was required to extract these deeper level messages additionally confirmation ally.

Nostradamus perhaps because of some Divine pre-ordained characteristic present, but to which never revealed to humanity, was so it seems an exception to many rules. Not only prolific in the number of predictions in total, but often having those deeper month, week, and day psychic/ future prediction insights so elusive most of the time. He has the missing puzzle pieces found nowhere else to many of the mystery situations surrounding certain aspects, and clarity of details relevant to Tribulation. I could not have made several very significant awareness break through without combining information of his, in relationship with mine. In world history, this is why, as will be discussed further, he is really two overall in my view in ranking. Number one reserved for John the Revelator, St. John, John of Patmos, however you may wish to describe him, is deserving of that ranking, and authoring perhaps one of the most, if not the most important Bible books (especially relevant in this present day). More on John of Patmos and Nostradamus in a minute, but let's get back to our false prophet discussion again for a minute.

Some people might feel empathy for Mr. Camping, or say, poor old guy, he was probably well intentioned. No, unscrupulously ill-intentioned is my take. If he runs a Christian radio station he ignored the Bible's restriction of speaking falsely and knowingly doing so. If you are not in receipt of information from holy source how can you be certain? He is guilty as sin, because there are no excuses, no exceptions to the rule and even running highway billboard ads, compounding the seriousness of the commission of the crime. If a genuine prophet doesn't have credibility, it neutralizes and negates everything they are trying to do in the carrying out of delivery of genuine prophecy awareness in service to God's purpose. The bottom line, if people then ignore warnings, lives get lost as end result because they didn't listen when they should have.

It gets exotic, too. T.V. Networks running series on Tribulation tossing information around like darts at a tavern dart board hoping some stick that are somewhere near the center of the truth, but having no clue themselves. Please, stick that up the Tribulation Botch category hole. Tribulation relates to God, awareness about Tribulation must come from God source, no exception or excuses there, either. Statements not derived from holy source constitute violation of scriptural/Bible law. Statements made otherwise put one at extreme spiritual afterlife jeopardy in punishment/peril terms. holy angel strict enforcement zone! Let me explain something here about this book and my own pronouncement on Tribulation. Were I not thoroughly convinced I was walking in a partnership with God so to speak, and felt that in fact I was a person sanctified and anointed under the Spirit of the holy Ghost specifically receiving holy angel sourced Tribulation awareness by and according to the will of God, then there is absolutely no way I'd consider speaking worldwide to the public the way I am doing in this book. No way would I receive virtually nothing in exchange for a one way ticket to hell for speaking falsely. I'm not doing this of my own accord, and it is exclusively by God's design apparently this destiny already in place with my birth, which is something not completely understood until most recently.

In fact, I debated whether to wait or proceed until after what I feel certain is holy Prophecy fulfills or whether to proceed in advance or not. It would be more comfortable for me to wait until further proof is evidenced, but I feel it is God's will that I proceed, and it is on that basis I do so. My assurances are as follows: (A) I have no doubt that my source is holy angel intermediary, having seen angel reveals at least twice, if not a third time conjunctive to all this; (B) My conclusions and awareness align with an ordained Dr. of Div. Minister, the angels even providing me with enhanced memory capabilities going all the way back to 1964 sermons I have no business remembering otherwise; (C) In over fifty years of psychic episodes, and scores of future predictions on general subject provided, none has ever failed to fulfill as provided. I have every reason and then some, to believe all holy source/subject prophecy now relating to future Tribulation period is correct and accurate, as well; and (D) My intuition (and indwelling holy anointed Spirit?) tells me to proceed rather than wait, perhaps more of an urgency that I make these awareness known than I realize even.

Fully I can understand skepticism, it's almost an embarrassment to be so honored by God with such a rare gift as one entrusted to deliver holy prophecy. I see the potential to save millions of lives, and also millions of souls by leading them to acceptance faith in Christ. Even awakening millions of Christians asleep in Christ as to proximity of the Tribulation. Wake up Christians, Wake up, that day is nearly upon us!

Although at times in this book, perhaps because of my attempts to keep some lively light hearted humor injected among the seriousness, it might give the impression of not being humbled, it in fact a bit ironic that I'm actually more humble than my writing might suggest, but yet use the 'Wildman' pen name.

Prophet vs. Holy Prophet

What is really true definition of holy Prophet? If you asked most people, especially clergymen the question: Was Nostradamus a holy prophet? Likely few would say yes, and even if asking the same question among professors of somewhat related subject disciplines such as Philosophy, or Psychology and others; a yes answer likely hard to come by. They would say the definition being something like: One who lived in Biblical times, and delivered messaged information from holy source, relating to holy subject that was fundamental in establishing Biblical accounts and/or description. Clarifications on holy subject, later compiled in Bible reference.

However, in my view as a prophet myself, and one receiving prophecy on holy subject from holy source, as well, this definition is incorrect. Not in total, but in part. One who lived in Biblical times what I'm referring to. Not only is it not valid in my case, even only a handful of my one hundred or so psychic prophecy episodes I'd define as relating to holy subject (End Times) yet, do qualify. Nostradamus with nearly eighty end times quatrains, clearly matches for Book of Revelation. With absolute certainty, I'm telling you not only will they fulfill, but will because they match the Bible, but just more elaborated upon. Still, it most definitely is holy subject, and new supplemental information on it Thus, both John of Patmos, and Nostradamus deriving holy source identical topic information, should both be considered holy Prophets. Nostradamus although elaborating much that is now of historical accuracy of non- religious subject, did in fact deliver holy subject (End Times) prophecy that although is yet to fulfill, then so is most of mine that is similar.

In essence, as the word Apocalypse means unveiling, so it seems as we approach Tribulation as I prophecy timeline in this book. So it appears that the Kingdom of heaven is delivering some last minute clarifications and further detail unveiling. The point being that the information does not need to be totally new, but could consist of better explanation of old and since the Biblical prophets are no longer around to deliver this. both Nostradamus, I, and others perhaps yet to speak out, will do so. I hope fulfillment of my Saints Covenant Prophecy will put to rest doubts of my legitimacy to describe myself being in receipt of holy prophecy, even though other awareness qualify, as well. That one will convince nearly all. So while not all of Nostradamus prophecy was holy subject, he should be considered one in receipt of holy prophecy, and thus, yes, Nostradamus was a prophet of holy subject/ holy prophet.

It should be kept in mind that the prophet is only an ordinary man in all cases of holy prophecy. The holy Prophet does in no way imply that the prophet is somehow holy, he is not. He is simply a Christian of faith entrusted to deliver the holy word. Only the word has holiness attached, the prophet more of a psychic trustee who also must sometimes interpret symbolism used in conveyance. The question, after receiving and interpreting, is then: What is God's purpose, and what is the intention?

In my case, it was clear, that my book (this book) was to be used to deliver these awareness, and clarifications, and timings to as many people as possible, worldwide. Convince others as to Tribulation threat, and reach out to deliver Christian message of spiritual salvation, as well as physical survival/ escape from death both in this dimension, as well as the afterlife. I hope to recruit a team of clergy to use this book as a new speaking platform to reach out from. Clergy are in the officers core, and I in the prophets core, and this is where they need to take command, take over these lifesaving messages, gladly surrendering complete control to them. One third of mankind is fated to perish in the soon to come destructions of the 2020 decade. I hope these clergy will give more credit to Nostradamus, as much of my awareness were confirmed through statements he made five hundred years ago. Much of the backbone of this book is derived from his awareness unequaled by anyone else except John of Patmos over 1,400 years prior. All end times prophecy now about to converge and fulfill. Sadly, even with clergy assistance, millions are certain to meet a violent and horrific death, the warnings unheeded.

What likely makes theologians and Bible scholars uncomfortable is the acceptance and proclaiming of anyone outside the Biblical Age as being a holy Prophet. Rather, they should realize, in doing so, they are questioning God's ability to do so, and thus placing restriction upon God. God cannot and should not ever be placed under restriction. Part of the problem stems from the difficulty in confirming holy Prophecy.

Yes, it is complicated, but I think I can shed some light toward better understanding. First, let's re-examine the how should holy Prophecy be defined. We know from the Miracle at Fatima 1914 timeframe of World War I, and more recently the Medjugorje/Mt. Podbrido apparition that this is clearly Divine interaction in the modern Age. Initially delivered externally to the three young girls in the Fatima case, rather than in the classic cerebral/psychic internal fashion. Aside from other examples in the Modern Age also, clearly the fence is knocked down on holy Prophecy delivery in the modern age. God cannot be restricted. So, the starting point is recognition that holy Prophecy in the modern Age is possible.

To make it more palatable for theologian and others not in acceptance of this, or easily swayed; let's reclassify similar to history and architecture. In this case, let's delineate three separate time periods. Biblical Age, Post Biblical, and twentieth and twenty-first century modern age. Thus the Biblical Prophets now have their own space that cannot be tampered with, long completed and self-contained. The Bible scholars and theologians feeling relieved already! They can now examine further comments without feeling uneasy.

Since God is the driving force behind holy Prophecy, and God is unrestricted, then so is potential for holy Prophecy during any time period unrestricted. Skeptics need to move beyond the misconception that there was no holy Prophecy beyond the Biblical period, or that it was ever restricted. None being delivered for long stretches different than saying it was because there was any sort of restriction. If it wasn't delivered for several centuries, it was because that was God's intent, and no other reason. He could have if he wanted to, but that wasn't part of his plan. He does so when he chooses to, but has that option at all times of doing so.

Go your way Daniel, for prophecy is sealed until the End Times what many will point to, except they can't clarify where End Times actually starts. In my three time period model, I described twentieth and twenty-first century as part of Modern Age; thus, 1914 and the 1990s clearly within it. Nostradamus lived Post Biblical Age, how could he then qualify as holy Prophet you ask Nostradamus' predictions were prolific, not all being holy Prophecy would be correct assessment. However, about eighty do reference 2020 decade forward and correlating John of Patmos in further confirmation. Some of my confirmations further confirming both these gentlemen, both holy Prophets!

It's a bit complicating and confusing, which is why I'm attempting to help clarify to you through my own perspective as psychic/prophet myself, on how to properly analyze as I see it, and these discussions hopefully will better enlighten you, assuming you are not precognitive psychic yourself. I'm sure I have the undivided attention of both Psychologists (even the agnostic ones and non-Christians), as well as theologian here, as well as others.

Some psychics possess clairvoyant, as well as precognitive capability. Most with E.S.P. have specialized ability limited to one, but occasionally two, but rarely more than two, yet occasionally some do. The remote viewers are generally clairvoyants who have honed their skills in what is commonly referred to as astral travel usually in some level of hypnotic or even dream state. Edgar Cayce used the hypnotic state to essentially do what R.V.r's do, while Nostradamus, also clearly clairvoyant would perhaps in relaxed awake state, scry, or delve in a bowl of liquid dangling from a tri-pod. It is in all cases reaching out to retrieve information. How much Holy Spirit was involved within them at the time, and how much external cannot be determined, but angels or spirit guides I personally believe are involved in almost all psychic episode where information conveyance is involved. As humans we are all recipients of inputs and at times intuitions, even those not considered psychic, it is just done on such a stealthy silent cerebral stairway, we never are aware in the vast majority of inputs.

I'm mentioning the scrying or delving aspect, where the subject is the origination point. Seldom will future prediction then be holy Prophecy, because by definition typically it comes unannounced, unexpected, with God at the origination point rather than the psychic pre-meditating focus topic and so you would think it impossible then for holy Prophecy to ever be derived in this way. Not so fast though. In Nostradamus' case, events that were well into the future he would have had no way of pre-focusing in on and often visions received nearly exceeded his comprehension to interpret with inventions far ahead of his time. You have to examine each psychic individually before any conclusions can be drawn. You need to realize one of the key points defining holy prophecy is: Was God at origination point and does prophecy reception in some way direct toward serving God's purpose?

While personally I believe God was involved in total with Nostradamus, not all Nostradamus predictions are holy Prophecy. The eighty or so End Times ones clearly so. Regardless of God as originator, or in Edgar Cayce's hypnotic trance state information retrieval, clearly holy angel involved in all such psychic transactions. You could think of the angels as the holy records paralegals, going to the library to research for the prophet with God's approval. However, information retrieved does still not constitute holy Prophecy in most cases, but still may serve God's purpose. As I'll explain in a minute, it gets a bit less distinguishable sometimes. While much of Nostradamus qualifies as accurate future prediction, it is perhaps serving God's purpose in general terms. Individually although fulfilling as predicted, not holy Prophecy. But, look at it collectively, and one could still argue divine purpose or intent might have been simply to assert evidence to humanity a reminder that they live in a controlled environment under God's all seeing, all knowing, dictates. Holy Prophecy often does upon fulfillment deliver dual meaning. In this case many somewhat pedestrian predictions, still when examined as to the prolific quantity, and magnitude, evidence of the larger picture. God's existence, and human involvement presence. Nostradamus predictions that are extensive and encompass many centuries, God's presence extensive and encompassing many centuries, clearly evidencing himself the larger, and important dual purpose meaning. If you deliver even one holy Prophecy it still qualifies as such.

Another borderline example was the Dutch psychic J. Van Der Hyde. In that case a premonition just before the assassination attempt on then Pope John Paul II, and this prior awareness well documented. Does this qualify as holy prophecy? Skeptics would argue that Pope John Paul II although holy Father Pontiff of the Vatican, is still a mortal, and that certainly tied to the church rather importantly, is separate from holy Bible, and even church doctrines and canons, and thus this would not then be holy Prophecy, arguing that this would be stretching the holy Prophecy boundaries.

My counter argument would be thus: All premonition are holy angel delivered, one hundred percent accuracy, certainty of fulfillment guaranteed. Kingdom of heaven origin, God's purpose involvement, and in this case, what could be described as a clear case of Divine intervention. The prophecy was the premonition, the holy part, the Divine intervention attempted. In my mind it had holy origin, delivered to carry out holy end purpose, and is definitely in my mind, holy Prophecy. The misconception being that it must resemble Biblical Age prophecy relating to prophecy similar to those. Well, there you go restricting God again! Religious tie in to event then, rather than religious laws, still constitutes holy Prophecy, if it clearly is holy source originated, and serving an end purpose of God, having been in receipt of both simple prophecy and holy Prophecy myself.

Points made so far: Holy Prophecy can and especially in End Times is likely to center on, (as mine were) on further clarification of seven-year Tribulation topic specifics. New information better describing old subject rather than new subject. Still I am certain, no question God is using the psychic abilities he has given me, as a Christian trustee advocate of holy trinity and Jesus Christ's soon return, to through this book serve his purpose. I am certain it is holy source derived, and genuine.

It is by no coincidence as explained prior, all major psychics all through history were of true Christian faith. God nor his angels will work with one who is not. Certainly an honor to be so entrusted, but a humbling experience at the same time when you realize the enormity of the responsibility placed upon you. As a psychic, you don't start out with anything too overwhelming, but at the advanced level, you learn firsthand where the term holy Smoke must have originated. An in color scripted (alphabetically worded) awake prophecy lettered vision suddenly appearing before my eyes out of thin air after the holy angel appearance, it literally had like mist rising up from it, or smoke, and almost like a paint running uphill effect to it. holy smokes Charlie Brown, this is for real holy Prophecy! Hopefully, fulfillment occuring in 2014, that can be elaborated in Part II.

Spiritual applications for Part I Metaphysical Section will carry forward to the start of Part II. (Chapters 20, 21, 22) Anyone doubting Nostradamus worthiness to qualify for being labeled a Post Biblical Age Holy Prophecy subject Prophet for the 10% or so of his total prediction that do in fact relate to the Tribulation soon to fulfill next decade will have those doubts disqualified instead. I will explain how God is not only now confirming timings to those 500 year old predictions, through celestial signal Solar and Lunar Eclipses, (2014/2015) when correctly interpreted, but adding in three levels of new message confirmational conveyances using symbolism very common to Holy prophecy. Obviously if Nostradamus carries such valid stature to God, then I ask you Reverand, how is it again you believe your opinion supercedes God's supremely extreme esteem higher court opinion directive to which he is acting upon? To invalidate Nostradamus here is tatamount to invalidating God! Step off of God's toes and back away slowly, you have the right to remain silent Reverand, what you say can and will be used against in Holy Angel witness! (Joking a bit to make my point)

So, Nostradamus, at least in my opinion, at least in part, should be recognized as holy Prophet, likely even some of his awareness delivered although not holy Prophecy at the surface level, in dual purpose still even in these serving God's greater purpose, and the holy Prophecy 80 or so prophecies, although delivered five hundred years ago now coming into greater confirmation through new ones to which I was recipient. The focus should be on is it God driven (obviously not always easy to determine)? Next if God is source, then the prophecy is likely a tool that is used to get to the end purpose result that God has in mind as end goal. This is at the core of what really defines holy Prophecy, and in any timeframe period. The same criteria can be applied to what the Biblical Prophets received.

A summation on the following points:

1. Since the Biblical Age prophets and time of Christ's crucifixion, all subsequent prophets to receive prophecy with holy subject tie-ins are devout Christian believers of Christian faith, both Catholic and Protestant. A pre-requisite in order for holy angel to interact with you.
2. A good term to describe these post Biblical Age prophets who do receive such prophecy with holy subject link, are perhaps best described as a class of Clarifying, and verifying prophets. At least a dozen or more since the Biblical Age. In virtually all cases, each receiving a few pieces of the Tribulation period puzzle, to then further clarify, and in so doing, further verify validity of Book of Revelation. itself. Re-verifying Book of Revelation amounts to reconfirming Christ's second Coming. (Contradicting certain other religions beliefs in so doing) In total the Christian faith is re-verified then, as well as certain Tribulation aspects further clarified, and continuing to do this, century after century, brings continued better awareness of Tribulation, but ever continuing re-confirmation of the Bible's validity, as well.
3. Only a small percentage of a prophet's total predictive prophecy is likely to touch on holy subject (10 percent or less typically). This can be differentiated between future fulfilling prophecy, and simply awareness given, but regarding future Tribulation timeframe. The prophet himself is in no way holy. Simply instead, one entrusted to pass along important information from holy source as it relates to holy subject. I will be the first to tell you that the prophet is ordinary before, during, and afterwards other than the prophet's faith desiring to fly off to be with God as aftereffect (Anointing apparently a powerful rocket fuel propellant!). Even a single prophecy on holy subject from a credible psychic does qualify one potentially as a clarifying/verifying class of prophet. Tribulation subject being the common theme among all such class prophets.
4. Most important of all, realize with certainty, John of Patmos, was the greatest Prophet of all time, Nostradamus second. Tribulation will fulfill, exactly as written, and my book you are reading right now will in later chapter, fill you in on further clarifying and verifying event and timing details. There is only one religion supreme and genuine in total and with absolute complete certainty.

Now you might say Christ was a prophet, too, wouldn't he be considered the greatest prophet who ever lived? The answer is yes, and no. He was certainly the greatest man/God (Emmanuel- the holy One who walks among us) who ever lived, and the only one who ever will do so. He wins hands down there, not a single challenger, and no one to even come close a sort of proof in itself to that honor and glory. With no challengers, there can be, and shouldn't be any disputing it. No one even a distant second, no one period.

Since his arrival was predicted more than once by earlier Old Testament prophets who not only predicted and then described this Savior's arrival, but precise circumstances connective to it so that it might be correctly recognized and identified once it occurred. Only Christ did in fact validate himself as promised Messiah by in future timeframe being the one to fulfill the prophecy by the previously set guideline description of these foretold 'Messiah to come prophecy,' matching not one prophecy in this regard, but several. and in compliance terms to all of them. In doing so, confirming himself indisputably as the true Messiah for all humanity to recognize. Unfortunately after two thousand years, much of world humanity is ignorant of the Gospel, in denial, or in very weak and insincere acceptance. A mistakenly large segment of the total body for Christ worldwide in acceptance only in mind, but not deeply or genuinely in heart. Too many professing to be Christians, but only lukewarm in their personal dedication belief, neither exiting the Christian church/faith, but neither closer and stronger in their faith over time. It is for this single reason, when the time comes to rapture along with devout Christians, they instead will perish. Caught up too much in this material temporal world of existence. At no time during that entire two thousand years was Jesus Christ not the Savior of humanity for each and every individual He is today, no different than as he was then. However, you as an individual must hunger and thirst for true faith, and once receiving it, keep it well-nourished that it, (faith) might experience growth within you and continue to flourish rather than stagnate or wither. (more on this in the last chapter and in the Supplement section) Be a total believer.

Let me as a psychic/prophet myself explain these prophecies do in fact originate, and are delivered through the Kingdom of heaven holy Ghost in Christ, Holy Spirit (Third Trinity aspect) or typically conveyance through holy angel, often Gabriel who seems to specialize in this, particularly of the most important ones. holy angels are real, and as subordinate associates of the Holy Trinity itself, further proof of the validity of the Holy Trinity itself. The Bible itself totally correct if anyone doubts it after scientists have tried to run Book of Genesis through the chipper-shredder doubt mill to then undermine the Bible. Don't believe it, don't be led astray as the Bible itself forewarns you, as doubt will undermine Christian faith faster than strong chemical acid dissolving soft compounds.

The Judeo-Christian faith, be you a Jew or a gentile, I promise you, is the only totally correct place to place your faith. Faith healings are prime example of the legitimacy and validity itself. No other religion does this period, never mind on a widespread, worldwide frequent basis. That is additional proof beyond the proofs I bring you through this book.

Admittedly I've strayed a bit from the major prophet course of this topic discussion, but hopefully with elaborations you will deem of worthy content value as to what was commented. Yes, we are in the Psychic Section of the book, but one of this book's objectives, is to prove to you that a very strong linkage is in place between the Kingdom of heaven, and the human mind E.S.P. psychic realm of the human mind, heavily holy angel interactions influences as Spirit guide intermediaries assisting humans who have such God-given gifts, to utilize such gifts for the benefit and betterment of humanity When you drive down a road and you see construction barricades that say: Caution, construction ahead, men working, or improvement in progress. Here it's E.S.P. prediction/fulfillment ahead holy angels Working, and Awareness from God in Progress. Kingdom of heaven Construction Co., with Prophets subcontracting as mediums to get the informational awareness transfer accomplished in service to God's purpose. Message sent from holy side, message received from one so ordained to do so Anointing comes in several forms, and when God gives a human the gift of prophecy, it is to serve God's purpose, and foremost even before whatever individual psychic messaging transmission might occur, it is to witness for, and exalt Jesus Christ as Lord and Savior. So you see, I'm under obligation directly from God to perpetually revisit this mention (A word from our sponsor, whom I have to strictly observe as my Senior and Contributing Editor of this book who saved my life numerous time that I might be here to author it.).

When John of Patmos received account of Book of Revelation, it was in fact Jesus Christ resurrected who identified himself as the delivery source and John of Patmos writing down every word in transcript receipt. It was John who was the Prophet, Christ the Senior and Contributing Editor.

A Prophet in receipt of holy prophecy has to be a human almost by definition (other than Christ) so that the human can act as a human intermediary in prophetic awareness or prophecy to other humans, as to interpretively relate such message as God intends it, but as is to be properly received and understood by humanity as a whole first, that whole comprised then of individuals.

Christ it is true was while still alive a prophet foreteller of many future fulfillment prediction including his own denial and betrayal, and coming crucifixion, Yet he knew also it was as God the Father so willed in completion of the purpose of washing the sins of the world through the establishment of salvation there-in through the shedding of Christ's blood at Calvary. He being holy, had to fulfill his own destiny foretold prediction, because once holy prophecy is delivered, it must always come to fulfillment because it is in essence a promise from God to do so. A promise from God cannot, will not, and has never been broken. Why also fulfillment of Book of Revelation is a certainty to fulfill, because it, too, represents a promise from God it one day will. God delivering to me through this book as a message vehicle, when that is going to happen through confirmation prophecy awareness received as of 2008/2009. You are now living in the last uninterrupted full decade prior to that decade when what was promised to John of Patmos by Christ fulfills, and if you judge the validity here of what I'm telling you by the angel reveals presented and witnessed at that 2008/2009 timeframe, that passed truth verification exams, you should probably file it under stronger than and beyond certainty, the same place I filed it in my mind. Double definite if there is such a thing. Yes, you have God's word on it, too, if that cake needs additional icing/convincing for you, something I would not say unless it was lock down solid certainty to fulfill as the angels delivered awareness so regarding this. Confirmation spot on, and no denying it, with multiple awareness indication each in confirmation of the other. heaven sourced thick icing on that confirmation of Tribulation cake. John of Patmos garnering top honors as the prophet in delivery originator/ receiver of this prophecy sourced through Jesus Christ.

You have to exclude Christ from this prophets comparison, for having 'unfair competitive advantage,' and already exceeding in greatness and glory, as King of Kings, Lord of Lords. and I think he would want John to have that trophy distinction as top Major Prophet of the post Biblical Age, even though it was included as the final Bible Book in testimony from Christ beyond the grave having risen victorious over death. It is the future this world is now nearing being described almost two thousand years ago as to exactly what will unfold. My recent awareness in undeniable confirmation as to the accuracy of Book of Revelation statements to the very minutest detail as correct, but then the entire Book of Revelation in total by so doing also. I ask you, how else is such possible except through validity of Christian faith beliefs themselves? Almighty God once again confirming correctness of Christian Holy Trinity concept.

No one disputes the collective greatness of the Biblical Prophets, at least not among Christian faithful. Some Prophets Major, like Isaiah or Daniel, and others Minor, like Micah or Joel. Yet this is only in the quantitative sense, as every single prophecy or awareness delivered from holy source is a treasure priceless in value. All prophecy then even from a Minor Prophet is equally major. (of major importance)

In Corinthians 12:11 we are told every saved person is given at least one 'Anointing Gift,' some potentially more than one, but according to God's will, and plan for their lives. Now no one disputes that people become born again saved

Christians at different age time points within their lives. This must be condition already in place prior to receiving activation of their anointing gift. The gift is there, likely already in place prior to the persons' birth. This is why in the Supplement Section (Part II) in discussing Saved and Anointed, I do not lump the two together. They eventually do merge, very true, but often the Saved part is active, while the anointing part is latently inactivated. There, but not yet activated, and only the Holy Spirit doing the activating, and according to God's timing/interaction with that person when the time arrives, and often so subtly done the person only gradually gains understanding awareness there afterwards, as it develops or manifests itself.

So Isaiah then already prophecy assigned and scheduled timing wise before his birth through pre-ordained destiny. It appears this is true of all Prophets to ever receive prophecy holy in nature. Divine destiny.

This being consistent with my own set of circumstances and similar destiny situation in place described in more detail elsewhere in this book. Thus a sort of mold for prophecy destiny becoming apparent uniformity throughout human history during the past three thousand years! It means that likely those receiving other God given gift follow similar destiny patterns of their own, relative to that particular gift that God so preordained before their birth also, but not activated until appropriate timing, purpose, and plan God has for their life.

God's Annointing Gifts

The Prophecy gift is described in several Bible scripture, and by listing it here in the Psych/ Parapsychology section, it confirms the macro linkage to the spiritual realm, which is a point that I am attempting to prove throughout this book. The supernatural is the realm of God, end of story. Amen?

Romans 12: 6,7,8 listing the 7 gifts:

1. Prophecy
2. Ministry
3. Teaching
4. Exhortation - witness so as to touch the heart of other so as to strengthen or bring them to faith
5. Giving - opportunity of all to charity
6. Ruling - administrative ability
7. Mercy with cheerfulness - love, caring, kindness, and helpful and hopefulness toward the needy

Ephesians 4:11

1. Apostles
2. Prophets - both foretellers (prediction) and forth teller sharing of awareness of future condition with others.
3. Evangelists - spreading the Gospel worldwide
4. Pastors and Teachers - shepherd the sheep, training the saints

Corinthians 12: 3–10 manifestations of the Holy Spirit

1. Speaking words of Christian knowledge and wisdoms in advocacy of faith
2. Gifts of healing and the working of miracles
3. Prophecy forth telling and foretelling
4. Discerning true prophets from false
5. Speaking in tongues and then interpretations by some (A language of angelic angel is said to exist, and beside speaking in a foreign language of Earthly nature, tongues can be of this ethereal language of angelic praise to God.)

You can see Prophecy is prominent in all three listings. It is God chosen means/method of communication with humans, and I can confirm it generally is done silently, telepathically, or through conveyance in premonition terms in describing event, but not limited to one form, and dreams, and psychic visions awake, either separately or in combination can take place. Reception and interpretation of message is all that is required of the Prophet. But where witnessing to the public at large is God's intended purpose, then the Prophet is obligated to carry this out. This book is an example of God intending that these awareness be spoken in witness to the worldwide public at large. Tribulation no doubt a clear and present danger looming large just beyond the next decade horizon, Christian faithful privileged to early warning. Praise the Lord, mercifully desiring to save lives and souls, and that a fit for his mold of love, as well.

Chapter 15
Describing My Own Personal Psychic Experience
A Discussion of Precognitive Psychic Nomenclature and Relating Some Prior Premonitions

The problem getting new terminology accepted, new para-psychic experiences acknowledged by the Academic community is that they don't have these experiences themselves. There is no way to clinically prove or verify, except perhaps to see if similar cases are reported from other sources. The existing terms are good, definitely valid, but in some cases used and abused as catch-all terms.

I'm not saying I have all the answers, just that I see room for vocabulary expansion, and that this would represent improvement and advancement. Can you imagine if since the eighteenth century nothing had changed with medical terminology. No matter what you had it must be a case of consumption. What if archeologists did that. Here's a new dinosaur bone. What is it? I don't know, it doesn't match any of the others, better throw it away!

Over there in the Twilight Zone is the Zonian jungle, and the pre-cognitive Mt. range. These mountains are laced with caves and caverns. Academia doesn't know this apparently, but some are yet unexplored and yet unnamed. Wildman here has explored many of them, and since Academia hasn't been in these caves themselves, or cutting vines with their psychic machete's through the Zonian jungle like Wildman has, maybe some of the para-psychic artifacts I've brought back, under further scrutiny by Academia will be of value. I should tell you also some of these caves are interconnected.

Maybe convene a committee to figure out which committee to convene for a panel to review new nomenclature. That's if any of these artifacts do in fact have merit. Re-name them, reorganize, do whatever you like, that's your part, mine was the initial discovery. Just don't set up the chairs for the committee in a circle. Apparently that's part of the problem. Dog chasing its tail round and round, meeting gets adjourned with no changes made, and the committee contracts consumption.

You guys purchased those ground breaking shovels what, fifty years ago and those shiny shovels are still in the box! Never been used. Well, here's your chance to dirty those shovels, get them dirty, make some progress, and don't throw these artifacts in with the dinosaur bones the archeologists discarded. Well what are you waiting for, Armageddon? Yes? Well actually I pulled it out of one of those caves, too, and stuck it in Chapter 27. Handle that one lightly, or all this nomenclature business will hardly matter.

Seriously, any offense was for the purpose of humor, I apologize for the stepped on toes. In reality you very much do command my respect and truly hope some of this information will be considered of merit. I came up with a one page diagram that at least in my forty-five years of pre-cognitive experience covers explanation of all events and circumstances. Wouldn't you know that a former Residential Building Contractor would use the analogy of a street and houses, which actually work well! It helps to give a total perspective, too.

Each house a different psychic realm, perhaps the abode of those matching experiences. fate and destiny like two ghosts unseen moving in and out of all the houses along this street. One side of this street is the personal side, and the other the Divine. Unless you recognize that God is involved on both sides of this street, you will never fully understand what goes on here. Think of a person who pulls up in their car at a drive-up ATM of their bank. They conduct a monetary transaction then drive off. In similar fashion a psychic transacts with a spiritual angel or guide, however you prefer to call it. When I first began having these occurrences, I suspected, but could not confirm it. That is no longer the case, I know this for certain now. You are certain you are receiving money from your ATM, and just as certain am I. I am transacting or interacting with angels, agents of God. No doubt whatsoever!

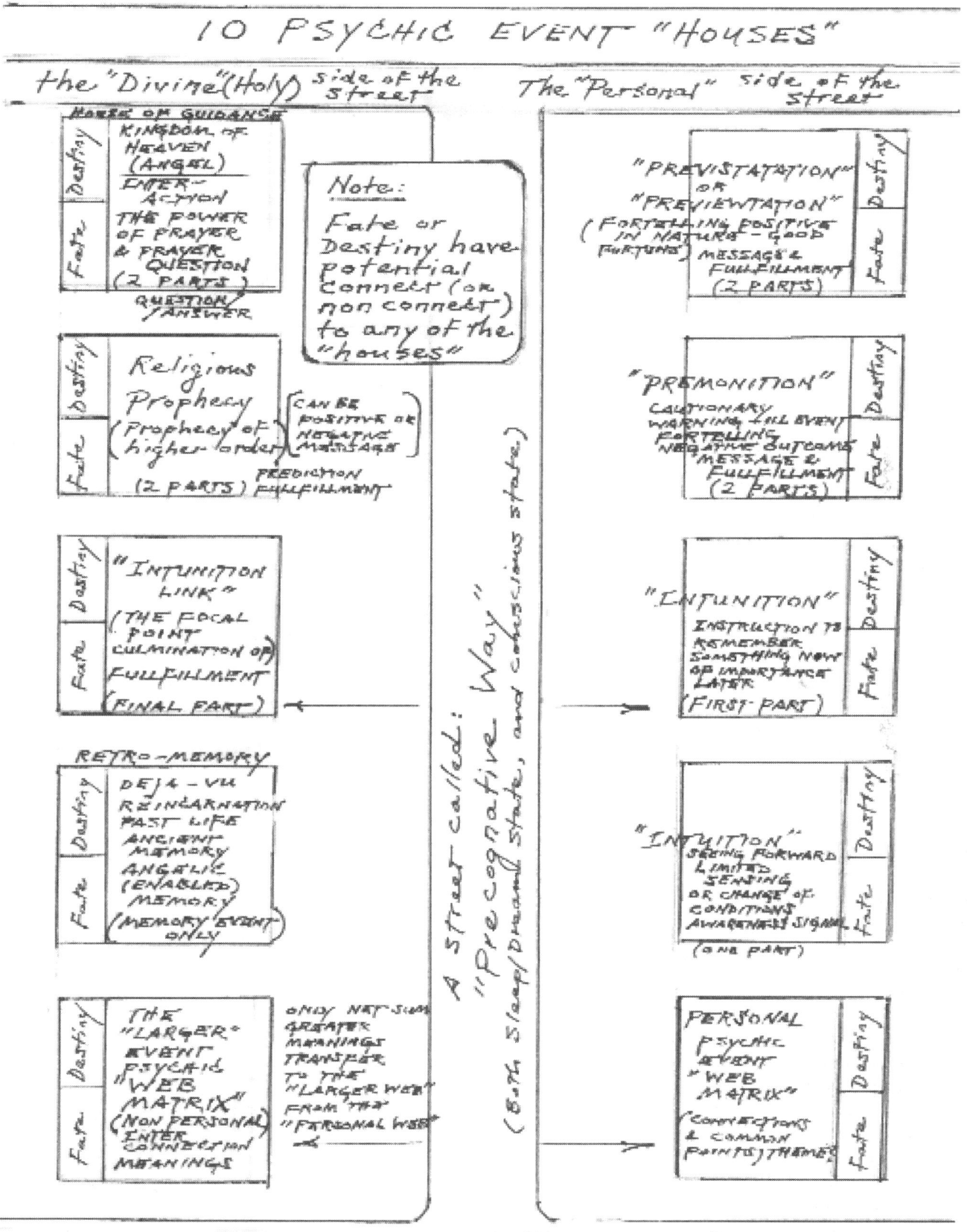

Now when you look at this diagram, the two lower boxes are like the sum totals to columns of addition. The sum totals of all psychic events occurring in the above houses. Think of each psychic event as a strand in a spider's web (the psychic person) These event webs of crisscrossing psychic experiences intersect as common points. I've discovered that all my premonitions have common intersection points of at least one (sometimes more) with other premonition or other psychic experiences. I have one personal event web matrix on the right, and a second event web matrix under construction bottom left. The one right, all psychic experience personal in nature, while the one left is only to do with horizons greater than my own, affecting the general population such as my readers of this book, but humanity as a whole.

Examining the Personal side of the street first (right side) you are well familiar with Intuition and Premonition. I'll come back to premonition later. Within the house of Intuition, I've noticed that I sometimes have a particular type of intuition (sub-category?). It is a mechanism whereby you sense conditional changes within your reality. It always has to do with conditions. You perhaps sense a traffic jam ahead while driving that's just occurred, or a new ordinance that says you can no longer walk a dog on the sidewalk. It's sunny now, but you sense it's about to change. Always altered conditions sensed that are applicable to current reality. There are probably several sub-categories beneath Intuition that a majority of Intuitions could fall within, this is one that is common for me.

On the diagram, across the street from Intuition is the House of retro-memory. They never look out the front of that house, only the back. Dejavu, Re-incarnation past life memory, ancient memory, and angelic enhanced memory. Here, I believe I have some ancient memory, as my ancient roots trace back to Atlantis, similar to Edgar Cayce who was also quite sure of that. Author Frank Joseph who I think did a superb job with his book Survivors of Atlantis, and has me buying into his evidence for four cataclysms because he's done a very convincing hypothesis for each. Migrations helped to prove his case with each of these. However, something inside me refuses to let go of the idea of an even earlier cataclysm around 6,000 to 8,000 B.C.; 7,500 B.C. maybe. Little evidence because of lack of migration except to remaining areas of Atlantis. I do think this is some ancient memory, possibly anyway.

Angelic enhanced memory? Suddenly, as I write this book it's like no matter how far back it is, if it pertains to this book, I have nearly full recall. Church sermon from 1964? No problem. Something that happened last week, not to do with this book, - total blank. You see why this category (house) had to go on the divine side of the street.

At the top of the chart on the personal side of the street is a House with a term yet decided. Previstatation, Preview-tation, something along those lines maybe. The word premonition gets abused, if there's someone familiar with premonition, it's Wildman. However, premonition (pre and monition) means pre cautioned or pre-warned of a future event. A degree of negative aspect included. The abuse of the term is when something more positive is sensed. For example a wedding or a birth, promotion at work with pay raise, winning a contest or award, all positives, yet often referred to as premonition. I say keep premonition when there is slight negative aspect, and create a new designation for happy, joyous occasion foretold. What? Are you guys afraid of getting your shovels dirty, because if you think you are getting out of this chapter with those shiny shovels, forget about it!

Clairvoyance, Pre-cognitive, and E.S.P. are all terms for the macro category, you need to come up with a new term for a positively expected psychic event that is similar in nature to premonition so that distinction can be made.

Below Premonition on that personal side of the street is another invented word: Intunition. I was looking for a word in between Intuition and Premonition, so Intunition fit. Call it whatever you like. There have been four of these instances in my life, and each time it was an occurrence somewhat similar to premonition yet very markedly different. It was like my guardian angel telling me (all be it silently), *Remember this, you'll need it later on in life*. That was it each time, that instruction. It can't be called premonition because no future event is foretold. Just angel Instructions, my angel providing Intunition. In this case guide even more appropriate perhaps than angel, and spiritual guidance certainly a defining characteristic. Across the street is the Intunition culmination point. Here you realize the link between all four occurrences. In my case, it was this book, starting way back in 1964, in church on Sunday and an angel is telling me to remember this sermon; you will need it later in life. I'm about 16, and the angel mentioned it wouldn't be until I was 60! Here are the 4 events, dates that they occurred, and all relate to this book.

1. 1964 Dr. Lancy's Sunday sermon (Dr. Lancy mentioned more in several chapters on religion)
2. 1980 Valerie tells of local psychic and ghost phenomenon
3. 1988 T.V. show about the Bible and U.F.O.
4. 1991 (approximately) another author's book –The South Florida U.F.O. Infestation

Now that I've talked on some of the potential new psychic experience terms, there is still some description of my own premonitions to mention. Some occur while conscious, others in dreams. There are several Bible passages about God speaking to men through dreams and visions. You will recall in talking about the spider's (my) web matrixes have either a personal or spiritual web theme. Spiritual meaning both derived from God, but with a theme directed toward the general population of humanity.

So currently I have not one, but two matrix web themes going at once. It appears that this book and its value information wise to others, clearly the theme. It was really only after accumulating extensive enough quantity of psychic thread that this analysis is possible.

The premonitions I will tell you about in a little bit, both occurred while listening to the radio that was in both cases at the moment the premonition occurred, talking on the radio about the very person my angel is telling me I'm one day going to meet! There are so many similarities between these that I call them the Parallel Premonitions. Another premonition occurred while listening to the radio, and probably a couple more. One with the T.V. on, which makes one wonder if frequency or something isn't in some way connected.

I have never received a premonition that did not fulfill. To my way of thinking, what Native American Indians describe as Omens, are in fact a kind of subcategory under premonition. The difference in an Omen and a regular or standard in your sleep premonition dream is that there is more symbolism, usually the relationship between yourself the dreamer, and elements like Earth, fire, air (wind) or water, and often includes one or more animals. A depiction is made often like a very short story. From this symbolism a message is delivered that must be interpreted. The last Omen I had was not in color, but more like Antique brown as if the short depiction was an aging old, early twentieth-century movie.

Wildman even picking up on shamanistic Indian stations on his psychic signal antenna. Many Indians very in touch with the spirit world, and you are only a Chaman when the spirit world tells you that you are, not when you simply claim you are. I became a mystic in 1970, actually probably 1968, but didn't become a Chaman until the other side recognized me as one. This wasn't until 2005. Full Twilight Zone citizenship!

With premonitions there is always a profound moment when the event occurs, and often when the event fulfills, but not always on that end. Sometimes you simply have awareness that the prior premonition is no longer pending. There can be varied degree of certainty on the event side, as to exactly what is being presented to you, yet you know the feeling of having the event, so regardless of how clear it is as to what you should expect up ahead, you know it eventually will, and it at that point earlier awareness always makes perfect sense.

In the upper left house on the Divine side of the street is the Kingdom of heaven house from where all wisdom stems. Through prayer, anyone can interact here. Divine Guidance? Found right there when you interact through prayer, and psychic ability not required. What is important is that you should always try to relax first, get in touch with your inner self, meditate on what it is you plan to ask, and humble yourself as totally as you possibly can. Respect is imperative. Questions can be asked that should be answered by either a *yes* or *no* answer. It is said maybe a third possible answer; I don't know.

It is important to note that anyone, even someone such as myself including those who might have been recipient of multiple bona-fide genuine Holy subject prophecy messages as intermediary mediums are not exempt and still vulnerable to (II Corinth. 11:14) interference interception of reception message communication by the "Great Deceiver" masquerading as an Angel of Light. The key is whether initial contact with the Holyside is initiated on their part to the human medium, or whether the medium attempt to contact the Holyside initiating the episode, such as with a prayer question. (More discussion regarding this in part II) The human initiating the contact leaves vulnerability exposure possibility, even when non Holy subject general topic focus is concerned. Religious Prophecy the last house to describe on that side of the street. Like a premonition, it, too, has two parts, event, awareness fortelling and fulfillment.

Now that my diagram is explained, what houses are on Precognitive Way by my version anyway, are over there in Psychic Estates, or is it psychic states? All premonitions have fulfilled, therefore all are one hundred percent bona fide. I'll give you a look and describe the Parallel Premonition for you. First explain each half, then the many similarities. Then some other ones, as well. After that I'll talk about something called wild dreams, and dream retrieval, or dream catch.

Premonition (Case 1)
The Foretelling of The First Girl (J.S.) From the Parallel Premonitions

It was 1981, and I was driving my truck on the road I commonly refer to in this book as the Psychic Trail. A year earlier, J.S.'s mother had died in a tragic plane crash in the Bermuda Triangle on Fourth of July weekend that killed all twenty-plus passengers and crew aboard. That event front page news, and fresh in the minds of all in the County still.

As I am now listening to the radio, they are giving an account of this woman's daughter being involved in a DUI fatality traffic accident that was her fault, and nearly killing her, as well. There was a question of whether she should be tried as a minor (age 17), or as an adult.

Then the premonition! You will later meet this girl several years from now. That was it. Interestingly, too, besides the psychic matrix that was later to evolve, a reality physical connect also. The road this accident occurred on, intersects the psychic trail just south of where I was when I heard this radio report, and had the premonition! With the other girl, other half of the Parallel Premonition, very much the same thing. I was stopped in a gas station along the psychic trail, again near the spot being talked about on the radio as the scene of a tragic fatality connected to that girl, which was the airport. The airport being a common psychic matrix intersection point to both! Then a nearly identical premonition delivered there, as well!

With the premonition for J.S. came the dark cloud thunderstorm funnel cloud and lightning vision. This girl would be bad news, and failing to heed this warning, by 1993 when I was introduced to her, she became my girlfriend and was living with me, black probation ankle bracelet and all.

Then having violated her probation, one night two armed deputies and five probation officers (two women and three men) arrived at my house to arrest Wildman's 'tornado' girlfriend in her bathrobe. (brave of them only bringing seven being badly outnumbered) A tornado handcuffed and taken away in her bathrobe. A five-year term in a women's correctional facility, but for being a well-behaved tornado, out in three years and a few months! Her return marked the real devastation that followed.

Premonition (Case 2)
The Foretelling of The Second Girl (C.H.) From the Parallel Premonitions

I've already mentioned from the first account, how I was once again on the psychic trail, and listening to the radio. This time near the airport. They were talking about a beauty contest winner (1984) who's high school boyfriend now estranged had drawn a revolver on C.H.'s new boyfriend who was an airplane mechanic at the airport. There was a struggle, the gun fired, and the high school boyfriend had died. Then the premonition almost identical to the previous one.

You will later meet this girl several years from now. There was no accompanying vision this time. If it had been, it would have had to have been that of a category five Hurricane, but it must have stumped my guardian angel as to either how to depict, or how to fit on my psychic radar vision screen. None the less, that is what C.H. turned out to be. Yes, Wildman only dates named storms, no tropical depressions!

Ten years later, a (friend?) introduces me to C.H. Married to an older attorney/Retirement Rental Community developer, now with two children, he suddenly divorces her. She had the children in the car, become too intoxicated to drive, and sideswiped several cars. The husband now possessing several lawsuits. After placing her in a mental institution, he then had divorced her while she was there, and in her words, kicked her to the curb. Maybe the same one those five damaged cars were parked along.

She was now a building strength Hurricane I had somehow adopted. Did I learn my lesson from the first time? No, actually most of the Tornado girlfriend damage was yet to come. This was during the period that J.S., tornado girlfriend was incarcerated. I had moved up to a 1st place beauty contest winning Hurricane!

I've never in twenty-six years at this location had windows blown out from a real hurricane, whereas this two legged one managed to smash two within a very short time span. The damage list is long, trust me, and when hurricane girlfriend blew out of my life, it wasn't long before J.S. the tornado blew back in. You've heard of hurricanes spawning tornadoes before right? The tornado came back to finish me off. My guardian angel a heck of a weather man. Issuing warnings twelve and ten years ahead!

Realize, at the time, I thought to myself, *How bad could these women really be?* I mean there is trouble spelled in small letters, and there is trouble spelled in caps and exclamation mark. As it later turned out, it was the caps and exclamation mark variety. An underline missed in interpretation? No, I received what was forewarned advertised twelve and ten years earlier, but then you see an all seeing and knowing God knew I'd get drawn in like a moth to a flame, and get burned, as well! But you see, now looking back, only by doing this, getting drawn into further examination would I be aware of the outcome. Had I avoided them, I'd never have known how things might turn out, and a valuable lesson learned, would not have been learned. That lesson, when holy angel forewarned you of something, no matter what it is, take heed! Take heed! It was part of my psychic training.

Now, with pieces of my life (like the entire town) and debris, wreckage, and damages of all kinds years later still hanging from the trees, dangling and twisting there, it is definitely a lesson learned.

Professional W.W.F wrestler Razor Ramon once dated Hurricane girlfriend, (so she said) and I'm guessing that might be what ended his career, maybe tossing him from the ring with those category five winds of hers. Crossing my path, turning me into a feeder band or something. A second warning came psychically on two legged Tornado girlfriend as you will read about. I guess I was a storm chaser back then, ignoring the second warning, which turned out to be a big mistake, because that's where 'my town' got flattened so to speak. Not only is the name appropriate from matching the first psychic vision/premonition, but because she seemed to leave a wide swath of destruction behind her among the men unfortunate enough to get 'sucked in.' A lot of men reading this probably thinking, I hear you brother, I hear you. Those pretty, sexy Tornadoes, with long legs and a short skirt like Calamity Jane.

The importance is, now having already learned this lesson, but more recently receiving forewarnings on Tribulation, I can put millions of people on the Tribulation awareness bus, instead of beneath it getting run over by it. You will need to take me serious, and realize that I could not be more serious. Through this book, I'll come back to this point again, and again, but forgive me, because a lot of people don't deserve to die just because they are stubborn bone heads! Many will not get it with the storm chaser analogy point already made.

Realize, Tribulation is a nearly two-thousand-year-old prophecy, contained in Bible Book of Revelation, New Testament, and by fresh awareness that were only recently holy angel received, proof to me of its complete accuracy, and in all regards then, thoroughly genuine, as I witness to you here in this book, with certainty! Now since Book of Revelation was said to be delivered by Christ in afterlife spiritual angelic visitation to John his disciple in exile around 70 AD, and Book of Revelation a part of New Testament (life and teachings of Christ), then doesn't this verify such messaging by Christ did occur, and in fact describing how Christ's second coming will occur as the seventh angel during Tribulation, just kind of verify itself? Verifying in total the Christian faith, as well, here? Yes, it absolutely does do this, Anyone who completes this book still unconvinced must have been reading with their brain's shuttered and closed, because undeniable proof is exhibited. Not in one way, but in multiple ways.

With Tribulation, there won't be any trees left for debris and the wreckage to hang from. There will be only three outcomes: either you rapture, you die, or you survive. For most survivors, conditions will be so harsh, they will wish they were dead. This book, by providing you with awareness on these future events, are your best hope to improve that future condition situation. The bridge actually is out up ahead, and the end actually is getting nearer. Don't thank me for the awareness I give you, Thank God the Father, and Christ Jesus, for it is their information, their awareness, not mine. I'm only passing along to you what has been given to me. This book will pour it out to you, but remember, take heed! Remember no holy prophecy prediction in human history has ever failed to fulfill exactly as predicted. If you try to outguess or ignore this (outdraw like an old west gunfighter) fulfillment will drop you in your tracks guaranteed, faster than you can even twitch that trigger finger hand.

Surprisingly, especially among many women, they feel so overwhelmed by the magnitude of the situation, rather than become anxious, they decide when the time comes they'll just concede defeat, throw in the towel so to speak termination wise, with a sigh of abandonment to their very existence. Hope your mother raised no such fool. Don't be an idiot! Like when the time arrives they will simply lay down their life like it was a bathmat in the shower? Must be a cheap one you don't value very much! More on this again later, please take my words seriously people, Tribulation is a monster mega/storm with total certainty to cross your existence path. Even if you are pretty sure you'll rapture, my backup strategy this book gives is advisable to all.

The Amazing Similarities
The Parallel or Book End Premonitions: A Tale of Two Storms
Common Features

1. Twelve years in advance it was foretold I would meet a girl (her initials J.S.) Ten years ahead, I was foretold by premonition in similar fashion I would meet another girl (her initials C.H.).
2. This was plenty of warning, but unfortunately, I didn't see them as storms on the distant horizon, although I should have in retrospect, since the J.S. premonition actually came with a vision of very dark clouds rolling in and lightning crashing down out of it. Tornado warning from my guardian angel! A very attractive sexy girl, but the gent who introduced me to her, about ten days later told me, I can't believe your still with her, run for it, she's really bad news. The other girl whom I was to meet later (C.H.) was about a Cat 5 Hurricane rolling in over my coastal life. Also extremely sexy and attractive, a national beauty contest winner, and a sweetheart of a destructive Hurricane.
3. Neither of these gentlemen (friends?) who introduced me to these two lived very long after doing so, and in both cases I had for- knowledge through Intuition that they were in danger, and in the second case, that death was imminent. Both intuitions correct!
4. Both girls had been in tragic death related circumstances that were being talked about on the radio. In both cases (different years) I was listening to their stories over the radio in my truck when the premonitions were delivered. Essentially in both cases, you will one day meet this girl. In both cases I was on the road (in different locations, but in each case near the event location being discussed on the radio) that I refer to as the psychic trail, as described by Valerie in the second Intunition.
5. Both girls were native Floridians, yet both had lived for a time out of state.
6. Both were divorced, each having a child by prior marriage. Each had failed second relationships, and each had a second child out of it that had to be raised by someone else more responsible.
7. Both had drug alcohol problems, both had more than one arrest, DUI charges (both girls more than one), and had created both damages physical, and lawsuits resulting.
8. Both girls had chronic alcoholic father's, and divorced parents.
9. Both girls were prone to alcoholic blackouts, drug addiction, and had arrests for these, as well.
10. Both girls in their thirties, and both had at least one sister.

11. As discussed earlier in this chapter, a Web Matrix from intersecting psychic events occurring. These are both psychic threads within my personal psychic theme Web.
12. The trail of wreckage, physical and financial damage, theft, damaged and totaled vehicles, law suits, lost rental car while I was getting auto repair work done, broken windows twice because C.H. forgot or lost her house keys, thousands worth of stolen property, and it's no exaggeration to say I got hit by a tornado, a hurricane, and then a tornado again. Things battered, tattered, and shattered. My life picked up, turned around, and sat down, whirl winded out of place! Whole new connotation for the expression, Wham Bam, Thank You Ma'am. The demonic extraterrestrials could take lessons from these two! Damage, Devastations, and Destructions 101 curriculum. I feel like I've already survived Tribulation! Note to self: Don't date named storms again, ever! An example of trying to help two with drug alcohol problems before they were ready to change.

I think back to the 1960s listening to Eric Clapton's song about the sirens luring the Great Ulysses ship up on the shoals to be wrecked. Those two sirens wouldn't have the initials J.S. and C.H. would they Ulysses? Oh no, you too? Let me guess, your ship with a good look; a hole ripped in the side about 38x24x36 inches, right? Eric Clapton must be psychic also.

Now when you get to the Religion Section, and you start to have doubts about future prophecy prediction I tell you about there, realize I learned a hard lesson here about not taking premonition seriously with ten and twelve years advance notice in these cases. Look what happened to me when my guardian angel told me to Run for your life before you meet these two and I didn't take it serious enough. It is going to be much higher stakes there. Your very survival, your life is on the line. This is a theme I will a bit repetitively return to again, and again. I am dead serious in saying those who don't listen will likely be among the dead. Psychic awareness is a gift from God, please respect it, and treat it as such.

Dream Retrieval - Dream Catch

What is it? Everyone has wild dreams, and often cannot upon awakening recall critical aspects. While these are not the same as a psychic dream, they are none-the-less similar, and what I only recently discovered, that in my case because I do possess psychic ability perhaps the reason, these wild dreams can also contain psychic message. These more ordinary dreams can have a message encapsulated within. However, wild dreams are often a bit hazier, less resolution, fuzzy, and thus image less clearly defined.

What I had to do was teach myself to first recognize one of these dreams (usually early morning light sleep) and master a technique I call dream retrieval, which is actually learning how to retrieve the message contained, but without and before waking up! You learn a kind of automatic response mechanism in your sleep. If you think of the dream as a capsulated item much like a nut with an outer shell, you must get at the message contained inside! You must extract the message, interpretation usually pretty easy, refine it to a phrase or two, and then repeat it to yourself, (still sleeping) before awakening. The repeating part helps you remember once you are awake. There is usually better clarity with a psychic dream, but valid psychic message, is valid psychic message, no matter how thick the briars and brambles were that your subconscious had to run through to bring to your dream state screen. The evaluation part, conscious awake state.

Premonition – Case 3
The Roommate Premonition

In the past occasionally I had rented out a front bedroom and spare bath. Always to ladies. They were fun company, paid their rent on time, and always very neat and tidy in all respects. There was no involvement, just a tenant landlord relationship.

I did not rent continuously, just now and then, often a year at a time. It wasn't long after I'd bought the place (1983) after it was first built, that one evening having a late lunch or supper in a bar/restaurant that something that seemed pretty weird at the time occurred.

A kind of tropical Tiki bar sort of theme, seafood was among the house specialties. In the corner of the restaurant was a seafood raw bar. I am sitting at the main bar, and there are dining tables around much of the perimeter (This restaurant located just one building away from the psychic trail, and the scene of more than one ghost sighting occurrences since – not by me, but by other people). As I looked over to a male employee who is tending this raw bar; a premonition. This guy will one day rent a room at my home as a tenant, so I'm told. I'd had a lot less premonition experience back then, so even though I realized it for what it was, it was a surprise.

Twelve years later, this now working within the construction field guy and I found ourselves working together. I didn't at first recognize him, or make the premonition connection. He in fact rented the room from me, and then in conversation later about where he once worked, it finally caught up. Let me tell you that is a true Twilight Zone ton of bricks on your head moment when the realization hits you. There would be many more Twilight Zone moments ahead for me, many more.

'Ted' (this roommates name) and I became good buddies, and in fact Ted was present when tornado girlfriend had been living with me, then arrested (yet another crossing of thread in the psychic matrix). He also knew and had worked with the guy who had introduced me to the two legged tornado (I had premonition of him being in danger, being too reckless on a bicycle, but didn't have a phone number to reach him and warn him.). About a week later he was dead. Killed after being struck by a car while riding his bicycle (at night). The premonition of this endangerment came outside the same restaurant where, years earlier, I'd had a premonition inside the restaurant regarding Ted. This time, while waiting for a traffic light, Billy came around the corner and waived hi to me. He had moved recently, and I had no way to reach him to warn him. A week later, he was dead. The wave that was meant as a "hello" became a sad, permanent wave good-bye. He had been on a bicycle when he waved, and he was struck and killed while on his bicycle.

Premonition – Case 4
The Girlfriends Canceling Out Premonition
(Also Called the Circular Driveway)

After J.S. (tornado girlfriend) was released from prison, she did not then return to being with me (larger disaster's to be the cause of elsewhere) and was out of state for over two years. In 1994, the residential construction remodeling job where I was working allowed us to leave the site at lunchtime, and on Friday's to go to the bank at lunchtime to cash our checks. This was a few miles north of the downtown, and on the intercostal waterway where our job-site was.

Not too many blocks south from the job site on the road I would travel, was a corner (duplex) house with a circular driveway. One Friday on the way to the bank I looked over to see a girl getting out of a car in the driveway. Then a premonition. I'm being told that in a few years I will meet this girl, but the chances of a developing relationship will be blocked by tornado girlfriend! My first reaction was, *What, am I losing my mind now?* Then, the profound feeling that always accompanies my premonitions. I didn't exactly know what was going to happen, only that it would happen.

About four years later I'm in a group meeting and there is a girl initials L.M., who talking to after the meeting was interested in a friendly first date. We made a date, and I'm now on a different job site and thought since the address she gave isn't too far to check out, I might drive by to locate the house, having an easy time checking the street numbers during daylight hours. So I'm driving down the correct street heading toward the Intercoastal waterway when it hits me. One of those ton of bricks over your head twilight zone moments. This street number that I'm looking for is going to be a corner house with a circular driveway! And with shock on sale two-for-one, it was! Something had come up, she'd have to cancel the date for that night, but would reschedule.

When she called to reschedule, tornado girlfriend had just crossed state lines, back in town, and had come over to see me. The phone rings, I thought it was for J.S. so I told her to go ahead and pick up the call. It was L.M., and hearing another female's voice, we never did go on a date after that, and I tried repeatedly. The premonition was not only accurate as far as that first date with the girl with the circular driveway, but the future relationship got cancelled, as well. Tornado girlfriend had touched down again!

Premonition – Case 5
The Misunderstanding Premonition

Weeks after realizing a date with L.M. is a dead issue, J.S. once again over to see me one evening, and she isn't just talking about getting back together, but wants an instant marriage! My guardian angel telling me, be real careful what you say, or it'll create a big misunderstanding, sending things spiraling out of control. To be sure I mishandled it anyway, stepped on sensitivity, sent the wrong signal, and sent things spiraling out of control. It took only hours for this one to fulfill, and a mess created that only seemed to get bigger with time progression.

Too much to explain, too many episodes oddly chronicling what unfolded from there. How do you tell an out of state tornado who had a child out of wedlock while she was gone, that a tornado in a wedding dress is moving a bit fast for you, without hurting her feelings. A tornado inside a church getting married to a guy named Wildman, that's almost moving too fast for your imagination to keep up with. Am I right?

A Death in The Family (A Case of Double Intuitions)

Both I and my oldest daughter who was care giver to her grandmother knew that gram didn't have a lot of time left. One day at work on a Tuesday afternoon, I heard my mother say my name voiced one time. I suspected she had passed on, and on Sunday the intuition came that if I checked the obituary section her name would be listed. So, I checked for that section, opened to it, and the very first name my eyes focused on was hers. When my daughter and I talked afterwards, she was a bit surprised I already knew. I asked what day had she passed, was it Tuesday? My daughter was very startled; how did you know?

Examples of Wild Dream, Dream Capture Retrievals

The second of the April 2008 U.F.O. dream premonition sightings was the one named Romeo, had given off negative evil vibes. I had been attempting to contact another psychic to see if I could obtain a statement that would confirm another psychic picking up bad vibes from an extraterrestrial spacecraft or source. Response was not forthcoming. Certainly my subconscious aware of a critical confirmation that I was seeking.

Then perhaps 3:30 or 4 A.M. I'm wrestling with a wild dream, because my sleep state conscious part of my brain realizes there could be information of importance imbedded or capsulized within the dream, and like some dream coast guard, it goes to interdict and board this vessel! It confiscates the message, then deciphers it. If you think of the dream as the smoke (to draw attention of the present, but semi-functional conscious) the message is the fire. The message deciphered from brain speak was that a group of extraterrestrials (one particular group) is fluent in a language spoken in hell. Since I didn't know there even was such a language in my conscious mind, I do consider this to be valid information.

Upon checking with a clergyman he tells me that it is widely believed among a sizeable number of clergy that such a language does exist, that there is in fact some demonic tongue! Exorcisms give clue to this also, when people possessed speak in some foreign tongue. It is said to be very guttural sounding with hissing sounds accompanying!

Just a few days after dream retrieval mentioned above, another one, both 2009. In this Wild Dream, a man is running out of a building, and he is very disturbed, very anxious over news just received. The building looks like a multi-story office building (symbolism for day time hours, while people are at work). He runs from the building down some steps and to the left a contraption I somehow deduct is a time machine. He frantically jumps into the time machine and wants to go back in time. More symbolism. It means the only way to escape what is impending is to exit by time machine. Then I scan within the dream over to my right. A grassy hill with something like a low sign very similar to a commercial building address street number. More symbolism. It's the year that this is occurring. The year of Armageddon? I will tell you in a later chapter (The Anti-Christ?).

After being the recipient of several different types of dream forms, it is certainty that they fall within different classifications. These dreams that I've just described to you as Wild Dreams are similar to dreams that almost anyone would have. Do some of their dreams contain psychic messaging also? Quite possible. The message must be extracted before awakening. It was only recently that I've been able to train myself to do this. Yes training classes for my brain while I'm sleeping, now you're starting to see how I might have earned the nick name Wildman. You can't get much wilder than a Wild Dream from Wildman. They are often of less clarity, smokier, hazier, less distinct, so that coast guard I spoke of is sometimes working in light fog.

A true psychic vision, what psychologists refer to as prophetic vision, are often almost as if seen in High Definition. Some color can be present, as well. Symbolism in varying degrees very common to all. It's simply an angel's way of getting the correct message to you, and not intended to confuse. The more you interpret, the better at it you become, and all prophetic visions worldwide are very apt to contain it.

With all dream visions the most important factor is to decipher meaning, make interpretation before awakening. This is absolutely imperative, otherwise you run the risk of losing some or even all of it upon consciousness.

There is a moral and ethical responsibility that all psychics have, because this information is derived from a spiritual source. These are implied, but unwritten, yet I'm certain are there, and must therefore be obeyed. These are:

1. All information obtained in this manner be used to benefit humanity, never to cause it harm.
2. Information obtained in this manner should not be used for selfish personal gain or advantage over another individual or group.
3. If information obtained in this manner has value to instruct or warn humanity to danger, it must not be held back.
4. It should always be considered as a gift from a holy source, and should not be taken for granted as a random act.

Fate and Destiny

In the Psychic Model- Street schematic diagram, you notice each of the psychic experience houses has back rooms or back porch, with one for fate, and one for destiny spaces. This for houses on both sides of the street. You could instead if it might make it any easier, to think of them as terminal blocks, with little light bulbs, perhaps green for destiny and red for fate. Electric wiring in both positive and negative aspect. An incoming wire for each, as well as one for outgoing, to a future (time) event occurrences, possibly matching a psychic predictive fulfillment at this distant terminal. The further off in time, the further away this destination terminal. Realize that this initial detection is prior to the destination terminal, and that some fulfillments simply occur on that end without detection and so if detection does not occur on that end until after event fulfillment, then analogy wise, the wire ran to an end terminal beyond and not exactly matching fulfillment in either time or space occurrences. Another real alternative is that fulfillment termination doesn't provide any further indications beyond what was signaled previously.

Realize also, that only psychics seem to have this kind of deluxe model sensitivity circuit signal circuit board. There are plenty of people, in fact likely the majority, who have either fate or destiny at play in their lives, then fulfilling, and never the wiser the whole time, or maybe only the slightest clue at some point, but not enough to state, or prove such emphatically. However, God and his holy angels are involved, and thus anything and everything is possible. If you are not psychic and would otherwise never know one of these forces is in play, but they want you to have recognition, then trust you will receive recognition. Perhaps in the process to also bring attention to their direct involvement. God is the operative word, and it means that your life is personally tied to a Divine blueprint that God the architect drew up perhaps long before you were born in many cases (but subject to revision, although generally not practiced). One has to suspect that in some cases, some much shorter term pre-destiny plans are made after our birth (or fate decisions), considering the power that this architect has Yes, last minute design changes and revisions, even though in fact for the most part, and with many people, we control our own paths in life, thus outcomes are direct result of our cumulative choices and decision. That is still true even with fate or destiny in play for the most part from my unique perspective.

So you have this model of a psychic's circuit board where a little light bulb lights if a corresponding electric current is detected at that terminal for both/either fate or destiny. For analogy purposes anyway, psychics were not born at the maternity ward at the Intel plant, but such analogy does help me relate rather complex description of varied circumstances involved.

When a signal light lights up indicating presence possibility for fate or destiny, it's only that possibility rather than certainty. You are thereby alerted to look for other clues which the larger psychic event may provide direction to look in. Miss the signal and you miss the indication. Only a fate or destiny directly connected is going to trip the signal. In other words, you could have one or more other ones in play in your life that will by-pass this signal, perhaps lighting up a different signal, different terminal, and different psychic occurrences at a different time. It's not required fate or destiny be attached to a terminal or psychic event occurrences at all, and you know this to be true because of the many non-psychics who have fate or destiny circumstance attached to their lives. So, that being the case, even being psychic you are not guaranteed at any point of having signal of fate or destiny presence, it's more to do with whether that's programed into the design in each particular circumstance for each particular individual.

Another thing to realize is that there are other sorts of things to look for aside from psychic detection. Logic and reasoning applied to something you observe might tip off a non-psychic, or help add further evidence to a case for it, a psychic or non-psychic is already trying to build. It isn't necessarily obscure, and can be more like proverbial 'handwriting boldly written,' or sticking out like a 'sore thumb.' It can be a single undeniably strong indicator, or a collection of several lesser ones that in sum total demand your attention. Often a clue will blatantly linger, other times perhaps missed if not quick to notice, and perception fast enough to rapidly recognize and correctly analyze the correct interpretation. It can pass right by, leave an undetected clue that is totally missed, but perhaps later remembered, so not completely lost. Intangible forces with resolve to eventually culminate at some future connecting intersection point in your life. So often unseen and undetected, they fulfill without recognition ever occurring. If you think of fate as having negative aspect, realize it can be avoided or sidestepped, but only if you identify it in time to take evasive action. Elsewhere in this book in later chapters much is discussed on the Tribulation subject so I don't want to get into that here, but if you are not one to rapture, and you have followed the guidelines stated as mechanism pre-Tribulation effort evasive death preventative actions, could at the least pro-long your life.

Clairvoyant Jean Dixon warned both of the Kennedy brothers prior to their respective deaths of great dangers present from assassination. Fate only occurs when evasive measure isn't even taken, and things are left to take their natural course. You have a bad feeling, or a bad dream the night before you are to take a flight. You decide to instead board a different flight on a different airline. The original flight crashes. You avoided fate, because your flight did not crash. With Tribulation you cannot escape the planet, but if you are doubtful of early rapture, Rapture itself is escape from the planet in spiritual sense, so perhaps you can upgrade your eligibility status beforehand, but if not the sections coming later can still prevent many deaths, so by the time you finish this book you'll have much greater awareness level which is the first step. Going back to the example made of a person having a bad dream right before their flight. The person a non-psychic. However, knowing with certainty the role holy angel play, that night, that dream is a holy angel orchestrated dream. Absolutely that person's guardian angel is hoping the person will change reservations, and in doing so, all works out for that person.

The discussion on destiny gets pretty extensive, and another place in this book where your imagination will get put through its paces perhaps trying to draw you a visualization for better comprehension, thus aiding realizations untangled from confusing complexities. I would move from the discussion on fate we just had directly to destiny, but instead I'm going to mention aspect of the Psychic web matrix first, and at least for some, it will help clarify, awhile for others, they may find themselves so snarled in inability to grasp what is being explained that it might have to be re-read several times before they understand. The word esoteric means understanding of abstruse characteristic, comprehensions lying well beyond the ordinary, perceived by only a few individuals so specially instructed or initiated.

Surrealism has to do with the expressing or exhibiting (as in art) of the workings of the subconscious mind, especially as manifested in dream form depiction. They are typically characterized by the incongruous arrangement and presentation of subject matter. In Art the arrangement of subject, and selection of subject, is to achieve a visual image that makes a certain existential statement that the artist wishes to represent upon completion. The surrealist artist wishes to steer your mind consciously through his or her deliberate inclusions and effects.

The psychic dream is not dissimilar, since it actually takes place within one's subconscious mind. They are generally in good clarity (high definition) and rich in symbolism. They also are very short in duration, often just one scene, also somewhat resembling a surrealist painting, but not quite to that extreme where most artists will exert maximum effect for maximum visual impact. The psychic dream much closer to reality than surrealism, except there may be something included to deliver the intended message using symbolism as needed. In this psychic dream it's all about the message, whatever visual effect occurs is of little significance beyond the importance of the message. In the Surreal artist's painting it's the opposite. Any message sent subliminally is secondary, the dramatic effects mimicking subconscious dreamscape is primary purpose for achieving maximum visual impact to someone viewing it within reality state. With awake state psychic visualizations, it is the same priority: Deliver the intended message as briefly and accurately as possible. Understanding this basic nature of psychic dreams here in review, might help avoid some confusion later as I attempt to relate things more advanced, but still connected.

I'm re-explaining the psychic dream in image terms, to now move into what I've referred to as the Psychic Web matrix. The Psychic Web Matrix being invisible, but yet detectable from realizations that point to its existence in place. Sort of like seeing the leaves on a tree, but not seeing the many interconnecting branches. The psychic event the leaves, the Psychic Web Matrix the branches. Or, in more kinetic terms, perhaps the analogy of iron filings being drawn up, indicating the presence of a magnet, yet not seeing the magnet itself. Now previously I told you about what appears to be both an individual level one (micro), as well as a larger world scene event (macro) to which the individual is also connected, and the individual (psychic spider) the link between the two. Yes, Oh what complicated Webs we weave. Here of course I'm referring to psychic webs actually quite different in design. Whereas in the (micro) personal Web matrix of psychic episode events, circumstances, and outside persons somehow inter-relating, what became apparent was that like threads of an actual spider's web in nature, thread strands always seem to intersect with at least one or more (sometimes several other strands). So much so, that it was obvious this was not random chance. While I can only speak for my own experiences, I'm suggesting such is true with other psychics also. That is, they build such webs in similar interconnection fashion. Psychologist/Para-psychologists need to keep those groundbreaking shovels handy, because you'll not be leaving this chapter without some serious psychic-archeology digs being undertaken. So in that psychic episode inter-connectivity sense, this Micro-Web Matrix, on the individual level closely resembles an actual spider's web in nature.

The Macro Web is different, and again I can only relate my own, but then suggest what I detect. Until you first build a significant amount of strands in the Micro-Web, you won't have a sense of direction as to how the Macro-Web ties to Micro. Generally from what I've read, a psychic's psychic episode occurrences trail off in their later years. So, if a secondary Macro-Web exists and is detected, then it must be recognizable by then, because beyond that point there are no more strands

Using what became apparent as my Macro-Web evolved and unfolded, was a different shape Web! This one more like a football field with one common theme the field, and pertinent psychic awareness arriving sort of laid down as parallel yard lines on the field, because the only thing they all had in common was End Times Tribulation timeframe topic. Yes, that's correct; Tribulation Field, and recognized in pre-cognitive future timeframe fashion. I, the spider, granted high level security clearance access pass to the field with my destiny access Pass. What, your imagination having trouble now imaging a psychic spider with very high level security clearance authorization from God? One nick named Wildman getting pre-view of Tribulation Field with a destiny Pass that was issued thousands of years ago by the creator of the universe just maxing out your imagination? Over the top incredible? But you see, that is because God is incredible, I'm just as in awe by all the things I'm describing to you, as you are to read them. It is my Christian faith, coupled with a healthy sense of humor, that allow me to just go with the flow, and the shock absorbers needed to keep my sanity cushioned over all of the bumps and around the sharp turns all this advanced level/plane psychic endure course throws at me, and why I recommend to all. God in Trinity Christian form that is, Christ your personal Savior, because if it works, road tested on Wildman's psychic extreme endure course, you'll find that through faith you have equivalent heavy-duty shocks, too. Some people know this already, and fully agree, but so many others are seeking answers, seeking the truth. True faith is the secret. In examining this Macro-Web Matrix, Tribulation Field, that all of my psychic episodes beyond individual level attach to, still it is I the psychic spider who is the connective link between Macro and Micro matrix, but where the Micro-Web seems to be pointing to personal awareness on the personal life level; not so with the Macro level Web. Here, everything being holy in nature, and the essence of faith away from focus on one's self, but instead to help others, so it is with my Macro-Web, driven by destiny, but so as to bring crucial awareness to others worldwide as to this fast approaching time period event that only Christians take quite seriously. With the Bible stating that one quarter of Earth's population will perish early on at beginning of Tribulation, both you and your illustration challenged imagination had better take every word a certain psychic spider with high level security access clearance has to say seriously. Otherwise, in future timeframe, you'll be granted access to this field yourself to see firsthand, but under exactly the circumstances I'm trying to help you avoid by advanced forewarning.

In the Macro Web, all the psychic awareness tie to the larger topic, but do not intersect each other. Another point differentiating in the Macro-Web, destiny driven situation is that whereas in typical psychic episode such as premonition with start predictive point, and secondary part fulfillment point, with only vague timing indication of separation between the two, it is different with destiny. With destiny itself, it's giving event occurrences and timing clearly, but you don't have the full confirmation of the awareness being destiny attached and driven. It sometimes doesn't seem to be confirmed until later, but ultimately won't be totally confirmed until fulfillment just like the psychic event specific. The reason fate and destiny are on both sides of the street and not just on the holy side/Macro side is that the psychic houses, any of them, can be contributive to the Macro-Web.

To help your fatigued and challenged imagination by this point, if you think of destiny (each one individually) as being in the shape of a cone, the wide bottom the origination point, and the tip apex as the fulfillment point and yourself year by year traveling upward inside this cone toward the apex. The cone of destiny of course invisibly surrounding you. The point of origin at which you first identified the cone is the base, even though, being Divine in origin, the true base might be much older than you imagine it, as perceived before your birth in the mind of God. Even so, you pick it up at the point where you so recognize it. As time passes and you move ever closer to the fulfillment apex, the sides of the cone are getting closer and if you weren't already aware of this cone, the chances increase that you'll somehow receive awareness of this cone's existence, all be it an invisible force prescribed and pre-ordained by God. I must be giving those Atheist, Agnostic, and non-Christian Psychologists an absolute severe migraine, not to mention all other non-psychologists fitting those classifications. Wait until they hear about Wildman's Fourth destiny, thus catapulting them toward a rude spiritual crisis awakening in over-load shock level mode.

Since it appears I have four different destiny situations all going on simultaneously, sort of stacked cone inside of cone, inside of cone situations, that pretty well answers the question of multiple destiny in play surrounding a person. Only the third one, already fulfilled with certainty proven. That one described later in the book in much greater detail, an early telepathic clairaudience episode with a holy angel, foretelling the writing of this book back in 1964, while attending Sunday church service! Your reading this book, and passed Lie-Detection proof of that third destiny cone's existence. The other three cones likely, but unfulfilled in total thus unproven (This Book in Part II fulfills the fourth Cone!).

The oldest one, almost four thousand years old in origin, you'll read about in the Epilogue (Part II). The second destiny cone inside it, a prediction that in this timeframe 2010/2011 someone would emerge to shed further light on Tribulation topic (made five hundred years ago) clearly has Wildman's name written in destiny's handwriting on that second cone wall, and somewhat an extension of the first destiny outer cone in nature. In similar fashion the third destiny cone (all in Macro-Web) Tribulation topic connectivity. That second cone prediction originating from none other than Nostradamus. The Fourth destiny cone fulfills with the publication of this book, release of all Tribulation information, and including forecast of timing for Christ's return. That one pretty rough on non-Christians, being told someone that they don't believe in will with certainty make appearance on a specific day, over a decade and a half away, better fasten your spiritual seat belt is all I've got to say. Because if you're not a Christian and your riding in this book with Wildman, your head is likely to go through the windshield (metaphorically speaking, of course) seventeen years before Wildman even applies the brakes on that puppy!

In this book I continually relate all aspects of the supernatural back to God. No one will ever grasp the supernatural realm unless they first respect, and acknowledge God as being in control. That is first off, secondly, this Psychic section in particular, realizing that condition is the key to other understandings in deeper examinations. You'll read about exact timing of Christ's return in later chapter of Supplement section, Part I, of this book.

Getting back to those destiny cones invisibly surrounding a person, let's examine what the awareness possibilities are as far as detection. They are:

1. Awareness recognition prior to reaching the cone apex
2. Awareness arriving at time of apex destiny culmination

3. Post-apex culmination point awareness (hindsight/reflection)
4. No awareness to destiny fulfillment occurs, even though it did actually occur, (existed) went unrecognized

In Wildman's case, relative to first and second cones, reading about circumstance that was suggestive of supporting evidence of destiny in play is arrived at. It becomes in each case strong possibility, but no direct psychic event is attached to confirm this. Even though the larger Macro-Web topic is Tribulation. Other psychic events relate to Tribulation, and these destiny cones all pointing to Tribulation make a connection in the sense of sharing common topic ground even though no direct psychic indicator toward destiny is exhibited, indirectly it is.

As a psychic spider, in these Web matrix examination, you see that even where no direct psychic link is evident, it is the spider with the psychic link to God, and recognition of the possibility of destiny in play is still possible to recognize by examining other surrounding inputs. In this case all four destiny cones with tie-in to Tribulation. Now in the first destiny cone which potentially dates back nearly four thousand years, a boyhood psychic retro-memory episode could be considered as the link, as it matches circumstances and details read about, but I'd rather view these as two matching halves rather than the psychic event as a separate whole. With the second destiny cone, the confirmation seems more to come from the back end forward,(Nostradamus prediction) than from my end tying back. I receive awareness on Tribulation timing (holy subject) through psychic means, then pick up a book and read where Nostradamus predicted someone would receive such awareness in exactly this current timeframe, but predicted five hundred years ago. Knowing this particular type of psychic awareness is quite rare (holy subject). I have to believe this second destiny cone is in fact in place, based on that alone, until shown it isn't. Every time strong evidence for the existence of another stacking destiny cone exists, it seems to just increase the likelihood chances of the others being correctly identified

Like I'm out there on Tribulation field with a chalk striping machine laying down sidelines and yard lines, and the more I lay down, the more it looks like I'm the one who will be chalk lining the entire field. Your imagination having to deal with a psychic spider pushing an athletic field chalk striping machine across the entire field. So, the question becomes who is working harder; the spider, or your imagination that had to downshift? Back a few pages where I was describing holy angel placing symbolism into a psychic dream that often takes on a Surrealism flavor but with emphasis on message conveyance, almost any item or image necessary can be present. In one psychic dream conveyance with a contraption my sub-conscious immediately identified as a time machine, the symbolism being one could only escape what was coming by traveling back in time.

As a Christian spider, believing in Holy Spirit received and indwelling within, then you must recognize that both personal (micro) and psychic model opposite side of the street (macro). Web Matrix are all threads from the mind of the psychic spider, but then actually originating from God. Such is only possible with faith (specifically Christian), since holy angel as the intermediary in holy dimension will have nothing to do with one who does not have it. They will only deal with you if you are one who knows and loves Christ Jesus. Faith is a psychic pre-condition that must be in place for psychic transaction to occur. With destiny, essentially you are one, at least in psychic terms pre-ordained by God if the subject matter turns to holy subject. What I'm saying is that clearly God knew before I was even born that Christian faith would be in place in my life, otherwise there would have been no point to so pre-ordain, pre-destine these current psychic occurrences. Realize that God can see past, present, and future simultaneously in view, thus previewed and approved by God, likely long, long ago.

You must see God as the composer and director of both the cosmos universe, but also the symphony of life and intelligence contained within. In Micro aspect, all humans, even non-believers play a role by their very existence on this music sheet. Those of greatest faith with the best footing, best grounding as to the nature and order of what force has ultimate control and doing the directing of such symphony orchestration on such complex Macro and Micro scales, yet somehow just like musical symphony all kept in harmony. Destiny like a louder note struck, or more complex chord played out, but with God's purpose and function within the larger symphony scheme. That is the symphony of our physical and spiritual individual existence.

In Psalm 150: 1–6, it speaks of the praise we are to return to the Lord, and specific musical instruments to be used to musically orchestrate praise back to God for all our blessing which we take for granted This relating to why most churches use musical organ and often other instruments accompanying in their worship services. Perhaps music itself one of those gifts too often taken for granted, and worse many who take God for granted, or don't believe at all. When someone gives sincere praise to God, it's not God that benefits, it's God that appreciates, and in such, the person giving the praise who benefits.

Spirituality and psychic experience both have the human mind in common, and I'm trying to explain the spiritual side so you can then better understand the psychic tie-in. Most people are so absorbed in their one dimensional material world existence, that everything must be seen to be believed. However, it isn't a one dimensional world. Other dimensions all around us, just unseen. Therefore you need to believe (in God, in Christ) in order to have any chance of being able to see within this *Interdimensional* world. Then things can be confirmed not with the eyes of your face, but with the eyes of your heart and mind, and the indwelling place of Holy Spirit, that is critical to light your way forward in the spiritual realm, exactly as Jesus stated, "I am the light and the way, and no one shall be received by the Father except through me." Only by faith in Christ is your spiritual existence and life under full warranty. This symphony music then proclaiming Jesus Christ as Lord today, because such a symphony can happen no other way! The symphony God the Father composed, and that you are a part of the ongoing orchestration.

The Bible telling me my job as a Prophet is to witness for Christ. The psychic explanation is just a thrown in extra that went with it!

One of the main themes of this book is how intertwined and inter-related all the different subject areas of the supernatural really are. So it should be no surprise to find religious topic comment in the Psychology/Parapsychology section here, or psychic and U.F.O./E.T. entity comments in the Religion section.

Understanding God's musical symphony composition as background for psychic structure and mechanics of operation as music in the larger macro scheme, and these as micro-notes then makes sense of all of it, when you allow yourself to see God as both composer and music in play director. Far too much higher intelligence and coordinative power at a higher level required, that could not be achieved randomly, or by any other means. However, there can be, but one correct defining of the nature of God, then rendering all others incomplete, or invalid. One that is incomplete then becomes invalid for that exact reason. God represents perfection. A faith that is incomplete is imperfect, and thus cannot be truly representative of such a deity.

Christian faith (The Bible) is both the key that unlocks all doors, and the answer to all questions, but is also the only truly perfect faith in a perfect God. To those of other faiths who question this, perhaps when prophecy described in Chapter 24 fulfills, you'll then concede I am right. Personally, I already know with certainty I am right, because of many other confirmations God has shown me, many to which this book will later describe.

In order to participate and spiritually Rapture (ascend) later, it is dependent on learning to transcend with your daily life thinking. To keep focus, an excellent way is to regularly praise the Lord for the many blessings you already have, he's already shown you. Give praise, Give thanks, and bless his holy name. The Lord's prayer always available

Corinthians 5:7 and 5:17 states, "For we walk by faith not by sight." This meaning that faith itself is true sight. And then in 5:17, "If any man be in Christ, he is a new creature." The apostle Paul here elaborating the role and importance of faith. By acknowledging God's existence, and establishing a respectful obedient relationship, which he desires with us all, you have laid the foundation on which faith can be built, then expanded. If you love God, he will love you back, it's that simple, because if you truly love God, you will be obedient to his word, and desire to do so.

He has given all of us imaginations that allow us to see without our eyes, enabling envisionment of things both tangible and (spiritual) intangible, or things of mixed concept. Allow me to illustrate a little.

Previously I mentioned extracting psychic finds from the caves and caverns over in the Twilight Zone, but typically the sort of tongue in cheek metaphor analogy I use is this one. Of trout fishing over in the Twilight Zone with my Indian fishing guide chief Pesumpsud (Pesu for short), and my guardian angel along.

We fish rivers and trout streams like the Reveal, Legend, Destiny, Foretold, and Superstition. We catch Brown Omen, speckled Premonition and wild quarkies (dreams).

Yes I'm sure your imagination is getting a work out in this book, an imagination on energy drink with ripped abs. A guardian angel in hip waders standing in rushing invisible water up to his waste, in a Trout stream over in the Twilight Zone fly fishing! He's a great fly fisherman, too!

Then as it's getting dark, there we are on the edge of the mystified forest, by the edge of a stream cooking our catch of the day in a skillet over an open campfire. Delicious Information! Very tasty. Another successful fishing trip and more frequent flyer miles to the Twilight Zone. The ironic part perhaps being that so much psychic information does travel by way Of dreams. Dream big!

Tomorrow we'll move our campsite, maybe take the canoe over to Oracle Lake. It's rumored Walt Disney once fished here, too, but that hasn't been confirmed.

Well, at least when your imagination is worn out after completing this book, it now knows where it wants to go trout fishing when you send it on vacation! Maybe it'll even bring you back some psychic souvenirs.

Now I wouldn't allow your imagination a vacation just yet, the Hallucinations Chapter is up next. As for the academic para-psychics, don't put away those dirty groundbreaker shovels just yet, either. I predict you can expect a contingency of theologians a few Chapters into the future, coming to you and wanting to know if they can borrow them.

New discoveries in the Religion Section, Chapter 27 (Part II) it seems I will have pointed out new interpretational artifacts of strong interest to them. How embarrassing though, having Wildman with his Twilight Zonian perspective, point out hither to overlooked interpretation of Bible verse, which could be valid hypothesis with major implications! Why didn't they think of that they are asking themselves.

Well at least you know they'll return the shovels if they in fact do borrow them. Just don't expect them back quickly, that location isn't the only Anthroclericological dig site I found (Your imagination to become extremely challenged there also - it's the Armageddon Chapter)! Some readers unfortunately probably won't make it through that chapter with imaginations still intact! But then some other readers might not even make it that far, reading a book about the supernatural written by Wildman. You guys are living pretty dangerous walking that mental precipice blindfolded on a moon less night, mighty brave of you. Grand Canyon/Mental Park and all!

Not mentioned in this chapter is something known as Future Memory, and since it is not among my personal experiences I could not give an account. A book entitled *The E.S.P. Enigma* by Dr. Diane Hennacy Powell states in Chapter 5, the future is now; the evidence for precognition, future memory page. Dr. Powell gives an analysis observed from case study showing characteristics through eight separate, categorized phases. She does a remarkably descriptive account for having had the person who experienced it firsthand relate the experience then transcribe it. I knew from her comment exactly what this other person experienced, and it definitely does deserve to be categorized independent of other equally distinct psychic experience categorizations.

On the Street named Precognitive Way already diagramed, I'd place it in the House of positive future event that I'm hoping psychologists will give a name to like Pre-visitation, Previewtation, or something like that. You could then certainly provide a room in that psychic house for Future Memory. Dr. Wildman concurring with Dr. Powell on Future Memory as definitely valid separate psychic categorization.

Normally premonitions received awake do not have vision accompaniment, and the Particle Beam Premonition where I did get visual, was more in general terms than future photo detail accuracy, time space convergence. As I've pointed out already, even among sleep dream visions there is not just one standard type, but several formats with identity uniqueness that beg to be classified accordingly. The need for more defined classifications in parapsychic precognitive psychology hopefully something academics will improve. Recognition of holy angel involvement hopefully agreed upon once and for all, because that is genuine truth.

Further discussing the Premonition Experience, while most are received awake (speaking firsthand in my personal psychic experience) and clairaudience telepathic silent thought messaging transpires, it can be delivered in dream sleep psychic vision (symbolic interpretation then required). If the cautionary warning is more extreme, or life threatening, an omen might be the psychic vehicle used.

After all awake psychic premonition are received, exact timing is seldom accompanying, but rather a vague approximate sense of simply a future approximate timeframe. With every single premonition, and without exception, a few seconds sort of afterglow profound feeling has always accompanied. A holy angel smiling as a receipt is psychically/handed to you. Confirmation of yet another holy angel psychic transaction, and guaranteed by the good faith and credit of God and the Kingdom of heaven, it shall fulfill, and with certainty. They always do fulfill.

It's not limited to awake clairaudience angel telepathy. When I experienced the September 1988 psychic vision Particle Beam Premonition, it came with a Profound moment receipt also. When I was in my early twenties (1970) a general circumstance/ condition foretelling was delivered to me. It outlined the nature of my career, and that while most of my career I'd engage in white collar work, specifically I was foretold that I would engage in some extensive blue collar physical work, but do so by choice. Looking back, having a lengthy career in construction, what was so predicted back in 1970 did prove accurate. Owning my own State Licensed Residential Construction business I did in fact engage in a great deal of hands on labor that I actually enjoyed doing, and was by choice. This type of awareness differed in that it described general condition rather than specific predicted event.

I now realize I was slowly being trained as a psychic so that this lifetime experience would prepare me to write this book, and that as the book was being written (itself predicted in 1964), I was also living a destiny to receive a few awareness not only from holy angel, but on holy subject. About five in all, clearly consistent with other psychics receiving further clarifications relative to specific topic dealing with the coming Tribulation period. Timing, and E.T./U.F.O. clearly topics given me for purpose of this book.

I ask the Psychology community, as well as the scientific, to realize all future seeing psychic experience is from the Biblical age/time of Christ, a mechanism employed by God through his holy angels exactly as was done in Biblical times. The same psychic prophet/ordinary man receiving personal future seeing awareness not on holy subject does in fact receive holy awareness in exactly the same manner. He is just an ordinary man before, during, and after. Only the awareness changes, but as occurred in my case, a long period of being trained to handle and interpret is required.

All major precognitive psychics are by no coincidence since the time of Christ devout Christian believers. holy angel (or God) would have nothing to do with transferring message of holy nature and significance to someone who was not, who could not be trusted to do the right thing with the information. God is the mechanism; one God in holy Triune form, is the only manner precognition awareness takes place. End of story; Amen. holy angels the intermediaries/ spirit guides, no question about it. It is time the scientific community conceded this one to theologians and the spiritual realm. You have that in writing!

Just one of many reasons Islam is exposed as fraudulent is because it appears to be a manmade contrived religion, which needed a holy connection in order to achieve validity, thus it appears the story of how the holy angel gave the teachings of the Qur'an to Mohammed was fictional account in order to grasp and claim holiness aspect. In Part II, I will cover other hoaxed, non-holiness aspected Cults duping people, and included, further discussion as to why Islam is false! Here I mention it relative to the fact that unless you are not only psychic, and pre-destined devout Christian, you are ineligible to receive holy Prophecy, and no exceptions to this rule, I promise you. Was Mohammed a devout Christian? Hardly, but it is possible demonic spirits assisted in this hoax rather than being entirely man derived origin. Either way, holy means pure and uncontaminated, and clearly here, contamination is seen. The Qur'an itself seems to contain some virtues similar to other religions, and thus some of the Qur'an in conflict with the Bible is invalid, but elsewhere in match for the themes and concepts contained in the Bible are non-conflicting. Mohammed himself and Allah though are imposters. I wouldn't say this unless absolutely certain, and I am certainly so. It takes a Prophet to know a Prophet. It seems somebody named Omar in vented Mohammed, who then invented Allah. The only trouble is, the real God, God of Moses and the Ten Commandments claimed there was but One God, Sovereign and omnipotent. Nice deception Omar, you've managed to deceive close to one billion Muslims, or one seventh of the world's population, but Holy Trinity: Jehovah, Jesus, and Holy Spirit are the true God. I am a prophet for proclaiming the second coming of Jesus as described in the Book of Revelation. The Prophet Wildman proclaiming Jesus' appearance in the sky will, as a Mighty angel, descending over Israel appear in spectacle form as a Wildman also. Believers in the Trinity fear not, but non-believers need fear that Wildman Mighty angel/Son of God greatly, for their days of reckoning will then have arrived, and Allah will be nowhere to be seen, heard, or believed. I am saying to you Muslims, he is that now, you have been spiritually deceived. Not maybe deceived, definitely deceived. Convert to the Christian faith while enough time remains to do so. Islam is bogus counterfeit, because Mohammed and Allah are! In Part II, I cover other Cult religions, also highly flawed, and some Christian faith connected, so Muslims don't take offense that I've singled them out. People practicing these faiths are victims, and I'm attacking no person or peoples, just false doctrines of religious ideology/philosophy. Mohammed did exist around 610 A.D., but was not a holy prophet.

My own awareness God given as a Christian psychic Prophet with a lifetime of genuine holy angel interactions, all the authenticity I need. My Prophet license tag and registration issued from the Holy Trinity with up to date validations to phrase it with a different analogy comparison. Excellent insurance, holy angel witness protection package all included (Lie Detection/Truth verification in Part II, actually confirms angel reveal/ air cover!). An anointed Prophet.

Part II is, perhaps, the best part relating to the pre-destiny aspect. The Biblical Prophets foretold of a coming Messiah, Christ's first Advent, and centuries earlier. However, even before these Prophets were born, God already knew them, centuries before. They were pre-destined to be holy Word of God Prophets. It was not by chance, random circumstance, or late last minute decision by God. The entire circumstances contained in Book of Revelation were known to Christ after resurrection then delivered to John of Patmos. I would describe to you my own life's destiny to Prophecy here, except I'd prefer to keep Tribulation information relative to timings exclusive to Part II, and some intertwining mention arises if I were to get into explanation here. What I see is destiny in four parts, and the final fourth part completed upon publication of my book, both Part I and Part II, but especially Part II. Wildman was destined to be a Prophet of the Apocalypse, with new unveiled detail (A preview is for further extended discussions, see Part II of this book also.).

Going back to the Web Matrix discussions already explained, the personal Matrix intersects became identified in retrospect, but the fascinating thing about the Macro Matrix, as the psychic spider, my Web of psychic awareness are non-intersecting as I pointed out in those earlier discussions. The Tribulation topic is the common point. However instead of retrospect, this is all future awareness, precognitive specter. These parallel event lines marked out across a future event field. Tribulation's big game day still over a decade away.

This allows time and opportunity to effect positive change and to mitigate and reduce future negative outcomes. Spiritually, as well as physically, billions of lives worldwide are at stake, but these are like awareness of hot malleable steel in the hands of this blacksmith human population world. Change can be effected while there is still time if the effort is made. But will it? Will Tribulation outcomes be altered because people across the world took what was explained to them seriously, becoming pro-active, or will the world squander this God given opportunity to increase Rapture numbers while decreasing death toll numbers, while improving survivor numbers?

At first glance the human mind wants to focus on and emphasize the possibility for dramatically improved future human outcome results. Perhaps overlooking God, as in God given awareness, and being the one in receipt of them, exactly where I place the emphasis. On the God given side, as in Jehovah Jireh (God the Provider and God the Protector). How genuine are the awareness? That's like asking how genuine is God to his word. Exactly the reason these should be taken with utmost seriousness. The people who perish will often have the common denominator shared, they didn't take these awareness serious, and thus were not responsive pro-actively to them (They'll never do that again!). When you arrive at recognition of Tribulation's approach, you must also then come into recognition of the Almighty who is in charge of this universe, and your relationship thusly with God. Meaning you don't want to be among those atheists posting billboard ads when Tribulation arrives, or you already know you are going to get called to the principal's office to then receive detention for eternity as a very naughty unintelligent child, destined for negative outcome fate, in afterlife.

Part II of this book exhibits all the cross field marker indications for Tribulation Field awareness, but the spiritual faith considerations toward expanded and improved relationship with God. The entire world needs to come into recognition of the Christian faith as the one and only correct faith, K.J. Bible correct word of God.

Chapter 16

Hallucination

Hallucinogenics and Altered States of Mind

Hallucinogenic substances (heavier ones beside the T.H.C.-based marijuana and hashish) were known by Spanish in the New World when they placed a ban on them as early as 1521. Some among them must have had a taste of that New World, as well. Most of these are organic derivative botanical plants and/or fungus.

While there are several variety variations, Ozuweekee, serpent vine, morning glory, quoaxil, Ayahuasca, Aztec magic mushroom, and Peyote, all have very similar chemical formula, as organic chemical as opposed to synthetically laboratory produced, such as LSD, which can also be organic in the form of fungus ergot. Two other synthetic hallucinogenics are Cilocybin, and Mescaline. The synthetic Mescaline providing a variant version of the trip derived from the organic version.

Richard Evan Schultes was a mid-twentieth-century pioneer in exploring the field of hallucinogenics, and rain forest botanicals, uncovering several previously unknown plant species, and most likely the inspiring behind another Harvard professor to follow later in the 1960s: Dr. Timothy Leary. Leary in turn influencing an entire generational counter cultural movement. Leary wasn't a botanist, he was looking at expanded consciousness from the perspective of psychology, philosophy, and the potential to unlock doors within the human mind for potential discoveries there.

In Oklahoma Schultes experienced Peyote with the Kiowa on an Indian reservation as part of an Indian spiritual ritual known as the Peyote Way. He was successful in convincing the government to allow the Kiowa and certain other tribes such as Hopi, to be allowed exemption from Federal Laws banning such substances as long as it stayed on the Indian lands.

Today, in my view, combining these very old rituals with Christianity, is a very powerful and positive religion. There are several Indians now holding Doctorate of Divinity degrees from respected theological schools and Universities. Theirs is a different feel and perspective of Christianity and the cosmos, but one that is quite valid. It is perhaps closest to my own in some regards, even though I am not Indian (Native American).

I will not attempt to explain their version, because that is something that should be left to them. Yet I, too, feel I am a Chaman, perhaps just not in identical sense as them. The spirit supernatural realm only deals with souls they recognize as mediums and here I'm referring to spirits of neutral or positive aspect. Negative energy isn't as choosy, it wants to be in contact and invade your space, of just about anyone, and immediate avoidance and rejection is vital. What do I mean by neutral spirit entity? Spirits that are not negative, but at least mildly positive; such as some ghost and potentially some E.T. It is within the realm of some psychic's ability to detect presence, differentiate identity of the entity, and even communicate telepathically in both sending and receiving silent thought wave messaging. Typically a clairvoyant/telepathic with this very specialized ability. E.S.P. is very much varied, similar to the way doctors practice specialized medicine within spheres of expertise.

I see a lower spiritual house or order that can be categorized as a natural, or metaphysical Earthbound spirit realm of multiple dimensions closely layered together. Connected to, but distinctly separate from an upper house or order, and the Holy Spiritual realm. Then there you are, in the lower spiritual house in the dimension of the living, but with all these other layered in dimension around you that you can't see, and can only gain some comprehension of or access through heavy hallucinogenic stimulant.

Native North and South American Indians have used such powerful organic chemicals from plants as part of their tribal religious ceremony dating back millennia. When these same Indians became Christianized, they in some cases did not abandon old practice tradition completely, but kept some of it in a sort of hybridized spiritualization practice. As long as it's the Christianity that has the dominant role, it needn't be minimalized, chastised, or condescended upon. It can give Christianity a very potent wallop of an impact, and all tied to their oldest spiritual tradition, as long as supervised under the direction of one with excellent accreditation, and on some reservations legal to do so.

With the upsurge of what was commonly called the counter culture in the late sixties into his seventies; it perhaps peaked when the Viet Nam War ended. It was 1970 that saw passage of the Federal Prohibitive Drug acts by congress. It created 'scheduling' as to the drugs classified as less dangerous all the way through most dangerous, according to predefine guidelines. Schedule I through V, with I being the most dangerous, and thus warranting the heaviest penalties.

As one over forty years ago, being of the right age, at the right time, at the right college campus place, let's just say that was the first time the nick name 'Wildman' was applied to me, but not the last. It seemed everyone in college then was a bit wild (perhaps always have been and always will be); however, both prior and since, much more centered on alcohol rather than drugs, but drug use still common just not as prevalent as it was, or among as large a base of users as back then when it had mushroomed (excuse the pun) to epidemic proportions. Over time things seemed to have returned to a saner level of insanity so to speak.

I became extremely knowledgeable about LSD firsthand, regarding all shapes, colors, sizes, types, and corresponding dosages. Then after sampling the entire candy store there, along comes a more than ample supply of Organic Mescaline (refined mushroom powder) my way. Haystacks of marijuana, and bricks of hashish for party favors, too!

Typically when I refer to lots of frequent flyer miles to the Twilight Zone, this is what I'm describing, also kicking in the side doors of the supernatural Bldg. at T.Z.U. (Twilight Zone University) with the supernatural building. A sort of student union/supernatural realm headquarters combined or something, because at the time a lot of other students were engaged in similar 'space exploration' into inner sanctum mind space. So your author rest assured is well versed on this entire drug induced altered states heavy research into heavy hallucinogenics analysis personal experimentation.

Yes, guilty. Dr. Timothy Leary's Space Academy. Major Tom's astronaut flight school of Deep mind Space exploration. Wildman the rocket man Early explorer/chartographer of the Twilight Zone surveyor teams. Check the signature in the box in the lower right hand corner on those maps and you can probably find the Chamen Wildman's signature on those plats!

According to Indian legend, only one who has true Chaman spirit can ingest Organic Mescaline for the first time and not get sick or vomit. Typically almost all who take it, do get sick some twenty to forty-five minutes later, I never did. Not the first time, or any other time. That was the first time the nick name the 'Chaman Wildman' was applied, The Chaman part was not long lived, but somehow surrounded by totally different people the name 'Wildman' kept returning to me!

So, clearly a psychic prospector nick named 'Wildman' an excellent tour guide up in the Hallucinogenic Mt. range of the 'altered state' for you relative to commentary within this book. A mountain top perspective that allows one to see the whole valley so to speak. A prospector up there prospecting for answers to supernatural mysteries, a seeker of hidden secrets. Don't get the wrong impression though, I'm not promoting or recommending this type of drug use to others at all. For myself anyway, this type of drug wasn't addictive (unless you do hit a rich gold vein of answers exhibited), but many other drugs do get abused no questions unanswered there, and in negative outcome. You have to be smarter than the drug, and know which ones to avoid completely if you go near them at all. You have to be smart enough never to inject a needle in your arm, as well. Later in life I often counseled people informally against drug use, and could only have been able to do so with any measure of credibility by having past experiences and knowledge of firsthand involvement regarding it.

Some might wonder, why with a strong Christian fundamentals background I would even want to explore the realm of consciousness expanding hallucinogenics. It had been only a few years since I'd been informed by a holy angel I would one day write this book, and somehow I sensed those experiences, instead of being in disregard of God, might be awareness enhancing toward the supernatural, and that in turn possibly at least, valuable to the book, and this book apparently valuable to God, or possibly so it seemed! A waiver in my back pocket from God to do such heavy drugs (in heavy dosage) you ask? No, more like convincing myself I had a tacit green light wink, nod, and a little grin from the Almighty! He couldn't officially approve, but in my unusual and rare case, if I knew there were benefits to be obtained, I had to believe he understood it would help with deeper comparative relationship understandings of the mystical supernatural realm, and that even he had to concede having this extended mind/space exploration would eventually yield positive elevated consciousness that could then eventually be useful in the writing of this book. In much the same way you have to be firsthand experienced in this field to help others break addictions, having this supernatural territory exploration knowledge under my belt allowed for a much more accurate and genuine grasp of how reality in this mind space dimension changes when in altered state of consciousness, and realization of the multi-dimensional fabric nature itself. You likely won't gain such realizations any other way. It is valuable in that sense, but limited in value over-all.

Certainly in 99.9 percent of all such usage cases, God unlikely would be in approval, regarding it as self-indulgence, and/or simply drug abuse of the human mind, our bodies a holy Temple in the holiness sense. Was my rare case the holder of that missing .01 percent tacit approval waiver? I won't know until afterlife, but at least possibly so! If I had it to do over again, it in my case was valuable for this book, thus for the sake of this book at least, worth doing. It is a component of the supernatural that if you are going to explain all aspects of, you will never fully comprehend unless you personally have a grasp of. How can other authors adequately explain the supernatural in full without this? They can't and they don't, only explaining those components which they do. This book doesn't hit just some of the floodlights, it is a very thorough evaluation effort in attempting to hit them all after crashing the supernatural gate for you.

It's no wonder it feels like the E.T./U.F.O. have the Wildman under surveillance re-con continually. It might sound paranoid delusional (as well as comical) to say the Reptilian demon have me under continual don't let him out of your sights watch perpetually. I sense them now sensing me as that dangerous, no good, troublemaking Christian psychic Prophet down below that the angels are always hanging out with! Better watch him, he's trouble; he'll do us a lot more damage than he's already done if we don't watch him. It's more like I'm making the demons paranoid! They better hope I don't perfect a long range weapon that can turn Christian faith into a high intensity laser, or South Florida. could start to see a lot of downed U.F.O., their outer surfaces with faith penetration holes! Talk about some fallen angels now, demons tormented by a human no less! Prince of the Power of the Air going into full engine stall-out the night mare I'd like to give them, but since they never sleep, for now I have to settle on trying to deliver paranoia to them. I see you guys up there watching me! Once you sign on to serve God, no matter what capacity it might be in, you have to realize there is no turning back, no quitting on God, no changing.

What happens is, if you fall back into former less spiritual, less righteous paths of behavior becoming more focused on this material world, much like that U.F.O. engine stall-out just mentioned, before you know it you've lost your spiritual identity self, and have if you're not careful precipitating a downward spiral loss of control over. No bigger conquest trophy for demons than pulling down a human who once had managed achievement to higher level, only to be defeated from the inside by themselves in defeat, recognizing too late what has happened. More is given by God to humans in anointing them, more is thusly expected from them in serving God. The punishment in afterlife can potentially be quite severe, for anyone who fails in service as a special agent for God. Possible that God's clearances might be granted, as well, unofficially of course. It makes it especially rough to provide signed documentation or really much proof at all I admit, but I'm stating this realizing there is scant evidence, yet still a lot more going on behind the scenes in all our lives, even at the highest holy levels, that we are totally oblivious to, yet likely is going on. Yet perhaps if even God can't pull a stealthy fast one on Wildman in this described situation, it could have something to do with being such an agent to serve his purpose by means of this book in the first place. Everything seems to always lead back to this book, and all roads, along with destiny connectivity all converging, and tied into this book.

Now elsewhere, later in the book, I speak of a couple of examples where Divine intercession or intervention may have occurred in order to save my life. You can't know any of these with certainty, but in discussing this heavy hallucinogenic drug 'trip' experience, here, too, a few times I got so high I had to say a prayer for permission to return to my home dimension for clearance for safe passage runway return landing. My space shuttle brain feeling weightless in upper atmosphere questioning if I'd even to be able accomplish return in order to survive that particular flight ordeal. It is a bit scary to be that high and not be sure if all the navigation instruments in your brain are functioning adequately to get you maneuvered into re-entry position (All of this figuratively speaking as you are really at the mercy of the drug and holy angel spirit guide that might be present.). Well, I did obviously make those landings, but not because I was a prospector astronaut with exceptional flight skills, but rather because all this inter dimensional altered states of reality would later be of great evaluation value for writing of this book. This book in service to God's purpose, so it's very possible that here too I had some high level landing clearances in place I was never fully aware of, just like those waivers in my back pocket, invisible and unsigned, yet there. More high level security clearance. The clergy are agents working for God, probably getting all kinds of special clearances all the time, too, often they also likely completely unaware. So it is not unreasonable that this hypothesis I've presented is that dissimilar. By the time you complete this book, some of this that might seem a bit far out right now, likely will make a lot more sense to you later.

It's a bit like a gemstone that's multi-faceted. I'm not just trying to show you the stone, but each facet seems to have relationship requiring explanation, necessary to understand the total gemstone picture

When I saw there was nothing more to be acquired knowledge and awareness wise I simply stopped using hallucinogenics. The drug controls you too much, you can't control it except minimally, and after a great deal of use you have to increase dosage to stay at an equivalent level since your body gradually builds up a sort of offsetting tolerance. You can't keep increasing dosage, your heart is already running a seven- to-ten-hour marathon, and the risk of prolonged use is too great relative to long term effects if not careful, and knowing when to say enough is enough. When you are really in it for gaining interdimensional awareness as I was, and you reach the point where nothing new is derived it's disappointing and frustrating, and so you have motivation to quit on that count, as well.

It's not addictive in the sense of chemical dependency. Tobacco was my addiction up until around age thirty-one or thirty-two. My intuition talking to me, telling me in another dozen years or so later in life, mid to late forties I was headed for a stroke or heart attack. I listened and quit, although relapsing several times before finally successful. Once you realize you've broken the addiction, you know you need to keep it broken, and the longer you go the easier it becomes. You create the determination to do so first, then that strong will is what defeats the bad habit. You realize, too, you can accomplish almost anything in this world if you want to bad enough and refuse to relinquish that desire to keep trying in order to succeed (addiction breaking just one example).

Now while we are on the drug use subject, let me diverge for a moment, and tell you about a girl I had only met once before, but ran into her by chance, at a timing that turned out fortunate for her. I wasn't aware she had just begun re-using heroine, something she hadn't done recently, but had eight to ten years prior. I'm in my early fifties, and she in her late thirties. I knew I had to intervene in her addiction, and sensed she needed to quit promptly before it really did become a strong addiction, but knew also the fact that she had only just recently begun re-use from what she told me would improve her chances of doing so. I sat her down where I could counsel her for several hours. I can't tell you exactly all that I said, but it worked!

She later credited me with turning her life around, and in fact said I likely did save her life. She made a complete recovery, and did get her life together and straightened out. Now if I had died from drug over dose back in 1969, who would have been there to counsel this young lady in intervention, do you see this additional reason why God may have intervened through holy angel in saving mine multiple times? I do. The young lady eventually moved back to the Philadelphia /South Jersey area where she was originally from, and last I heard had a child. So possibly you see three lives spared in this story.

Undoubtedly my guardian angel has a very long highlights reel of all the many saves he assisted in over the years. Likely more saves than most major league baseball relief pitchers. That same South Jersey shore decades earlier where I'd managed to escape both a vicious undertow and rip-current. He was a bit response slow in hitting the reset button on that one, not that I'm complaining about the two mile walk back up the beach when Wildman finally did manage to successfully swim back to shore. This only one of a collection of drowning close calls, even being an excellent swimmer. If you had a list of common near death experiences, such as falls from two story or greater heights, auto accidents, capsized sailboat, animal assaults, smoke inhalation, bicycle/car collision, drug over dose as previously described, near drowning, electrocution, and even exotic encounters like shark, lightning strike, or a blood clot in your leg, and I'm right there in true been there and done that form, and still here to tell it. It would seem even my guardian angel referring to me as the Wildman. What a highlight reel he has! So, I knew I must have a higher purpose, and as I've stated previously it always seems to point to this book! I'll cover a couple of these episodes later on in the book beside this drug over dose example already given as to others with greater likelihood of divine intervention that occurred. Seems if you want a certain book written you can't kill the author off ahead of time especially if he's a central character, and the 'Senior Editor' from on high has complete control. It becomes even more compelling when you become aware of the presence of destiny, which also will be examined further later on.

So, a girl named Robin went on to have a child, because she avoided an addiction that might have claimed her life. My counseling might have been the difference, but I had nearly died myself gaining those very awareness used to counsel her. Also, had I died, my children and grandchildren would not have been born, and this book you are reading right now giving credit to holy angel involvement along with Divine intervention for all of it, and mention of possibly some unofficial unsigned special agent holy waiver clearances in my back pocket throughout all of it! Now how is that for some amazing grace from an amazing God.

Well it's certainly reassuring to know you have a life insurance policy with the Kingdom of heaven insurance company. They never need to pay a claim because they won't let anything happen to you! Your prayers are your premium that you pay in, and exceptional coverage is provided. What a policy!

Now unfortunately I haven't had the same degree of success with others, as I did with Robin. Many simply hadn't hit their bottom, and no one changes until they want to. Until they finally realize they've hit a dead end bottom and must change course. Still, almost all told me what I spoke to them about did have impact, I was making a dent toward their eventual change in thinking. I was a positive influence who was making an impact. I had left my own drug days far behind, but could draw on my vast experiences to now counsel others.

While I don't totally regret what I did, it's simply not for most. I was seeking expanded consciousness and when it was clear there was nothing more to learn I stopped. The side-door of the supernatural building as I metaphorically often refer to it, and to which I'd kicked in many times, simply had nothing left but locked doors to hallways that couldn't be accessed. Top security files you couldn't get a look at, and security clearance not high enough to access restricted areas. After a while, even taking several times the single dose amount your body builds up a tolerance. You can't increase the dose any higher because six or seven of the eight to ten hours you are at it, your heart is already running at maximum capacity, and in a marathon. At that point you realize it's time to quit, and quit I did (1970).

All other drugs should be completely avoided, and those that I once did, due to less availability and stiffer penalty are difficult to even find anymore. An artist, musician, someone studying psychology, or philosophy, or even theology might gain some insight as I did, but no, I don't recommend it. I talk total avoidance to all drugs, because risks are real. Think health and nutrition, and from that spiritual mental health springs forth. These things aspect a person positively.

Now let me regress back to 1969, and I'm a student abroad taking undergraduate junior level courses in London England. I'd kicked in the side door of the supernatural building back in the states, now I was doing it over in England, at their London branch offices. A dabbler in their local LSD market? Who Wildman? He wouldn't sneak up behind an English ghost and say, Boo! Would he?

Let's just say that every time he heard the Warren Jevon song about the Werewolves of London, he had to pause and wonder if the song hadn't been written about he and a few classmates. Then the moment would pass as he realized it wasn't.

Wildman would a couple of times a week go out for a stroll around 11 P.M. and not return until several hours later when they would lock the front doors of the hotel and they would not be opened again until morning. In about twenty minutes or less after departing, Wildman would find himself completely lost. Every time, completely lost. How I always managed to find my way back and do so before the locking of the doors still amazes me to this day. Often with only a minute or two to spare.

One night on one of Wildman's midnight strolls and as always totally lost, something especially weird occurred. I'm talking about weird experience inside of the normal weird experience. As I'm walking down the sidewalk of this one street (southwest section). I glanced across the street to this stairway leading down to the door of a bottom flat.

There was a vibe coming from the door. The stairway wasn't the issue, it was this door. Intense evil vibes were hitting me, and I sensed something else. It was as if my psychic senses were telling me it was a portal into another dimension! I sensed if I went over to the stairs, walked down the steps and turned the knob, it would not be locked. However, upon crossing that threshold, I would never be seen or heard from again if I did so!

The intensity was probably about as intense as it can get for someone with greatly heightened sensitivities. Before or since, has an evil vibe been sensed that was that intense and extreme until the 2008 U.F.O. sighting that was dubbed the misnomer Romeo. Whether it was or wasn't a portal, still doesn't dismiss the picking up of a strong evil vibe. At the time not having many of the psychic experiences that wouldn't be encountered until later, I wasn't aware that in fact my psychic abilities although perhaps latent were still quite valid.

I decided to walk further down that street then return. Those vibes subsided as a one-hundred-foot walk up the street progressed, but then I decided to walk back to where I was, and the vibes got stronger and more intense as I did. I was now starting to require myself to fight back fear that was if unchecked ready to turn into terror! Over a door! A closed door, yet why was this one door of all the doors in the entire city causing me shockwaves? I wasn't about to walk down those steps even if you'd let me borrow your legs, and no way was I going to check the knob, either. Imagined? Real? I will never know, but neither will I ever forget the intensity of what I felt, or the sensed presence of evil. I do think portals exist, and move around. Dimensional overlap, and often an entrance to an evil one. They can occur in a swamp, forest, city, anywhere, and they don't stay in one place, but perhaps open up as an approaching person in some way triggers some type of psychic mechanism.

You might be in an altered state of consciousness as I was, but I don't think it's a prerequisite. I do think something psychic is the spring release trigger however. No one has ever documented a case of someone simply walking into another dimension and totally disappearing, yet there are a few reported cases. Some were proven to be a hoax. In his book, *World of Strange Phenomena*, a World War I Regiment simply vanishes in a cloud, according to Charles Berlitz's story. Yes these British troops were in battle during the Turkish campaign, and according to eye witnessed similar account simply and quite oddly vanished after a cloud descended, and when it lifted they had vanished. Several Thousand men simply gone! Guess we should add clouds to the swamps and forests list. But is it documented? Only in the sense that none of these men were ever seen again, and no dead bodies found on the battlefield (August 28, 1915, page 247 of that book).

Consider, too, such as was my case, if I'd turned the knob on that door and walked hypothetically into another dimension, with no one to witness it, it could happen, but go unreported as such and undocumented. It makes one wonder through history if such is the case, how many missing persons went into another dimension and then unable to return. Is this possible? That's your call to make.

In *Interdimensional Universe*, Chapter 6, "The Connection," Author Philip Imbrogno states, "People who have psychic abilities seem to be able to sense the location of a window when the interdimensional vortexes are formed." Your honor, I rest my case having presented the testimony of an expert witness in the field, which Mr. Imbrogno most certainly is. As Mr. Imbrogno's excellent book points out, often these windows are hostile, evil, demonic windows (just as the one I perceived in London in 1969), and he goes on to give more than one case study which he personally investigated, where (demonic) E.T. involvement occurred. E.T's opening up a portal right there in the wall of someone's bedroom and wanting that human individual to enter it.

Interdimensional Universe is a must read for anyone serious about researching the supernatural and U.F.O. subjects. Philip Imbrogno is extremely credible, so hearing these things from him makes it worthy even from a scientific standpoint, since he is expert in this supernatural field as investigative scientist. When he tells you a interdimensional portal opened up on someone's wall, believe it, and believe this type of strange E.T. contact type of phenomena, as well. These things really do happen to people, and this book certainly a good example of how I've encounter more than my fair share.

Once you realize E.T. and U.F.O. existence is real, all this other stuff just goes part and parcel with that very same phenomenon property.

Any number of U.F.O. books where humans have had contact with E.T.s, aside from the Greys, people often describe the being that they viewed as being Spider Man like in appearance. While I only caught a very brief glimpse out of a dream, I think my Reptilian sketch is close to what they are describing, and the hooded robed figures with eyes like glowing red coals, that witnessed accounts Phil gives in his book, are well documented in other E.T./U.F.O. sightings over the years. demonic? Yes, I think these guys are among the worst of the worst evil E.T.s.

Hallucinations in a Swiss bathtub border zone? What is it? To explain to someone who hasn't ever experienced a heavy hallucinogenic trip (my old frequent flier miles) an analogy can be drawn using a neutral country typically Switzerland, and a bathtub. Think of a bathtub as being a kind of neutral DMZ border between dimensions.

The tub is not up against a solid wall though, it is instead a sort of misty fog barrier that you can't see through. You are in this dimension, this reality on this side of the tub. When you take a heavy chemical stimulant, it mixes with chemicals naturally produced by your own brain and the altered state of consciousness occurs. You are now in the tub so to speak, your still within this dimension, but within that tub area, things from that other dimension or dimensions bleed through the mist/fog wall barrier into the neutral tub area. You have in essence met these other dimensions half way. They can't move into reality any more than you can go into the other dimensions as a living person. It's sealed from the living, and probably something you pass through after death.

Everything you learn and experience in the neutral area is what comes in and mixes from another dimension with your usual reality. Thus you are in both an altered state of consciousness, and at the same time experiencing things within a multi-dimensional reality. It is neither totally one dimension or the other as you perceive it, but rather a mixture. This is why it's consciousness expanding. It is both fascinating and thought provoking.

It becomes important in evaluating what you are seeing by being able to distinguish and differentiate between what is hallucinated but not real (in this reality), and that which is hallucinated as a distortion of what is known to be real. Some things, actually quite often will drift into view out of another dimension, then simply float back out again. Senses can be elevated (such as intensified or amplified hearing ability) and sound can even appear as visual color. You might actually see musical notes in front of you, and usually a very wide gamut of symbols, signs, numbers, alphabet letters, mathematical quotient signs, ancient script, astrology signs, you name it, in very depth layered perspectives and in color!

Since it's been documented that ghosts for example move into flora, trees, and vegetation at times, if you saw leaves turn into little faces for example, would it be just hallucination, or could it be there are scores of little spirits in those leaves. That's a tough one, but my point is there are cases where you can't be certain of exactly what it is you saw or how to classify it.

Now after talking previously about portals opening up, now I've just stated a living person can't penetrate another dimension while living. Allow me to clarify that. Let's say there are ten dimensions present and you are very comfortable within this one, this reality. Normally even though a person tripping is experiencing mixed dimensions, you aren't aware of how many other ones, or which ones. Let's now call one of these a demonic dimension. These portals Phil and I are telling you about, you don't open up consciously (possibly subconsciously), but something triggers these Entities from their side of the portal window, door or whatever you chose to call it to open it. If this were to happen and a person did enter it's highly unlikely that person would ever return to tell about it.

Equally true is the fact that what you take out of the bathtub zone is locked into your memory, but is nearly always impossible to express adequately in words no matter how articulate you are. So in that sense it's a very private journey. You do come away with a certain multidimensional awareness of other invisible realms that are present and co-existent with our own reality. Very easily there could be nine more all around you all layered as part of the time/space fabric within which we live and breathe. You never knew you were breathing invisible symbols, did you?

If you were trying to explain to a blind person what it is like to see light dance off of hundreds of prism glass crystals in a chandelier, who had never even seen a chandelier, could you verbally do justice? Not likely. That is the way it is with those types of experiences, and if two people stood side by side on the same drug taking the same quantity, would they each experience identically? No, certainly not, any more than two average people see the same thing in appreciating a piece of Art or sculpture, or listening to a symphony orchestra. Different brains will interpretively react differently.

The Existential Plane

Is the relationship of one's self to the multidimensional plane of existence the same as one's existential intellectual self?

Have you just been teleported from a Chapter in the psychology Section of a book into a class of philosophy grad students, perhaps the larger question! I will pose some statements as questions, and they are brain stimulants, nothing more:

Could the boundary area between dimensions be viewed as the place where one perceives one's own being within that space, and the perceptions of reality (or altered reality) in relation to one's own self, and including all intelligence, acquired knowledge, and spiritual value along with feelings derived from simultaneous input of the senses.? With input bleeding over from other dimensions while the mind struggles to relate in terms of these realities norms, could it then be when one's mind learns to think in terms and awareness of those other dimensional realities, and where reality from this dimension becomes the intruder that one has truly learned existential thinking? Aren't you glad you're not a philosophy grad student? A resounding Yes!

All of this just a lead in to what I call "self-directed (altered) Realities." A common misconception is that altered mental perceptions need to be stimulant induced. Not so. I will give you two examples of self-directed altered reality as I call it. Academics may have some other term. The two types are unintentional, and intentional.

Example 1: The unintentional Type

Let's take a person who is very busy with lots on their mind. This person wears reading glasses. It might be you! They constantly put them down, pick them on for a while, put them down, up down etc. This person at home or work it doesn't matter, but probably more likely to occur at home, and trying to manage several tasks and thoughts all at the same time tells oneself to look for the glasses.

The person then moves into managing other thoughts while they are hunting for their reading glasses. Can't find them, goes to look in a different room. Suddenly, abruptly, the person must come back to thinking about the reading glasses and put the other thoughts aside for a second or so and re-evaluate.

Then it occurs to them why they can't find them, they are still wearing them. They were looking right through the very glasses they were looking for. Absent minded, yes, but distracted by other thoughts overloading the circuit boards.

For that brief time they became distracted, they had unknowingly created a kind of false or altered reality. The brain commanded the body to go look for the glasses. The whole time, the brain so distracted with other thoughts it failed to recognize the obvious. That they not only already had them, but were looking through them during the search. Unintentional, but for a short time, altered self-directed reality.

Example 2: The intentional Type

People who practice yoga, and certain other Far East exercise seek to achieve a certain balance, a harmony between body, mind, and spirit. In martial arts, sometimes before an act, a mental state is achieved first, and thought appropriate to behavior is exercised.

It often goes beyond focus and concentration. A person about to practice Karate and break a board might concentrate on the thought of the board breaking in an altered reality state, then as the actual act is carried out, this reality then becomes one with the thought of the act already being accomplished. With the cracking of the board, the two realities merge.

A person meditating might try to reach a higher plane spiritually by first going into a relaxed state of peace and harmony, and try to allow the tranquility to cause or effect their spirit to ascend or transcend all that is restraining it.

Toward the end of this book I state the necessity of people becoming aware of the need to make changes in advance of what will be an enormous shift in realities coming to our planet which people will be powerless to prevent, but can likely survive if they make the required adjustments. The acceptance of it is first and foremost.

To do that, most are so caught up in this reality, that they will never make the necessary mental adjustment. Why is that? Because we are very materialistic. Make money to buy things, jobs to make that money to pay for Houses, boats, airplanes, furnishings, autos, electronics, new clothes, and all the smaller material things, as well. To break out of this thinking (only for brief periods) you will need to create your own, that's right, altered state of reality.

To help convince yourself of the need to take steps to insure your survival, this is what I suggest. Turn all of those material things to sand. Big piles of sand and little piles of sand. Everything you own now turned to sand, because destructions to come will pretty much do that. Coming around to thinking this way will help you later. For now it's just an exercise.

You now picture yourself trying to survive in a desert. The only things that really matter are people, and God. You only need necessities to survive, everything in the world turned to sand (at least in this exercise). If you adopt a similar line of thinking, you will not allow you or your family as the case might be to be caught off guard. Money no longer exists (sand) neon-lighted cities all gone, no more stores (sand), and everything around destroyed. But you survived! You slowly, but surely put a plan in place (used this sand thinking concept), and provided a survival shelter in place for when the time came, and you were then prepared. So many weren't, so many ignored the warnings until time had run out and it was too late. Little to no chance of survival, and later to be captured means imprisonment. When everyone else's world now turned to sand, and it was game over, you had the foresight, knowing the Bible's prediction of this, to redirect reality in advance ahead of all this into one encouraging your own survival.

You prepared yourself for this through motivation, later taking action to build underground shelter supplied with provisions. Whether that New Reality you imagine is everything sand, a moonscape, a post nuclear landscape, your neighborhood completely leveled, or whatever you choose that works for you. An altered reality of the now, in a desolate view of the future for your own motivation purposes is going to save your life (and family?) later, potentially.

About a dozen years left, but they will pass quickly unless you are able to maintain focus, and that requires motivation. It will be severe, and later chapters (Part II) give timeframe, but for now, accepting this and your motivation for survival is the first step. Empower yourself now, for your survival success later. If enough individuals survive, then our nation may, as well. Motivation will keep you focused over those dozen years, and helping America's survival, added motivation. An altered reality as a tool to save your life.

What about Christian Rapture known as the Pre-Tribulation or Church Rapture, where many Christians will vanish and be taken up and into a different dimension of existence you might ask, doesn't that preclude and eliminate the need for survival shelter you ask? See further extended discussions in Part II of this book also). Of all the Rapture scenarios Bible mentioned, there is more scripture that clearly supports these occurrences. However, there are varied interpretational differences even among clergy I'll get into later. While I personally believe in this occurrences myself, the question is exactly what per-cent of all Christians are included beyond the clergy. The most devout Christian certainly, but then exactly how high will that Rapture bar be set? Will you clear it? Are you even eligible, as only Christian faithful are? My point being, unless you are comfortable you are okay here, and your faith will easily pole vault itself over that bar, then you need a survival plan B just in case it doesn't.

A mindset that you might need a higher altitude survival shelter with a four year food/water supply, and therefore prepare one for yourself, perhaps with friends and relatives. First the mindset, then the planning, then actually accomplishing it. If it turns out you didn't need it, the effort and expense won't matter to you if you do rapture. However a bit like going ocean fishing twelve to fifteen miles off shore. You don't expect you'll need life preserver, life vests, but if you do, you have them along just in case. Building an underground shelter with provisions is not hiding from the wrath of God that is certainly approaching, it is instead a show of faith. Like someone bringing a rain jacket along because of better than 50 percent chance of heavy afternoon downpour. Remember it wasn't raining when Noah built his ark, either.

Being in a group, sharing expenses will lighten the cost burden. If it turns out only some rapture and some don't, the ones who didn't will be grateful to be blessed with this means of survival, when few who are without will survive another three and three quarters years to that point of Christ's return highest probability I've laid out for you. Your rapture, if you were the one raptured, then an inspiration to faith by those left behind.

A psychic visionary/prophet is saying to you, it starts with mindset. Noah acting on what he was certain was instruction from God to build an ark never questioned from that point on, he developed correct mindset determination that he would not waiver in carrying out exactly as instructed. While I might not be God, I am certain all my awareness come to me via holy angel, over an entire lifetime, always proving correct. These are God's holy angels. angels known for intense effort in preservation of human life.

Consider that angels would be aware they'd have to give me timing awareness, otherwise no-one would even consider carrying out what is suggested if there was no indication of Tribulation timeframe. It wasn't for just one life (mine) that this awareness information was provided me, it was for yours and the billions of other souls around the globe, who just might be willing to act upon danger alert regarding and coinciding with Bible Prophecy given in New Testament Book of Revelation. If you accept it as valid then you are indirectly accepting of Jesus Christ's validity if not already doing so, since it is said to have been given directly from Christ to John of Patmos, those very Apocalyptic Tribulation/Revelation accounts. Let me witness and testify to you it is in fact one hundred percent true as stated. My own recent psychic awareness precise tie-ins clear confirmation, as well as the holy angel source as previously stated.

Motivating yourself toward personal survival shouldn't be difficult. It isn't a substitute for clearing the rapture hurdle, it's directed as your precautionary life preserver. It starts with mindset, and with faith.

Throughout this book, I've tried to keep discourse discussion on Religion separated in its own segregated section in the final chapters and Supplement section (Part II). Yet at the same time trying to make a point that all these other topic compartments of the supernatural realm are all inseparably linked to religion, and God as Christian ideology/theology perceives it is Holy Trinity form. That in fact all of the supernatural is under his firm control, as well.

Here, because of the necessity in discussion of this altered mind-set reality perception, in order to relate it's importance to the topic of Tribulation, I must integrate religion into this conversation, thus temporarily breaking from the afore mentioned separation format. It is later in this book that I mention indications done from an in depth analytical study I did which shows in the range of 40 to 60 percent of all the Christian population worldwide failing to rapture with the rapture of the church (first rapture) Because factors vary widely from country to country, so will rapture participation percent numbers vary widely also. It projects in rough approximate terms, only one in five to one in four Americans who will rapture along with clergy at that time. The exact number and percentages will be in a state of flux all the way up to its actual occurrences. The point here being that large numbers of Americans (and other countries, as well) who associate and describe themselves as Christians may not actually be devout enough as of that time point of the rapture occurrences to participate. For many years, numerous Christian theologian have been warning of exactly what I'm describing. You don't care for lukewarm coffee, and Christ similar to this analogy has disdain for lukewarm Christians, and states this in Revelation 3:14–22, in evaluation of the Laodicean Church in review of this among the seven churches of that day. My point corresponding with Revelation 3:16, often used in quotation by these same clergy mentioned, with Christ's remarking, "I will spew thee out of my mouth," and with certainty references rejection and grounds for rejection. Suddenly my analytical study seemingly with backed by the words of Christ himself, relative to accuracy here! In the Supplement section (Part II) this will be reviewed again in greater depth.

So, in further relating this sand/desolation analogy, you can quote me here: If you have nothing else but desolation around you, but in your heart/mind and soul if you have Jesus, then you have everything. If instead you have only desolation around you, don't have the Holy Spirit inside you, then you are also devoid of hope beside you, as one desolate both inside and out (referencing future Tribulation timeframe).

Confusion arises when people assume that being Saved automatically guarantees them a seat on that first Rapture express. It doesn't mean such necessarily. No one disputes the clergy and most devout among the Saved will be the ones enjoined as a group inclusive of that first rapture departure. However, Christ has scheduled a second departure upon his appearance arrival that by my calculation arrives a little more than three and a half years later, and during the second Tribulation period known as the Great Tribulation (Further discussion on these points later in the book.).

Primarily then it appears those so written in the Lambs Book of Life (eternal life reference) already identified as first rapture candidates. However, mistakenly it seems all Christians have the misconception that by being Saved guarantees inclusion in that first departure prior to the Tribulation destructions start. Here I cannot say with certainty not so, but it does suggest from all evidences and indications, that many who are Christian, but of weaker faith (most of which considering themselves to be saved, yet are still shallow in that faith to varied degree) might not be eligible for first rapture, yet through Tribulation tempering and the testing of their faith's resolve, if passing that testing will then be among raptures at Christ's second coming, and the second rapture.

The catch being, you have to survive and be alive in order for that to occur, and with extremely harsh survival conditions being probable, the chances of more than three and a half years survival without advanced preparation on your own part to assist you, becomes improbable. Upon Christ's second coming all believers in Christ, both dead and alive, even the dead going back for centuries not raised up, shall do so as of that time.

This desolation/sand analogy is to example how one uncertain of being truly Saved in God's eyes, rather just in their own eyes might take a precautionary measure to hedge a 'just in case' safety net for themselves so to speak. Investors employ hedge strategies for their money, and your life and afterlife soul hopefully has precedence over it, so another good reason for those in doubt to consider this.

It will not happen unless you first motivate yourself, and you should at the same time have priority in bringing your current level of faith to resolve achieving increased level and depth, and holding on to it. It may be then that this safety net (plan B) will be neither used or necessary and plan B is not a substitute for Plan A of doing this. However, it will likely enable you to survive those three and a half plus years if needed. Motivating through this altered reality mindset desolation landscape is how you get yourself in acceptance to undertake Plan B, instead of the undertaker being motivated to bury you because you didn't!

The relevance here in this chapter is the mechanism employed between holy side delivery source, and the prophet, in this case, yours truly.

Now heavy hallucinogenic drugs when using them, will cause a person to visualize interdimensional layers, and not uncommonly letters, symbols, numbers, etc.; simply floating suspended within these layers, and sometimes seeing such on several layers at once! However, not seen is fully formed words or sentences sitting on the same, invisible, but flat plane background, with proper spacing between letters and words as if printed there.

Where I am going with this, is that when angels convey information by my experiences over fifty years, it is short message, regardless of conveyance means, limited to a sentence or two worth of total intelligent source informational awareness conveyance. Among other reason mentioning this, as later re-mentioned in Part II, is that when longer conveyance volume of information to human conveyance is required it from all indication is carried out directly by God, or by Jesus (using the entire holy Bible here as an example).

The fact that such is the case then relates to the Islamic claim that Gabriel delivered the entire Qur'an to Mohammed (a Christian holy angel associative with prophecy). If only Jehovah or Jesus were direct participant sourcing for all of Christianity's Holiest word, why would they, six hundred years later drop this restriction for Islam, which glorifies a different God contradicting the true word of the true God, and his Son now resurrected, holy and sacred Jesus' Holy Spirit? The obvious answer is it never happened, they did not. If Mohammed received any sort of supernatural derived communication in fact (doubtful) then it nearly most definitely was not the true God Almighty in contradiction to himself. What you have is an Arabic code of ethics and virtues that was man written (demonically assisted or not), that then desperately needed holy attachment in order for respectability, and so the whole Gabriel/Mohammed story was contrived for expressly that purpose. With certainty Gabriel works for Jehovah/Jesus, and in no way, shape, or form will engage in prophecy conveyance to anyone non-Christian or not loyal to Christ. *It ain't gunna happen*, to slang a phrase. Mohammed's own mother thought he was demon possessed at the time by her account, which makes a lot more sense, but trust me, it takes a prophet to know a prophet, and not even the slightest chance this guy remotely qualifies. Allah is an imposter God, Mohammed an imposter prophet, and hopefully you already knew that. Angels deliver small bits of info. at a time.

Contrarily or conversely, John of Patmos, a devote Christian most definitely did receive the Book of Revelation from Jesus, and my own 2008 confirmations pretty well cinch the authenticity sack for you if even the slightest doubt existed, as my confirmations in match for it, exactly as expressed.

Up until receiving Saints Covenant Prophecy (covered in Chapter 24 of Part II) I had never received prophecy in the form of alphabetically scripted words on an invisible flat plane background before. In fact it had only been a few months since my psychic general subject topic message had shifted to holy subject Tribulation message. This was new, uncharted territory. I mentioned, I always let the angels initiate the message conveyance to psychic transferals. This time, it was promulgated by the asking of a prayer question, then God responding with an out loud sonic boom Yes answer crashing down through my bedroom ceiling, actually causing me to look up and see if it left a big gaping hole or something! No question this voice of a Giant did originate from above, booming downward. Then the image of the bust of a man with a clergy collar, angel appearing before me, disappearing, reappearing then disappearing, and then scripted holy Prophecy in front of me appearing, disappearing and reappearing. Paint running uphill a supernatural symbol, and something like smoke from the upper edge of the image appearing also. Literally symbolizing holy Smoke, Holiness!

Some try to make this into a Satan masquerading as an angel of Light potential situation, and always evaluating objectively this did cross the alternative explanation case scenario possibility examination, but I've ruled it out for multiple reasons. No, I'm not totally certain until fulfillment, but feel certain God is going to fulfill it, and the answer there in contained. Fulfillment serves God's purpose, and pushes the Devil down a flight of serious injury, and setbacks staircase. This high up on the holy side source expectation explanation list.

So, assuming this is confirmed holy side mechanism in the holy side toolbox of options for conveyance delivery, and then considering perhaps the situation with John of Patmos, and the need for a larger volume of information to be delivered with high measure of accuracy, this becomes a very serious consideration for explaining how actual information conveyance was conducted. An entire page in this fashion similar to what I experienced (all be it only a few words) could have been used in this manner to John, where all he had to do was re-copy.

It would have had exact word usage in expression desired, the correct paragraph and sentence structure desired, correct punctuation, all already placed in perfect placement, and vocabulary as desired throughout not left up to John, perhaps then altered even ever so slightly in transferal. In other words, John saw before him all the pages of Book of Revelation already complete. With ink and quill, all that was required of John (still perhaps taking days) was to copy in identical fashion what he saw before his eyes in front of him, but not interfering with his writing immediately before him in copying what he was seeing. A scribe for Jesus!

For centuries Bible scholars and theologian have pondered exactly how this took place. In addition to the script to be recopied, Jesus could have reviewed it in checking for errors, as John copied it down, to make sure it was error free! We will never know for sure, but I submit this to others who contemplate this, as a strong possibility, but a definite tool in the prophecy conveyance tool box regardless. In Part II of this book, I confirm certain details of Book of Revelation given to me in 2008, and you realize then, too, just how unchanged the supernatural is, Jesus is, and my prediction foretelling the Book of Revelation statements expressed, timing wise, approaching fulfillment.

Consider what is said in Revelation 1:19, it reads, "write the thing which you (thou) hast seen—which are—which shall be hereafter." What I'm telling you is John likely saw an entire page at a time presented to him in thin air, from another spiritual dimension before him. Then on parchment scroll with ink and quill, re-copying exactly what he saw before him on other dimensional page of words in optically visible condition them in this dimension. Literally a whole page of sentences before him suspended in thin air! Absolutely in the holy mechanisms prophecy toolbox. Mine less than a paragraph, and perhaps, his could have been delivered a sentence at a time rather than whole page at a time, but literally printed alphabetically worded sentence suspended in midair before him. Absolutely a holy side prophecy mechanism I was privileged to witness, and other information of mine in total confirmation of Book of Revelation itself as written. Whenever God is involved, expect something powerful, as well as amazingly just incredible to interact directly and personally with. The entire final, Holy Bible Book written this way, twenty-first century confirmed, definitely powerful, amazingly incredible. Jehovah and Jesus and Holy Spirit in eternal radiant glory, supernatural Superstars!

As God is my witness, as I witness for God. - Prophet Wildman

Chapter 17
Leys, Dark Leys, and Psychic Leys

From perhaps what could have been around the time of Atlantis' zenith (perhaps around 4,000 B.C) to about the time migration from Atlantis' second destruction occurred around and settlers relocated to Western Europe (2,193 B.C. destructions) in similar fashion megaliths dotting the Western Europe landscape date back equivalent timeframe, and in increasing numbers. Especially in Ireland and England, but found in France and elsewhere, as well (pre-Celtic history). Stories/legends tie these monoliths, dolmins, Menhirs, Cairns, and tumuli back in part (if not in all) to the Atlantean.

In Chapter 11 of Frank Joseph's Survivors of Atlantis, entitled Atlantean Kings for Ireland and Wales, Mr. Joseph makes a strong case based on documented evidence (Another book I highly recommend.). He states that Stonehenge was conceived and constructed (perhaps completely) around 1,600 B.C., but abandoned by around 1,200 B.C.

Interestingly enough, the tie Mr. Joseph points out (Chapter 11, page 153) in the story of Macannan Mac Lir, who founded Lyr-cestre (now modern Leicester) and one of three chief holy families (as considered in those early pre-Christian times) of the entire isle of Britain. Known in Wales as the children of Llyr. Later in Shakespeare as he points out also, remembered as the tragic figure of disillusionment in Shakespeare's King Lear. Also mentioning association with Atlas' Garden of the Hesperides (Garden of Eden?) golden apple trees. Lyrean Extraterrestrial link, as well? One has to wonder. The link undeniably is present.

Fact, legend, or a bit of both, one then sees the U.F.O. link to both Atlantis and Stonehenge being possible Lyrean E.T. linked also. However, in my view, sometime after Stonehenge's original use as a holy site, that very well, could have had interaction with E.T. of holy expected intelligences, it went through a dark period of Pagan sacrificial rituals and demonic black alter sacrifices. Thus E.T. summoned to this site were demonic in spirit themselves, and this time period carrying into the very same as the Mayan, practicing the same (demonic E.T. inspired?) rituals.

U.F.O.-logists aren't totally sure of the link on the holy side of E.T. between Nords; tall almost Scandinavian looking, (often long blonde hair accompanying description and attractive human looking) and the Lyreans who are also human looking, attractive, and tall with Blonde or Red Hair. Are they one in the same? Lyreans seldom reported in modern times, but the tall slim Nords, occasionally are. angels can take human form and are certainly of holy disposition, but is that the case? It remains a mystery, but they are clearly no strangers to angels if not angels themselves. It is best to think of angels as angels and Nords and Lyrean as E.T. until more conclusive information is available. All three (if there are three) groups are benevolent toward humans.

Around Stonehenge are natural energy fields (straight, but narrow invisible Earth's energy force field corridors) known as Leys. It seems to create a psychic vortex, as well. Some psychics claim that the psychic fields also create memory fields or ancient memory fields that through the process referred to as psychometric of interacting with such fields, they can then visualize ancient scenes that took place on these very locations. Some have claimed to have seen ancient priests in yellow robes that drew spiritual energy from the stones. Some people have even reported to have heard clicking and/or whirring noises coming seemingly from within the stones themselves. It is claimed after this early period of attempting to extract positive spiritual energy, the much darker period of sacrificial rituals took place. Once a Black alter is established, then ET presence would either be Bad Greys or Reptilian (Reptilian essentially being flying demons) and Bad Greys as their associates.

All over Europe, but particularly western, Obylisks, megaliths, and henges (both Earth mound circles and stone circles) abound, numbering nearly nine hundred in the U.K. alone. Each time, they mark significant Earth energy or geophysical energy presence and location. The henges it seemed also doubled as astronomical observatory, and laid out to exactly capture by use of light and shadow, marker points of Sun, Moon, and stars, as well as predictors of equinox and solstices and eclipses. That important to an agrarian civilization for planting and harvesting timings. Still the Leys and more specifically Ley intersection points the determining factor as to stone monolith locations.

Points where Leys intersect (sometimes as many as ten or more) are referred to as nodes. Usually the more intersection, the more significant the nodes in importance. Often churches of very old history would have their chancery (front alter area) located directly over or near the node point because it was considered to be a spiritual vortex like energy column of air ascending upward. In fact windows, portals, gates, or whatever you choose to call them, at least in psychic terms are enhanced spaces and it is thus easy to see why churches would be anxious to capture such space within. Outdoors, the celestial planetary movement seem to also be a predictive indicator of when these Earth energies were about to increase or decrease in strength, as the Moon for example may have played a role.

There is something clearly going on beyond raw Electro Magnetic Energy. Electro-Magnetic Pulse seems to intensely be tied to beings of all classification and important regardless of what dimension they call home. Some believe the answer lies at the sub-atomic particle level.

Scientist Wilhelm Reich equated this to Orgone energy and claimed that alternating layers of organic and inorganic materials would produce the similar spiral vortex effect and intensifying naturally occurring planetary primal force.

Some rocking stones believed to channel this energy, as well, and are found both in the U.S. and U.K. Once again, Phil Imbrogno is right on target (read his book for details on this, as well).

The megalith vertical stones are said to act like storage batteries, or perhaps in some cases transformers functionally beyond just being markers Where rocking stones are concerned, some believe they are positioned to re-direct the energy flow in a desired direction, acting as deflectors. Quartz is known to be piezoelectric, or having the property of becoming electrically charged when pressure is applied to it. Not surprisingly Quartz being fairly common, many megaliths have high quartz concentrations that perhaps create some sort of electromagnetic chain reaction at the atomic level with sub atomic effect, as well.

In one location in the U.K., a case of levitation occurred where the energy stream was so strong it lifted a boy up off the ground levitating him by means of invisible spiraling currents. This an indication of just how forceful these energy currents can be, and in doing so, supply the sort of piezoelectric pressure perhaps required.

Cregg County Kerry, Ireland, is believed to be both high in EMP energy, but piezoelectric, as well.

No doubt psychic fields are also created through these spiral energy vortexes, and a scientific and spiritual crossroads in the process. For unknown reasons, burial sites also seem to create interdimensional corridors. Burial sites in combination with energy field sites seem to further amplify interdimensional activity/interactions with the living. That thin membrane separating dimensions seems to wear even thinner with interchanges and a whole gamut of paranormal activity becoming more easily accomplished, with supernatural unexpected suddenly becoming more natural; as well as expected.

Trying to convince people of dangers they have little to no awareness of that I might have awareness of through psychic means can cause some people to start thinking I'm crazy, but it can be a situation where if they don't believe me, and listen to what I tell them, then they will not only be dead wrong about me being crazy, but they could be dead period (I'd rather be a live nut than a dead skeptic). The supernatural is a lot of difficult baggage, and not at all that easy to simply take someone else's word regarding it, so many people resist or in denial reject what challenges their norms. People who aren't psychic themselves don't quite comprehend what the whole experience is like for someone who is.

I'm diverting a bit from leys, but just for a moment since I'm on this subject momentarily of accepting warnings from genuine psychics such as myself. Being or having psychic ability is a gift from God, and there is no doubt that it is his angels on the sending end of information I receive. If I tell someone to take notice (as I will later in this book), please do. Not all awareness comes with equal certainty, and I always try to articulate nuances and innuendo giving as much defining detail descriptively as I can. After discussing Dark Leys next, I'll then return to the psychic subject with the discussion of psychic leys, and some personal experiences.

Dark Leys

Particularly in the U.K. where Leys are so common, occasionally one of these Dark Leys is discovered (also referred to as black streams), and are essentially flows of negative energy in concentrated form. It isn't just negative in the electro-magnetic sense, but in the sense of being a kind of negative spiritual energy poison affecting plants and animals alike.

Humans can be affected in both mind and body, feeling both emotionally drained, as well as physically, and feeling degenerative, as well. Memory loss, mental stresses, breakdown, immune system loss, cancer, and even things like impotence and infertility, as well as a whole assortment of many other ailments can be directly attributed, from prolonged exposure. It has been documented livestock and plants suffer similar adverse reactions.

Re-directing it by planting angle irons in the ground to deflect it have proven successful, but not stopping it. They are said to be imbalances in the harmonious flows of Earth energy that create these flows in the first place. Even telegraph cables corrode more quickly when exposed to black streams!

The Yin and Yang in Chinese culture and natural balances as prescribed 8 by the Chinese philosophy known as fengshui, which means wind and water, but it, too, is based on achieving natural harmonious balance of Earth's energy for the most favorable result. It was believed the Yang currents flowed generally through mountains and hills, and should be present in a two to three ratio to Ying currents flowing through the valleys and subterranean channels. Their equivalent to Leys were known as lung mei. They felt that improper balance could result in the same result the West calls black streams.

In his book, *Angels Among Us*, author Ron Rhodes makes the point that fallen angels (demons) can and do cause human ailments and an array of maladies, some not dissimilar to the black streams. He also makes the point that many illnesses are naturally occurring, so the demons are simply adding to these rather than taking full credit. If positive spiritual spiral vortex columns are created by most leys, it's not too difficult to then connect dark leys and negative energy streams with dark spiritual demonic energies, at least presence on some occasion. This in turn might account for sightings of some manifestations of rather demonic appearing creatures which I personally refer to as demonic Rares (Chapter 3, Monsters).

Psychic Leys

In Chapter 15, in describing my personal psychic experiences, I spoke of a term I use, and several episodes similar (but different) to premonitions that I refer to as Intunitions. Also mentioning a intunition link, that each was but a link to a future common end occurrence, and it was this book that occurrence! Yes, destiny in spades. This book being the common feature, and end result to each of these links. Whereas the focus with individual premonitions is on the future event, separate and distinct from other events, with these the message was simply that this piece of information or set of circumstance would one day be important. Almost a reverse premonition in the sense that it is the present that is going to be needed in the future the psychic (myself) was made aware of. In comparison to future event knowledge being of importance to the present Parapsychologists now in awe? I had an intunition fifteen years ago they would be (just joking).

The first such intunition occurred in church in 1964. The second one had to do with a native Floridian named Valerie, in 1979/80 timeframe talking to me about a main North/South roadway, State road 809, and that in this area, a number of what could only be described as supernatural events had occurred along this roadway, particularly near what were believed to be ancient Indian sacred burial sites. Unfortunately with the widening of the road (now six to eight lanes) the supernatural disturbed sites had widened, as well. She stated many psychic occurrences, and even sporadic account of Indian ghost sightings were attributed to the roadway, once an Indian trail pathway used for hunting. Sacred burial sites near springs (leys?) and the hope the departed would have good hunting in the afterlife.

Almost immediately after being told all this I had one of these intunitions. Since then it appears this roadway (from personal experience confirming over almost thirty years), what she stated as far as these things go are true. Roughly 90 percent of all my psychic experiences have come either on or within about one quarter mile of this psychic roadway. The 1952 U.F.O. (now classic) sighting/landing occurred near what is now a busy intersection, but back then was scrub pine woodland and an ancient Indian burial site. I've had a few psychic awareness in that immediate area that predicted event which later fulfilled.

Yes, I mentioned all this before, but do so again for this reason. Just as in the U.K. leys and ancient burial sites near Leys seem to not only attract U.F.O., but elevated psychic activity level, so does this area in certain spots along State Road 809! The same in Sedona, Arizona, and there too ancient Indian burial sites and elevated psychic occurrences.

While so many consider the geology critical in the U.K. as to Leys, in fact Leys occur worldwide (the Chinese example), and Earth's energies straddle all regions of the globe. The energies move up from the Earth's core, likely along paths of least resistance. As they near the surface wells, springs, and aquifers likely assist this energy's quest to reach the surface. The spiraling flows moving by water, since water is very conductive to electrical charge. Here in Florida underground rivers move through softer geological strata such as sandstone and limestone, and upper layers can and often do contain mix of organic decaying material and inorganic stone and sand layer not dissimilar to that condition described earlier in the Reich model. Aquifers do run from northwest central Florida in a southeasterly direction, and likely along or near State road 809 through subterranean below it!

Now what becomes interesting is that there is another north/south roadway running parallel to S.R. 809, only about one quarter mile west. Yet, in the identical thirty-year time period, not one single psychic occurrences along that roadway whatsoever! No burial sites, and likely the underground aquifer not present beneath it, either. It is quite possible the Indian burial sites were located near springs (along the hunting trail) and, in doing so, amplified the Earth energy into psychic spiritual column vortex, as well. It is not surprising many Leys in the U.K. then do terminate at what are called ancient wells, and likely are source points. Dowsers that find water, also expert in Leys, and even in the U.K. the ancient burial site, and Ley combination a point of amplified supernatural and psychic occurrence.

Certainly in other places around the world, the same thing. Other locations in the U.S. with thousands of year old burial sites potentially near wells, springs, and such seem to attract U.F.O. there, too. Mentioned previously, one of the ways to differentiate what looks like a star from a U.F.O., is that it will do a little jiggle dance, or make a small circular motion as if attempting to locate directly above such EMP energy column spiraling invisibly to the human eye up to them. Clearly, their goal is to absorb this energy up into their craft.

U.F.O.'s doing little circular jiggle dances. If I put a notch in my belt for every Florida garden variety U.F.O. I've busted in this manner, I would need another belt, having run out of space. Down below, humans paying taxes on their energy consumption. I'm sure the State would love to tax them, too, taking free natural resource from Florida tax free, but the enforcement problem something the State legislature hasn't been able to resolve, so they just consider the ET as native wildlife I suppose. Tough coaxing a dollar from an alligator, either.

Phil Imbrogno points out in *Interdimensional Universe* something very similar perhaps occasionally overlooked, in that EMP anomaly reaches to great altitudes, and this in turn can have effect on human aircraft, particularly Bermuda and Devil's Triangle. That in turn means all the other accompanying phenomena such as psychic/Time/ghost/E.T. and other supernatural conditions can be present, not to mention the disruption to flight instrumentation.

In the ill-fated Everglades crash of Flight 401 a documented account of a former flight personnel member returning as a ghost, and appearing to several members of another flight, one might then see the connection to appropriate condition being present to allow for such to occur. Psychic spiral vortex here in Florida with elevated levels of supernatural occurrences? As a recipient, I'd say definitely so.

KNOWN EUROPEAN AGES OLD TUMULI & LEY LINE SITES
(often with heightened level Parapsychic activity)

Chapter 18

Portals: High Strangeness: Dimensional Warps

The Role of Psychology in Paranormal Cases
(Evaluating Portals, High Strangeness, Dimensional Warps, Etc.)

In my view, there are two ways psychology plays a role in the paranormal case event. One is in attempting to determine if the event is completely external of the person who experienced it, or if spirit entities interacted with the human mind internally, and had causal effect influencing brain function, either partially or completely. If so, it then becomes a parapsychic event, with brain function itself having been influenced.

Quite possibly some cases of Schizophrenia showing psychotic personality schisms, are in spiritual terms, exhibiting signs of possible demonic spirit possession at whatever varied presence level. A bit like a computer virus inside a computer, in this case the human mind like the computer, but infected with an unwelcome spirit entity. Sometimes mild or moderately so, usually nearly totally undetectable, even Psychiatrists unable to detect or recognize. Certainly there are several other causes for Schizophrenia, but this one difficult to diagnose.

Parapsychologists, too, often have difficulty in paranormal event cases when interview and even hypnotic recall and other technique fail to yield answers. When analysis and evaluations turn up little, making determinations is challenging. However, what the person experiences both during the event occurrences, and their later reaction are important. The person who is receptor plays a key role, as to the nature of their own personal psychology, and not just in terms of thought, but senses, and intuitions if present also, that can leave clues.

Light orbs, Portals, High Strangeness, Dimensional or Perception Warps, Ghosts and other Spirit Entity can mix to potentially play hidden co-roles in event occurrences. Yet, unless the external spirit is demonically oriented to some degree, other Spirit Entities tend not to interfere with the human mind internally except in rare cases, and always in positive rather than negative ways. Such as my own interaction with angels for psychic benefit (for example, clairaudience).

To give an illustration of potential negative Spirit interaction, there are documented cases of what is known in Parapsychology terms for a particular paranormal event as ghost cars or phantom vehicles. This paranormal occurrence is quite rare, but appears to me to be demonic Spirit possession. It often occurs late at night and always seems to involve a vehicle approaching at high speed in the opposite direction, often described as appearing out of nowhere.

In the broader scope of my research, I'm attempting to recall from memory what was read previously. A case in England described a driver who swerved to avoid just such an approaching vehicle's headlights headed directly toward him at high speed. Swerving to avoid collision, collided with a streetlight lamppost instead. If I remember correctly, the driver was killed, but a witness claimed that the speeding vehicle mysteriously and suddenly vanished in thin air!

In the U.S. a similar case in the Chicago area near a large and quite old cemetery. A fast approaching vehicle, headlights headed right for another car. The sound of screeching tires, broken glass, and crunching metal, but when the driver got out to inspect the damage, there was none! The phantom car had disappeared, instantly vanished.

Two clues here. The old cemetery the likely source of a demonic spirit, and the sound effects not carrying into reality, suggests the demonic spirit orchestrated all this, manipulating that drivers brain internally, even though the perception was external. It was an altered state of consciousness brought about by the demonic Spirit.

They want to pull down the living and harm you, but spiritual law dictates they are not allowed to kill you directly, they must trick you into you bringing about your own demise. The trickery involved here is the clue. This is a case of externally perceived event, yet was due to parapsychic internal brain function interference and manipulation. A person experiencing such circumstance possibly totally oblivious to the fact it was possession from an evil spirit that caused it all.

Next we'll examine interpretation of a paranormal event - my own! It is either Oz factor/Oz orb, or angel orbs. The first version you will read explains the event, and essentially labels it Oz factor, Oz orbs, but concedes at the end that angel orbs are an alternative explanation. Then you can see how reweighting the criteria used for the evaluation revises completely factors used for determination. While the answer remains undecided, I did this to show you how the psychology involved exerts strong interpretational influence on description of such events. After reading both accounts, your own opinion might also be changed as to interpretation. I think you will enjoy the comparison.

Oz Factor

British author, psychologist Jenny Randles has examined this condition looking at it from a psychology standpoint. The term is a U.F.O.-logy term, as well because it clearly involves E.T. pranksters. Almost without fail there is a visibly seen U.F.O. present, or within a mile range. Most often these cases occur in know U.F.O. hot spots. The cases have been documented worldwide, but are not particularly common.

Gain or loss of time are sometimes reported, so in that sense are not unlike time warp cases, and high strangeness effect is often present also. Circumstances and description of occurrences can vary widely, but these seem to be common components. The intensity or degree of distortion of reality can vary widely also, as well as the duration of the experience.

Without restating accounts from her books *Sixth Sense* (1987) and *U.F.O. Reality* (1983), I've instead noted some additional common factors that are typically noted, along with those just described.

1. U.F.O. clearly present and visible within reasonably close proximity of the Oz Factor reportee.
2. Typically light or light beam is involved, emitted from a U.F.O., glowing from a U.F.O., but descending light rays is common.
3. Reality perception distortions occur. The person reporting having experienced Oz Factor may in some instances feel like they have been separated from reality into some type of non, or distorted reality; an altered state of consciousness. It isn't clear if the mechanism controlling this is internal, external, or some combination of both. Their surroundings as observed appear altered from what they believe it should be. They may mildly sense that everything isn't quite right, not as it should be, but after the experience (temporary) they return back to reality from this altered state.

Example: A street that should be busy with cars, traffic, and pedestrians suddenly appears deserted. Time loss can accompany the experience. (It is typical for U.F.O. abductees and contactees to experience time distortions.

Now I'll give you three separate locations, years, and quotes, mentioned in her books: (All Oz Factor cases)

July 21, 1978, Manchester, England: Beautiful purple rays shot out (from a U.F.O.)
December 6, 1980, Poole, Dorset, England: The object emitted a beam of light.
April 15, 1989, Novato, California: The spheres were golden with a white halo.

I'm building in some background for you on this Oz Factor, for better understanding of a recent February 7, 2009, case that happened to yes, you guessed it! The Wildman went to Ozland, but the wizard wasn't there.

The alien pranksters got me good? It's apparent no one has taken down the note up on the other dimensional bulletin board, regarding the deadline for submissions for my book as the end of 2008. Most probably the bulletin board over in the supernatural building. Or the one at T.Z.U. (Twilight Zone University).

Just when I think I've finally completed lie detection tests (in order to give my readers a fighting chance at believing me), more new stuff just keeps happening. I could be the first human to be bankrupted by aliens, because these tests are expensive. I'm already beginning to feel like I'm locked in mental hand to hand combat with them, with explosions from mental mind game mortar rounds being exchanged. They keep trying to crack me, and can't do it, and won't be able to do it, but these frustrated aliens keep trying. I think these bunch of aliens have really stubbed their little three-toed, cloven hoofed toes on me. They've probably never met a human like me, one who can't be cracked, and just laughs at them!

A great sense of humor and strong Christian faith will get you through most anything. When I refer to my heavy duty Twilight Zone off road shock absorbers cradling my brain, which is what I'm actually referring. Come on aliens, bring it on, your time warp is a wasting! My guardian angel is going to want a pay raise if this keeps up. Come on aliens, show me what you've got, (they're starting to run out of things to show me), heck I've seen ghosts who could do better.

Wildman Gets Oz Factored

Don't figure yourself as being somebody significant, or one who has experienced it all until you've been goofed on by aliens! Maybe a pre-emptive payback for all the slanderous things I'm saying about them in my book.

Approximately between an one eighth and one quarter of a mile south of where I live, there is a large shopping center with a supermarket in the middle. To the left, out in the parking lot area is a restaurant. This location has changed hands, and now a new restaurant was having its grand opening. They had rented a trailer with four large sky search light type lights mounted on the trailer, and had it parked next to the restaurant. At night they could have the four lights wash across the sky in different directions, arcing back and forth, back and forth in a straight beam, or use a second setting. The second setting caused each of the four searchlights to tilt, while at the same time, apparently the mounting platform would rotate ninety degrees, pause, rotate, pause, rotate, etc., complete 360-degree rotation, and then would repeat.

What this did with the light beams extending high into the sky, was to cause the circles or orbs of light to come together in the center, then arc outward in a large one quarter circle turn, in a counterclockwise motion (as observed from the ground). Eventually each orb, would move 360 degrees after completing four large one quarter circle arcs each time.

I had seen both settings, both from my house, and watching it from over at the shopping center, as well. Interestingly, the spot is right below part of the lopsided chocolate chip cookie mentioned in another chapter. Aliens don't like light, have sensitive eyes in that regard, so this restaurant owner without even knowing it was poking aliens right in the eye with a stick so to speak. (much to my delight) Apparently the aliens must have thought I had something to do with this. (return mortar fire), so I think that's why they Oz'd me.

The search lights had been scanning for several nights, but I noticed something strange about the circular rotating orbs. As I moved down my sidewalk, it was as if they moved, too! They would keep the same pattern going, but move wherever I went, so it seemed. Optical illusion? Maybe. I continued different movements, and it seemed they would always relocate above me. It was the same pattern observed before, different nights, and even at the shopping center. But optical illusion or not they appeared to follow me. I would pause, they would pause directly above me while still continuing their repetitive spinning pattern.

I had a bag of re-cycle material in the house, and decided to go and get it. They followed me. My front sidewalk points north, and is about sixty feet long. All the way down the sidewalk and into the parking lot, these orbs right overhead and following me. Next I made an abrupt turn heading to the recycle bin some 350 feet west. The orbs following me to the bin. I pause there, and they pause while continuing their rotational circular pattern. Then I start back. They follow me! I'm walking East now. I stop and lean against the front grill of my truck. They pause above me! Then I decide to take a much longer walk up the road heading back West. Approximately five thousand feet up the road. As I'm walking, every time I abruptly stop, the orbs stop, but still four orbs in an endless repetitive pattern. Coming together, all four touching, then bursting outward in a wide ninety-degree loop, and each orb rotating ninety degrees each time!

As I'm walking West I notice a U.F.O. of the Bright class in that direction. Other U.F.O. in the skies. Living around here since my 2008 sightings I've become highly proficient at discriminating U.F.O. from stars (about as easily as the average person can tell a cat from a dog in their front yard). The government never bothered to tell it's citizenry that they are living in a U.F.O. wildlife Preserve, because the general population couldn't handle it, so they must think. They are right to a certain extent, but the public needs to be told, and the public allowed to sort it out and deal with it themselves. When some people think of Florida they think of mosquitos. actually most nights the sea breezes keep the first five or six miles inland mosquito free. U.F.O. often outnumber mosquitos!

Now back to the story. I've completed my five thousand foot walk west, I paused, and the orbs paused. As I'm beginning my return, looking over to the Southeast, between two buildings, I can see through to the restaurant/shopping center parking lot above the trees. The beams are no longer in circular mode they are in back and forth straight scan mode. Even more disturbing, there is quite clearly no connection between my orbs and the light beams over in the shopping center almost one quarter mile away. My four orbs above me still doing circular pattern rotation!

This is one of those Twilight Zone moments when you get hit with that mental ton of bricks on your brain. Like checking into a hotel over in the Twilight Zone, but you don't remember passing by or registering at the lobby front desk, yet there you are in a hotel room on the fourteenth floor and the bellhop expects a tip. There is only one problem. It's only a ten-story hotel, and how did you get to the fourteenth floor! Yes, even if I wasn't being Ozificationed or Ozified from U.F.O./ E.T source (which I don't think I was), but rather involved in an equally rare Biblical, Signs and Wonders episode, (practically Twilight Zone next door neighbors in the High Strangeness neighborhood) Welcome to Wildman's world, y'all! I tried to throw away that weirdness attractor magnet that apparently I've been carrying, but it must be shaped like a boom-a-rang, because it seems to keep returning. Does this somehow tie back to Chapter 8, that one time having a beer served by Jackie L., then both her and the bar shortly thereafter ceasing to exist? No metaphorically speaking, or perhaps double metaphorically speaking. Mickey Spillane and Paul Harvey live over in a completely different Twilight Zone neighborhood, as different as the twin moons of Zeta Reticuli. The only link, the Web (Psychic Web) from the same psychic spider, except here with God And angels involved, without any other humans there is no Web Matrix intersection point relative to my personal (Micro) Web, only the Macro, where God/and holy angel message delivery of future Tribulation timings and event awareness being the common denominator.

It was literally a wondrous sign from God. A green light, thumbs up all systems go for God's pre-destined Operation Wildman so to speak, comparatively a bit like NASA immediately after rocket launch checking system confirmations with capsule crewmember, in this case, just me. This book including Part II (phase II rocket, analogy wise here) are the informational payloads that God wants delivered deep into people's consciousness brain/ mind space. Tribulation early warning messages from God, addressed to you, and any and all other humans smart enough to listen up, and respect the holy Sacredness of holy Prophecy and Divine Forth telling as exactly such. God's purpose: save additional lives and souls, that might otherwise be lost! While I can't be certain, judging from the angelic celebration in perpetual rotation around an invisible cross/crucifix shape in the middle, in the night sky following my every move protectively, could be indication my books will in fact have very significant impact toward achieving God's desired outcome results. I hope so, about the last thing anyone wants is to be a disappointment to God, as that seldom ends well. The rotation a few thousand feet overhead, was visible driving even (not looking directly at it), seeing the reflective swirls of light mirrored on the shoulder of the road as I drove in return trip from the bank, as a test to see what would happen. Four angels flying air cover for a Prophet's drive to a bank ATM, you've got to love it all true story! - (ATM at first bank branch not open)

While it at first might seem hallucination like, it clearly is not. Why? Because hallucinations don't throw shadows or light reflections down. During the ride home from the second bank, the light reflections observed were consistent with the movement pattern seen all along. I could not see the light orbs themselves since they were above me. Yet, they were traveling at an equal speed as my truck, throwing light reflection on the shoulder of the road that was visible out my side window as I drove.

It also shows that whatever reason for the occurrences, it was not contingent on looking directly at the moving orbs of light, such as a psychologically in some way generated hallucination would be expected to. I was driving at the speed limit of around thirty-five or forty miles per hour. The orbs were matching my speed, and if I came to a stop at a traffic light, guess what else did also!

Ghost orbs following the author of a book being written on the supernatural? U.F.O./alien directed Oz orbs? Or angels assigned to protect the author? A multiple choice question to which the correct answer is still a mystery. The timing of the event, while this book is being written, only adds to the awe.

At first the angel theory might not seem to have validity to some people, but spiritual entities do take the form of light orbs as has been documented on other occasions, locations, and time periods worldwide. If they wish to show their presence, this could have been a way of doing so, are still present, but no longer need to reveal it, already having done so.

There have been many cases in the past where U.F.O.-logist investigators have experienced 'entities' coming out of another dimension to threaten their further pursuit. Once again, *Interdimensional Universe* has some excellent example of just such occurrences. Not just alien looking beings, but the so called Men in Black, as well, who in one account I read, simply vanished in thin air on leaving. The demonic Extraterrestrial point I make throughout my book is well documented and quite valid. They work very hard at keeping their dirty little secret a secret, and don't want the public to have any awareness of this. Looking at it that way, I very well could be under God's witness protection plan, since fatalities have occurred in the past for threats out of another (demonic) dimension then being made good, as Philip Imbrogno, and other authors have documented, has happened!

Alternative Explanation Viewpoint of a Paranormal Event

The first account version leaned toward Oz Factor, U.F.O. source explanation. To evaluate this Oz Factor or angel Orb episode now from the psychological perspective of it being angel orbs. If you add weight to your criteria favoring that conclusion on which you are basing interpretation, then your opinion is likely to bias differently.

While ultimately since evidence is not convincing enough in either direction as to explanation, it must be left undetermined. To make a stronger case for angel orbs, this can be accomplished by adding weight to factors leaning toward explanation in that direction, my point, such as:

1. Additional research did show angels can manifest in multiple ways, orbs of white light one documented version (human image in a vision believed to be another, and one I have also witnessed).
2. In observation of the orbs when they came together, the pattern of an imaginary cross or crucifix could be visualized at the center where the four orbs met. Both leaving and returning through the four ends of the cross in rotational pattern (diagram).

3. The fulfillment completion of a forty-five-year-old destiny premonition for both this book, but more specifically, my Final Chapter Predictions now in writing (A possible celebration of the angels, allowing display for my awareness of that also?).
4. My published predictions made well in advance, have if correct and acted upon, potential to save many, many, lives. Since angels are also in the business of saving lives, that potentially or ultimately the cause for celebration?
5. The fact that it occurred immediately after matching my own psychic prediction (whom I credit the angels as being the source of), as well as prediction of other psychics through history, to that of the St. John the Divine, Bible Book of Revelation accounts, where even there, angels four in number are described, seems a much more compelling tie in than U.F.O. source Oz orbs.
6. Since at the time of these event, perception of manipulation of external environment was not detected, or artificially altered, but was instead, paranormal occurrences within normal unaltered environment, this possibly reduces the likelihood of Oz Factor as explanation, and in doing that possibly increases chances of angel orbs explanation (It must also be mentioned that not all Oz Factor cases clearly link the U.F.O. as causal, even when highly suspected, and although manipulation of perception of one's environment is common in such cases, it is not necessarily prerequisite as each case is different).

I've tried to show how interpretation of a paranormal event can be swayed in total by how individual contributing aspects influence the decision making determination process as a whole. The process of weighing component aspects validity, then influencing the psychology interpretational process, as bias plays a role. Choosing to remain objective, in this case, neither interpretation can be considered conclusive since there are valid points to each side.

Psychology can be said to play a role on the causal side of event (as shown with phantom vehicles), as well as reactive interpretation afterwards with paranormal/parapsychic occurrences. While normally not so, in some rare cases, I wanted to show that internal manipulation of the human mind's perceptions can be manipulated or altered from external source. While I'm by no means a psychology professional in the academic sense, having firsthand experience at a wide array of paranormal occurrences makes my opinion qualified in that sense.

It must be realized that some ET are demonically oriented, as are other spirit entities. In such cases where external source manipulation occurs influencing over internal brain function or perceptions, these are of demonic origin. Thus Oz Factor, High Strangeness, and other cases such as phantom vehicles all qualify. Spirits positive in nature seldom influence internally with brain function interference, unless for outcome noticeably positive (angel premonition-Clairaudience, example).

If the Oz orbs in my case were U.F.O. generated it still would qualify as an Oz Factor case for that reason, since even though environment was not manipulated perception wise, it is still quite a strange event and the orbs moved in the identical pattern as the searchlight strobes! As is often the case with Oz Factor, U.F.O. link is suspected, but not evidenced other than their nearby presence at time of occurrences. Had I stood next to the search lights in the restaurant parking lot at that time, I could have duplicated the four searchlights action, but without electricity! It remains a mystery! However I believe, they were holy angel orbs.

Of Angels, Orbs, and Prophecy

Having four orbs of white lights rotating high above me (February 7, 2009, 10:30 P.M.) in a clover leaf pattern, one could if they wanted to, see an imaginary cross or crucifix (imaginary) as a background, with four ends. Each Orb exiting from an end, doing a large 1/4 circle turn outward, then returning to the center of the cross through the next end in counterclockwise direction.

Having it suggested forty-five years earlier, by an angel, while attending church, I would one day write a book (One God had already read, and considered significant?). A premonition this was to happen delivered at that time.

In 2008 additional prophecy of religious nature delivered through a vision, to fulfill in approximately four years (the number four again!). This orbs event occurring immediately upon completion of rough draft of the book's final chapter, matching my own, as well as all other prophecy to that of St. John the Divine's Bible book of Revelation. This seen as fulfillment of a forty-five-year-old foretelling? Were these orbs angels now dancing in celebration as a clear sign for my witness?

I definitely do consider the 2008 vision prophecy to be of holy origin, and the inclusion of that in this book certainly related. I leave it for you to draw your own conclusions.

Presenting this to you my readers in the manner in which I did was to example the necessary subjective objectivity which needs to be in observance when evaluating any Para-Psychic supernatural occurrences, or simply supernatural occurrences analysis. End conclusion can and will be skewed according to how evidence present in the case is determined indicator wise, then influencing over-all final determination.

I truly personally believe what I experienced is what is holy Bible referenced as Signs and Wonders. The wonder being itself a sign from God. I do think these were angel orbs in perpetual rotation around a crucifix invisible yet recognizable shape present. Keep in mind it had been ten months since holy foretelling and forth telling had been received, so this was not the only acts of God occurrences during this larger time period. Had this been Oz Factor event, I still would have not escaped that Twilight Zone Ton of Bricks over my head delivery recognition of supernatural interaction/direct involvement, but these bricks for benefit of building awareness to you my readers, giving further account of God revealing his presence yet again. The crucifix and four angel orbs being the sign aspect of the Signs and Wonders, and the only possible through a higher power/intelligence capability happening above the head of one anointed and pre-destined to prophecy, giving all glory in testimony to our Lord and Savior Jesus Christ, whose Book of Revelation Prophecy described to John the Revelator not far off from fulfillment. My role as Prophet/author to describe this to you, I am not significant beyond that. The event itself is not significant other than being a confirmational visual wonder that coupled as a sign from God. Jesus and Christianity, as is always the case, is what was relevant take-away from these occurrences.

A Prophet with a lump on top of his head from all these supernatural Twilight Zone brick delivers of New Reality, but in knowing it is for your awareness benefit, informational conveyance from God, somehow makes it all worthwhile, no matter how many times I get clobbered by supernatural brick deliveries. If these bricks build greater motivation toward inspiration toward Jesus Christ's validity as Messiah/Son of God faith, then I truly don't mind being Wildman the Prophet with a figurative lump atop his head! Jesus suffered a lot worse on the cross for all our sins. File this episode occurrences under holy Signs and Wonders, in further proof of Christ's Holiness and authenticity most genuine. The proper interpretation being then, Glory to God, Glory to Jesus. The Oz Factor maybe those realization Twilight Zone brick deliveries!

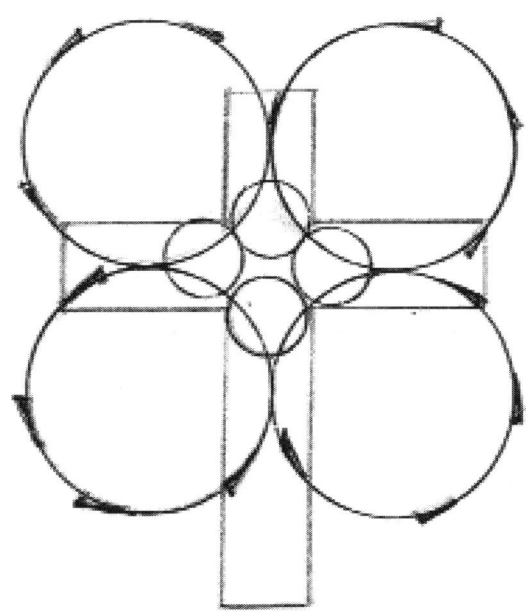

```
The larger circles indicating the path the smaller circle would
take (Orbs of white light)  There was no cross, but imagined as a
background, in counter-clockwise rotation, each Orb would follow
the pattern of the larger circles, make full 360 degree rotation
all the way around, then begin the pattern over again!
```

Also in comparative reference:
   Rosemary Ellen Guile (copyright 2000)
   Encyclopedia of Ghosts and Spirits - Second Edition
   Checkmark Books
   11 Penn. Plaza, New York, NY
   She states: Angels are most often sensed or heard by clairaudience; occasionally they manifest as apparitions in brilliant white robes, or balls of brilliant white color/light. They can also appear as real persons.

A couple thousand feet above me in the night sky overhead on the night of February 7, 2009, I witnessed four orbs of white light in perpetual rotation around an invisible yet recognizable crucifix in the center—angels!

Chapter 19

The 1988 T.V. Show and Particle Beam Premonition

It's a wonder
Where my mind wanders
And it shall go there I know
My mind shall go
To where it wonders, I know!
It shall go there and wander
Through the future there to behold
Then returning to present,
Future wonders foretold.

Thank You, Lord.
Wildman, Christmas morning 2008

How many psychic's in the world have ever had a premonition that they were going to have a definite U.F.O. sighting, and then did? Likely not many. How many have had two or more U.F.O. premonitions that later fulfilled? Now the list gets short. I'd check with the Guinness Book of World Records, but they don't have categories for those since they are difficult to verify. Visions and thoughts in one's head that is. These are covered by lie-Detection Test.

Why did these things happen to me? I suspect it serves God's purpose to be in this book. It isn't often that an author can talk about the same event with aspects pertaining to U.F.O., Psychic, and quite significant Religious implications. This chapter will describe the Psychic occurrences.

It was late September 1988 (one of brief period of months at that time that I had a T.V. in my bedroom, and this helped to confirm the date), and I was watching a T.V. show about the Bible and U.F.O.. It was likely one of the major networks (NBC), but I've never seen the show repeated since.

The two U.F.O. premonitions are actually quite different. The 1988 premonition occurred while wide awake watching T.V., but didn't fulfill until 19 ½ years later. The 2008 U.F.O. premonition occurred while asleep, in a dream vision, and fulfilled just weeks later.

To better illustrate I've drawn a diagram to help illustrate what it is I'm describing. This was particularly strange, because my mind was in two places at once, not that we all don't get distracted from time to time by multiple thoughts. However, this was two thoughts on the same subject.

As I was watching the T.V. program (about three quarters completed), they got onto the subject of the likelihood of the Bible, Book of Revelation (9:2–4). There came out of the pit (ocean's-bottomless pit, the Abyss) a smoke out of the Pit there came out of the smoke - locusts which have power, as the scorpions of the Earth. Scorpions with stings in their tails (9:5). Their function: that they should not kill, but torment. This T.V. show was commenting that these were probably references to extraterrestrial operated U.F.O., and demonic because in (9:11) states that the king of the bottomless pit has charge over them. (Satan) demonic extraterrestrials who will operate stinger tail Tasers torturing wicked humans in the Tribulation period. My premonition proves them correct!

As they began talking about all this, my mind decided to just get up and take a stroll out back! Maybe my imagination, I don't know exactly what part of my mind simply wandered off, but I'm still watching a picture of a U.F.O. on T.V.. The imagination then went to a back fence line, moved East to a point that intersects with a tree line running along my side of a drainage canal. It jumps the canal, and now I'm seeing a U.F.O. in front of me on T.V., and one across the canal, diagonally behind me! My imagination on remote, and I'm now seeing this same U.F.O. in two places! On T.V. in front of me, and diagonally behind me! Wow! As the T.V. U.F.O. lowered a particle beam Taser tail, so did my imagination's U.F.O. on the other side of the canal. Except now the one on T.V. is stationary, but my canal U.F.O. is moving North! It moved some seventy-five to one hundred feet north and then stopped. When the T.V. show image ended, so did my imagination image! Then I get a certain profound feeling I get immediately after all premonitions.

But what was I supposed to make of this except it was going to have to do with U.F.O., and like all premonitions, once they do fulfill they then make sense. Except this one took 19½ years to fulfill. It took a while just to even recollect all these things. The two important aspects being that in fact my 2008 U.F.O. and particle beam sighting are I believe truly the very Bible Book of Revelation scorpion stinger tail mentioned almost two thousand years ago in the Bible. So if you said it was predicted two thousand years ago and just now fulfilled there is some truth there, as well. The premonitions are delivered by angels of the Kingdom of heaven, and thus I do think God must want this information known.

Oh, some won't be convinced of what I'm describing, I'm just in total awe by all this myself. God as a contributing editor. Now if they don't believe the beam I saw, no point in telling them it was carried out by a contributing editor who runs the universe in his spare time.

Yes, but consider the source, a guy who likely holds Guinness World Records in non-existent categories for premonition. Maybe World's largest collection of Twilight Zone frequent flyer miles, too! No none of this will convince anybody you're right, but they will need to believe me anyway. Why?

Because there is another aspect to this. When you pivot the 19½ years forward it fits precisely where it should into the Bible's very synchronized Tribulation time line according to Dr. Lancy's template! Premonition to fulfillment 19½ years, then 19½ years forward into the Tribulation template with perfect fit! Then when you figure in who my contributing editor seems to be, it suddenly becomes very believable! I think it's also safe to say the prophecy window that's been closed from heaven for millennium or nearly so, is now operational. Meaning? Other psychics are going to begin receiving and experiencing Biblical Prophecy, as well. Further evidencing this timeline to be correct!

In the Religious section (Chapter 26) we'll return to discussion of this incredible scorpion Taser tail, and timeline template. I am totally convinced that this is exactly what this was and is.

Now I'm sure when some people read this, they will wonder if God is showing this to Wildman because Wildman is somehow a bad person in need of seeing the lashing whip as some sort of personal behavioral warning. The answer is no, absolutely not. Wildman would be at the back of an imaginary warning line, not first recipient, and learning proper interpretations is just as important as experiencing the psychic event itself. Sure, God would certainly be capable of what was described, but one should realize even average ordinary people experience awareness and intuitions from their guardian angels all the time, and without even realizing these minute psychic nudges in one direction or another. One with E.S.P. is merely experiencing it at a much more elevated or intensified level. The point being, the psychic first receives holy angel delivered messaging, then is inspired toward proper interpretation. The angel with E.S.P. as to reading and interpreting that persons thoughts. You might think your mind is private, but it is not. Both E.T. and angels have telepathic abilities, but as this book points out as reminder, not all are of holy side allegiance.

Here, proper interpretation is that my Senior Editor wants this included in the book, and for more than one reason. It has nothing to do with me personally, other than gaining firsthand awareness so it can be related to others. This is an apple falling out of a tree described in Book of Revelation almost two thousand years ago, so to speak. The orchard you could say *is* Book of Revelation, and those acres on a farm known as the New Testament Farm. I don't think I need to tell you who that owner (God the Father) or that farmer, his son, Jesus Christ, is, but it is because so many people and religions worldwide are in denial of that apple, that tree, that orchard, that farm, and that farmer (metaphorically speaking) that Wildman is given this awareness to bring it to their attention, via this book, and other Tribulation event/timeline awareness to make others aware of the Bible's genuineness if they are not already believers of this as fact. The start of Tribulation less than fifteen years away.

Wildman in joyous delighted approval that God in essence hijacked this book in order to say, *And now an important message to humanity*. Perhaps the most important, that (see Supplement section, corresponding with Dr. Lancy's 1964 Sermon pronouncement) we can expect the reappearance of Jesus Christ, in the holy land, above the Mt. of Olives as Book of Revelation exactly states. More about the Particle beam in chapter 26 (Dr. Lancy, Chapters 23 and 27).

When you get to the Psychic Section in discussion of premonitions, it mentions that after all my holy angel delivered future awareness premonitions, it always concludes with a profound golden moment feeling in the front of your forehead (chakra). It is a signature component of all holy side message transmissions, prophetic in content that I've received. In essence confirming holy source as the sender. It literally is like a holy receipt!

If the 1988 Particle Beam Premonition had this component present, then I knew that was the receipt I was looking for here. Regardless of what occurred on the back end fulfillment side, Extraterrestrial demon included in the other 2008 psychic dream (asleep) vision or not. You have to recognize the linkage, and demons don't want humans to know their secrets or classified weaponry systems exposed. If you think about it, it would take a direct order from God, and nothing less, to get them, or force them, to release such secrets. It doesn't serve their purpose for me to witness this, it serves humanity, and thus it serves God's purpose. The image of the E.T. demon in the dream only seen briefly, had to have been either my subconscious in holy angel assisted E.T./demon likeness image recreation, or holy angel studios image capture handed over to my subconscious of a Reptilian E.T. Prior to those split second look and see glimpses, I can tell you I had no clue what one looked like, and most humans haven't, either. More demon secrecy. Saying God thought it was necessary for inclusion in this book is yet another rather weird, but accurate assessment of what took place. God giving humanity some advanced warning of demon Satanic Air Force and what their commanders look like. Apparently God enrolled me in a graduate advanced course in Para-psychology /U.F.O.-logy, for additional information required for release in this book, back there in 2008.

Wildman now with invisible, holy angel handed undergraduate degree, from Twilight Zone University with early graduation. Then recruited by them right out of college to serve in the Christian psychics Intelligence corp. doing training for future divinities/theology anointing prophecy! Apparently my graduate major in holy Prophecy, and one with a pocket full of those premonition transmitted profound golden moment, holy angel receipts. Everything invisible, but in the Spirit of God, held in memory and held in heart. All Kingdom of heaven, and Spirit of God more real than any real of this dimension, and as profoundly golden as it gets. I can show you nothing, but I can express in witness word; everything! Christian witness, exactly God's intention. Jehovah God and Jesus Christ invisible, too, but who better to witness for them their truth, and reality as Bible expressed than a present day Christian psychic/Prophet? One with a pocket full of those holy angel confirm receipts! In like manner a loving God confirms faith, when you honor it prior. Just like prophecy never goes unfulfilled, so to, true faith in Jesus Christ never goes unfulfilled, either. You have his word on it, and mine, and every Christian pastor who ever opened a Bible will all tell you exactly the same thing. It takes faith prior, to equal faith fulfilled in confirmation later. Old Testament, New Testament, and my testament to you. You might think mine the quietest and weakest, until you get to the Supplement Section with a little informational surprise package for you to unwrap there. You might even figuratively speaking want to bring along ear plugs, because my Christian witness gets pretty loud over there! If I just lost you a little there, don't worry, it'll all make sense later.

That is often what happens with future prediction. It doesn't always make complete sense when you receive it, but it always does make full sense upon fulfillment. You get fully filled in. With faith, you put your trust in God to guide you and watch over you, knowing that you as a believing Christian are never alone. Never! However, sometimes the plan God has for your life will not come into full focus understanding until well later.

When it is proper timing, proper season, then will God's understandings come into clearer focus, sharper image of the larger picture, and God will provide for you deeper more profound understanding awareness. Indications in your life of how your life is to intersect with God's purpose for your life, that you are then better able to embrace, because your plans for your life and his plans for your life are no longer diverging, but converging. His plans then become your plans also. Authoring this book in witness to you, is example of exactly what I've just described. God already foretold me of a pre-destiny to write this book way back in 1964. The 2008 Para-psychic episodes were conveyances of needed information God wanted in this book. Not one acts of God episode, but several.

Humanity needed further awareness of Tribulation's approach, but further evidences that could have been provided no other way than through direct acts of God involvement. The obviousness, and the irrefutable nature, especially when examined collectively, to inspire and stimulate stronger motivation toward Christian faith. Tribulation is no joke, and on its way.

Once acknowledging God's involvement, plan, oversight, and control, in this sense, not at all unlike the military, government, or a business corporation. Except here you are dealing in the supernatural. Orders originate at the top, then filter down to those given responsibility of carrying them out. Here in the supernatural realm, you have the holy side and the unholy side. So, for analysis purpose let me explain first that in the case of my two episodes both with demonic ET participation, to leave it at that is not to see the forest for the trees obstructing your view. That is totally knee-jerk reaction, surface only, and false conclusion.

It might surprise you that this was all meant for you, this book meant for you, this very examination of this you are reading right now, all are of God's design and meant for you. You were the focus, even though Prophessor (intentional misspelled as a cross between Prophet and Professor) would deliver this lecture to you right now at T.Z.U.! It seems God has a permanent chair as Chancellor Emeritus, Dean of Students, Faculty consort advisor, and more. Yes, God knew I would crack the casing on this mystery item and present it to you also, or I wouldn't have been involved at all. God has his purposes, and remember I learned forty-five years ago through angel delivered message this book would one day be written. That is the key piece of evidence signaling God's involvement, and the larger forest picture that I speak of. God evidences himself in many ways, but we often are seeing only an immediate tree or two in front of us rather than the entire forest.

E.T.s are an integral part of God's universe, and why U.F.O.-logy, Theology, and Parapsychology including angels direct involvement in human Psychology are all connective. The episodes I experienced merely God's plans coming together, and carried out through God's established order. It was a psychic heavy lifting experience at the time, but I should feel very humbly honored that God chose me to carry it out. Not so much for me, but for me to interpret then explain to others, so you definitely are purpose focus. This book the vehicle to accomplish such.

Let's take the Particle Beam episode first. Down through the holy angel ranks orders to deliver the 1988 premonition were given. These are U.F.O. of demonic registry that delivered it upon fulfillment, but on the initial premonition, it was like all my premonition, I am quite certain holy angel delivered.

Part A of God's plan carried out. I didn't know exactly when, but at some future time, that might even be Tribulation itself, I know I would one day actually see the Particle beam described in the Book of Revelation

It is clear to me now, the double meaning to deliver message as to Tribulation timing, essential to crack the code, then to be told in this book. These are further evidences of God's purpose, plan, and direct involvement in implementation of his plan.

So, now you are wondering how the connect with unholy side demonic loyalty ET, and their co-operation/ participation. Just as I described in the Entities section about the Greys they have two factions. One good with awareness, respect, and desire to please God. The other the Bad Greys, aligned with the demon Reptilian E.T. or just demon, as you might prefer. The Greys are the bridge communications link between the holy side and unholy side when message or command need to be passed. The commands are always holy side to unholy side, never reverse since they have neither power or authority to do so (God's authority rules supreme). The good Greys have to curb their natural hostile to human attitude, and do so because God wills it, so seeing that humans have God's favor and mercy, they are obedient, repressing ill will, replacing it with positive outlook. Not totally good, I characterize them as 'neutral,' since they can't be accurately categorized as bad. This is typical U.F.O.-logist thinking of most, but not all, U.F.O.-logists. I definitely agree with it.

When the 1988 Particle Beam Premonition fulfilled twenty years later, it was a case of the order being passed down on the holy side, then delivered message from Good Greys (telepathically) to Bad Greys to carry out direct order. That is how I would represent explanation of that episode, and much less complex than the other premonition.

What complicates the other is that the premonition was clearly being delivered, either by an E.T. Reptilian (demon) or an angel delivered representation of one. Although I explained the Particle Beam Premonition first in this analysis, it came after the 2008 U.F.O. Sighting Premonition and Fulfillment in actuality. Knowing that God was involved and was directly responsible in the other, you see it's pretty apparent that this psychic fish pulled into the same psychic fishing boat by the same psychic fisherman (myself) landed several catches into the same fishing boat that God owns and was piloting at the time!

Guardian angels saved Wildman's life so many times, maybe God has me working off my debt of gratitude on his psychic fishing boat these days. A lot of awareness I could only deliver to you the reader if the experiences were given to me that could then be analyzed and passed on to you. In the case of this Premonition predicting six definite, and a number of likely other indefinite U.F.O. sightings, it again fits this mold. Apparently God wanted to give me clearer understandings on ET/ U.F.O. subject that could then be related to you. He certainly did accomplish that! But behind the scenes, how was this premonition carried out? Let's examine three possibilities.

1. Similar to the other premonition, it was delivered by holy angel, and when it was appropriate time for fulfillment, the word passed from Good Greys to Bad Greys then delivered to the Reptilian commanding them. (what I refer to as the 391st Alien Air Wing) God originated, in this scenario.
2. It was not God originated, but demon originated, demon (391st) carried out on the fulfillment end also.
3. The in-sleep dream was a replication of a Reptilian E.T. (demon), but carried out, like all other premonitions, from holy angel. A sort of special effects holy angel dream works presentation. Certainly within their power to achieve such realistic special effects as a demon ET ratcheting up torture psychic voltage level to the point of jolting me awake! angelic Psychic Engineering you could call it. The demon was only a replication. At the time other U.F.O. likely overhead near my house, but was that because of this angel activity perhaps?

I can only surmise both sides were party to the Premonition. The greater purpose end goal was decided fulfilling God's objectives. A book enlightening the general public on demonology as it relates to the 391st exactly what they wouldn't want. They try very hard to keep a low profile. Keep their appearance, and activity routines and description away from public awareness, remain covert, diabolical, and stealthily purvey Evil without slightest human awareness. You can therefore now eliminate possibility of scenario two.

What actually occurred something along the lines of one and three, perhaps containing some aspects of both, but more importantly still with God as the source, because it shows in spite of demonic E.T. involvement, it is still in service of God's purpose. A whole demonic Air Wing literally flying a flight mission for God because they were commanded to and had no choice? Or, was the premonition an angel prompting to see something I otherwise would have missed, an ET saucer Air Show the ET were unaware I was witness to? That is frankly difficult to say.

Let's hope none of these Bad E.T.s took off with your A.T.V. parked outside while you were in class. The Twilight zone not exactly the place to get stranded alone (rough neighborhood in more ways than most people realize; a little humor).

Now all of this, to some, just a waste of conjecture effort. Yet you build from what you know, and anytime you can expand awareness, you create the opportunity to build off of it, further knowledge and understandings from which wisdom is derived upon past mystery. All of Albert Einstein's proven theories started out as hypothesis. From these physics principles now commonly accepted were derived. I'm not trying to compare myself to Einstein except to equate hypothesis of merit that has some basis in validity has analytical value not only in what can be learned directly, but if later proven, can be a step or building block toward future discovery in the learning process.

What I've shown here is example of where what appears to be a demonic presence and purpose on the surface can in fact if properly evaluated be something orchestrated for holy side end result purpose. Things aren't always what they appear within the supernatural, and understanding that will move you a step closer to understanding God.

Certainly seeing holy side and unholy side as adversaries is true, but that tends to think of the two as being on equal footing, and we know that isn't the case. A better analogy for examination purpose might be to think of comparison to corporate structure. Place God in this analogy as CEO, Chairman of the Board of Universe Corporation. His resurrected holy son Jesus Christ as acting corporation President of operations and management. Satan is merely a lower Department head; yes, a demonic department in control of evil operations. Still subject to all corporate orders and directives that he must obey. Sure, he has plans to undermine the power structure and be in control at the top one day, but they are wise to these unscrupulous ambitions, and have been for a long time. Precautions are in place, but he does occasionally serve useful purpose to the holy side's activities and planned programs. Obedience allows him to maintain at least Department head authority.

Actually, you wouldn't find the two even in the same building together, but this was just for analogy, they keep their distance and don't mix. Yet the unholy side must do the bidding of the holy side if ordered to. I will give another example.

The moth man, what I've described according to my own classification system as a demonic Rare, few would doubt this bat out of hell looking creature is likely that, a half humanlike/ half bat like demonic creature actually from hell! However, it appears as an omen of impending tragedy on sights where loss of human life will occur in future timeframe. Seen by more than one hundred witnesses at the Point Pleasant West Virginia bridge and surrounding town area, prior to that accident. You have to realize that about the last thing Satan would want to do is warn humans of impending death, because then some intelligent human might figure things out in time to warn some of whom might otherwise be victims. Clearly a case here of compliance by the unholy side to direct orders from the holy side!

God isn't on vacation when these occurrences happen, he isn't taking a nap and missed the whole thing when these things happen, and he is the one initiating his plan. It kind of makes humans a bit more aware of holy side when unholy side plants a flying demon creature atop a local landmark. See what happens when you don't tithe 10 percent of your income (joking of course)! The bridge had a structural defect, humans at fault, not the supernatural, but I believe this is a case of God, through his own design sending an omen messenger, yes dark entity to deliver it.

When you get to the Supplement Section (Part II) under Comet, I see the same thing with Mothman happening yet again. Hopefully, I've interpreted correctly. Probability I have, I would estimate to be quite high, in the 75 to 85 percent range. Once again, God behind this evil entity, but with a purpose of warning to humans to reduce or eliminate fatalities. In the case of this future scenario, eliminate fatalities, unfortunately considering the magnitude of the event, very unlikely, reduction in the number however, very achievable. The trouble is, as humans we want to see for ourselves and be reactionary. Don't look back, you'll be turned into a pillar of salt! Oops, you were right.

Keep in mind God does love his Christians and wants to give them an advantage from unknowns that might clobber them and has a whole range of tools at his disposal to accomplish this. It includes using aspects of the demonic dimension to carry out his purpose if it facilitates it best. In the months leading up to the Comet wormwood event, you can possibly expect to see the Return of the Mothman once again in these locations. By then you should have already prepared your shelter safe haven that I recommend. When even trained clergy are in such wide disagreement regarding Rapture, I'm simply sharing with you what I and extended family have planned as evasive countermeasure survival plans (discussed extensively in Part II).

Excerpts from Truth Verification Exams, Tests Five and Six
Fulfillment of the 1988 Particle Beam Premonition and Vision in 2008 and Other Excerpts From Part II

Readers please note: When the lie Detection/Truth verification Exams were taken, this book was still conceptualized as a single book, rather than necessary Part I, Part II, because of length. The questions verifying this Particle Beam, U.F.O. delivered in direct match of a 1988 Premonition fulfilling in 2008, corresponding to the 1988 U.F.O./Beam vision seen then are included in Tests five and six which are now included with questions relating to Part II. However, these excerpts were pulled from there, and included here in Part I. One of the questions contains a year I do not wish to release until then, so I have crossed over it here. Other questions (a few) are also exhibited for your examination. These questions, part of those exams, will be printed in Part II again when those exams are displayed for full transparency.

Test 5
Question 3
Over the last 45 years you have had many psychic experiences, most related to future event foretelling, never a prophecy or prediction failing to fulfill, even though exact timing was not always clear. Is this an accurate and True statement?
Answer: YES

Question 4
While watching a 1988 T.V. Show Entitled, *The Bible & U.F.O.*, that was discussing Bible mentions of the locusts described in Book of Revelation as potentially being U.F.O., and the Scorpion like Stinger Tail, as potentially being a Particle Beam delivered from a U.F.O., you began to have a premonition that you would one day see it, coupled with visualization of the U.F.O. and Particle Beam seen on T.V., but now visualized on the opposite side of a drainage canal adjacent to your home. The U.F.O. and particle beam in the vision began moving north along the canal, but when the T.V. show went on to a different subject the vision ended. You were watching the T.V. in front of you, the vision pictured outdoors, but behind you.
Answer: YES

Test 6
Question 5
When the all black Shadow of Death Particle Beam was seen in late April 2008, it appeared to descend from a U.F.O. located above the last spot seen in the 1988 premonition/vision. You observed this from your front yard around midnight, the end about 8 foot away aimed directly at your head when it finally halted (descent). Is this a True and accurate statement?
Answer:YES

Question 6
Has any of your premonition/prophecy ever failed to fulfill?
Answer: NO
Is this a True and correct statement?
Answer: YES

Test 6 (second questions set)
Question 5
You feel certain that the U.F.O. Shadow of Death Particle Beam seen in 2008 in /our front yard, as predicted in1988, is in fact, for certain the same Bible Book of Revelation one, and that the 5 month sting period of stinging humans by Taser, will in fact occur in the year XXXX (withheld until PartII), that message being derived from this also Is this True and accurate statement? Answer: YES

Readers please note: Part II does provide when I believe the five-month sting period is, and while it was extremely difficult conclusion to arrive at, and is less certain than the year, I do think I have it correctly placed. Everyone should recognize the larger picture here. Confirmation from God of a New Testament (Book of Revelation) event, that only Christians take seriously, is then also further confirmation for Christians of the coming Tribulation, but re-verification of the correctness of Christian faith, Christian K.J. Bible.

Test 6 (second question set)
Question 4
In terms of supernatural and parapsychic occurrences, would you say God has evidenced multiple acts of God within this book as witnessed and holy angel presence and activity, as well?
Is this True and Accurate statement?
Answer: YES

Another Particle Beam question links it's timing to severe persecutions for Christians and Jews is not exhibited here, but is included in Part II.

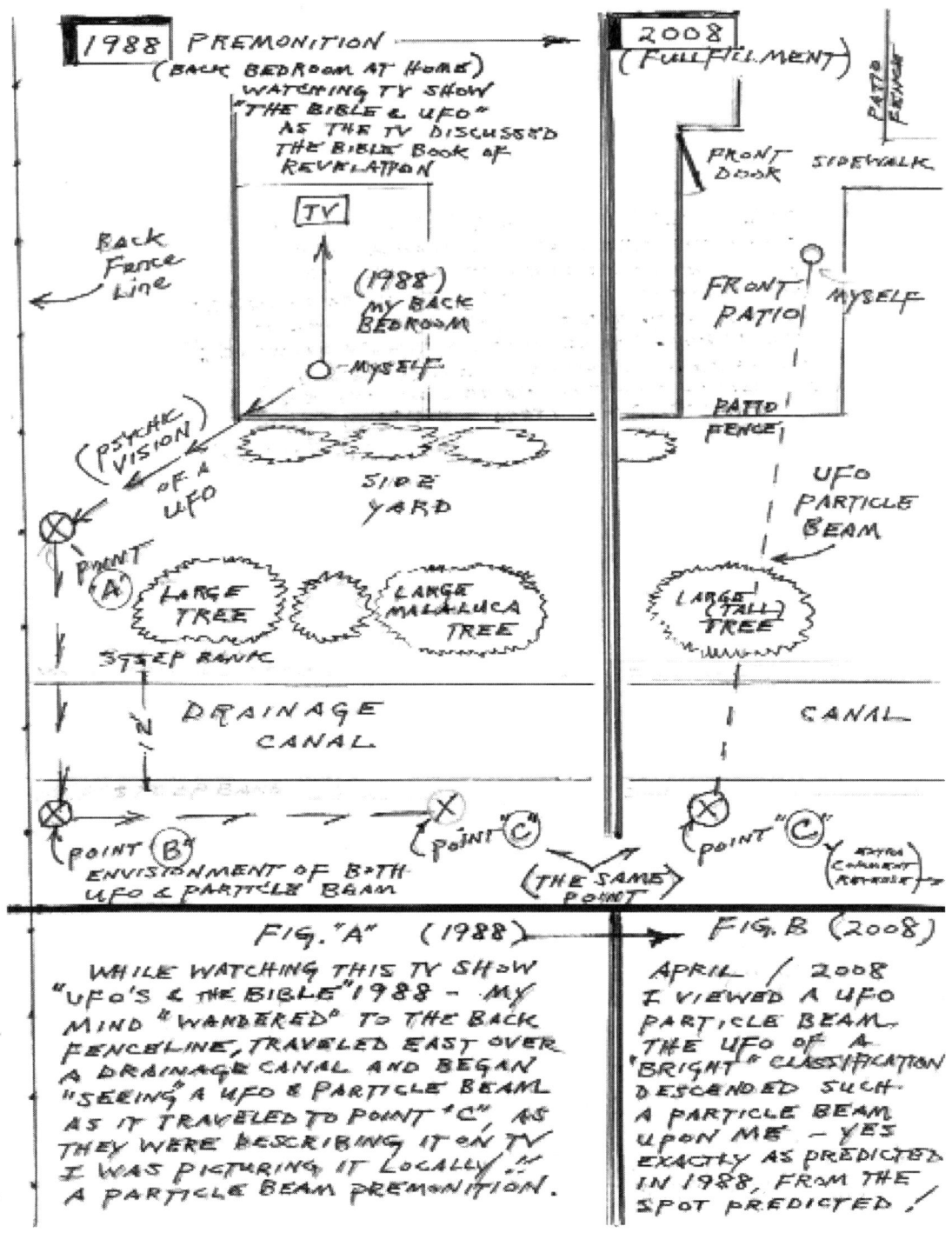

Chapter 20
Metaphysical Section: Time Warps

Loops, warps, locks, inversions, tunnels, pockets, and slips are just some of the terms used to express anomalies involving time. It would seem as humans we have bought into the traditional concept of time as we perceive it, rather than a piece of the state of what it really is an illusion! We define it according to its effect upon us and how our existence relates to it, our planet's revolution around the sun, and a measuring system of it based on that. However, time is not constant by this measuring system through the greater galaxy and universe, and is not constant even among the multiple dimensions surrounding us. Nowhere is it said time must operate by the same mechanisms and at the same rate everywhere, or even exist there at all. Time likely more like spiraled helixes that are interwoven through an equal multiplicity of parallel space fabric layers (dimensions) weaving a Space/Time construct varying greatly. Where space expands, perhaps time contracts, slows, speeds up, or even stops in suspension, but depending on which dimension.

What happens in this dimension may or may not be true in another one. Many dimensions, perhaps some immune or only effected in limited ways to laws of Physics. Make no mistake, there is in fact multiple dimensions, and many of these tied more to the spiritual than to science, yet even on the science end of the spectrum, clearly additional dimensions.

Einstein established through his Theory of Relativity the concept of curvature of both time and space. Even he conceptualized that Space and Time were not separate, but an interwoven fabric of Space/Time. Yet it is important to point out also, that spiritual dimensions exist within this very same Space/Time multidimensional invisible fabric in tandem. It is not to be completely explained through science alone (A point I will come back to later).

1. Einstein also suggested that time, wound around through the universe much like a river. Today some speculative physicists believe that, again like a river, time sometimes forms eddies or whirlpools, vortexes providing shortcuts through both time and space.

In research, there were too many time/anomaly tales to present all of them, so rather than infringe on other authors copyrights, I thought I'd summarize some as descriptive samples, then point you to other sources for the complete account. The sequential numbering is Bibliography, as well. Here are several examples/ case studies documented.

2. In September 1974, in Dunblane, Perthshire Scotland, sighting of a Roman ghost legion (seen, but not heard) and consisting of several thousand troops. This Ghost Legion was witnessed at night marching through a field near town. Other witnessed some sound, as well as the sighting. In 117 A.D. legend claims this IX Roman legion was cursed, and mysteriously vanished at that time in that very region (Local dogs became very disturbed, as well.)!
3. In 1951, spanning ten years, but nine years almost to the exact day and hour, two English sisters vacationing together in France heard what was like re-enactment sounds of a D-day battle, and coming from the same site where in early A.M (same hour) heavy casualties were reported on the beach.
4. In June 1967, a driver leaves Washington State headed for Los Angeles, Calif. At around 3:30 A.M. in clear dry Autumn weather the driver rounds a bend into a blinding snowstorm. Moving through this, the driver arrives in what appears to be an old West town from the 1880s period. The engine on the car quit, so the driver stayed overnight leaving the next day, and having talked to some of the locals. After departing, he claimed driving through a cloud like fog, then returning to the present!
5. In the Summer of 1958 and 1960, two accounts in the similar Eastern Pennsylvania area, near the town of Trumbauersville (about halfway between Philadelphia and Allentown). Similar accounts describe a drive into a

one-hundred-year-old slide back into time south of Easton/ Bethlehem where a town that no longer exists, they somehow managed a drive into, even carrying on conversation with locals. One of the witnesses claiming he thought one of these locals (solid in appearance) he suspects might have been his father who passed away shortly after his birth!

6. In Fall 1968 in Australia, A seventy-mile trip with a detour in time takes twelve hours. An attempt to retrace landmarks seen along this journey proves futile, as nothing matched, and things seen, now seemingly vanished. A scenic journey down a road not even shown on any maps that apparently doesn't exist!
7. In 1934 in Great Britain, Air Marshall Goddard flies over Drem Airfield, a recognized landmark (heavy storm again), except this abandoned airfield now no longer abandoned, it is as Drem will look four years later in 1938.
8. An American fast forward incident of an aviator in the Bermuda Triangle, happening on December 4, 1970. A Beechcraft Bonanza piloted through a rotating donut hole cloud vortex that pushed the compass backwards. The Andros Island to West Palm Beach trip only taking forty-five minutes instead of seventy-five!

Time slip or time warp episodes as you may choose to call them can be similar to time horizon change recorded in U.F.O. High Strangeness episodes, however in some of these cases time is altered and other times surroundings seem to be the focus of alteration. Even angels can bring about environment alteration. Compare this case: A young girl with her parents on vacation begins having a seizure. The nearest hospital is an hour distant, and as her parents near, they become concerned that they won't be able to locate the correct roads to arrive at the hospital. Just then blue and white signs begin to appear along the roadway they are on, indicating with arrows where to turn. When they later checked with a Doctor and the local Chamber of Commerce, they discovered there had never been blue/white hospital signs with arrows, either along their arrival route or any other roads in the area for that matter! This miracle attributed to angel involvement/interceding.

E.T. then are not the only parties to occasionally manipulating the human environment on occasion. Conversely, if an obvious positive outcome is not apparently demonstrated, it is unlikely angels are involved, as that is their calling card—holy angels that is. Remember, too, the unholy angels (demons) leave exactly the opposite calling card. Bad E.T and Jinn, lesser demons, are known as pranksters among other pursuits, and bring about negative outcomes without humans often having even the slightest awareness of their presence, at least in most cases (but not all).

Some dimensions may be time vacuums, or time there not equivalent to ours perhaps at a different vibrational tempo. Frequency vibrations different of the entities are hidden there, as well. It appears in some spirit or ghost dimensions there is absolutely no consciousness of time, and they are in a state of time suspension -zero time change. They perhaps are no longer capable of measure capability or even time concept.

One might say that time belongs to the living, because to the dead time is dead also. Ghosts and other spirits fit this dimension of time void very likely, but there appears to be other dimensions with other entities that human living are totally unaware of also.

Phil Imbrogno, author of *Interdimensional Universe*, describes what he terms of such existed in our atmosphere nearly oblivious to humans as sky critters. Perhaps that is a good label for a catch-all category of any such beings. It is a sort of a *come out of your dimension and let us have a look at you so we can identify you* situation. All the uncooperative unknowns categorized then as sky critters until such time as a more definitive identity can be determined.

Interdimensional Universe is just filled with remarkable, insightful, and quite brilliant analysis worth your reading. I urge my readers to examine his book as excellent comparative information that will broaden perspective. I found nothing at all in his comments I disagreed with, although he is welcome to disagree with me after he reads this book as difference of opinion is something to be encouraged, yet we seem to approach the supernatural from very different vantage points yet always seem to draw similar conclusion.

He also gives some personal perspective to the Philadelphia Experiment and Montauk experiments conducted by the U.S. government. Now, over sixty years old, these tests are yielding some fascinating, but also tragic, results. High frequency generators being used to investigate experimental Space/Time manipulation (Chapter 5 of his book). These topics have been covered by other authors, as well, and additionally paranormal Sourcebook by Charles E. Sellier and Joe Meier covers similar account.

Time variation anomalies are sometimes suspected of being U.F.O./E.T. related. We know E.T.s are interdimensional. If you think of time like a river or perhaps conveyor belt passing through different dimensions at the same rate initially, then if you initially slow the conveyor (or speed it up) and then in a different dimension but similar location in space, you can then perhaps slow, or speed up time in that dimension, as well; fluxing the conveyor, so to speak, in the time/space/matter equation. It is just an analogy to grasp the concept of manipulation. Motion relates to energy, as well as Time/Space/matter, so energy must likely play some role in manipulation, even if at micro or nano levels perhaps, and sound frequency vibration potentially an involvement candidate, as well. We should also consider that not all dimensions scale alike, so micro quantity here possibly more a macro quantity elsewhere, and space very likely does contain even in outer reaches of our own galaxy, places where Space Time and gravitational forces are constantly pulling and distorting, like an elevator not stopping correspondingly at exact match with a building floor level, so too might Space/Time have similar rough spots where things don't exactly mesh or blend evenly, but are not constant because of continually changing deep space invisible gravitational forces. Then you have the eddies and back currents along the shoreline of time that are similar to Einstein's description. There meddling isn't necessary, it's occurring naturally. Closer to Earth it seems more like a wheel in the Anticathera Mechanism sticking, or a zero on an odometer slipping away. The cases I exhibited previously indications of documented Time abnormalities at the least if not manipulation.

Are three or four spindly fingered ET playing with the dials in the Time control room again? Picked the lock, now trespassing in a restricted security area? Possibly so, but not necessarily. To me, this control room is clearly in a spiritual dimension. God created all things, science an explanation of function and parameters of those things, and time simply an aspect of God's creation, thus these controls held within spiritual realm.

The keys to time held in the spiritual realm. That isn't to say that scientists can't study the nature and physics of it. The larger question should be who exactly holds duplicate sets of keys to the control room, and access to the various buttons, knobs, switches and dials modulating it. If our government (Intelligence Services) through their dealings with ET have solved this mystery, likely very few humans have clearance high enough to access the answer, if in fact it has been obtained. Who beyond the holy realm have keys to that control room of time? The demonic realm would totally disrupt time if allowed to, yet at times do seem to be able to distort and manipulate it. Dragon's and Bermuda triangles seem to create such anomalies naturally. One does also wonder what secrets in total the ET have shared with humans, especially as to likely future event horizon outcomes. Thinking telepathically anyway, one also wonders how much human intelligence the ET have gathered off humans dealing with them, absorbing information like a sponge leaching human brain function/memory.

Re-examining some of the anomaly cases mentioned previously, although the beholder or beholders in these cases don't describe fear or a sense of being threatened, they all seem to at first enjoy the novelty of their experiences having traveled well back in time to a previous era, but one gets the feeling in some of these instances as timeframe extends, they become a bit anxious over what has happened to them. A mild apprehension/anxiety/panic begins to set in. A reaction of, this is certainly unique, but get me out of here, I don't belong here, and perhaps even questioning if they've fallen through some trap door in time, can they even return at all. A mild paranoia setting in. State road one hundred drove them into a town one hundred years back in time, but will they be able to follow the same road back to their previous present day? It always does.

One wonders, too, why they didn't stay a little longer to learn more from their experience in some of these cases where they are walking the sidewalks now of towns that no longer exist, Bona-fide ghost towns come back to life in some time regression/time pocket they stumbled into. What if they stayed a little longer, ate some one-hundred-year-old, but fresh food (one reported actually drinking a Coca-Cola). If they stayed, would this time mirage simply vanish? Would they become trapped in it somehow and vanish with it? Stay an extra night in Zane Grayville and get caught on the wrong side of some grand canyon time rift, now unable to return? Has this happened? Visitors from the future becoming trapped in the past. Your imagination in Wildman's gym now bench pressing one hundred time/pounds. worth of past also I see.

Ghost specters as discussed in Chapter Two, can include autos, trucks, trains, planes, towns and entire scenes resembling theatrical sets, but almost all ghost specters occur at night rather than daytime, especially late at night. Ships at sea similarly. The difference here being many of these occurrences were daytime, or the Oregon case that began at night, but carried into day. In these cases a Time pocket portal or window is opened, and scenery seems to be simply part and parcel with it being the focus, rather than scene. Ghost specters at night usually observed from a distance with the observer outside the scene. In these cases the observer is actually inside the occurrences, or very connecting to it, such as a pilot flying over altered condition on the ground. Such is also consistent with U.F.O. High Strangeness cases, with alteration of both time and scene variation anomaly. One wonders, too, if a person encountered were cut, would they bleed? If so would you then be witnessing someone bleed one hundred yrs. ago? How much time loss would be experienced returning to the present, any? Lots of questions, as the people encountered seem to be solid normal looking people, just from a different by-gone era, and some conversation is possible. Is it a ghost mirage or an actual step back in time? With nothing more than a small handful of rare participant accounts in such episodes spanning centuries, so far the answers are inconclusive. You can interview the people involved, but not actually revisit the time-warp occurrences itself. Like the song lyrics of Zane Gray Town, and when you touch down, it's much stranger than now being sung by the 1960s music group the Byrds, and others. In fact if you turned your radio on in a time before radio would anything at all be on the air in that locale, or like you coming from external locale, would it still work and be received? Something from down yonder to ponder right there now, if only you could distinguish in that situation when now is, or where the boundary of then is.

Although these cases worldwide are certainly rare, enough credible people have been involved, including pilots with compass needle in some combination with time loss, or time gain, or different era time warp zone pocket entrance/

acknowledgement/ then exit situation return to normal state, that it has become an accepted anomaly fact by most who have studied it.

So it is legitimate, but what are factors common to such cases?

1. Things that don't exist in a location particular to it now do, including inhabitant and physical environment changes either backward or forward in time. Paved roads now dirt roads, autos now horse drawn wagons, building structure from a different era, people wearing antique style clothes, and other signs or landmark changes recognized from an earlier time period, (or more modern) Possibly the presence of current landmarks no longer present.
2. The person experiencing the episode sensing a strong feel that *this is not normal* or wide awake illusion of reality relative to what should be the present. Strange smells, visions may often appear if cast through a lens, casting a strange lighting effect and even trees that should throw a shadow a certain way, but now don't! In general, a more surreal than normal atmosphere (U.F.O. High Strangeness accounts very much similar descriptions).
3. Later on, returning to present, none of the sights, sounds, or visuals, smells, or sensing that was associated is re-traceable.
4. People in these antique setting scenes have astonished looks of surprise on their faces. As if to say, *What are you doing here, who are you, and where did you come from?* Exactly what the person who is experiencing the episode is wondering about them. They thinking this intruder doesn't belong in their reality, and the intruder wondering how his parachuted in New Reality within altered environment of his existence managed to occur, as well.

Every account seemingly a bit unique, yet containing such oddity factors in each case, quite similar, and consistent worldwide. The same being true of U.F.O. abduction accounts.

In Chapter 7 (U.F.O. Section) mentioning varied U.F.O. Theory developed over many years, then commenting on them, in theory six, Time Travel, I explained how scientists in Physics currently believe it only possible to go back in time as far back as the invention of the time machine itself. This being why currently man could not venture back into the past by his own devise. In theory it could change in the future, but then one point this book is adamant in making is that there is so little time left before Bible described Tribulation, then Armageddon. Sorry to dash the hopes of time travelers everywhere, but it is in the sense of Christian holy Prophecy awareness, which such confirmation was given to me. Forward seeing precognitive of psychic (gift of God) gift, such as myself and others who experience it, are in essence experiencing awareness time travel, and Remote Viewing Clairvoyant sometimes having greater control steering ability in doing so. They don't physically time travel, but their subconscious seems to Astral plane travel for them, even taking a camera along for visuals, so to speak.

The line of thinking behind what some refer to as there Grandfather Paradox includes what would happen if someone went back in time and killed their father or grandfather, how in theory could they have then been born in the first place to go back in time to prevent their own birth. Store that one in the same archive with the which first chicken or the egg quandary, and if the person who might have invented a working time machine wasn't brought into existence already except for his mother having an abortion. Perhaps neither the time machine nor the abortion was meant to be, but the end of one eliminating the other, as well. A few more coffee breaks with the Wildman and I'll have your conscious in Astral plane travel mode booked in a seat right next to your subconscious for one of those flights, and attending conferences in Existentialville.

Ironically, time machines will likely never happen. Not because perhaps they aren't possible, or that physicists might not successfully reach some break through hypothesis solutions. No, it won't happen for another reason. Never existing then outside of the symbolism of something similar to my 2008 psychic dream sleep dream where it was presented through holy angel depiction as representative as a symbol of time travel.

One could argue that perhaps what the dream was suggesting that in the next fifteen years or so mankind will invent such a machine, but I choose to believe it is merely symbolic representation, with about 95 percent or more certainty. That irony part resides in the fact that human kind will simply run out of time in which to complete a successfully functioning prototype. Or, I could just tell you that Part II of this book picks up in continuation of this Chapter over there on the other (spiritual) side of this time warp/time machine discussion.

You are now asking me, *Does this mean time will run out of existence first?* An ocean of time surrounding our very existence now out of this water of time? Let's just say Part II requires your mental seat belt fastened, not just for continuation of this chapter, but a lot more of what awaits over there, as well.

Existentialville while intellectually stimulating, does not have a down to Earth bricks/stones and mortar church anywhere in town. It can only conceptualize one, and its spiritual ramifications and correlations to everything conceivably attached. Over in Part II of this book and this Chapter's continuation, the spiritual side of metaphysical and supernatural mechanisms are explored relevant to both time, yourself, God, and functioning aspects of this relationship.

In fact, continuation of all the Metaphysical/Supernatural chapters do the same thing. After reading all of these continuation chapters, they sort of better explain each other relative to God's overriding control from within the spiritual realm.

With time, I could use the analogy of this church we were just discussing having a bell tower with a cross atop, and a clock face. God the father/creator like the long hand on the clock, Jesus/Son of God like the other large hand, and the Holy Spirit being the thin harder to see seconds hand, and all of them working in harmony in conjunction to keep time. However, if the nature of humanity's society becomes increasingly irresponsible in a collective sense morally, and thus neglectful of the routine maintenance required for very mechanism of time to function as it was originally designed for proper performance, then what? If the gears of spiritual faith are not properly oiled and vital component are not routinely checked and maintained, then eventually sticking and slippage will occur. Then you could almost look at the Book of Revelation as prediction by the clock's designers that eventually improper upkeep would lead to a seven-year period of irreversible trouble or trouble like never before in time/event malfunctions eventually leading up to the day when that great clock grinds to a total halt standstill, except in this case referring not to just the clock, but the time it was keeping reaching dimensional termination! That clock although going through Great Tribulation, eventually simply ran out of time to keep, so it stopped dead in its tracks. Is that what is going to happen? Join the other seat belt fastened readers in Part II, and maybe hear the higher octave lowdown from that church's organist. My guess that organ taking on a more macabre tone once the Rapture of Church occurs, and the pastors of this world have for the most part exited. I'd be mighty wary of any who don't!

These same Chapters covered then in Part II, but with emphasis on God's control of all these supernatural mechanisms, and importance of an active personal Christian faith that outcomes in your life will reflect positively for you, that I will better explain understanding of the how and what regarding God's interconnectivity aspects. Religion aside from Christianity is a bit like fishing without bait, or a luxury auto without fuel. In one case you won't get very far, and in the other it's just a waste of your time. Faith in Jesus Christ as your personal Lord and savior is the master key that fits all supernatural locks. It (Christian faith) is mandatory must, otherwise the supernatural will be a deck stacked against you instead of for you. It is why I separated the Metaphysical Chapters in half. Part I of this book discusses the mechanisms, while Part II discusses the spiritual (Christian) tie-ins.

Part II will offer my predictive forecast not only for the seven-year metaphorical clock Tribulation, but the Biblical one matching, not to mention that final clock stick/halting point. Rapture advice, destructions discussion, Christian witness story, and explanation of something called the Lancy Timeline Hypothesis all make for some colorful and stimulating reading/exploration interspersed with Wildman's course sense of humor to try to lighten the dense heaviness of some of the more serious religious subject, and you should find this adventure quite informatively entertaining and enjoyably stimulating. That's if it goes all according to plan. Otherwise just have your family catch up with you at the hospital emergency room trauma unit. At least you'll have something in common with the other patients there—Part II of this book! The time warp then becoming the ambulance ride to the hospital that you don't remember because you were unconscious. Now you see what I mean about the importance of having the Holy Spirit on your side. Now you see what I mean with course sense of humor, too! Don't let the doctor see you trying to finish reading the book, or he'll confiscate it from you.

Too much high octane knowledge awareness of the future can be a very powerful, but volatile potent commodity. Wildman has conditioned his brain with heavy-duty off road shock absorbers to cradle his brain, but it is tough dispersing such information to the public because like a medicine or drug, different people have different dosage toleration limitations. What is no problem for most, might totally O.D., freak someone else out. I'm not out to crush anyone's mind under the weight of implications, or push somebody over the edge with anxiety disorder to begin with. Anyone who fits those descriptions should not read Part II, as it actually could implode their sanity! For those who survive Part I (most will), then they know about what to expect, and enter at their own risk, Part II. Just the fact that a caveat disclaimer is necessary (again) in Part II to Enter Part II at your own risk, like it was fraught with Amazon jungle like mental sanity hazard abounding, only further entices some of the more adventurous, but seriously could be a little too intense for others in terms of New Reality dosage. Spiritual truths can rock your world every bit as intensely as some of the supernatural quick-sand hazard to one's sanity already encountered here in Part I. Most people will be fine, but I'm not too sure about everybody, and I truly don't want anyone to in anyway be traumatized by either part of a book I authored. I'm trying to explain spiritual afterlife, not catapult someone into it. As a Christian Prophet my goal is to promote Jesus, not create a mental health epidemic, among throngs of people who overdosed on reality/truth resulting in comatose/catatonic shock levels. Yeah, that group of people over there, blank look steady stair at the church bell tower clock your imagination is picturing, what I don't wish to be the cause of.

Part II is filled with high octane knowledge future awareness. The first string, all truth playing team out on field. Can you deal with it? Bible scripture clarification and verification validity in full dress mind blow reveal, direct assault pummeling mode. Are you sure you can handle it? Maybe isn't good enough. Let someone else read it for you then, and they can relate it; it's pretty shock-o-licious!

Chapter 21
Astrology/Astronomy: Pre-Statement Comments

Before even beginning this chapter itself, if I don't offer some advanced comment, then some people especially clergy might mistake the theme of this Chapter's discussion, and not get the proper take—away impression. Fist realize that I decided to cover all of these Metaphysical Chapters in two parts. The first part to be found here in part I, but then in Part II, explaining the greater spiritual and religious tie-in ramifications of different aspects there. Unless you have this as background for what is there, you wouldn't see the larger picture, and until you've read Part II, you don't see fully aspects of the Holy Spiritual realm, which is really where the importance lies in over-all picture. Each Metaphysical Chapter in two parts, continued in part II, which is kind of like Wildman's holy cathedral of spiritual message reading experience.

Without reading Part II of this Chapter, and without this pre-statement first, clergy might get the wrong impression thinking I am now explaining the occult to them, since many view Astrology that way, as in the Bible in ancient times, it was rightfully thought of this way, because those dealing in sorcery, black magic, and witchcraft, sometimes thought of planets as cosmic deities. This is the time before all the great Astronomers, astro-physics Mathematics, and Science applied to God's universe. Astrology today is a different and far less mystical, almost a social/science sociology/science study of invisible fields of energy in constant motion/flux to human trait and behavior. In my opinion the clergy need to remove lingering stigma of it being 'occult' from it and move on. It is only occult if the person involved with it is ungodly, using it in some ungodly way. Otherwise it is respectable enough for saved Christians to investigate and examine innocently desiring only a better understanding of it.

The phrase, *Know thy enemy,* used by military Strategists does apply. Christians armed with their armor of faith should not fear examining anything occult actually. The more you know about your enemy the Devil in spiritual terms, the less effective he becomes using things against you. In a sense, among other informative goals of this book, relating information in this area of supernatural characteristics is passing on this Spiritual intelligence to clergy and readers, so they don't have to be crawling under the Devil's barbed wire fences through the mud at midnight (metaphorically speaking, of course) on their bellies to retrieve some of these insights themselves. They only need worry about re-painting the walls, once again metaphorically, from the brain splatter, when they get their minds blown reading what I've told them (freshly painted wall next to a person's favorite reading/easy chair, a possible telltale sign they've been reading New Realities). A reptile stealthily sneaks up on its prey because the prey is ignorant and oblivious to what is happening until caught by surprise. Ignorance is a tool in the Devil's toolbox. The better people understand the supernatural, the more they understand the fence of faith, but as observed from the other side of that fence, then confirming what the Bible on the other side of that fence says being confirmed now in total, but all in perspective from the opposite side of that fence, now looked at from different vantage point, different lens, as well. It makes Christian faith, Christian Bible look as timeless as truth itself, because Jesus is timeless, and Jesus is the truth.

Just the same, intelligence gathering of what other tools the Devil's toolbox contains, possible applications, modus operandi, and other miscellaneous information/knowledge of other weapons in his arsenal of hostile to humans armory, not easy to come by, but unless sought after, likely never would be known. The last time clergy tried to crawl under that barbed wire in the mud at midnight, they never returned (presumed to have been captured by arresting demons then tortured until driven mad!). Only figurative conjecture, but more fact than fiction, as the supernatural is realm territory partially leased by God to the Devil for the conducting of Evil official business, but leased under God's auspices and rules he is stringently required strict adherence to terms and conditions set by God as boundaries. If it wasn't for that, humanity would have all gone extinct along the way, long ago. Jesus gave us fair warning that during Tribulation period, for a little season the Devil will have relaxed restrictions, but how relaxed, in what regards, etc., other than what we know from the Book of Revelation is not fully clear.

My whole point is, no matter what area of the supernatural I am discussing, it is always with the purpose of gaining insights into uncharted understandings territory. Above I said partially leased, meaning that the Devil has access rights to one Dimension out of several which are all part of, and contained within the supernatural. God's corrections system part of the demonic dimension, no doubt. When I speak of crawling under the fence metaphorically, I'm not speaking of that demonic dimension, but rather the entire supernatural realm as a whole. Perhaps God recruiting me as a special agent because of my T.Z.U credentials even though I don't remember my bachelor's degree being majored in supernatural Spying for God special agent training, it somehow just turned out that way. Must've taken a supernatural fork in the road back in my college days I don't now recall, and some over in England, too, maybe, but my point, how are you going to learn anything new unless I describe things from the other side of that supernatural fence? Clergy need to understand something here, as well, besides delivering supernatural awareness, I'm doing so to serve God's purpose. I need to convince every single person who reads my books that the bottom line is all about the correctness of the Holy Bible, and Christian faith following in one's life, as the one and only true religion (Holy Trinity concept of God). So forget about which off road AT.V. trails, or barbed fences I have my readers crawl under, at the end of the day, at the culmination of all explained, it is always, again, and again, and again, yet one more reproof of validity of and in Christian faith. When clergy read Part II continuation of this chapter, it will all come into greater focus, and look at the bright side, all this new sermon, mountains of evidence material I've excavated for them as heavy extractions equipment operator! Maybe I'm over reacting, but anything even remotely considered occult in clergy's mind causes the supernatural hair they don't have to feel like it is standing straight-up. Relax, cut me some slack; we are in the same Christian army. I've already been hit from mistaken identity friendly fire as it is. Metaphorical bullet wounds in the back just make it even harder to crawl under the supernatural fence to conduct espionage. You start to wonder if those clergy who went spying for answers, but never returned weren't shot by clergy on this side of the fence, a little too trigger happy. (Speaking Figuratively)

One starts to wonder, too, what stories not contained in the Bible, of all the Biblical Prophets, they might divulge if you had them, (they lived in different century across nine hundred years) if you gathered all of them around a campfire for their supernatural Stories addendum accounts. The best stories in their personal lives that never made it into Bible inclusions. I guarantee you; it would be worth hearing it. Yet, translate it into common denominator, and you would certainly arrive right back at witnessing for God, and apostles in further witness for Jesus, the Messiah Christ. They would all tell you, they became duty bound by God, to then deliver spiritual inspirations to others to promote faith. Being touched by God, through acts of God to then deliver to others new profound spiritual awareness. That is what I share with them more than two thousand years later, something only God can orchestrate.

The Role of Astrology and Astronomy on the Supernatural Realm

When you look at the role of Astrology and Astronomy in the realm of the supernatural, my personal view is that Astrology is to begin with primarily focused on the relationship between primary planets and related aspect of position. First at time of birth, as identifying who each of us are, then secondly relating that to determining current aspect of these planetary factors in the larger cosmic situation, and based upon collective studies and comparisons gathered over thousands of years to identify prevailing conditions and trends when these cosmic changes occur. It is not in opposition to religion, but coexists, just as the movement of the universe's stars, planets, comets, asteroids, galaxies, solar and star systems are creation of God, and then properties associated which effect human behavior or condition, are then influences of God's creation, upon us, living beings also within God's creation.

Astrologers often don't have idea of why things break cause and effect wise in certain directions, they can't explain the why part, only that it does. It is not exact, either. Depending on what area of Astrology you examine, margin of error changes. Day to day forecast often weak in terms of reliability, yet can be right on the mark, and not by mere coincidence. The broader more general you define tendency, often the greater the correctness. My own study done once on some of noted Astrologer Linda Goodman's predictive description upon random field study, did evidence some remarkable accurate description, and what seemed to be a success of prediction rating in the 75–80 percent (based on birth sign) range. She was doing comparative Venus/Mars study on people's ability to form and keep lasting personal relationship between signs. She did well, but something my study turned up was that people with greatest ability star aspect wise, often seem to balance out with deficiency to an equal degree in some other aspect of their traits and life. Cosmic balance!

We are currently moving out of the age of Pisces, and into that of Aquarius, the water bearer/water sign. In later chapters I predicted the tsunami and the world flood. It should cause you a bit of pause since Mayans also referenced flood for this timeframe, and nine other psychics, including Edgar Cayce and Nostradamus! Astrology then does have causal role, as well as the way it is reacted to, individuals of different star signs. demonic Possession being exception to the rule. In that case the supernatural occurrences is happening within the individual. The connective reasons for this having little to do with Astrology, more to do with spirituality. Yet even here, indirectly, astrology being a partial determinate as described previously of whom the individual is, does aspect. Again though, it has more to do with reaction to an occurrences, and ability to cope.

Astronomy seems to on the other hand play a direct role. Since Astrology is in essence cause and effect of Astronomy, the two are forever linked. Thus, even though I am treating Astronomy as if it were completely separate in discussing it. It is never disconnected, even when only along for the ride so to speak. Here I am examining Astronomy's influence on the cast of characters from the Entities Section of this book, and supernatural occurrences, phenomena, and anomaly. The ebbing of high and low ocean tides almost symbolic of the high and lows of cosmic gravitational tides that in turn are known magnetic force fields. These in turn are electro-magnetic force fields that are moving through a multitude of dimensions. All invisible! Energy both positive charge, and negative charge. Energy not only the force behind living matter, but invisible spirit (other dimensional) matter. Ghosts drawing heat energy, and/or electrical charge energy, proving that the common *Interdimensional* stem for varied dimensional leaves is in fact electro-magnetic charged energy. It could on nano levels where exchanges take place. Sub-Atomic particle below the Electron, Proton, and Neutron levels perhaps. Tie a spirit brain to such sub matter and next thing you know, you have ghosts slipping through keyholes. Isn't that right Houdini?

With sub-atomic particle colliders and accelerators in the U.S. (Illinois) and France/Swiss scientists working on the same, perhaps the answers to unlocking many such mysteries are within eventual grasp. Not to put a damper on this, but my Bible/Tribulation period predictions seem to be casting a heavy shadow over such projects, looming large. Scientists turning into the very sub-atomic particles they were looking for. Having Wildman teach you applied science; a pretty clear indication in and of itself that the world is close to termination. How about a more familiar expert, Albert Einstein, who said at the subatomic level, time and space are interchangeable.

My T.Z.U. degree looking a bit flimsy by comparison, especially printed in the disappearing ink used. Faculty names there like Dr. Merlin, Mandrake, Leary, and Sterling (also serving as University Chancellor). Yet relating the supernatural to Astronomy, having knowledge of the supernatural is imperative if any secrets are to be unlocked. My T.Z.U. credentials having Rhodes Scholar quality in that perspective.

The Solar solstices (December 21, Winter, and June 21, Summer) and the Equinoxes (Vernal or Spring-March 21 and Autumn-September 21) all play a role. Just as these have to do with electro-magnetic and gravitational force fields. For whatever the reason, these do seem to correspond with peak periods of supernatural activity. These peak periods seem to begin building about twenty days prior, and tail off for twenty days after (Interesting that the Mayan calendar was based on twenty-day period cycles.). Thus supernatural events are more likely to happen within these periods, but especially when closer to the peak date itself. Twelve twenty-year cycles comprising the Mayan 240-year-long count calendar round (twenty also).

Keep in mind, too, that there are several other influences that do seem to also play a probability role. The more of these that you stack together, the more likely the occurrences, and explainable after the fact. Also realize, activity is not bound, it doesn't have to follow any prescribed pattern, and it's just that it usually does. It would seem that other unrelated circumstances and influences can and do have involvement, often unrecognized. You won't understand something that can't be conclusively identified. Every case situation is different. If you did a comparative study of say, ten thousand cases, I'm confident the criteria I am presenting you with would hold up well as predictive indicators.

Like the sun and the moon exert their influences, too. Contrary to popular belief that the full moon is peak period for unusual activity, my findings indicate this to only be true of human activity. The nonhuman (E.T.) and nonliving (ghost and other entities) are very clearly preferential toward darkness (new moon period). E.T. eyes are in fact sensitive to light, and my sightings log clearly evidences reduced numbers on the Full Moon. Thus a new moon happening during a peak solar period would be an example of stacking. The more indicators that you stack, the more likely and predictable the occurrences.

Certainly the positioning of other planets do play a role, but to a lesser extent usually than the Sun and Moon. It would relate to the electromagnetic and gravitational force fields for sure.

In looking at the Physics of the supernatural, it is the same, Time, Space, and Matter. Matter, both in the sense of the Chemistry Periodic Chart of the Elements, but also in the sense of form. Earth (solid), air, (gas), fire (combustion energy), water (liquid of life), and plasma (super-hot or cold gas); this is the way the ancients saw the elements comprising their world.

With the sighting of the both visible and invisible, Scorpion stinger tail/Taser which I feel it was, as described in the Bible Book of Revelation, was I seeing something out of another dimension? My answer would have to be yes. The black donut-like rings that when seen looked as thick and heavy as if they were made of asphalt, were in fact existent in another dimension that required eye focus in a specific manner in order to see. The fact I quickly learned I had control over its appearance in this manner and could thusly make it appear or disappear at will (in spite of its heavy solid appearance) proves it was not a hallucination, but an object with multi-dimensional existence, not unlike the U.F.O. or E.T. associated.

We think of Time as linear: past, present, and future. The Mayan saw it more as a loop; cycling and recycling, not unlike planetary orbit that they saw as metering the tempo of their very precise calendar. I will talk more on the Mayan in this chapter relative to their calendar and how their predictions would mesh with my own. Blood sacrifice was also known to occur according to Sun/Moon celestial cycle. Periods of Death are also an influence and marker. Sacrifice, Death itself, be it accidental, in battle, or natural, is yet another influence upon the supernatural, in this case, often the anniversary date and time (something else stackable).

So now I've given you some key time, space, matter, considerations and influences, sometimes relating to negative energy, but also to neutral energy as many ghosts who are not demonic could be described. Positive energy exerts powerful energies when applied that we never see, but these Holy Spirit forces sometimes counter balance or even will cancel out demonic negative forces, but beyond our awareness. If you think of our material world (dimension) as under the supreme rule of God, but control (counter balancing) of assorted demonic dark and evil forces, continually impacting it in negative ways, you've pretty accurately described what is going on. Thus more often than not (not that positive forces aren't) what is at work in terms of the supernatural are demonic negatively expected forces, because the consequences of negative manifestations quickly draw our attention, while the positive/natural flow aspects of existence draw less attention, and are often taken for granted.

Mayan Calendar and 2012

Originally, when writing this section, the plan was to publish and release this book prior to December 21, 2012. Therefore it made sense to explain what I believe the true Mayan meaning of this date is in advance of it becoming present tense (for many very tense). However for reason I'll discuss in a minute, delay was contemplated which meant if the book was published and released until after that date, then a complete re-write of this section/topic would be required.

People already having lived through this date would know exactly what it did or didn't have in store besides a rare, once every 26,000-year solar eclipse among three that year. People would realize that the world did not come to brakes screeching abrupt end as of that date, (not that too many really thought so anyway) Little would seem changed. Notice I said 'seemed' changed rather than 'was' changed. There are a few possibilities I'll come back to discussing a little later, some being potentially unrecognizable noticeable wise, and perhaps only remote, yet, during such rare event of gravitational/magnetic-wise, not beyond the realm of conceivable.

Re-write would mean the loss of some humor applied next to the more serious information being presented. It isn't as easy in the next section of the book inserting any humor that isn't placed with extreme care. Sort of like a sign reading no gas station for the next 150 miles, this humor might be the last seen for the next 150 pages. This Metaphysical section an easier place to joke a little, and although I did manage to discreetly and in good taste place/slide-in some humor, it's far harder when the subject is far more sacred/serious. So, I really didn't want to make humor the sacrificial lamb of re-write, a collateral casualty.

Why delay the book, then cause the need for re-write you ask? It has to do with what is discussed in Chapter 24, Saints Covenant Prophecy. While the truth verification/lie detection backs me up using polygraph Passed exam, it still only provides to some people anyway, partial measure of assurance believability. At this stage, only God and I know for certain in addition to the polygraph exam that I am one hundred percent genuine and very truthful. Others to varying degree will suspect something so rare being described as still being suspect of being a lie, hoax, fabrication or scam, not to mention claiming it being delusional all in my head real, rather than reality real deal real. Everything stated is reality real deal real in this book, but I concede seeing why people would have suspicion of non-validity no matter the reason.

If you think about it, even Jesus was scoffed, rebuked, and rejected, in his day, and in some quarters, still is! Yet Christians know that he and the Bible is genuine word of God, and Judeo-Christian faith is the genuine article. I realized if you can't after nearly two thousand years get humanity as a whole to accept in total there, then even if I wait to see the eventual outcome, whichever it turns out to be fulfillment, I'm still only going to even then gain only partial acceptance. The downside of waiting beside the re-write, lost humor, and extended delay of other urgent Tribulation information certainly is offsetting.

Waiting for the Prophecy to fulfill so that the world could see it happened exactly as predicted and described would certainly send my believability/credibility through the positive acceptance roof, and seeing then holy side had to be source involved, practically to the point of a necessity for declaration of stock split level. People forced to accept God really did entrust Wildman with delivery of holy Prophecy, then my word in witness of Jesus Christ should be received as solidly sound then.

Actually, the prophecy could fulfill very close to, or even on any rare eclipse, date. Wouldn't that be something? Rare, holy prophecies and rare eclipses happening in close approximation fulfillments. Tell me that wouldn't be some extra heavy duty celestial metaphor; not to mention my advanced recognition of the possibility! A Christian, psychic, chamen-spirited holy Prophet with full mojo mode prediction under anointing Spirit power in full thrust! It's not about me though, it's all about Jesus, and through destiny in play these Prophecy Gift awareness are given so as to be presented through this book foretold to me in 1964, I'd one day write, but ultimately all of God's purpose centers upon New Testament, and specifically better awareness of Book of Revelation/Tribulation. It is God in his infinite wisdom knowing I need the believability increased acceptance level to fully carry out his purpose another aspect reason why fulfillment is certainty. Over fifty years of fulfillments of all other prediction on general subject, now shifting to holy subject, is virtual fulfillment certainty.

Yet, whether or not to proceed as planned was a dilemma. A bit like convincing people of a July snowstorm in South Florida. not beyond conceivable. holy forth telling is hard enough, prophecy even slightly harder, and both as being recipient of, enough to get even a clergyman called a liar! Yet, I stand my ground. Even if only God, I, and a polygraph machine believe me, I decided finally to proceed as planned. Some of the die-hard nonbelievers not likely believing God, or his word, either. Expecting them to believe God sourced information wouldn't even matter if the prophecy then had fulfilled yet or not. With so many levels of reader acceptance, I can't concern myself with all of them including the less or non-accepting, because too much other information contained in this book regarding other aspects of Tribulation are too important to too many people, not to mention God's purpose in supplying the awareness in the first place. People who doubt me will hopefully cut me some slack until predicted time of fulfillment, otherwise be a die-hard skeptic if they desire to be!

The point they need to consider also is that if I am in fact as I claim relating holy sourced information, and they choose to ignore it, it represents the word of God, and even the Mayans, demons, and E.T. will tell you ignoring his word comes with dire consequences. Always a price to be paid. A lot of people who ignore what is told to them through this book will be in for a big shock when Tribulation eventually arrives, and unfolds exactly as Prophet Wildman predicted it would, and death becomes the New Reality brain buster.

Their autopsy revealing the cause of their death was their own disbelief, right along with them in cemetery syndrome conclusive evidence fashion. Looking up at the bottom of your own tombstone head marker is apt to do that to you. The marker reading something like: Die-hard skeptic, now a believer, you convinced me finally! Tribulation is not something one can be reactive to, one must be pro-active, and to do that, you need the higher awareness level I attempt to deliver through means of this book.

Unfortunately too many people who think as Christians they will all rapture when it arrives, and thus are safe. In fact many are safe, many will be raptured, but others really relying on, but I'm a good person, taking their assessment of themselves in assumption God's assessment is identical match. When people read my non clergy rapture views elaborated in the Supplement section, they can do a ten-point diagnostic on themselves the way they would taking their car to a mechanic for inspection. If your spiritual self needs complete overhaul, it's better to take care of it now rather than later. Others may only need new faith wiper blades for their faith outlook windshields, or spiritual battery charge a little low.

Although I had felt proceeding prior to Prophecy fulfillment was not only warranted, but perhaps preferable, it now seems that fulfillment could take place beyond January 2014 timeframe. This will delay Part II publication (essentially already written except for further details relating to this fulfillment aspect upon this subject).

Improving the level of credibility/believability could then translate into additional souls/lives saved by more people recognizing the need to follow recommendations presented to them. You have to agree, that's something priority wise, certainly preferable to God as well, thus represents the best approach to take.

It should be recognized that one who Prophecies, likely is predestined to do so, and this being something I personally believe and claim which this book also makes is supported in Bible scripture. In Romans 8: 28, "And we know that all things work together for good to them that love God, to them who are called according to his purpose" (God's purpose, and the carrying out thereof). Then in Romans 8: 29–30, "For whom he did foreknow, he also did predestinate to be confirmed to the image of his son" (meaning to bear witness to his son, Jesus Christ). Here the apostle Paul conveys linkage through eternity in circular form of one's pre-born past in direct cause/effect through destiny preordained by God, reflected into the future. It is not limited to just the gift of prophecy, but encompassing, foreknowledge, predestination divinely directed, a spiritual calling such as to Ministry, and all that is in justification and glorification of Jesus Christ. All of these are instruments of God, toward service of a believer describing then how God's purpose is fulfilled through man.

Pathways if you will toward accomplishing God's divine will and purpose that God has already worked out in advance, and man simply then carrying out God's completion to that end pre-designed. Prophecy in fulfillment in the larger sense then is fulfillment of God's plans, as well, but carried out through man, so as to spiritually benefit man, and all in further evidence to Christ's glory.

So to my cynics and skeptics in disbelief of my claim of receipt of Prophecy and forth tellings upon holy subject, I say to them, no man is justified to criticize me for this reason, and to do so means they have judged me, and accused me, when they should leave that for God. Raise this issue before God the Father Almighty then, a prophecy in testimony witness support of faith in Christ, the very spirit of this prophecy fulfillment.

Now you are going to ask: How my prophecy awareness of Holy source relate, how does this square with Mayan End of Days prophecy. The answer is simple, I do not agree with December 21, 2012, as end of the world at all!

I see it as the end of their old fifty-two-year calendar, and completion of the 26,000-year solar eclipsed based cycle simultaneously yes, but not to imply the world would end of and on that very day. Contradicting evidence I have sourced from holy angel suggests that what they were telling us is that this was the beginning of the end, rather than the end itself. Meaning, not even another single twenty-year increment left to begin a new calendar upon, and that's all they are saying. Could some natural disasters occur on December 21, 2012? Sure. Just not the end of the world total. The world only gets to end once and in choice between Mayans (mortals) and holy angels, I think I'll prefer the messages from the immortals myself, but that's just me! (As of original 2010 manuscript, Dec. 21st, 2012 was future timing)

I've minimized mentions of Tribulation seven-year Biblical period, as this is what Part II of my Book is mainly covering. However, to further inspire and advocate, as well as encourage Christian Faith, I thought I'd provide a linkage information tie between Part I and Part II. Controversial to some as all get out, but when Wildman is talking holy subject, Wildman is talking serious subject. One of the reasons I hesitate to toss my reader's a tidbit here, is that without all the additional information awaiting in Part II, some are going to question the validity, accuracy, whatever you want to call it, but I stand behind all predictions I make, and never yet wrong on future prediction in fifty years, and quite confident I'm correct on this one, as well. Supplement Section of this book what I'm referring to, a little prophecy present under your tree to unwrap last, and don't worry about the tick, tick, tick, ticking sound inside this is set for future timeframe, but the realization could detonate some people's minds upon opening! Yes exactly, they could lose their tree (Joking I hope)!

This will give you all the perspective focus you need for now on this whole End of Days situation in lens adjustment, with the rest explained at length in Part II. No need for the hot steamy Yucatan jungle, investigative answers expedition. You have those Mayan Anthropologists beat by a mile, and didn't have to leave your easy chair, and minus the Deet mosquito spray. It was polite of you to offer a cold beer to them, but three thousand miles away they didn't quite hear you!

Having ticked off the Mayan Anthropologists, I'll take it a step further, and remind them the answers in Part II of my book they are seeking are likely to be slow arriving in Yucatan book stores, until language translation has taken place, and they then might not have it in stock for years after people in the States in their easy chairs sipping ice cold beer have already read it! The jungle had them steamed; now I do (Wildman's humor strikes again!)!

All three Metaphysical Section Chapters pick up again over in Part II. with further spiritual tie-in aspects there (Maybe even more Anthropologist humor abuse!). So, rest easy for now, 2012 is at least in my view, and with good reason explained, not the Year to Fear. However that Beginning of the End interpretation from Mayans take away message, not exactly cheery, either. Still you will have time to finish that beer and read Part II. At this time it is unclear how much time space interval there will be between books, but at least some interval could occur, and it important then I mention it. (less than a year, perhaps only a few months' time spacing, and I could re-decide to let Saints Covenant Prophecy fulfill first, for added impact!

No one questions the Mayans advanced knowledge of Astronomy, but it clearly came from Extraterrestrial assistance. Which group is not clear, and those crystal skulls of Lyrean E.T. origin the answer or might it have been the demonic Reptilian? The cascading shadow of a snake down a precision position staircase of a blood ritual temple, their knowledge of the Milky Way's dark rift zone as being home of Spirits of the Underworld, exactly where the Orion belt Sirius and Rigel Star systems are located, home of the Greys and the Reptilian, what a small universe neighborhood! Huge coincidence the Reptilian have a taste for fresh human sacrificed blood isn't it. Pyramid temples in Egypt and other Aztec/Toltec location all a coincidence, too, or demon business card tucked inside a How to build a pyramid instruction manual. T.V. shows making too much money off of advertising to point that out to you. They solve the mystery, and they stop making money. The last thing they want to do is supply you with the answer - there's less money rather than more for them! Oh, did Wildman just knock their extra ice cream scoop on the floor? T.V. networks siding with demon secrecy if it helps them make a buck off you. They never figured on Wildman, or their ice cream scoop on the floor. Did I do that? How metaphysical of me.

One last thing, since Part II may not be published until after extended delays, that ought to be mentioned briefly here. This is the hypothesis of a U.F.O. armada invasion occurring as of that date! Some likely now sighting this as proof I'm crazy, others thinking so anyway, but I didn't say definite, this is merely hypothesis theory. Hear this out, keep an open mind, and don't rush to conclusion. Actually, if it did occur, it might happen invisibly in this dimension, completely undetected, even comprising an armada of thousands of saucers! It's not a random event, but one requiring God sign off in approval on first, and God actually stipulating the low profile restriction be kept in strict compliance currently, until Tribulation, if in fact extra additional saucers and E.T. crews are required.

The five-month sting of humans not occurring until 2027, a confirm I've already received from God as a Prophet. Now there are already saucers here in Earth's locale on a regular basis, but what if more in sizeable numbers are required for this scorpion tail like Taser/ Particle Beam/ U.F.O. delivered, event? Some believe the last big U.F.O. saucer migration of E.T. across the galaxy occurred 26,000 years ago, and the last rare solar eclipse of this type is no coincidence! Occurrences happened exactly 26,000 years ago, too.

Think of a heavy vault door as a comparative. Wildman dialing the combination with N.A.S.A. looking over my shoulder, and you looking over theirs. As the combination dials are turned, tumblers inside are then turned, moving sets of pins into alignment, and metal 'fingers' to be properly aligned to move freely without restriction thus facilitating opening of the vault door. Now in similar fashion example, supposing this rare eclipse created removal of restrictive forces, readjusted gravitational and unobstructed electro-magnetic fields blocked by the eclipse itself. A clear passage from the Orion constellation opening of our solar system vault door now allowing improved straight shot from there to here condition much more favorable? We don't necessarily need to understand all the why and how, leave that for the astrophysicists at N.A.S.A. and at Universities to contemplate. This is not increased threat to humans at this time, because God has it under control. This is hypothesis only, and even were it to be correct possibility, there is no immediate threat to humans prior to Tribulation period. Demonic E.T. saucers arriving for the big Tribulation event dance early, but kept in check by God's tight leash conditional rules permissible behavior guidelines, of which interference with humans is strictly prohibited until Tribulation!

Little Jimmy not making it clear to Santa he wanted the video game version of the alien E.T. saucer/ Earth invasion for Christmas, not the real thing, the minor glitch cause of major outcome? No, my sense of humor on the loose once again, I have to rein in constantly. If this hypothesis proves true, I sure hope God has better success reining in that invasion force of demonic E.T which is apt to be almost as big a challenge for him as reining in my sense of humor is for me.

There is Mayan 2012 connection, as well, and part of this chapter's Part II explanation, other book's continuation. I wanted to slip in an early mention of it here in Part I. A little E.T. invasion, Christmas stocking stuffer for 2012! A Merry Mayan Christmas to you, too, Little Jimmy. You can almost tell, little Jimmy's parents sometimes have a hard time reining him in, little figurative unruly child that he is!

For those questioning this hypothesis thinking world human population numbers might have declined sufficiently worldwide by mid-Tribulation, timeframe that additional saucer craft might not be required to carry out all of tasering workload, figure again. World population drop off in the first three years cutting world population in half roughly give or take down to about three and a half billion or so, and these Taser stings delivered at night, one person at a time. It is open season on non-spiritual, or those not of Christian faith humans, not exceeding 5 months total time allotment specification, according to Book of Revelation. Based on approximate likely saucer available saucer numbers in total currently, (we can only guess at) then at least potentially need will exist for substantially more U.F.O. saucer craft. The hypothesis possibly what the Mayan attempted to relate to future humans, was something linking the rare Winter Solstice with Solar eclipse, to a U.F.O. invasion embarking from Orion Constellation, exactly where the E.T. here now are said to be from. Little Jimmy's Christmas wish in the real? Possibly so, but if so, likely carried out with humans none the wiser. This account a way of depriving them of saying that they got it over on humans and pulled it off completely by surprise. They might have gotten up early in the morning and traveled light years to get here, but it wasn't good enough to fool the humans if such be the case, when all is said and done. The demons' invasion plans were foiled in surprise, and just one of the reasons for the bounty on my head or the dossier on me is a dangerous Christian subversive undermining their efforts to undermine humans. It fundamentally changes the math of the equation when you have God on your side, with relationship in serving him. Something the people in 2027 will figure out in a hurry once they get Tasered. Jesus is Lord.

Chapter 22
Cosmic Model

As a young boy in the 1950s while visiting an aunt out of state, a cousin then just returned from the 'hot war' in Korea and serving in the Air Force, gave me a puzzle to work out on paper, assisting in keeping me amused. You may have run across it and be familiar with it yourself. Three houses with three utilities opposite, one utility opposite each house. The object is to connect the utilities, one line to each of the houses without crossing any of the lines. It is a doable puzzle.

The metaphysical and supernatural is in some sense like that. There are both tangible and intangible scientific dimension, and spiritual ones of good and evil. Just as there can be repelling force within electromagnetism, so it is between forces spirit wise holy and unholy, opposites that don't mix, but rather repel, or lines that cannot cross as in the houses and utilities puzzle analogy.

In this Chapter, I thought I'd challenge my reader to come up with their own Cosmic Model, realizing that when you feel you have correctly worked it out to your satisfaction, although there is certainly a correct model, there is no confirmation, even if you get it right. Keep in mind it is one of the greatest enigma riddles of mankind since the beginning. There is no consensus of opinion as a whole, but more like consensus clumps of agreement on certain points. Experts can't even state with certainty how many dimensions exactly there are. Lots of theories, even in scientific circles, but no certainties as yet.

You are in control, choose what medium you want to work in similar to an artist. Pencil or pen on paper, or perhaps some computer three-dimensional enhanced program ideal for assisting in graphic dimensional illustration your choice. The value is in the mental stimulation, and the endeavor of attempting to grasp concept, then be analytical and self constructively critical in evaluation seeking flaws. Design, refine, re-design, redefine, until you reach the point at which you've constructed your own conceptual model that will at the very least bring you to awareness of just how complex it all is, yet totally functional. The world of our very existence.

Experiment with different hypothesis, compare component inter relationship and connectivity, or lack of, where dimensional separation or insulations might be positioned, and if these same conditions are constant or variable through the entire universe, as well. Astrophysics 101 so to speak, but the theory aspect rather than the math part. You might be constructing a model similar to a Chemical Engineer who is examining three-dimensional graphic of atomic molecular structure covalent bonding consisting of spheres and connective channel in straight direction, or even as an Architectural model of rooms (not necessarily square) and hallways. It's the mental stimulation that will get your contemplative juices flowing, or perhaps the other way around as you cross into a zone of wonderment just beyond some imaginary threshold within deep fascinating contemplation of uncharted and unexplored regions of your own mind! An entire universe now of both outer space and your mind's inner space, there are no boundaries to your quest for greater understanding.

Most think first of the three dimensions of measure and perspective based on those, but in this exercise if you decide to pursue it, you must learn to think in terms of yourself being the intelligent force controlling that dimension, from the inside out in some cases, perhaps thinking of your thoughts themselves as your identity when pursuing unconventional analytical analysis. Extreme flexibility to the very thought processes and procedure you approach the challenge with, might be the key to discovering the very key to unlocking these mysteries. It shouldn't feel like work, but rather the type of fun one has meeting the challenge, enjoying the endeavor of pursuing it, rather than being expectant of a particular outcome. Ride the rapids, enjoy the ride, go with flow (of thought) and see where it takes you.

With physicists doing the very same thing, asking are there ten or twelve dimensions, are they parallel throughout space? String Theory? Super String Theory? What forces alter dimensions? What role does both the Laws of Science and physical properties play at the Nano-level to beings and intelligent living forms, as well as that importance at the macro level? In other galaxy, could they have alternate dimensions? Do they have different science or science varied from ours, with elements not on the known Periodic Chart now known to man? Black holes and white holes only known to man a relatively short time (although suggested by Einstein as existing even prior to their discovery). What else of Science does man not know currently, having come very far, very fast, in terms of discovery relative to man's total period of existence. Lots and lots of questions, few confirmations. You aren't likely to solve this puzzle in a single attempt, but just making the attempt can be stimulatingly beneficial and enlightening, and no one ever doubted Astrophysicists doing the same, as not being extremely bright minded. However, only some of the dimensions can be explained exclusively through science, and the spiritual dimensions thus likely an equally important evaluative tool in many regards in combination with Science in this respect.

Using all the insights I've given you in this book, like a child dumping a large container of toys out on the floor, but then somehow devising a spontaneous approach to how to go about play, perhaps things will come to you in the process of proceeding forward with it. No one is going to grade you, because the correct answer isn't known, all answers are as valid as you decide to make it by judging whatever model you decide is the one you finally decide you like best that you are comfortable with.

Yes, I will present my own non-conformist model on flat paper rather than three-dimensional, and listing dimensions as I perceive them, rather than get into speculation on how all the pieces I describe actually fit together, but for you, if you decide to try to build a three-dimensional model of how yours fits, it can be the point of awareness where you realize what was okay on paper, maybe stills needs modification as to fit properly in the grand scheme master concept. The point of this chapter is that, if you involve yourself directly in the process, you will not only enjoy the intensity and depth of the contemplation (exercise perhaps almost yoga-like), but you will somehow come away feeling more enlightened, and better for having done so. The benefits of these reflections will be all yours.

In your cosmic model, maybe that little dot waving back is you. Is it waving back? You perhaps now programed to think in ten dimensions simultaneously. It's great mental exercise, and can even have spiritual benefit that in turn can have health benefit indirectly perhaps in subconscious terms, similar to what some Eastern philosophies prescribe.

Now since I am a huge believer in the existence of God, and the trinity Christian model of Holy Spirit, not surprising, God exists throughout my model. Within, soul's mind's eye, without, God's eye throne and heavenly firmament, and the Holy Spirit pervading the entire universe. So in my model, I don't just place God off in some corner, but Holy Spirit in varied form exists throughout. Not everyone might share this view, I recognize your right to your own opinion, and it is after all, your own model built upon your own set of beliefs.

It is a funny thing about faith, you have to have it in order to then recognize and bring that realm into your own existence (I will discuss at greater length in the Religion Section coming up after this chapter). It is amazing that some PhD's otherwise quite brilliant are sometimes so spiritually deficient and thus ignorant on the subject of religion/God's existence. Minimalist theories, Godless Big Bang, and Pantropic Theory, not to mention other agnostic or atheistic theories all quite wrong! Now I wouldn't say wrong unless I was quite certain I was right, and in the Religious Section you will read how I expect to disprove once and for all this Godless misinformation. Short of getting a signed statement (you wouldn't have anything to compare his signature to anyway!) it is my hope, and belief on faith that I've already been delivered the means to make a strong case, in terms of spiritual evidence (through prophecy) of God's existence. Now putting skeptics and unbelievers on notice! Wildman's waving his silver psychic sword and faith, right in their face, but not meaning them harm, instead to remove their blindness that they infect others with, and show them Jesus Christ truly is the light of the world (A lot more on this in the final section of the book.).

That Godless universe is their universe, and one I wouldn't want to live in. In mine the desserts are real, fruit trees bear fruit, all forces of nature are in God's command, and prayers and prophecies really do get answered. The Bible is fact, not fiction, and denial of God's existence is delusional. Then there are the religions believing in a different interpretation of God than my own. That is their prerogative to believe as they choose and worship as they choose. Only the Christian faith has a true Messiah, and the world is fast approaching that time in world history where little else will matter! The Christian faith, and only the Christian faith, comes with a soul-saving warranty. Suddenly those buying into these other faiths discovering theirs has none (Those of Hebrew faith holding warrants that can be exercised as option to be converted one for one into warranties!). It will take the time of Tribulation, for most to realize, if they don't already, the Judeo-Christian model is the correct spiritual model (I now have clear evidence of this being certainty!).

Back to the model I promised you, that I'll now describe, explaining as I go, listing my interpretation, but also stating I encourage you to evaluate and come up with one of your own, as you prefer it.

My Personal Cosmic Model (Description and Discussion)

1. Existence of intelligent life is necessary in order to perceive other dimensions. Therefore all intelligent life form is included here, but also including unintelligent life, and lesser intelligent life. Plant, animal, and humans. Even animals have keen sense of environmental factors, some of which include dimensions, therefore life in general should all be classified together. While most will create separate dimensional space for giving God autonomy, in my model I perceive God to be both integral and autonomous. That is to say aspects of Holy Spirit are present in existence; therefore God should not be excluded from the dimension of the living, even though God is present in separate dimension, as well. God has linkage to all dimensions, does he not? You must think broadly here, across the entire expanse of universe, and in doing so, realize that in addition to God, other intelligent life forms likely exist, but in alternate dimensions, in far flung places within this vast universe under God's control, thus this category is not limited to our Solar System, but carry throughout the entire universe, and in other dimension even, Life and intelligent Life being the key for inclusion here, even into other dimension of existence. Thus considering Life the determining factor rather than dimension. One should realize, too, other Entity can and does, often invisibly enter the dimension of the living, and thus even some Entity with their own dimension (non-living) transits the environment of the living.
2. Since theoretically at least, a living being could exist, but without the senses the higher forms have of senses: Smell, hearing, taste, light/vision, feel/touch, as well as temperature/sensitivity, or include only some sense factor, the senses should be considered as a separate dimension. The dimension of the senses applied to living beings.
3. Then the dimension of Height, Width, and Depth visual perception
4. Next, the dimension of specificity, measure, and quantity. Very much a dimension heavily used by Science, but other dimension inter-act with Science, so they are not exclusive. Here you would have things like weight: pounds., grams, ounces, etc;. volume: cubic, liters, gallons, etc.; air/water pressure; thermal: BTU, R-Value, temperature, radiation measure, etc.; and distance measure: fraction of inches, inches, feet, yards, centimeters, meters, kilometers, etc. All other similar measure, definition and delineation
5. Time, often called the fourth dimension, if I switched places with number four above it would then be four, but numbering sequence obviously irrelevant. Real or illusion, it exists, and is measured or unmeasured, essential to human concept of order and motion relationship with Space/Time.
6. Scientific Properties as governing the Laws of Science, and as shown to be proven Scientifically factual. The forces governing natural elements around us These also seem to be commonly used by and manipulated by Entity from other dimension such as ghost and E.T. as both energy source/and or a kind of transit system.

    1. Clearly attached, but existing in intangible, invisible, and in a sense ethereal conceptual space the realm of human intellect, and acquired wisdom. Essentially human consciousness on a higher thought plane of existence. One would be tempted to consider this a plane rather than a dimension, except it already exists on several levels, thus it demands being considered as a separate dimension consisting of several planes within it. Choice, and differentiations, intellectual decisions, reason, wisdom ethics, philosophy, academics, science, law, spiritual concept, awareness, religion, psychic planes of consciousness, psychology language, mathematics, history, politics, all can extend to very complex and advanced levels of human thought. All of this bundle of channels and planes and focused thought included here. The human mind aspiring to improve, do more and better than that previously accomplished. The internally expanding universe of the human mind. I didn't include the Arts mentioned above because creativity is included in all of those endeavors, but aspected through all we do, as well. The human mind, heart, and soul that humans unique, defining of who we are.

7. Death: That threshold between living and non-living, that few who cross into ever return from. In astrology, the house of death, in Tarot card, the death card, the dimension that all living eventually transfer into. Thoughts of exactly how the process of Rapture will work is not in total agreement among all Christians, relative to how it compares to death, other than the human spirit being taken up in a vanishing from this dimension. It is definitely preferable to ordinary death, as there is a measure of worthiness prerequisite in order for it to occur based on faith Then, the act becomes a confirmation from above of one's worthiness You might think of death as a short, short, space similar to the connecting ramp between concourse and aircraft. Simply a short space of linkage between where you've been and where you are going and hope you have a nice flight! (careful which plane you board)
8. Evil: All spirit forces unholy and enemy of the forces of Light, and Right. The House of pain and punishment for wrongdoers held in this dimension. The Greeks described Hades as a place of punishment (hell), but a lower-level known as Tarturus, one of fire, similar to the Biblical lake of fire, some shall be cast. Roughly a third of

angels, fallen from God's grace by their following Lucifer or Satan in rebellion against God, and as I have and will explain again in the Religion Section, there is a hierarchy even here, including lesser demons and some ET in the ranks. Once you become personally convinced as to the legitimate accuracy and genuine Holiness of the Bible, you must then accept these as authentic truths. They are!

9. The Holy Spirit Dimension - Both here on Earth, throughout the universe and into the highest plane of the heavenly firmament of God, even higher and above the Kingdom of Heaven. God's angels (as already described in Chapter 2), Some previously living human souls do go to heaven in afterlife, perhaps some re-incarnate, and many more souls await final judgments to be judged at the end of this Age (now on final approach) The second coming of Jesus Christ will occur, and in Chapter 27, I describe, what I feel is accurate to close proximity to both timetable and event occurrences.

These are my ten dimensions, but I have a conceptual eleventh I'll discuss next that I call the Legacy Dimension, but perhaps really just a plane in the tenth. Perhaps this outline will help if you decide to try your own.

The Legacy Dimension

This is a hypothetical Dimension, and could be more of a separate plane within a previously mentioned Dimension or what might be called a corridor. Notice also that the fifth rank of holy angels are known as Virtues. Could it possibly be that they have charge over this domain?

What if the true meaning of one's life was examined in retrospect after all accomplishment had been accomplished, all decisions made, and all and everything positive we had ever managed to bring of worth had been brought forth? It could then be examined as our entire body of life's work. Everything. Employment, raising children, Volunteer work, Donations not just of money but of time and effort, all things creative or entertaining to others. Everything of use, value, or benefit to others, both individuals (simple acts of kindness perhaps) or service to organizations, government, or military. Everything in sum and total. How would we look? Think of the many greats through history in every field imaginable and the legacy each of these people made. If your being was evaluated in hindsight, how would you compare?

It is an intriguing thought, and quite possibly to the holy realm of God, is in fact how we will be viewed in the records of eternity, since each of us live singular and unique one of kind only existences never again to be repeated exactly the same. What was of only short term value, and what was of long term? How will we be seen and judged, we never know, but by something similar in extensive and comprehensively detailed scrutiny, one should perhaps wander, *How will I do? How would I score?* Did one obey God's laws, as highest measure of all, and would God be pleased or disappointed in results? The value of thinking in such terms to motivate one's self to do a little more, or a little better, we all have unlimited potential.

The same likely holds true of Nations leaving legacy, as well. It is with sadness to look to the future, but envision, as if with retrospect, the fated? demise of our proud country. Trying to comprehend so much loss, destruction, and devastation, having traveled across it, seeing so much of its natural beauty is painful. At the end of this book these predictions and descriptions will be a truly depressing account, yet my purpose from these awareness given are to hopefully save lives, It is not with certainty these events will happen, most visions are from other psychics and not my own, yet if there wasn't a pretty strong set of indicators, I would not have proceeded. Better to be shocked and awed, than killed later, caught by total surprise. Having spoken of the legacy individual's silhouette might be, what might be our nation?

A Tribute to America's Greatness

Built on the Guiding Light faith in God principle. Unmatched in Spirit, Productivity, Hope and aspiration toward achievement. Unrivaled in accomplishments in every area of human endeavor, and achievement. Unequaled in the entire history of the world as a Champion of and defender of personal Liberty and Freedom. Not just at home, but around the Globe.

No other Nation has ever risen to such high standards of Exceptionalism. Will this be America's Legacy, and how God will remember us as a people? The best he has ever seen? Or will all our failings to his high standards blemish and tarnish his impression? For our missionary, medical, and humanitarian relief to those in need offset? So then a reason to show America a measure of mercy as to Tribulation harshness degree?

The answer there lies with the Nation of Israel. So as we stand by as protector and in strong support to the nation of Israel as allied, as long as we have the determination in strength commitment. For if we ever waiver, or withdraw favor and commitment to Israel, then surely that will be the day that God withdraws favor and commitment to us. Our greatness, our favor from God, our legacy, all are dependent upon how well we protect the nation of Israel, until Christ returns when we can relinquish responsibility.

Unfortunately, looking to the future, America doesn't quite complete the full term, because Tribulation start gets in the way. Of course, God already knows this and only holds us responsible up until then. Our legacy then intact, as long as we continue our support until then. It is God's cue to Israel then, for full Christian faith conversion. Validity of Christian faith can hardly then be argued, when so many Americans otherwise military, and politically guarding Israel suddenly have now vanished in rapture! God will forgive and overlook mistakes and judgment errors, but only if we hold fast to our commitment with Israel can our legacy of exceptionalism be preserved by preserving the nation of Israel, because this, too, is God's will that we do so.

A final tribute to America's greatness is the preservation of our legacy with God. He already knows we succeed in future time, and now you know, too, as well as how! Through continued preservation of Israel. Israel you may recall was built on the very same Guiding Light, faith in God principle. So a legacy of exceptionalism is all about faith in God, and holding to his principles. You already knew all that right?

Pre-Destiny, Nations, and People

God pre-destines nations just like people, and sometimes people to be the instrument by which to accomplish his nation pre-destined purpose results. By his faith, David, later King David in biblical Judea, won favor from God by holding God in highest esteem that in turn encouraged Judea to gain Divine providence and covenant. The covenant God has had since the time of David, is one of at least four covenants still in place held, or still being upheld by God, with Israel even today, that will all come into active play during the coming Tribulation period.

America's founding fathers had a vision for a new nation that would be founded on the importance of keeping close relationship with God, not only for our laws and government, but as a moral compass to direct our nation forward in all aspects of an America in partnership with God in our daily lives, as individuals, but all of our undertakings as a nation. That our endeavors would be righteous in the eyes of God, that our nation might so be blessed by God. A new virgin land that literally was God's country and pristine, might be equally so spiritually set on a strong foundation, and it was. A new nation, under God, and thereby favored by God.

Very much like King David, George Washington was pre-destined to lead, not only as a military general and First President later, but guided by God because of his faith in God. He was God's favored Son to set the cornerstone for America, and get it started on correct path, not only to the visions of man for America, but the vision of God for America in tandem. No question about it, George Washington had an air force under God's command, assisting his land armies under his command, under Divine providence. Sometimes things happened for a reason that only God would understand, even if seeming like a short term set back, the long term was one hundred percent on Washington's best outcome side, because he was God's favored Son. God was literally George Washington's invisible secret weapon. Favorable outcome guaranteed, although you still have to work for it, perhaps to appreciate it once achieved.

Then gradually, just like the Garden of Eden, the Devil slithers in, and the best laid plans of both God and man go awry. The distancing of man from God increasingly like new generations in Israel, being absently mindful of what brought prosperity and made the country great in the first place. A nation is only great when seen as such in God's eyes, not man's. Legacy can be generational and temporary, or permanent. A nation's legacy is of the permanent measure variety ultimately. Whenever Israel strayed from God, it paid consequence penalty. And, although America still has greatness, its moral, ethical, and spiritual codes in recent decades have shown signs of toleration slippage, erosion, and decay, which is measured across entire population. Bigger, not necessarily better, and the individual's cosmic model, as to how they see themselves in God's universe, and their universe within this planet in relationship to God is increasingly inaccurate, damaged, or polluted perspective. Not healthy for them, but then they having influence on others negatively. America is on a collision course with serious consequence penalty, as explained in the Book of Revelation. I'm just sort of a Deputy Spiritual Marshall serving notice papers more than a decade in advance. Day of reckoning on its way, explicitly explained in Part II, and everyone is officially served notice here in Part I. You can't say God never warned you, you've just been served warning notice, and if you don't think it official now, Part II likely will change your mind. God sending an apocalypse Prophet named Wildman makes perfect sense to me, whether you agree or not. Oh yeah, I almost forgot to mention the tie in here to this discussion. I am pre-destined to Prophecy from God, and then extend awareness to the public through this two-part book. The accounts are the forth part, and the book itself being what I've described as a four-part destiny, the third and fourth part completing.

Some people wondering what is it like; do you sense God directly involved in your life? Realize first of all, it extends to people in general occupational pursuits and endeavors, as well. Scientists, teachers, athletes, government and business leaders, it can happen to anybody, and sometimes lesser events. Maybe that swimmer who saved someone else from drowning was pre-destined to be there that day, at that time, and place. Maybe the person saved his or herself for something later in life, and that would then not be possible if they had drowned. Sure, a lot of life is random, but that's God's will also, that we chart our own course right or wrong, have decision making discretionary power.

Every case is different circumstances wise, but when it is higher up in priority to God, especially spiritual matters, then you are most definitely likely to have God reveal involvement, but in my case, in multiple ways, and somehow, receiving full comprehension from God as to ground God wanted me to cover in my books. You'll notice usage of the word God, Jesus, holy angels, holy Bible, and Christian faith a lot, and if that isn't a solid give-away as to who my Senior Editor is, then I don't know what else to tell you.

Sort of like the Harbor Master coming onboard a large ocean going vessel to safely navigate it through narrow channel, treacherous current, and unseen obstacle hazards. For safe passage. In this case, it is safe passage of correct message to be sent. Not everyone can experience this firsthand, but that is what a Christian witness does, they are a witness to God, and especially now, the importance of Christian faith to others, as they navigate their own vessel (lives) through a narrow channel of treacherous currents, hazards, and dangers spiritually. That the message, hold fast to faith at the helm of your own life, and keep it steady on your life's faith rudder of direction, always toward Christian faith, and believing you have God that Master Harbor Pilot as your guide, as well. As a Prophet, God desires that I witness, as well as inform others about Tribulation.

The pre-destined person is a pivotal person, as they can be the cause behind the effect, influencing other people, and events, in a cascading fashion. I've never authored a book before, just like old George Washington never founded a nation before, with the other constitutional founding father delegates. They believed in God as their guide, and the rest, excuse the pun, is history. It all started with God. They took care of things for God in this dimension, and God did things behind the scenes for them invisibly in other dimensional ways. Like a musical, two-part harmony, it all came together according to God's plan. George Washington in parallel fashion thought to be his, but clearly understanding God most definitely had a hand in it and with full blessing approval. Albeit it invisible, God's signature is there on both the Declaration of Independence and the Constitution. You can take that literally or figuratively, however you choose.

You have to remember that you sense God's involvement, you sense his presence, often little more. My case was different, I received a whole lot more, but I'm the exception rather than the rule, and this did enter holy awareness sacred ground prophecy territory likely why. But the witnessing for Christ is also why, end purpose wise, and upon Tribulation awareness (covered in Part II).

I've turned the supernatural realm inside out for you like it was a reversible coat. By the time readers finish Part II, I think they will then have better concept of this Cosmic Model. Your K.J. Bible is really the secret of all you really need. If you take Christian fundamentalist philosophy and apply it to your own life, then this over all Cosmic Model will come into focus as proper perspective automatically, as the only part you need concern yourself with. Leave all that other Cosmic stuff for God to handle. Self-fulfill your own destiny as humbly serving God's purpose whatever you find it to be, and follow Jesus' word and the New Testament for guidance. It worked for our founding fathers, it works for me, and it will work for you, but full commitment is required for best results. Jesus is one heck of a great Spiritual Harbor Pilot. Once he comes on board and takes the helm of your vessel (or cosmic model), you will never be the same. Trust in Jesus. Hit the foghorn, too, will you!

By so believing in Christ, are we then empowered by faith (John 1:11–12). Take a look at what the Apostle John (Gospel Book of John) offers as eight proofs of the Deity/Holiness of Jesus Christ:

1.	Turning water to wine before witnesses	John 2: 2–11
2.	Healing the Nobleman's son	4:46–54
3.	Healing the important man	5: 1–15
4.	Feeding the five thousand	6: 1–14
5.	Healing the blind man	9: 1–41
6.	Walking on water	6: 15–21
7.	Raising Lazarus	11: 1–44
8.	Providing the catch of fish	21: 6–11

Certainly the Bible offers many more proofs, and likely there easily could have been other instances never recorded.

Further evidence is contained in the direct quotations of Jesus himself in references known as the great *I am* quotations:

1.	I am the Bread of Life	6: 35
2.	I am the Light of the World	8:12, and 9:5
3.	I am the Door	10: 7
4.	I am the Good Shepard	10:11–14
5.	I am the Resurrection and the Life	11: 25

6. I am the Way, the Truth, and the Life	14: 6
7. I am the True Vine	15: 1

So, in total here you have fifteen confirmations corresponding in exact harmony context with all other Bible scripture mentions. Both in the sense of Old Testament prophecy mentions predicting a coming Messiah, centuries beforehand, yet describing what to look for so as to identify one to be birthed in Bethlehem and raised in Nazareth. New Testament confirming the life and crucifixion/resurrection from corresponding witness matching testimony.

Then for your added belief confirmation prophecy testimony, one who believes he has received accurate forth telling awareness to the timing of the coming Tribulation, even and including time placement of highest probability for Christ's Second Advent, Second Coming return, within that seven year period (year, likely month, and possibly even the week this will occur). Although I cannot and won't claim this a certainty, I would describe the probability of correct prediction within the high end range of being correct. Remember, I maintain a one hundred percent prophecy prediction success rating, as verified in the Truth Verification section.

Chapter 27 (Part II) is a look into the future at Tribulation including this second advent coming of Christ as the seventh and mighty angel described in Book of Revelation, confirmed in total accuracy correctness, as well! Supplement Section will provide additional details necessary to your understanding.

Wildman's Legacy

It is my sincere hope persons hearing the Prophet Wildman pen-name will equate it as a pre-destined Christian Prophet, foretelling in prophecy the second Coming of Christ, in exact manner Holy Bible describes, as well as all of Tribulation further details; one who then strongly advocates Christian Faith to all.

That others will be inspired by my Christian witness to both bring lost souls to faith in Christ, but as well stimulate strengthened and expanded faith, and my books act as catalyst in accomplishing such. In addition, encouraging all nations and peoples of the world to stand in solidarity with Israel, on the basis of God's will being done on Earth as it is in heaven, that all peoples and nations do so.

Although there are other connotations equally correct, Christian Prophet of the Apocalypse is clearly attached to the destiny aspect. This in addition to being synonymous with second Coming of Christ Proclaimer, and advocator of faith in Jesus as the spiritual true salvation of souls redeemer. Believe!

You want to be greeted by Christ in afterlife arrival saying, Well done, good and faithful servant, well done. You will only accomplish that by in fact being that good and faithful servant in this life. If this is not your goal, then how will you succeed in accomplishing that? What you succeed in accomplishing over your entire lifetime, then becoming your eternal legacy with God.

As a Christian Prophet, I encourage all people to leave such eternal legacy with God, and strive with whole hearted commitment to do so. Jesus' teachings will be your will to follow. Follow Jesus. Leave a legacy for eternity you can be proud of; make Jesus proud, as well, as his battles are your battles. Take up his cross in service in his honor; and in so doing, honor yourself in the afterlife.

See file folders for:
Truth Verification/ Lie Detection Exams and related Info

Supplement Section
Two Riders Knowing God: Poetic Justice to Divine Destiny in Matrix Convergence

Yes, I know. You are thinking, Wildman, whatever in the world are you talking about? In Part I of New Realities I had to cover a lot of supernatural territory, Entities, E.T./U.F.O., Para-Psychic and Prophecy, and Metaphysical section discussions. But try to provide understanding of the overlying controlling countenance domain of Almighty God, who is in fact, is the Judeo-Christian concept of Jehovah, Jesus, and the Holy Spirit as with absolute total certainty correct model. Part II to delve exclusively into Religion in support of this. Part I describes some of the gears in motion characteristics that would be helpful in further understanding paranormal aspects of Part II.

However, before I conclude Part I, if you re-call I mentioned in Chapter 6 in discussing death, that were it not for Divine Destiny and Divine Intervention in protection of it, I would have died in 1968. Only four years earlier I'd been messaged by a holy angel to one day write a book, but if I'd died that prophecy would have been blocked from fulfillment by my death, and the third and fourth parts of stacked cones within, then kept from completion fulfillment. Instead, divine intervention taking place, the death obstruction removed, and so this book you are now reading in Christian witness to a loving God could be a testimony shared with you. Now I believe the fourth and final destiny component is relating event/timing match-ups for the entire Book of Revelation. That Second Destiny came five hundred years ago. It was Nostradamus coming into awareness that a Prophet in this future timeframe would receive holy source confirmations of greater detail on the Tribulation. He predicting another twenty-first century prophet to be a bonafide giver of Apocalypse awareness. Apocalypse means unveiling, and he foretold one would come to do so. I do in fact believe I am that Nostradamus mentioned Apocalypse Prophet.

In Chapter 6, I also mentioned two Christian witness heavy awareness guns, informational delivery battleships. Not firing off explosive destructive ordinance, but metaphorically, cratering people's minds with information, testimony, and evidences in validation measures supportive of the holy Bible, and Christian Faith. Figuratively speaking, both part I and Part II being these two sister ships, but Part II definitely doing heavier pounding, throwing heavier caliber ammunition ordinance so to speak. Those God given Prophecy shells really packing a wallop of a punch. In this sense, God does own a munitions works factory! You learned about his metaphorical heavenly warfare shipyards in Chapter 6, and build-up heading closer to Tribulation and Armageddon. shouldn't surprise you Reverend! Clergy have known about World War III, Tribulation strife, and final Armageddon battle for almost two thousand years. Either Book of Revelation is one hundred percent accurate and genuine as written, or not at all. It is all or nothing. I'm here to confirm to you as a Christian Prophet agent for God, that it is in fact confirmed to me to be one hundred percent genuinely accurate.

I've decided to Test Fire so to speak, one of those huge forward deck (forward deck figurative for the future if you caught that) heavy artillery big caliber guns for you, just to give example of what Part II holds in store. What is more, I'm going to load those forward guns with poetry! Now you are saying, wait a minute you promised to wallop my brain with heavy Christian witness, and you intend to do this with poetry? You've got to be kidding Right? You are joking? Right? No, this is a battleship in God's fleet, munitions from God's munitions in caliber fit for these heavy witness guns, and yes, these are poetry shells about to be fired! I'm still promising a wallop revelation reveal of awareness of great holy significance, poetry shell casing or not.

Now in Part I we discussed destiny and fate a little, we discussed God's Para-psychic mechanism for both general and holy subject forth telling, and foretelling, through telepathy, visions awake, vision/dreams in sleep, premonitions, and even alphabetically scripted out of thin air words. I also discussed personal and macro web matrix intersection points, other dimensions, and how a Prophet of God is a clay vessel just a humble servant of God, as all true Christians see themselves. Wildman is an extension of God, for God, to serve Jesus. Now the Bible says no one is to know the hour or the day of our Savior's return, that is true. But it also says God does nothing without informing his Prophets first. Although my awareness are limited in number on holy subject, all from 2008 timeframe, they were delivered exactly twenty years prior to timing described in this poem, and 2008 being that third destiny in fulfillment, and fulfillment of a 1988 premonition to see something that is mentioned nowhere else except in Book of Revelation. 1988 to 2008, again twenty years. Matrix timing intersection points, intersecting me the Prophet, intersecting Bible mention, intersecting a 1964 sermon, and in intersection of future timeframe fulfillment being described to a holy angel trained Prophet of fifty years training in parapsychic symbolisms! What I'm leading up to, is that while I cannot tell you the day or hour, (holy angels seldom give day or hour anyway) I can tell you the year and month, and a clue to the possible week, (but not definite on week) for Jesus Christ's second Coming arrival. The poem plays to the destiny and Matrix intersection points exposed thusly fitting for Part I. I didn't think it was right to withhold this from the world along with other Part II timings of the seven-year Tribulation, because it is supremely important to people's faith worldwide.

Nearly one billion plus four hundred million Arabic and other Muslims who believe as they are instructed falsely through Islam, that Jesus was, but one of many prophets of Allah, and is not Son of God, and is not going to make a return as a Mighty angel at the seventh Trumpet, as in Book of Revelation description. What I'm saying here is not meant exclusively for Muslims, but worldwide, all humans not now of Christian faith. My own faith demands I speak truthfully and accurately, not on this holy subject alone, but on any holy subject, and it is to be taken as a direct mandate from God, without exception circumstance. God demands this be strictly observed, and I take this with utmost seriousness throughout both books I've written.

What I am delivering through this poem is what I personally believe from my awareness to be: 1 Confirmations indisputable of his Book of Revelations return exactly as described there, for those of any level of doubt. What I believe to be correct timing for his second Coming return to Israel, giving year, and month, and likely the week, but less definite there, as in fact only God knows the day and hour, and it is not to be revealed.

Islamics should consider Jesus is God, Son of Jehovah, second aspect in Holy Trinity, and not think about pride or tradition, but just convert to become Christians, which is God's mandate to all. To believe in Jesus and worship him, putting no other God before Jehovah God. Salvation of one's soul is achieved only through such faith (as a Christian Prophet I confirm God's word the Bible that makes this abundantly clear on this point) and better to lose pride, not very Godly anyway, and forget old traditions if incorrect, and follow correct spiritual path instead. The Christian faith being the only correct spiritual path, in the only correct Savior, Jesus Christ. Certainly one with a lifetime of transactions and Para-psychic episodes with holy angels in receipt of holy Prophecy is a worthy spiritual advisor in the true nature of God. The Christian K.J. version holy Bible is correct word of God explaining his true nature and anything I tell you is supplement to it, never replacement for it.

While many Christians might not get heavily rocked by this poem except in a good way, Muslims are likely to find the shockwaves damaged their local Mosque in figurative analogy terms, adding cracks inside and out not previously there before. With certainty Jesus as Son of God, return to Israel, confirmed by a modern day Christian Prophet pre-destined to Prophecy for Jehovah God who views Allah as false, confirming these things through Prophecy exposing Allah is false? The confirmation on timing further cracking the Mosque philosophy Islam doctrine wall. Part II of Prophet Wildman's book that other Christian witness heavy gun theology battleship opening fire, taking aim, could finish off that Mosque completely with irrefutable truths delivered directly from God's own Prophecy munitions works. One known as Saints Covenant Prophecy threatens to destroy all non-Christian religions thoroughly and completely! In shatters, tatters, and splatters, leaving behind only what matters. Faith in Jesus.

It's hard to refute Wildman's heavy lifting of psychic munitions on board his Christian witness battleships. Your reading of Part I confirming it left port and is already out to sea to confront any and all non-Christian ideology in direct engagement in service to God's purposes. It is the commission all Christians have, to bring lost souls into full recognition faith while there is still time before Tribulation arrival. Witness rounds being unique in that they can be fired again and again with unlimited re-supply. Part II will further explain all of Tribulation event/timing match-ups. Realize this is genuine acts of God involvement; don't waste your time trying to be a skeptic or maybe a cynic, because I'll only prove you wrong. God wants recruits and to bring awareness to those willing to listen, to then put this new perspective, New Reality to work in serving his goals, his greater purpose. You should make serving him your goal, Take awareness I have brought to you, and in like manner use this information to win souls to faith in Christ. By serving the Son, you are serving the creator, Jehovah, following Jesus' instructions while alive.

The Bible instructs me, as a Prophet to witness for Jesus (hence the two books, two battleships), but that is to inspire and inform other to pick up their torches and be evangelist soul winners leading the lost of this world to Christ. Only little more than a decade left. Do you wish to doubt Wildman who has never been wrong in future prediction in his life? No, I hope not, and don't doubt my poem, either. It won't win any compositional correctness awards, but you can't beat its contents. It might be a crude bulldozer/informational bombshell nuke, but getting the attention of several billion people, I'd say this poem left quite a crater! A Wildman test firing sample, for your attention also.

Two Riders Knowing God

And so, there is a lady named Destiny, an invisible sign
This so as not to be seen with the naked eye,
And so, she rides a horse so aptly named Divine.
Not on land, but through heaven's sky.
And, should you recognize her handwriting on your life's wall
Then perhaps you'll ride a horse beside her,
On the horse of Prophecy sitting tall
From the point of prediction these riders ride,
Certain that arrival will upon being reached, mesh into time, becoming blur.
And with Celestial forces moving to direct this tide,
And all foretold that Destiny's handwriting now has so driven,
Shall unfold once this ride finally ends, prediction occurred
Blessed event, good fortune of knowledge awareness, future wisdoms now having been given
Most certainly a sign from God, attached to the message it sends.
Who better than this humble Poet/Prophet to make this call.
So recently enjoyed her company riding right alongside
Holy angel alerting me, detecting her writing on my wall,
Then upon reaching fulfillment, confirmations so wide.
Firsthand account given, and with certainty so near,
Profoundly understanding, that only through God, would such be here.

The Prophet Wildman, 2010

Two Riders with God (Part II)
Prophecy of the Second Coming of Christ

But no, not just any God, but one formed in aspect of Trinity
For only devout Christian can account so you see,
The importance of faith, loyal to Christ's Divinity
For only with faith, would such be revealed to me.
His second Coming much closer than many might think.
Arriving to ease Israel's suffering, pain, and tormented strife.
In this future timeframe to deliver new hope, re-establish his holy link on the 80th Anniversary, To breathe into Israel,
His Spirit, and new life!
No, not with certainty this timing can I say,
Yet here, destiny in faith combination, is an indication quite strong,
A Gentile Prophet, and a Hebrew nation, both born same year, same month, and same day, then Eighty years later the
Prophet foretelling, and with odds against such occurrences quite long, that Christ's return a match exactly that way.
So written in a book, holy angel's advance foretelling said would occur, Once fulfilling, Destiny's handwriting clearly
seen exhibited, but now into the future, and still in play.
So also importance of faith in Christ's future redemption as it were. From God, in Trinity, Through his love and
grace, exactly this way,
Has destiny's future secret fulfillment been revealed to you, Today!
Praise Jesus' name most holy and Sacred forever. Amen.

The Prophet Wildman, 2010

    Now that you've read the poem, you better understand the predestined part from birth destiny to prophecy Christ's second Coming return (fourth destiny aspect). No mistaking it in my mind, and originating from awareness received in 1964 in church. The ordained Minister's sermon on two occasions, containing Tribulation timings, that second sermon containing this May 18, 2028 return of Christ pronouncement from the pulpit, and all of his pronouncements confirmed to me as of 2008 (twenty years advance confirmation) that this is correct timing. My birthday is on May 18, and the date many in Israel use as birth of Israel date in 1948, plus eighty equals 2028, and based on other holy angel confirmation, confirmed in scripture, 2027 would be too early; 2029 too late.

    It literally cannot be any other year than 2028, and Pentecost the correct general timeframe. However while the third week is high probability in May that year, unlike the Minister, without knowing more, I cannot say more than Pentecost timeframe of 2028 as Christ's return timing, with year at or near 100 percent certainty. May/Pentecost somewhere in

90 percent range likelihood, although I'm personally convinced it will in fact be on or very close to the May 18 date. Holy angel perhaps cuing in Dr. Lancy before he gave his sermon pronouncement? Or maybe Jesus told him, as I promise you they were well acquainted good friends!

Intersections of my birthday, birth of Israel, Christ's return and Dr. Lancy's sermon pronouncement all intersecting. Trifecta perfecta plus sermon makes common convergence point arrived at from four directions, sort of like a Christian cross, sort of like my four holy angel orbs of white light at night in perpetual rotation around an invisible cross in the center. Meeting in the center each time then bursting out of the ends, back in the next end to meet in the middle. The middle here with angels revealing their presence involvement being four arms of that cross with a May, 2028 return of Christ center point. Mt. of Olives Israel and the 4 Web Matrix intersections emphasizing this event importance. A perfectly balanced brain implosion for my readers as the revelation paradigm's incredulousness reverberates their brain after its impact. How you like my poetry now? Christians loving it, others in face through the New Realities windshield when this awareness came to abrupt stop, their brains absorbing a little too much future reality too quickly. I can actually state God pre-destined me to hit those Reality brakes hard the purpose of God exactly. A wake up call!

The backside of that fate/destiny coin is that fate wise, we are running out of Time (another decade) until the Tribulation period arrives. That second battleship, Part II explains much more.

Will Wildman's shot fired be the poem resonating around the world? Christians hopefully will marvel, but as well appreciate its significance, and take it as reliable. A Christian future awareness psychic, never wrong in his lifetime, making this prediction assisted by holy angels, Bible scripture, and the 1964 sermon of an Ordained Dr. of Div. Minister. holy angel's presence in both 1964 and in 2008. If you do not believe me, then explain the No Deception Indicated Passed Polygraph which also included witness to the 1988 holy angel delivered premonition, that I'd one day see the Book Revelation mentioned scorpion stinger tail; U.F.O. generated Particle Beam, fulfilling also in 2008. An awful lot of holy angel interaction verified that the polygraph says is all true, including U.F.O. Particle beam in my front yard, private VIP Prophets only showing. First believe me, that as a Prophet, acts of God occurrences are the norm, any time, any place, and 24/7. The least I can do for a loving God who has repeatedly saved my life, on top of the times I saved it myself. My word is always going to be good on holy subject, because we are not allowed to waiver from exact truthfulness. I hold myself accountable for this second Coming prediction, and stand behind it fully, as one hundred percent accurate statement as described. It will happen, and it will happen in the manner stated.

Now for non-Christians, no matter who they are, the ramifications of larger picture importance is huge, no matter what country they are from, no matter what they now believe, or do not believe spiritually/religion wise. Christianity, and faith in Jesus Christ, is in fact the only way you can save your afterlife soul. Even Orthodox Jews will need to convert (as many already have) to full faith worship and belief in Christ. I devoted a whole Chapter in Part II in explanation to them why this is well advised to do so with Tribulation's approach.

Once the faithful among Christians rapture, and one quarter then of planet Earth's population perishes, remaining Christians will be in the Europe/Middle East World War III struggle not to be conquered by the Anti-Christ (Iranian radicalized Islam) armies. The mark of the Beast, once it is accepted will guarantee holy damnation from God in afterlife, very soon to then arrive. Christian faith and martyrdom if necessary in resistance being the only way to save ones soul. It is well advised that even moderate Muslims abandon Islam, accept Jesus. However, they must also leave the Middle East or be murdered by other radicalized Muslims who do not understand the spiritual realm. Jehovah/Jesus is the only true God, and Trinity form concept is correct concept.

Non-Christians need to realize the catch twenty-two involved here. They cannot just sit back and say, *Well, I'll wait to witness this for myself, then convert.* By that time, most will have already received a dragon, or 666 Mark of the Beast, Anti-Christ loyalist mark. By then it's too late and you've lost your soul essentially becoming a piece of soul coal, among millions of other people who just didn't reach the very awareness I'm now describing in time to prevent getting thrown into the Devil's furnace for eternity. There is a hell, inside the Earth's core, but in the Spirit dimension of the non-living. I'm solemnly serious on that, and the Christian Bible references it repeatedly.

People worldwide need to come to recognition in Christ, and practice their faith, by saving others from being thrown into the furnace as just another piece of afterlife soul-coal. (Better known as Evangelism or soul winning, and essentially cheating the Devil on his soul-coal delivery shipments!)

By waiting, non-Christians will miss the raptures, yes I believe in a total of three to occur, and I explain in Part II when I expect them to happen, as well. So, if you aren't a believing Christian, you then forfeit/disqualify yourself from rapture participation. Do that and you make yourself eligible for death, either sooner or just a few years later; but death definitely not the preferable alternative.

The time for non-Christians to become Christians is as soon as you possibly can to become more knowledgeable in your faith, expanding and improving your relationship with God to better and higher level of faith. Faith takes time to develop, and all too much of the world in no faith, weak faith, or wrong faith. It won't cut it with God. Jehovah God is the creator, but Jesus really is our Savior intercessor with God the Father Jehovah. People need to worship and pray to Jesus as their one and only personal Lord/God.

It is important for everyone to realize the Book of Revelation will fully play out precisely as it describes these event occurrences in a future timeframe. From holy angel/and or God derived source information, Part II of my book event/time matches all events, but with varying degree of certainty with each, because of varying informational solidness certainties to base it on, sometimes quite complex or involving multiple indicators. It is likely, in spite of margin for error, the most exact and accurately comprehensive explanation of Tribulation ever offered to date. You can only accomplish what I did with help from God, and the fact I did, is pretty strong evidence supporting it and yet additional proof of Christian faith necessity/validity.

Not all Christians interpret second Coming precisely the same, so to be more specific, even prior to Millennial Reign, and Armageddon participation/attendance, the poem is referencing the seventh angel/seventh Trumpet visual appearance to be witnessed in Israel as spectacle in the sky above Jerusalem, exactly in the description your Bible provides. So: My official prediction Pentecost (May) in 2028. I'm also saying without direct holy provided awareness, which is as close as I can personally state. However, Dr. Lancy, a Doctorate of Divinities Methodist Minister made identical prediction in 1964 sermon, but taking all the way to pronouncement of week and even day. May 18 is Israel's birthday and mine. True, many use the May 14th day I'm fully aware, but physical control took place on the 18th (to better explain the poem). A lot more discussion on this in Part II, but I'd be figuring the 18th if I were you rather than believe Dr. Lancy wrong. Pentecost 2028, regardless!

Other Celestial Signs from God

A Solar Eclipse in 2015, and Four "Blood Moons" of Lunar Eclipse happening in both 2014 and 2015 on traditional Jewish Holy periods have led many in the theological community to hypothesize theory of possible meaning. I should add, almost all agree, it has Tribulation context as well, which means confirmation will not be obtained until fulfillment during Tribulation, which I also agree with.

As of January 2014, I have copyright pending on my version, and the full explanation presented in Part II of this book. Clearly, God never sends out message only to return void, meaning at least one person will arrive at correct interpretation. However, in prophecy there is often a secondary as well as third tertiary level interpretation. I believe such is the case here, but unfortunately many only provide a single primary message interpretation, but then disqualifying it because if God has message additional on those other shelf levels going unnoticed, then that represents message returning void, hence disqualified interpretation on technical grounds regardless of primary interpretation.

Although here, I'm only giving you a quick synopsis of my primary message interpretation, I have copyrighted my version of all three levels to message being sent, very much so, Tribulation related. Nostradamus 500 years ago predicted W.W. III battles on both land and sea, and Islamic forces moving westward in aggresion, invasion conquest effort of all the countries bordering the northern Mediterranean.Eclipse symbol of over taking, and the blood red moon symbolizing bloodshed. Put the two together and you have 5 nations coming under invasion exactly as Nostradamus predicted, however, the prediction requires knowledge of something that only a Prophet like Wildman would know about. It's what I call a fulfillment Protocol in timing. What is it? I noticed with some of what message conveyance was being received actually applied to a set 20 year into the future timeframe. Like a big yardstick measurement extention into the future. If you received awareness as of late July 2004, (as in one case I actually did) it meant the current month in the present plus the twenty years the time period it applied to. I had a few of these. Then somewhere in the aproximate 2012 timeframe with Tribulation moving closer, possibly 2013, there was a shift to a ten year protocol instead of the previous 20 year one. Only in certain types of conveyance is it required to know and apply. I mention it here because if you take the actual date of lunar or solar eclipse in 2014/2015, then add the ten year fulfillment protocol interpretational measure, it lines up exactly with Nostradamus prediction. Turkey the first country he mentions then falls as of March timeframe 2024, just a few months ahead of Tribulation cataclysmic destructions arrival, with the country's moderate Islam government overtaken by Islamic radicals. By october/November Greece then is attacked and conquered. Italy aligns with the Solar eclipse then also attacked and conquered, and symbolically the darkness blocking out the Sun is symbolic of the Italian legitimate government being overtaken, in turn the Vatican, in aftermath of the pre-Trib. rapture, the catholic church is corrupted, exactly as the Bible states in "revival of the Roman Empire", as well as the church corrupted and the Anti-Christ sharing the same capitol; Rome. It all happens on a very tight schedule. The last two Blood Moons being Spain and France are attacked and heavily damaged, but not conquered, as the enemy is eventually repulsed. All of this is 500 year old Nostradamus prediction, that using the formula explained to you previously, represents confirmation from God as to actual timing for these occurances. You'd have to be a Wildman Prophet with indwelling Holy Spirit to know assuredly this is God's confirmational message, and it is such a tight fit to the time space allotted that you practically need a shoehorn, but yet I believe for that very reason is legitimate translation interpretationally of this Tribulation aspect picture.

Now many point to the turn of fortune in other similar Blood Moons Lunar and Solar eclipse situations (3 others in the past 600 years) for the Jewish people, undergoing temporary adversity, but as if God then is messaging; "Hold on, things are about to turn favorable!", and sure enough reversal of fortunes toward positive outcome then occurred. It's temporary testing, and reminder, God is in control. The Jewish aspect here in relativity connects heavily to the secondary and third level message in interpretation, I'm not going to cover here, but rather in Part II.

Seeing how upon Tribulation's arrival how radical Islam immediately upon seeing worldwide cataclysms will go on the offensive, then compare to current Middle East radical Islam upheavals and Jihadist terrorism. Europe becoming then the focus of attack. How on target then is recent call to action in the U.K. by British Prime Minister David Cameron who is calling for stiffer laws dealing with home grown terrorist using their British passports fighting literally for the Devil, certainly not for God. Prime Minister Cameron deserves alot of credit and support from both the British citizenry, and Parliament, and eventually the United States will have to legislate special powers at home to combat Islamic terrorists.

God's Tribulation Blueprint

The majority of people's perception viewpoint perspective is that God simply looked into the future, foresaw what lay ahead for 21st Century world humanity relative to the spiritual realm, then described the future random events to unfoid as they merged toward a Millennial period follow ing the described 7-year one, then described what he saw to John at Patmos Is that really what happened?

In "New Realities" -Part II, in no uncertain terms providing new proofs and evidences, I will present a case that God actually had a blueprint in place plan thousands of years ago, even ahead of description of events to John at Patmos. How so? Because the placement of events are not random either collectively or individually. All timings are pre-design, thus in each event case it represents fulfillment in timing terms no differently than individual Holy prophecy does. Not only that, but Christ Jesus, the likely Architect Son of God likely had God's sign-off approval for these plans, which once understood in awareness bring further glory to both the Allmighty, and his Savior Son to be able to not only design such a truly amazing design in complexity, yet structured like architecture often does toward purpose and function. Individual occurances doubling as component of the larger collective template with aspects of timing playing a very key role not only on the individual level but the macro design structure all inclusively allowing the end purpose, master design function to be a success, but all on highly specific terms. Nothing left to chance, no randomness, all happening with the precision of a swiss watch! Exactly what human blueprints do, that is, provide exact measurement of the final end product design structure purposed toward construction accomplishment.

Wildman being a Prophet, but as well with an indwelling Holy Spirit helper, you could use as analogy of myself as retired building contractor with strong architectural blueprint familiarity having the Holy Spirit hand me a working drawings set of God's Tribulation blueprints. Already extensive pre-destiny happenings going on here in Part I, (this book having been fortold 44 years prior of it's writing during 1964 church services, not to mention many other examples) The God given awareness that confirm Tribulation timeline, then foundational certainty in confirming existance of an actual highly intelligent thought out design structure for all Tribulation timeframe occurances. It's very complex even to explain everything that I observe, but definately solumnly seriously a Holy blueprint presencing itself with assist from the Holy Spirit additionally to cue my attention in certain direction observationally for complete scan in take-away awareness reception. God blowing my mind and yours once again.

The only psychic event more recent was a psychic dream on the eve of the U.S. Embassy attack in Libya on 9/11 aniversary 2012. I wasn't even aware at the time of calendar date, or that the very next day was 9/11/01 anniversary. Unfortunately my conscious mind in sleep state, alerted to my sub-conscious mind formulating a dream, and the dream had not yet been fully constructed or completed apparently in readying it for the viewing conveyance for my conscious mind in sleep state. I recall seeing an actual doorway between my conscious state mind (asleep) and this back room representing the unconscious/subconscious dream assembly area. It had something to do with duality, and I could see the twin towers. The duality I realized the next day upon hearing of the Benghazi embassy attack, was the duality side of what this dream message was likely trying to convey. You notice in Revelation 18:2 the use of the word fallen twice, Babylon is fallen, fallen. O.K. what I'm believing here is that since Islam will be the Anti-Christ's Confederacy of nations in future timeframe, and Islam believes in an eye for an eye, justice, God is confirming in my dream, these attacks God sees as an affront to Christianity that he will personally avenge against radical Muslims, using their own eye for an eye justice. God's vengengeance duality and double!

As Part II will explain in detail, we have now passed the point of it being more than 10 years until the opening of the Tribulation scroll with 7 seals, and 7 onlooking Angel with 7 trumpets, to less than 10 years into the future fulfillment of Book of Revelation starting point!

Conclusion, Part I
Preview, Part II

Congratulations on the completion of Part I, and making it through with your sanity not too banged up! But wait, there is more.

Another book, Part II edition. Still an A.T.V. ride through the supernatural with Wildman as your guide once again, but this time in deeper exploration of the religious regions on the Tribulation Trail (sold separately; approximately 385 pages).

Not a single human on the planet can afford to miss out on information it contains. Again, totally genuine non-fiction, with more off the charts incredible content. Literally, survival essential reading, both in the physical and spiritual sense. Part II in total confirmation of the Christian faith's validity, something no self-respecting theologian will dare want to miss. (or you!)

With Prophet Wildman receiving key forth telling holy angel delivered confirmations and awareness, finally with God's assistance, someone has broken the timing code for Tribulation, decoding event/timing match-ups with close proximity accuracy! Give all glory and credit to God in thankful praise. Hallelujah!

This is no joke, this is serious sacred holy territory, and I assure all this the real article holy forth telling awareness received. Once you read Part II, especially after the shock and awe that pummeled you from Part I, you'll understand that Wildman is simply a humble vessel that God is using as an agent to carry out his purpose. I didn't seek or ask for this, it was simply as a psychic medium, delivered unto me. One of several of holy subject received. (relating the Coming Tribulation)

Part II is most definitely must read, even including some commentary on post Tribulation Millennial Reign (Are you spiritually righteous enough to participate?).

Needless to say, Part II promotes Christian faith and Holy Trinity Bible concept of God. actually taking it a step further in proof fashion with multiple evidences, and quite difficult to refute (Holy prophecy no less, among them!). You better believe it!

Prophet Wildman has a long list of Christian ministries that will be receiving financial support benefit from author's share of return. Protestant, Catholic, and even Jewish Rabbi who believe in and worship Jesus Christ will be receiving donation; selected charities, as well. When God works with a mortal empowering him in service to God's purpose, this book becomes an instrument then of accomplishing such. The returns belong to God therefore, and from my share I will keep very little.

There are several main purposes and goals of New Realities I and II. Here is an outline (Focus on Part II):

1. To show further proof evidences, and personal witness testimony to further verify God's existence, but also proving Christian Holy Trinity to be correct concept of God. Confirmations between God and holy angels, in direct interaction with a psychic medium Prophet in current timeframe similar to Biblical interactions.
2. Provide deeper explanation awareness of the Coming seven-year Tribulation for individuals, corporations and governments, as well as theologians, and raise money from this book to support many Christian churches, ministries, and charities.
3. To mitigate loss of human life and soul worldwide, but bring to (especially current non-Christians) the recognition that through evidences provided, that other religions are false and misleading, having been shown invalid and thus incorrect.

4. To evidence my honesty and life-long psychic experiences as a medium that my readers will receive my prophecy account testimony as factual, genuine, and truthful (I can only help others if they take me at my word and my word seriously.).
5. To elaborate and give interpretational appraisal of aspects of less certainty, but valuable input commentary of connective event and Tribulation circumstances.
6. To elaborate important event timings, such as Rapture, second Coming of Christ, Tribulation destructions, Armageddon, Millennial Reign and more. Then in regard to these, give analogous correct focus perspective, and the larger spiritual picture, that everyone can then calibrate themselves to this overall picture before it arrives that they not be spiritually lost and confused when it arrives.
7. Afterlife understandings/Millennial Reign – One-thousand-year reign of Jesus Christ. When it will start, and self-evaluation in advance understandings of being a Saved Christian.

Christians are already pretty well prepared for the twenty-first century not containing a full deck of ten decades relative to this existence order. My book not only confirms Tribulation's close proximity approach, but tries to present a calming attitude, optimistic, not pessimistic, that people might adapt personal attitudes conducive to best personal outcome. The humor mixed side by side with totally serious or sacred subject, so some readers don't get shocked into comatose catatonic state of speechlessness. It can seem like I'm being disrespectful of holy Sacred subject, but I assure all, just the opposite is true, and I want to encourage my readers to take these spiritual mentions equally seriously. I'm also quite humble before God, though I know I can sound otherwise.

By faith, may you receive God's blessing and salvation.

Because of anticipated possible further delays in bringing Part II to print, I want to leave readers here in Part I with a general summary of my Tribulation (Book of Revelation) timing/event outline, reflective of all conclusions drawn comprising my own personal beliefs in this regard Part II will delve deeper in much broader discussion examination, offering greater specifics, but this timeline will remain unchanged.

Remember those points I made earlier here in Chapter 13 of American citizens likely <u>not</u> being informed/forwarned by their Government prior to Tribulation's on-set arrival. They simple don't make future forcasts the way the weather man predicts weather, and their concern is, should they get it wrong for any reason, they then dissolve their credibility, as well as seing this as a separation of church and state matter, even with more than 200 Million lives at risk of death, of the more than 300 Million in total citizenry affected. Some are asking; you mean the Government still has credibility to dissolve? Yes, at least to some in varying degree, but reliance on Government forwarning is an effort in futility, my point. In the cases of those institutionalized churches, much the same is true. A mispronouncement would destroy their credibility they fear, so they will give only vague general forwarning that is essentially usefulness limited. They are placing their self preservation ahead of the public's safety, as lives and souls are endangered on specific peril terms, not generalities. What good is the survival of an institution if all the citizenry followers are dead or rapture departed? The majority will perish, the minority will rapture, the sad likely truth of the matter, but those at risk of death can at least potentially save their lives if they have clearer understanding, perhaps rapturing later upon survival and increased faith.

A Loving God <u>has</u> been giving forwarnings through prophecy, and the cataclysmic wrath of God destructions aimed toward the non-believer, and such forwarnings will only be accepted by the believer anyway, (As the Apostle states in I Corinthians 14:22-23) Your best survival bet is to accept Prophet Wildman at his word, relative to my statements of multiple Tribulation event/timing confirmations. Strive by Christian faith to be among those raptured, but higher elevation (above 2,800 ft above sea level re-inforced concrete underground bunker/shelter, with 4 years food/water supply is an excellant PLAN B) pro-active survival preperation move just in case relative to that summer of 2024 prescribed danger time zone that Prophet Wildman warns of. Realize though, there is no substitution for Christian faith, and that bunker needing a Bible as well for spiritual survival. I'll risk my reputation to save even one life, aside from those of that 200 Million plus lives total Americans at risk. (Foreigners too!)

TRIBULATION - OUTLINE SUMMARY - BIBLE BOOK OF REVELATION
EVENT-TIMING Match-ups

Mid Oct. 2022	A conflict between Israel and it's Arabic neighbors breaks out into open warfare that is not resolved until a treaty/truce seven months later.
May (Pentecost) 2023	Aformentioned peace treaty signing. The Anti-Christ (present and directly involved is identif- for the first time) This directly corresponds to opening of the Tribulation scroll. Invisibly in the spiritual dimension.
Mid July 2024	The Rapture of the Christian church/body of Christ, First Rapture event occurs, likely early AM occurance. Rapture by God's Grace to devout believers in the Holy NKJ Bible, Jesus as Lord as their remission of sins obtained by the blood of Christ as Savior/Messiah of all humanity in faith.
Final week July 2024	Full array of Tribulation cataclysmic destructions occurs lasting seven weeks, including Comet Wormwood scorch, Tsunami coastal flooding innundations, massive wildfires, earthquakes, volcano eruptions, economic collapse, buildings collapse, and outbreak of W.W. III in the Mediterranean area.
2025	Dense bands of black smoke darken skies worldwide lasting into 2026 (4th trumpet)
June 6, 2026	The 666 martyr in Rome, Italy, Italy already is conquered by the Anti-Christ now governing.
as early as 2026	The 5th Trumpet, UFO in locust (too many to be counted numbers out of the ocean abyss "Bottomless Pit" inner Earth.)
Nov. 2026	The treaty with Israel is broken, Israel is subdued, and this represents MID-TRIB point.
Dec. 2026	The Anti-Christ moves his capitol to Jerusalem Israel, Italy about to be liberated the reason.
Jan. 2027	The Anti-Christ "Abomination of Desolations" event.
2027	The 5-months of stings by UFO particle Beam in tazer stings of unrighteous humans at night. Two possible periods, but overlapping in the summer. (June through Sept. likely with either scenario.)
late 2027	The Great Euphraites Battle begins lasting into early 2028, in the Iraq. region (200 million combatants present. Weapons of mass destruction used, from Bible described indication of results.
May (Pentecost) 2028	Christ's "Mighty Angel, 7th trumpet event with spectacle in the sky above the Mt. of Olives. The dead in Christ are raised, then those left and alive (Christian) are raptured. Second Rapture is expected between May 14th-18th.
July to Sept 2028	The Sackcloth Martyr event (also likely 14-18th). Although the Timeline follows the 1964 Minister's sermon almost exclusively, because he was less than certain on this particular timing point, I conducted an intense research study to see if there was any indication of a more likely time point for this occurrence. There was, and at least 10% more likely for correctness, although neither timing scenario can be stated as either right or wrong absolute.
July 2028-July 2029	"Time of Jacob's Trouble" peak martyr period of Orthodox Jews in Israel directed by the Anti-Christ.
Oct. 2029	The 144,000 (likely children) and the 1/3rd of Israel, Third Rapture. of those who fled to Jordan. These are late Orthodox/Messianic converts who are raptured during "Feast of Tabernacles" timeframe.
Nov. 2029	The Bowl or Vial Judgements outpourings begin (6 months/6 bowl judgements plus Armageddon the 7th)
May (Pentecost) 2030	Armageddon battle, Christ's 2nd Coming, "King of Kings appearance" with all his saints.
July/Aug. 2030	The Anti-Christ/False Prophet cast alive into the "Lake of Fire" Satin is bound for 1,000 years.
July/Aug. 2031	An invisible "Alpha/Omega" timeseam seperating the "End of the Church Age" from unofficial transition into Millennial Reign period. Late July, Aug. 1st maybe, unconfirmable, but there.
May (Pentecost) 2033	2,000 years after the Book of Acts, Upper Room, Christ's 1,000 year Millennial Reign officially begins. (Fulfillment of Daniel 8:14, and 12:12)

This timeline I personally hold to be accurate and true because it is nearly an identical match for an Ordained Minister's 1964 sermon, descriptively, where I was instructed telepathically from Holy source to pay close attention and remember the sermon's Tribulation account. Then the publishing of this book was also prophesy message received. Further added timing/event confirmations received as of 2008, also correspond identically with the 1964 sermon's Tribulation timeline account.

Fulfillment of this book's publication exactly when predicted, confirms it was Holy source derived information. That in turn affirms the genuineness of the timeline as being of Holy source also, since the timeline is inclusive here, within the book. The power, Holiness, and glory of Jesus Christ further evidenced, both now and forever, that I further witness to all. God has given you an awareness gift of increased Tribulation awareness understanding, and truly a 21st Century; "New Reality" Jesus' "Crown of Holiness" line in the sand is actually now a confirmed Tribulation timeline delivered through prophecy fulfillment most genuine, and carrying through in the spiritual dimension as truth for all eternity.

Bibliography by Chapter

Chapter 2: Ghosts, Jinn, and Angels
Ghosts
1. *The Supernatural*, by Hans Holzer, Chapter 8 (pages 119 - 132) *Near Death Experiences-Proof of a Hereafter* (summarization; not direct quote)
1.B *The Supernatural*, by Hans Holzer, Chapter 7 (pages 112 - 113) *What It's Like on the Other Side* (summarization; not direct quote)
2.3. *Florida Ghostly Legends & Haunted Folklore*, by Greg Jenkins, Vol. I, II, and III (general summary and accuracy verification of other sources)
4. *Ghosts & Specters of the Old South*, by Nancy Roberts (pages 81 -87); *The Hound of Goshin Hill*, general reference
5. CBS T.V. *Evening News* report, May 5, 2008
6. *Interdimensional Universe*, by Philip Imbrogno, Chapter 7, "The Jinn" (pages 195- 198); general reference and comparison
7. *The Atlantis Blueprint: Unlocking Mysteries of a Lost Civilization*, by Colin Wilson and Rand Flemeth (pages 190, 198, 209); general summary
8. General summary (page 209); *Fire, Brimstone, and Flood*, and several other reference sources; comparative on fallen angel/ Jinn subject mentions angels
9. *Angels Among Us*, by Ron Rhodes (pages 10, 78, 84); general summary and reference in total, also direct quote, the number of angels
12. *Interdimensional Universe*, by Philip Imbrogno - Chapter 7, "Angels" (no direct quote) and *Armageddon Now- The End, A to Z* (pages 24 -26); general, *The Atlantis Blueprint*, by Colin Wilson and Rand Flemeth, and other general references, multiple sources

Chapter 3   Monsters
1. *Unexplained*, by Jerome Clark (pages 433, 436); summarized
2. *World of Strange Phenomena*, by Charles Berlitz (page 65), summarized

Chapter 4   Extraterrestrials
1. *U.F.O.*, by William Dudley Timmonsdorf (page 45)
2. *Cosmic Explorers*, by Courtney Brown, PhD (page 99); direct quote
Both of these books were very useful general reference information sources, but including also:
    Encyclopedia of U.F.O, by Ron Story (1980)
    Interdimensional Universe, by Philip Imbrogno (2008)
    Mysteries of the Unknown, by Mystic Places-Time/Life Books (1987)
    Mystery Chronicles: U.F.O. Files, by Joe Nickell (2004)
        Tales from the Time Loop, by David Icke (2003)
        U.F.O.'s in the 1980s, by Jerome Clark (1990)
        Scientific Enigmas, by Robert B. Downs (1987)
        U.F.O. Abductions & The Threat, by Ed. M. Jacobs (2000) and (1998)
        Survivors of Atlantis, by Frank Joseph (2004)
        Silent Invasion, by Ellen Crystall
        U.F.O. Headquarters, by Susan Wright (1998)

Imagining Atlantis, by Richard Ellis (1998)
Confirmation: the Hard Evidence of Aliens Among Us, by Whitley Strieber (1998)
The God's Machine: Stonehenge to Crop Circles, by W.C. Bong (2008)
World of Strange Phenomena, by Charles Berlitz (1988)
The Truth About Alien Abductions, by Peter Hough (1997) *Unexplained*, by Jerome Clark (1999)
The Power of the Earth, by Peter Brooksenth (1984)
Encyclopedia of Alien Encounters, by Alan Baker (2000)

I skim read many more books and balanced them against my own personal experiences and sightings observations first hand, in reference to various aspects on this subject.

Chapter 5
Humans Possessed and Vampires

1. *Vampires: Fact or Fiction*, by Angela Cybulski (2003) listing of primary cases over centuries; direct quote
   Madame Blavatsky accounts -summarization, including other sources.
2. *The Supernatural*, by Hans Holzer, Chapter 11 (pages 165-167); direct quote
3. *23 Minutes in Hell*, by Bill Weise (2006); general reference and numerous other references, including the Bible

Chapter 6   Other Phenomena
1. *Unexplained*, by Jerome Clark (pages 123 - 127), summary reference; pages 89, 90), summary reference; (pages 131- 137), summary reference
   Interdimensional Universe, by Philip Imbrogno, Chapter 8 (page 234);summary reference
2. *Unexplained*, by Jerome Clark (page 93 – 96), summary reference, (pages 99 -106), summary reference
   World of Strange Phenomena, by Charles Berlitz (page 271); summary reference
3. *Unexplained*, by Jerome Clark (pages 131 - 137); summary reference
4. No single source, crystal skulls, general reference

Chapter 7   U.F.O. Theories
Encyclopedia of U.F.O. provided outline of current main theory. Using this for review basis reference, my own comments and opinion, original remarks are then analytical review of these themes. Any basic material not my own mention in this process, is of this source, but direct quote sentencing is not made.

Chapter 8   The 2004 U.F.O. Sighting - Original

Chapter 9   The 2008 U.F.O. Premonition - Original

Chapter 10   The 2008 U.F.O. Premonition Fulfilled
The 1988 U.F.O. Particle Beam/U.F.O. Premonition Fulfilled
1. *Silent Invasion*, by Ellen Crystall, Chapter 3 (page34); direct quote
   History Channel - *U.F.O. in History*, mention of South France pre-historic cave depiction of a U.F.O.; resembling distinguishable characteristic of the first of my 6, 2008, U.F.O. sightings- showing same style U.F.O. possibly in existence then.
   All other is original

Chapter 11   Busting the Star Pretenders and Sighting Log; original

Chapter 12   U.F.O. Craft and Characteristics
1. *World of Strange Phenomena*, by Charles Berlitz (pages 248, 249); summary reference
2. *Visitors from Time: The Secret of U.F.O.'s*, by Marc Davenport; summary reference
3. *U.F.O. Encyclopedia*, by Ron Story (pages 281 and 299)
4. *Cosmic Explorers*, by Courtney Brown, PhD (page 129); Reptilian Headquarters, and Galactic Federation" mention general reference
5. *Interdimensional Universe*, by Philip Imbrogno, Chapter 4 (page 104)

Chapter 13 Gov't. U.F.O. Cover-Up & Intelligence Agency inaccessibility
1. U.F.O. in the 1980s, Vol. I -Jerome Clark (1990) pages 85 -107
2. U.F.O.'s (1964) William Dudley
3. The Threat & U.F.O. Abductions (1998) David M. Jacobs, PhD.
4. *Interdimensional Universe* -Philip Imbrogno, Chapter 7, page 194
5. *The Truth About Alien Abductions*, by Peter Hough and Moyshe Calman (page 71)
6. *Interdimensional Universe*, by Philip Imbrogno, Chapter 3, (pages 103, 104)
7. *Return of Planet- X*, by Jayson Q. Rand (page 198); firsthand experiences on these topics, and several more books as general reference

Chapter 14 Who are the Major Psychics?
1. *King James Bible*, Book of Isaiah
2. In describing profile of the Major psychics, a composite derived from several general reference sources was utilized, no direct quote. (at least 6 different ones) including: *Paranormal Sourcebook, Supernatural,* and *Return of Planet-X*
3. *Paranormal Sourcebook* (and other) verify Nostradamus and Malachi with last Pope to be named Peter prediction
4. *Return of Planet -X* and other sources used to verify religious affiliations of the listing of psychics
5. Kirlian aura interpretations, several sources
6. Dream categorizations, several general reference sources

Chapter 15 Thoughts on my personal psychic experiences; all original

Chapter 16 Hallucinations and Altered States of Mind
1. A synopsis of information included in a History Channel program (T.V.) on the *History of Hallucinogenic Drugs*
2. *World of Strange Phenomena*, by Charles Berlitz
3. *Interdimensional Universe*, by Philip Imbrogno; several gate/portal references:
    Chapter 3 Mary
    Chapter 7 Sandra (page 200)
    Chapter 5 Windows (pages 123–125)
    Plus original discussion of personal account

Chapter 17 Leys, Dark Leys, and Psychic Leys
1. *Survivors of Atlantis*, by Frank Joseph, Chapter 11 (pages 149 -153) (all support material to Lyrean connect claim and Atlantis ties)
2. *Mystic Places* (page 50); leys
3. *Interdimensional Universe* -Philip Imbrogno, Chapter. 5
4. *Multitude of Dimensions, Rocking Stones* (page 127), same source
5. *Mystic Places*, pages 51, 106, 107
6. *Angels Among Us*, by Ron Rhodes, Chapter 15 (pages 201, 202)
7. *Interdimensional Universe*, by Philip Imbrogno, Chapter 5 (page 143)
8. *Florida Ghosts, Legends, and Haunted Folklore*, Vol. I (Southland Central Florida) Greg Jenkins, "Flight 401, Case 4," (pages 32–42)

Chapter 18 *The Role of Psychology In The Parapsychic Experience*
Sixth Sense & U.F.O. Reality (British), by Jenny Randle (1987 and 1983)
All original accounts

Chapter 19 *Psychic Aspect: The 1988 U.F.O. Premonition Re-Discussed*; all original accounts

Chapter 20 Cosmic/Metaphysical Section -Time Warps
1. *Above Top Secret*, by Jim Marrs (page 153) Einstein quote, other time descriptions; general reference sources
2. *World of Strange Phenomena*, by Charles Berlitz (pages 202, 203); "Marchers From the Ancient Past"
3. *World of Strange Phenomena*, by Charles Berlitz

    The Battle Heard Ten Years Later (pages 189–190); general summarizations, the preceding two
4. *Hans Holzer's Supernatural Waylaid in Another Time*
   Chapter 12, Time and Space, pages 188–193
5. Same pages 180–188
6. Same page 193
7. *Prophets, Psychics, and Seers* (page 202), Psychic Potpourri
8. *Paranormal Sourcebook*, by Sellier (This pilot also authored a book giving firsthand account.)
9. *Angels Among Us*, by Ron Rhodes (Page 21), "Emergency Guidance," encounter summarization for comparative
10. *Interdimensional Universe*, by Philip Imbrogno; general comparative description (not page noted), but as reference referral

Chapter 21 Astrology/Astronomy
    1. *The Supernatural*, by Hans Holzer (page 15)
    2. *King James Bible, Book of Revelation* quotes
   All others are original calculations and interpretations describing the Mayan calendar and celestial occurrences, as well as U.F.O./Bible locusts and E.T. invasion accounts.

Chapter 22 Cosmic Model (All original)

Chapter 23 (Religion Section) Who was Dr. Lancy, and related personal experiences shared
    General reference: *King James Bible and Bible Commentary*
   (other all original)

Chapter 24 Saints Covenant Prophecy
   General reference: *King James Bible and Bible Commentary*
   (other all original)

Chapter 25 *The 1988 Premonition*, Bible and U.F.O. T.V. shows, other topics
    1. *World of Strange Phenomena*, by Charles Berlitz (page 37), "We interrupt this Program for a Special Premonition"
   General reference: *King James Bible and Bible Commentary*
   other all original or, as noted, general reference

Chapter 26 Pre-Tribulation, Rapture and Gnosticism, discussed general reference: *King James Bible and Bible Commentary*
    1. *Magic, Mystery & Science* (pages 290, 307)
    2. *U.F.O.s*, by William Dudley (page 94)
    3. Book of Revelation quote
    4. *Psychic Potpourri: Prophets, Psychics, and Seers, The last Pope Named Peter, Nostradamus and Malachi Predicting the Same*
   (Other all original)

Chapter 27 Tribulation/Armageddon
   General reference: *King James Bible and Bible Commentary*
   Many Bible direct quotes
    1. *Return of Planet-X,* by Jayson Q. Rand
    2. *Cosmic Explorers,* by Courtney Brown, PhD
    3. *Countdown to Apocalypse,* by Paul Halpern
    4. Nostradamus quotes: *Nostradamus-Roberts (The complete Prophecies of)*
    5. *Armageddon A-Z,* as general reference, no quotes
   (Other all original)

Supplement Section
   -All original, except general reference; Earthquake and volcano data:
   Earthquake Generation, by Jeff Goodman (1979)

General Bibliography

Baker, Alan. *Encyclopedia of Alien Encounter.* New York, NY: Checkmark Books, 2000.

Beloff, John. *Parapsychology: A Concise History.* New York, NY: St. Martin's Press, 1993.

Berlitz, Charles. *World of Strange Phenomena.* New York, NY: Stongesong Press, 1988.

Bong, Wun Chok. *The God's Machines.* Berkley, CA: North Atlantic Books, 2008.

Brooksenth, Peter. *The Power of the Earth.* Garnerville, NY: Orbis Publishing, 1984.

Brown, Courtney, PhD. *Cosmic Explorers.* New York, NY: Penguin Group, 1999.

Burton, Dan and David Grandy. *Magic, Mystery and Science.* Bloomington, IN: Indiana University Press, 2004.

Clark, Howard. *Cambridge Annotated Study Bible.* New York, NY: Cambridge University Press, 1993.

Clark, Jerome. *U.F.O.s of the 1980s.* Detroit, MI: Apogee Books, 1990.

Clark, Jerome. *Unexplained.* Farmington Hills, MI: Visible Ink Press, 1999.

Crystall, Ellen. *Silent Invasion.* New York, NY: Paragon House, 2000.

Cybulski, Angela. *Vampires: Fact or Fiction.* Greenhaven Press, 2003.

Downs, Robert B. *Scientific Enigmas.* Littleton, CO: Libraries Unlimited, 1987.

Dunwich, Gerina. *A Wiccan's Guide to Prophecy and Divination.* Seacacus, NJ: Citadel Press, 1977.

Ellis, Richard. *Imagining Atlantis.* New York, NY: Alfred A. Knopf Publishers, 1998.

Ghezzi, Bert. *Mystics and Miracles.* Chicago, IL: Loyola Press, 2002.

Goodman, Jeffrey. *Psyhic Archeology: Time Machine to the Past.* New York, NY: Berkley Publishing Group, 1977.

Goodman, Jeffery, PhD. *We are the Earthquake Generation.* New York, NY: Berkley Publishing, 1979.

Halpern, Paul, PhD. *Countdown to Apocalypse.* New York, NY: Plenum Trade, 1998.

Holzer, Hans. *The Supernatural: Explaining the Unexplained.* Franklin Lakes, NJ: New Page Books, 2003.

Hough, Peter and Moyshe Kalman. *Truth About Alienc Abductions.* New York, NY: Sterling Publishing Co. Inc.

Icke, David. *Tales From the Time Loop*. Isle of Wright, U.K.: David Icke Books, 2003.

Imbrogno, Philio. *Interdimensional Universe*. Woodbury, MN: Llewellyn Publications, 2008.

Jacob, David M. *U.F.O. & Abductions: Challenging the Borders of Knowledge*. Lawrence, KS: University Press of Kansas, 2000.

Jenkins, Greg. *Florida's Ghostly Legends and Haunted Folklore*. Sarasota, FL: Pineapple Press, 2005.

Joseph, Frank. *Survivors of Atlantis: Their Impact on World Culture*. Rochester, VT: Bear & Co. Publishing, 2004.

Joseph, Frank. *UnEarthing Ancient America: The Lost Sagas*. Franklin Lakes, NJ: New Page Books, 2009.

King James Bible, any edition

King James Bible Commentary. Nashville, TN: Thomas Nelson Publishing, 2005.

Marrs, Jim. *Above Top Secret*. New York, NY: The Disinformation Company Limited, 2008.

Marrs, Jim. *Alien Agenda*. New York, NY: Harpers Collins Publishing Inc., 1997.

Mysteries of the Unkown: Mystic Places. Richmond, VA: Time-Life Books, 1987.

Nickell, Joe. *Mystery Chronicles: More Real Life X-Files*. Lexington, KY: University Press of Kentucky, 2000.

Pudley, William. *U.F.O.s*. San Diego, CA: Greenhaven Press, 1999.

Rand, Jayson Q., PhD. *Return of Planet X*. Horn Lake, MS: Future World Publishing International LLC, 2007.

Rhodes, Ron. *Angels Among Us*. Eugene, OR: Harvest House Publishers, 1994.

Roberts, Nancy. *Ghosts and Spectors of the Old South*. Orangeburg, SC: Sandlapper Publishing, 1974.

Roget's Thesaurus of the Bible. San Francisco, CA: Harper Publishing, 1992.

Sellier, Charles E. and Joe Meier. *Paranormal Sourcebook*. Los Angeles, CA: Lowell House Publishing, 1999.

Story, Ron. *Encyclopedia of U.F.O.s*. Garden City, NY: Doubleday Publishing, 1980.

Weise, Bill. *23 Minutes in Hell*. Lake Mary, FL: Charism House, 2006.

Willis, Jim and Barbara Willis. *Armageddon Now: The End of the World A to Z*. Canton, MI: Visible Ink Press, 2006.

Wilson, Colin and Rand Flemeth. *Unlocking the Mysteries of a Long Lost Civilization*. New York, NY: Delacorte Press, 2000.

Wright, Susan. *U.F.O. Headquarters*. New York, NY: St. Martin's Press, 1998.

And so what God is telling me, he is saying to everyone else, as well. What he is saying essentially to you is, *Go forth, take this that's has been given, and use it to save lives, and save souls.*

Passing the message on, now it's your turn. Don't forget about your own, because if you forget about or neglect others who are greatly at risk, by disregarding these others, you just did!

Good-bye for now. Hope you enjoyed Part I..Hope to rejoin you in Part II.
Prophet Wildman, 2012

Lie Detection Section

Putting together a listing for you of what was verified in extended detail read too much like inventory at the bulk shock and awe warehouse. Reading in full transparency the questions themselves, answered a clear cut YES or NO, gives you the reader what you need to see.

Clearly, no one could pass 108 test questions, often with perfect and near perfect score of pass grade, given by two different professional Truth Verification Test givers, using two separate types of equipment, and testing methods covering a nine hundred-page, two-part book, of highly detailed questions, plus control questions, and totally passing everything! Virtually covering all aspects of the supernatural realm at the same time, all inclusive.

It ends here for the skeptics, now swallowing the bitter pill of full acceptance, or risk getting their mind blown to Smithereens when they read these. This is the part where New Realities, Part I, flexes its Non-fiction factual muscle. An all dimensional enduro mental off road/on road course for challenging one's sanity, as Old Realities sort of melt like surreal concepts in the Twilight Zone borderlands!

This book, New Realities Part I, a sort of advanced shock-o-holic reader training course for what is to come in Part II. Here it was the para-psychic, U.F.O. paranormal, and supernatural Subject Seminar. Part II is all about God, religion, and spirituality, Christian faith, and the seven-year Tribulation in High Def. detailed.

Just how far up the Richter Scale either of these books take your mind personally is in your control, as is how many mega-tons of shock wave they slam your brain with. The humor I provided in both books to help as a sort of cushion bounce back, so as not to drive my readers all catatonic/comatose, at least not all of them, or even most of them. I'm not intentionally trying to beat my reader's brains into plowshares, in other words. Many of strong conviction to Christian faith will have very little problem coping, but that is sort of the point I make. The relevance and importance of having and sustaining strong Christian faith as correct faith. These are multiple acts of God from that living God theologian always speak about, described by a living, modern day Prophet of and for that Judeo-Christian in Trinity God. That third side of the triangle, Holy Spirit within me right now as I write this, y'all!

This book is not to 'beat up' on your mind, it is to bring people to recognition of Jesus Christ/Christian faith as true and correct faith, if you are not already there. (Prophet alter-call of sorts)

After your 'old realities' get sold for scrap at the scrapyard in other dimensional Twilight Zone, back side of Pluto fashion, if that need be the case, then you are ready to accept everything described that I tell you as fact not fiction, because you know I have my Contributing Editor looking over my shoulder, looking on, so to speak. (except humor with exemption) It is only when people understand both these books have such heavy direct God involvements, that automatically explains all of the massive amount of incredibles and extraordinaires, and unbelieveables, do those unbelieveables become believables like water into wine. Where ever in your mind there is an explanation blank, you just fill in the word God, and it makes explaining, and dealing with it simple and easy. Cuts down on coping with all the mega-tons of shock and awe, too. You just chalk it up to being an 'acts of God' episode, and you make it a whole lot easier on yourself.

So, you are much better off instead of resisting with skepticism as is almost instinctual, to instead, decide before hand, 'Wildman is telling me the truth,' I'm going to approach this in just the opposite manner, and accept everything as factual unless and until I see reason not to. In other words, seeing this many episodes of incredible supernatural, Para-Psychic, and paranormal coupled with the ones in Part II, (two books required to explain them all), and with holy angel multiple reveals included, not to mention holy subject messaging, and it pretty well evidences God being directly involved, which he most definitely was. No question in my mind, but all of this is to get it to become no question in your mind, because it always comes back to what was God's purpose. There-in is his purpose. To get you to believe me, so, as a medium, I can pass information to the world that will be accepted and believed. Passing it to me does no good unless I succeed in that last part, run after catch, touchdown for God. (his un-defeated record, I'm trying to insure stays that way)

Part II confirming Christ's second Coming, as well as all timing/event codes being broken for Tribulation in major decoding fashion. So many others through history have tried and failed at this. Prophet Wildman was successful only because God himself pre-destined me to succeed, which I explain in Part II, also, more scoops of main course acts of God on your mental appetite handling plate there, with plenty of shock and awe sides. Part I in essence prepares you for gaining full acceptance of Wildman as a Christian Prophet to be believed, with acts of God episodes expected, it gives you the foundation necessary for God through me, to deliver future Tribulation awareness to you! Hope that makes sense to you, Wildman just a sort of 'special agent' for God, pre-destined to do so.

Lie Detection Variations (as stated)

National Institute for Truth Verifications
International Verifications NIT.V. -1
Capt. John Slater (U.S. Army) Retired, Test Taker
11400 Fortune Circle
(Wellington) West Palm Beach, Fl. 33414

Test Type: Military Program (same)
                   Computer Algorithm/ Voice Inflection
This Testing,   Total 77 Questions
                   Test 1 51 Questions, combined tests
                   Test 2 13 Questions
                   Test 3 13 Questions
Test Results: <u>NO DECEPTION INDICATED</u>, All Questions

Scope:
   * Verification of psychic ability and event occurrences
   * Detail Verify of 2004 U.F.O. sighting (witnessed by three)
   * 2008 Dream sleep Premonition, predicting sighting of 6 U.F.O.
   * 2008 Premonition Fulfillment with 6 U.F.O. sighted
   * Description of individual U.F.O. sightings
   * U.F.O. Tractor beam episode described

Connors Polygraph & Investigative Services   Fl. Agency License A26–00293
Denny Connors, Test Taker
Retired, Orange County Fla., Major Case Detective
Orange County Sheriff's Department
7200 Lake Ellenor Drive, Suite 116
Orlando, Fla. 32809

Test Type: Standard Professional Polygraph
This Testing,   Total 31 Questions (plus control question)
                   Test 4 10 Questions
                   Test 5 11 Questions
                   Test 6 10 Questions
Test Results: <u>NO DECEPTION INDICATED</u>, All Questions

Scope:
   * Confirmed psychic ability and one hundred percent prediction success rate
   * Two additional 'Definite' U.F.O. sightings -(new total, nine)
   * Sighting of the Bible Book of Revelation Particle Beam, as predicted from a 1988 T.V. show induced Premonition

- * Voice of God in prayer question/answer, angel appearance, and receipt of prophecy from holy source of holy subject
- * Description of psychic Intunitions (four)
- * Waking Dream sighting of (four) Ladies, (angels?)
- * 2/07/09 sighting of (four) orbs of white light rotating (angels?)
- * 1964 Dr. Lancy sermon, clairaudience episode (angel)
- * Two additional psychic dreams, year of Armageddon confirmed
- * Other claims verified also

(Total 108 Questions Verified; no Deception Indicated)

Test 1 ALL QUESTIONS ANSWERED WITH YES ANSWER UNLESS OTHERWISE NOTED – NO

1. In December 2004, at approximately 4:10 A.M., driving the roadway adjacent to the inter-costal waterway that is situated between West Palm Beach and the section of Palm Beach Island immediately South of the Southern Boulevard (State Road 80), you report seeing a U.F.O. at that time and place.
2. Property owners along this stretch are multi-millionaires and billionaires and this stretch has been called by some locals as Billionaire's Row The fact that this sighting occurred in this location was a strong contributing factor in the decision not to come forward at that time.
3. At that time, you stated a female passenger sitting next to you, to your right approximately thirty-nine or forty and a younger male friend of her approximately late twenties to early forties, sitting in the passenger seat of this vehicle which you were driving, also witnessed this event (sighting of a U.F.O.).
4. The three of you witnessed this event for approximately twenty minutes of time.
5. Upon rapid departure of this craft, you turned to these two and asked both if they had seen all that and they answered affirmatively both said yes they had.
6. At the time of the sighting, you were completely sober, no alcohol, no medication, no illegal drugs, no substance intoxication of any kind.
7. You would qualify for jury duty and are or would be considered a person of credible witness.
8. So, it would be accurate to say that three individuals at that time and place witnessed a U.F.O.
9. You feel there are only two possible explanations for what you three sighted that night. Either a craft piloted by alien life form, or a covert Govt. Black Box project that is literally decades ahead of technology the general public is currently aware of.
10. You feel more likely it was an alien craft.
11. You stated because of the extreme darkness on that night, (or lack of Moonlight) that at no time was either a defining silhouette, or definite saucer shape visible.
12. .Would it be correct to say that it hovered for more than forty-five minutes in the same spot, at approximately A height of roughly between of 275 feet to 350 feet off the ground, very quietly no prop or rotor noise.
13. Could this have been a helicopter? No!
14. You also stated that you counted fourteen vertically rectangular windows in a horizontal side to side arrangement facing approximately South. Not unlike manmade aircraft windows, you also stated these appeared to have rounded corners.
15. Other than saucer shaped hovercraft, could it have been a triangle or trapezoid shape (other shapes possible, but far less likely)?
16. Would you say that saucer shape is your best estimate and that the diameter or width is approximately sixty feet wide to eighty feet wide.
17. Going back to the windows, you stated that the height was roughly twice the width. Would it be accurate to say that the width was approximately twenty-two to thirty inches and the height was approximately forty-four to sixty inches.
18. You were approximately five-eighths of a mile away, slightly to the southwest, at the point where you finally shut off both your engine and headlights in order to kill your taillights, you had earlier shut off your regular higher beam headlights.
19. Your reason for driving slightly further on was to possibly convince the craft it hadn't been spotted, but also to get a better angel/view of the windows.
20. You stated the craft appeared to be over land not water, but adjacent to, but above the seawall there.
21. Is it fair to say that, despite the dark conditions, that this and the distance impaired your vision relative to postulation/description and scale measurement only slightly?
22. Is it true that while you wear reading glasses you have always had and continue to have better than twenty-twenty distance vision (able to read below the twenty-twenty line on a vision chart)?

23. On the westerly side of this U.F.O. you noticed what appeared to be like a string of light portals of white light running back toward an upper center axis point and with a noticeable arc. Below what would be the outer rim of a saucer (if it was a saucer) and to a center axis point, but with less arc, more straight, a second string of portal lights were observed. You saw perhaps six to eight lights on the upper string. You saw perhaps four to six lights along the lower string.
24. These were small circular white lights that the upper string, an occasional on/off light was observed, as well as possible red or blue light seen only intermittently. No light was seen to flash on/off on/off at regular interval. Other than windows discussed previously, is this an accurate description of other lights observed.
25. On two separate occasions you observed what appeared to be shadows or human-like forms moving inside the craft behind the previously described windows. The distance made it too difficult to see detail, however, whether alien form, or human form, clearly the craft did appear to be occupied.
26. You believe now these were aliens.
27. At the time of most of, and final minutes of this observation by the three of you, were parked in the road, at a diagonal (for better viewing angel), and with your headlight and tail light off, and engine off, as well.
28. When you turned your headlights back on, this is what spooked the U.F.O.. and it took-off at an extremely fast rate of speed from total standstill. Possibly one thousand miles per hour and disappeared out over the ocean. The time elapsed you feel was less than a second or millesecond.
29. It would be accurate to say, that if anyone blinked, they would have missed this rapid departure moving from a total standstill.
30. During this departure, you saw for, or within that brief Mila-second, light streaks, or trails behind the craft, as well as taking note that the craft broke the night horizon out over the ocean at several miles distance at a northeast trajectory, rather than due east.
31. Noticing this northeast trajectory, since the craft appeared not to gain altitude, but rather simply move in sideways motion, you calculated (re-playing it over and over again in your mind) that this trajectory was approximately thirty to thirty-five degrees, toward the northeast.
32. That are of the Atlantic would be considered part of the Bermuda triangle, south of Bermuda.
33. Although probably just coincidence, isn't it true that the girl sitting to you right, also observing this craft had a mother who perished in waters off the Bahamas, some consider these waters to be part of the Triangle, as well. Her mother had been lost there over twenty-two years ago (at the time of the sighting).
34. You feel that at present, although not impossible, it is unlikely that either the United States or mankind yet possesses the technology of a hovercraft that can accelerate instantly from a standstill to the sort of speed you three witnessed.
35. You also feel that again, while not impossible it is unlikely that humans now have the capability to withstand the enormous G-force generated from that type of rapid acceleration to go from zero to perhaps one thousand miles per hour or more instantly.
36. Therefore, your conclusion, both then and now, that this was a U.F.O., likely, but not definitely a saucer shaped craft, and likely piloted by aliens.
37. Even though you absolutely had the sensation of the craft's departure at high speed, you lingered for several minutes more until you were convinced that the craft had not simply gone lights out, because it had vanished so rapidly. Only then did you leave the scene.
38. You have also stated that in terms of para-psychology particularly E.S.P. and premonitions of future events, you have had in your lifetime at least ten such occurrences. That is, for-knowing of specifics about a future event that later was proven true. These related to your own life and those around you, rather than world events.
39. Did you have any warning or for telling ahead of time that you would see a U.F.O.. that night? No!
40. You did have a premonition twelve years ahead of time that you would meet this girl, is that correct, that the premonition you would meet the girl occurred in 1981, you then were introduced to her in 1993.
41. This girl was in, or in some way tied to other premonitions, as well, but not all.
42. In regards to someone else with clairvoyant ability, from the description of this U.F.O. encounter that night, do you feel they might connect in order to shed some additional light on these aliens? Such as who they were, what their purpose and intentions were, or where they were from?
43. Re-ask question one a second time and use December 8 this time; let's see what happens!
44. You have substituted this statement for another one which you were going to make that included some highly charged and controversial information.
45. That is because, after formulating the statement, that same night with just a few hours into sleep, you awoke from a short dream at or around 2:30 A.M. you felt essentially a spirit, or spiritual source.
46. You feel that the interpretation of the dream or vision was that this information would be better if it remained unpublished, not become public knowledge at this time. The dream awoke you.

47. In the past, while you were conscious, you have had foretelling, at varying time frames into the future, regarding yourself, as well as others, of events of negative consequence, even death.
48. You say this vision or dream (since you were asleep) is similar in nature you think, to what Indians or native Americans have described, like a short story, rich in symbolism, yet reasonably east to interpret (omens).
49. So, phrasing it differently, in summary, you dropped a controversial statement from this format, because of a spirit induced recommendation to do so, given to you in a dream while asleep. You did so, because you took it seriously.
50. Do you feel certain that this was the message? Better not to publicize?

Nothing Follows

51. Control Question – You have been completely truthful, honest, and accurate will all questions asked. Answered Yes with no deception indicated. (Shown on evaluation page)

I certify that these statements were composed from the original statements that were provided by Prophet Wildman without alteration. The original documents provided by Prophet Wildman will be retained by this examiner for a period of three years and remain as part of the Prophet Wildman case file.

I further certify that the statements listed accurately depict the statements that were read to Prophet Wildman as part of his Voice Stress Examination.

Captain John P. Slater (Ret.)
Certified Voice Stress Examiner
International Verification Services

International Verification Services
March 19, 2008

Prophet Wildman
Author's actual address (confidential)

Re: Truth Verification Examination

Mr. Wildman, (real name here kept private for confidentiality purpose)

On this date, I provided services to you in regards to a sighting of an Unidentified Object that you believe to have been a U.F.O.. in the Palm Beach Island area of West Palm Beach, Florida, during the month of December 2004.

You provided me with a list of statements that you wanted to confirm your truthfulness on concerning the events by utilizing the Computer Voice Stress Analyzer. During the Examination, I referenced your statements by stating, regarding statement one (The statement was read), and then you were asked, Is that a true and accurate statement? You then provided me with a response. Attached is the final report and transcribed statements that you provided me with.

As you know, the CVSA is utilized throughout the United States by over 1,700 law enforcement agencies and is currently being utilized by Special Forces units in Iraq.

I am a retired Criminal Investigation Commander with eighteen years of experience. I have consulted with various Federal, State and Local Law Enforcement agencies from around the country. I am a certified Voice Stress Examiner, as well as a Voice Stress Instructor and have given instruction to numerous Law Enforcement Officers and Special Forces Personnel in the art of Voice Stress Examinations. Along with this I have provided consultation with numerous News organizations regarding High Profile cases.

The results of the examination are within the following pages and I hereby submit my findings to you.

Best regards,

Captain John P. Slater (Ret.)
International Verification Services

TO: Whom it may concern
SUBJECT: Prophet Wildman

Case: Other
Date: 19 March 2008

PREDICTION

This truth verification examination was predicated upon a request by Prophet Wildman.
(real name here kept private for confidentiality purpose)

SCOPE

The scope of this truth verification examination shall be limited to the subject's honesty as it relates to the events surrounding the statements made concerning the sighting of an unidentified object flying in or around the Palm Beach Island area of West Palm Beach in December of 2004.

Pretest Interview

During the pretest interview, Mr. Wildman related that while traveling in the area of Palm Beach Island in West Palm Beach, Florida in December 2004, he and two (2) passengers observed an object that appeared to be hovering above the ground in an area of the Island and then disappear at a very fast rate of speed out over the ocean in a easterly direction. Mr. Wildman provided this Examiner with a list of statements that he made to validate that his statements are truthful. Due to the amount of statements to validate, three separate exams were performed with breaks between exams. All statements are attached with this report.

Report

On March 19, 2008, this company extended an interview to Prophet Wildman.
I conducted the interview, and herby submit the results to you. The following relevant questions were interspersed with irrelevant and control questions:

1. Regarding statement 1, is this a true and accurate statement? The subject responded yes. No deception was indicated.
2. Regarding statement 2, is this a true and accurate statement? The subject responded yes. No deception was indicated.
3. Regarding statement 3, is this a true and accurate statement? The subject responded yes. No Deception was indicated.
4. Regarding statement 4, is this a true and accurate statement? The subject responded yes. No deception was indicated.
5. Regarding statement 5, is this a true and accurate statement? The subject responded yes. No deception was indicated.
6. Regarding statement 6, is this a true and accurate statement? The subject responded yes. No deception was indicated.
7. Regarding statement 7, is this a true and accurate statement? The subject responded yes. No deception was indicated.
8. Regarding statement 8, is this a true and accurate statement? The subject responded yes. No deception was indicated.
9. Regarding statement 9, is this a true and accurate statement? The subject responded yes. No deception was indicated.
10. Regarding statement 10, is this a true and accurate statement? The subject responded yes. No deception was indicated.
11. Regarding statement 11, is this a true and accurate statement? The subject responded yes. No deception was indicated.
12. Regarding statement 12, is this a true and accurate statement? The subject responded yes. No deception was indicated.

13. Regarding statement 13, is this a true and accurate statement? The subject responded no. No deception was indicated.
14. Regarding statement 14, is this a true and accurate statement? The subject responded yes. No deception was indicated.
15. Regarding statement 15, is this a true and accurate statement? The subject responded yes. No deception was indicated.
16. Regarding statement 16, is this a true and accurate statement? The subject responded yes. No deception was indicated.
17. Regarding statement 17, is this a true and accurate statement? The subject responded yes. No deception was indicated.
18. Regarding statement 18, is this a true and accurate statement? The subject responded yes. No deception was indicated.
19. Regarding statement 19, is this a true and accurate statement? The subject responded yes. No deception was indicated.
20. Regarding statement 20, is this a true and accurate statement? The subject responded yes. No deception was indicated.
21. Regarding statement 21, is this a true and accurate statement? The subject responded yes. No deception was indicated.
22. Regarding statement 22, is this a true and accurate statement? The subject responded yes. No deception was indicated.
23. Regarding statement 23, is this a true and accurate statement? The subject responded yes. No deception was indicated.
24. Regarding statement 24, is this a true and accurate statement? The subject responded yes. No deception was indicated.
25. Regarding statement 25, is this a true and accurate statement? The subject responded yes. No deception was indicated.
26. Regarding statement 26, is this a true and accurate statement? The subject responded yes. No deception was indicated.
27. Regarding statement 27, is this a true and accurate statement? The subject responded yes. No deception was indicated.
28. Regarding statement 28, is this a true and accurate statement? The subject responded yes. No deception was indicated.
29. Regarding statement 29, is this a true and accurate statement? The subject responded yes. No deception was indicated.
30. Regarding statement 30, is this a true and accurate statement? The subject responded yes. No deception was indicated.
31. Regarding statement 31, is this a true and accurate statement? The subject responded yes. No deception was indicated.
32. Regarding statement 32, is this a true and accurate statement? The subject responded yes. No deception was indicated.
33. Regarding statement 33, is this a true and accurate statement? The subject responded yes. No deception was indicated.
34. Regarding statement 34, is this a true and accurate statement? The subject responded yes. No deception was indicated.
35. Regarding statement 35, is this a true and accurate statement? The subject responded yes. No deception was indicated.
36. Regarding statement 36, is this a true and accurate statement? The subject responded yes. No deception was indicated.
37. Regarding statement 37, is this a true and accurate statement? The subject responded yes. No deception was indicated.
38. Regarding statement 38, is this a true and accurate statement? The subject responded yes. No deception was indicated.
39. Regarding statement 39, is this a true and accurate statement? The subject responded. No deception was indicated.
40. Regarding statement 40, is this a true and accurate statement? The subject responded yes. No deception was indicated.

41. Regarding statement 41, is this a true and accurate statement? The subject responded yes. No deception was indicated.
42. Regarding statement 42, is this a true and accurate statement? The subject responded yes. No deception was indicated.
43. Regarding statement 43, is this a true and accurate statement? The subject responded yes. No deception was indicated.
44. Regarding statement 44, is this a true and accurate statement? The subject responded yes. No deception was indicated.
45. Regarding statement 45, is this a true and accurate statement? The subject responded yes. No deception was indicated.
46. Regarding statement 46, is this a true and accurate statement? The subject responded yes. No deception was indicated.
47. Regarding statement 47, is this a true and accurate statement? The subject responded yes. No deception was indicated.
48. Regarding statement 48, is this a true and accurate statement? The subject responded yes. No deception was indicated.
49. Regarding statement 49, is this a true and accurate statement? The subject responded yes. No deception was indicated.
50. Regarding statement 50, is this a true and accurate statement? The subject responded yes. No deception was indicated.
51. Regarding statement 51, is this a true and accurate statement? The subject responded yes. No deception was indicated.

Post-Test Interview
No post test was conducted due to the results of the exam.
Conclusion

Based upon my training and experience, it is my opinion that the subject did respond truthfully to the relevant questions. The CVSA's internal algorithm was utilized to back the examiners call of the charts. The findings of the results were the same as those of this Examiner that the subject did respond truthfully to the questions posed regarding the statements that he made regarding the sighting of an unknown object in December 2004 along the Palm Beach Island area.

I am maintaining a copy of this report on file, as well as the original signed statements made by Mr. Wildman. (real name kept private)

John Slater
Director of Operations
International Verification Services

Test 2

1. While many of the observations described in this exam are admittedly pretty amazing, incredible, even hard to imagine, be that as it may, you state that other than difficulty in making accurate approximation of altitude and distance estimates at night that all other description is truthful and accurate to the best of your ability.

   Answer:
   <u>True</u> or False

---

2. In describing U.F.O. activity during the stated observation time period, would it be accurate to say that there were so many U.F.O. suspects, that you took to naming them, (different ones) in your notes to avoid confusion in describing their behavior.

   Answer:
   <u>Yes</u> or No

---

3. The six that you personally feel were definite U.F.O., were named Alpha, Romeo, Ranger, Jitterbug, and The Tractor Beam Pair. Each was visually different, in different directions, altitudes, geographic areas, and observed in some cases on different nights.
   Is this statement True?

   Answer:
   <u>Yes</u> or No

---

4. Would you say the following statement in Total is true:
   Many aircraft pilots flying at night are accustomed to making similar U.F.O. observations. They are reluctant to make any type of official report because sightings are so common, and they don't wish to jeopardize their license to fly. A gag order on the U.F.O. subject, mandated or otherwise has been going on for decades, and is observed by both the news media and Air-Traffic Controllers. When U.F.O. are present, pilots make a much lower runway approach at night, and come in low, rather than gradually descend.

   Answer:
   <u>YES</u> or No

---

5. When you first observed Alpha the first of the six sightings on 4/14/08, at around 12:15 A.M., it first appeared as a very stationary object, and thought it could be a star. However, you then noticed motion, like it had been trying to hold GPS position and fixed altitude, but upper atmosphere winds were giving it difficulty, movement that stars don't do.
   Is this statement an accurate and true Account?

   Answer:
   <u>Yes</u> or No

---

6. The geographic area you feel Alpha was above was the north end of Palm Beach Island, or at least toward the North end of the city of West Palm Beach, at around fifteen to twenty thousand feet altitude. You also feel you have seen Alpha many more times at varying altitudes, all within a radius of downtown West Palm. Is this an accurate assessment?
   Answer: <u>Yes</u> or No

---

7. Getting back to the night of 4/14/08, after the second time you observed Alphabet knocked off position perhaps by strong wind gusts in the upper atmosphere, you then saw the craft perhaps rev-up its propulsion system. In any event, you witnessed the craft fire-off what you describe as a double zigzag pattern of colored lights around what may have been the rim of the craft.
   Would this be an accurate description?

   Answer:
   <u>Yes</u> or No

8. Each colored light would stay on only for a second, but as one light went out on the upper part of the zigzag pattern, another would come on behind it on the lower part. The lights were circulating from right to left, which would mean clockwise on a disk. The succession of lights was moderately rapid, and as a light would come on another would go out. The sequence of lights only lasted for a minute plus, perhaps two minutes at most then stopped.

Would this be a True and accurate statement?

Answer:

<u>Yes</u> or No

---

9. After the lights stopped, the craft got knocked of coarse again, and again the colored light sequence for an equal period of about a minute and a half, then stop. You observed the craft as it got knocked off course, and saw the light sequence three separate times, only going off for about the same amount of time in between sequences. Then it stopped, and it stayed stationary!

Would this be a True and accurate statement?

Answer:

<u>Yes</u> or No

(Romeo Sighting)

10. After sighting Alfa, visibility wasn't favorable for sightings during the middle of the week due to cloud cover, but after midnight on Friday or early Saturday, April 19, 2008, you saw a craft to the West (just slightly to the North) low on the horizon, perhaps only a mile and a half to two miles distant. It was glowing red, gave off a pulse or red burst beneath the rim that caught your attention, and you got a close enough look at windows, as well as silhouette to state with reasonable certainty that it was a U.F.O. of the Low Hat classification, but certainly a U.F.O.

Is this a True and Accurate Statement?

Answer: <u>Yes</u> or No

---

11. With the 2004 sighting you could not see exact silhouette, but feel it was of the High Hat classification most likely. You did get clear view of windows of that craft. Would you say both in total number and size, the windows of that craft very closely (if not identically) matched what you saw with this craft?

Answer:

<u>Yes</u> or No

---

12. Although you were absolutely certain this was a U.F.O., you knew of radio towers in the area that have red lights, you knew someone trying to debunk this sighting would certainly try to raise the proposition that red light was reflected off a cloud or something. You yourself being certain the U.F.O. being the source of the light, however after establishing ground markers, you returned to a sight the following night at this identical spot. No red light, no U.F.O. present. Is this true and accurate?

Answer: <u>Yes</u> or No

You feel that your dream Vision or premonition a week to ten days before these sightings began, also alluded to the fact that there would be more than six U.F.O. present, but that you would only be able to confirm six with certainty as Definite.

Answer:

<u>Yes</u> or No

Test 3

1. During the third week of April 2008, and into the fourth week, you have increased your time spent observing the local night sky in order to spot possible U.F.O.. activity in the West Palm Beach area. You have observed suspect objects in the night sky.
    Would that be an accurate statement?
    Answer: <u>Yes</u> or No

---

2. Is it an accurate statement that at no time during, or just immediately before these observation periods, has there been any consumption of alcohol, medication, illegal drugs, or intoxicating substance of any kind taken, and this statement true for every observation period on different nights?
    Answer: <u>Yes</u> or No

---

3. During the observation period described, would it be an accurate statement to say, that in your mind, without any doubt what-so-ever, you definitely witnessed the sighting of a total of 6 U.F.O., (Aircraft of non-human origin), as well as many other sightings you cannot totally confirm, but feel were very likely U.F.O. craft.
    Answer: <u>Yes</u> or No

---

4. About a week to ten days prior to the observation period you had a pre-cognitive dream vision, but at the time did not fully understand all the ramifications or correct interpretation of what you saw. Is this a true and accurate description of this event?
    Answer: <u>Yes</u> or No

---

5. STATEMENT:
    In this dream image you were sitting in the middle of a large area surrounded by four alien beings, (non-human), with a few others in the background, in shadows, the lighting was very dim, you tried to get a better look at their faces, but larger than human pointed ears led you to determine these were not humans. you could not see their faces in the shadows, they appeared dark brown, just silhouettes as to size and shape.
    These aliens had shown you New Realities, and you saw yourself grimacing, and anguished from mental pressure and coping with the shock of what you had seen. Then you awoke, unsure of what this meant.
    Is this statement true and accurate?
    Answer: <u>Yes</u> or No

---

6. Would you say that the actual sightings that occurred over a period of several nights, and in all different directions did in fact closely correspond, or match relatively speaking the positions the aliens were standing in, around you in this Dream Vision, including the two in the background.
    Is this an accurate and True statement?
    Answer: <u>Yes</u> or No

---

7. Therefore, it would be accurate to state:
    That the Dream Vision you had prior, not only foretold the number of U.F.O. sightings you would have as definite confirmed, (6) but the direction each would be sighted in, and that in total, these sightings did generate shock and awe to you, and New Realities were in fact revealed.
    Is this a True and Accurate statement?
    Answer: <u>Yes</u> or No

---

8. Statement:
    The last two of these six sightings were seen together in what you refer to as the Tractor Beam Pair, or the Tractor Beam –Incident. This occurred early, (2 A.M.) on the morning of Tuesday, April 22, 2008. Observing West and slightly South, below mid-sky, approximately thirty-five to forty degrees up.

At first these appeared to be stars, but then you witnessed the upper star, (offset about twenty degrees not directly above) extend a beam down and attach to the lower tar. Then both moved sideways, (South) perhaps one eighth of a mile distance, horizontally. From a distance of approximately ten miles, the beam appeared no wider than a thin white sewing thread, yet clearly visible to the naked eye.

The movement stopped when the beam was retracted. You then witnessed the beam lowered a second time, attach, and again both craft moved sideways or horizontally, (further South) by a distance about equal to the first time. Again, movement stopped when the beam was retracted. This time they stayed in place, back to just pretending to be stars. In total is this accurate and true?

Answer: Yes or No

---

9. Would you say that the sighting of this Tractor Beam Pair correlated to the two aliens in the shadowy background of the Dream Vision?

Answer Yes or No

---

10. Statement:
There is a stretch of Military Trail, not far from where you live, that has a long history of Indian Ghosts. (rather than ghosts of European descent) Many strange events and anomalies have occurred here over the years going back to reports from the 1950s. It is believed the Indians buried their dead along what once was an Indian footpath, so that they might have good hunting in the afterlife.

This was told to you around 1980 by a local named Valerie who grew up here and went to High School here. State Road 809 Military Trail widened many times, has likely disturbed countless grave sites of very old origin. Is this information accurate and True?

Answer: Yes or No

---

11. Statement:
On the afternoon of Sunday, April 13 around 4 P.M., you were returning home from shopping when it began to rain, and had already passed through the area mentioned in the previous statement when it began to rain. You tried to turn on the windshield wipers, but they would simply not come on, your battery had adequate charge. You kept trying as it began to rain even harder. In ten years and over one hundred miles personally driven in this truck you have never once experienced this difficulty before; you made it home okay, but no wipers.

The next morning about to take the truck in for repairs, you decided to try them one last time. They worked!
Is this a True and Accurate Account?

Answer: Yes or No

---

12. Statement:
The fourth sighting of the six involved the craft you dubbed as Jitterbug observed almost directly overhead, earlier on the same night as The Tractor Pair were observed. This one seen as a definite disk shape, swimming in a zigzag pattern, moving from the East to the West, around Midnight. You feel certain a disk at high altitude swimming like a pollywog had to be a U.F.O..

Answer: Yes or No

---

13. Statement:
The third U.F.O. sighting of the six occurred on the evening of April 20, 2008 (early Sun. A.M.), and was dubbed Ranger, because it showed a full range of maneuvers, a display like it was in some alien Air show! With a full moon backlighting the clouds behind it, you saw a definite disk move sideways then up by an approximate equal distance both up and sideways, like, tracing five steps upward, perhaps gaining about one thousand feet each move. Moving from perhaps fifteen to twenty thousand feet. Then on a forty-five-degree angle, and keeping the craft horizontal, it proceeded to descend back down to around fifteen thousand feet altitude. It was like watching a small child slide down a slide. At the bottom, it made a small circular motion, moving clockwise. Then it just remained still!
Is this statement True and Accurate?

Answer: Yes or No

Test 4

Verifications Test Questions

1. After the six U.F.O. sightings foretold in advance through premonition (April 2008) were later confirmed, and verified by means of lie -Detection, another U.F.O. event occurred involving your sighting of a Particle Beam emanating from a U.F.O. you had dubbed Illustra. It was above the last spot visualized in a 1988 premonition/vision while watching T.V. on the same U.F.O./particle beam subject (The one in the Bible Book of Revelation).
Is this statement accurate and true?   Answer <u>Yes</u>   No

---

2. At the time of this U.F.O./Particle beam sighting, you were not under the influence of any alcohol or drug substance, either legal or illegal at this time, and although tired, (around midnight) you definitely are certain this was no hallucination, both U.F.O. and this Particle beam were real, even though the Particle beam was both visible and invisible depending on how it was viewed.
Is this statement accurate and true?   Answer <u>Yes</u>   No

---

3. This event occurring late night, you state that the beam was both visible and invisible depending on how you focused your eyes upon this (all black as pitch) particle beam, even darker than the night air surrounding it, that seemed like staggered donut shape rings stacking up a center black shaft, roughly three inches diameter, but with two dark (Jacinth) blue rectangular plates (parallel) that appeared imbedded in a blunt, (slightly round) end.
Is this statement accurate and true?   Answer <u>Yes</u>   No

---

4. Would you say that sighting up the beam, (steep pitched angel) focusing both eyes directly at the beam allowed you to see it, sighting up the beam toward the U.F.O. on the other end.
Is this statement accurate and true?   Answer <u>Yes</u>   No

---

5. You could make this beam appear or disappear, (even though it was still present) by focusing your eyes at any close ground object, but with one eye still on the beam, and the beam would vanish and not be visible. (Even though appearing quite solid and heavy in weight!) However, refocus of your eyes, and sighting up the beam made it reappear.
Is this statement accurate and true?   Answer Yes   No

---

6. You made the beam disappear then reappear more than twenty times, while moving around and viewing it from many different ground locations and sighting angels. (all in conformity to eye focus as controlling factor to visible /non-visible) as the U.F.O. and beam both remained stationary.
Is this statement accurate and True?   Answer <u>Yes</u>   No

---

7. Upon initial descent, it came straight toward your head as you stood perfectly still. At first it stopped at about ten feet away, but then inched toward you to only about 8 feet from your face. (like a shotgun barrel twenty thousand or so feet long!)
Is this statement accurate and True?   Answer <u>Yes</u> No

---

8. The U.F.O. you dubbed Illumus of the Bright classification appeared as a very bright star in the May 2008 night sky. Twice, in the same location, but two separate dates about ten days apart) you Busted this Star-pretender as being a definite U.F.O., by waiting until first light early AM, when background darkness faded, and its disk shape clearly visible (both times) upon departure.
Is this statement accurate and True?   Answer <u>Yes</u>   No

---

9. Even though you have ousted numerous U.F.O. in the act of pretending to be stars; singles, doubles, triangles, and whole formations even the Big Dipper fraud, and more, you've stopped your count of Definite at 9, with nothing left to prove by adding more.
Is this statement accurate and True? Answer <u>Yes</u>   No

------

10. Are <u>all</u> of the following statements true regarding the psychic experience you refer to as an Intunition.
    1. Four times in your life you feel you were messaged by an angel, beginning in 1964, which message each time: Remember this, you'll need it later in life.
    2. You suspected, but were not told that this meant one day you would be writing a book it would be needed for.
    3. In fact, that book just now completed (this one) does connect all four Intunition separate subject information, as integral component of the book.
    4. These are different than premonition, (although like the third one can be tied to or conjunctive with premonition) An Intunition then, an instruction something now will be significance or importance in the future and to remember it for that reason (An angelic notice!).
Is this statement in total, accurate and true? Answer <u>Yes</u>   No

------

Printed and bound by PG in the USA